Nmap Network Scanning

Official Nmap Project Guide to Network Discovery and Security Scanning

Gordon "Fyodor" Lyon

From port scanning basics for novices to the type of packet crafting used by advanced hackers, this book by Nmap's author and maintainer suits all levels of security and networking professionals. Rather than simply document what every Nmap option does, Nmap Network Scanning demonstrates how these features can be applied to solve real world tasks such as penetration testing, taking network inventory, detecting rogue wireless access points or open proxies, quashing network worm and virus outbreaks, and much more. Examples and diagrams show actual communication on the wire. This book is essential for anyone who needs to get the most out of Nmap, particularly security auditors and systems or network administrators.

Nmap Network Scanning: Official Nmap Project Guide to Network Discovery and Security Scanning

by Gordon "Fyodor" Lyon

Book URL: *http://nmap.org/book/*
ISBN-13: 978-0-9799587-1-7
ISBN-10: 0-9799587-1-7
Library of Congress Control Number (LCCN): 2008940582
Library Of Congress Subject Headings:
1. Computer networks--Security measures
2. Computer security

Published by Insecure.Com LLC. For information on bulk purchases, special sales, rights, book distributors, or translations, please contact us directly:

Insecure.Com LLC
370 Altair Way #113
Sunnyvale, CA 94086-6161
United States
Email: sales@insecure.com; Phone: +1-650-989-4206; Fax: +1-650-989-4206

Revision History:
First Edition: December 2008
Defcon Pre-Release: August 2008
Zero-Day Release: May 2008

Table of Contents

List of Figures

List of Tables

List of Examples

Preface

1. Introduction

On September 1, 1997, I released a security scanner named Nmap in the fifty-first issue of *Phrack* magazine. My goal was to consolidate the fragmented field of special-purpose port scanners into one powerful and flexible free tool, providing a consistent interface and efficient implementation of all practical port scanning techniques. Nmap then consisted of three files (barely 2,000 lines of code) and supported only the Linux operating system. It was written for my own purposes, and released in the hope that others would find it useful.

From these humble beginnings, and through the power of Open Source development, Nmap grew into the world's most popular network security scanner[1], with millions of users worldwide. Over the years, Nmap has continued to add advanced functionality such as remote OS detection, version/service detection, IP ID idle scanning, the Nmap Scripting Engine, and fast multi-probe ping scanning. It now supports all major Unix, Windows, and Mac OS platforms. Both console and graphical versions are available. Publications including *Linux Journal, Info World, LinuxQuestions.Org*, and the *Codetalker Digest* have recognized Nmap as "security tool of the year". It was even featured in several movies[2], including *The Matrix Reloaded, The Bourne Ultimatum*, and *Die Hard 4*.

Nmap ("Network Mapper") is a free and open source utility for network exploration and security auditing. Many systems and network administrators also find it useful for tasks such as network inventory, managing service upgrade schedules, and monitoring host or service uptime. Nmap uses raw IP packets in novel ways to determine what hosts are available on the network, what services (application name and version) those hosts are offering, what operating systems (and OS versions) they are running, what type of packet filters/firewalls are in use, and dozens of other characteristics. It was designed to rapidly scan large networks, but works fine against single hosts.

While Nmap is extremely powerful, it is also complex. More than 100 command-line options add expressiveness for networking gurus, but can confound novices. Some of its options have never even been documented. This book documents all Nmap features and, more importantly, teaches the most effective ways of using them. It has taken nearly four years to write, with constant updating as Nmap has evolved.

This book is dedicated to the Nmap community of users and developers. Your passion, ideas, patches, feature requests, flame wars, bug reports, and midnight rants have shaped Nmap into what it is today.

—Gordon "Fyodor" Lyon <fyodor@insecure.org>

2. Intended Audience and Organization

This book documents the free Nmap Security Scanner, from port scanning basics for novices to the types of packet crafting used by advanced hackers. It should benefit Nmap users (or potential users) of all experience levels.

---

[1]Based on download frequency, number of Google hits, and Freshmeat.Net software "popularity" ranking.

[2] *http://nmap.org/movies.html*

Starting with the basics, this book gives an overview of Nmap by example in Chapter 1. Then Chapter 2 covers obtaining, compiling and installing Nmap. Chapters 3 through 5 cover features in the order you might use them when conducting a penetration test. First comes host discovery ("ping scanning"), which determines the available hosts on a network. Next, port scanning is covered in depth. In Chapter 5, all the Nmap scanning techniques are detailed, with advice and examples. Scanning a large network can take a long time, so Chapter 6 is full of performance optimization advice. Chapter 7 details service and application version detection, in which Nmap queries ports to determine exactly what is running rather than simply guessing based on the port number. Chapter 8 covers one of Nmap's most loved features: remote OS detection. Chapter 9 details one of Nmap's newest features: the Nmap Scripting Engine. NSE allows users and developers to easily extend Nmap with new features by writing simple scripts to be efficiently executed against target machines. My favorite chapter is number 10: *Detecting and Subverting Firewalls and Intrusion Detection Systems*. For balance, that is followed by a chapter on defending against Nmap scans. Chapter 12 then fully documents the Zenmap multi-platform Nmap GUI and results viewer. The next two chapters cover output formats and data files. The final and longest chapter is the *Nmap Reference Guide*, a quick resource for looking up specific Nmap options.

Scattered throughout the book are detailed instructions for performing common tasks such as scanning a network for a certain single open TCP port or detecting wireless access points by scanning from the wired side. First each problem is described, then an effective solution is provided. A final discussion section describes the solution in more depth and may provide alternative solutions and insights into similar problems.

3. Conventions

Nmap output is used throughout this book to demonstrate principles and features. The output is often edited to cut out lines which are irrelevant to the point being made. The dates/times and version numbers printed by Nmap are generally removed as well, since some readers find them distracting. Sensitive information such as hostnames, IP addresses, and MAC addresses may be changed or removed. Other information may be cut or lines wrapped so that they fit on a printed page. Similar editing is done for the output of other applications. Example 1 gives a glimpse at Nmap's capabilities while also demonstrating output formatting.

Example 1. A typical Nmap scan

```
# nmap -A -T4 scanme.nmap.org
Starting Nmap ( http://nmap.org )
Interesting ports on scanme.nmap.org (64.13.134.52):
Not shown: 994 filtered ports
PORT    STATE  SERVICE VERSION
22/tcp  open   ssh        OpenSSH 4.3 (protocol 2.0)
25/tcp  closed smtp
53/tcp  open   domain  ISC BIND 9.3.4
70/tcp  closed gopher
80/tcp  open   http       Apache httpd 2.2.2 ((Fedora))
|_ HTML title: Go ahead and ScanMe!
113/tcp closed auth
Device type: general purpose
Running: Linux 2.6.X
OS details: Linux 2.6.20-1 (Fedora Core 5)

TRACEROUTE (using port 80/tcp)
HOP RTT    ADDRESS
[Cut first seven hops for brevity]
8    10.59 so-4-2-0.mpr3.pao1.us.above.net (64.125.28.142)
9    11.00 metro0.sv.svcolo.com (208.185.168.173)
10   9.93  scanme.nmap.org (64.13.134.52)

Nmap done: 1 IP address (1 host up) scanned in 17.00 seconds
```

Special formatting is provided for certain tokens, such as filenames and application commands. Table 1 demonstrates the most common formatting conventions.

Table 1. Formatting style conventions

Token type	Example
literal string	I get much more excited by ports in the `open` state than those reported as `closed` or `filtered`.
Command-line options	One of the coolest, yet least understood Nmap options is `--packet-trace`.
Filenames	Follow the `-iL` option with the input filename such as `C:\net\dhcp-leases.txt` or `/home/h4x/hosts-to-pwn.lst`.
Emphasis	Using Nmap from your work or school computer to attack banks and military targets is a *bad* idea.
Application commands	Trinity scanned the Matrix with the command **nmap -v -sS -O 10.2.2.2**.
Replaceable variables	Let `<source>` be the machine running Nmap and `<target>` be `microsoft.com`.

4. Other Resources

While this book is an important reference for Nmap, it isn't the only one. The Nmap web page at *http://nmap.org* is not just for downloads. It also provides substantial documentation from Nmap developers and third parties. For example, you can find the *Nmap Reference Guide* translated into a dozen languages there. Other books, videos, and articles covering Nmap are also available.

The official web site for this book is at *http://nmap.org/book/*. Go there for errata, updates, and many sample chapters.

Any serious Nmap user should subscribe to the *nmap-hackers* mailing list for announcements about Nmap and Insecure.Org. Traffic is very light (about six posts per year) because it is reserved for only the most important announcements. Developers and particularly devoted users can also subscribe to the *nmap-dev* mailing list. Traffic is much higher (hundreds of posts per month), but it is a great place to learn about and try new features before they are released and to pick up tips from advanced users. Subscription information and archives for both lists are available at *http://seclists.org*.

While Nmap can be useful, it won't solve all of your security problems. Every few years I do a survey of thousands of Nmap users to determine what other tools they like. The list is posted at *http://sectools.org*, which has become one of my most popular web sites. Read through the list and you are sure to find many gems you had never even heard of. Most of the tools are free and open source.

5. Request for Comments

While I tried my best to make this book comprehensive, accurate, and up-to-date, we all make mistakes. If you find any problems or just have suggestions for making this book better, please let me know by email at `<fyodor@insecure.org>`. The open source principle of many readers and contributors is just as viable for documentation as for software. As the next section attests, dozens of people have already generously contributed their time and skills to make this book a success.

If you have a question or comment about Nmap (rather than this book itself), it is best sent to the Nmap development list as described at Section 15.17, "Bugs" [411].

6. Acknowledgements

When I first floated the idea of writing an Nmap book to the *nmap-hackers* mailing list, I was inundated with suggestions and offers to help. This outpouring of enthusiasm convinced me to proceed. My complete naivety about how much work was involved also contributed to my decision. It has been quite an undertaking, but what kept me going chapter by chapter was a private review group called the *nmap-writers*. They provided invaluable feedback, advice, and detailed review notes throughout the process. In particular, I would like to thank the following people:

- **David Fifield** is listed first (everyone else is alphabetical) because he was a tremendous help during the book writing process. He solved a number of technical DocBook problems, created many of the final illustrations from my terrible drafts, dramatically improved the index, helped with proofreading, and even wrote Chapter 12, *Zenmap GUI Users' Guide* [307].

- **Matt Baxter** allowed the use of his beautiful TCP/IP header diagrams (in Section 7, "TCP/IP Reference" [xxvi]). Several other diagrams in this book were done in that style to match.

- **Saurabh Bhasin** contributed detailed feedback on a regular basis.

- **Mark Brewis** could always be counted on for good advice.

- **Ellen Colombo** was a big help from the beginning.

- **Patrick Donnelly** helped improve Chapter 9, *Nmap Scripting Engine* [205].

- **Brandon Enright** printed out the whole book and reviewed it chapter by chapter.

- **Brian Hatch** has always been a big help.

- **Loren Heal** was a continual source of ideas.

- **Dan Henage** provided advice and proofread numerous chapters.

- **Tor Houghton** reviewed every chapter, probably giving me more feedback than anyone else.

- **Doug Hoyte** documented the many Nmap features he added, and also handled most of the book indexing.

- **Marius Huse Jacobsen** reviewed many chapters, providing detailed feedback.

- **Kris Katterjohn** performed thorough reviews of several chapters.

- **Eric Krosnes** sent useful technical review feedback and also regularly nagged me about book progress. This was helpful since I didn't have a traditional editor to do so.

- **Vlad Alexa Mancini** created the Nmap eye logo for the cover (and the Nmap web site).

- **Michael Naef** kindly reviewed many chapters.

- **Bill Pollock** of No Starch Press was always happy to provide advice and answer book publishing questions based on his decades of experience.

- **David Pybus** was one of the most frequent contributors of ideas and proofreading.

- **Tyler Reguly** helped by reviewing multiple chapters just when it was most needed.

- **Chuck Sterling** provided both high level advice and detailed proofreading of several chapters.

- **Anders Thulin** provided detailed reviews of many chapters.

- **Bennett Todd** sent dozens of suggestions.

- **Diman Todorov** wrote an initial draft of Chapter 9, *Nmap Scripting Engine* [205].

- **Catherine Tornabene** read many chapters and sent extremely detailed feedback.

6.1. Technology Used to Create This Book

As an author of open source tools myself, I'm a big believer in their power and capability. So I made an effort to use them wherever possible in creating this book. I wasn't about to write it in Microsoft Word and then handle layout with Adobe FrameMaker!

Nmap Network Scanning was written with the GNU Emacs text editor in the DocBook XML format.

The free online chapters are created from the XML using Norman Walsh's XSL Stylesheets and the xsltproc XSL processor.

The print version also uses Norman's stylesheets and xsltproc, but the output is to the XSL-FO format[3]. An XSL-FO processor is then used to build a PDF. I would like to use Apache FOP[4] for this, but a footnote-related bug[5] prevents this, so I switched to the RenderX XEP Engine. XEP is proprietary, but at least it runs on Linux. I hope to switch back to FOP after the footnote bug is fixed.

Cover layout was done with Scribus and (due to printing company format requirements) Adobe InDesign. Raster graphics for the cover and internal illustrations were created with The Gimp, while Inkscape was used for vector graphics.

Subversion was used for revision control and the free web chapters are serviced by Apache httpd.

7. TCP/IP Reference

This book assumes basic familiarity with TCP/IP and networking concepts. You won't find a primer on the OSI seven-layer model or a rundown of the Berkeley Socket API within these pages. For a comprehensive guide to TCP/IP, I recommend *"The TCP/IP Guide"* by Charles Kozierok or the old classic *"TCP/IP Illustrated, Volume I"* by W. Richard Stevens.

While TCP/IP familiarity is expected, even the best of us occasionally forget byte offsets for packet header fields and flags. This section provides quick reference diagrams and field descriptions for the IPv4, TCP, UDP, and ICMP protocols. These beautiful diagrams from *http://www.fatpipe.org/~mjb/Drawings* are used by permission of author Matt Baxter.

---

[3] *http://en.wikipedia.org/wiki/XSL_Formatting_Objects*
[4] *http://xmlgraphics.apache.org/fop/*
[5] *https://issues.apache.org/bugzilla/show_bug.cgi?id=37579*

Figure 1. IPv4 header

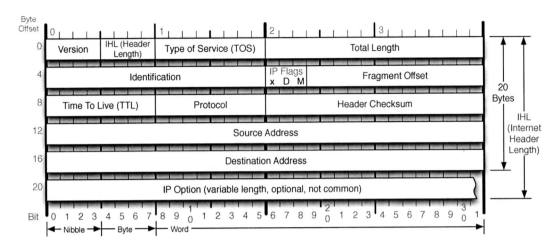

Version
Version of IP Protocol. 4 and 6 are valid. This diagram represents version 4 structure only.

Header Length
Number of 32-bit words in TCP header, minimum value of 5. Multiply by 4 to get byte count.

Protocol
IP Protocol ID. Including (but not limited to):

1 ICMP	17 UDP	57 SKIP
2 IGMP	47 GRE	88 EIGRP
6 TCP	50 ESP	89 OSPF
9 IGRP	51 AH	115 L2TP

Total Length
Total length of IP datagram, or IP fragment if fragmented. Measured in Bytes.

Fragment Offset
Fragment offset from start of IP datagram. Measured in 8 byte (2 words, 64 bits) increments. If IP datagram is fragmented, fragment size (Total Length) must be a multiple of 8 bytes.

Header Checksum
Checksum of entire IP header

IP Flags
x D M

x 0x80 reserved (evil bit)
D 0x40 Do Not Fragment
M 0x20 More Fragments follow

RFC 791
Please refer to RFC 791 for the complete Internet Protocol (IP) Specification.

Figure 2. TCP header

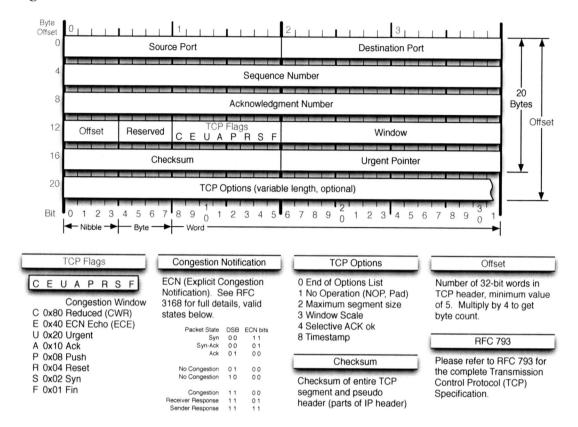

Figure 3. UDP header

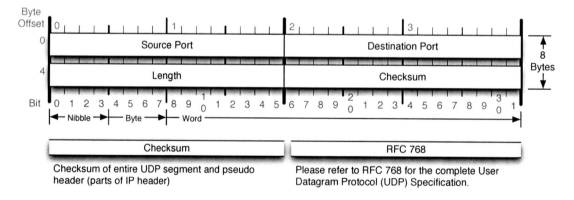

Figure 4. ICMP header

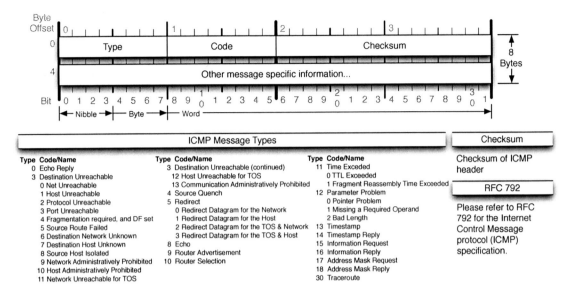

ICMP Message Types

Type	Code/Name
0	Echo Reply
3	Destination Unreachable
	0 Net Unreachable
	1 Host Unreachable
	2 Protocol Unreachable
	3 Port Unreachable
	4 Fragmentation required, and DF set
	5 Source Route Failed
	6 Destination Network Unknown
	7 Destination Host Unknown
	8 Source Host Isolated
	9 Network Administratively Prohibited
	10 Host Administratively Prohibited
	11 Network Unreachable for TOS

Type	Code/Name
3	Destination Unreachable (continued)
	12 Host Unreachable for TOS
	13 Communication Administratively Prohibited
4	Source Quench
5	Redirect
	0 Redirect Datagram for the Network
	1 Redirect Datagram for the Host
	2 Redirect Datagram for the TOS & Network
	3 Redirect Datagram for the TOS & Host
8	Echo
9	Router Advertisement
10	Router Selection

Type	Code/Name
11	Time Exceded
	0 TTL Exceeded
	1 Fragment Reassembly Time Exceeded
12	Parameter Problem
	0 Pointer Problem
	1 Missing a Required Operand
	2 Bad Length
13	Timestamp
14	Timestamp Reply
15	Information Request
16	Information Reply
17	Address Mask Request
18	Address Mask Reply
30	Traceroute

Checksum

Checksum of ICMP header

RFC 792

Please refer to RFC 792 for the Internet Control Message protocol (ICMP) specification.

Chapter 1. Getting Started with Nmap

1.1. Introduction

Nmap ("Network Mapper") is a free and open source utility for network exploration and security auditing. Many systems and network administrators also find it useful for tasks such as network inventory, managing service upgrade schedules, and monitoring host or service uptime. Nmap uses raw IP packets in novel ways to determine what hosts are available on the network, what services (application name and version) those hosts are offering, what operating systems (and OS versions) they are running, what type of packet filters/firewalls are in use, and dozens of other characteristics. It was designed to rapidly scan large networks, but works fine against single hosts. Nmap runs on all major computer operating systems, and both console and graphical versions are available.

This chapter uses fictional stories to provide a broad overview of Nmap and how it is typically used. An important legal section helps users avoid (or at least be aware of) controversial usage that could lead to ISP account cancellation or even civil and criminal charges. It also discusses the risks of crashing remote machines as well as miscellaneous issues such as the Nmap license (GNU GPL), and copyright.

1.2. Nmap Overview and Demonstration

Sometimes the best way to understand something is to see it in action. This section includes examples of Nmap used in (mostly) fictional yet typical circumstances. Nmap newbies should not expect to understand everything at once. This is simply a broad overview of features that are described in depth in later chapters. The "solutions" included throughout this book demonstrate many other common Nmap tasks for security auditors and network administrators.

1.2.1. Avatar Online

Felix dutifully arrives at work on December 15th, although he does not expect many structured tasks. The small San Francisco penetration-testing firm he works for has been quiet lately due to impending holidays. Felix spends business hours pursuing his latest hobby of building powerful Wi-Fi antennas for wireless assessments and war driving exploration. Nevertheless, Felix is hoping for more business. Hacking has been his hobby and fascination since a childhood spent learning everything he could about networking, security, Unix, and phone systems. Occasionally his curiosity took him too far, and Felix was almost swept up in the 1990 Operation Sundevil prosecutions. Fortunately Felix emerged from adolescence without a criminal record, while retaining his expert knowledge of security weaknesses. As a professional, he is able to perform the same types of network intrusions as before, but with the added benefit of contractual immunity from prosecution and even a paycheck! Rather than keeping his creative exploits secret, he can brag about them to client management when presenting his reports. So Felix was not disappointed when his boss interrupted his antenna soldering to announce that the sales department finally closed a pen-testing deal with the Avatar Online gaming company.

Avatar Online (AO) is a small company working to create the next generation of massive multi-player online role-playing games (MMORPGs). Their product, inspired by the Metaverse envisioned in Neil Stevenson's

---

Snow Crash, is fascinating but still highly confidential. After witnessing the high-profile leak[1] of Valve Software's upcoming game source code, AO quickly hired the security consultants. Felix's task is to initiate an external (from outside the firewall) vulnerability assessment while his partners work on physical security, source code auditing, social engineering, and so forth. Felix is permitted to exploit any vulnerabilities found.

The first step in a vulnerability assessment is network discovery. This reconnaissance stage determines what IP address ranges the target is using, what hosts are available, what services those hosts are offering, general network topology details, and what firewall/filtering policies are in effect.

Determining the IP ranges to scan would normally be an elaborate process involving ARIN (or another geographical registry) lookups, DNS queries and zone transfer attempts, various web sleuthing techniques, and more. But in this case, Avatar Online explicitly specified what networks they want tested: the corporate network on 6.209.24.0/24 and their production/DMZ systems residing on 6.207.0.0/22. Felix checks the ARIN IP allocation records anyway and confirms that these IP ranges belong to AO[2]. Felix subconsciously decodes the CIDR notation[3] and recognizes this as 1,280 IP addresses. No problem.

Being the careful type, Felix first starts out with what is known as an Nmap list scan (-sL option). This feature simply enumerates every IP address in the given target netblock(s) and does a reverse-DNS lookup (unless -n was specified) on each. One reason to do this first is stealth. The names of the hosts can hint at potential vulnerabilities and allow for a better understanding of the target network, all without raising alarm bells[4]. Felix is doing this for another reason—to double-check that the IP ranges are correct. The systems administrator who provided the IPs might have made a mistake, and scanning the wrong company would be a disaster. The contract signed with Avatar Online may act as a get-out-of-jail-free card for penetrating their networks, but will not help if Felix accidentally roots another company's server! The command he uses and an excerpt of the results are shown in Example 1.1.

---

[1] *http://www.smh.com.au/articles/2003/10/03/1064988378345.html*

[2] These IP addresses are actually registered to the United States Army Yuma Proving Ground, which is used to test a wide variety of artillery, missiles, tanks, and other deadly weapons. The moral is to be very careful about who you scan, lest you accidentally hit a highly sensitive network. The scan results in this story are not actually from this IP range.

[3] Classless Inter-Domain Routing (CIDR) notation is a method for describing networks with more granularity than class A (CIDR /8), class B (CIDR /16), or class C (CIDR /24) notation. An excellent description is available at *http://public.pacbell.net/dedicated/cidr.html*.

[4] It is possible that the target nameserver will log a suspicious bunch of reverse-DNS queries from Felix's nameserver, but most organizations don't even keep such logs, much less analyze them.

Example 1.1. Nmap list scan against Avatar Online IP addresses

```
felix> nmap -sL 6.209.24.0/24 6.207.0.0/22

Starting Nmap ( http://nmap.org )
Host 6.209.24.0 not scanned
Host fw.corp.avataronline.com (6.209.24.1) not scanned
Host dev2.corp.avataronline.com (6.209.24.2) not scanned
Host 6.209.24.3 not scanned
Host 6.209.24.4 not scanned
Host 6.209.24.5 not scanned
...
Host dhcp-21.corp.avataronline.com (6.209.24.21) not scanned
Host dhcp-22.corp.avataronline.com (6.209.24.22) not scanned
Host dhcp-23.corp.avataronline.com (6.209.24.23) not scanned
Host dhcp-24.corp.avataronline.com (6.209.24.24) not scanned
Host dhcp-25.corp.avataronline.com (6.209.24.25) not scanned
Host dhcp-26.corp.avataronline.com (6.209.24.26) not scanned
...
Host 6.207.0.0 not scanned
Host gw.avataronline.com (6.207.0.1) not scanned
Host ns1.avataronline.com (6.207.0.2) not scanned
Host ns2.avataronline.com (6.207.0.3) not scanned
Host ftp.avataronline.com (6.207.0.4) not scanned
Host 6.207.0.5 not scanned
Host 6.207.0.6 not scanned
Host www.avataronline.com (6.207.0.7) not scanned
Host 6.207.0.8 not scanned
...
Host cluster-c120.avataronline.com (6.207.2.120) not scanned
Host cluster-c121.avataronline.com (6.207.2.121) not scanned
Host cluster-c122.avataronline.com (6.207.2.122) not scanned
Host cluster-c123.avataronline.com (6.207.2.123) not scanned
Host cluster-c124.avataronline.com (6.207.2.124) not scanned
...
Host 6.207.3.253 not scanned
Host 6.207.3.254 not scanned
Host 6.207.3.255 not scanned
Nmap done: 1280 IP addresses scanned in 331.49 seconds
felix>
```

Reading over the results, Felix finds that all of the machines with reverse-DNS entries resolve to Avatar Online. No other businesses seem to share the IP space. Moreover, these results give Felix a rough idea of how many machines are in use and a good idea of what many are used for. He is now ready to get a bit more intrusive and try a port scan. He uses Nmap features that try to determine the application and version number of each service listening on the network. He also requests that Nmap try to guess the remote operating system via a series of low-level TCP/IP probes known as OS fingerprinting. This sort of scan is not at all stealthy, but that does not concern Felix. He is interested in whether the administrators of AO even notice these blatant scans. After a bit of consideration, Felix settles on the following command:

nmap -sS -p- -PS22,80,113,33334 -PA80,113,21000 -PU19000 -PE -A -T4 -oA avatartcpscan-121503 6.209.24.0/24 6.207.0.0/22

These options are described in later chapters, but here is a quick summary of them.

`-sS`

> Enables the efficient TCP port scanning technique known as SYN scan. Felix would have added a U at the end if he also wanted to do a UDP scan, but he is saving that for later. SYN scan is the default scan type, but stating it explicitly does not hurt.

`-p-`

> Requests that Nmap scan *every* port from 1-65535. The default is to scan only ports one through 1024, plus about 600 others explicitly mentioned in the `nmap-services` database. This option format is simply a short cut for `-p1-65535`. He could have specified `-p0-65535` if he wanted to scan the rather illegitimate port zero as well. The `-p` option has a very flexible syntax, even allowing the specification of a differing set of UDP and TCP ports.

`-PS22,80,113,33334 -PA80,113,21000 -PU19000 -PE`

> These are all *ping types* used in combination to determine whether a host is really available and avoid wasting a lot of time scanning IP addresses that are not in use. This particular incantation sends a TCP SYN packet to ports 22, 80, 113, and 33334; a TCP ACK packet to ports 80, 113, and 21000; a UDP packet to port 19000; and a normal ICMP echo request packet. If Nmap receives a response from the target host itself to any of these probes, it considers the host to be up and available for scanning. This is more extensive than the Nmap default, which simply sends an echo request and an ACK packet to port 80. In a pen-testing situation, you often want to scan every host even if they do not seem to be up. After all, they could just be heavily filtered in such a way that the probes you selected are ignored but some other obscure port may be available. To scan every IP whether it shows an available host or not, specify the `-PN` option instead of all of the above. Felix starts such a scan in the background, though it may take a day to complete.

`-A`

> This shortcut option turns on *Advanced* and *Aggressive* features such as OS and service detection. At the time of this writing it is equivalent to `-sV -sC -O --traceroute` (version detection, Nmap Scripting Engine, remote OS detection, and traceroute). More features may be added to `-A` later.

`-T4`

> Adjusts timing to the `aggressive` level (#4 of 5). This is the same as specifying `-T aggressive`, but is easier to type and spell. In general, the `-T4` option is recommended if the connection between you and the target networks are faster than dialup modems.

`-oA avatartcpscan-121503`

> Outputs results in every format (normal, XML, grepable) to files named `avatartcpscan-121503.<extension>` where the extensions are .nmap, .xml, and .gnmap respectively. All of the output formats include the start date and time, but Felix likes to note the date explicitly in the filename. Normal output and errors are still sent to stdout[5] as well.

---

[5]stdout is the "C" notation for representing the standard output mechanism for a system, such as to the Unix xterm or Windows command window in which Nmap was initiated.

```
6.209.24.0/24 6.207.0.0/22
```

These are the Avatar Online netblocks discussed above. They are given in CIDR notation, but Nmap allows them to be specified in many other formats. For example, `6.209.24.0/24` could instead be specified as `6.209.24.0-255`.

Since such a comprehensive scan against more than a thousand IP addresses could take a while, Felix simply starts it executing and resumes work on his Yagi antenna. A couple hours later he notices that it has finished and takes a peek at the results. Example 1.2 shows one of the machines discovered.

Example 1.2. Nmap results against an AO firewall

```
Interesting ports on fw.corp.avataronline.com (6.209.24.1):
(The 65530 ports scanned but not shown below are in state: filtered)
PORT      STATE   SERVICE     VERSION
22/tcp    open    ssh         OpenSSH 3.7.1p2 (protocol 1.99)
53/tcp    open    domain      ISC BIND 9.2.1
110/tcp   open    pop3        Courier pop3d
113/tcp   closed  auth
143/tcp   open    imap        Courier Imap 1.6.X - 1.7.X
3128/tcp  open    http-proxy  Squid webproxy 2.2.STABLE5
Device type: general purpose
Running: Linux 2.4.X|2.5.X
OS details: Linux Kernel 2.4.0 - 2.5.20
Uptime 3.134 days
```

To the trained eye, this conveys substantial information about AO's security posture. Felix first notes the reverse DNS name—this machine is apparently meant to be a firewall for their corporate network. The next line is important, but all too often ignored. It states that the vast majority of the ports on this machine are in the `filtered` state. This means that Nmap is unable to reach the port because it is blocked by firewall rules. The fact that all ports except for a few chosen ones are in this state is a sign of security competence. Deny-by-default is a security mantra for good reasons—it means that even if someone accidentally left SunRPC (port 111) open on this machine, the firewall rules would prevent attackers from communicating with it.

Felix then looks at every port line in turn. The first port is Secure Shell (OpenSSH). Version 3.7.1p2 is common, as many administrators upgraded to this version due to potentially exploitable buffer management bugs affecting previous versions. Nmap also notes that the SSH protocol is 1.99, suggesting that the inferior legacy SSHv1 protocol is supported. A truly paranoid sysadmin would only allow SSH connections from certain trusted IP addresses, but one can argue for open access in case the administrator needs emergency access while far from home. Security often involves trade-offs, and this one may be justifiable. Felix makes a note to try his brute force password cracker and especially his private timing-based SSH user enumeration tool against the server.

Felix also notes port 53. It is running ISC BIND, which has a long history of remotely exploitable security holes. Visit the BIND security page[6] for further details. BIND 9.2.1 even has a potentially exploitable buffer overflow, although the default build is not vulnerable. Felix checks and finds that this server is not vulnerable to the libbind issue, but that is beside the point. This server almost certainly should not be running an externally-accessible nameserver. A firewall should only run the bare essentials to minimize the risk of a disastrous compromise. Besides, this server is not authoritative for any domains—the real nameservers are

---

[6] *http://www.isc.org/products/BIND/bind-security.html*

on the production network. An administrator probably only meant for clients within the firewall to contact this nameserver, but did not bother locking it down to only the internal interface. Felix will later try to gather important information from this unnecessary server using zone transfer requests and intrusive queries. He may attempt cache poisoning as well. By spoofing the IP of `windowsupdate.microsoft.com` or another important download server, Felix may be able to trick unsuspecting internal client users into running a trojan-horse program that provides him with full network access behind the firewall.

The next two open ports are 110 (POP3) and 143 (IMAP). Note that 113 (auth) between them is `closed` instead of `open`. POP3 and IMAP are mail retrieval services which, like BIND, have no legitimate place on this server. They are also a security risk in that they generally transfer the mail and (even worse) authentication credentials unencrypted. Users should probably VPN in and check their mail from an internal server. These ports could also be wrapped in SSL encryption. Nmap would have then listed the services as `ssl/pop3` and `ssl/imap`. Felix will try his user enumeration and password guessing attacks on these services, which will probably be much more effective than against SSH.

The final open port is a Squid proxy. This is another service that may have been intended for internal client use and should not be accessible from the outside (and particularly not on the firewall). Felix's initially positive opinion of the AO security administrators drops further. Felix will test whether he can abuse this proxy to connect to other sites on the Internet. Spammers and malicious hackers often use proxies in this way to hide their tracks. Even more critical, Felix will try to proxy his way into the *internal* network. This common attack is how Adrian Lamo[7] broke into the New York Times internal network in 2002. Lamo was caught after he called reporters to brag about his exploits against the NY Times and other companies in detail[8].

The following lines disclose that this is a Linux box, which is valuable information when attempting exploitation. The low three-day uptime was detected during OS fingerprinting by sending several probes for the TCP timestamp option value and extrapolating the line back to zero.

Felix then examines the Nmap output for another machine, as shown in Example 1.3.

---

[7] *http://en.wikipedia.org/wiki/Adrian_Lamo*
[8] *http://www.securityfocus.com/news/340*

Example 1.3. Another interesting AO machine

```
Interesting ports on dhcp-23.corp.avataronline.com (6.209.24.23):
(The 65526 ports scanned but not shown below are in state: closed)
PORT        STATE      SERVICE        VERSION
135/tcp     filtered   msrpc
136/tcp     filtered   profile
137/tcp     filtered   netbios-ns
138/tcp     filtered   netbios-dgm
139/tcp     filtered   netbios-ssn
445/tcp     open       microsoft-ds   Microsoft Windows XP microsoft-ds
1002/tcp    open       windows-icfw?
1025/tcp    open       msrpc          Microsoft Windows msrpc
16552/tcp   open       unknown
Device type: general purpose
Running: Microsoft Windows NT/2K/XP
OS details: Microsoft Windows XP Professional RC1+ through final release
```

Felix smiles when he spies this Windows XP box on the Network. Thanks to a spate of MS RPC vulnerabilities, those machines are trivial to compromise if the OS patches aren't up-to-date. The second line shows that the default state is `closed`, meaning the firewall does not have the same deny-by-default policy for this machine as for itself. Instead they tried to specifically block the Windows ports they consider dangerous on 135-139. This filter is woefully inadequate, as MS exports MS RPC functionality on many other ports in Windows XP. TCP ports 445 and 1025 are two examples from this scan. While Nmap failed to recognize 16552, Felix has seen this pattern enough to know that it is probably the MS Messenger Service. If AO had been using deny-by-default filtering, port 16552 would not be accessible in the first place. Looking through the results page, Felix sees several other Windows machines on this DHCP network. Felix cannot wait to try his favorite DCOM RPC exploit against them. It was written by HD Moore and is available at *http://www.metasploit.com/tools/dcom.c*. If that fails, there are a couple newer MS RPC vulnerabilities he will try.

Felix continues poring over the results for vulnerabilities he can leverage to compromise the network. On the production network, he sees that `gw.avataronline.com` is a Cisco router that also acts as a rudimentary firewall for the systems. They fall into the trap of only blocking privileged ports (those under 1024), which leaves a bunch of vulnerable SunRPC and other services accessible on that network. The machines with names like `clust-*` each have dozens of ports open that Nmap does not recognize. They are probably custom daemons running the AO game engine. `www.avataronline.com` is a Linux box with an open Apache server on the HTTP and HTTPS ports. Unfortunately, it is linked with an exploitable version of the OpenSSL library. Oops! Before the sun sets, Felix has gained privileged access to hosts on both the corporate and production networks.

As Felix has demonstrated, Nmap is frequently used by security auditors and network administrators to help locate vulnerabilities on client/corporate networks. Subsequent chapters describe the techniques used by Felix, as well as many other Nmap features, in much greater detail.

1.2.2. Saving the Human Race

Figure 1.1. Trinity begins her assault

Trinity is in quite a pickle! Having discovered that the world we take for granted is really a virtual "Matrix" run by machine overlords, Trinity decides to fight back and free the human race from this mental slavery. Making matters worse, her underground colony of freed humans (Zion) is under attack by 250,000 powerful alien sentinels. Her only hope involves deactivating the emergency power system for 27 city blocks in less than five minutes. The previous team died trying. In life's bleakest moments when all hope seems to be lost, what should you turn to? Nmap, of course! But not quite yet.

She first must defeat the perimeter security, which on many networks involves firewalls and intrusion detection systems (IDS). She is well aware of advanced techniques for circumventing these devices (covered later in this book). Unfortunately, the emergency power system administrators knew better than to connect such a critical system to the Internet, even indirectly. No amount of source routing or IP ID spoofed scanning will help Trinity overcome this "air gap" security. Thinking fast, she devises a clever plan that involves jumping her motorcycle off the rooftop of a nearby building, landing on the power station guard post, and then beating up all of the security guards. This advanced technique is not covered in any physical security manual, but proves highly effective. This demonstrates how clever hackers research and devise their own attacks, rather than always utilizing the script-kiddie approach of canned exploits.

Trinity fights her way to the computer room and sits down at a terminal. She quickly determines that the network is using the private 10.0.0.0/8 network address space. A ping to the network address generates responses from dozens of machines. An Nmap ping scan would have provided a more comprehensive list of available machines, but using the broadcast technique saved precious seconds. Then she whips out Nmap[9]. The terminal has version 2.54BETA25 installed. This version is ancient (2001) and less efficient than newer releases, but Trinity had no time to install a better version from the future. This job will not take long anyway. She runs the command **nmap -v -sS -O 10.2.1.3**. This executes a TCP SYN scan and OS detection against 10.2.1.3 and provides verbose output. The host appears to be a security disaster—AIX 3.2 with well over a dozen ports open. Unfortunately, this is not the machine she needs to compromise. So she runs the same command against 10.2.2.2. This time the target OS is unrecognized (she should have upgraded Nmap!) and only has port 22 open. This is the Secure Shell encrypted administration service. As any sexy PVC-clad hacker goddess knows, many SSH servers from around that time (2001) have an exploitable vulnerability in the CRC32 compensation attack detector. Trinity whips out an all-assembly-code exploit and utilizes it to change the root password of the target box to Z10N0101. Trinity uses much more secure passwords under normal circumstances. She logs in as root and issues a command to disable the emergency backup power system for 27 city blocks, finishing just in time! Here is a shot of the action—squint just right and you should be able to read the text.

Figure 1.2. Trinity scans the Matrix

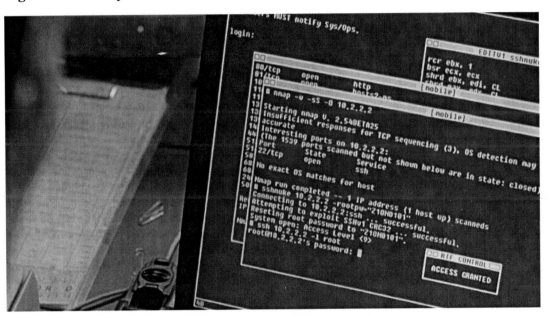

In addition, a terminal-view video showing the whole hack is available on the Internet[10]. At least it will be until the MPAA finds out and sends sentinels or lawyers after the webmasters.

1.2.3. MadHat in Wonderland

This story differs from the previous ones in that it is actually true. Written by frequent Nmap user and contributor MadHat, it describes how he enhanced and customized Nmap for daily use in a large enterprise.

---

[9]A sexy leather-clad attacker from the previous team actually started the session. It is unclear at what point she died and left the remaining tasks to Trinity.

[10] *http://nmap.org/movies.html*

In true open source spirit, he has released these valuable scripts on his Web site[11]. IP addresses have been changed to protect the corporate identity. The remainder of this section is in his own words.

After spending the past couple of decades learning computers and working my way up from tech support through sysadmin and into my dream job of Information Security Officer for a major Internet company, I found myself with a problem. I was handed the sole responsibility of security monitoring for our entire IP space. This was almost 50,000 hosts worldwide when I started several years ago, and it has doubled since then.

Scanning all of these machines for potential vulnerabilities as part of monthly or quarterly assessments would be tough enough, but management wanted it done daily. Attackers will not wait a week or month to exploit a newly exposed vulnerability, so I can't wait that long to find and patch it either.

Looking around for tools, I quickly chose Nmap as my port scanner. It is widely considered to be the best scanner, and I had already been using it for years to troubleshoot networks and test security. Next I needed software to aggregate Nmap output and print differences between runs. I considered several existing tools, including HD Moore's Nlog[12]. Unfortunately none of these monitored changes in the way I desired. I had to know whenever a router or firewall access control list was misconfigured or a host was publicly sharing inappropriate content. I also worried about the scalability of these other solutions, so I decided to tackle the problem myself.

The first issue to come up was speed. Our networks are located worldwide, yet I was provided with only a single U.S.-based host to do the scanning. In many cases, firewalls between the sites slowed the scanning down significantly. Scanning all 100,000 hosts took over 30 hours, which is unacceptable for a daily scan. So I wrote a script called nmap-wrapper which runs dozens of Nmap processes in parallel, reducing the scan time to fifteen hours, even including OS detection.

The next problem was dealing with so much data. A SQL database seemed like the best approach for scalability and data-mining reasons, but I had to abandon that idea due to time pressures. A future version may add this support. Instead, I used a flat file to store the results of each class C address range for each day. The most powerful and extensible way to parse and store this information was the Nmap XML format, but I chose the "grepable" (-oG option) format because it is so easy to parse from simple scripts. Per-host timestamps are also stored for reporting purposes. These have proven quite helpful when administrators try to blame machine or service crashes on the scanner. They cannot credibly claim a service crash at 7:12AM when I have proof that the scan ran at 9:45AM.

The scan produces copious data, with no convenient access method. The standard Unix **diff** tool is not smart enough to report only the changes I care about, so I wrote a Perl script named nmap-diff to provide daily change reports. A typical output report is shown in Example 1.4.

[11] http://www.unspecific.com/nmap/
[12] http://www.securiteam.com/tools/3T5QMQ0NFK.html

Example 1.4. nmap-diff typical output

```
> nmap-diff.pl -c3
  5 IPs showed changes

  10.12.4.8 (ftp-box.foocompany.biz)
        21/tcp    open    ftp
        80/tcp    open    http
       443/tcp    open    https
      1027/tcp    open    IIS
    + 1029/tcp    open    ms-lsa
     38292/tcp    open    landesk-cba
  OS: Microsoft Windows Millennium Edition (Me)
      Windows 2000 Professional or Advanced Server
      or Windows XP

  10.16.234.3 (media.foocompany.biz)
        80/tcp    open    http
    +  554/tcp    open    rtsp
    + 7070/tcp    open    realserver

  192.168.10.186 (testbox.foocompany.biz)
    + 8082/tcp    open    blackice-alerts
  OS: Linux Kernel 2.4.0 - 2.5.20

  172.24.12.58 (mtafoocompany.biz)
    +   25/tcp    open    smtp
  OS: FreeBSD 4.3 - 4.4PRERELEASE

  172.23.76.22 (media2.foocorp.biz)
        80/tcp    open    http
      1027/tcp    open    IIS
    + 1040/tcp    open    netsaint
      1755/tcp    open    wms
      3372/tcp    open    msdtc
      6666/tcp    open    irc-serv
      7007/tcp    open    afs3-bos
  OS: Microsoft Windows Millennium Edition (Me)
      Windows 2000 Professional or Advanced Server
      or Windows XP
```

Management and staff were impressed when I demonstrated this new system at an internal company security symposium. But instead of allowing me to rest on my laurels, they began asking for new features. They wanted counts of mail and web servers, growth estimates, and more. This data was all available from the scans, but was difficult to access. So I created yet another Perl script, nmap-report, which made querying the data much easier. It takes specifications such as open ports or operating systems and finds all the systems that matched on a given day.

One problem with this approach to security monitoring is that employees do not always place services on their IANA-registered official ports. For example, they might put a web server on port 22 (SSH) or vice versa. Just as I was debating how to address this problem, Nmap came out with an advanced service and version detection system (see Chapter 7, *Service and Application Version Detection* [145]). nmap-report now has a rescan feature that uses version scanning to report the true services rather than guessing based on port number. I hope to further integrate version detection in future versions. Example 1.5 shows nmap-report listing FTP servers.

Example 1.5. nmap-report execution

```
> nmap-report -p21 -rV
[...]
172.21.199.76 (ftp1.foocorp.biz)
   21/tcp   open   ssl|ftp Serv-U ftpd 4.0

192.168.12.56 (ftp2.foocorp.biz)
   21/tcp   open   ftp      NcFTPd

 192.168.13.130 (dropbox.foocorp.biz)
   21/tcp   open   ftp      WU-FTPD 6.00LS
```

While being far from perfect, these scripts have proven themselves quite valuable at monitoring large networks for security-impacting changes. Since Nmap itself is open source, it only seemed fair to release my scripts to the public as well. I have made them freely available at *http://www.unspecific.com/nmap*.

1.3. The Phases of an Nmap Scan

Now that we've seen some applications of Nmap, let's look at what happens when an Nmap scan runs. Scans proceed in phases, with each phase finishing before the next one begins. As you can see from the phase descriptions below, there is far more to Nmap than just port scanning.

Target enumeration. In this phase, Nmap researches the host specifiers provided by the user, which may be a combination of host DNS names, IP addresses, CIDR network notations, and more. You can even use (-iR) to ask Nmap to choose your targets for you! Nmap resolves these specifiers into a list of IPv4 or IPv6 addresses for scanning. This phase cannot be skipped since it is essential for further scanning, but you can simplify the processing by passing just IP addresses so Nmap doesn't have to do forward resolution. If you pass the -sL -n options (list scan with no reverse-DNS resolution), Nmap will print out the targets and perform no further scanning. This phase is discussed in Section 3.2, "Specifying Target Hosts and Networks" [47] and Section 3.5.1, "List Scan (-sL)" [57].

Host discovery (ping scanning). Network scans usually begin by discovering which targets on the network are online and thus worth deeper investigation. This process is called *host discovery* or *ping scanning*. Nmap offers many host discovery techniques, ranging from quick ARP requests to elaborate combinations of TCP, ICMP, and other types of probes. This phase is run by default, though you can skip it (simply assume all target IPs are online) using the -PN (no ping) option. To quit after host discovery, specify -sP -n. Host discovery is the subject of Chapter 3 [47].

Reverse-DNS resolution. Once Nmap has determined which hosts to scan, it looks up the reverse-DNS names of all hosts found online by the ping scan. Sometimes a host's name provides clues to its function, and names make reports more readable than providing only IP numbers. This step may be skipped with the -n (no resolution) option, or expanded to cover all target IPs (even down ones) with -R (resolve all). Name resolution is covered in Section 3.4, "DNS Resolution" [56].

Port scanning. This is Nmap's fundamental operation. Probes are sent, and the responses (or non-responses) to those probes are used to classify remote ports into states such as open, closed, or filtered. That

---

brief description doesn't begin to encompass Nmap's many scan types, configurability of scans, and algorithms for improving speed and accuracy. An overview of port scanning is in Chapter 4 [73]. Detailed information on algorithms and command-line options are in Chapter 5 [95]. Port scanning is performed by default, though you can skip it and still perform some of the later traceroute and partial Nmap Scripting Engine phases by specifying their particular command-line options (such as `--traceroute` and `--script`) along with a ping scan (`-sP`).

Version detection. If some ports are found to be open, Nmap may be able to determine what server software is running on the remote system. It does this by sending a variety of probes and matching the responses against a database of thousands of known service signatures. Version detection is enabled by the `-sV` option. It is fully described in Chapter 7 [145].

OS detection. If requested with the `-O` option, Nmap proceeds to OS detection. Different operating systems implement network standards in subtly different ways. By measuring these differences it is often possible to determine the operating system running on a remote host. Nmap matches responses to a standard set of probes against a database of more than a thousand known operating system responses. OS detection is covered in Chapter 8 [171].

Traceroute. Nmap contains an optimized traceroute implementation, enabled by the `--traceroute` option. It can find the network routes to many hosts in parallel, using the best available probe packets as determined by Nmap's previous discovery phases. Traceroute usually involves another round of reverse-DNS resolution for the intermediate hosts. More information is found in Section 15.4, "Host Discovery" [378].

Script scanning. The Nmap Scripting Engine (NSE) uses a collection of special-purpose scripts to gain even more information about remote systems. NSE is powered by the Lua programming language and a standard library designed for network information gathering. Among the facilities offered are advanced version detection, notification of service vulnerabilities, and discovery of backdoors and other malware. NSE is a large subject, fully discussed in Chapter 9 [205]. NSE is not executed unless you request it with options such as `--script` or `-sC`.

Output. Finally, Nmap collects all the information it has gathered and writes it to the screen or to a file. Nmap can write output in several formats. Its default, human-readable format (interactive format) is usually presented in this book. Nmap also offers an XML-based output format, among others. The ins and outs of output are the subject of Chapter 13 [337].

As already discussed, Nmap offers many options for controlling which of these phases are run. For scans of large networks, each phase is repeated many times since Nmap deals with the hosts in smaller groups. It scans each group completely and outputs those results, then moves on to the next batch of hosts.

1.4. Legal Issues

When used properly, Nmap helps protect your network from invaders. But when used improperly, Nmap can (in rare cases) get you sued, fired, expelled, jailed, or banned by your ISP. Reduce your risk by reading this legal guide before launching Nmap.

1.4.1. Is Unauthorized Port Scanning a Crime?

The legal ramifications of scanning networks with Nmap are complex and so controversial that third-party organizations have even printed T-shirts and bumper stickers promulgating opinions on the matter[13], as shown in Figure 1.3. The topic also draws many passionate but often unproductive debates and flame wars. If you ever participate in such discussions, try to avoid the overused and ill-fitting analogies to knocking on someone's home door or testing whether his door and windows are locked.

Figure 1.3. Strong opinions on port scanning legality and morality

While I agree with the sentiment that port scanning *should not* be illegal, it is rarely wise to take legal advice from a T-shirt. Indeed, taking it from a software engineer and author is only slightly better. Speak to a competent lawyer within your jurisdiction for a better understanding of how the law applies to your particular situation. With that important disclaimer out of the way, here is some general information that may prove helpful.

The best way to avoid controversy when using Nmap is to always secure written authorization from the target network representatives before initiating any scanning. There is still a chance that your ISP will give you trouble if they notice it (or if the target administrators accidentally send them an abuse report), but this is usually easy to resolve. When you are performing a penetration test, this authorization should be in the Statement of Work. When testing your own company, make certain that this activity clearly falls within your job description. Security consultants should be familiar with the excellent Open Source Security Testing Methodology Manual (OSSTMM)[14], which provides best practices for these situations.

---

[13]These are from the now-defunct AmericanSushi.Com.

[14] *http://www.osstmm.org/*

While civil and (especially) criminal court cases are the nightmare scenario for Nmap users, these are very rare. After all, no United States federal laws explicitly make port scanning illegal. A much more frequent occurrence is that the target network will notice a scan and send a complaint to the network service provider where the scan initiated (your ISP). Most network administrators do not seem to care or notice the many scans bouncing off their networks daily, but a few complain. The scan source ISP may track down the user corresponding to the reported IP address and time, then chide the user or even kick them off the service. Port scanning without authorization is sometimes against the provider's acceptable use policy (AUP). For example, the AUP for the huge cable-modem ISP Comcast presently says[15]:

> Network probing or port scanning tools are only permitted when used in conjunction with a residential home network, or if explicitly authorized by the destination host and/or network. Unauthorized port scanning, for any reason, is strictly prohibited.

Even if an ISP does not explicitly ban unauthorized port scanning, they might claim that some "anti-hacking" provision applies. Of course this does *not* make port scanning illegal. Many perfectly legal and (in the United States) constitutionally protected activities are banned by ISPs. For example, the AUP quoted above also prohibits users from transmitting, storing, or posting "any information or material which a reasonable person could deem to be objectionable, offensive, indecent, pornographic, ... embarrassing, distressing, vulgar, hateful, racially or ethnically offensive, or otherwise inappropriate, regardless of whether this material or its dissemination is unlawful." In other words, some ISPs ban any behavior that could possibly offend or annoy someone. Indiscriminate scanning of other people's networks/computers does have that potential. If you decide to perform such controversial scanning anyway, never do it from work, school, or any other service provider that has substantial control over your well-being. Use a dialup or commercial broadband provider instead. Losing your DSL connection and having to change providers is a slight nuisance, but it is immeasurably preferable to being expelled or fired.

While legal cases involving port scanning (without follow-up hacking attacks) are rare, they do happen. One of the most notable cases involved a man named Scott Moulton who had an ongoing consulting contract to maintain the Cherokee County, Georgia emergency 911 system. In December 1999, he was tasked with setting up a router connecting the Canton, Georgia Police Department with the E911 Center. Concerned that this might jeopardize the E911 Center security, Scott initiated some preliminary port scanning of the networks involved. In the process he scanned a Cherokee County web server that was owned and maintained by a competing consulting firm named VC3. They noticed the scan and emailed Scott, who replied that he worked for the 911 Center and was testing security. VC3 then reported the activity to the police. Scott lost his E911 maintenance contract and was arrested for allegedly violating the Computer Fraud and Abuse Act of America Section 1030(a)(5)(B)[16]. This act applies against anyone who "intentionally accesses a protected computer without authorization, and as a result of such conduct, causes damage" (and meets other requirements). The damage claimed by VC3 involved time spent investigating the port scan and related activity. Scott sued VC3 for defamation, and VC3 countersued for violation of the Computer Fraud and Abuse Act as well as the Georgia Computer Systems Protection Act.

The civil case against Scott was dismissed before trial, implying a complete lack of merit. The ruling made many Nmap users smile:

> "Court holds that plaintiff's act of conducting an unauthorized port scan and throughput test of defendant's servers does not constitute a violation of either the Georgia Computer

---

[15] *http://www.comcast.net/terms/use.jsp*
[16] *http://www4.law.cornell.edu/uscode/18/1030.html*

Systems Protection Act or the Computer Fraud and Abuse Act."—Civ. Act. No. 1:00-CV-434-TWT (N.D. Ga. November 6, 2000)

This was an exciting victory in the civil case, but Scott still had the criminal charges hanging over his head. Fortunately he kept his spirits high, sending the following note[17] to the *nmap-hackers* mailing list:

> I am proud that I could be of some benefit to the computer society in defending and protecting the rights of specialists in the computer field, however it is EXTREMELY costly to support such an effort, of which I am not happy about. But I will continue to fight and prove that there is nothing illegal about port scanning especially when I was just doing my job.

Eventually, the criminal court came to the same conclusion and all charges were dropped. While Scott was vindicated in the end, he suffered six-figure legal bills and endured stressful years battling through the court system. The silver lining is that after spending so much time educating his lawyers about the technical issues involved, Scott started a successful forensics services company[18].

While the Moulton case sets a good example (if not legal precedent), different courts or situations could still lead to worse outcomes. Remember that many states have their own computer abuse laws, some of which can arguably make even pinging a remote machine without authorization illegal[19].

Laws in other nations obviously differ as well. For example, A 17-year-old youth was convicted in Finland[20] of attempted computer intrusion for simply port scanning a bank. He was fined to cover the target's investigation expenses. The Moulton ruling might have differed if the VC3 machine had actually crashed and they were able to justify the $5,000 damage figure required by the act.

At the other extreme, an Israeli judge acquitted[21] Avi Mizrahi in early 2004 for vulnerability scanning the Mossad secret service. Judge Abraham Tennenbaum even praised Avi as follows:

> In a way, Internet surfers who check the vulnerabilities of Web sites are acting in the public good. If their intentions are not malicious and they do not cause any damage, they should even be praised.

In 2007 and 2008, broad new cybercrime laws took effect in Germany[22] and England[23]. These laws are meant to ban the distribution, use, and even possession of "hacking tools". For example, the UK amendment to the Computer Misuse Act makes it illegal to "supply or offer to supply, believing that it is likely to be used to commit, or to assist in the commission of [a Computer Misuse Act violation]". These laws have already led some security tool authors to close shop or move their projects to other countries. The problem is that most security tools can be used by both ethical professionals (white-hats) to defend their networks and black-hats to attack. These dangerous laws are based on the tool author or user's intent, which is subjective and hard to divine. Nmap was designed to help secure the Internet, but I'd hate to be arrested and forced to defend my intentions to a judge and jury. These laws are unlikely to affect tools as widespread and popular

---

[17] *http://seclists.org/nmap-hackers/2001/0026.html*

[18] *http://www.forensicstrategy.com/*

[19] An excellent paper on this topic by lawyer Ethan Preston is available at *http://grove.ufl.edu/~techlaw/vol6/issue1/preston.html*. He has also written an excellent paper relating to the legal risks of publishing security information and exploits at *http://www.mcandl.com/computer-security.html*.

[20] *http://insecure.org/stf/fin.html*

[21] *http://www.theregister.co.uk/2004/03/01/mossad_website_hacker_walks_free/*

[22] *http://www.beskerming.com/commentary/2007/08/12/249/German_Security_Professionals_in_the_Mist*

[23] *http://www.theregister.co.uk/2008/01/02/hacker_toll_ban_guidance/*

as Nmap, but they have had a chilling effect on smaller tools and those which are more commonly abused by computer criminals (such as exploitation frameworks).

Regardless of the legal status of port scanning, ISP accounts will continue to be terminated if many complaints are generated. The best way to avoid ISP abuse reports or civil/criminal charges is to avoid annoying the target network administrators in the first place. Here are some practical suggestions:

- Probably at least 90% of network scanning is non-controversial. You are rarely badgered for scanning your own machine or the networks you administer. The controversy comes when scanning other networks. There are many reasons (good and bad) for doing this sort of network exploration. Perhaps you are scanning the other systems in your dorm or department to look for publicly shared files (FTP, SMB, WWW, etc.). Or maybe you are just trying to find the IP of a certain printer. You might have scanned your favorite web site to see if they are offering any other services, or because you were curious what OS they run. Perhaps you are just trying to test connectivity, or maybe you wanted to do a quick security sanity check before handing off your credit card details to that e-commerce company. You might be conducting Internet research. Or are you performing initial reconnaissance in preparation for a break-in attempt? The remote administrators rarely know your true intentions, and do sometimes get suspicious. The best approach is to get permission first. I have seen a few people with non-administrative roles land in hot water after deciding to "prove" network insecurity by launching an intrusive scan of the entire company or campus. Administrators tend to be more cooperative when asked in advance than when woken up at 3AM by an IDS alarm claiming they are under massive attack. So whenever possible, obtain written authorization before scanning a network. Adrian Lamo would probably have avoided jail if he had asked the New York Times to test their security rather than telling reporters about the flaws afterward. Unfortunately they would likely have said no. Be prepared for this answer.

- Target your scan as tightly as possible. Any machine connected to the Internet is scanned regularly enough that most administrators ignore such Internet white noise. But scanning enough networks or executing very noisy/intrusive scans increases the probability of generating complaints. So if you are only looking for web servers, specify -p80 rather than scanning all 65,536 TCP ports on each machine. If you are only trying to find available hosts, do an Nmap ping scan rather than full port scan. Do not scan a CIDR /16 (65K hosts) when a /24 netblock suffices. The random scan mode now takes an argument specifying the number of hosts, rather than running forever. So consider -iR 1000 rather than -iR 10000 if the former is sufficient. Use the default timing (or even -T polite) rather than -T insane. Avoid noisy and relatively intrusive scans such as version detection (-sV). Similarly, a SYN scan (-sS) is quieter than a connect scan (-sT) while providing the same information and often being faster.

- As noted previously, do not do anything controversial from your work or school connections. Even though your intentions may be good, you have too much to lose if someone in power (e.g. boss, dean) decides you are a malicious cracker. Do you really want to explain your actions to someone who may not even understand the terms packet or port scanner? Spend $40 a month for a dialup, shell, or residential broadband account. Not only are the repercussions less severe if you offend someone from such an account, but target network administrators are less likely to even bother complaining to mass-market providers. Also read the relevant AUP and choose a provider accordingly. If your provider (like Comcast discussed above) bans any unauthorized port scanning and posting of "offensive" material, do not be surprised if you are kicked off for this activity. In general, the more you pay to a service provider the more accommodating they are. A T1 provider is highly unlikely to yank your connection without notice because someone reported being port scanned. A dialup or residential DSL/cable provider very well might. This can happen even when the scan was forged by someone else.

- Nmap offers many options for stealthy scans, including source-IP spoofing, decoy scanning, and the more recent idle scan technique. These are discussed in the IDS evasion chapter. But remember that there is always a trade-off. You are harder to find if you launch scans from an open WAP far from your house, with 17 decoys, while doing subsequent probes through a chain of nine open proxies. But if anyone does track you down, they will be mighty suspicious of your intentions.

- Always have a legitimate reason for performing scans. An offended administrator might write to you first (or your ISP might forward his complaint to you) expecting some sort of justification for the activity. In the Scott Moulton case discussed above, VC3 first emailed Scott to ask what was going on. If they had been satisfied with his answer, matters might have stopped there rather than escalating into civil and criminal litigation. Groups scanning large portions of the Internet for research purposes often use a reverse-DNS name that describes their project and run a web server with detailed information and opt-out forms.

Also remember that ancillary and subsequent actions are often used as evidence of intent. A port scan by itself does not always signify an attack. A port scan followed closely by an IIS exploit, however, broadcasts the intention loud and clear. This is important because decisions to prosecute (or fire, expel, complain, etc.) are often based on the whole event and not just one component (such as a port scan).

One dramatic case involved a Canadian man named Walter Nowakowski, who was apparently the first person to be charged in Canada with theft of communications (Canadian Criminal Code Section S.342.1) for accessing the Internet through someone's unsecured Wi-Fi network. Thousands of Canadian "war drivers" do this every day, so why was he singled out? Because of ancillary actions and intent. He was allegedly caught[24] driving the wrong way on a one-way street, naked from the waist down, with laptop in hand, while downloading child pornography through the aforementioned unsecured wireless access point. The police apparently considered his activity egregious enough that they brainstormed for relevant charges and tacked on theft of communications to the many child pornography-related charges.

Similarly, charges involving port scanning are usually reserved for the most egregious cases. Even when paranoid administrators notify the police that they have been scanned, prosecution (or any further action) is exceedingly rare. The fact that a 911 emergency service was involved is likely what motivated prosecutors in the Moulton case. Your author has scanned hundreds of thousands of Internet hosts while writing this book and received no complaints.

To summarize this whole section, the question of whether port scanning is legal does not have a simple answer. I cannot unequivocally say "port scanning is never a crime", as much as I would like to. Laws differ dramatically between jurisdictions, and cases hinge on their particular details. Even when facts are nearly identical, different judges and prosecutors do not always interpret them the same way. I can only urge caution and reiterate the suggestions above.

For testing purposes, you have permission to scan the host `scanme.nmap.org`. You may have noticed that it was used in several examples already. Note that this permission only includes scanning via Nmap and not testing exploits or denial of service attacks. To conserve bandwidth, please do not initiate more than a dozen scans against that host per day. If this free scanning target service is abused, it will be taken down and Nmap will report `Failed to resolve given hostname/IP: scanme.nmap.org`.

---

[24] *http://www.ctv.ca/servlet/ArticleNews/story/CTVNews/1069439746264_64848946/*

1.4.2. Can Port Scanning Crash the Target Computer/Networks?

Nmap does not have any features designed to crash target networks. It usually tries to tread lightly. For example, Nmap detects dropped packets and slows down when they occur in order to avoid overloading the network. Nmap also does not send any corrupt packets. The IP, TCP, UDP, and ICMP headers are always appropriate, though the destination host is not necessarily expecting the packets. For these reasons, no application, host, or network component *should* ever crash based on an Nmap scan. If they do, that is a bug in the system which should be repaired by the vendor.

Reports of systems being crashed by Nmap are rare, but they do happen. Many of these systems were probably unstable in the first place and Nmap either pushed them over the top or they crashed at the same time as an Nmap scan by pure coincidence. In other cases, poorly written applications, TCP/IP stacks, and even operating systems have been demonstrated to crash reproducibly given a certain Nmap command. These are usually older legacy devices, as newer equipment is rarely released with these problems. Smart companies use Nmap and many other common network tools to test devices prior to shipment. Those who omit such pre-release testing often find out about the problem in early beta tests when a box is first deployed on the Internet. It rarely takes long for a given IP to be scanned as part of Internet white noise. Keeping systems and devices up-to-date with the latest vendor patches and firmware should reduce the susceptibility of your machines to these problems, while also improving the security and usability of your network.

In many cases, finding that a machine crashes from a certain scan is valuable information. After all, attackers can do anything Nmap can do by using Nmap itself or their own custom scripts. Devices should not crash from being scanned and if they do, vendors should be pressured to provide a patch. In some usage scenarios, detecting fragile machines by crashing them is undesirable. In those cases you may want to perform very light scanning to reduce the risk of adverse effects. Here are a few suggestions:

- Use SYN scan (-sS) instead of connect scan (-sT). User-mode applications such as web servers can rarely even detect the former because it is all handled in kernel space (some older Linux kernels are an exception) and thus the services have no excuse to crash.

- Version scanning (-sV) risks crashing poorly written applications. Similarly, some pathetic operating systems have been reported to crash when OS fingerprinted (-O). Omit these options for particularly sensitive environments or where you do not need the results.

- Using -T2 or slower (-T1, -T0) timing modes can reduce the chances that a port scan will harm a system, though they slow your scan dramatically. Older Linux boxes had an identd daemon that would block services temporarily if they were accessed too frequently. This could happen in a port scan, as well as during legitimate high-load situations. Slower timing might help here. These slow timing modes should only be used as a last resort as they can slow scans by an order of magnitude or more.

- Limit the number of ports and machines scanned to the fewest that are required. Every machine scanned has a minuscule chance of crashing, and so cutting the number of machines down improves your odds. Reducing the number of ports scanned reduces the risks to end hosts as well as network devices. Many NAT/firewall devices keep a state entry for every port probe. Most of them expire old entries when the table fills up, but occasional (pathetic) implementations crash instead. Reducing the ports/hosts scanned reduces the number of state entries and thus might help those sorry devices stay up.

1.4.3. Nmap Copyright

While Nmap is open source, it still has a copyright license that must be respected. As free software, Nmap also carries no warranty. These issues are covered in much greater detail in Section 15.19, "Legal Notices" [412]. Companies wishing to bundle and use Nmap within proprietary software and appliances are especially encouraged to read this section so they don't inadvertently violate the Nmap license. Fortunately the Nmap Project sells commercial redistribution licenses for companies which need one.

1.5. The History and Future of Nmap

Many ancient and well loved security tools, such as Netcat, tcpdump, and John the Ripper, haven't changed much over the years. Others, including Nessus, Wireshark, Cain and Abel, and Snort have been under constant development since the day they were released. Nmap is in that second category. It was released as a simple Linux-only port scanner in 1997. Over the next 10+ years it sprouted a myriad of valuable features, including OS detection, version detection, the Nmap Scripting Engine, a Windows port, a graphical user interface, and more. This section provides a timeline of the most important events over a decade of Nmap history, followed by brief predictions on the future of Nmap. For all significant Nmap changes (thousands of them), read the Nmap Changelog[25]. Old releases of Nmap can be found at *http://nmap.org/dist/*, and ancient versions at *http://nmap.org/dist-old/*.

- **September 1, 1997** — Nmap is first released in *Phrack* Magazine Issue 51, article 11[26]. It doesn't have a version number because new releases aren't planned. Nmap is about 2,000 lines long, and compilation is as simple as **gcc -O6 -o nmap nmap.c -lm**.

- **September 5, 1997** — Due to popular demand, a slightly modified version of the *Phrack* code is released, calling itself version 1.25. The gzipped tarball is 28KB. Version 1.26 (48KB) is released 19 days later.

- **January 11, 1998** — Insecure.Org is registered and Nmap moves there from its previous home at the DataHaven Project[27] ISP.

- **March 14, 1998** — Renaud Deraison writes to inform me that he is writing a security scanner, and asks if he can use some Nmap source code. Of course I say yes. Nine days later he sends me a pre-release version of Nessus, noting that it "is designed for sysadmins, not 3l33t H4ck3rZ".

- **September 1, 1998** — Inspired by Nmap's first anniversary, I begin work on adding remote OS detection for the upcoming Nmap 2.00. On October 7 I release the first private beta version to a handful of top Nmap developers. We quietly work on this for several months.

- **December 12, 1998** — Nmap version 2.00 is publicly released, introducing Nmap OS detection for the first time. An article describing the techniques was released in *Phrack* 54, Article 9[28]. By this point Nmap is broken up into many files, consists of about 8,000 lines of code, is kept in a private CVS revision control system, and the tarball size is 275KB. The *nmap-hackers* mailing list is started, and later grows to more than 55,000 members.

---

[25] *http://nmap.org/changelog.html*
[26] *http://nmap.org/p51-11.html*
[27] *http://www.dhp.com*
[28] *http://nmap.org/phrack54-09.txt*

- **April 11, 1999** — Nmap 2.11BETA1 is released. This is the first version to contain a graphical user interface as an alternative to the traditional command-line usage. The bundled Unix-only GUI named NmapFE was originally written by Zach Smith. Some people like it, but most prefer command-line execution.

- **April 28, 2000** — Nmap 2.50 is released[29]. By this point the tarball has grown to 461KB. This release includes timing modes such as `-T aggressive`, direct SunRPC scanning, and Window and ACK scan methods.

- **May 28, 2000** — Gerhard Rieger sends a message[30] to the *nmap-dev* list describing a new "protocol scan" he has developed for Nmap, and he even includes a patch. This is so cool that I release[31] Nmap 2.54BETA1 with his patch less than 12 hours later.

- **December 7, 2000** — Nmap 2.54BETA16 is released[32] as the first official version to compile and run on Microsoft Windows. The Windows porting work was done by Ryan Permeh and Andy Lutomirski.

- **July 9, 2001** — The Nmap IP ID idle scan is introduced with Nmap 2.54BETA26. A paper describing the technique is released concurrently. This extremely cool (though not always practical) scan technique is described in Section 5.10, "TCP Idle Scan (-sI)" [117].

- **July 25, 2002** — I quit my job at Netscape/AOL and start my dream job working on Nmap full time.

- **July 31, 2002** — Nmap 3.00 is released[33]. The tarball is 922K. This release includes Mac OS X support, XML output, and uptime detection.

- **August 28, 2002** — Nmap is converted from C to C++ and IPv6 supported is added as part of the Nmap 3.10ALPHA1 release[34].

- **May 15, 2003** — Nmap is featured in the movie *The Matrix Reloaded*, where Trinity uses it (followed by a real SSH exploit) to hack a power station and save the world. This leads to more publicity for Nmap than it had ever seen before or has seen since then. Details and screen shots are available at *http://nmap.org/movies.html*.

- **July 21, 2003** — I finish a first implementation of Nmap service/version detection (Chapter 7, *Service and Application Version Detection* [145]) and release it to a couple dozen top Nmap developers and users as Nmap 3.40PVT1. That is followed up by 16 more private releases over the next couple months as we improve the system and add signatures.

- **September 16, 2003** — Nmap service detection is finally released[35] publicly as part of Nmap 3.45. A detailed paper is released concurrently.

- **February 20, 2004** — Nmap 3.50 is released[36]. The tarball is now 1,571KB. SCO Corporation is banned from redistributing Nmap because they refuse to comply with the GPL. They have to rebuild their Caldera

---

[29] *http://seclists.org/nmap-hackers/2000/0140.html*
[30] *http://seclists.org/nmap-hackers/2000/0217.html*
[31] *http://seclists.org/nmap-hackers/2000/0219.html*
[32] *http://seclists.org/nmap-dev/2000/q4/0013.html*
[33] *http://insecure.org/stf/Nmap-3.00-Release.html*
[34] *http://seclists.org/nmap-dev/2002/q3/0041.html*
[35] *http://seclists.org/nmap-hackers/2003/0030.html*
[36] *http://insecure.org/stf/Nmap-3.50-Release.html*

release ISOs to remove Nmap. This release includes the packet tracing and UDP ping options. It also includes the OS classification system which classifies each of the hundreds of detected operating systems by vendor name, operating system name, OS generation, and device type.

- **August 31, 2004** — The core Nmap port scanning engine is rewritten for Nmap 3.70[37]. The new engine, named `ultra_scan` features dramatically improved algorithms and parallelization support to improve both accuracy and speed. The differences are particularly dramatic for hosts behind strict firewalls.

- **June 25, 2005** — Google sponsors 10 college and graduate students to work on Nmap full time for the summer as part of Google's Summer of Code[38] initiative. Projects include a second generation OS detection system (Zhao Lei), a new cross-platform GUI named Umit (Adriano Monteiro Marques), and many other cool projects described at *http://seclists.org/nmap-hackers/2005/0008.html*.

- **September 8, 2005** — Nmap gains raw ethernet frame sending support with the release of version 3.90[39]. This allows for ARP scanning (see Section 3.6.6, "ARP Scan (-PR)" [64]) and MAC address spoofing as well as evading the raw IP packet ban introduced by Microsoft in Windows XP SP2.

- **January 31, 2006** — Nmap 4.00 is released[40]. The tarball is now 2,388KB. This release includes runtime interaction to provide on-demand completion estimates, a Windows executable installer, NmapFE updates to support GTK2, and much more.

- **May 24, 2006** — Google sponsors 10 more Nmap summer developers as part of their SoC program. Zhao and Adriano return as part of 2006 SoC to further develop their respective projects. Diman Todorov is sponsored to help develop the Nmap Scripting Engines. These and seven other talented students and their projects are described at *http://seclists.org/nmap-hackers/2006/0009.html*.

- **June 24, 2006** — After two years of development and testing, the 2nd generation OS detection system is integrated into Nmap 4.20ALPHA1[41]. This new system is based on everything we've learned and the new ideas we've conceived since the 1st generation system debuted 8 years earlier. After a bit of time to grow the DB, the new system proves much more accurate and granular than the old one. It is described in Chapter 8, *Remote OS Detection* [171].

- **December 10, 2006** — The Nmap Scripting Engine is released[42] as part of Nmap 4.21ALPHA1. NSE allows users to write (and share) simple scripts to automate a wide variety of networking tasks. The system is a huge success, and is described in Chapter 9, *Nmap Scripting Engine* [205].

- **December 20, 2006** — Nmap's Subversion source code repository opens to the public[43]. Until this time, only a handful of developers had access to the private source repository. Everyone else had to wait for releases. Now everyone can follow Nmap development day by day. There is even an `nmap-svn` mailing list providing real-time change notification by email. Details are provided in Section 2.1.5, "Obtaining Nmap from the Subversion (SVN) Repository" [28].

---

[37] *http://seclists.org/nmap-hackers/2004/0010.html*

[38] *http://code.google.com/soc*

[39] *http://seclists.org/nmap-hackers/2005/0012.html*

[40] *http://insecure.org/stf/Nmap-4.00-Release.html*

[41] *http://seclists.org/nmap-dev/2006/q2/0444.html*

[42] *http://seclists.org/nmap-dev/2006/q4/0184.html*

[43] *http://seclists.org/nmap-dev/2006/q4/0253.html*

- **May 28, 2007** — Google sponsors six summer Nmap developers as part of their SoC program. Meanwhile, Adriano's Umit GUI for Nmap is approved as an independent program for SoC sponsorship. Among the sponsored students was David Fifield, who continued long after the summer ended and became one of Nmap's top developers. The Nmap students and their projects are listed at *http://seclists.org/nmap-hackers/2007/0003.html.*

- **June 27, 2007** — *Die Hard 4: Live Free or Die Hard* is released in theaters. It includes a brief scene of hacker Matthew Farrell (Justin Long) demonstrating his Nmap skills. Then he leaves his computer to join Bruce Willis in fighting a diabolical terrorist mastermind. One week later, *The Bourne Ultimatum* is released and also contains an Nmap scene! The CIA uses Nmap in this movie to hack a newspaper's mail server and read the email of a reporter they assassinated (nice guys)! Screen shots of Nmap movie cameos are all available on the Nmap movies page[44].

- **July 8, 2007** — The Umit graphical front end is improved and integrated into the Nmap 4.22SOC1 release[45] for testing. Umit is later renamed to Zenmap, and the venerable NmapFE GUI is removed. Zenmap is covered in Chapter 12, *Zenmap GUI Users' Guide* [307].

- **December 13, 2007** — Nmap 4.50 is released[46] to celebrate Nmap's 10th anniversary!

- **June 1, 2008** — Nmap 4.65 is released[47] and includes, for the first time, an executable Mac OS X installer. The Nmap source tarball is now four megabytes. This release includes 41 NSE scripts, 1,307 OS fingerprints, and 4,706 version detection signatures.

- **August 18, 2008** — The Nmap project completes its fourth Summer of Code, with our highest success percentage ever (six out of seven sponsored students). They greatly improved Zenmap, the Nmap Scripting Engine, OS detection, and Ncat, as described at *http://seclists.org/nmap-dev/2008/q4/0193.html.*

- **September 8, 2008** — Nmap 4.75 is released[48] with almost 100 significant improvements over 4.68. These include the Zenmap network topology and scan aggregation features (see Chapter 12, *Zenmap GUI Users' Guide* [307]). It also includes port-frequency data from my Worldscan project, which I presented[49] at Black Hat and Defcon in August.

While it is easy to catalogue the history of Nmap, the future is uncertain. Nmap didn't start off with any grand development plan, and most of the milestones in the preceding timeline were not planned more than a year in advance. Instead of trying to predict the shape of the Internet and networking way out in the future, I closely study where it is now and decide what will be most useful for Nmap now and in the near future. So I have no idea where Nmap will be 10 years from now, though I expect it to be as popular and vibrant as ever. The Nmap community is large enough that we will be able to guide Nmap wherever it needs to go. Nmap has faced curve balls before, such as the sudden removal of raw packet support in Windows XP SP2, dramatic changes in network filtering practices and technology, and the slow emergence of IPv6. Each of those required significant changes to Nmap, and we'll have to do the same to embrace or at least cope with networking changes in the future.

---

[44] *http://nmap.org/movies.html*

[45] *http://seclists.org/nmap-dev/2007/q3/0030.html*

[46] *http://insecure.org/stf/Nmap-4.50-Release.html*

[47] *http://seclists.org/nmap-dev/2008/q2/0558.html*

[48] *http://seclists.org/nmap-hackers/2008/0004.html*

[49] *http://insecure.org/presentations/*

While the 10-year plan is up in the air, the coming year is easier to predict. As exciting as big new features are, they won't be a focus. None of us want to see Nmap get bloated and disorganized. So this will be a year of consolidation. The Zenmap and NSE systems are not as mature as the rest of Nmap, so improving these is a big priority. New NSE scripts are great because they extend Nmap's functionality without the stability risks of incorporating new source code into Nmap proper. Meanwhile, Zenmap needs usability and stability improvements, as well as better results visualization. Another focus is the Nmap web site, which will become more useful and dynamic. A web discussion system, Nmap demo site, and wiki are planned.

Nmap may also grow in its ability to handle web scanning. When Nmap was first developed, different services were often provided as separate daemons identified by the port number they listen on. Now, many new services simply run over HTTP and are identified by a URL path name rather than port number. Scanning for known URL paths is similar in many ways to port scanning (and to the SunRPC scanning which Nmap has also done for many years). Nmap already does some web scanning using the Nmap Scripting Engine (see Chapter 9, *Nmap Scripting Engine* [205]), but it would be faster and more efficient if basic support was built into Nmap itself.

Some of the coolest Nmap features in the past, such as OS detection and version scanning, were developed in secret and given a surprise release. You can expect more of these in coming years because they are so much fun!

Chapter 2. Obtaining, Compiling, Installing, and Removing Nmap

2.1. Introduction

Nmap can often be installed or upgraded with a single command, so don't let the length of this chapter scare you. Most readers will use the table of contents to skip directly to sections that concern them. This chapter describes how to install Nmap on many platforms, including both source code compilation and binary installation methods. Graphical and command-line versions of Nmap are described and contrasted. Nmap removal instructions are also provided in case you change your mind.

2.1.1. Testing Whether Nmap is Already Installed

The first step toward obtaining Nmap is to check whether you already have it. Many free operating system distributions (including most Linux and BSD systems) come with Nmap packages, although they may not be installed by default. On Unix systems, open a terminal window and try executing the command **nmap --version**. If Nmap exists and is in your PATH, you should see output similar to that in Example 2.1.

Example 2.1. Checking for Nmap and determining its version number

```
felix~>nmap --version

Nmap version 4.76 ( http://nmap.org )
felix~>
```

If Nmap does *not* exist on the system (or if your PATH is incorrectly set), an error message such as nmap: Command not found is reported. As the example above shows, Nmap responds to the command by printing its version number (here 4.76).

Even if your system already has a copy of Nmap, you should consider upgrading to the latest version available from *http://nmap.org/download.html*. Newer versions often run faster, fix important bugs, and feature updated operating system and service version detection databases. A list of changes since the version already on your system can be found at *http://nmap.org/changelog.html*. Nmap output examples in this book may not match the output produced by older versions.

2.1.2. Command-line and Graphical Interfaces

Nmap has traditionally been a command-line tool run from a Unix shell or (more recently) Windows command prompt. This allows experts to quickly execute a command that does exactly what they want without having to maneuver through a bunch of configuration panels and scattered option fields. This also makes Nmap easier to script and enables easy sharing of useful commands among the user community.

One downside of the command-line approach is that it can be intimidating for new and infrequent users. Nmap offers more than a hundred command-line options, although many are obscure features or debugging controls that most users can ignore. Many graphical frontends have been created for those users who prefer

---

a GUI interface. Nmap has traditionally included a simple GUI for Unix named NmapFE, but that was replaced in 2007 by Zenmap, which we have been developing since 2005. Zenmap is far more powerful and effective than NmapFE, particularly in results viewing. Zenmap's tab-based interface lets you search and sort results, and also browse them in several ways (host details, raw Nmap output, and ports/hosts). It works on Linux, Windows, Mac OS X, and other platforms. Zenmap is covered in depth in Chapter 12, *Zenmap GUI Users' Guide* [307]. The rest of this book focuses on command-line Nmap invocations. Once you understand how the command-line options work and can interpret the output, using Zenmap or the other available Nmap GUIs is easy. Nmap's options work the same way whether you choose them from radio buttons and menus or type them at a command-line.

2.1.3. Downloading Nmap

Nmap.Org is the official source for downloading Nmap source code and binaries for Nmap and Zenmap. Source code is distributed in bzip2 and gzip compressed tar files, and binaries are available for Linux (RPM format), Windows (NSIS executable installer) and Mac OS X (.dmg disk image). Find all of this at *http://nmap.org/download.html*.

2.1.4. Verifying the Integrity of Nmap Downloads

It often pays to be paranoid about the integrity of files downloaded from the Internet. Popular packages such as Sendmail (example[1]), OpenSSH (example[2]), tcpdump, Libpcap, BitchX, Fragrouter, and many others have been infected with malicious trojans. Software distributions sites at the Free Software Foundation, Debian, and SourceForge have also been successfully compromised. This has never happened to Nmap, but one should always be careful. To verify the authenticity of an Nmap release, consult the PGP detached signatures or cryptographic hashes (including SHA1 and MD5) posted for the release in the Nmap signatures directory at *http://nmap.org/dist/sigs/?C=M&O=D*.

The most secure verification mechanism is detached PGP signatures. As the signing key is never stored on production servers, even someone who successfully compromises the web server couldn't forge and properly sign a trojan release. While numerous applications are able to verify PGP signatures, I recommend GNU Privacy Guard (GPG)[3].

Nmap releases are signed with a special Nmap Project Signing Key, which can be obtained from the major keyservers or *http://nmap.org/data/nmap_gpgkeys.txt*. My key is included in that file too. The keys can be imported with the command **gpg --import nmap_gpgkeys.txt**. You only need to do this once, then you can verify all future Nmap releases from that machine. Before trusting the keys, verify that the fingerprints match the values shown in Example 2.2.

---

[1] *http://cert.org/advisories/CA-2002-28.html*
[2] *http://cert.org/advisories/CA-2002-24.html*
[3] *http://www.gnupg.org/*

Example 2.2. Verifying the Nmap and Fyodor PGP Key Fingerprints

```
flog~> gpg --fingerprint nmap fyodor
pub 1024D/33599B5F 2005-04-24
    Key fingerprint = BB61 D057 C0D7 DCEF E730 996C 1AF6 EC50 3359 9B5F
uid                  Fyodor <fyodor@insecure.org>
sub 2048g/D3C2241C 2005-04-24

pub 1024D/6B9355D0 2005-04-24
    Key fingerprint = 436D 66AB 9A79 8425 FDA0 E3F8 01AF 9F03 6B93 55D0
uid                  Nmap Project Signing Key (http://insecure.org/)
sub 2048g/A50A6A94 2005-04-24
```

For every Nmap package download file (e.g. `nmap-4.76.tar.bz2` and `nmap-4.76-win32.zip`), there is a corresponding file in the `sigs` directory with `.gpg.txt` appended to the name (e.g. `nmap-4.76.tar.bz2.gpg.txt`). This is the detached signature file.

With the proper PGP key in your keyring and the detached signature file downloaded, verifying an Nmap release takes a single GPG command, as shown in Example 2.3. If the file has been tampered with, the results will look like Example 2.4.

Example 2.3. Verifying PGP key fingerprints (Successful)

```
flog> gpg --verify nmap-4.76.tar.bz2.gpg.txt  nmap-4.76.tar.bz2
gpg: Signature made Fri 12 Sep 2008 02:03:59 AM PDT using DSA key ID 6B9355D0
gpg: Good signature from "Nmap Project Signing Key (http://www.insecure.org/)"
```

Example 2.4. Detecting a bogus file

```
flog> gpg --verify nmap-4.76.tar.bz2.gpg.txt nmap-4.76-hacked.tar.bz2
gpg: Signature made Fri 12 Sep 2008 02:03:59 AM PDT using DSA key ID 6B9355D0
gpg: BAD signature from "Nmap Project Signing Key (http://www.insecure.org/)"
```

While PGP signatures are the recommended validation technique, SHA1 and MD5 (among other) hashes are made available for more casual validation. An attacker who can manipulate your Internet traffic in real time (and is extremely skilled) or who compromises Nmap.Org and replaces both the distribution file and digest file, could defeat this test. However, it can be useful to check the authoritative Nmap.Org hashes if you obtain Nmap from a third party or feel it might have been accidentally corrupted. For every Nmap package download file, there is a corresponding file in the `sigs` directory with `.digest.txt` appended to the name (e.g. `nmap-4.76.tar.bz2.digest.txt`). An example is shown in Example 2.5. This is the detached signature file. The hashes from the digest file can be verified using common tools such as sha1sum, md5sum, or gpg, as shown in Example 2.6, "Verifying Nmap hashes" [28].

Example 2.5. A typical Nmap release digest file

```
flog> cat sigs/nmap-4.76.tgz.digest.txt
nmap-4.76.tgz:    MD5 = 54 B5 C9 E3 F4 4C 1A DD  E1 7D F6 81 70 EB 7C FE
nmap-4.76.tgz:   SHA1 = 4374 CF9C A882 2C28 5DE9  D00E 8F67 06D0 BCFA A403
nmap-4.76.tgz: RMD160 = AE7B 80EF 4CE6 DBAA 6E65  76F9 CA38 4A22 3B89 BD3A
nmap-4.76.tgz: SHA224 = 524D479E 717D98D0 2FB0A42B 9A4E6E52 4027C9B6 1D843F95
                        D419F87F
nmap-4.76.tgz: SHA256 = 0E960E05 53EB7647 0C8517A0 038092A3 969DB65C BE23C03F
                        D6DAEF1A CDCC9658
nmap-4.76.tgz: SHA384 = D52917FD 9EE6EE62 F5F456BF E245675D B6EEEBC5 0A287B27
                        3CAA4F50 B171DC23 FE7808A8 C5E3A49A 4A78ACBE A5AEED33
nmap-4.76.tgz: SHA512 = 826CD89F 7930A765 C9FE9B41 1DAFD113 2C883857 2A3A9503
                        E4C1E690 20A37FC8 37564DC3 45FF0C97 EF45ABE6 6CEA49FF
                        E262B403 A52F4ECE C23333A0 48DEDA66
```

Example 2.6. Verifying Nmap hashes

```
flog> sha1sum nmap-4.76.tgz
4374cf9ca8822c285de9d00e8f6706d0bcfaa403  nmap-4.76.tgz
flog> md5sum nmap-4.76.tgz
54b5c9e3f44c1adde17df68170eb7cfe  nmap-4.76.tgz
flog> gpg --print-md sha1 nmap-4.76.tgz
nmap-4.76.tgz: 4374 CF9C A882 2C28 5DE9  D00E 8F67 06D0 BCFA A403
```

While releases from Nmap.Org are signed as described in this section, certain Nmap add-ons, interfaces, and platform-specific binaries are developed and distributed by other parties. They have different mechanisms for establishing the authenticity of their downloads.

2.1.5. Obtaining Nmap from the Subversion (SVN) Repository

In addition to regular stable and development releases, the latest Nmap source code is always available using the Subversion (SVN) revision control system[4]. This delivers new features and version/OS detection database updates immediately as they are developed. The downside is that SVN head revisions aren't always as stable as official releases. So SVN is most useful for Nmap developers and users who need a fix which hasn't yet been formally released.

SVN write access is strictly limited to top Nmap developers, but everyone has read access to the repository. Check out the latest code using the command **svn co --username guest --password ""** **svn://svn.insecure.org/nmap/**. Then you can later update your source code by typing **svn up** in your working directory. The "guest" username is required due to an svnserve authorization bug.

While most users only follow the /nmap directory in svn (which pulls in /nbase, /nsock, and /zenmap on its own), there is one other interesting directory: /nmap-exp. This directory contains *experimental* Nmap branches which Nmap developers create when they wish to try new things without destabilizing Nmap proper. When developers feel that an experimental branch is ready for wider-scale testing, they will generally email the location to the *nmap-dev* mailing list.

---

[4] *http://subversion.tigris.org*

Once Nmap is checked out, you can build it from source code just as you would with the Nmap tarball (described later in this chapter).

If you would like real-time (or digested) notification and diffs by email when any changes are made to Nmap, sign up for the nmap-svn mailing list at *http://cgi.insecure.org/mailman/listinfo/nmap-svn*.

2.2. Unix Compilation and Installation from Source Code

While binary packages (discussed in later sections) are available for most platforms, compilation and installation from source code is the traditional and most powerful way to install Nmap. This ensures that the latest version is available and allows Nmap to adapt to the library availability and directory structure of your system. For example, Nmap uses the OpenSSL cryptography libraries for version detection when available, but most binary packages do not include this functionality. On the other hand, binary packages are generally quicker and easier to install, and allow for consistent management (installation, removal, upgrading, etc.) of all packaged software on the system.

Source installation is usually a painless process—the build system is designed to auto-detect as much as possible. Here are the steps required for a default install:

1. Download the latest version of Nmap in .tar.bz2 (bzip2 compression) or .tgz (gzip compression) format from *http://nmap.org/download.html*.

2. Decompress the downloaded tarball with a command such as:

   bzip2 -cd nmap-<VERSION>.tar.bz2 | tar xvf -

   With GNU tar, the simpler command **tar xvjf nmap-<VERSION>.tar.bz2** does the trick. If you downloaded the .tgz version, replace bzip2 with gzip in the decompression command.

3. Change into the newly created directory: **cd nmap-<VERSION>**

4. Configure the build system: **./configure**

   If the configuration succeeds, an ASCII art dragon appears to congratulate you on successful configuration and warn you to be careful, as shown in Example 2.7.

Example 2.7. Successful configuration screen

```
flog~/nmap> ./configure
checking build system type... x86_64-unknown-linux-gnu
[hundreds of lines cut]
configure: creating ./config.status
config.status: creating Makefile
config.status: creating nsock_config.h
config.status: nsock_config.h is unchanged
  ( )   /\  _                    (
   \ |  ( \ ( \.(               )               _____
    \ \ \ `  `   ) \           (  ___          / _    \
   (_`   \+   . x  ( .\        \/   \____-----------/ (o)   \_
  - .-    \+  ;         ( O     _____/
       )        _____ ` ` _ )    \
  (__         +- .( -'.- <. - _  VVVVVVV VV V\      \/
  (_____      ._._: <_ - <- _  (-- _AAAAAAA__A_/   |
   .  /./.+-  . .- /  +--  - .    _____//_     _____
    (__ ' /x  / x _/ (                            \___'      \  /
   , x / ( '  . / .  /                              |         \ /
    / / _/ /   +                                   /          \/
    ' (__/                                        /            \
              NMAP IS A POWERFUL TOOL -- USE CAREFULLY AND RESPONSIBLY
Configuration complete. Type make (gmake on some *BSD machines) to compile.
```

5. Build Nmap (and the Zenmap GUI if its requirements are met): **make**

   Note that GNU Make is required. On BSD-derived Unix systems, this is often installed as *gmake*. So if **make** returns a bunch of errors such as "Makefile, line 1: Need an operator", try running **gmake** instead.

6. Become a privileged user for system-wide install: **su root**

   This step may be skipped if you only have an unprivileged shell account on the system. In that case, you will likely need to pass the --prefix option to configure in step four as described in the next section.

7. Install Nmap, support files, docs, etc.: **make install**

   Congratulations! Nmap is now installed as /usr/local/bin/nmap! Run it with no arguments for a quick help screen.

As you can see above, a simple source compilation and install consists of little more than running **./configure;make;make install** as root. However, there are a number of options available to configure that affect the way Nmap is built.

2.2.1. Configure Directives

Most of the Unix build options are controlled by the configure script, as used in step number four above. There are dozens of command-line parameters and environmental variables which affect the way Nmap is built. Run **./configure --help** for a huge list with brief descriptions. These are not applicable to building Nmap on Windows. Here are the options which are either specific to Nmap or particularly important:

`--prefix=<directoryname>`

This option, which is standard to the configure scripts of most software, determines where Nmap and its components are installed. By default, the prefix is `/usr/local`, meaning that nmap is installed in `/usr/local/bin`, the man page (`nmap.1`) is installed in `/usr/local/man/man1`, and the data files (`nmap-os-db`, `nmap-services`, `nmap-service-probes`, etc.) are installed under `/usr/local/share/nmap`. If you only wish to change the path of certain components, use the options `--bindir`, `--datadir`, and/or `--mandir`. An example usage of `--prefix` would be to install Nmap in my account as an unprivileged user. I would run **./configure --prefix=</home/fyodor>**. Nmap creates subdirectories like `/home/fyodor/man/man1` in the install stage if they do not already exist.

`--without-zenmap`

This option prevents the Zenmap graphical frontend from being installed. Normally the build system checks your system for requirements such as the Python scripting language and then installs Zenmap if they are all available.

`--with-openssl=<directoryname>`

The version detection system and Nmap Scripting Engine are able to probe SSL-encrypted services using the free OpenSSL libraries. Normally the Nmap build system looks for these libraries on your system and include this capability if they are found. If they are in a location your compiler does not search for by default, but you still want them to be used, specify `--with-openssl=<directoryname>`. Nmap then looks in `<directoryname>/libs` for the OpenSSL libraries themselves and `<directoryname>/include` for the necessary header files. Specify `--without-openssl` to disable SSL entirely.

`--with-libpcap=<directoryname>`

Nmap uses the Libpcap library[5] for capturing raw IP packets. Nmap normally looks for an existing copy of Libpcap on your system and uses that if the version number and platform is appropriate. Otherwise Nmap includes its own recent copy of Libpcap, which has been modified for improved Linux functionality. The specific changes are described in `libpcap/NMAP_MODIFICATIONS` in the Nmap source directory. Because of these Linux-related changes, Nmap always uses its own Libpcap by default on that platform. If you wish to force Nmap to link with your own Libpcap, pass the option `--with-libpcap=<directoryname>` to configure. Nmap then expects the Libpcap library to be in `<directoryname>/lib/libpcap.a` and the include files to be in `<directoryname>/include`. Nmap will always use the version of Libpcap included in its tarball if you specify `--with-libpcap=included`.

`--with-libpcre=<directoryname>`

PCRE is a Perl-compatible regular expression library available from *http://www.pcre.org*. Nmap normally looks for a copy on your system, and then falls back to its own copy if that fails. If your PCRE library is not in your compiler's standard search path, Nmap probably will not find it. In that case you can tell Nmap where it can be found by specifying the option `--with-libpcre=<directoryname>` to configure. Nmap then expects the library files to be in `<directoryname>/lib` and the include files to be in `<directoryname>/include`. In some cases, you may wish to use the PCRE libraries

---

[5] *http://www.tcpdump.org*

included with Nmap in preference to those already on your system. In that case, specify
`--with-libpcre=included`.

`--with-libdnet=<directoryname>`
> Libdnet is an excellent networking library that Nmap uses for sending raw ethernet frames. The version in the Nmap tree is heavily modified (particularly the Windows code), so the default is to use that included version. If you wish to use a version already installed on your system instead, specify `--with-libdnet=<directoryname>`. Nmap then expects the library files to be in `<directoryname>/lib` and the include files to be in `<directoryname>/include`.

`--with-localdirs`
> This simple option tells Nmap to look in `/usr/local/lib` and `/usr/local/include` for important library and header files. This should never be necessary, except that some people put such libraries in `/usr/local` without configuring their compiler to find them. If you are one of those people, use this option.

2.2.2. If You Encounter Compilation Problems

In an ideal world, software would always compile perfectly (and quickly) on every system. Unfortunately, society has not yet reached that state of nirvana. Despite all our efforts to make Nmap portable, compilation issues occasionally arise. Here are some suggestions in case the source distribution compilation fails.

Upgrade to the latest Nmap
> Check *http://nmap.org/download.html* to make sure you are using the latest version of Nmap. The problem may have already been fixed.

Read the error message carefully
> Scroll up in the output screen and examine the error messages given when commands fail. It is often best to find the first error message, as that often causes a cascade of further errors. Read the error message carefully, as it could indicate a system problem such as low disk space or a broken compiler. Users with programming skills may be able to resolve a wider range of problems themselves. If you make code changes to fix the problem, please send a patch (created with **diff -uw <oldfile> <newfile>**) and any details about your problem and platform to *nmap-dev* as described in Section 15.17, "Bugs" [411]. Integrating the change into the base Nmap distribution allows many other users to benefit, and prevents you from having to make the changes with each new Nmap version.

Ask Google and other Internet resources
> Try searching for the exact error message on Google or other search engines. You might also want to browse recent activity on the Nmap development (*nmap-dev*) list—archives and a search interface are available at *http://seclists.org*.

Ask *nmap-dev*
> If none of your research leads to a solution, try sending a report to the Nmap development (*nmap-dev*) mailing list, as described in Section 15.17, "Bugs" [411].

Consider binary packages

> Binary packages of Nmap are available on most platforms and are usually easy to install. The downsides are that they may not be as up-to-date and you lose some of the flexibility of self-compilation. Later

sections of this chapter describe how to find binary packages on many platforms, and even more are available via Internet searching. Obviously you should only install binary packages from reputable sources.

2.3. Linux Distributions

Linux is the most popular platform for running Nmap. In one user survey, 86% said that Linux was at least one of the platforms on which they run Nmap. The first release of Nmap in 1997 *only* ran on Linux.

Linux users can choose between a source code install or using binary packages provided by their distribution or Insecure.Org. The binary packages are generally quicker and easier to install, and are often slightly customized to use the distribution's standard directory paths and such. These packages also allow for consistent management in terms of upgrading, removing, or surveying software on the system. A downside is that packages created by the distributions are necessarily behind the Nmap.Org source releases. Most Linux distributions (particularly Debian and Gentoo) keep their Nmap package relatively current, though a few are way out of date. Choosing the source install allows for more flexibility in determining how Nmap is built and optimized for your system. To build Nmap from source, see Section 2.2, "Unix Compilation and Installation from Source Code" [29]. Here are simple package instructions for the most common distributions.

2.3.1. RPM-based Distributions (Red Hat, Mandrake, SUSE, Fedora)

I build RPM packages for every release of Nmap and post them to the Nmap download page at *http://nmap.org/download.html*. I build two packages: The nmap package contains just the command-line executable and data files, while the zenmap package contains the optional Zenmap graphical frontend (see Chapter 12, *Zenmap GUI Users' Guide* [307]). The zenmap package requires that the nmap package be installed first. One down side to installing the RPMs rather than compiling from source is that the RPMs don't support OpenSSL for version detection and Nmap Scripting Engine probing of SSL services.

Installing via RPM is quite easy—it even downloads the package for you when given the proper URLs. The following example downloads and installs Nmap 4.68, including the frontend. Of course you should use the latest version at the download site above instead. Any existing RPM-installed versions are upgraded. Example 2.8 demonstrates this installation process.

Example 2.8. Installing Nmap from binary RPMs

```
# rpm -vhU http://nmap.org/dist/nmap-4.68-1.i386.rpm
Retrieving http://nmap.org/dist/nmap-4.68-1.i386.rpm
Preparing...                ########################################### [100%]
   1:nmap                   ########################################### [100%]
# rpm -vhU http://nmap.org/dist/zenmap-4.68-1.noarch.rpm
Retrieving http://nmap.org/dist/zenmap-4.68-1.noarch.rpm
Preparing...                ########################################### [100%]
   1:zenmap                 ########################################### [100%]
```

As the filenames above imply, these binary RPMs were created for normal PCs (x86 architecture). I also distribute x86_64 binaries for 64-bit Linux users. These binaries won't work for the relatively few Linux users on other platforms such as SPARC, Alpha, or PowerPC. They also may refuse to install if your library versions are sufficiently different from what the RPMs were initially built on. One option in these cases would be to find binary RPMs prepared by your Linux vendor for your specific distribution. The original install CDs or DVD are a good place to start. Unfortunately, those may not be current or available. Another option is to install Nmap from source code as described previously, though you lose the binary package maintenance consistency benefits. A third option is to build and install your own binary RPMs from the source RPMs distributed from the download page above. Example 2.9 demonstrates this technique with Nmap 4.68.

Example 2.9. Building and installing Nmap from source RPMs

```
> rpmbuild --rebuild http://nmap.org/dist/nmap-4.68-1.src.rpm
[ hundreds of lines cut ]
Wrote: /home/fyodor/rpmdir/RPMS/i386/nmap-4.68-1.i386.rpm
[ cut ]
> su
Password:
# rpm -vhU /home/fyodor/rpmdir/RPMS/i386/nmap-4.68-1.i386.rpm
Preparing...                ########################################### [100%]
   1:nmap                   ########################################### [100%]
#
```

It is not necessary to rebuild Zenmap in this fashion because the Zenmap RPM is architecture-independent ("noarch"). For that reason there are no Zenmap source RPMs.

Removing RPM packages is as easy as **rpm -e nmap zenmap**.

2.3.2. Updating Red Hat, Fedora, Mandrake, and Yellow Dog Linux with Yum

The Red Hat, Fedora, Mandrake, and Yellow Dog Linux distributions have an application named Yum which manages software installation and updates from central RPM repositories. This makes software installation and updates trivial. Since distribution-specific Yum repositories are normally used, you know the software has already been tested for compatibility with your particular distribution. Most distributions do maintain Nmap in their Yum repository, but they don't always keep it up to date. This is particularly problematic if you (like most people) don't always quickly update to the latest release of your distribution. If you are running a two-year old Linux release, Yum will often give you a two-year-old version of Nmap. Even the latest version of distributions often take months to update to a new Nmap release. So for the latest version of Nmap on these systems, try the RPMs we distribute as described in the previous section. But if our RPMs aren't compatible with your system or you are in a great hurry, installing Nmap from Yum is usually as simple as executing **yum install nmap** (run **yum install nmap zenmap** if you would like the GUI too, though some distributions don't yet package Zenmap). Yum takes care of contacting a repository on the Internet, finding the appropriate package for your architecture, and then installing it along with any necessary dependencies. This is shown (edited for brevity) in Example 2.10. You can later perform **yum update** to install available updates to Nmap and other packages in the repository.

Example 2.10. Installing Nmap from a system Yum repository

```
flog~#yum install nmap
Setting up Install Process
Parsing package install arguments
Resolving Dependencies
--> Running transaction check
---> Package nmap.x86_64 2:4.52-1.fc8 set to be updated
--> Finished Dependency Resolution
Dependencies Resolved
===========================================================================
 Package               Arch        Version         Repository        Size
===========================================================================
Installing:
 nmap                  x86_64      2:4.52-1.fc8    updates           1.0 M

Transaction Summary
===========================================================================
Install      1 Package(s)
Update       0 Package(s)
Remove       0 Package(s)

Total download size: 1.0 M
Is this ok [y/N]: y
Downloading Packages:
(1/1): nmap-4.52-1.fc8.x8 100% |=========================| 1.0 MB    00:02
Running Transaction Test
Transaction Test Succeeded
Running Transaction
  Installing: nmap                            ########################### [1/1]

Installed: nmap.x86_64 2:4.52-1.fc8
Complete!
```

2.3.3. Debian Linux and Derivatives such as Ubuntu

LaMont Jones does a fabulous job maintaining the Nmap .deb packages, including keeping them reasonably up-to-date. The proper upgrade/install command is **apt-get install nmap**. This works for Debian derivatives such as Ubuntu too. Information on the latest Debian "stable" Nmap package is available at *http://packages.debian.org/stable/nmap* and the development ("unstable") Nmap and Zenmap packages are available from *http://packages.debian.org/unstable/nmap* and *http://packages.debian.org/unstable/zenmap*.

2.3.4. Other Linux Distributions

There are far too many Linux distributions available to list here, but even many of the obscure ones include Nmap in their package tree. If they don't, you can simply compile from source code as described in Section 2.2, "Unix Compilation and Installation from Source Code" [29].

2.4. Windows

While Nmap was once a Unix-only tool, a Windows version was released in 2000 and has since become the second most popular Nmap platform (behind Linux). Because of this popularity and the fact that many Windows users do not have a compiler, binary executables are distributed for each major Nmap release. While it has improved dramatically, the Windows port is not quite as efficient or stable as on Unix. Here are some known limitations:

- You cannot generally scan your own machine from itself (using a loopback IP such as 127.0.0.1 or any of its registered IP addresses). This is a Windows limitation that we haven't yet worked around. If you really want to do this, use a TCP connect scan without pinging (-sT -PN) as that uses the high level socket API rather than sending raw packets.

- Nmap only supports ethernet interfaces (including most 802.11 wireless cards and many VPN clients) for raw packet scans. Unless you use the -sT -PN options, RAS connections (such as PPP dialups) and certain VPN clients are not supported. This support was dropped when Microsoft removed raw TCP/IP socket support in Windows XP SP2. Now Nmap must send lower-level ethernet frames instead.

Scans speeds on Windows are generally comparable to those on Unix, though the latter often has a slight performance edge. One exception to this is connect scan (-sT), which is often much slower on Windows because of deficiencies in the Windows networking API. This is a shame, since that is the one TCP scan that works against localhost and over all networking types (not just ethernet, like the raw packet scans). Connect scan performance can be improved substantially by applying the Registry changes in the nmap_performance.reg file included with Nmap. By default these changes are applied for you by the Nmap executable installer. This registry file is in the nmap-<version> directory of the Windows binary zip file, and nmap-<version>/mswin32 in the source tarball (where <version> is the version number of the specific release). These changes increase the number of ephemeral ports reserved for user applications (such as Nmap) and reduce the time delay before a closed connection can be reused. Most people simply check the box to apply these changes in the executable Nmap installer, but you can also apply them by double-clicking on nmap_performance.reg, or by running the command **regedit32 nmap_performance.reg**. To make the changes by hand, add these three Registry DWORD values to HKEY_LOCAL_MACHINE\SYSTEM\CurrentControlSet\Services\Tcpip\Parameters:

MaxUserPort
>   Set a large value such as 65534 (0x0000fffe). See MS KB Q196271[6].

TCPTimedWaitDelay
>   Set the minimum value (0x0000001e). See MS KB Q149532[7].

StrictTimeWaitSeqCheck
>   Set to 1 so TCPTimedWaitDelay is checked.

---

[6] http://support.microsoft.com/kb/Q196271
[7] http://support.microsoft.com/kb/Q149532

Note

I would like to thank Ryan Permeh of eEye, Andy Lutomirski, and Jens Vogt for their hard work on the Nmap Windows port. For many years, Nmap was a Unix-only tool, and it would likely still be that way if not for their efforts.

Windows users have three choices for installing Nmap, all of which are available from the download page at *http://nmap.org/download.html*.

2.4.1. Windows 2000 Dependencies

Nmap supports Windows 2000, but a couple dependencies from Microsoft must be installed first. Those are the Windows Installer 3.1 (v2)[8] and the Security Update for Windows 2000 (KB835732)[9]. After installing these, follow the general instructions in the following two sections to install Nmap.

2.4.2. Windows Self-installer

Every Nmap release includes a Windows self-installer named `nmap-<version>-setup.exe` (where `<version>` is the version number of the specific release). Most Nmap users choose this option since it is so easy. Another advantage of the self-installer is that it provides the option to install the Zenmap GUI. Simply run the installer file and let it walk you through panels for choosing an install path and installing WinPcap. The installer was created with the open-source Nullsoft Scriptable Install System[10]. After it completes, read Section 2.4.5, "Executing Nmap on Windows" [39] for instructions on executing Nmap on the command-line or through Zenmap.

2.4.3. Command-line Zip Binaries

Note

Most users prefer installing Nmap with the self-installer discussed previously.

Every stable Nmap release comes with Windows command-line binaries and associated files in a Zip archive. No graphical interface is included, so you need to run `nmap.exe` from a DOS/command window. Or you can download and install a superior command shell such as those included with the free Cygwin system available from *http://www.cygwin.com*. Here are the step-by-step instructions for installing and executing the Nmap .zip binaries.

Installing the Nmap zip binaries

1. Download the .zip binaries from *http://nmap.org/download.html*.

2. Uncompress the zip file into the directory you want Nmap to reside in. An example would be `C:\Program Files`. A directory called `nmap-version` should be created, which includes the Nmap executable and data files. Microsoft Windows XP and Vista include zip extraction—just right-click on the file in

---

[8] *http://microsoft.com/downloads/details.aspx?FamilyID=889482FC-5F56-4A38-B838-DE776FD4138C*

[9] *http://microsoft.com/downloads/details.aspx?FamilyID=0692C27E-F63A-414C-B3EB-D2342FBB6C00*

[10] *http://nsis.sourceforge.net/Main_Page*

Explorer. If you do not have a Zip decompression program, there is one (called unzip) in Cygwin described above, or you can download the open-source and free 7-Zip utility[11]. Commercial alternatives are WinZip[12] and PKZIP[13].

3. For improved performance, apply the Nmap Registry changes discussed previously.

4. Nmap requires the free WinPcap packet capture library. We build our own WinPcap installer which is available in the zip file as `winpcap-nmap-<version>.exe`, where `<version>` is the Nmap version rather than the WinPcap version. Alternatively, you can obtain and install the latest version from *http://www.winpcap.org*. You must install version 4.0 or later.

5. Due to the way Nmap is compiled, it requires the Microsoft Visual C++ 2008 Redistributable Package of runtime components. Many systems already have this installed from other packages, but you should run `vcredist_x86.exe` from the zip file just in case you need it.

6. Instructions for executing your compiled Nmap are given in Section 2.4.5, "Executing Nmap on Windows" [39].

2.4.4. Compile from Source Code

Most Windows users prefer to use the Nmap binary self-installer, but compilation from source code is an option, particularly if you plan to help with Nmap development. Compilation requires Microsoft Visual C++ 2008, which is part of their commercial Visual Studio suite. Any of the Visual Studio editions should work, including the free Visual C++ 2008 Express[14].

Compiling Nmap on Windows from Source

1. Download the latest Nmap source distribution from *http://nmap.org/download.html*. It has the name nmap-`<version>`.tar.bz2 or nmap-`<version>`.tgz. Those are the same tar file compressed using gzip or bzip2, respectively. The bzip2-compressed version is smaller.

2. Uncompress the source code file you just downloaded. Recent releases of the free Cygwin distribution[15] can handle both the `.tar.bz2` and `.tgz` formats. Use the command **tar xvjf nmap-version.tar.bz2** or **tar xvzf nmap-version.tgz**, respectively. Alternatively, the common WinZip application can decompress the .tgz version.

3. Open Visual Studio and the Nmap solution file (`nmap-<version>/mswin32/nmap.sln`).

4. Choose "Build Solution" from the "Build Menu". Nmap should begin compiling, and end with the line "`-- Done --`" saying that all projects built successfully and there were zero failures.

5. The executable and data files can be found in `nmap-<version>/mswin32/Release/`. You can copy them to a preferred directory as long as they are all kept together.

---

[11] *http://www.7-zip.org*
[12] *http://www.winzip.com*
[13] *http://www.pkware.com*
[14] *http://www.microsoft.com/express/vc/*
[15] *http://www.cygwin.com/*

---

6. Ensure that you have WinPcap installed. You can obtain it by installing our binary self-installer or executing `winpcap-nmap-<version>.exe` from our zip package. Alternatively, you can obtain the official installer at *http://www.winpcap.org*.

7. Instructions for executing your compiled Nmap are given in the next section.

Many people have asked whether Nmap can be compiled with the gcc/g++ included with Cygwin or other compilers. Some users have reported success with this, but we don't maintain instructions for building Nmap under Cygwin.

2.4.5. Executing Nmap on Windows

Nmap releases now include the Zenmap graphical user interface for Nmap. If you used the Nmap installer and left the Zenmap field checked, there should be a new Zenmap entry on your desktop and Start Menu. Click this to get started. Zenmap is fully documented in Chapter 12, *Zenmap GUI Users' Guide* [307]. While many users love Zenmap, others prefer the traditional command-line approach to executing Nmap. Here are detailed instructions for users who are unfamiliar with command-line interfaces:

1. Make sure the user you are logged in as has administrative privileges on the computer (user should be a member of the `administrators` group).

2. Open a command/DOS Window. Though it can be found in the program menu tree, the simplest approach is to choose "Start" -> "Run" and type **cmd<enter>**. Opening a Cygwin window (if you installed it) by clicking on the Cygwin icon on the desktop works too, although the necessary commands differ slightly from those shown here.

3. Change to the directory you installed Nmap into. Assuming you used the default path, type the following commands.

```
c:
cd "\Program Files\Nmap"
```

4. Execute **nmap.exe**. Figure 2.1 is a screen shot showing a simple example.

Figure 2.1. Executing Nmap from a Windows command shell

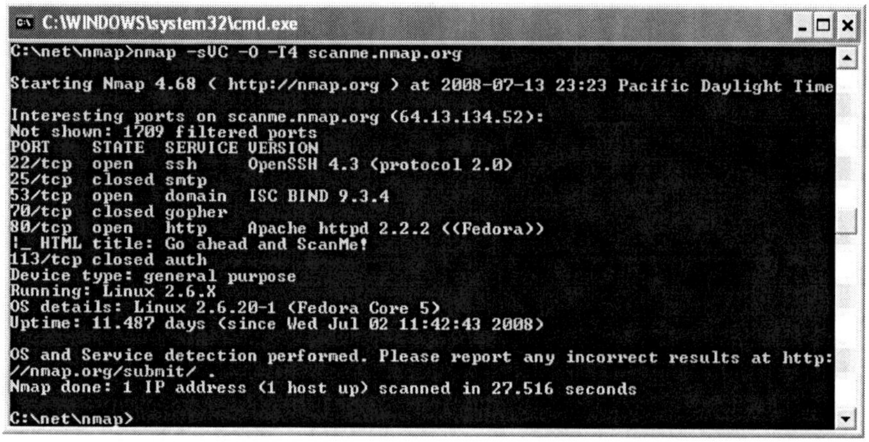

```
C:\WINDOWS\system32\cmd.exe                                              _ □ x
C:\net\nmap>nmap -sUC -O -T4 scanme.nmap.org

Starting Nmap 4.68 ( http://nmap.org ) at 2008-07-13 23:23 Pacific Daylight Time

Interesting ports on scanme.nmap.org (64.13.134.52):
Not shown: 1709 filtered ports
PORT     STATE  SERVICE  VERSION
22/tcp   open   ssh      OpenSSH 4.3 (protocol 2.0)
25/tcp   closed smtp
53/tcp   open   domain   ISC BIND 9.3.4
70/tcp   closed gopher
80/tcp   open   http     Apache httpd 2.2.2 ((Fedora))
|_ HTML title: Go ahead and ScanMe!
113/tcp  closed auth
Device type: general purpose
Running: Linux 2.6.X
OS details: Linux 2.6.20-1 (Fedora Core 5)
Uptime: 11.487 days (since Wed Jul 02 11:42:43 2008)

OS and Service detection performed. Please report any incorrect results at http:
//nmap.org/submit/ .
Nmap done: 1 IP address (1 host up) scanned in 27.516 seconds

C:\net\nmap>
```

If you execute Nmap frequently, you can add the Nmap directory (c:\Program Files\Nmap by default) to your command execution path. The exact place to set this varies by Windows platform. On my Windows XP box, I do the following:

1. From the desktop, right click on My Computer and then click "properties".

2. In the System Properties window, click the "Advanced" tab.

3. Click the "Environment Variables" button.

4. Choose Path from the System variables section, then hit edit.

5. Add a semi-colon and then your Nmap directory (c:\Program Files\Nmap by default) to the end of the value.

6. Open a new DOS window and you should be able to execute a command such as **nmap scanme.nmap.org** from any directory.

2.5. Sun Solaris

Solaris has long been well-supported by Nmap. Sun even donated a complete SPARCstation to the project, which is still being used to test new Nmap builds. For this reason, many Solaris users compile and install from source code as described in Section 2.2, "Unix Compilation and Installation from Source Code" [29].

Users who prefer native Solaris packages will be pleased to learn that Steven Christensen does an excellent job of maintaining Nmap packages at *http://www.sunfreeware.com* for all modern Solaris versions and architectures. Instructions are on his site, and are generally very simple: download the appropriate Nmap package for your version of Solaris, decompress it, and then run **pkgadd -d <packagename>**. As is generally the case with contributed binary packages, these Solaris packages are simple and quick to install. The advantages of compiling from source are that a newer version may be available and you have more flexibility in the build process.

2.6. Apple Mac OS X

Thanks to several people graciously donating shell accounts on their Mac OS X boxes, Nmap usually compiles on that platform without problems. Because not everyone has the development tools necessary to compile from source, there is an executable installer as well. Nmap is also available through systems such as MacPorts and Fink which package Unix software for Mac OS X.

2.6.1. Executable Installer

The easiest way to install Nmap and Zenmap on Mac OS X is to use our installer. The Mac OS X section of the Nmap download page[16] provides a file named `nmap-<version>.dmg`, where `<version>` is the version number of the most recent release. The `.dmg` file is known as a "disk image". Installation instructions follow:

1. Download the file `nmap-<version>.dmg`. Double-click the icon to open it. (Depending on how you downloaded the file, it may be opened automatically.)

2. The contents of the disk image will be displayed. One of the files will be a Mac meta-package file named `nmap-<version>.mpkg`. Double-click it to start the installer.

3. Follow the instructions in the installer. You will be asked for your password since Nmap installs in a system directory.

4. Once the installer is finished, eject the disk image by control-clicking on its icon and selecting "Eject". The disk image may now be placed in the trash.

See the instructions in Section 2.6.4, "Executing Nmap on Mac OS X" [42] for help on running Nmap and Zenmap after they are installed.

The programs installed by the installer are universal binaries that will run on Mac OS X 10.4 (Tiger) or later. Users of earlier versions will have to compile from source or use a third-party package.

2.6.2. Compile from Source Code

Compiling Nmap from source on Mac OS X is no more difficult than on other platforms once a proper build environment is in place.

Compile Nmap from source code

Compiling Nmap on Mac OS X requires Xcode[17], Apple's developer tools that include GCC and the rest of the usual build system. Xcode is not installed by default, but is available as an optional install on the Mac OS X installation discs. If you do not have the installation discs or if you want a newer version, you can download Xcode free of charge by following these steps.

---

[16] *http://nmap.org/download.html#macosx*
[17] *http://developer.apple.com/tools/xcode/*

1. Apple restricts downloads of Xcode to members of the Apple Developer Connection. Browse to *http://connect.apple.com* and fill out some forms to create an account. Skip to the next step if you already have an account.

2. Return to *http://connect.apple.com* and log in with your account credentials.

3. Hit the `Download` link and then choose `Developer Tools`.

4. Download and install the most recent `Xcode`.

These exact steps may change, but it is hoped that this general approach will continue to work.

Once you have installed Xcode, follow the compilation instructions found in Section 2.2, "Unix Compilation and Installation from Source Code" [29]. Note that on some older versions of Mac OS X, you may have to replace the command **./configure** with **./configure CPP=/usr/bin/cpp**.

Compile Zenmap from source code

Zenmap depends on some external libraries that do not come with Mac OS X, including GTK+ and PyGTK. These libraries have many dependencies of their own. A convenient way to install all of them is to use a third-party packaging system as described in Section 2.6.3. Once the dependencies are installed, follow the instructions in Section 2.2, "Unix Compilation and Installation from Source Code" [29] to install Zenmap as usual.

2.6.3. Third-party Packages

Another option for installing Nmap is to use a system which packages Unix software for Mac OS X. The two discussed here are Fink[18] and MacPorts[19]. See the respective projects' web sites for how to install the package managers.

To install using Fink, run the command **fink install nmap**. Nmap will be installed as `/sw/bin/nmap`. To uninstall use the command **fink remove nmap**.

To install using MacPorts, run **sudo port install nmap**. Nmap will be installed as `/opt/local/bin/nmap`. To uninstall, run **sudo port uninstall nmap**.

These systems install the `nmap` executable outside the global `PATH`. To enable Zenmap to find it, set the `nmap_command_path` variable in `zenmap.conf` to `/sw/bin/nmap` or `/opt/local/bin/nmap` as described in Section 12.10.1, "The nmap Executable" [330].

2.6.4. Executing Nmap on Mac OS X

The terminal emulator in Mac OS X is called Terminal, and is located in the directory `/Applications/Utilities`. Open it and a terminal window appears. This is where you will type your commands.

---

[18] *http://www.finkproject.org*
[19] *http://www.macports.org*

By default the root user is disabled on Mac OS X. To run a scan with root privileges prefix the command name with sudo, as in **sudo nmap -sS `<target>`**. You will be asked for a password, which is just your normal login password. Only users with administrator privileges can do this.

Zenmap requires the X11 application to be installed. If it was not installed by default it may be available as an optional install on the Mac OS X installation discs.

When Zenmap is started, a dialog is displayed requesting that you type your password. Users with administrator privileges may enter their password to allow Zenmap to run as the root user and run more advanced scans. To run Zenmap in unprivileged mode, select the "Cancel" button on this authentication dialog.

2.7. FreeBSD / OpenBSD / NetBSD

The BSD flavors are well supported by Nmap, so you can simply compile it from source as described in Section 2.2, "Unix Compilation and Installation from Source Code" [29]. This provides the normal advantages of always having the latest version and a flexible build process. If you prefer binary packages, these *BSD variants each maintain their own Nmap packages. Many BSD systems also have a *ports tree* which standardizes the compilation of popular applications. Instructions for installing Nmap on the most popular *BSD variants follow.

2.7.1. OpenBSD Binary Packages and Source Ports Instructions

According to the OpenBSD FAQ[20], users "are HIGHLY advised to use packages over building an application from ports. The OpenBSD ports team considers packages to be the goal of their porting work, not the ports themselves." That same FAQ contains detailed instructions for each method. Here is a summary:

Installation using binary packages

1. Choose a mirror from *http://www.openbsd.org/ftp.html*, then FTP in and grab the Nmap package from `/pub/OpenBSD/<version>/packages/<platform>/nmap-<version>.tgz`. Or obtain it from the OpenBSD distribution CD-ROM.

2. As root, execute: **pkg_add -v nmap-`<version>`.tgz**

Installation using the source ports tree

1. If you do not already have a copy of the ports tree, obtain it via CVS using instructions at *http://openbsd.org/faq/faq15.html*.

2. As root, execute the following command (replace `/usr/ports` with your local ports directory if it differs):

   cd /usr/ports/net/nmap && make install clean

---

[20] *http://www.openbsd.org/faq/*

2.7.2. FreeBSD Binary Package and Source Ports Instructions

The FreeBSD project has a whole chapter[21] in their Handbook describing the package and port installation processes. A brief summary of the process follows.

Installation of the binary package

The easiest way to install the binary Nmap package is to run **pkg_add -r nmap**. You can then run the same command with the `zenmap` argument if you want the X-Window front-end. If you wish to obtain the package manually instead, retrieve it from *http://freshports.org/security/nmap* and *http://freshports.org/security/zenmap* or the CDROM and run **pkg_add <packagename.tgz>**.

Installation using the source ports tree

1. The ports tree is often installed with the system itself (usually in `/usr/ports`). If you do not already have it, specific installation instructions are provided in the FreeBSD Handbook chapter referenced above.

2. As root, execute the following command (replace `/usr/ports` with your local ports directory if it differs):

   cd /usr/ports/security/nmap && make install clean

2.7.3. NetBSD Binary Package Instructions

NetBSD has packaged Nmap for an enormous number of platforms, from the normal i386 to PlayStation 2, PowerPC, VAX, SPARC, MIPS, Amiga, ARM, and several platforms that I have never even heard of! Unfortunately they are not very up-to-date. A list of NetBSD Nmap packages is available from *ftp://ftp.netbsd.org/pub/NetBSD/packages/pkgsrc/net/nmap/README.html* and a description of using their package system to install applications is available at *http://netbsd.org/Documentation/pkgsrc/using.html*.

2.8. Amiga, HP-UX, IRIX, and Other Platforms

One of the wonders of Open Source development is that resources are often directed towards what people find exciting rather than having an exclusive focus on profits as most corporations do. It is along those lines that the Amiga port came about. Diego Casorran performed most of the work and sent in a clean patch which was integrated into the main Nmap distribution. In general, AmigaOS users should be able to simply follow the source compilation instructions in Section 2.2, "Unix Compilation and Installation from Source Code" [29]. You may encounter a few hurdles on some systems, but I presume that must be part of the fun for Amiga fanatics.

Nmap supports many proprietary Unix flavors such as HP-UX and SGI IRIX. The Nmap project depends on the user community to help maintain adequate support for these systems. If you have trouble, try sending a report with full details to the *nmap-dev* mailing list, as described in Section 15.17, "Bugs" [411]. Also let us know if you develop a patch which improves support on your platform so we can incorporate it into Nmap.

---

[21] *http://www.freebsd.org/doc/en_US.ISO8859-1/books/handbook/ports.html*

2.9. Removing Nmap

If your purpose for removing Nmap is simply to upgrade to the latest version, you can usually use the upgrade option provided by most binary package managers. Similarly, installing the latest source code (as described in Section 2.2, "Unix Compilation and Installation from Source Code" [29]) generally overwrites any previous from-source installations. Removing Nmap is a good idea if you are changing install methods (such as from source to RPM or vice versa) or if you are not using Nmap anymore and you care about the few megabytes of disk space it consumes.

How to remove Nmap depends on how you installed it initially (see previous sections). Ease of removal (and other maintenance) is a major advantage of most binary packages. For example, when Nmap is installed using the RPM system common on Linux distributions, it can be removed by running the command **rpm -e nmap zenmap** as root. Analogous options are offered by most other package managers—consult their documentation for further information.

If you installed Nmap from the Windows installer, simply open the Control Panel, select "Add or Remove Programs" and select the "Remove" button for Nmap. You can also remove WinPcap unless you need it for other applications such as Wireshark.

If you installed Nmap from source code, removal is slightly more difficult. If you still have the build directory available (where you initially ran **make install**), you can remove Nmap by running **make uninstall**. If you no longer have that build directory, type **nmap -V** to obtain the Nmap version number. Then download that source tarball for that version of Nmap from *http://nmap.org/dist/* or *http://nmap.org/dist-old/*. Uncompress the tarball and change into the newly created directory (nmap-<version>). Run ./**configure**, including any install-path options that you specified the first time (such as --prefix or --datadir). Then run **make uninstall**. Alternatively, you can simply delete all the Nmap-related files. If you used a default source install of Nmap versions 4.50 or higher, the following commands remove it.

```
# cd /usr/local
# rm -f bin/nmap bin/nmapfe bin/xnmap
# rm -f man/man1/nmap.1 man/man1/zenmap.1
# rm -rf share/nmap
# ./bin/uninstall_zenmap
```

You may have to adjust the above commands slightly if you specified --prefix or other install-path option when first installing Nmap. The files relating to zenmap, nmapfe, and xnmap do not exist if you did not install the Zenmap frontend.

Chapter 3. Host Discovery ("Ping Scanning")

3.1. Introduction

One of the very first steps in any network reconnaissance mission is to reduce a (sometimes huge) set of IP ranges into a list of active or interesting hosts. Scanning every port of every single IP address is slow and usually unnecessary. Of course what makes a host interesting depends greatly on the scan purposes. Network administrators may only be interested in hosts running a certain service, while security auditors may care about every single device with an IP address. An administrator may be comfortable using just an ICMP ping to locate hosts on his internal network, while an external penetration tester may use a diverse set of dozens of probes in an attempt to evade firewall restrictions.

Because host discovery needs are so diverse, Nmap offers a wide variety of options for customizing the techniques used. Despite the name ping scan, this goes well beyond the simple ICMP echo request packets associated with the ubiquitous ping tool. Users can skip the ping step entirely with a list scan (-sL) or by disabling ping (-PN), or engage the network with arbitrary combinations of multi-port TCP SYN/ACK, UDP, and ICMP probes. The goal of these probes is to solicit responses which demonstrate that an IP address is actually active (is being used by a host or network device). On many networks, only a small percentage of IP addresses are active at any given time. This is particularly common with private address space such as 10.0.0.0/8. That network has 16.8 million IPs, but I have seen it used by companies with fewer than a thousand machines. Host discovery can find those machines in a sparsely allocated sea of IP addresses.

This chapter first discusses how Nmap ping scanning works overall, with high-level control options. Then specific techniques are covered, including how they work and when each is most appropriate. Nmap offers many ping techniques because it often takes carefully crafted combinations to get through a series of firewalls and router filters leading to a target network. Effective overall ping scanning strategies are discussed, followed by a low-level look at the algorithms used.

3.2. Specifying Target Hosts and Networks

Everything on the Nmap command-line that isn't an option (or option argument) is treated as a target host specification. The simplest case is to specify a target IP address or hostname for scanning.

Sometimes you wish to scan a whole network of adjacent hosts. For this, Nmap supports CIDR-style addressing. You can append /<numbits> to an IPv4 address or hostname and Nmap will scan every IP address for which the first <numbits> are the same as for the reference IP or hostname given. For example, 192.168.10.0/24 would scan the 256 hosts between 192.168.10.0 (binary: 11000000 10101000 00001010 00000000) and 192.168.10.255 (binary: 11000000 10101000 00001010 11111111), inclusive. 192.168.10.40/24 would scan exactly the same targets. Given that the host scanme.nmap.org is at the IP address 64.13.134.52, the specification scanme.nmap.org/16 would scan the 65,536 IP addresses between 64.13.0.0 and 64.13.255.255. The smallest allowed value is /0, which scans the whole Internet. The largest value is /32, which scans just the named host or IP address because all address bits are fixed.

CIDR notation is short but not always flexible enough. For example, you might want to scan 192.168.0.0/16 but skip any IPs ending with .0 or .255 because they may be used as subnet network and broadcast addresses. Nmap supports this through octet range addressing. Rather than specify a normal IP address, you can specify a comma-separated list of numbers or ranges for each octet. For example, 192.168.0-255.1-254 will skip all addresses in the range that end in .0 or .255. Ranges need not be limited to the final octets: the specifier 0-255.0-255.13.37 will perform an Internet-wide scan for all IP addresses ending in 13.37. This sort of broad sampling can be useful for Internet surveys and research.

IPv6 addresses can only be specified by their fully qualified IPv6 address or hostname. CIDR and octet ranges aren't supported for IPv6 because they are rarely useful.

Nmap accepts multiple host specifications on the command line, and they don't need to be the same type. The command **nmap scanme.nmap.org 192.168.0.0/8 10.0.0,1,3-7.0-255** does what you would expect.

3.2.1. Input From List (`-iL`)

Passing a huge list of hosts is often awkward on the command line, yet it is a common need. For example, your DHCP server might export a list of 10,000 current leases that you wish to scan. Or maybe you want to scan all IP addresses *except* for those ones to locate hosts using unauthorized static IP addresses. Simply generate the list of hosts to scan and pass that filename to Nmap as an argument to the `-iL` option. Entries can be in any of the formats accepted by Nmap on the command line (IP address, hostname, CIDR, IPv6, or octet ranges). Each entry must be separated by one or more spaces, tabs, or newlines. You can specify a hyphen (`-`) as the filename if you want Nmap to read hosts from standard input rather than an actual file.

3.2.2. Choose Targets at Random (`-iR <numtargets>`)

For Internet-wide surveys and other research, you may want to choose targets at random. This is done with the `-iR` option, which takes as an argument the number of IPs to generate. Nmap automatically skips certain undesirable IPs, such as those in private, multicast, or unallocated address ranges. The argument 0 can be specified for a never-ending scan. Keep in mind that some network administrators bristle at unauthorized scans of their networks. Carefully read Section 1.4, "Legal Issues" [13] before using -iR.

If you find yourself really bored one rainy afternoon, try the command **nmap -sS -PS80 -iR 0 -p 80** to locate random web servers for browsing.

3.2.3. Excluding Targets (`--exclude`, `--excludefile <filename>`)

It is common to have machines which you don't want to scan under any circumstances. Machines can be so critical that you won't take any risk of an adverse reaction. You might be blamed for a coincidental outage even if the Nmap scan had nothing to do with it. Or perhaps you have legacy hardware that is known to crash when scanned, but you haven't been able to fix or replace it yet. Or maybe certain IP ranges represent subsidiary companies, customers, or partners that you aren't authorized to scan. Consultants often don't want their own machine included in a scan of their client's networks. Whatever the reason, you can exclude hosts or entire networks with the `--exclude` option. Simply pass the option a comma-separated list of excluded targets and netblocks using the normal Nmap syntax. Alternatively, you can create a file of excluded hosts/networks and pass that to Nmap with the `--excludefile` option.

3.2.4. Practical Examples

While some tools have simple interfaces that only allow a list of hosts or maybe let you specify the start and end IP addresses for a range, Nmap is much more powerful and flexible. But Nmap can also be more difficult to learn—and scanning the wrong IP addresses is occasionally disastrous. Fortunately, Nmap offers a dry run using the list scan (`-sL` option). Simply execute **nmap -sL -n `<targets>`** to see which IPs would be scanned before you actually do it.

Examples may be the most effective way to teach the Nmap host specification syntax. This section provides some, starting with the simplest.

nmap scanme.nmap.org, nmap scanme.nmap.org/32, nmap 64.13.134.52
These commands all do the same thing, assuming that scanme.nmap.org resolves to 64.13.134.52. They scan that one IP and then exit.

nmap scanme.nmap.org/24, nmap 64.13.134.52/24, nmap 64.13.134.0-255
These all ask Nmap to scan the 256 IP addresses from 64.13.134.0 through 64.13.134.255. In other words, they ask to scan the class C sized address space surrounding scanme.nmap.org.

nmap 64.13.134.52/24 --exclude scanme.nmap.org,insecure.org
Tells Nmap to scan the class C around 64.13.134.52, but to skip scanme.nmap.org and insecure.org if they are found within that address range.

nmap 10.0.0.0/8 --exclude 10.6.0.0/16,ultra-sensitive-host.company.com
Tells Nmap to scan the whole private 10 range except that it must skip anything starting with 10.6 as well as ultra-sensitive-host.company.com.

egrep '^lease' /var/lib/dhcp/dhcpd.leases | awk '{print $2}' | nmap -iL -
Obtain the list of assigned DHCP IP addresses and feed them directly to Nmap for scanning. Note that a hyphen is passed to `-iL` to read from standard input.

nmap -6 2001:800:40:2a03::3
Scans the IPv6 host at address 2001:800:40:2a03::3.

3.3. Finding an Organization's IP Addresses

Nmap automates many aspects of network scanning, but you still must tell it which networks to scan. I suppose you could specify `-iR` and hope Nmap hits your target company randomly, or you could try the brute force method of specifying `0.0.0.0/0` to scan the whole Internet. But either of those options could take months or years, and possibly get you into trouble. So it is important to carefully research target netblocks before scanning them. Even if you are conducting a legitimate penetration test and the client gave you a list of their netblocks, it is important to double check them. Clients sometimes have out-of-date records or simply write them down wrong. An authorization letter signed by your client won't help if you accidentally break into the wrong company.

In many cases, you start with only a company's domain name. This section demonstrates a few of the most common and effective ways to turn that into a list of netblocks owned, operated by, or affiliated with the target company. Typical Linux command-line utilities are demonstrated, but similar tools are available for other platforms.

At the ShmooCon conference in 2006, a fellow came up to me and complained that Nmap documentation specified many example ways to scan `target.com`. He noted that ICANN had reserved the domain name `example.com` for this purpose, and pressured me to revise the man page accordingly. While he was technically right, it was a strange thing to obsess about. His motivation became clear when he handed me his business card:

Figure 3.1. A business card explains everything

Apparently, many Nmap users copied examples straight from the man page and ran them without changing the target specifier. So target.com was flooded with scans and corresponding IDS alerts. In honor of that incident, the goal of this section is to determine IP ranges assigned to and used by Target Corporation.

3.3.1. DNS Tricks

The primary purpose of DNS is to resolve domain names into IP addresses, so it is a logical place to start. In Example 3.1, I use the Linux **host** command to query some common DNS record types.

Example 3.1. Using the host command to query common DNS record types

```
> host -t ns target.com
target.com name server ns4.target.com.
target.com name server ns3.target.com.
target.com name server ns1-auth.sprintlink.net.
target.com name server ns2-auth.sprintlink.net.
target.com name server ns3-auth.sprintlink.net.
> host -t a target.com
target.com has address 161.225.130.163
target.com has address 161.225.136.0
> host -t aaaa target.com
target.com has no AAAA record
> host -t mx target.com
target.com mail is handled by 50 smtp02.target.com.
target.com mail is handled by 5 smtp01.target.com.
>host -t soa target.com
target.com has SOA record extdns02.target.com. hostmaster.target.com.
```

Next I resolve the IP addresses for the hostnames above (using host again) and I try a few common subdomain names such as `www.target.com` and `ftp.target.com`. Starting with names like `ns3.target.com` and `smtp01.target.com`, I try changing the digits to find new machines. All of this leaves me with the following target.com names and addresses:

Table 3.1. First pass at listing target.com IPs

Hostname	IP Addresses
ns3.target.com	161.225.130.130
ns4.target.com	161.225.136.136
ns5.target.com	161.225.130.150
target.com	161.225.136.0, 161.225.130.163
smtp01.target.com	161.225.140.120
smtp02.target.com	198.70.53.234, 198.70.53.235
extdns02.target.com	172.17.14.69
www.target.com	207.171.166.49

While a substantial hostname list can be generated in this manner, the mother lode of hostnames comes from a zone transfer. Most DNS servers now reject zone transfer requests, but it is worth a try because many still allow it. Be sure to try every DNS server you have found through domain NS records and port scanning corporate IP ranges. So far we have found seven Target nameservers: `ns3.target.com`, `ns4.target.com`, `ns5.target.com`, `ns1-auth.sprintlink.net`, `ns2-auth.sprintlink.net`, `ns3-auth.sprintlink.net`, and `extdns02.target.com`. Unfortunately, all of those servers either refused the transfer or did not support the TCP DNS connections required for a zone transfer. Example 3.2 shows a failed `target.com` zone transfer attempt using the common **dig** (domain information groper) tool[1], followed by a successful one against an unrelated organization (`cpsr.org`).

---

[1]Nmap's `zone-transfer` NSE script could have been used instead (see Chapter 9, *Nmap Scripting Engine* [205]).

Example 3.2. Zone transfer failure and success

```
> dig @ns2-auth.sprintlink.net -t AXFR target.com
; <<>> DiG 9.5.0b3 <<>> @ns2-auth.sprintlink.net -t AXFR target.com

; Transfer failed.

> dig @ns2.eppi.com -t AXFR cpsr.org
; <<>> DiG 9.5.0b1 <<>> @ns2.eppi.com -t AXFR cpsr.org

cpsr.org               10800   IN      SOA     ns1.findpage.com. root.cpsr.org.
cpsr.org.              10800   IN      NS      ns.stimpy.net.
cpsr.org.              10800   IN      NS      ns1.findpage.com.
cpsr.org.              10800   IN      NS      ns2.eppi.com.
cpsr.org.              10800   IN      A       208.96.55.202
cpsr.org.              10800   IN      MX      0 smtp.electricembers.net.
diac.cpsr.org.         10800   IN      A       64.147.163.10
groups.cpsr.org.       10800   IN      NS      ns1.electricembers.net.
localhost.cpsr.org.    10800   IN      A       127.0.0.1
mail.cpsr.org.         10800   IN      A       209.209.81.73
peru.cpsr.org.         10800   IN      A       208.96.55.202
www.peru.cpsr.org.     10800   IN      A       208.96.55.202
[...]
```

A common mistake when gathering forward DNS results like these is assuming that all systems found under a domain name must be part of that organization's network and safe to scan. In fact, nothing prevents an organization from adding records pointing anywhere on the Internet. This is commonly done to outsource services to third parties while keeping the source domain name for branding. For example, www.target.com resolves to 207.171.166.49. Is this part of Target's network, or is it managed by a third party we might not want to scan? Three quick and easy tests are DNS reverse-resolution, traceroute, and whois against the relevant IP address registry. The first two steps can be done by Nmap, while the Linux whois command works well for the third. These tests against target.com are shown in Example 3.3 and Example 3.4.

Example 3.3. Nmap reverse-DNS and traceroute scan against www.target.com

```
# nmap -PN -T4 --traceroute www.target.com

Starting Nmap ( http://nmap.org )
Interesting ports on 166-49.amazon.com (207.171.166.49):
Not shown: 998 filtered ports
PORT     STATE SERVICE
80/tcp   open  http
443/tcp  open  https

TRACEROUTE (using port 80/tcp)
HOP RTT     ADDRESS
[cut]
9    84.94  ae-2.ebr4.NewYork1.Level3.net (4.69.135.186)
10   87.91  ae-3.ebr4.Washington1.Level3.net (4.69.132.93)
11   94.80  ae-94-94.csw4.Washington1.Level3.net (4.69.134.190)
12   86.40  ae-21-69.car1.Washington3.Level3.net (4.68.17.7)
13   185.10 AMAZONCOM.car1.Washington3.Level3.net (4.71.204.18)
14   84.70  72.21.209.38
15   85.73  72.21.193.37
16   85.68  166-49.amazon.com (207.171.166.49)

Nmap done: 1 IP address (1 host up) scanned in 20.57 seconds
```

Example 3.4. Using whois to find owner of www.target.com IP address

```
> whois 207.171.166.49
[Querying whois.arin.net]
[whois.arin.net]

OrgName:    Amazon.com, Inc.
OrgID:      AMAZON-4
Address:    605 5th Ave S
City:       SEATTLE
StateProv:  WA
PostalCode: 98104
Country:    US
[...]
```

In Example 3.3, the reverse DNS (two places) and interesting traceroute results are bolded. The Amazon.com domain name makes it highly likely that the web site is run by Amazon rather than Target itself. Then the whois results showing "Amazon.com, Inc." as the IP space owner removes all doubt. The web site is Target branded, but displays "Powered by Amazon.com" at the bottom. If we were hired by Target to test their security, we would need separate permission from Amazon to touch this address space.

Web databases can also be used to find hostnames under a given domain. For example, Netcraft has a web site DNS search feature at *http://searchdns.netcraft.com/?host*. Typing .target.com in to the form brings 36 results, as shown in Figure 3.2. Their handy table shows the netblock owner too, which catches cases such as Amazon running www.target.com. We already knew about some of the discovered hosts, but we would have been unlikely to guess names such as sendasmoochie.target.com.

Figure 3.2. Netcraft finds 36 Target web servers

Found 36 sites

	Site	Site Report	First seen	Netblock	OS
1.	www.target.com	🗐	October 1995	Amazon.com, Inc.	unknown
2.	weeklyad.target.com	🗐	January 2005	Akamai Technologies	Linux
3.	sites.target.com	🗐	August 2005	Target Corporation	F5 Big-IP
4.	redcard.target.com	🗐	November 2005	Target Corporation	F5 Big-IP
5.	www.target.com.au	🗐	June 2000	APNIC	Windows 2000
6.	targetrewards.target.com	🗐	August 2005	Target Corporation	F5 Big-IP
7.	cinemared.target.com	🗐	August 2005	Target Corporation	F5 Big-IP
8.	recipes.target.com	🗐	November 2005	Allrecipes.com, Inc.	Windows Server 2003
9.	bookmarked.target.com	🗐	September	Implex.net	Linux

Google can also be used for this purpose with queries such as `site:target.com`.

3.3.2. Whois Queries Against IP Registries

After a set of initial "seed" IPs are discovered, they must be researched to ensure they belong to the company you expect and to determine what netblocks they are part of. A small company might have a tiny allocation of 1–16 IP addresses, while larger corporations often have thousands. This information is kept in regional databases, such as ARIN (American Registry for Internet Numbers) for North America and RIPE for Europe and the Middle East. Modern whois tools take an IP address and automatically query the appropriate registry.

Small and mid-sized companies normally don't have IP space allocated by the likes of ARIN. Instead, they are delegated netblocks from their ISPs. Sometimes you get this ISP information from IP queries. This generally leaves you with a big netblock and you don't know which portion of it is allocated to your target. Fortunately, many ISPs now subdelegate customer ranges using Shared Whois (SWIP) or Referral Whois (RWhois). If the ISP has done this, you learn the customer's exact netblock size.

One of the IP addresses previously discovered for target.com was `161.225.130.163`. Example 3.5 demonstrates a whois query (automatically directed against ARIN) to determine the owner and IP allocation information for this IP.

Example 3.5. Using whois to find netblock containing 161.225.130.163

```
> whois 161.225.130.163
[Querying whois.arin.net]
[whois.arin.net]

OrgName:     Target Corporation
OrgID:       TARGET-14
Address:     1000 Nicollet TPS 3165
City:        Minneapolis
StateProv:   MN
PostalCode:  55403
Country:     US

NetRange:    161.225.0.0 - 161.225.255.255
CIDR:        161.225.0.0/16
NetName:     TARGETNET
NetHandle:   NET-161-225-0-0-1
Parent:      NET-161-0-0-0-0
NetType:     Direct Assignment
NameServer:  NS3.TARGET.COM
NameServer:  NS4.TARGET.COM
Comment:
RegDate:     1993-03-04
Updated:     2005-11-02

OrgTechHandle: DOMAI45-ARIN
OrgTechName:   Domainnames admin
OrgTechPhone:  +1-612-696-2525
OrgTechEmail:  Domainnames.admin@target.com
```

Not surprisingly, Target owns a huge Class B netblock, covering all 65,536 IPs from 161.225.0.0 through 161.225.255.255. Since the OrgName is Target, this isn't a case where we are seeing results from their ISP.

The next step is to similarly look up all previously discovered IPs which don't fall within this range. Then you can begin with more advanced queries. The command **whois -h whois.arin.net \?** gives the ARIN query syntax. It would be nice if you could search for all netblocks matching a given address, OrgID, or OrgTechEmail, but IP registries generally don't allow that. However, many other helpful queries are allowed. For example, **whois -h whois.arin.net @target.com** shows all the ARIN contacts with email addresses at target.com. The query **whois -h whois.arin.net "n target*"** shows all the netblock handles starting with target. It is not case sensitive. Similarly, **whois -h whois.arin.net "o target*"** shows all of the organizational names starting with target. You can look up the address, phone number, and contact email associated with each entry to determine whether they are part of the company you wish to scan. Often they are 3rd parties who happen to have a similar name.

3.3.3. Internet Routing Information

The core routing protocol of the Internet is the Border Gateway Protocol (BGP). When scanning mid-sized and large organizations, BGP routing tables can help you find their IP subnets all over the world. For example, suppose you want to scan IP addresses belonging to Microsoft Corporation. A DNS lookup for microsoft.com provides the IP address 207.46.196.115. A whois query as discussed in the previous section shows that the whole 207.46.0.0/16 block belongs to Microsoft at their appropriate "One Microsoft Way" address in Redmond. That provides 65,536 IP addresses to scan, but BGP tables expose many more.

Entities such as Microsoft are assigned autonomous system (AS) numbers for routing purposes. A handy tool for determining the AS number advertised for a given IP address is available at *http://asn.cymru.com/*. Typing 207.46.0.0 into this form provides Microsoft's AS number 8075. Next, I want to find all of the IP prefixes which route to this AS. A handy tool for doing so is available at *http://www.robtex.com/as/*. Typing in AS8075 and hitting Go on that page leads to a summary screen showing 42 prefixes found. Those prefixes represent 339,456 IP addresses and can be enumerated by clicking the BGP tab.

While obtaining BGP information from canned web forms such as these is convenient, obtaining routing data from actual routers is more fun and may allow more powerful custom queries. Several organizations provide such a service. For an example, telnet to route-views.routeviews.org or visit *http://routeviews.org*. Of course these services provide read-only access to the data. If you need to manipulate global routing tables as part of a diabolical plan to take over the Internet, that is beyond the scope of this book.

3.4. DNS Resolution

The key focus of Nmap host discovery is determining which hosts are up and responsive on the network. That narrows down the field of targets, since you can't hack a host which doesn't exist. But don't let discovery end there. You wouldn't date girls (or guys) just because they're breathing, and selecting boxes on the network to penetrate deserves special care too. A great source of information (about networked hosts, not potential dates) is DNS, the domain name system. Even security conscious organizations often assign names which disclose the function of their systems. It's not uncommon to see wireless access points named wap or wireless, firewalls named fw, firewall, or fw-1, and development web servers with not-yet-published content named dev, staging, www-int, or beta. Locations or department names are also often disclosed, as in the company whose Chicago office firewall is named fw.chi.

By default, Nmap performs reverse-DNS resolution for every IP which responds to host discovery probes (i.e. those that are online). If host discovery is skipped with -PN, resolution is performed for all IPs. Rather than use the slow standard DNS resolution libraries, Nmap uses a custom stub resolver which performs dozens of requests in parallel.

While the defaults generally work well, Nmap offers four options for controlling DNS resolution. They can substantially affect scanning speed and the amount of information gathered.

-n (No DNS resolution)
> Tells Nmap to *never* do reverse DNS resolution on the active IP addresses it finds. Since DNS can be slow even with Nmap's built-in parallel stub resolver, this option reduces scanning times.

-R (DNS resolution for all targets)
> Tells Nmap to *always* do reverse DNS resolution on the target IP addresses. Normally reverse DNS is only performed against responsive (online) hosts.

--system-dns (Use system DNS resolver)
> By default, Nmap resolves IP addresses by sending queries directly to the name servers configured on your host and then listening for responses. Many requests (often dozens) are performed in parallel to improve performance. Specify this option to use your system resolver instead (one IP at a time via the

`getnameinfo` call). This is slow and rarely useful unless you find a bug in the Nmap parallel resolver (please let us know if you do). The system resolver is always used for IPv6 scans.

`--dns-servers <server1>[,<server2>[,...]]`   (Servers to use for reverse DNS queries)
By default, Nmap determines your DNS servers (for rDNS resolution) from your resolv.conf file (Unix) or the Registry (Win32). Alternatively, you may use this option to specify alternate servers. This option is not honored if you are using `--system-dns` or an IPv6 scan. Using multiple DNS servers is often faster, especially if you choose authoritative servers for your target IP space. This option can also improve stealth, as your requests can be bounced off just about any recursive DNS server on the Internet.

This option also comes in handy when scanning private networks. Sometimes only a few name servers provide proper rDNS information, and you may not even know where they are. You can scan the network for port 53 (perhaps with version detection), then try Nmap list scans (`-sL`) specifying each name server one at a time with `--dns-servers` until you find one which works.

3.5. Host Discovery Controls

By default, Nmap will include a ping scanning stage prior to more intrusive probes such as port scans, OS detection, Nmap Scripting Engine, or version detection. Nmap usually only performs intrusive scans on machines that are shown to be available during the ping scan stage. This saves substantial time and bandwidth compared to performing full scans against every single IP address. Yet this approach is not ideal for all circumstances. There are times when you *do* want to scan every IP (`-PN`), and other times when you want to perform host discovery and nothing more (`-sP`). There are even times when you want to print out the target hosts and exit prior to even sending ping probes (`-sL`). Nmap offers several high-level options to control this behavior.

3.5.1. List Scan (`-sL`)

List scan is a degenerate form of host discovery that simply lists each host on the network(s) specified, without sending any packets to the target hosts. By default, Nmap still performs reverse-DNS resolution on the hosts to learn their names. Nmap also reports the total number of IP addresses at the end. List scan is a good sanity check to ensure that you have proper IP addresses for your targets. If the hosts sport domain names you do not recognize, it is worth investigating further to prevent scanning the wrong company's network.

There are many reasons target IP ranges can be incorrect. Even network administrators can mistype their own netblocks, and pen-testers have even more to worry about. In some cases, security consultants are given the wrong addresses. In others, they try to find proper IP ranges through resources such as whois databases and routing tables. The databases can be out of date, or the company could be loaning IP space to other organizations. Whether to scan corporate parents, siblings, service providers, and subsidiaries is an important issue that should be worked out with the customer in advance. A preliminary list scan helps confirm exactly what targets are being scanned.

Another reason for an advance list scan is stealth. In some cases, you do not want to begin with a full-scale assault on the target network that is likely to trigger IDS alerts and bring unwanted attention. A list scan is unobtrusive and provides information that may be useful in choosing which individual machines to target. It is possible, though highly unlikely, that the target will notice all of the reverse-DNS requests. When that is a concern, you can bounce through anonymous recursive DNS servers using the `--dns-servers` option as described in the section called "DNS proxying" [286].

A list scan is specified with the `-sL` command-line option. Since the idea is to simply print a list of target hosts, options for higher level functionality such as port scanning, OS detection, or ping scanning cannot be combined with `-sL`. If you wish to disable ping scanning while still performing such higher level functionality, read up on the `-PN` option. Example 3.6 shows list scan being used to enumerate the CIDR /28 network range (16 IP addresses) surrounding the main Stanford University web server.

Example 3.6. Enumerating hosts surrounding www.stanford.edu with list scan

```
felix~> nmap -sL www.stanford.edu/28

Starting Nmap ( http://nmap.org )
Host www9.Stanford.EDU (171.67.16.80) not scanned
Host www10.Stanford.EDU (171.67.16.81) not scanned
Host scriptorium.Stanford.EDU (171.67.16.82) not scanned
Host coursework-a.Stanford.EDU (171.67.16.83) not scanned
Host coursework-e.Stanford.EDU (171.67.16.84) not scanned
Host www3.Stanford.EDU (171.67.16.85) not scanned
Host leland-dev.Stanford.EDU (171.67.16.86) not scanned
Host coursework-preprod.Stanford.EDU (171.67.16.87) not scanned
Host stanfordwho-dev.Stanford.EDU (171.67.16.88) not scanned
Host workgroup-dev.Stanford.EDU (171.67.16.89) not scanned
Host courseworkbeta.Stanford.EDU (171.67.16.90) not scanned
Host www4.Stanford.EDU (171.67.16.91) not scanned
Host coursework-i.Stanford.EDU (171.67.16.92) not scanned
Host leland2.Stanford.EDU (171.67.16.93) not scanned
Host coursework-j.Stanford.EDU (171.67.16.94) not scanned
Host 171.67.16.95 not scanned
Nmap done: 16 IP addresses (0 hosts up) scanned in 0.38 seconds
```

3.5.2. Ping Scan (`-sP`)

This option tells Nmap to *only* perform a ping scan, then print out the available hosts that responded to the scan. No further testing (such as port scanning or OS detection) is performed, except for Nmap Scripting Engine (`--script`) host scripts and traceroute probing (`--traceroute`) if you specified those options. This is one step more intrusive than a list scan, and can often be used for the same purposes. It performs light reconnaissance of a target network quickly and without attracting much attention. Knowing how many hosts are up is more valuable to attackers than the list of every single IP and host name provided by list scan.

Systems administrators often find this option valuable as well. It can easily be used to count available machines on a network or monitor server availability. This is often called a ping sweep, and is more reliable than pinging the broadcast address because many hosts do not reply to broadcast queries.

Example 3.7 shows a quick ping scan against the CIDR /24 (256 IPs) surrounding one of my favorite web sites, Linux Weekly News.

Example 3.7. Discovering hosts surrounding `www.lwn.net` with a ping scan

```
# nmap -sP -T4 www.lwn.net/24

Starting Nmap ( http://nmap.org )
Host 66.216.68.0 seems to be a subnet broadcast address (returned 1 extra ping)
Host 66.216.68.1 appears to be up.
Host 66.216.68.2 appears to be up.
Host 66.216.68.3 appears to be up.
Host server1.camnetsec.com (66.216.68.10) appears to be up.
Host akqa.com (66.216.68.15) appears to be up.
Host asria.org (66.216.68.18) appears to be up.
Host webcubic.net (66.216.68.19) appears to be up.
Host dizzy.yellowdog.com (66.216.68.22) appears to be up.
Host www.outdoorwire.com (66.216.68.23) appears to be up.
Host www.inspectorhosting.com (66.216.68.24) appears to be up.
Host jwebmedia.com (66.216.68.25) appears to be up.
[...]
Host rs.lwn.net (66.216.68.48) appears to be up.
Host 66.216.68.52 appears to be up.
Host cuttlefish.laughingsquid.net (66.216.68.53) appears to be up.
[...]
Nmap done: 256 IP addresses (105 hosts up) scanned in 12.69 seconds
```

This example only took 13 seconds, but provides valuable information. In that class C sized address range, 105 hosts are online. From the unrelated domain names all packed into such a small IP space, it is clear that LWN uses a colocation or dedicated server provider. If the LWN machines turn out to be highly secure, an attacker might go after one of those neighbor machines and then perform a local ethernet attack with tools such as Ettercap or Dsniff. An ethical use of this data would be a network administrator considering moving machines to this provider. He might e-mail a few of the listed organizations and ask their opinion of the service before signing a long-term contract or making the expensive and disruptive datacenter move.

The -sP option sends an ICMP echo request and a TCP ACK packet to port 80 by default. Since unprivileged Unix users (or Windows users without WinPcap installed) cannot send these raw packets, a SYN packet is sent instead in those cases. The SYN packet is sent using a TCP connect system call to port 80 of the target host. When a privileged user tries to scan targets on a local ethernet network, ARP requests (-PR) are used unless the --send-ip option is specified.

The -sP option can be combined with any of the techniques discussed in Section 3.6, "Host Discovery Techniques" [60] for greater flexibility. If any of those probe type and port number options are used, the default probes (ACK and echo request) are overridden. When strict firewalls are in place between the source host running Nmap and the target network, using those advanced techniques is recommended. Otherwise hosts could be missed when the firewall drops probes or their responses.

3.5.3. Disable Ping (-PN)

Another option is to skip the Nmap discovery stage altogether. Normally, Nmap uses this stage to determine active machines for heavier scanning. By default, Nmap only performs heavy probing such as port scans, version detection, or OS detection against hosts that are found to be up. Disabling host discovery with the -PN option causes Nmap to attempt the requested scanning functions against *every* target IP address specified. So if a class B sized target address space (/16) is specified on the command line, all 65,536 IP addresses are scanned. Proper host discovery is skipped as with a list scan, but instead of stopping and printing the target list, Nmap continues to perform requested functions as if each target IP is active.

There are many reasons for disabling the Nmap ping tests. One of the most common is intrusive vulnerability assessments. One can specify dozens of different ping probes in an attempt to elicit a response from all available hosts, but it is still possible that an active yet heavily firewalled machine might not reply to any of those probes. So to avoid missing anything, auditors frequently perform intense scans, such as for all 65,536 TCP ports, against every IP on the target network. It may seem wasteful to send hundreds of thousands of packets to IP addresses that probably have no host listening, and it can slow scan times by an order of magnitude or more. Nmap must send retransmissions to every port in case the original probe was dropped in transit, and Nmap must spend substantial time waiting for responses because it has no round-trip-time (RTT) estimate for these non-responsive IP addresses. But serious penetration testers are willing to pay this price to avoid even a slight risk of missing active machines. They can always do a quick scan as well, leaving the massive -PN scan to run in the background while they work. Chapter 6, *Optimizing Nmap Performance* [135] provides more performance tuning advice.

Another frequent reason given for using -PN is that the tester has a list of machines that are already known to be up. So the user sees no point in wasting time with the host discovery stage. The user creates their own list of active hosts and then passes it to Nmap using the -iL (take input from list) option. This strategy is rarely beneficial from a time-saving perspective. Due to the retransmission and RTT estimate issues discussed in the previous paragraph, even one unresponsive IP address in a large list will often take more time to scan than a whole ping scanning stage would have. In addition, the ping stage allows Nmap to gather RTT samples that can speed up the following port scan, particularly if the target host has strict firewall rules. While specifying -PN is rarely helpful as a time saver, it is important if some of the machines on your list block all of the discovery techniques that would otherwise be specified. Users must strike a balance between scan speed and the possibility of missing heavily cloaked machines.

3.6. Host Discovery Techniques

There was a day when finding whether an IP address was registered to an active host was easy. Simply send an ICMP echo request (*ping*) packet and wait for a response. Firewalls rarely blocked these requests, and the vast majority of hosts obediently responded. Such a response has been required since 1989 by RFC 1122, which clearly states that "Every host MUST implement an ICMP Echo server function that receives Echo Requests and sends corresponding Echo Replies".

Unfortunately for network explorers, many administrators have decided that security concerns trump RFC requirements and have blocked ICMP ping messages.Example 3.8 uses an ICMP-only Nmap ping scan against six popular Web sites, but receives only two responses. This demonstrates that hosts can no longer be assumed unavailable based on failure to reply to ICMP ping probes. The "-sP -PE" options in this example specify an ICMP-only ping scan. The -R option tells Nmap to perform reverse-DNS resolution against all hosts, even down ones.

Example 3.8. Attempts to ping popular Internet hosts

```
# nmap -sP -PE -R -v microsoft.com ebay.com citibank.com google.com \
                    slashdot.org yahoo.com

Starting Nmap ( http://nmap.org )
Host origin2.microsoft.com (207.46.250.252) appears to be down.
Host pages.ebay.com (66.135.192.87) appears to be down.
Host ld1-www.citicorp.com (192.193.195.132) appears to be down.
Host 216.239.57.99 appears to be up.
Host slashdot.org (66.35.250.150) appears to be down.
Host w3.rc.dcn.yahoo.com (216.109.127.30) appears to be up.
Nmap done: 6 IP addresses (2 hosts up) scanned in 3.76 seconds
```

Fortunately, Nmap offers a wide variety of host discovery techniques beyond the standard ICMP echo request. They are described in the following sections. Note that if you specify any of the -P options discussed in this section, they *replace* the default discovery probes rather than adding to them.

3.6.1. TCP SYN Ping (-PS<port list>)

The -PS option sends an empty TCP packet with the SYN flag set. The default destination port is 80 (configurable at compile time by changing DEFAULT_TCP_PROBE_PORT_SPEC in nmap.h), but an alternate port can be specified as a parameter. A list of ports may be specified (e.g. -PS22-25,80,113,1050,35000), in which case probes will be attempted against each port in parallel.

The SYN flag suggests to the remote system that you are attempting to establish a connection. Normally the destination port will be closed, and a RST (reset) packet will be sent back. If the port happens to be open, the target will take the second step of a TCP three-way-handshake by responding with a SYN/ACK TCP packet. The machine running Nmap then tears down the nascent connection by responding with a RST rather than sending an ACK packet which would complete the three-way-handshake and establish a full connection.[2]

Nmap does not care whether the port is open or closed. Either the RST or SYN/ACK response discussed previously tell Nmap that the host is available and responsive.

On Unix boxes, only the privileged user root is generally able to send and receive raw TCP packets. For unprivileged users, a workaround is automatically employed whereby the connect system call is initiated against each target port. This has the effect of sending a SYN packet to the target host, in an attempt to establish a connection. If connect returns with a quick success or an ECONNREFUSED failure, the underlying TCP stack must have received a SYN/ACK or RST and the host is marked available. If the connection attempt is left hanging until a timeout is reached, the host is marked as down. This workaround is also used for IPv6 connections, as raw IPv6 packet building support is not yet available in Nmap.

Example 3.8 failed to detect four out of six machines because they did not respond to ICMP echo requests. Repeating the experiment using a SYN probe to port 80 (HTTP) garners responses from all six, as shown in Example 3.9.

---

[2]The RST packet is sent by the kernel of the machine running Nmap in response to the unexpected SYN/ACK, not by Nmap itself.

Example 3.9. Retry host discovery using port 80 SYN probes

```
# nmap -sP -PS80 -R -v microsoft.com ebay.com citibank.com google.com \
                       slashdot.org yahoo.com

Starting Nmap ( http://nmap.org )
Host origin2.microsoft.com (207.46.249.252) appears to be up.
Host pages.ebay.com (66.135.192.87) appears to be up.
Host ld1-www.citicorp.com (192.193.195.132) appears to be up.
Host 216.239.57.99 appears to be up.
Host slashdot.org (66.35.250.150) appears to be up.
Host w3.rc.dcn.yahoo.com (216.109.127.30) appears to be up.
Nmap done: 6 IP addresses (6 hosts up) scanned in 0.48 seconds
```

In addition to detecting all six machines, the second run is much faster. It takes less than half a second because the machines are scanned in parallel and the scan never times out waiting for a response. This test is not entirely fair because these are all popular web servers and thus can be expected to listen on TCP port 80. However, it still demonstrates the point that different types of hosts respond to different probe types. Nmap supports the usage of many scan types in parallel to enable effective scanning of diverse networks.

3.6.2. TCP ACK Ping (`-PA<port list>`)

The TCP ACK ping is quite similar to the SYN ping. The difference, as you could likely guess, is that the TCP ACK flag is set instead of the SYN flag. Such an ACK packet purports to be acknowledging data over an established TCP connection, but no such connection exists. So remote hosts should always respond with a RST packet, disclosing their existence in the process.

The `-PA` option uses the same default port as the SYN probe (80) and can also take a list of destination ports in the same format. If an unprivileged user tries this, or an IPv6 target is specified, the connect workaround discussed previously is used. This workaround is imperfect because connect is actually sending a SYN packet rather than an ACK.

The reason for offering both SYN and ACK ping probes is to maximize the chances of bypassing firewalls. Many administrators configure routers and other simple firewalls to block incoming SYN packets except for those destined for public services like the company web site or mail server. This prevents other incoming connections to the organization, while allowing users to make unobstructed outgoing connections to the Internet. This non-stateful approach takes up few resources on the firewall/router and is widely supported by hardware and software filters. As just one example of the prevalence of this method, the Linux Netfilter/iptables firewall software offers the `--syn` convenience option, which the man page describes as follows.

> Only match TCP packets with the SYN bit set and the ACK and RST bits cleared. Such packets are used to request TCP connection initiation; for example, blocking such packets coming in an interface will prevent incoming TCP connections, but outgoing TCP connections will be unaffected. It is equivalent to --tcp-flags SYN,RST,ACK SYN.

When firewall rules such as this are in place, SYN ping probes (`-PS`) are likely to be blocked when sent to closed target ports. In such cases, the ACK probe excels by cutting right through these rules.

Another common type of firewall uses stateful rules that drop unexpected packets. This feature was initially found mostly on high-end firewalls, though it has become much more common over the years. The Linux Netfilter/iptables system supports this through the `--state` option, which categorizes packets based on connection state as described in the following man page excerpt:

> Possible states are INVALID meaning that the packet is associated with no known connection, ESTABLISHED meaning that the packet is associated with a connection which has seen packets in both directions, NEW meaning that the packet has started a new connection, or otherwise associated with a connection which has not seen packets in both directions, and RELATED meaning that the packet is starting a new connection, but is associated with an existing connection, such as an FTP data transfer, or an ICMP error.

The ACK probe is unlikely to work against firewalls taking this approach, as such an unexpected packet will be classified in the INVALID state and probably dropped. Example 3.10 shows an attempted ACK ping against Microsoft. Their stateful firewall drops the packet, leading Nmap to wrongly conclude that the host is down. The SYN probe has a much better chance of working in such cases. This raises the question of which technique to use when the firewall rules of the target networks are unknown or inconsistent. The proper answer is usually both. Nmap can send SYN and ACK probes to many ports in parallel, as well as performing other host discovery techniques at the same time. This is further discussed in Section 3.7, "Putting It All Together: Host Discovery Strategies" [66].

Example 3.10. Attempted ACK ping against Microsoft

```
# nmap -sP -PA www.microsoft.com

Starting Nmap ( http://nmap.org )
Warning: Hostname www.microsoft.com resolves to 5 IPs. Using 207.46.192.254.
Note: Host seems down. If it is really up, but blocking ping probes, try -PN
Nmap done: 1 IP address (0 hosts up) scanned in 2.22 seconds
```

3.6.3. UDP Ping (`-PU<port list>`)

Another host discovery option is the UDP ping, which sends an empty (unless `--data-length` is specified) UDP packet to the given ports. The port list takes the same format as with the previously discussed `-PS` and `-PA` options. If no ports are specified, the default is 31,338. This default can be configured at compile-time by changing `DEFAULT_UDP_PROBE_PORT_SPEC` in `nmap.h`. A highly uncommon port is used by default because sending to open ports is often undesirable for this particular scan type.

Upon hitting a closed port on the target machine, the UDP probe should elicit an ICMP port unreachable packet in return. This signifies to Nmap that the machine is up and available. Many other types of ICMP errors, such as host/network unreachables or TTL exceeded are indicative of a down or unreachable host. A lack of response is also interpreted this way. If an open port is reached, most services simply ignore the empty packet and fail to return any response. This is why the default probe port is 31,338, which is highly unlikely to be in use. A few services, such as the Character Generator (chargen) protocol, will respond to an empty UDP packet, and thus disclose to Nmap that the machine is available.

The primary advantage of this scan type is that it bypasses firewalls and filters that only screen TCP. For example, I once owned a Linksys BEFW11S4 wireless broadband router. The external interface of this device filtered all TCP ports by default, but UDP probes would still elicit port unreachable messages and thus give away the device.

3.6.4. ICMP Ping Types (–PE, –PP, and –PM)

In addition to the unusual TCP and UDP host discovery types discussed previously, Nmap can send the standard packets sent by the ubiquitous ping program. Nmap sends an ICMP type 8 (echo request) packet to the target IP addresses, expecting a type 0 (echo reply) in return from available hosts. As noted at the beginning of this chapter, many hosts and firewalls now block these packets, rather than responding as required by RFC 1122. For this reason, ICMP-only scans are rarely reliable enough against unknown targets over the Internet. But for system administrators monitoring an internal network, this can be a practical and efficient approach. Use the –PE option to enable this echo request behavior.

While echo request is the standard ICMP ping query, Nmap does not stop there. The ICMP standard (RFC 792) also specifies timestamp request, information request, and address mask request packets as codes 13, 15, and 17, respectively. While the ostensible purpose for these queries is to learn information such as address masks and current times, they can easily be used for host discovery. Nmap does not currently implement information request packets, as they are not widely supported (RFC 1122 insists that "a host SHOULD NOT implement these messages"). Timestamp and address mask queries can be sent with the –PP and –PM options, respectively. A timestamp reply (ICMP code 14) or address mask reply (code 18) discloses that the host is available. These two queries can be valuable when administrators specifically block echo request packets, but forget that other ICMP queries can be used for the same purpose.

3.6.5. IP Protocol Ping (–PO<protocol list>)

The newest host discovery option is the IP protocol ping, which sends IP packets with the specified protocol number set in their IP header. The protocol list takes the same format as do port lists in the previously discussed TCP and UDP host discovery options. If no protocols are specified, the default is to send multiple IP packets for ICMP (protocol 1), IGMP (protocol 2), and IP-in-IP (protocol 4). The default protocols can be configured at compile-time by changing DEFAULT_PROTO_PROBE_PORT_SPEC in nmap.h. Note that for the ICMP, IGMP, TCP (protocol 6), and UDP (protocol 17), the packets are sent with the proper protocol headers while other protocols are sent with no additional data beyond the IP header (unless the --data-length option is specified).

This host discovery method looks for either responses using the same protocol as a probe, or ICMP protocol unreachable messages which signify that the given protocol isn't supported by the destination host. Either type of response signifies that the target host is alive.

3.6.6. ARP Scan (–PR)

One of the most common Nmap usage scenarios is to scan an ethernet LAN. On most LANs, especially those using private address ranges granted by RFC 1918, the vast majority of IP addresses are unused at any given time. When Nmap tries to send a raw IP packet such as an ICMP echo request, the operating system must determine the destination hardware (ARP) address corresponding to the target IP so that it can address the ethernet frame properly. This requires it to issue a series of ARP requests. This is shown in Example 3.11, where a ping scan is attempted against a local ethernet host. The --send-ip option tells Nmap to send IP

---

level packets (rather than raw ethernet) even though it is a local network. Wireshark output of the three ARP requests and their timing has been pasted into the session.

Example 3.11. Raw IP ping scan of an offline target

```
# nmap -n -sP --send-ip 192.168.33.37

Starting Nmap ( http://nmap.org )
  0.000000 00:01:29:f5:27:f2 -> ff:ff:ff:ff:ff:ff ARP Who has 192.168.33.37?
  0.999836 00:01:29:f5:27:f2 -> ff:ff:ff:ff:ff:ff ARP Who has 192.168.33.37?
  1.999684 00:01:29:f5:27:f2 -> ff:ff:ff:ff:ff:ff ARP Who has 192.168.33.37?
Note: Host seems down. If it is really up, but blocking ping probes, try -PN
Nmap done: 1 IP address (0 hosts up) scanned in 2.04 seconds
```

This example took more than two seconds to finish because the (Linux) OS sent three ARP requests, one second apart, before giving up on the host. Given that ARP replies usually come within a couple milliseconds, multi-second waits are excessive. Decreasing this timeout period is no priority for OS vendors because the vast majority of packets are sent to hosts that actually exist. Nmap, on the other hand, must send packets to 16 million IPs when given a target such as 10.0.0.0/8. A two second wait for each becomes a huge delay even though many targets are pinged in parallel.

There is another problem with raw IP ping scans on LANs. When a destination host is found to be unresponsive as in the previous example, the source host generally adds an incomplete entry for that destination IP in its kernel ARP table. ARP table space is finite, and some operating systems react badly when it fills up. When Nmap is used in raw IP mode (`--send-ip`), Nmap sometimes has to wait several minutes for ARP cache entries to expire before it can continue with host discovery.

ARP scanning resolves both problems by putting Nmap in control. Nmap issues the raw ARP requests and handles retransmission and timeout periods at its own discretion. The system ARP cache is bypassed. Example 3.12 shows the difference. This ARP scan takes just over a tenth of the time taken by its IP equivalent.

Example 3.12. ARP ping scan of an offline target

```
# nmap -n -sP -PR --packet-trace --send-eth 192.168.33.37

Starting Nmap ( http://nmap.org )
SENT (0.0060s) ARP who-has 192.168.33.37 tell 192.168.0.100
SENT (0.1180s) ARP who-has 192.168.33.37 tell 192.168.0.100
Note: Host seems down. If it is really up, but blocking ping probes, try -PN
Nmap done: 1 IP address (0 hosts up) scanned in 0.23 seconds
```

In Example 3.12, neither the `-PR` or `--send-eth` options have any effect. This is because ARP is the default scan type when scanning ethernet hosts that Nmap detects are on a local ethernet network. This includes traditional wired ethernet as well as 802.11 wireless networks. Not only is ARP scanning more efficient as discussed above, it is also more accurate. Hosts frequently block IP-based ping packets, but they generally cannot block ARP requests or responses and still communicate on the network. Even if different ping types (such as `-PE` or `-PS`) are specified, Nmap uses ARP instead for any of the targets which are on the same LAN. If you absolutely don't want to do an ARP scan, specify `--send-ip` as shown in Example 3.11, "Raw IP ping scan of an offline target" [65].

Giving Nmap control to send raw ethernet frames also allows Nmap to control the source MAC address. If you have the only PowerBook in the room at a security conference and a massive ARP scan is initiated from a MAC address registered to Apple, heads may turn in your direction. You can spoof your MAC address with the `--spoof-mac` option, as discussed in Section 10.4.8, "MAC Address Spoofing" [270].

3.6.7. Default Combination

If none of these host discovery techniques are chosen, Nmap uses a default which is equivalent to the `-PA` `-PE` arguments for Windows or privileged (root) Unix users. Attentive readers know that this means a TCP ACK packet to port 80 and an ICMP echo request query are sent to each machine. An exception to this is that an ARP scan is used for any targets which are on a local ethernet network. For unprivileged Unix shell users, the default is equivalent to `-PS` (a TCP `connect` call against port 80 of the target hosts). For security auditing, I recommend using a more comprehensive set of ping types, such as those discussed in the section called "Designing the ideal combinations of probes" [70].

3.7. Putting It All Together: Host Discovery Strategies

3.7.1. Related Options

Previous sections describe the major options used to control the Nmap host discovery phase and customize the techniques used. However, there are many more general Nmap options which are relevant here. This section provides a brief description of how these option flags relate to ping scanning. See Chapter 15, *Nmap Reference Guide* [373] for complete descriptions of each option.

`-v` (same as `--verbose`)
    By default, Nmap usually only prints active, responsive hosts. Verbose mode causes Nmap to print down hosts, as well as extra information about active ones.

`--source-port <portnum>` (same as `-g`)
    Setting a constant source port works for ping scanning (TCP and UDP) as it does with other Nmap features. Some naive firewall administrators make a ruleset exception in order to keep DNS (port 53) or FTP-DATA (port 20) working. Of course this opens a hole big enough to drive an Nmap ping scan through. Section 10.4.2, "Source Port Manipulation" [266] provides further details on this technique.

`-n, -R`
    The `-n` option disables all DNS resolution, while the `-R` option enables DNS queries for all hosts, even down ones. The default behavior is to limit DNS resolution to active hosts. These options are particularly important for ping scanning because DNS resolution can greatly affect scan times.

`--dns-servers <server1>[,<server2>[,...]]` (Servers to use for reverse DNS queries)
    By default Nmap will try to determine your DNS servers (for rDNS resolution) from your resolv.conf file (Unix) or the Registry (Win32). Alternatively, you may use this option to specify alternate servers. This option is not honored if you are using `--system-dns` or an IPv6 scan. Using multiple DNS servers is often faster and more stealthy than querying just one. The best performance is often obtained by specifying all of the authoritative servers for the target IP space.

`--data-length <length>`

This option adds `<length>` random bytes of data to every packet, and works with the TCP, UDP, and ICMP ping scan types (for privileged users scanning IPv4). This helps make the scan less conspicuous and more like the packets generated by the ubiquitous ping diagnostics program. Several intrusion detection systems (IDS), including Snort, have alerts for zero-byte ping packets. This option evades those alerts. An option value of 32 makes an echo request look more like it came from Windows, while 56 simulates the default Linux ping.

`--ttl <value>`

Setting the outgoing TTL is supported for privileged users doing IPv4 ping scans. This can be useful as a safety precaution to ensure a scan does not propagate beyond the local network. It can also be used to simulate a native ping program even more convincingly. Some enterprise networks suffer from known routing loops which they can't easily fix. Reducing the outgoing TTL with `--ttl` helps to reduce router CPU load when loops are encountered.

Canned timing options (`-T3`, `-T4`, `-T5`, etc.)

Higher `-T` values speed up ping scanning, just as they speed other Nmap features. With a moderately fast and reliable connection between the source and target networks (i.e. anything more than a dial-up modem), the `-T4` option is recommended.

`--max-parallelism`, `--min-parallelism <value>`

These affect how many probes may be outstanding at once. With the default ping type (two probes), the parallelism value is roughly the number of machines scanned in parallel. Reducing the ping techniques to one probe per host (e.g. `-PE`) will double the number of hosts scanned at once for a given parallelism level, while increasing to four probes per host (e.g. `-PE -PS22,113,50000`) halves it. Most users simply stick to the canned timing options such as `-T4`.

`--min-rtt-timeout`, `--max-rtt-timeout`, `--initial-rtt-timeout <time>`

These options control how long Nmap waits for a ping response.

Input options (`-iL <filename>`, `-iR <number>`)

Host input options are supported as in the rest of Nmap. Users often combine the input-from-list (`-iL`) option with `-PN` to avoid ping-scanning hosts that are already known to be up. Before doing this in an attempt to save time, read Section 3.5.3, "Disable Ping (-PN)" [59]. The `-iR` option chooses hosts at random from allocated Internet IP space. It takes as an argument the number of random hosts you wish to scan. Use zero for a never-ending (until you abort or kill the Nmap process) scan.

Output options (`-oA`, `-oN`, `-oG`, `-oX`, etc.)

All of the Nmap output types (normal, grepable, and XML) support ping scanning. Chapter 13, *Nmap Output Formats* [337] further describes how they work.

`--randomize-hosts`

Shuffling the host scan order with this option may make the scan less conspicuous, though it also can make the scan output a bit more difficult to follow.

`--reason`

The normal Nmap output indicates whether a host is up or not, but does not describe which discovery test(s) the host responded to. For this detail, add the `--reason` option. The results can be confusing for host discovery since Nmap does not always try every probe. It stops as soon as it gets a first response.

So Nmap might report an ICMP echo response from a host during the run, but then a RST response might be received first during a second run and lead Nmap to report that.

`--packet-trace`
> When you want even more details than `--reason` provides, try `--packet-trace`. This option shows every packet send and received by Nmap, including details such as sequence numbers, TTL values, and TCP flags.

`-D <decoy1,decoy2,...>`
> Decoys are fully supported for privileged IPv4 ping scans, camouflaging the true attacker.

`-6`
> The TCP `connect`-based ping scans (`-PS`) support the IPv6 protocol, including multi-port mode (such as `-PS22,80,113`.

`-S <source IP address>,-e <sending device name>`
> As with other functions of Nmap, the source address and sending device can be specified with these options.

General options
> By default, unless `-sP` or `-sL` are specified, Nmap moves onto more intrusive scanning after the host discovery stage. Thus many dozens of general port scanning, OS detection, and version detection options can be used. See the reference guide or relevant chapters for further information.

3.7.2. Choosing and Combining Ping Options

Effective scanning requires more than knowing all of the options described in this and previous sections. Users must understand how and when to use them to suit the target network topology and scanning goals.

TCP probe and port selection

The TCP ping options are some of the most powerful discovery techniques in Nmap. An administrator may be able to get away with blocking ICMP echo request packets without affecting most users, but a server absolutely must respond to SYN packets sent to the public services it provides. Meanwhile, ACK packets often get through non-stateful firewalls. I would recommend using both of SYN and ACK probes, using lists of ports based on any knowledge you might have of the target networks as well as more generally popular ports. A quick scan of more than 10,000 IP addresses across the Internet showed the ports in Table 3.2 to be particularly valuable. Of hosts with a default-drop filter (the hardest type to reach), these are the 14 ports most likely to be accessible (open or closed).

Table 3.2. Most valuable TCP probe ports, in descending order of accessibility.

Port number / Service	Reasoning
`80/http`	The prevalence of Web servers on the Internet leads many newbies to believe that the Web *is* the Internet.
`25/smtp`	Mail is another Internet "killer app" that companies allow through their firewalls.
`22/ssh`	SSH seems to have finally surpassed Telnet as the standard for remote terminal administration.

Port number / Service	Reasoning
443/https	SSL is a popular way for web sites to protect confidential directory information.
21/ftp	This file transfer protocol lives on, though many firewall administrators would not mourn its passing.
113/auth	The auth (identd) service allows servers (usually mail or IRC) to request the username of clients connected to them. Administrators often leave this port unfiltered to avoid long timeouts that can occur when firewall rules prevent servers from connecting back to port 113. Using this port for ping scanning can sometimes lead to false positives, as some administrators have been known to configure their firewalls to forge RST packets back in response to auth queries to any IP on their network, even when no machine exists at that IP. Administrators do this to avoid server timeouts while still preventing the ports from being accessed.
23/telnet	Many devices still offer this administrative interface, though it is a security nightmare.
53/domain	Domain name servers are extremely widespread.
554/rtsp	Real Time Stream Control Protocol is used by media servers, including QuickTime and RealServer.
3389/ms-term-server	Microsoft Terminal Services allows users (and sometimes hackers) to access applications and data on a remote computer.
1723/pptp	Point-to-Point Tunneling Protocol is often used to implement VPN solutions on Microsoft Windows.
389/ldap	The Lightweight Directory Access Protocol is often used to store contact directories and the like.
636/ldapssl	LDAP over SSL is popular for accessing confidential information.
256/FW1-secureremote	Checkpoint Firewall-1 devices often have this administration port open.

In addition to popular ports such as the ones in the list above, choosing at least one high-numbered port is recommended. Many poorly configured firewalls only have default-deny for the privileged ports, meaning those below 1,024. I usually pick a high numbered port out of the air, such as 40,000 or 10,042, to catch machines behind this sort of firewall.

In choosing the ports to probe, remember to emphasize platform diversity. If you are limiting your ping scan to two ports, HTTP (80) and SSH (22) are probably better than HTTP (80) and HTTPS (443) because the latter two are related web services, and many machines that have HTTPS will often have HTTP available anyway. Finding two accessible ports on the same machine is no better for ping scanning purposes than finding one. The goal is to choose ports so that a broad set of hosts will match at least one of them.

Note that the valuable port table does not include many client-oriented ports such as the ubiquitous Windows SMB port 135. The primary reason is that this table only looked at hosts behind default-deny firewalls, where the vast majority of ports are filtered. In those situations, Windows ports such as 135-139 and 445 are usually blocked. When these machines are not behind a firewall, the open ports are unimportant for ping scanning because the thousands of closed ports work just as well.

UDP port selection

In selecting UDP ports, remember that an open port is unlikely to respond to the probes. Unfiltered ports are desired. To avoid open ports, you might consider excluding common UDP services like DNS (port 53) and SNMP (161). On the other hand, firewall rules are often so broad that those probes (particularly to port 53) might get through and hit a closed port. So I would recommend choosing at least port 53 and an arbitrarily selected high-numbered port such as 37,452.

ICMP probe selection

For ICMP, the standard ping (echo request) is usually worth trying. Many administrators specifically allow this because it is useful for debugging or because RFC 1122 requires it. I would also use at least one of the address mask or timestamp requests. These are valuable for networks where administrators intentionally block echo request packets, but forget about other ICMP queries.

Designing the ideal combinations of probes

How all of these ping types are combined into a ping scan strategy depends on characteristics of the target network and on the scan goals. For internal networks, the default ping type usually works well. The default is also fine for most casual scanning, where missing an occasional host is no big deal. Adding more probes can help catch those occasional stealthy machines, at the expense of making the ping scan take a bit longer. Time taken is roughly proportional to the number of probes sent to each machine. For security scans of target networks over the Internet, adding more probes is usually advisable. Try to include a diverse set of the techniques discussed previously. Here is a set of ping options that should catch the vast majority of hosts: `-PE -PA -PS21,22,23,25,80,113,31339 -PA80,113,443,10042`. Adding in `--source-port 53` might be worthwhile as well. How much better will the results be, and how much longer will it take? That depends on the target network, of course, but the Nmap random target selection option (`-iR`) makes it easy to perform a quick test. Example 3.13 shows Nmap generating 50,000 random IP addresses and then performing a default ping scan. You should remember that the default is a TCP ACK packet to port 80, and an ICMP echo request packet.

Example 3.13. Generating 50,000 IP addresses, then ping scanning with default options

```
# nmap -n -sL -iR 50000 -oN - | grep "not scanned" | awk '{print $2}' \
  | sort -n > 50K_IPs
# head -5 50K_IPs
3.100.147.9
3.100.148.119
3.10.160.33
3.10.201.11
3.101.154.139
# nmap -sP -T4 -iL 50K_IPs
# nmap -sP -T4 -iL 50K_IPs -S -oA 50KHosts_DefaultPing
Starting Nmap ( http://nmap.org )
Host dialup-4.177.9.75.SanDiego1.Level3.net (4.177.9.75) appears to be up.
Host dialup-4.181.100.97.SanJose1.Level3.net (4.181.100.97) appears to be up.
Host firewall2.baymountain.com (8.7.97.2) appears to be up.
[thousands of lines cut]
Host 222.91.121.22 appears to be up.
Nmap done: 50000 IP addresses (3348 hosts up) scanned in 1598.07 seconds
```

Scanning the 50,000 address took just under 27 minutes, and 3,348 hosts were detected. Most of the DNS names were already in cache due to a previous scratch run, though it still would have likely been faster had DNS resolution been disabled with -n. To determine the effects of using a wider range of ping techniques, the same 50K hosts were rescanned with 13 probes per port rather than the default of two. As shown in Example 3.14, Nmap was able to detect 1,125 (34%) more hosts. It took about 71 minutes, which is more than 2.5 times as long. Given all the new hosts detected, that extra time was well spent. Note that not all of the new hosts will be legitimate. Increasing the number of ping probes increases the chances that Nmap will hit network artifacts that make a non-existent host appear to be active. Firewalls that return a RST for SYN or ACK packets to port 113 are one example of this.

Example 3.14. Repeating ping scan with extra probes

```
# nmap -sP -PE -PP -PS21,22,23,25,80,113,31339 -PA80,113,443,10042 \
  -T4 --source-port 53 -iL 50K_IPs -oA 50KHosts_ExtendedPing
Starting Nmap ( http://nmap.org )
Host sim7124.agni.lindenlab.com (8.10.144.126) appears to be up.
Host firewall2.baymountain.com (8.7.97.2) appears to be up.
Host 12.1.6.201 appears to be up.
Host psor.inshealth.com (12.130.143.43) appears to be up.
[thousands of hosts cut]
Host ZM088019.ppp.dion.ne.jp (222.8.88.19) appears to be up.
Host 222.92.136.102 appears to be up.
Nmap done: 50000 IP addresses (4473 hosts up) scanned in 4259.28 seconds
```

When performing security audits for clients, I normally start TCP analysis with a port scan against the most common 1000 ports (the default) with comprehensive ping scan options like those shown in Example 3.14, "Repeating ping scan with extra probes" [71]. Such a scan does not take particularly long, allowing me to quickly start working. I also launch -PN (ping disabled) scans against all 65K TCP ports in the background while I work. When they finish, which may be days later, I compare them to my initial quick scan and investigate any new ports or machines found.

3.8. Host Discovery Code Algorithms

One of the greatest benefits of Open Source software like Nmap is that curious users are always able to study the source code when they want answers about its operation. The highest level ping scanning function is `nexthost` (in `targets.cc`, which calls `massping` to initialize a list of targets. `Massping` in turn passes the list off to `ultra_scan` (in `scan_engine.cc`). Ultra_scan is Nmap's general-purpose scanning function and does all the hard work of sending, receiving, and interpreting packets. For more on `ultra_scan` see Section 5.13, "Scan Code and Algorithms" [128].

While source code analysis is the only way to truly get the complete picture of Nmap operation down to every trivial detail, it is not always the easiest approach to understanding Nmap. In many cases, the most effective way to explore Nmap's behavior given a set of command-line options is to add the `--packet-trace` option, which prints out all of the packets sent and received by Nmap.

Because the source code and the `--packet-trace` option are excellent resources for learning the nitty-gritty details of Nmap operation, I'll only discuss how host discovery works at a high level here. When Nmap is executed, it may be passed networks containing hundreds of thousands or even millions of hosts. So Nmap breaks them into blocks that are small enough to deal with at one time (dozens up to a few thousand hosts). `ultra_scan` then works its way through the block, sending packets as fast as its congestion controls allow. Rather than sending all the probes requested by the user to each host all at once, Nmap sends the first probe to all the targets, then the second probe, and so on. When a conclusive response to a probe is received, that host is marked as up or down as appropriate and no further probes are sent to it. A target host which fails to respond to any probes, even after retransmissions, is marked as down. Nmap waits until every host has either received a conclusive response or has timed out. Eventually, Nmap runs out of new hosts in the block and the number of outstanding probes dwindles to zero as retransmissions complete. The ping scanning subsystem returns the results so that Nmap can begin port scanning or any other requested probing of the target machines. When Nmap finishes completely with a block of hosts, it prints the results and passes the next block to the ping scanner.

Multiple hosts, usually with multiple probes per host, are handled in parallel. The number of outstanding probes and timeout periods are modified in real-time based on network latency and reliability. The `ultra_scan` performance algorithms are further described in Section 5.13, "Scan Code and Algorithms" [128].

Chapter 4. Port Scanning Overview

4.1. Introduction to Port Scanning

While Nmap has grown in functionality over the years, it began as an efficient port scanner, and that remains its core function. The simple command **nmap <target>** scans the most commonly used 1,000 TCP ports on the host *<target>*, classifying each port into the state open, closed, filtered, unfiltered, open|filtered, or closed|filtered.

4.1.1. What Exactly is a Port?

Ports are simply a software abstraction, used to distinguish between communication channels. Similar to the way IP addresses are used to identify machines on networks, ports identify specific applications in use on a single machine. For example, your web browser will by default connect to TCP port 80 of machines in HTTP URLs. If you specify the secure HTTPS protocol instead, the browser will try port 443 by default.

Nmap works with two protocols that use ports: TCP and UDP. A connection for each protocol is uniquely identified by four elements: source and destination IP addresses and corresponding source and destination ports. All of these elements are simply numbers placed in the headers of each packet sent between hosts. The protocol is an eight-bit field, which specifies what type of packet is contained in the IP data (payload) section. For example, TCP is protocol number six, and UDP is 17. IPv4 addresses have a length of 32-bits, while ports are 16-bits long. IPv6 addresses are 128-bits in length. Further IP, TCP, and UDP header layout details can be found in Section 7, "TCP/IP Reference" [xxvi].

Because most popular services are registered to a well-known port number, one can often guess what services open ports represent. Nmap includes an nmap-services file, containing the well-known service for registered port and protocol numbers, as well as common ports for trojan backdoors and other applications that don't bother registering with the Internet Assigned Numbers Authority (IANA). Nmap prints this service name for reference along with the port number.

Because the port number field is 16-bits wide, values can reach 65,535. The lowest possible value, zero, is invalid. The Berkeley sockets API, which defines how programs are usually written for network communication, does not allow port zero to be used as such. Instead, it interprets a port zero request as a wildcard, meaning that the programmer does not care which is used. The system then chooses an available port number. For example, programmers rarely care what source port number is used for an outgoing connection. So they set it to zero and let the operating system choose one.

While port zero is invalid, nothing stops someone from specifying it in the header field. Some malicious trojan backdoors listen on port zero of compromised systems as a stealthy way to offer illegitimate access without appearing on most port scans. To combat this, Nmap does allow scanning of port zero when it is specified explicitly (e.g. -p0-65535).

The first class of valid ports, numbers one through 1,023, are known as reserved ports. Unix systems (unlike Windows) require that applications have special (root) privileges in order to bind to and listen on these ports. The idea is to allow remote users to trust that they are connecting to a valid service started by an administrator and not by some wicked, unprivileged user. If the registered port for SSH was 2,222 instead of 22, a malicious

---

user could start up a rogue SSH daemon on that port, collecting passwords from anyone who connects. As most common server applications listen on reserved ports, these are often the most fruitful to scan.

The ephemeral port range is another class of ports. This pool of ports is made available by the system for allocation as needed. When an application specifies port zero (meaning "any port"), the system chooses a port from this range. The range varies by operating system, and is usually configurable. It should contain at least a couple thousand ports to avoid running out when many concurrent connections are open. The Nmap connect scan can use hundreds at a time as it scans every specified port on each target machine. On Linux, you can view or set the range using the file `/proc/sys/net/ipv4/ip_local_port_range`. Example 4.1 shows that on my Linux system, the range is 32,768 to 61,000. Such a large range should be sufficient in almost all cases, but I expand it just to demonstrate how to do so.

Example 4.1. Viewing and increasing the ephemeral port range on Linux

```
felix/# cat /proc/sys/net/ipv4/ip_local_port_range
32768   61000
felix/# echo "10000 65000" > /proc/sys/net/ipv4/ip_local_port_range
felix/# cat /proc/sys/net/ipv4/ip_local_port_range
10000   65000
felix/#
```

SunRPC ports are often found in the ephemeral range. Other applications open ephemeral ports temporarily for a file transfer or other event. FTP clients often do this when requesting an active mode transfer. Some P2P and instant messaging clients do so as well.

The IANA has their own port classification scheme, which differs slightly from the vernacular of this book. Their authoritative port list at *http://www.iana.org/assignments/port-numbers* divides the space into the following three classes:

well-known ports
> These are reserved ports (within the range of 1 to 1,023, as discussed above) which have been registered with the IANA for a certain service. Familiar examples are ports 22, 25, and 80 for the services SSH, SMTP, and HTTP, respectively.

registered ports
> These ports fall within the range 1,024 to 49,151 and have been registered with the IANA in the same way the well known ports have. Most of these are not as commonly used as the well-known ports. The key difference is that unprivileged users can bind to these ports and thus run the services on their registered port. Users cannot do so on most platforms for well-known ports, since they reside in the reserved port range.

dynamic and/or private ports
> The IANA reserves the port numbers from 49152 through 65535 for dynamic uses such as those discussed in the ephemeral ports section. Proprietary services that are only used within a company may also use these ports.

When this book mentions registered or well-known ports without any reference to the IANA, it usually means ports registered with Nmap in the `nmap-services` file, regardless of whether they fall in the reserved port range.

Nmap's port registration file (`nmap-services`) contains empirical data about how frequently each TCP or UDP port is found to be open. By default, Nmap scans the 1,000 most popular ports of each protocol it is asked to scan. There are many options for specifying an alternate set of ports (by frequency or by listing them explicitly), as described in Section 4.3.2, "Selecting Ports to Scan" [83].

4.1.2. What Are the Most Popular Ports?

I spent the Summer of 2008 scanning tens of millions of Internet hosts and collecting data from enterprises to determine how frequently each port number is found open. It is important to be familiar with the most common service ports, and also interesting to see which ones made the list. The following two lists provide the top TCP and UDP ports as determined by our empirical scan data. The listed service is the one found in our `nmap-services` file. We try to list the most common service for each port there, though of course it is possible for a port to be used for different things.

Top 20 (most commonly open) TCP ports

1. Port 80 (HTTP)—If you don't even know this service, you're reading the wrong book. This accounted for more than 14% of the open ports we discovered.

2. Port 23 (Telnet)—Telnet lives on (particularly as an administration port on devices such as routers and smart switches) even though it is insecure (unencrypted).

3. Port 443 (HTTPS)—SSL-encrypted web servers use this port by default.

4. Port 21 (FTP)—FTP, like Telnet, is another insecure protocol which should die. Even with anonymous FTP (avoiding the authentication sniffing worry), data transfer is still subject to tampering.

5. Port 22 (SSH)—Secure Shell, an encrypted replacement for Telnet (and, in some cases, FTP).

6. Port 25 (SMTP)—The Standard Mail Transfer Protocol (also insecure).

7. Port 3389 (ms-term-server)—Microsoft Terminal Services administration port.

8. Port 110 (POP3)—Post Office Protocol version 3 for email retrieval (insecure).

9. Port 445 (Microsoft-DS)—For SMB communication over IP with MS Windows services (such as file/printer sharing).

10. Port 139 (NetBIOS-SSN)—NetBIOS Session Service for communication with MS Windows services (such as file/printer sharing). This has been supported on Windows machines longer than 445 has.

11. Port 143 (IMAP)—Internet Message Access Protocol version 2. An insecure email retrieval protocol.

12. Port 53 (Domain)—Domain Name System (DNS), an insecure system for conversion between host/domain names and IP addresses.

13. Port 135 (MSRPC)—Another common port for MS Windows services.

14. Port 3306 (MySQL)—For communication with MySQL databases.

---

15. Port 8080 (HTTP-Proxy)—Commonly used for HTTP proxies or as an alternate port for normal web servers (e.g. when another server is already listening on port 80, or when run by unprivileged UNIX users who can only bind to high ports).

16. Port 1723 (PPTP)—Point-to-point tunneling protocol (a method of implementing VPNs which is often required for broadband connections to ISPs).

17. Port 111 (RPCBind)—Maps SunRPC program numbers to their current TCP or UDP port numbers.

18. Port 995 (POP3S)—POP3 with SSL added for security.

19. Port 993 (IMAPS)—IMAPv2 with SSL added for security.

20. Port 5900 (VNC)—A graphical desktop sharing system (insecure).

Top 20 (most commonly open) UDP ports

1. Port 631 (IPP)—Internet Printing Protocol.

2. Port 161 (SNMP)—Simple Network Management Protocol.

3. Port 137 (NETBIOS-NS)—One of many UDP ports for Windows services such as file and printer sharing.

4. Port 123 (NTP)—Network Time Protocol.

5. Port 138 (NETBIOS-DGM)—Another Windows service.

6. Port 1434 (MS-SQL-DS)—Microsoft SQL Server.

7. Port 445 (Microsoft-DS)—Another Windows Services port.

8. Port 135 (MSRPC)—Yet Another Windows Services port.

9. Port 67 (DHCPS)—Dynamic Host Configuration Protocol Server (gives out IP addresses to clients when they join the network).

10. Port 53 (Domain)—Domain Name System (DNS) server.

11. Port 139 (NETBIOS-SSN)—Another Windows Services port.

12. Port 500 (ISAKMP)—The Internet Security Association and Key Management Protocol is used to set up IPsec VPNs.

13. Port 68 (DHCPC)—DHCP client port.

14. Port 520 (Route)—Routing Information Protocol (RIP).

15. Port 1900 (UPNP)—Microsoft Simple Service Discovery Protocol, which enables discovery of Universal plug-and-play devices.

16. Port 4500 (nat-t-ike)—For negotiating Network Address Translation traversal while initiating IPsec connections (during Internet Key Exchange).

17. Port 514 (Syslog)—The standard UNIX log daemon.

18. Port 49152 (Varies)—The first of the IANA-specified dynamic/private ports. No official ports may be registered from here up until the end of the port range (65536). Some systems use this range for their ephemeral ports, so services which bind a port without requesting a specific number are often allocated 49152 if they are the first program to do so.

19. Port 162 (SNMPTrap)—Simple Network Management Protocol trap port (An SNMP agent typically uses 161 while an SNMP manager typically uses 162).

20. Port 69 (TFTP)—Trivial File Transfer Protocol.

4.1.3. What is Port Scanning?

Port scanning is the act of remotely testing numerous ports to determine what state they are in. The most interesting state is usually open, meaning that an application is listening and accepting connections on the port. Many techniques are available for conducting such a scan. Chapter 5, *Port Scanning Techniques and Algorithms* [95] explains the circumstances under which each is most appropriate.

While many port scanners have traditionally lumped all ports into the open or closed states, Nmap is much more granular. It divides ports into six states. These states are not intrinsic properties of the port itself, but describe how Nmap sees them. For example, an Nmap scan from the same network as the target may show port 135/tcp as open, while a scan at the same time with the same options from across the Internet might show that port as filtered.

The six port states recognized by Nmap

open
> An application is actively accepting TCP connections or UDP packets on this port. Finding these is often the primary goal of port scanning. Security-minded people know that each open port is an avenue for attack. Attackers and pen-testers want to exploit the open ports, while administrators try to close or protect them with firewalls without thwarting legitimate users. Open ports are also interesting for non-security scans because they show services available for use on the network. Before you get too excited about an open port, note that it is possible that the application is protected with a TCP wrapper (tcpd) or that the application itself is configured to only service approved client IP addresses. Such cases still leave more attack surface than a closed port.

closed
> A closed port is accessible (it receives and responds to Nmap probe packets), but there is no application listening on it. They can be helpful in showing that a host is online and using an IP address (host discovery, or ping scanning), and as part of OS detection. Because closed ports are reachable, they may be worth scanning later in case some open up. Administrators may want to consider blocking such ports with a firewall so they appear in the filtered state, discussed next.

filtered
> Nmap cannot determine whether the port is open because packet filtering prevents its probes from reaching the port. The filtering could be from a dedicated firewall device, router rules, or host-based firewall software. These ports frustrate attackers because they provide so little information. Sometimes they respond with ICMP error messages such as type 3 code 13 (destination unreachable: communication

administratively prohibited), but filters that simply drop probes without responding are far more common. This forces Nmap to retry several times just in case the probe was dropped due to network congestion rather than filtering. This sort of filtering slows scans down dramatically.

unfiltered
: The unfiltered state means that a port is accessible, but Nmap is unable to determine whether it is open or closed. Only the ACK scan, which is used to map firewall rulesets, classifies ports into this state. Scanning unfiltered ports with other scan types such as Window scan, SYN scan, or FIN scan, may help resolve whether the port is open.

open|filtered
: Nmap places ports in this state when it is unable to determine whether a port is open or filtered. This occurs for scan types in which open ports give no response. The lack of response could also mean that a packet filter dropped the probe or any response it elicited. So Nmap does not know for sure whether the port is open or being filtered. The UDP, IP protocol, FIN, NULL, and Xmas scans classify ports this way.

closed|filtered
: This state is used when Nmap is unable to determine whether a port is closed or filtered. It is only used for the IP ID Idle scan discussed in Section 5.10, "TCP Idle Scan (-sI)" [117].

While Nmap attempts to produce accurate results, keep in mind that all of its insights are based on packets returned by the target machines (or firewalls in front of them). Such hosts may be untrustworthy and send responses intended to confuse or mislead Nmap. Much more common are non-RFC-compliant hosts that do not respond as they should to Nmap probes. FIN, NULL, and Xmas scans are particularly susceptible to this problem. Such issues are specific to certain scan types and so are discussed in the relevant sections of Chapter 5, *Port Scanning Techniques and Algorithms* [95].

4.1.4. Why Scan Ports?

Port scanning is not only performed for fun and amusement. There are numerous practical benefits to regularly scanning your networks. Foremost among these is security. One of the central tenets of network security is that reducing the number and complexity of services offered reduces the opportunity for attackers to break in. Most remote network compromises come from exploiting a server application listening on a TCP or UDP port. In many cases, the exploited application is not even used by the targeted organization, but was enabled by default when the machine was set up. Had that service been disabled, or protected by a firewall, the attack would have been thwarted.

Realizing that every open port is an opportunity for compromise, attackers regularly scan targets, taking an inventory of all open ports. They compare this list of listening services with their list of favorite exploits for vulnerable software. It takes just one match to compromise a machine, creating a foothold that is often used to infest the whole network. Attackers who are less discriminate about who they target will often scan for just the default port of an exploitable application. This is much faster than scanning every port, though the service will be missed when running on a non-default port. Such attackers are often derided as "script kiddies", because they often know little more about security than how to run an exploit script written by someone more skilled. Across many organizations, such attackers are bound to find vulnerable hosts. They can be quite a nuisance, though their sheer numbers and relentless pounding against Internet-accessible machines often drive people to patch systems quickly. This reduces the likelihood of more serious, targeted attacks succeeding.

An important defense against these crackers is for systems administrators to scan their own networks regularly with tools such as Nmap. Take the list of open ports, and shut down any services that aren't used. Ensure that those which must remain available are fully patched and that you are on the vendor's security notification list. Firewall rules should be added where possible, limiting access to only legitimate users. Hardening instructions are available on the Web for most popular applications, reducing the cracker's opportunity even further. Nmap cannot do most of this for you, but it creates the list of available services to start out with. Some administrators try to use **netstat** instead, but that doesn't scale well. It requires access to every machine, and some mobile machines are easy to miss. Plus, you can't run **netstat** on your average wireless access point, VoIP phone, or printer. In addition, there is always the risk that a compromised machine will have a trojaned **netstat** which gives out false information. Most of the modern rootkits installed by attackers include this functionality. Relying solely on Nmap is a mistake too. A combination of careful design, configuration auditing, and regular scanning is well advised.

While security is the most common reason for port scanning, administrators often find that it suits other purposes as well. Creating an inventory of machines and the services they offer can be useful for asset tracking, network design, policy compliance checks, software license tracking, availability testing, network debugging, and more.

4.2. A Quick Port Scanning Tutorial

One of my goals in developing Nmap is to keep the most common usage simple, while retaining the flexibility for custom and advanced scans. This is accomplished with the command-line interface by offering dozens of options, but choosing sane defaults when they are not specified. A newbie can start out with a command as simple as **nmap <target>**. Meanwhile, advanced users sometimes specify so many options that their terminal line wraps around.

A similar balance must be struck with command output. The most important results should stick out even to the occasional user who hasn't even read the man page. Yet the output should be comprehensive and concise enough to suit professional penetration testers who run Nmap against thousands of machines daily. Users smart enough to read this book or the Nmap source code benefit from greater control of the scanner and insights into what Nmap output really means.

This tutorial demonstrates some common Nmap port scanning scenarios and explains the output. Rather than attempt to be comprehensive, the goal is simply to acquaint new users well enough to understand the rest of this chapter.

The simplest Nmap command is just **nmap** by itself. This prints a cheat sheet of common Nmap options and syntax. A more interesting command is **nmap <target>**, which does the following:

1. Converts <target> from a hostname into an IPv4 address using DNS. If an IP address is specified instead of a hostname this lookup is skipped.

2. Pings the host, by default with an ICMP echo request packet and a TCP ACK packet to port 80, to determine whether it is up and running. If not, Nmap reports that fact and exits. I could have specified -PN to skip this test. See Chapter 3, *Host Discovery (Ping Scanning)* [47].

3. Converts the target IP address back to the name using a reverse-DNS query. Because of the way DNS works, the reverse name may not be the same as the <target> specified on the command-line. This query can be skipped with the -n option to improve speed and stealthiness.

---

4. Launches a TCP port scan of the most popular 1,000 ports listed in `nmap-services`. A SYN stealth scan is usually used, but connect scan is substituted instead for non-root Unix users who lack the privileges necessary to send raw packets.

5. Prints the results to standard output in normal human-readable format, and exits. Other output formats and locations (files) can be specified, as described in Chapter 13, *Nmap Output Formats* [337]. Example 4.2 displays the results when scanme.nmap.org is used as `<target>`.

Example 4.2. Simple scan: nmap scanme.nmap.org

```
# nmap scanme.nmap.org

Starting Nmap ( http://nmap.org )
Interesting ports on scanme.nmap.org (64.13.134.52):
Not shown: 994 filtered ports
PORT      STATE   SERVICE
22/tcp    open    ssh
25/tcp    closed  smtp
53/tcp    open    domain
70/tcp    closed  gopher
80/tcp    open    http
113/tcp   closed  auth

Nmap done: 1 IP address (1 host up) scanned in 4.99 seconds
```

The first output line in Example 4.2 simply gives the URL for downloading Nmap. The time Nmap started and version number are normally provided as well, though these were are generally removed from this book for consistency and to avoid line wrapping.

The next line provides the target IP address (IPv4 in this case), and reverse DNS name (also known as the PTR record) if it is available. Nmap promises to show the "interesting ports", though all ports scanned are accounted for. The ports considered most interesting because they are open or in a rarely-seen state for that host are itemized individually. When many ports are in a single non-open state, they are considered a default state, and aggregated onto a single line to avoid diluting the results with thousands of uninteresting entries. In this case, Nmap notes that 994 ports are filtered.

The interesting ports table comes next, and provides the key scan results. The columns vary depending on options used, but in this case provide the port number and protocol, state, and service protocol for each port. The service here is just a guess made by looking up the port in `nmap-services`. The service would be listed as `unknown` if any of the ports had no name registered in that file. Three of these ports are open and three are closed.

Finally, Nmap reports some basic timing stats before it exits. These stats are the number of targets specified, the number of those that the ping scan found to be up, and the total time taken.

While this simple command is often all that is needed, advanced users often go much further. In Example 4.3, the scan is modified with four options. `-p0-` asks Nmap to scan every possible TCP port, `-v` asks Nmap to be verbose about it, `-A` enables aggressive tests such as remote OS detection, service/version detection, and the Nmap Scripting Engine (NSE). Finally, `-T4` enables a more aggressive timing policy to speed up the scan.

Example 4.3. More complex: nmap -p0- -v -A -T4 scanme.nmap.org

```
# nmap -p0- -v -A -T4 scanme.nmap.org

Starting Nmap ( http://nmap.org )
Completed Ping Scan at 00:03, 0.01s elapsed (1 total hosts)
Scanning scanme.nmap.org (64.13.134.52) [65536 ports]
Discovered open port 22/tcp on 64.13.134.52
Discovered open port 53/tcp on 64.13.134.52
Discovered open port 80/tcp on 64.13.134.52
SYN Stealth Scan Timing: About 6.20% done; ETC: 00:11 (0:07:33 remaining)
Completed SYN Stealth Scan at 00:10, 463.55s elapsed (65536 total ports)
Completed Service scan at 00:10, 6.03s elapsed (3 services on 1 host)
Initiating OS detection (try #1) against scanme.nmap.org (64.13.134.52)
Initiating Traceroute at 00:10
64.13.134.52: guessing hop distance at 9
Completed SCRIPT ENGINE at 00:10, 4.04s elapsed
Host scanme.nmap.org (64.13.134.52) appears to be up ... good.
Interesting ports on scanme.nmap.org (64.13.134.52):
Not shown: 65530 filtered ports
PORT     STATE  SERVICE VERSION
22/tcp   open   ssh     OpenSSH 4.3 (protocol 2.0)
25/tcp   closed smtp
53/tcp   open   domain  ISC BIND 9.3.4
70/tcp   closed gopher
80/tcp   open   http    Apache httpd 2.2.2 ((Fedora))
|_ HTML title: Go ahead and ScanMe!
113/tcp closed auth
Device type: general purpose
Running: Linux 2.6.X
OS details: Linux 2.6.20-1 (Fedora Core 5)
Uptime guess: 2.457 days (since Thu Sep 18 13:13:24 2008)
TCP Sequence Prediction: Difficulty=204 (Good luck!)
IP ID Sequence Generation: All zeros

TRACEROUTE (using port 80/tcp)
HOP RTT    ADDRESS
[First eight hops cut for brevity]
9   10.36 metro0.sv.svcolo.com (208.185.168.173)
10  10.29 scanme.nmap.org (64.13.134.52)

Nmap done: 1 IP address (1 host up) scanned in 477.23 seconds
          Raw packets sent: 131432 (5.783MB) | Rcvd: 359 (14.964KB)
```

Nmap certainly provided the requested verbosity in Example 4.3! Fortunately the extra output is easy to understand. The first 13 new lines are runtime information letting the user know what is happening as she stares expectantly at the terminal, hoping for good news. What constitutes good news depends on whether she is a systems administrator who has to fix problems, a pen-tester who needs some issues to report on, or a black-hat cracker trying to exploit them. About a dozen similar lines were removed for brevity. The "discovered open port" lines provide as-it-happens notification of open ports so that she can start banging on them before the scan even finishes. The "scan timing" line provides a completion time estimate, so she knows whether to keep staring at the screen or have lunch. Since network conditions (latency, congestion, bandwidth, etc.) and packet filtering rules vary so much, the same scan options may take 30 seconds to complete against one host and 45 minutes against another. If you want the current time estimate while scanning, just press enter.

The port table shows no new ports. All the extra ports scanned are in the filtered state, raising the filtered port total from 994 to 65,530. While there are no new itemized ports, the entries have changed. A new VERSION column provides the application name and version details for the listening service. This comes from service detection, one of the features enabled by the −A option. Another feature of service detection is that all of the service protocols in the SERVICE column have actually been verified. In the previous scan, they were based on the relatively flimsy heuristic of an nmap−services port number lookup. That table lookup happened to be correct this time, but it won't always be.

Another feature added by −A is the Nmap Scripting Engine, which is discussed in depth in Chapter 9, *Nmap Scripting Engine* [205]. The only script shown here is HTML title. Dozens of other scripts exist, but none found useful output for this machine. The traceroute results were also added by −A. This option is more efficient and more powerful than most traceroute programs since probes are performed in parallel and Nmap uses scan results to determine a favorable probe type (TCP packets to port 80 in this case).

Most of the remaining new lines come from OS detection (also enabled by −A), which is discussed in depth in Chapter 8, *Remote OS Detection* [171]. The final line shows that all this extra info came at a price—the scan took almost 100 times longer than Example 4.2, "Simple scan: nmap scanme.nmap.org" [80] to complete (477 seconds compared to 5).

4.3. Command-line Flags

While the tutorial showed how simple executing an Nmap port scan can be, dozens of command-line flags are available to make the system more powerful and flexible. This section covers only options that relate to port scans, and often describes only the port-scanning-related functionality of those options. See Chapter 15, *Nmap Reference Guide* [373] for a comprehensive list of option flags and everything they do.

4.3.1. Selecting Scan Techniques

One of the first considerations when contemplating a port scan is deciding what techniques to use. Nmap offers about a dozen such methods and this section provides a brief summary of them. Full coverage comes in the next chapter. Only one scan method may be used at a time, except that UDP scan (−sU) may be combined with any one of the TCP scan types. As a memory aid, port scan type options are of the form −s*<C>*, where *<C>* is a prominent character in the scan name, usually the first. The one exception to this is the deprecated FTP bounce scan (−b). By default, Nmap performs a SYN Scan, though it substitutes a connect scan if the user does not have proper privileges to send raw packets (requires root access on Unix) or if IPv6 targets were specified.

Port scanning methods supported by Nmap

TCP SYN Stealth (−sS)
> This is far and away the most popular scan type because it the fastest way to scan ports of the most popular protocol (TCP). It is stealthier than connect scan, and it works against all functional TCP stacks (unlike some special-purpose scans such as FIN scan).

TCP Connect (`-sT`)

Connect scan uses the system call of the same name to scan machines, rather than relying on raw packets as most of the other methods do. It is usually used by unprivileged Unix users and against IPv6 targets because SYN scan doesn't work in those cases.

UDP (`-sU`)

Don't forget UDP ports—they offer plenty of security holes too.

TCP FIN, Xmas, and Null (`-sF`, `-sX`, `-sN`)

These special purpose scan types are adept at sneaking past firewalls to explore the systems behind them. Unfortunately they rely on target behavior that some systems (particularly Windows variants) don't exhibit.

TCP ACK (`-sA`)

ACK scan is commonly used to map out firewall rulesets. In particular, it helps understand whether firewall rules are stateful or not. The downside is that it cannot distinguish open from closed ports.

TCP Window (`-sW`)

Window scan is like ACK scan, except that it is able to detect open versus closed ports against certain machines.

TCP Maimon (`-sM`)

This obscure firewall-evading scan type is similar to a FIN scan, but includes the ACK flag as well. This allows it to get by more packet filtering firewalls, with the downside that it works against even fewer systems than FIN scan does.

TCP Idle (`-sI` `<zombie host>`)

Idle scan is the stealthiest scan type of all, and can sometimes exploit trusted IP address relationships. Unfortunately, it is also slow and complex.

IP protocol (`-sO`)

Protocol scan determines which IP protocols (TCP, ICMP, IGMP, etc.) are supported by the target machine. This isn't technically a port scan, since it cycles through IP protocol numbers rather than TCP or UDP port numbers. Yet it still uses the `-p` option to select scanned protocol numbers, reports its results with the normal port table format, and even uses the same underlying scan engine as the true port scanning methods. So it is close enough to a port scan that it belongs here.

TCP FTP bounce (`-b` `<FTP bounce proxy>`)

This deprecated scan type tricks FTP servers into performing port scans by proxy. Most FTP servers are now patched to prevent this, but it is a good way to sneak through restrictive firewalls when it works.

4.3.2. Selecting Ports to Scan

Nmap's port registration file (`nmap-services`) contains empirical data about how frequently each TCP or UDP port is found to be open. This data was collected by scanning tens of millions of Internet addresses, then combining those results with internal scan data contributed by large enterprises. By default, Nmap scans the 1,000 most popular ports of each protocol it is asked to scan. Alternatively, you can specify the `-F` (fast) option to scan only the 100 most common ports in each protocol or `--top-ports` to specify an arbitrary number of ports to scan.

When none of these canned port sets suit your needs, an arbitrary list of port numbers can be specified on the command-line with the −p option. The syntax of the −p option can be complex, and is best described with examples.

Port selection examples with the −p option

−p 22
> Scan a single port (in this case port 22) by specifying just that number as the −p argument.

−p ssh
> Port names may be specified rather than numbers. Note that a name may match multiple ports.

−p 22,25,80
> Multiple ports may be separated with commas. Note that no protocol is specified, so these same port numbers will be used for whatever scan methods are specified on the command-line. If a TCP scan such as SYN scan (−sS) is specified, TCP ports 22, 25, and 80 are scanned. Those correspond to the services SSH, SMTP, and HTTP, respectively. If a UDP scan is selected (−sU), those three UDP ports are scanned. If both are specified, those three ports are scanned for each protocol, for a total of six scanned ports. With IP protocol scan (−sO), those three IP protocols (corresponding to XNS IDP, Leaf-1, and ISO-IP) are scanned.

−p80−85,443,8000−8005,8080−8085
> Port ranges may be specified by separating the beginning and end port with a hyphen. Multiple ranges or individual ports can be specified with commas. This option scans ports 80, 81, 82, 83, 84, 85, 443, 8000, etc. Based on the port numbers, this user is probably scanning TCP and looking for web servers.

−p−100,60000−
> You can omit the beginning of a range to imply port one, or the end to imply the last port possible (65535 for TCP and UDP, 255 for protocol scan). This example scans ports one through 100, and all ports greater or equal to 60,000.

−p−
> Omit beginning and end numbers to scan the whole range (excluding zero).

−pT:21,23,110,U:53,111,137,161
> Separate lists of TCP and UDP ports can be given by preceding the lists with T: (for TCP) or U:. This example scans three TCP ports (FTP, Telnet, and POP3), and four UDP services (DNS, rpcbind, NetBIOS, and SNMP). Specifying both TCP and UDP ports only matters if you also tell Nmap to do a UDP scan (−sU) and one of the TCP scan methods, such as −sS, −sA, or −sF.

−p http*
> Wildcards may be used to match ports with similar names. This expression matches eight port numbers, including http (80), http-mgmt (280), https (443), and http-proxy (8080). Depending on your command shell, you may need to escape the asterisk so it isn't treated as a filename glob.

−p 1−1023,[1024−]
> Enclosing a range in brackets causes those port numbers to be scanned only if they are registered in nmap-services. In this example, all the reserved ports (1–1,023), plus all the higher ports registered in nmap-services. That was Nmap's default behavior before nmap-services was augmented with open port frequency data for more precise selection.

4.3.3. Timing-related Options

Port scanning is often the most time consuming part of an Nmap scan (which might also include OS detection, version detection, and NSE scripts). While Nmap tries to be quick and efficient by default, manual optimization often helps. Nmap offers dozens of options for tailoring scan intensity and speed to match your exact needs. This section lists the most important options for optimizing port scan times. Options which take an amount of time are given in milliseconds unless you append s (seconds), m (minutes), or h (hours) to the value. For further details on any of these options, see Section 15.11, "Timing and Performance" [394]. A much more thorough treatment, with examples and best-practices for improving Nmap performance is available in Chapter 6, *Optimizing Nmap Performance* [135].

Top port scan performance options

-T0 through -T5
> These timing templates affect many variables, offering a simple way to adjust overall Nmap speed from very slow (-T0) to extremely aggressive (-T5). A timing template may be combined with the more granular options describe below, and the most granular option takes precedence.

--min-rtt-timeout, --max-rtt-timeout, --initial-rtt-timeout
> The minimum, maximum, and initial amount of time that Nmap will wait for a port scan probe response.

--host-timeout
> Asks Nmap to give up on hosts that take more than the given amount of time to scan.

--min-rate, --max-rate
> Sets the floor and ceiling, respectively, to the number of probe packets Nmap sends per second.

--max-retries
> Specifies the maximum number of port scan probe retransmissions to a single port.

--min-hostgroup, --max-hostgroup
> Sets the minimum and maximum number of hosts that Nmap will port scan in parallel.

--min-parallelism, --max-parallelism
> Limits the minimum or maximum number of port scan probes (across all hosts scanned concurrently) that Nmap may have outstanding.

--scan-delay, --max-scan-delay
> Asks Nmap to wait at least the given amount of time between sending probes to any individual host. The scan delay can grow as Nmap detects packet loss, so a maximum may be specified with --max-scan-delay.

4.3.4. Output Format and Verbosity Options

Nmap offers the ability to write its reports in its standard format, a simple line-oriented "grepable" format, or XML. These reports are enabled with the -oN (normal), -oG (grepable), and -oX (XML) options. Each option takes a filename, and they may be combined to output in several formats at once. Several options are also available to increase output verbosity. This section lists the most important output-related options and how they apply to port scanning. For further details on any of these options, see Section 15.13, "Output" [403].

A much more thorough treatment of output options and formats, with many examples, is available in Chapter 13, *Nmap Output Formats* [337].

Top Nmap output options applicable to port scans

`-v`

Increases the verbosity level, causing Nmap to print more information about the scan in progress. Open ports are shown as they are found and completion time estimates are provided when Nmap thinks a scan will take more than a few minutes. Use it twice or more for even greater verbosity.

`-d`

Increases the debugging level, causing Nmap to print out details about its operation that can be useful for tracking down bugs or simply understanding how it works. Higher levels result in massive amounts of data. Using the option once sets the debugging level to one, and it is incremented for each additional `-d`. Or you may follow the `-d` with the desired level, as in `-d5`. If you don't see enough information, try a higher level. The maximum effective level is nine. If your screen is flooded with too much debugging data, reduce the level. Reducing scan intensity, such as the number of ports or targets scanned and the features used, can also help to isolate only the debug messages you want.

`--packet-trace`

Causes Nmap to print a summary of every packet sent or received. This is often used for debugging, but is also a valuable way for new users to understand exactly what Nmap is doing under the covers. To avoid printing thousands of lines, you may want to specify a limited number of ports to scan, such as `-p20-30`.

`-oN <filename>` (normal output)

Write output in Nmap's normal format to `<filename>`. This format is roughly the same as the standard interactive output printed by Nmap at runtime.

`-oX <filename>` (XML output)

Write output in Nmap's XML format to `<filename>`. Normal (human readable) output will still be printed to stdout unless you ask for XML to be directed there by specifying `-` as `<filename>`. This is the preferred format for use by scripts and programs that process Nmap results.

`-oG <filename>` (grepable format output)

Write output in Nmap's so-called grepable format to `<filename>`. This tabular format fits the output of each host on a single line, making it easy to grep for open ports, certain operating systems, application names, or other data. Normal output will still be printed to stdout unless you ask for the grepable output to be directed there by specifying `-` as `<filename>`. While this format works well for parsing with simple grep and awk command-lines, significant scripts and programs should use the XML output instead. The XML format contains substantial information that grepable format has no place for, and extensibility makes XML easier to update with new information without breaking tools that rely on it.

`-oA <basename>` (output to all formats)

As a convenience, you may specify `-oA <basename>` to store scan results in normal, XML, and grepable formats at once. They are stored in `<basename>`.nmap, `<basename>`.xml, and `<basename>`.gnmap, respectively. As with most programs, you can prefix the filenames with a directory path, such as `~/nmaplogs/foocorp/` on Unix or `c:\hacking\sco` on Windows.

`--resume <filename>`

    Resume an aborted scan by specifying the normal (`-oN`) or grepable (`-oG`) output file which was created during the ill-fated scan. Don't use any options other than `--resume`, as Nmap will use the ones specified in the output file. It then parses the file and resumes scanning (and logging to the file) at the host which the previous Nmap execution was working on when it ceased.

`--append-output`

    Tells Nmap to append scan results to any output files specified (with arguments such as `-oN` or `-oX`) rather than overwriting them.

`--open`

    Only show open ports in the Nmap interesting port tables.

4.3.5. Firewall and IDS Evasion Options

Nmap offers many options for sneaking past IDSs undetected or evading firewall rules. For an overview, see Section 15.12, "Firewall/IDS Evasion and Spoofing" [399]. For a comprehensive look at firewall and IDS evasion techniques, along with practical examples, see Chapter 10, *Detecting and Subverting Firewalls and Intrusion Detection Systems* [257].

4.3.6. Specifying Targets

To scan a single host (or a few of them), simply add their names or IP addresses to the end of your Nmap command line. Nmap also has a structured syntax to make scanning large networks easy. You can give Nmap a file listing targets, or even ask Nmap to generate them randomly. This is all described in Section 3.2, "Specifying Target Hosts and Networks" [47].

4.3.7. Miscellaneous Options

Here are some options that can be quite handy even though they don't fit into specific categories. The descriptions focus on how each option relates to port scanning. See the Chapter 15, *Nmap Reference Guide* [373] for more comprehensive coverage of each option.

`-6`

    Asks Nmap to scan the target using the IPv6 protocol. This process is described in Section 4.4, "IPv6 Scanning (-6)" [88].

`-r`

    Nmap randomizes the port scan order by default to make detection slightly harder. The `-r` option causes them to be scanned in numerical order instead.

`-PN`

    Tells Nmap to skip the ping test and simply scan every target host provided. Other options for controlling host discovery are described in Chapter 3, *Host Discovery (Ping Scanning)* [47].

`--reason`

    Adds a column to the interesting ports table which describes why Nmap classified a port as it did.

4.4. IPv6 Scanning (−6)

Since 2002, Nmap has offered IPv6 support for its most popular features. In particular, ping scanning (TCP-only), connect scanning, and version detection all support IPv6. The command syntax is the same as usual except that you also add the −6 option. Of course, you must use IPv6 syntax if you specify an address rather than a hostname. An address might look like 3ffe:7501:4819:2000:210:f3ff:fe03:14d0, so hostnames are recommended. Example 4.4 shows a typical port scanning session. The output looks the same as it usually does, with the IPv6 address on the "interesting ports" line being the only IPv6 give away.

Example 4.4. A simple IPv6 scan

```
# nmap -6 -sV www.eurov6.org

Starting Nmap ( http://nmap.org )
Interesting ports on ns1.euro6ix.com (2001:800:40:2a03::3):
Not shown: 996 closed ports
PORT    STATE SERVICE VERSION
21/tcp open  ftp     Pure-FTPd
22/tcp open  ssh     OpenSSH 3.5p1 (protocol 2.0)
53/tcp open  domain  ISC BIND 9.2.1
80/tcp open  http    Apache httpd

Nmap done: 1 IP address (1 host up) scanned in 56.78 seconds
```

While IPv6 hasn't exactly taken the world by storm, it gets significant use in some countries and most modern operating systems support it. To use Nmap with IPv6, both the source and target of your scan must be configured for IPv6. If your ISP (like most of them) does not allocate IPv6 addresses to you, free tunnel brokers are widely available and work fine with Nmap. I use the free IPv6 tunnel broker service at *http://www.tunnelbroker.net*. Other tunnel brokers are listed at Wikipedia[1]. 6to4 tunnels are another popular, free approach.

Systems that support IPv6 don't always have their IPv4 and IPv6 firewall rules in sync. Section 10.4.3, "IPv6 Attacks" [267] shows a real-life example of reaching ports through IPv6 that are filtered in IPv4.

4.5. SOLUTION: Scan a Large Network for a Certain Open TCP Port

4.5.1. Problem

You wish to quickly find all machines on a network that have a certain TCP port open. For example, after a new Microsoft IIS vulnerability is found, you might want to scan for all machines with TCP port 80 open and ensure that they aren't running a vulnerable version of that software. Or if you investigate a compromised box and find that the attacker left a backdoor running on port 31337, scanning your whole network for that port might quickly identify other compromised systems. A full (all ports) scan would be done later.

---

[1] *http://en.wikipedia.org/wiki/List_of_IPv6_tunnel_brokers*

4.5.2. Solution

The straightforward way is to run:

nmap -PN -p<portnumber> -oG <logfilename.gnmap> <target networks>

Here is a concrete example of searching 4096 IPs for web servers (port 80 open):

nmap -PN -p80 -oG logs/pb-port80scan-%D.gnmap 216.163.128.0/20

The "%D" in the filename is replaced with the numeric date on which the scan was run (e.g. "090107" on September 1, 2007). While this scan command works, a little effort choosing appropriate timing values for the network being scanned reduces scan time substantially. The scan above took 1,236 seconds, while the optimized version below provided the same results in 869 seconds:

nmap -T4 -PN -p80 --max-rtt-timeout 200 --initial-rtt-timeout 150 --min-hostgroup 512 -oG logs/pb-port80scan2-%D.gnmap 216.163.128.0/20

And much of that time is spent doing reverse-DNS resolution. Excluding that by adding −n to the command-line above reduces the 4096-host scan time to 193 seconds. Being patient for three minutes is far easier than for the 21 minutes taken before.

The commands above store grepable-format results in the specified file. A simple egrep command will then find the machines with port 80 open:

egrep '[^0-9]80/open' logs/pb-port80scan2-*.gnmap

The egrep pattern is preceded with [^0-9] to avoid bogus matching ports such as 3180. Of course that can't happen since we are only scanning port 80, but it is a good practice to remember for many-port scans. If you only want the IP addresses and nothing else, pipe the egrep output to **awk '{print $2}'**.

4.5.3. Discussion

Sometimes a story is the best way to understand decisions, such as how I decided upon the command lines in the solution section. I was bored at home, and started exploring the network of a popular magazine named *Playboy*. Their main site includes a huge trove of images, but most are locked away behind a paid subscription authentication system. I was curious as to whether I could find any other systems on their network which offer up images for free. I figured that they might have staging or development servers which rely on obscurity rather than password authentication. While such servers could theoretically listen on any port number, the most likely is TCP port 80. So I decide to scan their whole network for that open port as quickly as possible.

The first step is determining which IP addresses to scan. I perform a whois search of the American Registry for Internet Numbers (ARIN) for organizations named Playboy. The results are shown in Example 4.5.

Example 4.5. Discovering Playboy's IP space

```
core~> whois -h whois.arin.net n playboy
[Querying whois.arin.net]
[whois.arin.net]

OrgName:    Playboy
OrgID:      PLAYBO
Address:    680 N. Lake Shore Drive
City:       Chicago
StateProv:  IL
PostalCode: 60611
Country:    US

NetRange:   216.163.128.0 - 216.163.143.255
CIDR:       216.163.128.0/20
NetName:    PLAYBOY-BLK-1
NetHandle:  NET-216-163-128-0-1
Parent:     NET-216-0-0-0-0
NetType:    Direct Assignment
NameServer: NS1-CHI.PLAYBOY.COM
NameServer: NS2-CHI.PLAYBOY.COM
[...]
```

This shows 4096 IPs (the net range 216.163.128.0/20) registered to Playboy. Using techniques discussed in Section 3.3, "Finding an Organization's IP Addresses" [49] I could have found many more netblocks they control, but 4096 IPs are sufficient for this example.

Next I want to estimate latency to these machines, so that Nmap will know what to expect. This isn't required, but feeding Nmap appropriate timing values can speed it up. This is particularly true for single-port -PN scans, such as this one. Nmap does not receive enough responses from each host to accurately estimate latency and packet drop rate, so I will help it out on the command line. My first thought is to ping their main web server, as shown in Example 4.6.

Example 4.6. Pinging Playboy's web server for a latency estimate

```
# ping -c5 www.playboy.com
PING www.phat.playboy.com (209.247.228.201) from 205.217.153.56
64 bytes from free-chi.playboy.com (209.247.228.201): icmp_seq=1 time=57.5 ms
64 bytes from free-chi.playboy.com (209.247.228.201): icmp_seq=2 time=56.7 ms
64 bytes from free-chi.playboy.com (209.247.228.201): icmp_seq=3 time=56.9 ms
64 bytes from free-chi.playboy.com (209.247.228.201): icmp_seq=4 time=57.0 ms
64 bytes from free-chi.playboy.com (209.247.228.201): icmp_seq=5 time=56.6 ms

--- www.phat.playboy.com ping statistics ---
5 packets transmitted, 5 received, 0% loss, time 4047ms
rtt min/avg/max/mdev = 56.652/57.004/57.522/0.333 ms
```

The maximum round trip time is 58 milliseconds. Unfortunately, this IP address (209.247.228.201) is not within the 216.163.128.0/20 netblock I wish to scan. I would normally add this new netblock to the target list, but have already decided to limit my scan to the original 4096 IPs. These times are probably perfectly fine to use, but finding actual values from IPs on the target network would be even better. I use dig to obtain

Playboy's public DNS records from a nameserver shown in the previous whois query. The output is shown in Example 4.7.

Example 4.7. Digging through Playboy's DNS records

```
core~>dig @ns1-chi.playboy.com playboy.com. any
; <<>> DiG 8.3 <<>> @ns1-chi.playboy.com playboy.com. any
[...]
;; ANSWER SECTION:
playboy.com.            1D IN A      209.247.228.201
playboy.com.            1D IN MX     10 mx.la.playboy.com.
playboy.com.            1D IN MX     5 mx.chi.playboy.com.
playboy.com.            1D IN NS     ns15.customer.level3.net.
playboy.com.            1D IN NS     ns21.customer.level3.net.
playboy.com.            1D IN NS     ns29.customer.level3.net.
playboy.com.            1D IN NS     ns1-chi.playboy.com.
playboy.com.            1D IN NS     ns2-chi.playboy.com.
playboy.com.            1D IN SOA    ns1-chi.playboy.com. dns.playboy.com. (
                                     2004092010    ; serial
                                     12H           ; refresh
                                     2h30m         ; retry
                                     2w1d          ; expiry
                                     1D )          ; minimum


;; ADDITIONAL SECTION:
mx.chi.playboy.com.     1D IN A      216.163.143.4
mx.la.playboy.com.      1D IN A      216.163.128.15
ns1-chi.playboy.com.    1D IN A      209.247.228.135
ns2-chi.playboy.com.    1D IN A      64.202.105.36

;; Total query time: 107 msec
```

The DNS query reveals two MX (mail) servers within the target 216.163.128.0/20 netblock. Since the names `mx.chi` and `mx.la` imply that they are in different regions (Chicago and Los Angeles), I decide to test them both for latency. The **ping** results are shown in Example 4.8.

Example 4.8. Pinging the MX servers

```
core~> ping -c5 mx.chi.playboy.com
PING mx.chi.playboy.com (216.163.143.4) 56(84) bytes of data.

--- mx.chi.playboy.com ping statistics ---
5 packets transmitted, 0 received, 100% packet loss, time 4000ms

core~> ping -c5 mx.la.playboy.com
PING mx.la.playboy.com (216.163.128.15) 56(84) bytes of data.

--- mx.la.playboy.com ping statistics ---
5 packets transmitted, 0 received, 100% packet loss, time 4011ms
```

Well, that attempt was a miserable failure! The hosts seem to be blocking ICMP ping packets. Since they are mail servers, they must have TCP port 25 open, so I try again using hping2[2] to perform a TCP ping against port 25, as demonstrated in Example 4.9.

Example 4.9. TCP pinging the MX servers

```
core# hping2 --syn -p 25 -c 5 mx.chi.playboy.com
eth0 default routing interface selected (according to /proc)
HPING mx.chi.playboy.com (eth0 216.163.143.4): S set, 40 headers + 0 data bytes
46 bytes from 216.163.143.4: flags=SA seq=0 ttl=51 id=14221 rtt=56.8 ms
46 bytes from 216.163.143.4: flags=SA seq=1 ttl=51 id=14244 rtt=56.9 ms
46 bytes from 216.163.143.4: flags=SA seq=2 ttl=51 id=14274 rtt=56.9 ms
46 bytes from 216.163.143.4: flags=SA seq=3 ttl=51 id=14383 rtt=61.8 ms
46 bytes from 216.163.143.4: flags=SA seq=4 ttl=51 id=14387 rtt=57.5 ms

--- mx.chi.playboy.com hping statistic ---
5 packets transmitted, 5 packets received, 0% packet loss
round-trip min/avg/max = 56.8/58.0/61.8 ms

core# hping2 --syn -p 25 -c 5 mx.la.playboy.com
eth0 default routing interface selected (according to /proc)
HPING mx.la.playboy.com (eth0 216.163.128.15): S set, 40 headers + 0 data bytes
46 bytes from 216.163.128.15: flags=SA seq=0 ttl=52 id=58728 rtt=16.0 ms
46 bytes from 216.163.128.15: flags=SA seq=1 ttl=52 id=58753 rtt=15.4 ms
46 bytes from 216.163.128.15: flags=SA seq=2 ttl=52 id=58790 rtt=15.5 ms
46 bytes from 216.163.128.15: flags=SA seq=3 ttl=52 id=58870 rtt=16.4 ms
46 bytes from 216.163.128.15: flags=SA seq=4 ttl=52 id=58907 rtt=15.5 ms

--- mx.la.playboy.com hping statistic ---
5 packets transmitted, 5 packets received, 0% packet loss
round-trip min/avg/max = 15.4/15.8/16.4 ms
```

These are the results I was looking for. The LA host never takes more than 16 milliseconds to respond, while the Chicago one takes up to 62 milliseconds. This is not surprising, given that I am probing from a machine in California. It pays to be cautious, and latency can increase during heavy scanning, so I decide to let Nmap wait up to 200 milliseconds for responses. I'll have it start with a timeout of 150 ms. So I pass it the options

---

[2] *http://www.hping.org*

`--max-rtt-timeout 200 --initial-rtt-timeout 150`. To set a generally aggressive timing mode, I specify `-T4` at the beginning of the line.

Since I value minimizing completion time of the whole scan over minimizing the amount of time before the first batch of host results is returned, I specify a large scan group size. The option `--min-hostgroup 512` is specified so that at least 512 IPs will be scanned in parallel (when possible). Using an exact factor of the target network size (4096) prevents the small and less efficient 96-host block which would occur at the end if I specified `--min-hostgroup 500`. All of these timing issues are explained in much more depth in Chapter 6, *Optimizing Nmap Performance* [135].

There is no need to waste time with a prior ping stage, since a ping would take as long as the single-port scan itself. So `-PN` is specified to disable that stage. Substantial time is saved by skipping reverse-DNS resolution with the `-n` argument. Otherwise, with ping scanning disabled, Nmap would try to look up all 4096 IPs. I am searching for web servers, so I request port 80 with `-p80`. Of course I will miss any HTTP servers running on non-standard ports such as 81 or 8080. SSL servers on port 443 won't be found either. One could add them to the `-p` option, but even one more port would double the scan time, which is roughly proportional to the number of ports scanned.

The final option is `-oG` followed by the filename in which I want grepable results stored. I append the target network to the command, then press enter to execute Nmap. The output is shown in Example 4.10.

Example 4.10. Launching the scan

```
# nmap -T4 -p80 -PN --max-rtt-timeout 200 --initial-rtt-timeout 150 \
   --min-hostgroup 512 -n -oG pb-port80scan-%D.gnmap 216.163.128.0/20
Warning: You specified a highly aggressive --min-hostgroup.
Starting Nmap ( http://nmap.org )
Interesting ports on 216.163.128.0:
PORT    STATE    SERVICE
80/tcp filtered http

Interesting ports on 216.163.128.1:
PORT    STATE    SERVICE
80/tcp filtered http

Interesting ports on 216.163.128.2:
PORT    STATE    SERVICE
80/tcp filtered http

Interesting ports on 216.163.128.3:
PORT    STATE    SERVICE
80/tcp filtered http
[ ... ]
Interesting ports on 216.163.143.255:
PORT    STATE    SERVICE
80/tcp filtered http

Nmap done: 4096 IP addresses (4096 hosts up) scanned in 192.97 seconds
```

Nmap scans all 4096 IPs in about three minutes. The normal output shows a bunch of ports in the `filtered` state. Most of those IPs are probably not active hosts—the port simply appears filtered because Nmap receives no response to its SYN probes. I obtain the list of web servers with a simple **egrep** on the output file, as shown in Example 4.11.

Example 4.11. Egrep for open ports

```
# egrep '[^0-9]80/open' pb-port80scan-*.gnmap
Host: 216.163.140.20 () Ports: 80/open/tcp//http///
Host: 216.163.142.135 ()    Ports: 80/open/tcp//http///
```

After all that effort, only two accessible web servers are found out of 4096 IPs! Sometimes that happens. The first one, 216.163.140.20 (no reverse DNS name) brings me to a Microsoft Outlook Web Access (webmail) server. That might excite me if I was trying to compromise their network, but it isn't gratifying now. The next server (reverse name mirrors.playboy.com) is much better. It offers those gigabytes of free images I was hoping for! In particular it offers Linux ISO images as well as substantial FreeBSD, CPAN, and Apache archives! I download the latest Fedora Core ISOs at a respectable 6 Mbps. The abundance of bandwidth at Playboy is not surprising. Later I scan other Playboy netblocks, finding dozens more web servers, though some of their content is inappropriate for this book.

While this is an unusual reason for port scanning, single port sweeps are common for many other purposes expressed previously. The techniques described here can be easily applied to any single-port TCP sweep.

4.5.4. See Also

Version detection can be used to find specific applications listening on a network. For example, you could seek a certain vulnerable version of OpenSSH rather than find all hosts with port 22 open. This is also useful for single-port UDP scans, as the techniques in this solution only work well for TCP. Instructions are provided in Section 7.8, "SOLUTION: Find All Servers Running an Insecure or Nonstandard Application Version" [166].

Chapter 6, *Optimizing Nmap Performance* [135] looks at scan speed optimization in much more depth.

Chapter 5. Port Scanning Techniques and Algorithms

5.1. Introduction

As a novice performing automotive repair, I can struggle for hours trying to fit my rudimentary tools (hammer, duct tape, wrench, etc.) to the task at hand. When I fail miserably and tow my jalopy to a real mechanic, he invariably fishes around in a huge tool chest until pulling out the perfect gizmo which makes the job seem effortless. The art of port scanning is similar. Experts understand the dozens of scan techniques and choose the appropriate one (or combination) for a given task. Inexperienced users and script kiddies, on the other hand, try to solve every problem with the default SYN scan. Since Nmap is free, the only barrier to port scanning mastery is knowledge. That certainly beats the automotive world, where it may take great skill to determine that you need a strut spring compressor, then you still have to pay thousands of dollars for it.

The previous chapter described port scanning with Nmap in general terms, including a brief summary of Nmap's supported scan types in Section 4.3.1, "Selecting Scan Techniques" [82]. This chapter describes each of those scan types in depth. Typical usage scenarios and instructions are given for each scan type, as are on-the-wire packet traces illustrating how they work. Then the ultra_scan algorithm (which most scan methods use) is discussed, with an emphasis on aspects that can be tweaked to improve performance.

Most of the scan types are only available to privileged users. This is because they send and receive raw IP packets, (or even ethernet frames) which requires root access on Unix systems. Using an administrator account on Windows is recommended, though Nmap sometimes works for unprivileged users on that platform when WinPcap has already been loaded into the OS. Requiring root privileges was a serious limitation when Nmap was released in 1997, as many users only had access to shared shell accounts. Now, the world is different. Computers are cheaper, far more people have always-on direct Internet access, and desktop Unix systems (including Linux and Mac OS X) are prevalent. A Windows version of Nmap is now available, allowing it to run on even more desktops. For all these reasons, users rarely need to run Nmap from limited shared shell accounts. This is fortunate, as the privileged options make Nmap far more powerful and flexible.

When discussing how Nmap handles probe responses, many sections discuss ICMP error messages by their type and code numbers. The type and code are each eight-bit fields in ICMP headers that describe the message's purpose. Nmap port scanning techniques are concerned only with ICMP type 3, which are destination unreachable messages. Figure 5.1 shows the ICMP header layout of such a packet (it is encapsulated in the data section of an IP packet, as shown in Figure 1, "IPv4 header" [xxvii]).

Figure 5.1. ICMPv4 destination unreachable header layout

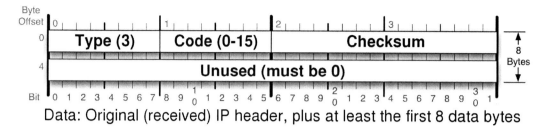

Data: Original (received) IP header, plus at least the first 8 data bytes

There are sixteen codes representing different destination unreachable messages. They are all shown in Table 5.1, though Nmap only cares about codes 0–3, 9, 10, and 13, which are marked with an asterisk.

Table 5.1. ICMP destination unreachable (type 3) code values

Code	Description
0*	Network unreachable
1*	Host unreachable
2*	Protocol unreachable
3*	Port unreachable
4	Fragmentation needed but don't-fragment bit set
5	Source route failed
6	Destination network unknown
7	Destination host unknown
8	Source host isolated (obsolete)
9*	Destination network administratively prohibited
10*	Destination host administratively prohibited
11	Network unreachable for type of service (TOS)
12	Host unreachable for TOS
13*	Communication administratively prohibited by filtering
14	Host precedence violation
15	Precedence cutoff in effect

5.2. TCP SYN (Stealth) Scan (−sS)

SYN scan is the default and most popular scan option for good reason. It can be performed quickly, scanning thousands of ports per second on a fast network not hampered by intrusive firewalls. SYN scan is relatively unobtrusive and stealthy, since it never completes TCP connections. It also works against any compliant TCP stack rather than depending on idiosyncrasies of specific platforms as Nmap's FIN/NULL/Xmas, Maimon and idle scans do. It also allows clear, reliable differentiation between open, closed, and filtered states.

SYN scan may be requested by passing the -sS option to Nmap. It requires raw-packet privileges, and is the default TCP scan when they are available. So when running Nmap as root or Administrator, -sS is usually omitted. This default SYN scan behavior is shown in Example 5.1, which finds a port in each of the three major states.

Example 5.1. A SYN scan showing three port states

```
krad# nmap -p22,113,139 scanme.nmap.org

Starting Nmap ( http://nmap.org )
Interesting ports on scanme.nmap.org (64.13.134.52):
PORT     STATE    SERVICE
22/tcp   open     ssh
113/tcp  closed   auth
139/tcp  filtered netbios-ssn

Nmap done: 1 IP address (1 host up) scanned in 1.35 seconds
```

While SYN scan is pretty easy to use without any low-level TCP knowledge, understanding the technique helps when interpreting unusual results. Fortunately for us, the fearsome black-hat cracker Ereet Hagiwara has taken a break from terrorizing Japanese Windows users[1] to illustrate the Example 5.1 SYN scan for us at the packet level. First, the behavior against open port 22 is shown in Figure 5.2.

Figure 5.2. SYN scan of open port 22

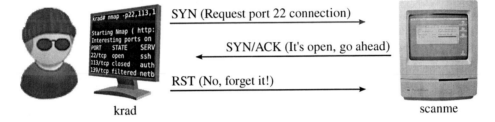

As this example shows, Nmap starts by sending a TCP packet with the SYN flag set (see Figure 2, "TCP header" [xxviii] if you have forgotten what packet headers look like) to port 22. This is the first step in the TCP three-way handshake that any legitimate connection attempt takes. Since the target port is open, Scanme takes the second step by sending a response with the SYN and ACK flags back. In a normal connection, Ereet's machine (named krad) would complete the three-way handshake by sending an ACK packet acknowledging the SYN/ACK. Nmap does not need to do this, since the SYN/ACK response already told it that the port is open. If Nmap completed the connection, it would then have to worry about closing it. This usually involves another handshake, using FIN packets rather than SYN. So an ACK is a bad idea, yet something still has to be done. If the SYN/ACK is ignored completely, Scanme will assume it was dropped and keep re-sending it. The proper response, since we don't want to make a full connection, is a RST packet as shown in the diagram. This tells Scanme to forget about (reset) the attempted connection. Nmap could send this RST packet easily enough, but it actually doesn't need to. The OS running on krad also receives the SYN/ACK, which it doesn't expect because Nmap crafted the SYN probe itself. So the OS responds to the unexpected SYN/ACK with a RST packet. All RST packets described in this chapter also have the ACK

---

[1] *http://www.microsoft.com/japan/security/bulletins/MS04-003e.mspx*

bit set because they are always sent in response to (and acknowledge) a received packet. So that bit is not shown explicitly for RST packets. Because the three-way handshake is never completed, SYN scan is sometimes called half-open scanning.

Figure 5.3 shows how Nmap determines that port 113 is closed. This is even simpler than the open case. The first step is always the same—Nmap sends the SYN probe to Scanme. But instead of receiving a SYN/ACK back, a RST is returned. That settles it—the port is closed. No more communication regarding this port is necessary.

Figure 5.3. SYN scan of closed port 113

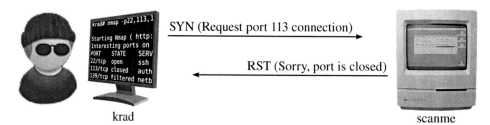

Finally, Ereet shows us how a filtered port appears to Nmap in Figure 5.4. The initial SYN is sent first, as usual, but Nmap sees no reply. The response could simply be slow. From previous responses (or timing defaults), Nmap knows how long to wait and eventually gives up on receiving one. A non-responsive port is usually filtered (blocked by a firewall device, or perhaps the host is down), but this one test is not conclusive. Perhaps the port is open but the probe or response were simply dropped. Networks can be flaky. So Nmap tries again by resending the SYN probe. After yet another timeout period, Nmap gives up and marks the port filtered. In this case, only one retransmission was attempted. As described in Section 5.13, "Scan Code and Algorithms" [128], Nmap keeps careful packet loss statistics and will attempt more retransmissions when scanning less reliable networks.

Figure 5.4. SYN scan of filtered port 139

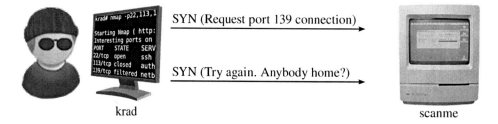

Nmap will also consider a port filtered if it receives certain ICMP error messages back. Table 5.2 shows how Nmap assigns port states based on responses to a SYN probe.

Table 5.2. How Nmap interprets responses to a SYN probe

Probe Response	Assigned State
TCP SYN/ACK response	open
TCP RST response	closed

Probe Response	Assigned State
No response received (even after retransmissions)	filtered
ICMP unreachable error (type 3, code 1, 2, 3, 9, 10, or 13)	filtered

While the pretty illustrations in this section are useful when you have them, Nmap reports exactly what it is doing at the packet level when you specify the --packet-trace option in addition to any other desired command-line flags. This is a great way for newbies to understand Nmap's behavior when Ereet is not around to help. Even advanced users find it handy when Nmap produces results they don't expect. You may want to increase the debug level with -d (or even -d5) as well. Then scan the minimum number of ports and hosts necessary for your purpose or you could end up with literally millions of output lines. Example 5.2 repeats Ereet's three-port SYN scan with packet tracing enabled (output edited for brevity). Read the command-line, then test yourself by figuring out what packets will be sent before reading on. Then once you read the trace up to "The SYN Stealth Scan took 1.25s", you should know from the RCVD lines what the port state table will look like before continuing on to read it.

Example 5.2. Using --packet-trace to understand a SYN scan

```
krad# nmap -d --packet-trace -p22,113,139 scanme.nmap.org

Starting Nmap ( http://nmap.org )
SENT (0.0130s) ICMP krad > scanme echo request (type=8/code=0) ttl=52 id=1829
SENT (0.0160s) TCP krad:63541 > scanme:80 A iplen=40 seq=91911070 ack=99850910
RCVD (0.0280s) ICMP scanme > krad echo reply (type=0/code=0) iplen=28
We got a ping packet back from scanme: id = 48821 seq = 714 checksum = 16000
massping done:  num_hosts: 1  num_responses: 1
Initiating SYN Stealth Scan against scanme.nmap.org (scanme) [3 ports] at 00:53
SENT (0.1340s) TCP krad:63517 > scanme:113 S iplen=40 seq=10438635
SENT (0.1370s) TCP krad:63517 > scanme:22 S iplen=40 seq=10438635
SENT (0.1400s) TCP krad:63517 > scanme:139 S iplen=40 seq=10438635
RCVD (0.1460s) TCP scanme:113 > krad:63517 RA iplen=40 seq=0 ack=10438636
RCVD (0.1510s) TCP scanme:22 > krad:63517 SA iplen=44 seq=75897108 ack=10438636
SENT (1.2550s) TCP krad:63518 > scanme:139 S iplen=40 seq=10373098 win=3072
The SYN Stealth Scan took 1.25s to scan 3 total ports.
Interesting ports on scanme.nmap.org (64.13.134.52):
PORT     STATE     SERVICE
22/tcp   open      ssh
113/tcp  closed    auth
139/tcp  filtered  netbios-ssn

Nmap done: 1 IP address (1 host up) scanned in 1.40 seconds
```

SYN scan has long been called the stealth scan because it is subtler than TCP connect scan (discussed next), which was the most common scan type before Nmap was released. Despite that moniker, don't count on a default SYN scan slipping undetected through sensitive networks. Widely deployed intrusion detection systems and even personal firewalls are quite capable of detecting default SYN scans. More effective techniques for stealthy scanning are demonstrated in Chapter 10, *Detecting and Subverting Firewalls and Intrusion Detection Systems* [257].

5.3. TCP Connect Scan (-sT)

TCP connect scan is the default TCP scan type when SYN scan is not an option. This is the case when a user does not have raw packet privileges or is scanning IPv6 networks. Instead of writing raw packets as most other scan types do, Nmap asks the underlying operating system to establish a connection with the target machine and port by issuing the `connect` system call. This is the same high-level system call that web browsers, P2P clients, and most other network-enabled applications use to establish a connection. It is part of a programming interface known as the Berkeley Sockets API. Rather than read raw packet responses off the wire, Nmap uses this API to obtain status information on each connection attempt. This and the FTP bounce scan (Section 5.12, "TCP FTP Bounce Scan (-b)" [127]) are the only scan types available to unprivileged users.

When SYN scan is available, it is usually a better choice. Nmap has less control over the high level `connect` call than with raw packets, making it less efficient. The system call completes connections to open target ports rather than performing the half-open reset that SYN scan does. Not only does this take longer and require more packets to obtain the same information, but target machines are more likely to log the connection. A decent IDS will catch either, but most machines have no such alarm system. Many services on your average Unix system will add a note to syslog, and sometimes a cryptic error message, when Nmap connects and then closes the connection without sending data. Truly pathetic services crash when this happens, though that is uncommon. An administrator who sees a bunch of connection attempts in her logs from a single system should know that she has been connect scanned.

Figure 5.5 shows a connect scan in action against open port 22 of scanme.nmap.org. Recall that this only required three packets in Figure 5.2, "SYN scan of open port 22" [97]. The exact behavior against an open port depends on the platform Nmap runs on and the service listening at the other end, but this six packet example is typical.

Figure 5.5. Connect scan of open port 22 (nmap -sT -p22 scanme.nmap.org)

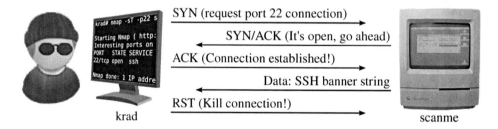

The first two steps (SYN and SYN/ACK) are exactly the same as with a SYN scan. Then, instead of aborting the half-open connection with a RST packet, krad acknowledges the SYN/ACK with its own ACK packet, completing the connection. In this case, Scanme even had time to send its SSH banner string (`SSH-1.99-OpenSSH_3.1p1\n`) through the now-open connection. As soon as Nmap hears from its host OS that the connection was successful, it terminates the connection. TCP connections usually end with another handshake involving the FIN flag, but Nmap asks the host OS to terminate the connection immediately with a RST packet.

While this connect scan example took twice as many packets as a SYN scan, the bandwidth differences are rarely so substantial. The vast majority of ports in a large scan will be `closed` or `filtered`. The packet traces for those are the same as described for SYN scan in Figure 5.3, "SYN scan of closed port 113" [98] and Figure 5.4, "SYN scan of filtered port 139" [98]. Only open ports generate more network traffic.

The output of a connect scan doesn't differ significantly from a SYN scan. Example 5.3 shows a connect scan of Scanme. The -sT option could have been omitted since Nmap is being run from a non-privileged account so connect scan is the default type.

Example 5.3. Connect scan example

```
krad~> nmap -T4 -sT scanme.nmap.org

Starting Nmap ( http://nmap.org )
Interesting ports on scanme.nmap.org (64.13.134.52):
Not shown: 994 filtered ports
PORT     STATE  SERVICE
22/tcp   open   ssh
25/tcp   closed smtp
53/tcp   open   domain
70/tcp   closed gopher
80/tcp   open   http
113/tcp  closed auth

Nmap done: 1 IP address (1 host up) scanned in 4.74 seconds
```

5.4. UDP Scan (-sU)

While most popular services on the Internet run over the TCP protocol, UDP services are widely deployed. DNS, SNMP, and DHCP (registered ports 53, 161/162, and 67/68) are three of the most common. Because UDP scanning is generally slower and more difficult than TCP, some security auditors ignore these ports. This is a mistake, as exploitable UDP services are quite common and attackers certainly don't ignore the whole protocol. Fortunately, Nmap can help inventory UDP ports.

UDP scan is activated with the -sU option. It can be combined with a TCP scan type such as SYN scan (-sS) to check both protocols during the same run.

UDP scan works by sending an empty (no data) UDP header to every targeted port. Based on the response, or lack thereof, the port is assigned to one of four states, as shown in Table 5.3.

Table 5.3. How Nmap interprets responses to a UDP probe

Probe Response	Assigned State
Any UDP response from target port (unusual)	open
No response received (even after retransmissions)	open|filtered
ICMP port unreachable error (type 3, code 3)	closed
Other ICMP unreachable errors (type 3, code 1, 2, 9, 10, or 13)	filtered

The most curious element of this table may be the open|filtered state. It is a symptom of the biggest challenges with UDP scanning: open ports rarely respond to these probes. The target TCP/IP stack simply

---

passes the (empty) packet up to the listening application, which usually discards it immediately as invalid. If ports in all other states would respond, then open ports could all be deduced by elimination. Unfortunately, firewalls and filtering devices are *also* known to drop packets without responding. So when Nmap receives no response after several attempts, it cannot determine whether the port is open or filtered. When Nmap was released, filtering devices were rare enough that Nmap could (and did) simply assume that the port was open. The Internet is better guarded now, so Nmap changed in 2004 (version 3.70) to report non-responsive UDP ports as open|filtered instead. We can see that in Example 5.4, which shows Ereet scanning a Linux box named Felix.

Example 5.4. UDP scan example

```
krad# nmap -sU -v felix

Starting Nmap ( http://nmap.org )
Interesting ports on felix.nmap.org (192.168.0.42):
(The 997 ports scanned but not shown below are in state: closed)
PORT      STATE          SERVICE
53/udp   open|filtered domain
67/udp   open|filtered dhcpserver
111/udp open|filtered rpcbind
MAC Address: 00:02:E3:14:11:02 (Lite-on Communications)

Nmap done: 1 IP address (1 host up) scanned in 999.25 seconds
```

This scan of Felix demonstrates the open|filtered ambiguity issue as well as another problem: UDP scanning can be *slow*. Scanning a thousand ports took almost 17 minutes in this case due to ICMP response rate limiting performed by Felix and most other Linux systems. Nmap provides ways to work around both problems, as described by the following two sections.

5.4.1. Disambiguating Open from Filtered UDP Ports

In the case of the Felix scan, all but the three open|filtered ports were closed. So the scan was still successful in narrowing down potentially open ports to a handful. That is not always the case. Example 5.5 shows a UDP scan against the heavily filtered site Scanme.

Example 5.5. UDP scan example

```
krad# nmap -sU -T4 scanme.nmap.org

Starting Nmap ( http://nmap.org )
All 1000 scanned ports on scanme.nmap.org (64.13.134.52) are open|filtered

Nmap done: 1 IP address (1 host up) scanned in 5.50 seconds
```

In this case, the scan didn't narrow down the open ports at all. All 1000 are open|filtered. A new strategy is called for.

Table 5.3, "How Nmap interprets responses to a UDP probe" [101] shows that the open|filtered state occurs when Nmap fails to receive any responses from its UDP probes to a particular port. Yet it also shows that, on rare occasions, the UDP service listening on a port will respond in kind, proving that the port is open.

The reason these services don't respond often is that the empty packets Nmap sends are considered invalid. Unfortunately, UDP services generally define their own packet structure rather than adhering to some common general format that Nmap could always send. An SNMP packet looks completely different than a SunRPC, DHCP, or DNS request packet.

To send the proper packet for every popular UDP service, Nmap would need a large database defining their probe formats. Fortunately, Nmap has that in the form of `nmap-service-probes`, which is part of the service and version detection subsystem described in Chapter 7, *Service and Application Version Detection* [145].

When version scanning is enabled with `-sV` (or `-A`), it will send UDP probes to every `open|filtered` port (as well as known `open` ones). If any of the probes elicit a response from an `open|filtered` port, the state is changed to `open`. The results of adding `-sV` to the Felix scan are shown in Example 5.6.

Example 5.6. Improving Felix's UDP scan results with version detection

```
krad# nmap -sUV -F felix.nmap.org

Starting Nmap ( http://nmap.org )
Interesting ports on felix.nmap.org (192.168.0.42):
Not shown: 997 closed ports
PORT     STATE         SERVICE    VERSION
53/udp   open          domain     ISC BIND 9.2.1
67/udp   open|filtered dhcpserver
111/udp  open          rpcbind    2 (rpc #100000)
MAC Address: 00:02:E3:14:11:02 (Lite-on Communications)

Nmap done: 1 IP address (1 host up) scanned in 1037.57 seconds
```

This new scan shows that port 111 and 53 are definitely open. The system isn't perfect though—port 67 is still `open|filtered`. In this particular case, the port is open but Nmap does not have a working version probe for DHCP. Another tough service is SNMP, which usually only responds when the correct community string is given. Many devices are configured with the community string `public`, but not all are. While these results aren't perfect, learning the true state of two out of three tested ports is still helpful.

After the success in disambiguating Felix results, Ereet turns his attention back to Scanme, which listed all ports as `open|filtered` last time. He tries again with version detection, as shown in Example 5.7.

Example 5.7. Improving Scanme's UDP scan results with version detection

```
krad# nmap -sUV -T4 scanme.nmap.org

Starting Nmap ( http://nmap.org )
Interesting ports on scanme.nmap.org (64.13.134.52):
Not shown: 999 open|filtered ports
PORT    STATE SERVICE VERSION
53/udp open  domain  ISC BIND 9.3.4

Nmap done: 1 IP address (1 host up) scanned in 3691.89 seconds
```

This result took an hour, versus five seconds for the previous Scanme scan, but these results are actually useful. Ereet's smile widens and eyes sparkle at this evidence of an open ISC BIND nameserver on a machine he wants to compromise. That software has a long history of security holes, so perhaps he can find a flaw in this recent version.

While Ereet will focus his UDP attacks on port 53 since it is confirmed open, he does not forget about the other ports. Those 1007 are listed as `open|filtered`. As we witnessed with the dhcpserver port on Felix, certain open UDP services can hide even from Nmap version detection. He has also only scanned the default ports so far, there are 64529 others that could possibly be open. For the record, 53 is the only open UDP port on Scanme.

While this version detection technique is the only way for Nmap to automatically disambiguate `open|filtered` ports, there are a couple tricks that can be tried manually. Sometimes a specialized traceroute can help. You could do a traceroute against a known-open TCP or UDP port with a tool such as **hping2**[2]. Then try the same against the questionable UDP port. Differences in hop counts can differentiate open from filtered ports. Ereet attempts this against Scanme in Example 5.8. The first **hping2** command does a UDP traceroute against known-open port 53. The `-t 8` option tells **hping2** to start at hop eight and is only used here to save space. The second command does the same thing against presumed-closed port 54.

---

[2] *http://www.hping.org*

Example 5.8. Attempting to disambiguate UDP ports with TTL discrepancies

```
krad# hping2 --udp --traceroute -t 8 -p 53 scanme.nmap.org
HPING scanme.nmap.org (ppp0): udp mode set, 28 headers + 0 data bytes
hop=8 TTL 0 during transit from 206.24.211.77 (dcr2.SanFranciscosfo.savvis.net)
hop=9 TTL 0 during transit from 208.172.147.94 (bpr2.PaloAltoPaix.savvis.net)
hop=10 TTL 0 during transit from 206.24.240.194 (meer.PaloAltoPaix.savvis.net)
hop=11 TTL 0 during transit from 205.217.152.21 (vlan21.sv.meer.net)

--- scanme.nmap.org hping statistic ---
12 packets transmitted, 4 packets received, 67% packet loss
round-trip min/avg/max = 13.4/13.8/14.1 ms

krad# hping2 --udp --traceroute -t 8 -p 54 scanme.nmap.org
HPING scanme.nmap.org (ppp0): udp mode set, 28 headers + 0 data bytes
hop=8 TTL 0 during transit from 206.24.211.77 (dcr2.SanFranciscosfo.savvis.net)
hop=9 TTL 0 during transit from 208.172.147.94 (bpr2.PaloAltoPaix.savvis.net)
hop=10 TTL 0 during transit from 206.24.240.194 (meer.PaloAltoPaix.savvis.net)
hop=11 TTL 0 during transit from 205.217.152.21 (vlan21.sv.meer.net)

--- scanme.nmap.org hping statistic ---
12 packets transmitted, 4 packets received, 67% packet loss
round-trip min/avg/max = 12.5/13.6/14.7 ms
```

In this example, Ereet was only able to reach hop eleven of both the open and closed ports. So these results can't be used to distinguish port states against this host. It was worth a try, and does work in a significant number of cases. It is more likely to work in situations where the screening firewall is at least a hop or two before the target host. Scanme, on the other hand, is running its own Linux iptables host-based firewall. So there is no difference in hop count between filtered and open ports.

Another technique is to try application-specific tools against common ports. For example, a brute force SNMP community string cracker could be tried against port 161. As Nmap's version detection probe database grows, the need to augment its results with external specialized tools is reduced. They will still be useful for special cases, such as SNMP devices with a custom community string.

5.4.2. Speeding Up UDP Scans

The other big challenge with UDP scanning is doing it quickly. Open and filtered ports rarely send any response, leaving Nmap to time out and then conduct retransmissions just in case the probe or response were lost. Closed ports are often an even bigger problem. They usually send back an ICMP port unreachable error. But unlike the RST packets sent by closed TCP ports in response to a SYN or connect scan, many hosts rate limit ICMP port unreachable messages by default. Linux and Solaris are particularly strict about this. For example, the Linux 2.4.20 kernel on Felix limits destination unreachable messages to one per second (in net/ipv4/icmp.c). This explains why the scan in Example 5.4, "UDP scan example" [102] is so slow.

Nmap detects rate limiting and slows down accordingly to avoid flooding the network with useless packets that the target machine will drop. Unfortunately, a Linux-style limit of one packet per second makes a 65,536-port scan take more than 18 hours. Here are some suggestions for improving UDP scan performance. Also read Chapter 6, *Optimizing Nmap Performance* [135] for more detailed discussion and general advice.

Increase host parallelism

If Nmap receives just one port unreachable error from a single target host per second, it could receive 100/second just by scanning 100 such hosts at once. Implement this by passing a large value (such as 100) to `--min-hostgroup`.

Scan popular ports first

Very few UDP port numbers are commonly used. A scan of the most common 100 UDP ports (using the `-F` option) will finish quickly. You can then investigate those results while you launch a multi-day 65K-port sweep of the network in the background.

Add `--version-intensity 0` to version detection scans

As mentioned in the previous section, version detection (`-sV`) is often needed to differentiate open from filtered UDP ports. Version detection is relatively slow since it involves sending a large number of application protocol-specific probes to every `open` or `open|filtered` port found on the target machines. Specifying `--version-intensity 0` directs Nmap to try only the probes most likely to be effective against a given port number. It does this by using data from the `nmap-service-probes` file. The performance impact of this option is substantial, as will be demonstrated later in this section.

Scan from behind the firewall

As with TCP, packet filters can slow down scans dramatically. Many modern firewalls make setting packet rate limits easy. If you can bypass that problem by launching the scan from behind the firewall rather than across it, do so.

Use `--host-timeout` to skip slow hosts

ICMP-rate-limited hosts can take orders of magnitude more time to scan than those that respond to every probe with a quick destination unreachable packet. Specifying a maximum scan time (such as 900000 for 15 minutes) causes Nmap to give up on individual hosts if it hasn't completed scanning them in that much time. This allows you to scan all of the responsive hosts quickly. You can then work on the slow hosts in the background.

Use `-v` and chill out

With verbosity (`-v`) enabled, Nmap provides estimated time for scan completion of each host. There is no need to watch it closely. Get some sleep, head to your favorite pub, read a book, finish other work, or otherwise amuse yourself while Nmap tirelessly scans on your behalf.

A perfect example of the need to optimize UDP scans is Example 5.7, "Improving Scanme's UDP scan results with version detection" [104]. The scan obtained the desired data, but it took more than an hour to scan this one host! In Example 5.9, I run that scan again. This time I add the `-F --version-intensity 0` options and the hour long scan is reduced to 13 seconds! Yet the same key information (an ISC Bind daemon running on port 53) is detected.

Example 5.9. Optimizing UDP Scan Time

```
krad# nmap -sUV -T4 -F --version-intensity 0 scanme.nmap.org

Starting Nmap ( http://nmap.org )
Interesting ports on scanme.nmap.org (64.13.134.52):
Not shown: 99 open|filtered ports
PORT    STATE SERVICE VERSION
53/udp open  domain  ISC BIND 9.3.4

Nmap done: 1 IP address (1 host up) scanned in 12.92 seconds
```

5.5. TCP FIN, NULL, and Xmas Scans (-sF, -sN, -sX)

These three scan types (even more are possible with the `--scanflags` option described in the next section) exploit a subtle loophole in the TCP RFC to differentiate between `open` and `closed` ports. Page 65 of RFC 793 says that "if the [destination] port state is CLOSED .... an incoming segment not containing a RST causes a RST to be sent in response." Then the next page discusses packets sent to open ports without the SYN, RST, or ACK bits set, stating that: "you are unlikely to get here, but if you do, drop the segment, and return."

When scanning systems compliant with this RFC text, any packet not containing SYN, RST, or ACK bits will result in a returned RST if the port is closed and no response at all if the port is open. As long as none of those three bits are included, any combination of the other three (FIN, PSH, and URG) are OK. Nmap exploits this with three scan types:

Null scan (-sN)
    Does not set any bits (TCP flag header is 0)

FIN scan (-sF)
    Sets just the TCP FIN bit.

Xmas scan (-sX)
    Sets the FIN, PSH, and URG flags, lighting the packet up like a Christmas tree.

These three scan types are exactly the same in behavior except for the TCP flags set in probe packets. Responses are treated as shown in Table 5.4.

Table 5.4. How Nmap interprets responses to a NULL, FIN, or Xmas scan probe

Probe Response	Assigned State
No response received (even after retransmissions)	open|filtered
TCP RST packet	closed
ICMP unreachable error (type 3, code 1, 2, 3, 9, 10, or 13)	filtered

The key advantage to these scan types is that they can sneak through certain non-stateful firewalls and packet filtering routers. Such firewalls try to prevent incoming TCP connections (while allowing outbound ones)

---

by blocking any TCP packets with the SYN bit set and ACK cleared. This configuration is common enough that the Linux iptables firewall command offers a special `--syn` option to implement it. The NULL, FIN, and Xmas scans clear the SYN bit and thus fly right through those rules.

Another advantage is that these scan types are a little more stealthy than even a SYN scan. Don't count on this though—most modern IDS products can be configured to detect them.

The big downside is that not all systems follow RFC 793 to the letter. A number of systems send RST responses to the probes regardless of whether the port is open or not. This causes all of the ports to be labeled `closed`. Major operating systems that do this are Microsoft Windows, many Cisco devices, and IBM OS/400. This scan does work against most Unix-based systems though. Since Nmap OS detection tests for this quirk, you can learn whether the scan works against a particular type of system by examining the `nmap-os-db` file. Test T2 sends a NULL packet to an open port. So if you see a line like `T2(R=N)`, that system seems to support the RFC and one of these scans should work against it. If the T2 line is longer, the system violated the RFC by sending a response and these scans won't work. Chapter 8, *Remote OS Detection* [171] explains OS fingerprinting in further detail.

Another downside of these scans is that they can't distinguish open ports from certain filtered ones. If the packet filter sends an ICMP destination prohibited error, Nmap knows that a port is filtered. But most filters simply drop banned probes without any response, making the ports appear open. Since Nmap cannot be sure which is the case, it marks non-responsive ports as `open|filtered`. Adding version detection (`-sV`) can disambiguate as it does with UDP scans, but that defeats much of the stealthy nature of this scan. If you are willing and able to connect to the ports anyway, you might as well use a SYN scan.

Using these scan methods is simple. Just add the `-sN`, `-sF`, or `-sX` options to specify the scan type. Example 5.10 shows two examples. The first one, a FIN scan against Para, identifies all five open ports (as `open|filtered`). The next execution, an Xmas scan against scanme.nmap.org doesn't work so well. It detects the closed port, but is unable to differentiate the 995 filtered ports from the four open ones, all 999 are listed as `open|filtered`. This demonstrates why Nmap offers so many scan methods. No single technique is preferable in all cases. Ereet will simply have to try another method to learn more about Scanme.

Example 5.10. Example FIN and Xmas scans

```
krad# nmap -sF -T4 para

Starting Nmap ( http://nmap.org )
Interesting ports on para (192.168.10.191):
Not shown: 995 closed ports
PORT       STATE          SERVICE
22/tcp     open|filtered  ssh
53/tcp     open|filtered  domain
111/tcp    open|filtered  rpcbind
515/tcp    open|filtered  printer
6000/tcp   open|filtered  X11
MAC Address: 00:60:1D:38:32:90 (Lucent Technologies)

Nmap done: 1 IP address (1 host up) scanned in 4.64 seconds

krad# nmap -sX -T4 scanme.nmap.org

Starting Nmap ( http://nmap.org )
Interesting ports on scanme.nmap.org (64.13.134.52):
Not shown: 999 open|filtered ports
PORT     STATE  SERVICE
113/tcp closed auth

Nmap done: 1 IP address (1 host up) scanned in 23.11 seconds
```

Demonstrating the full, firewall-bypassing power of these scans requires a rather lame target firewall configuration. Unfortunately, those are easy to find. Example 5.11 shows a SYN scan of a SCO/Caldera machine named Docsrv.

Example 5.11. SYN scan of Docsrv

```
# nmap -sS -T4 docsrv.caldera.com

Starting Nmap ( http://nmap.org )
Interesting ports on docsrv.caldera.com (216.250.128.247):
(The 997 ports scanned but not shown below are in state: filtered)
PORT     STATE  SERVICE
80/tcp   open    http
113/tcp closed  auth
507/tcp open    crs

Nmap done: 1 IP address (1 host up) scanned in 28.62 seconds
```

This example looks OK. Only two ports are open and the rest (except for 113) are filtered. With a modern stateful firewall, a FIN scan should not produce any extra information. Yet Ereet tries it anyway, obtaining the output in Example 5.12.

Example 5.12. FIN scan of Docsrv

```
# nmap -sF -T4 docsrv.caldera.com

Starting Nmap ( http://nmap.org )
Interesting ports on docsrv.caldera.com (216.250.128.247):
Not shown: 961 closed ports
PORT        STATE         SERVICE
7/tcp       open|filtered echo
9/tcp       open|filtered discard
11/tcp      open|filtered systat
13/tcp      open|filtered daytime
15/tcp      open|filtered netstat
19/tcp      open|filtered chargen
21/tcp      open|filtered ftp
22/tcp      open|filtered ssh
23/tcp      open|filtered telnet
25/tcp      open|filtered smtp
37/tcp      open|filtered time
79/tcp      open|filtered finger
80/tcp      open|filtered http
110/tcp     open|filtered pop3
111/tcp     open|filtered rpcbind
135/tcp     open|filtered msrpc
143/tcp     open|filtered imap
360/tcp     open|filtered scoi2odialog
389/tcp     open|filtered ldap
465/tcp     open|filtered smtps
507/tcp     open|filtered crs
512/tcp     open|filtered exec
513/tcp     open|filtered login
514/tcp     open|filtered shell
515/tcp     open|filtered printer
636/tcp     open|filtered ldapssl
712/tcp     open|filtered unknown
955/tcp     open|filtered unknown
993/tcp     open|filtered imaps
995/tcp     open|filtered pop3s
1434/tcp    open|filtered ms-sql-m
2000/tcp    open|filtered callbook
2766/tcp    open|filtered listen
3000/tcp    open|filtered ppp
3306/tcp    open|filtered mysql
6112/tcp    open|filtered dtspc
32770/tcp open|filtered sometimes-rpc3
32771/tcp open|filtered sometimes-rpc5
32772/tcp open|filtered sometimes-rpc7

Nmap done: 1 IP address (1 host up) scanned in 7.64 seconds
```

Wow! That is a lot of apparently open ports. Most of them are probably open, because having just these 39 filtered and the other 961 closed (sending a RST packet) would be unusual. Yet it is still possible that some or all are filtered instead of open. FIN scan cannot determine for sure. We will revisit this case and learn more about Docsrv later in this chapter.

5.6. Custom Scan Types with `--scanflags`

Truly advanced Nmap users need not limit themselves to the canned scanned types. The `--scanflags` option allows you to design your own scan by specifying arbitrary TCP flags. Let your creative juices flow, while evading intrusion detection systems whose vendors simply paged through the Nmap man page adding specific rules!

The `--scanflags` argument can be a numerical flag value such as 9 (PSH and FIN), but using symbolic names is easier. Just mash together any combination of `URG`, `ACK`, `PSH`, `RST`, `SYN`, and `FIN`. For example, `--scanflags URGACKPSHRSTSYNFIN` sets everything, though it's not very useful for scanning. The order these are specified in is irrelevant.

In addition to specifying the desired flags, you can specify a TCP scan type (such as `-sA` or `-sF`). That base type tells Nmap how to interpret responses. For example, a SYN scan considers no-response indicative of a `filtered` port, while a FIN scan treats the same as `open|filtered`. Nmap will behave the same way it does for the base scan type, except that it will use the TCP flags you specify instead. If you don't specify a base type, SYN scan is used.

5.6.1. Custom SYN/FIN Scan

One interesting custom scan type is SYN/FIN. Sometimes a firewall administrator or device manufacturer will attempt to block incoming connections with a rule such as "drop any incoming packets with only the SYN flag set". They limit it to *only* the SYN flag because they don't want to block the SYN/ACK packets which are returned as the second step of an outgoing connection.

The problem with this approach is that most end systems will accept initial SYN packets which contain other (non-ACK) flags as well. For example, the Nmap OS fingerprinting system sends a SYN/FIN/URG/PSH packet to an open port. More than half of the fingerprints in the database respond with a SYN/ACK. Thus they allow port scanning with this packet and generally allow making a full TCP connection too. Some systems have even been known to respond with SYN/ACK to a SYN/RST packet! The TCP RFC is ambiguous as to which flags are acceptable in an initial SYN packet, though SYN/RST certainly seems bogus.

Example 5.13 shows Ereet conducting a successful SYN/FIN scan of Google. He is apparently getting bored with scanme.nmap.org.

Example 5.13. A SYN/FIN scan of Google

```
krad# nmap -sS --scanflags SYNFIN -T4 www.google.com

Starting Nmap ( http://nmap.org )
Warning: Hostname www.google.com resolves to 4 IPs. Using 74.125.19.99.
Interesting ports on cf-in-f99.google.com (74.125.19.99):
Not shown: 996 filtered ports
PORT     STATE  SERVICE
80/tcp   open   http
113/tcp  closed auth
179/tcp  closed bgp
443/tcp  open   https

Nmap done: 1 IP address (1 host up) scanned in 7.58 seconds
```

Similar scan types, such as SYN/URG or SYN/PSH/URG/FIN will generally work as well. If you aren't getting through, don't forget the already mentioned SYN/RST option.

5.6.2. PSH Scan

Section 5.5, "TCP FIN, NULL, and Xmas Scans (-sF, -sN, -sX)" [107] noted that RFC-compliant systems allow one to scan ports using any combination of the FIN, PSH, and URG flags. While there are eight possible permutations, Nmap only offers three canned modes (NULL, FIN, and Xmas). Show some personal flair by trying a PSH/URG or FIN/PSH scan instead. Results rarely differ from the three canned modes, but there is a small chance of evading scan detection systems.

To perform such a scan, just specify your desired flags with --scanflags and specify FIN scan (-sF) as the base type (choosing NULL or Xmas would make no difference). Example 5.14 demonstrates a PSH scan against a Linux machine on my local network.

Example 5.14. A custom PSH scan

```
krad# nmap -sF --scanflags PSH  para

Starting Nmap ( http://nmap.org )
Interesting ports on para (192.168.10.191):
(The 995 ports scanned but not shown below are in state: closed)
PORT      STATE         SERVICE
22/tcp    open|filtered ssh
53/tcp    open|filtered domain
111/tcp   open|filtered rpcbind
515/tcp   open|filtered printer
6000/tcp  open|filtered X11
MAC Address: 00:60:1D:38:32:90 (Lucent Technologies)

Nmap done: 1 IP address (1 host up) scanned in 5.95 seconds
```

Because these scans all work the same way, I could keep just one of -sF, -sN, and -sX options, letting users emulate the others with --scanflags. There are no plans to do this because the shortcut options

---

are easier to remember and use. You can still try the emulated approach to show off your Nmap skills. Execute **nmap -sF --scanflags FINPSHURG target** rather than the more mundane **nmap -sX target**.

Warning

In my experience, needlessly complex Nmap command-lines don't impress girls. They usually respond with a condescending sneer, presumably recognizing that the command is redundant.

5.7. TCP ACK Scan (–sA)

This scan is different than the others discussed so far in that it never determines open (or even open|filtered) ports. It is used to map out firewall rulesets, determining whether they are stateful or not and which ports are filtered.

ACK scan is enabled by specifying the −sA option. Its probe packet has only the ACK flag set (unless you use --scanflags). When scanning unfiltered systems, open and closed ports will both return a RST packet. Nmap then labels them as unfiltered, meaning that they are reachable by the ACK packet, but whether they are open or closed is undetermined. Ports that don't respond, or send certain ICMP error messages back, are labeled filtered. Table 5.5 provides the full details.

Table 5.5. How Nmap interprets responses to an ACK scan probe

Probe Response	Assigned State
TCP RST response	unfiltered
No response received (even after retransmissions)	filtered
ICMP unreachable error (type 3, code 1, 2, 3, 9, 10, or 13)	filtered

ACK scan usage is similar to most other scan types in that you simply add a single option flag, −sA in this case. Example 5.15 shows an ACK scan against Scanme.

Example 5.15. A typical ACK Scan

```
krad# nmap -sA -T4 scanme.nmap.org

Starting Nmap ( http://nmap.org )
Interesting ports on scanme.nmap.org (64.13.134.52):
Not shown: 994 filtered ports
PORT     STATE      SERVICE
22/tcp   unfiltered ssh
25/tcp   unfiltered smtp
53/tcp   unfiltered domain
70/tcp   unfiltered gopher
80/tcp   unfiltered http
113/tcp  unfiltered auth

Nmap done: 1 IP address (1 host up) scanned in 4.01 seconds
```

One of the most interesting uses of ACK scanning is to differentiate between stateful and stateless firewalls. See Section 10.3.2, "ACK Scan" [260] for how to do this and why you would want to.

Sometimes a combination of scan types can be used to glean extra information from a system. As an example, start by reviewing the FIN scan of Docsrv in Example 5.12, "FIN scan of Docsrv" [110]. Nmap finds the closed ports in that case, but 39 of them are listed as open|filtered because Nmap cannot determine between those two states with a FIN scan. Now look at the ACK scan of the same host in Example 5.16, "An ACK scan of Docsrv" [115]. Two of those 39 previously unidentified ports are shown to be filtered. The other 37 (based on the default port line above the table) are in the state unfiltered. That means open or closed. If one scan type identifies a port as open or filtered and another identifies it as open or closed, logic dictates that it must be open. By combining both scan types, we have learned that 37 ports on Docsrv are open, two are filtered, and 961 are closed. While logical deduction worked well here to determine port states, that technique can't always be counted on. It assumes that different scan types always return a consistent state for the same port, which is inaccurate. Firewalls and TCP stack properties can cause different scans against the same machine to differ markedly. Against Docsrv, we have seen that a SYN scan considers the SSH port (tcp/22) filtered, while an ACK scan considers it unfiltered. When exploring boundary conditions and strangely configured networks, interpreting Nmap results is an art that benefits from experience and intuition.

Example 5.16. An ACK scan of Docsrv

```
# nmap -sA -T4 docsrv.caldera.com

Starting Nmap ( http://nmap.org )
Interesting ports on docsrv.caldera.com (216.250.128.247):
Not shown: 998 unfiltered ports
PORT       STATE     SERVICE
135/tcp    filtered msrpc
1434/tcp   filtered ms-sql-m

Nmap done: 1 IP address (1 host up) scanned in 7.20 seconds
```

5.8. TCP Window Scan (-sW)

Window scan is exactly the same as ACK scan except that it exploits an implementation detail of certain systems to differentiate open ports from closed ones, rather than always printing `unfiltered` when a RST is returned. It does this by examining the TCP Window value of the RST packets returned. On some systems, open ports use a positive window size (even for RST packets) while closed ones have a zero window. Window scan sends the same bare ACK probe as ACK scan, interpreting the results as shown in Table 5.6.

Table 5.6. How Nmap interprets responses to a Window scan ACK probe

Probe Response	Assigned State
TCP RST response with non-zero window field	open
TCP RST response with zero window field	closed
No response received (even after retransmissions)	filtered
ICMP unreachable error (type 3, code 1, 2, 3, 9, 10, or 13)	filtered

This scan relies on an implementation detail of a minority of systems out on the Internet, so you can't always trust it. Systems that don't support it will usually return all ports `closed`. Of course, it is possible that the machine really has no open ports. If most scanned ports are `closed` but a few common port numbers (such as 22, 25, and 53) are `open`, the system is most likely susceptible. Occasionally, systems will even show the exact opposite behavior. If your scan shows 997 open ports and three closed or filtered ports, then those three may very well be the truly open ones.

While this scan is not suited for every situation, it can be quite useful on occasion. Recall Example 5.12, "FIN scan of Docsrv" [110], which shows many `open|filtered` ports not found in a basic SYN scan. The problem is that we can't distinguish between open and filtered ports with that FIN scan. The previous section showed that we could distinguish them by combining FIN and ACK scan results. In this case, a Window scan makes it even easier by not requiring the FIN scan results, as shown in Example 5.17.

Example 5.17. Window scan of docsrv.caldera.com

```
# nmap -sW -T4 docsrv.caldera.com

Starting Nmap ( http://nmap.org )
Interesting ports on docsrv.caldera.com (216.250.128.247):
Not shown: 961 closed ports
PORT        STATE      SERVICE
7/tcp       open       echo
9/tcp       open       discard
11/tcp      open       systat
13/tcp      open       daytime
15/tcp      open       netstat
19/tcp      open       chargen
21/tcp      open       ftp
22/tcp      open       ssh
23/tcp      open       telnet
25/tcp      open       smtp
37/tcp      open       time
79/tcp      open       finger
80/tcp      open       http
110/tcp     open       pop3
111/tcp     open       rpcbind
135/tcp     filtered   msrpc
[14 open ports omitted for brevity]
1434/tcp    filtered   ms-sql-m
2000/tcp    open       callbook
2766/tcp    open       listen
3000/tcp    open       ppp
3306/tcp    open       mysql
6112/tcp    open       dtspc
32770/tcp   open       sometimes-rpc3
32771/tcp   open       sometimes-rpc5
32772/tcp   open       sometimes-rpc7

Nmap done: 1 IP address (1 host up) scanned in 7.30 seconds
```

These results are exactly what Ereet wanted! The same 39 interesting ports are shown as with the FIN scan, but this time it distinguishes between the two filtered ports (MS-SQL and MSRPC) and the 37 that are actually open. These are the same results Ereet obtained by combining FIN and ACK scan results together in the previous section. Verifying results for consistency is another good reason for trying multiple scan types against a target network.

5.9. TCP Maimon Scan (-sM)

The Maimon scan is named after its discoverer, Uriel Maimon. He described the technique in *Phrack* Magazine issue #49 (November 1996). Nmap, which included this technique, was released two issues later. This technique is exactly the same as NULL, FIN, and Xmas scan, except that the probe is FIN/ACK. According to RFC 793 (TCP), a RST packet should be generated in response to such a probe whether the port is open or closed. However, Uriel noticed that many BSD-derived systems simply drop the packet if the port is open. Nmap takes advantage of this to determine open ports, as shown in Table 5.7.

Table 5.7. How Nmap interprets responses to a Maimon scan probe

Probe Response	Assigned State
No response received (even after retransmissions)	`open|filtered`
TCP RST packet	`closed`
ICMP unreachable error (type 3, code 1, 2, 3, 9, 10, or 13)	`filtered`

The Nmap flag for a Maimon scan is `-sM`. While this option was quite useful in 1996, modern systems rarely exhibit this bug. They send a RST back for all ports, making every port appear closed. This result is shown in Example 5.18.

Example 5.18. A failed Maimon scan

```
# nmap -sM -T4 para

Starting Nmap ( http://nmap.org )
All 1000 scanned ports on para (192.168.10.191) are: closed
MAC Address: 00:60:1D:38:32:90 (Lucent Technologies)

Nmap done: 1 IP address (1 host up) scanned in 4.19 seconds
```

5.10. TCP Idle Scan (`-sI`)

In 1998, security researcher Antirez (who also wrote the **hping2** tool frequently used in this book) posted to the Bugtraq mailing list an ingenious new port scanning technique. Idle scan, as it has become known, allows for completely blind port scanning. Attackers can actually scan a target without sending a single packet to the target from their own IP address! Instead, a clever side-channel attack allows for the scan to be bounced off a dumb "zombie host". Intrusion detection system (IDS) reports will finger the innocent zombie as the attacker. Besides being extraordinarily stealthy, this scan type permits discovery of IP-based trust relationships between machines.

While idle scanning is more complex than any of the techniques discussed so far, you don't need to be a TCP/IP expert to understand it. It can be put together from these basic facts:

- One way to determine whether a TCP port is open is to send a SYN (session establishment) packet to the port. The target machine will respond with a SYN/ACK (session request acknowledgment) packet if the port is open, and RST (reset) if the port is closed. This is the basis of the previously discussed SYN scan.

- A machine that receives an unsolicited SYN/ACK packet will respond with a RST. An unsolicited RST will be ignored.

- Every IP packet on the Internet has a fragment identification number (IP ID). Since many operating systems simply increment this number for each packet they send, probing for the IPID can tell an attacker how many packets have been sent since the last probe.

By combining these traits, it is possible to scan a target network while forging your identity so that it looks like an innocent zombie machine did the scanning.

5.10.1. Idle Scan Step by Step

Fundamentally, an idle scan consists of three steps that are repeated for each port:

1. Probe the zombie's IP ID and record it.

2. Forge a SYN packet from the zombie and send it to the desired port on the target. Depending on the port state, the target's reaction may or may not cause the zombie's IP ID to be incremented.

3. Probe the zombie's IP ID again. The target port state is then determined by comparing this new IP ID with the one recorded in step 1.

After this process, the zombie's IP ID should have increased by either one or two. An increase of one indicates that the zombie hasn't sent out any packets, except for its reply to the attacker's probe. This lack of sent packets means that the port is not open (the target must have sent the zombie either a RST packet, which was ignored, or nothing at all). An increase of two indicates that the zombie sent out a packet between the two probes. This extra packet usually means that the port is open (the target presumably sent the zombie a SYN/ACK packet in response to the forged SYN, which induced a RST packet from the zombie). Increases larger than two usually signify a bad zombie host. It might not have predictable IP ID numbers, or might be engaged in communication unrelated to the idle scan.

Even though what happens with a closed port is slightly different from what happens with a filtered port, the attacker measures the same result in both cases, namely, an IP ID increase of 1. Therefore it is not possible for the idle scan to distinguish between closed and filtered ports. When Nmap records an IP ID increase of 1 it marks the port `closed|filtered`.

For those wanting more detail, the following three diagrams show exactly what happens in the three cases of an open, closed, and filtered port. The actors in each are:

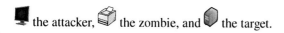 the attacker, ⌨ the zombie, and ⬡ the target.

Figure 5.6. Idle scan of an open port

Step 1: Probe the zombie's
IP ID.

Step 2: Forge a SYN packet
from the zombie.

Step 3: Probe the zombie's
IP ID again.

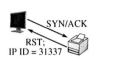

The attacker sends a SYN/ACK
to the zombie. The zombie, not
expecting the SYN/ACK, sends
back a RST, disclosing its IP ID.

The target sends a SYN/ACK in
response to the SYN that appears
to come from the zombie. The
zombie, not expecting it, sends
back a RST, incrementing its
IP ID in the process.

The zombie's IP ID has increased by 2 since step 1, so
the port is open!

Figure 5.7. Idle scan of a closed port

Step 1: Probe the zombie's
IP ID.

Step 2: Forge a SYN packet
from the zombie.

Step 3: Probe the zombie's
IP ID again.

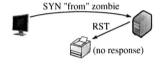

The attacker sends a SYN/ACK
to the zombie. The zombie, not
expecting the SYN/ACK, sends
back a RST, disclosing its IP ID.
This step is always the same.

The target sends a RST (the port
is closed) in response to the SYN
that appears to come from the
zombie. The zombie ignores the
unsolicited RST, leaving its
IP ID unchanged.

The zombie's IP ID has increased
by only 1 since step 1, so the port
is not open.

Figure 5.8. Idle scan of a filtered port

Step 1: Probe the zombie's
IP ID.

Step 2: Forge a SYN packet
from the zombie.

Step 3: Probe the zombie's
IP ID again.

Just as in the other two cases,
the attacker sends a SYN/ACK to
the zombie. The zombie discloses
its IP ID.

The target, obstinately filtering
its port, ignores the SYN that
appears to come from the zombie. The zombie, unaware that
anything has happened, does not
increment its IP ID.

The zombie's IP ID has increased
by only 1 since step 1, so the port
is not open. From the attacker's
point of view this filtered port is
indistinguishable from a closed
port.

Idle scan is the ultimate stealth scan. Nmap offers decoy scanning (-D) to help users shield their identity,
but that (unlike idle scan) still requires an attacker to send some packets to the target from his real IP address
in order to get scan results back. One upshot of idle scan is that intrusion detection systems will generally

send alerts claiming that the zombie machine has launched a scan against them. So it can be used to frame some other party for a scan. Keep this possibility in mind when reading alerts from your IDS.

A unique advantage of idle scan is that it can be used to defeat certain packet filtering firewalls and routers. IP source address filtering is a common (though weak) security mechanism for limiting machines that may connect to a sensitive host or network. For example, a company database server might only allow connections from the public web server that accesses it. Or a home user might only allow SSH (interactive login) connections from his work machines.

A more disturbing scenario occurs when some company bigwig demands that network administrators open a firewall hole so he can access internal network resources from his home IP address. This can happen when executives are unwilling or unable to use secure VPN alternatives.

Idle scanning can sometimes be used to map out these trust relationships. The key factor is that idle scan results list open ports from the zombie host's perspective. A normal scan against the aforementioned database server might show no ports open, but performing an idle scan while using the web server's IP as the zombie could expose the trust relationship by showing the database-related service ports as open.

Mapping out these trust relationships can be very useful to attackers for prioritizing targets. The web server discussed above may seem mundane to an attacker until she notices its special database access.

A disadvantage to idle scanning is that it takes far longer than most other scan types. Despite the optimized algorithms described in Section 5.10.4, "Idle Scan Implementation Algorithms" [122], A 15-second SYN scan could take 15 minutes or more as an idle scan. Another issue is that you must be able to spoof packets as if they are coming from the zombie and have them reach the target machine. Many ISPs (particularly dialup and residential broadband providers) now implement egress filtering to prevent this sort of packet spoofing. Higher end providers (such as colocation and T1 services) are much less likely to do this. If this filtering is in effect, Nmap will print a quick error message for every zombie you try. If changing ISPs is not an option, you might try using another IP on the same ISP network. Sometimes the filtering only blocks spoofing of IP addresses that are *outside* the range used by customers. Another challenge with idle scan is that you must find a working zombie host, as described in the next section.

5.10.2. Finding a Working Idle Scan Zombie Host

The first step in executing an IP ID idle scan is to find an appropriate zombie. It needs to assign IP ID packets incrementally on a global (rather than per-host it communicates with) basis. It should be idle (hence the scan name), as extraneous traffic will bump up its IP ID sequence, confusing the scan logic. The lower the latency between the attacker and the zombie, and between the zombie and the target, the faster the scan will proceed.

When an idle scan is attempted, Nmap tests the proposed zombie and reports any problems with it. If one doesn't work, try another. Enough Internet hosts are vulnerable that zombie candidates aren't hard to find. Since the hosts need to be idle, choosing a well-known host such as www.yahoo.com or google.com will almost never work.

A common approach is to simply execute a Nmap ping scan of some network. You could use Nmap's random IP selection mode (-iR), but that is likely to result in far away zombies with substantial latency. Choosing a network near your source address, or near the target, produces better results. You can try an idle scan using each available host from the ping scan results until you find one that works. As usual, it is best to ask permission before using someone's machines for unexpected purposes such as idle scanning.

We didn't just choose a printer icon to represent a zombie in our illustrations to be funny—simple network devices often make great zombies because they are commonly both underused (idle) and built with simple network stacks which are vulnerable to IP ID traffic detection.

Performing a port scan and OS identification (-O) on the zombie candidate network rather than just a ping scan helps in selecting a good zombie. As long as verbose mode (-v) is enabled, OS detection will usually determine the IP ID sequence generation method and print a line such as "IP ID Sequence Generation: Incremental". If the type is given as Incremental or Broken little-endian incremental, the machine is a good zombie candidate. That is still no guarantee that it will work, as Solaris and some other systems create a new IP ID sequence for each host they communicate with. The host could also be too busy. OS detection and the open port list can also help in identifying systems that are likely to be idle.

While identifying a suitable zombie takes some initial work, you can keep re-using the good ones.

5.10.3. Executing an Idle Scan

Once a suitable zombie has been found, performing a scan is easy. Simply specify the zombie hostname to the -sI option and Nmap does the rest. Example 5.19 shows an example of Ereet scanning the Recording Industry Association of America by bouncing an idle scan off an Adobe machine named Kiosk.

Example 5.19. An idle scan against the RIAA

```
# nmap -PN -p- -sI kiosk.adobe.com www.riaa.com

Starting Nmap ( http://nmap.org )
Idlescan using zombie kiosk.adobe.com (192.150.13.111:80); Class: Incremental
Interesting ports on 208.225.90.120:
(The 65522 ports scanned but not shown below are in state: closed)
Port        State       Service
21/tcp      open        ftp
25/tcp      open        smtp
80/tcp      open        http
111/tcp     open        sunrpc
135/tcp     open        loc-srv
443/tcp     open        https
1027/tcp    open        IIS
1030/tcp    open        iad1
2306/tcp    open        unknown
5631/tcp    open        pcanywheredata
7937/tcp    open        unknown
7938/tcp    open        unknown
36890/tcp   open        unknown

Nmap done: 1 IP address (1 host up) scanned in 2594.47 seconds
```

From the scan above, we learn that the RIAA is not very security conscious (note the open PC Anywhere, portmapper, and Legato nsrexec ports). Since they apparently have no firewall, it is unlikely that they have an IDS. But if they do, it will show kiosk.adobe.com as the scan culprit. The -PN option prevents Nmap from sending an initial ping packet to the RIAA machine. That would have disclosed Ereet's true address. The scan took a long time because -p- was specified to scan all 65K ports. Don't try to use kiosk for your scans, as it has already been removed.

By default, Nmap forges probes to the target from the source port 80 of the zombie. You can choose a different port by appending a colon and port number to the zombie name (e.g. `-sI kiosk.adobe.com:113`). The chosen port must not be filtered from the attacker or the target. A SYN scan of the zombie should show the port in the `open` or `closed` state.

5.10.4. Idle Scan Implementation Algorithms

While Section 5.10.1, "Idle Scan Step by Step" [118] describes idle scan at the fundamental level, the Nmap implementation is far more complex. Key differences are parallelism for quick execution and redundancy to reduce false positives.

Parallelizing idle scan is trickier than with other scan techniques due to indirect method of deducing port states. If Nmap sends probes to many ports on the target and then checks the new IP ID value of the zombie, the number of IP ID increments will expose how many target ports are open, but not which ones. This isn't actually a major problem, as the vast majority of ports in a large scan will be `closed|filtered`. Since only open ports cause the IP ID value to increment, Nmap will see no intervening increments and can mark the whole group of ports as `closed|filtered`. Nmap can scan groups of up to 100 ports in parallel. If Nmap probes a group then finds that the zombie IP ID has increased <N> times, there must be <N> open ports among that group. Nmap then finds the open ports with a binary search. It splits the group into two and separately sends probes to each. If a subgroup shows zero open ports, that group's ports are all marked `closed|filtered`. If a subgroup shows one or more open ports, it is divided again and the process continues until those ports are identified. While this technique adds complexity, it can reduce scan times by an order of magnitude over scanning just one port at a time.

Reliability is another major idle scanning concern. If the zombie host sends packets to any unrelated machines during the scan, its IP ID increments. This causes Nmap to think it has found an open port. Fortunately, parallel scanning helps here too. If Nmap scans 100 ports in a group and the IP ID increase signals two open ports, Nmap splits the group into two fifty-port subgroups. When Nmap does an IP ID scan on both subgroups, the total zombie IP ID increase better be two again! Otherwise, Nmap will detect the inconsistency and rescan the groups. It also modifies group size and scan timing based on the detected reliability rate of the zombie. If Nmap detects too many inconsistent results, it will quit and ask the user to provide a better zombie.

Sometimes a packet trace is the best way to understand complex algorithms and techniques such as these. Once again, the Nmap `--packet-trace` makes these trivial to produce when desired. The remainder of this section provides an annotated packet trace of an actual seven port idle scan. The IP addresses have been changed to `Attacker`, `Zombie`, and `Target` and some irrelevant aspects of the trace lines (such as TCP window size) have been removed for clarity.

```
Attacker# nmap -sI Zombie -PN -p20-25,110 -r --packet-trace -v Target
Starting Nmap ( http://nmap.org )
```

`-PN` is necessary for stealth, otherwise ping packets would be sent to the target from Attacker's real address. Version scanning would also expose the true address, and so `-sV` is *not* specified. The `-r` option (turns off port randomization) is only used to make this example easier to follow.

Nmap firsts tests Zombie's IP ID sequence generation by sending six SYN/ACK packets to it and analyzing the responses. This helps Nmap immediately weed out bad zombies. It is also necessary because some systems (usually Microsoft Windows machines, though not all Windows boxes do this) increment the IP ID by 256 for each packet sent rather than by one. This happens on little-endian machines when they don't convert the

IP ID to network byte order (big-endian). Nmap uses these initial probes to detect and work around this problem.

```
SENT (0.0060s) TCP Attacker:51824 > Zombie:80 SA id=35996
SENT (0.0900s) TCP Attacker:51825 > Zombie:80 SA id=25914
SENT (0.1800s) TCP Attacker:51826 > Zombie:80 SA id=39591
RCVD (0.1550s) TCP Zombie:80 > Attacker:51824 R id=15669
SENT (0.2700s) TCP Attacker:51827 > Zombie:80 SA id=43604
RCVD (0.2380s) TCP Zombie:80 > Attacker:51825 R id=15670
SENT (0.3600s) TCP Attacker:51828 > Zombie:80 SA id=34186
RCVD (0.3280s) TCP Zombie:80 > Attacker:51826 R id=15671
SENT (0.4510s) TCP Attacker:51829 > Zombie:80 SA id=27949
RCVD (0.4190s) TCP Zombie:80 > Attacker:51827 R id=15672
RCVD (0.5090s) TCP Zombie:80 > Attacker:51828 R id=15673
RCVD (0.5990s) TCP Zombie:80 > Attacker:51829 R id=15674
Idlescan using zombie Zombie (Zombie:80); Class: Incremental
```

This test demonstrates that the zombie is working fine. Every IP ID was an increase of one over the previous one. So the system appears to be idle and vulnerable to IP ID traffic detection. These promising results are still subject to the next test, in which Nmap spoofs four packets to Zombie as if they are coming from Target. Then it probes the zombie to ensure that the IP ID increased. If it hasn't, then it is likely that either the attacker's ISP is blocking the spoofed packets or the zombie uses a separate IP ID sequence counter for each host it communicates with. Both are common occurrences, so Nmap always performs this test. The last-known Zombie IP ID was 15674, as shown above.

```
SENT (0.5990s) TCP Target:51823 > Zombie:80 SA id=1390
SENT (0.6510s) TCP Target:51823 > Zombie:80 SA id=24025
SENT (0.7110s) TCP Target:51823 > Zombie:80 SA id=15046
SENT (0.7710s) TCP Target:51823 > Zombie:80 SA id=48658
SENT (1.0800s) TCP Attacker:51987 > Zombie:80 SA id=27659
RCVD (1.2290s) TCP Zombie:80 > Attacker:51987 R id=15679
```

The four spoofed packets coupled with the probe from Attacker caused the Zombie to increase its IP ID from 15674 to 15679. Perfect! Now the real scanning begins. Remember that 15679 is the latest Zombie IP ID.

```
Initiating Idlescan against Target
SENT (1.2290s) TCP Zombie:80 > Target:20 S id=13200
SENT (1.2290s) TCP Zombie:80 > Target:21 S id=3737
SENT (1.2290s) TCP Zombie:80 > Target:22 S id=65290
SENT (1.2290s) TCP Zombie:80 > Target:23 S id=10516
SENT (1.4610s) TCP Attacker:52050 > Zombie:80 SA id=33202
RCVD (1.6090s) TCP Zombie:80 > Attacker:52050 R id=15680
```

Nmap probes ports 20-23. Then it probes Zombie and finds that the new IP ID is 15680, only one higher than the previous value of 15679. There were no IP ID increments in between those two known packets, meaning ports 20-23 are probably closed|filtered. It is also possible that a SYN/ACK from a Target port has simply not arrived yet. In that case, Zombie has not responded with a RST and thus its IP ID has not incremented. To ensure accuracy, Nmap will try these ports again later.

```
SENT (1.8510s) TCP Attacker:51986 > Zombie:80 SA id=49278
RCVD (1.9990s) TCP Zombie:80 > Attacker:51986 R id=15681
```

Nmap probes again because four tenths of a second has gone by since the last probe it sent. The Zombie (if not truly idle) could have communicated with other hosts during this period, which would cause inaccuracies later if not detected here. Fortunately, that has not happened: the next IP ID is 15681 as expected.

```
SENT (2.0000s) TCP Zombie:80 > Target:24 S id=23928
SENT (2.0000s) TCP Zombie:80 > Target:25 S id=50425
SENT (2.0000s) TCP Zombie:80 > Target:110 S id=14207
SENT (2.2300s) TCP Attacker:52026 > Zombie:80 SA id=26941
RCVD (2.3800s) TCP Zombie:80 > Attacker:52026 R id=15684
```

Nmap probes ports 24, 25, and 110 then queries the Zombie IP ID. It has jumped from 15681 to 15684. It skipped 15682 and 15683, meaning that two of those three ports are likely open. Nmap cannot tell which two are open, and it could also be a false positive. So Nmap drills down deeper, dividing the scan into subgroups.

```
SENT (2.6210s) TCP Attacker:51867 > Zombie:80 SA id=18869
RCVD (2.7690s) TCP Zombie:80 > Attacker:51867 R id=15685
SENT (2.7690s) TCP Zombie:80 > Target:24 S id=30023
SENT (2.7690s) TCP Zombie:80 > Target:25 S id=47253
SENT (3.0000s) TCP Attacker:51979 > Zombie:80 SA id=12077
RCVD (3.1480s) TCP Zombie:80 > Attacker:51979 R id=15687
```

The first subgroup is ports 24 and 25. The IP ID jumps from 15685 to 15687, meaning that one of these two ports is most likely open. Nmap tries the divide and conquer approach again, probing each port separately.

```
SENT (3.3910s) TCP Attacker:51826 > Zombie:80 SA id=32515
RCVD (3.5390s) TCP Zombie:80 > Attacker:51826 R id=15688
SENT (3.5390s) TCP Zombie:80 > Target:24 S id=47868
SENT (3.7710s) TCP Attacker:52012 > Zombie:80 SA id=14042
RCVD (3.9190s) TCP Zombie:80 > Attacker:52012 R id=15689
```

A port 24 probe shows no jump in the IP ID. So that port is not open. From the results so far, Nmap has tentatively determined:

- Ports 20-23 are `closed|filtered`

- Two of the ports 24, 25, and 110 are `open`

- One of the ports 24 and 25 are `open`

- Port 24 is `closed|filtered`

Stare at this puzzle long enough and you'll find only one solution: ports 25 and 110 are open while the other five are `closed|filtered`. Using this logic, Nmap could cease scanning and print results now. It used to do so, but that produced too many false positive open ports when the Zombie wasn't truly idle. So Nmap continues scanning to verify its results:

```
SENT (4.1600s) TCP Attacker:51858 > Zombie:80 SA id=6225
RCVD (4.3080s) TCP Zombie:80 > Attacker:51858 R id=15690
SENT (4.3080s) TCP Zombie:80 > Target:25 S id=35713
```

```
SENT (4.5410s) TCP Attacker:51856 > Zombie:80 SA id=28118
RCVD (4.6890s) TCP Zombie:80 > Attacker:51856 R id=15692
Discovered open port 25/tcp on Target
SENT (4.6900s) TCP Zombie:80 > Target:110 S id=9943
SENT (4.9210s) TCP Attacker:51836 > Zombie:80 SA id=62254
RCVD (5.0690s) TCP Zombie:80 > Attacker:51836 R id=15694
Discovered open port 110/tcp on Target
```

Probes of ports 25 and 110 show that they are open, as we deduced previously.

```
SENT (5.0690s) TCP Zombie:80 > Target:20 S id=8168
SENT (5.0690s) TCP Zombie:80 > Target:21 S id=36717
SENT (5.0690s) TCP Zombie:80 > Target:22 S id=4063
SENT (5.0690s) TCP Zombie:80 > Target:23 S id=54771
SENT (5.3200s) TCP Attacker:51962 > Zombie:80 SA id=38763
RCVD (5.4690s) TCP Zombie:80 > Attacker:51962 R id=15695
SENT (5.7910s) TCP Attacker:51887 > Zombie:80 SA id=61034
RCVD (5.9390s) TCP Zombie:80 > Attacker:51887 R id=15696
```

Just to be sure, Nmap tries ports 20-23 again. A Zombie IP ID query shows no sequence jump. On the off chance that a SYN/ACK from Target to Zombie came in late, Nmap tries another IP ID query. This again shows no open ports. Nmap is now sufficiently confident with its results to print them.

```
The Idlescan took 5 seconds to scan 7 ports.
Interesting ports on Target:
PORT      STATE           SERVICE
20/tcp    closed|filtered ftp-data
21/tcp    closed|filtered ftp
22/tcp    closed|filtered ssh
23/tcp    closed|filtered telnet
24/tcp    closed|filtered priv-mail
25/tcp    open            smtp
110/tcp   open            pop3

Nmap finished: 1 IP address (1 host up) scanned in 5.949 seconds
```

For complete details on the Nmap idle scan implementation, read `idle_scan.cc` from the Nmap source code distribution.

While port scanning is a clever abuse of predictable IP ID sequences, they can be exploited for many other purposes as well. Examples are peppered throughout this book, particularly in Chapter 10, *Detecting and Subverting Firewalls and Intrusion Detection Systems* [257].

5.11. IP Protocol Scan (-sO)

IP protocol scan allows you to determine which IP protocols (TCP, ICMP, IGMP, etc.) are supported by target machines. This isn't technically a port scan, since it cycles through IP protocol numbers rather than TCP or UDP port numbers. Yet it still uses the -p option to select scanned protocol numbers, reports its results within the normal port table format, and even uses the same underlying scan engine as the true port scanning methods. So it is close enough to a port scan that it belongs here.

Besides being useful in its own right, protocol scan demonstrates the power of open-source software. While the fundamental idea is pretty simple, I had not thought to add it nor received any requests for such functionality. Then in the summer of 2000, Gerhard Rieger conceived the idea, wrote an excellent patch implementing it, and sent it to the *nmap-hackers* mailing list. I incorporated that patch into the Nmap tree and released a new version the next day. Few pieces of commercial software have users enthusiastic enough to design and contribute their own improvements!

Protocol scan works in a similar fashion to UDP scan. Instead of iterating through the port number field of a UDP packet, it sends IP packet headers and iterates through the eight-bit IP protocol field. The headers are usually empty, containing no data and not even the proper header for the claimed protocol. An exception is made for certain popular protocols (including TCP, UDP, and ICMP). Proper protocol headers for those are included since some systems won't send them otherwise and because Nmap already has functions to create them. Instead of watching for ICMP port unreachable messages, protocol scan is on the lookout for ICMP *protocol* unreachable messages. Table 5.8 shows how responses to the IP probes are mapped to port states.

Table 5.8. How Nmap interprets responses to an IP protocol probe

Probe Response	Assigned State
Any response in any protocol from target host	`open` (for protocol used by response, not necessarily probe protocol)
ICMP protocol unreachable error (type 3, code 2)	`closed`
Other ICMP unreachable errors (type 3, code 1, 3, 9, 10, or 13)	`filtered` (though they prove ICMP is open if sent from the target machine)
No response received (even after retransmissions)	`open|filtered`

Like open ports in the TCP or UDP protocols, every open protocol is a potential exploitation vector. In addition, protocol scan results help determine the purpose of a machine and what sort of packet filtering is in place. End hosts usually have little more than TCP, UDP, ICMP, and (sometimes) IGMP open, while routers often offer much more, including routing-related protocols such as GRE and EGP. Firewalls and VPN gateways may show encryption-related protocols such as IPsec and SWIPE.

Like the ICMP port unreachable messages received during a UDP scan, ICMP protocol unreachable messages are often rate limited. For example, no more than one ICMP destination unreachable response is sent per second from a default Linux 2.4.20 box. Since there are only 256 possible protocol numbers, this is less of a problem than with a 65,536-port UDP scan. The suggestions in Section 5.4.2, "Speeding Up UDP Scans" [105] apply to speeding up IP protocol scans as well.

Protocol scan is used the same way as most other scan techniques on the command line. Simply specify -sO in addition to whatever general Nmap options please you. The normal port (-p) option is used to select protocol numbers. Or you can use -F to scan all protocols listed in the nmap-protocols database. By default, Nmap scans all 256 possible values. Example 5.20 shows Ereet scanning a router in Poland followed by a typical Linux box on my local network.

Example 5.20. IP protocol scan of a router and a typical Linux 2.4 box

```
# nmap -sO 62.233.173.90 para

Starting Nmap ( http://nmap.org )
Interesting protocols on ntwklan-62-233-173-90.devs.futuro.pl (62.233.173.90):
Not shown: 240 closed ports
PROTOCOL STATE           SERVICE
1        open            icmp
4        open|filtered   ip
6        open            tcp
8        open|filtered   egp
9        open|filtered   igp
17       filtered        udp
47       open|filtered   gre
53       filtered        swipe
54       open|filtered   narp
55       filtered        mobile
77       filtered        sun-nd
80       open|filtered   iso-ip
88       open|filtered   eigrp
89       open|filtered   ospfigp
94       open|filtered   ipip
103      filtered        pim

Interesting protocols on para (192.168.10.191):
Not shown: 252 closed ports
PROTOCOL STATE           SERVICE
1        open            icmp
2        open|filtered   igmp
6        open            tcp
17       filtered        udp
MAC Address: 00:60:1D:38:32:90 (Lucent Technologies)

Nmap done: 2 IP addresses (2 hosts up) scanned in 458.04 seconds
```

5.12. TCP FTP Bounce Scan (–b)

An interesting feature of the FTP protocol (RFC 959) is support for so-called proxy FTP connections. This allows a user to connect to one FTP server, then ask that files be sent to a third-party server. Such a feature is ripe for abuse on many levels, so most servers have ceased supporting it. One of the abuses this feature allows is causing the FTP server to port scan other hosts. Simply ask the FTP server to send a file to each interesting port of a target host in turn. The error message will describe whether the port is open or not. This is a good way to bypass firewalls because organizational FTP servers are often placed where they have more access to other internal hosts than any old Internet host would. Nmap supports FTP bounce scan with the –b option. It takes an argument of the form *<username>*:*<password>*@*<server>*:*<port>*. *<Server>* is the name or IP address of a vulnerable FTP server. As with a normal URL, you may omit *<username>*:*<password>*, in which case anonymous login credentials (user: anonymous password:-wwwuser@) are used. The port number (and preceding colon) may be omitted as well, in which case the default FTP port (21) on *<server>* is used.

In Example 5.21, I attempt to bounce off the main Microsoft FTP server to scan Google.

Example 5.21. Attempting an FTP bounce scan

```
# nmap -PN -b ftp.microsoft.com google.com

Starting Nmap ( http://nmap.org )
Your FTP bounce server doesn't allow privileged ports, skipping them.
Your FTP bounce server sucks, it won't let us feed bogus ports!
```

Frequent users of the FTP bounce scan better get used to that error message. This vulnerability was widespread in 1997 when Nmap was released, but has largely been fixed. Vulnerable servers are still around, so it is worth trying when all else fails. If bypassing a firewall is your goal, scan the target network for open port 21 (or even for any FTP services if you scan all ports with version detection), then try a bounce scan using each. Nmap will tell you whether the host is vulnerable or not. If you are just trying to cover your tracks, you don't need to (and, in fact, shouldn't) limit yourself to hosts on the target network. Before you go scanning random Internet addresses for vulnerable FTP servers, consider that sysadmins may not appreciate you abusing their servers in this way.

Example 5.22 shows a successful bounce scan against a few interesting ports on Scanme. The verbose option (-v) was given to provide extra detail. The given server type of "JD FTP Server" means that this is an HP JetDirect print server.

Example 5.22. Successful FTP bounce scan

```
krad~> nmap -p 22,25,135 -PN -v -b XXX.YY.111.2 scanme.nmap.org

Starting Nmap ( http://nmap.org )
Attempting connection to ftp://anonymous:-wwwuser@@XXX.YY.111.2:21
Connected:220 JD FTP Server Ready
Login credentials accepted by ftp server!
Initiating TCP ftp bounce scan against scanme.nmap.org (64.13.134.52)
Adding open port 22/tcp
Adding open port 25/tcp
Scanned 3 ports in 12 seconds via the Bounce scan.
Interesting ports on scanme.nmap.org (64.13.134.52):
PORT     STATE    SERVICE
22/tcp   open     ssh
25/tcp   open     smtp
135/tcp filtered msrpc

Nmap done: 1 IP address (1 host up) scanned in 21.79 seconds
```

5.13. Scan Code and Algorithms

In 2004, Nmap's primary port scanning engine was rewritten for greater performance and accuracy. The new engine, known as `ultra_scan` after its function name, handles SYN, connect, UDP, NULL, FIN, Xmas, ACK, window, Maimon, and IP protocol scans, as well as the various host discovery scans. That leaves only idle scan and FTP bounce scan using their own engines.

While the diagrams throughout this chapter show how each scan type works, the Nmap implementation is far more complex since it has to worry about port and host parallelization, latency estimation, packet loss detection, timing profiles, abnormal network conditions, packet filters, response rate limits, and much more.

This section doesn't provide every low-level detail of the `ultra_scan` engine. If you are inquisitive enough to want that, you are better off getting it from the source. You can find `ultra_scan` and its high-level helper functions defined in `scan_engine.cc` from the Nmap tarball. Here I cover the most important algorithmic features. Understanding these helps in optimizing your scans for better performance, as described in Chapter 6, *Optimizing Nmap Performance* [135].

5.13.1. Network Condition Monitoring

Some authors brag that their scanners are faster than Nmap because of stateless operation. They simply blast out a flood of packets then listen for responses and hope for the best. While this may have value for quick surveys and other cases where speed is more important than comprehensiveness and accuracy, I don't find it appropriate for security scanning. A stateless scanner cannot detect dropped packets in order to retransmit and throttle its send rate. If a busy router half way along the network path drops 80% of the scanner's packet flood, the scanner will still consider the run successful and print results that are woefully inaccurate. Nmap, on the other hand, saves extensive state in RAM while it runs. There is usually plenty of memory available, even on a PDA. Nmap marks each probe with sequence numbers, source or destination ports, ID fields, or other aspects (depending on probe type) which allow it to recognize responses (and thus drops). It then adjusts its speed appropriately to stay as fast as the network (and given command-line options) allow without crossing the line and suffering inaccuracy or unfairly hogging a shared network. Some administrators who have not installed an IDS might not notice an Nmap SYN scan of their whole network. But you better believe the administrator will investigate if you use a brute packet flooding scanner that affects his Quake ping time!

While Nmap's congestion control algorithms are recommended for most scans, they can be overridden. The `--min-rate` option sends packets at the rate you specify (or higher) even if that exceeds Nmap's normal congestion control limits. Similarly, the `--max-retries` option controls how many times Nmap may retransmit a packet. Options such as `--min-rate 100 --max-retries 0` will emulate the behavior of simple stateless scanners. You could double that speed by specifying a rate of 200 packets per second rather than 100 pps, but don't get too greedy—an extremely fast scan is of little value if the results are wrong or incomplete. Any use of `--min-rate` is at your own risk.

5.13.2. Host and Port Parallelization

Most of the diagrams in this chapter illustrate using a technique to determine the state of a single port. Sending a probe and receiving the response requires a round trip time (RTT) between the source and target machines. If your RTT is 200 ms and you are scanning 65,536 ports on a machine, handling them serially would take at least 3.6 hours. Scan a network of 20,000 machines that way and the wait balloons to more than eight years. This is clearly unacceptable so Nmap parallelizes its scans and is capable of scanning hundreds of ports on each of dozens of machines at the same time. This improves speeds by several orders of magnitude. The number of hosts and ports it scans at a time is dependent on arguments described in Chapter 6, *Optimizing Nmap Performance* [135], including `--min-hostgroup`, `--min-parallelism`, `-T4`, `--max-rtt-timeout`, and many others. It also depends on network conditions detected by Nmap.

When scanning multiple machines, Nmap tries to efficiently spread the load between them. If a machine appears overwhelmed (drops packets or its latency increases), Nmap slows down for that host while continuing against others at full speed.

5.13.3. Round Trip Time Estimation

Every time a probe response is received, Nmap calculates the microseconds elapsed since the probe was sent. We'll call this the instanceRTT, and Nmap uses it to keep a running tally of three crucial timing-related values: srtt, rttvar, and timeout. Nmap keeps separate values for each host and also merged values for a whole group of hosts scanned in parallel. They are calculated as follows:

srtt
> The smoothed average round trip time. This is what Nmap uses as its most accurate RTT guess. Rather than use a true arithmetic mean, the formula favors more recent results because network conditions change frequently. The formula is:
>
> ```
> newsrtt = oldsrtt + (instanceRTT - oldsrtt) / 8
> ```

rttvar
> This is the observed variance or deviation in the round trip time. The idea is that if RTT values are quite consistent, Nmap can give up shortly after waiting the srtt. If the variance is quite high, Nmap must wait much longer than the srtt before giving up on a probe because relatively slow responses are common. The formula follows (ABS represents the absolute value operation):
>
> ```
> newrttvar = oldrttvar + (ABS(instanceRTT - oldsrtt) - oldrttvar) / 4
> ```

timeout
> This is the amount of time Nmap is willing to wait before giving up on a probe. It is calculated as:
>
> ```
> timeout = newsrtt + newrttvar * 4
> ```
>
> When a probe times out, Nmap may retransmit the probe or assign a port state such as filtered (depending on scan type). Nmap keeps some state information even after a timeout just in case a late response arrives while the overall scan is still in progress.

These simple time estimation formulas seem to work quite well. They are loosely based on similar techniques used by TCP and discussed in RFC 2988, *Computing TCP's Retransmission Timer*. We have optimized those algorithms over the years to better suit port scanning.

5.13.4. Congestion Control

Retransmission timers are far from the only technique Nmap gleaned from TCP. Since Nmap is most commonly used with TCP, it is only fair to follow many of the same rules. Particularly since those rules are the result of substantial research into maximizing throughput without degrading into a tragedy of the commons where everyone selfishly hogs the network. With its default options, Nmap is reasonably polite. Nmap uses three algorithms modeled after TCP to control how aggressive the scan is: a congestion window, exponential backoff, and slow start. The congestion window controls how many probes Nmap may have outstanding at once. If the window is full, Nmap won't send any more until a response is received or a probe times out. Exponential backoff causes Nmap to slow down dramatically when it detects dropped packets. The congestion window is usually reduced to one whenever drops are detected. Despite slow being in the name, slow start is a rather quick algorithm for gradually increasing the scan speed to determine the performance limits of the network.

All of these techniques are described in RFC 2581, *TCP Congestion Control*. That document was written by networking gurus Richard Stevens, Vern Paxson, and Mark Allman. It is only 10 pages long and anyone interested in implementing efficient TCP stacks (or other network protocols, or port scanners) should find it fascinating.

When Nmap scans a group of targets, it maintains in memory a congestion window and threshold for each target, as well as a window and threshold for the group as a whole. The congestion window is the number of probes that may be sent at one time. The congestion threshold defines the boundary between slow start and congestion avoidance modes. During slow start, the congestion window grows rapidly in response to responses. Once the congestion window exceeds the congestion threshold, congestion avoidance mode begins, during which the congestion window increases more slowly. After a drop, both the congestion window and threshold are reduced to some fraction of their previous value.

There is an important difference between TCP streams and Nmap port scans, however. In TCP streams, it's normal to expect ACKs in response to every packet sent (or at least a large fraction of them). In fact, proper growth of the congestion window depends on this assumption. Nmap often finds itself in a different situation: facing a target with a default-deny firewall, very few sent packets will ever be responded to. The same thing happens when ping scanning a block of network addresses that contains only a few live hosts. To compensate for this, Nmap keeps track of the ratio of packets sent to responses received. Any time the group congestion window changes, the amount of the change is multiplied by this ratio. In other words, when few packets receive responses, each response carries more weight.

A graphical description of how the group congestion window and threshold vary during a typical port scan is shown in Figure 5.9. The congestion window is shown in black and the congestion threshold is in gray.

Figure 5.9. Congestion window and threshold

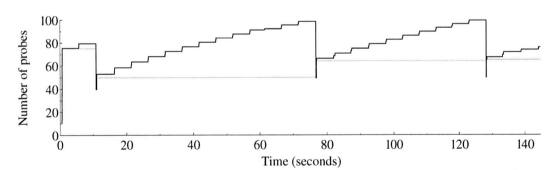

The congestion window starts low and the congestion threshold starts high. Slow start mode begins and the window size increases rapidly. The large "stairstep" jumps are the result of timing pings. At about 10 seconds, the congestion window has grown to 80 probes when a drop is detected. Both the congestion window and threshold are reduced. The congestion window continues to grow until about 80 seconds when another drop is detected. Then the cycle repeats, which is typical when network conditions are stable.

Drops during a scan are nothing to be afraid of. The purpose of the congestion control algorithms is to dynamically probe the network to discover its capacity. Viewed in this way, drops are valuable feedback that help Nmap determine the correct size for the congestion window.

5.13.5. Timing probes

Every technique discussed in this algorithms section involves (at some level) network monitoring to detect and estimate network packet loss and latency. This really is critical to obtaining fast scan times. Unfortunately, good data is often difficult to come by when scanning heavily firewalled systems. These filters often drop the overwhelming majority of packets without any response. Nmap may have to send 20,000 probes or more to find one responsive port, making it difficult to monitor network conditions.

To combat this problem, Nmap uses timing probes, also known as port scan pings. If Nmap has found at least one port responsive on a heavily filtered host, it will send a probe to that port every 1.25 seconds that it goes without receiving responses from any other ports. This allows Nmap to conduct a sufficient level of monitoring to speed up or slow down its scans as network conditions allow.

5.13.6. Inferred Neighbor Times

Sometimes even port scan pings won't help because no responsive ports at all have been found. The machine could be down (and scanned with -PN), or every single port could be filtered. Or perhaps the target does have a couple responsive ports, but Nmap has not been lucky enough to find them yet. In these cases, Nmap uses timing values that it maintains for the whole group of machines it is scanning at the same time. As long as at least one response has been received from any machine in the group, Nmap has something to work with. Of course Nmap cannot assume that hosts in a group always share similar timing characteristics. So Nmap tracks the timing variances between responsive hosts in a group. If they differ wildly, Nmap infers long timeouts for neighboring hosts to be on the safe side.

5.13.7. Adaptive Retransmission

The simplest of scanners (and the stateless ones) generally don't retransmit probes at all. They simply send a probe to each port and report based on the response or lack thereof. Slightly more complex scanners will retransmit a set number of times. Nmap tries to be smarter by keeping careful packet loss statistics for each scan against a target. If no packet loss is detected, Nmap may retransmit only once when it fails to receive a probe response. When massive packet loss is evident, Nmap may retransmit ten or more times. This allows Nmap to scan hosts on fast, reliable networks quickly, while preserving accuracy (at the expense of some speed) when scanning problematic networks or machines. Even Nmap's patience isn't unlimited though. At a certain point (ten retransmissions), Nmap will print a warning and give up on further retransmissions. This prevents malicious hosts from slowing Nmap down too much with intentional packet drops, slow responses, and similar shenanigans. Such an attack is known as tarpitting and is commonly used against spammers.

5.13.8. Scan Delay

Packet response rate limiting is perhaps the most pernicious problem faced by port scanners such as Nmap. For example, Linux 2.4 kernels limit ICMP error messages returned during a UDP (-sU) or IP protocol (-sO) scan to one per second. If Nmap counted these as normal drops, it would be continually slowing down (remember exponential backoff) but still end up having the vast majority of its probes dropped. Instead,

Nmap tries to detect this situation. When a large proportion of packets are being dropped, it implements a short delay (as little as 5 milliseconds) between each probe sent to a single target. If drops continue to be a major problem, Nmap will keep doubling the delay until the drops cease or Nmap hits the maximum allowed scan delay. The effects of scan delay while UDP scanning ports 1–50 of a response rate-limited Linux host are shown in Figure 5.10. At the beginning, the scan rate is unlimited by scan delay, though of course other mechanisms such as congestion control impose their own limits. When drops are detected, the scan delay is doubled, meaning that the maximum scan rate is effectively halved. In the graph, for example, a maximum scan rate of five packets per second corresponds to a scan delay of 200 milliseconds.

Figure 5.10. Scan rate as affected by scan delay

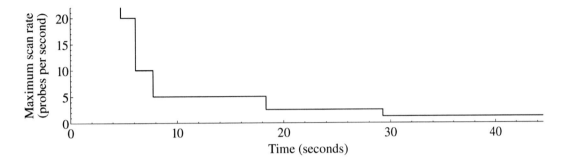

The maximum scan delay defaults to one second between probes. The scan delay is sometimes enabled when a slow host can't keep up, even when that host has no explicit rate limiting rules. This can reduce total network traffic substantially by reducing wasted (dropped) probe packets. Unfortunately even small scan delay values can make a scan takes several times as long. Nmap is conservative by default, allowing second-long scan delays for TCP and UDP probes. If your priorities differ, you can configure maximum scan delays with ‑‑max‑scan‑delay as discussed in Chapter 5, *Port Scanning Techniques and Algorithms* [95].

Chapter 6. Optimizing Nmap Performance

6.1. Introduction

One of my highest Nmap development priorities has always been performance. A default scan (**nmap <hostname>**) of a host on my local network takes a fifth of a second. That is barely enough time to blink, but adds up when you are scanning hundreds or thousands of hosts. Moreover, certain scan options such as UDP scanning and version detection can increase scan times substantially. So can certain firewall configurations, particularly response rate limiting. While Nmap utilizes parallelism and many advanced algorithms to accelerate these scans, the user has ultimate control over how Nmap runs. Expert users carefully craft Nmap commands to obtain only the information they care about while meeting their time constraints.

While Nmap performance is a high priority, accuracy is even more important. Authors of competing scanners have given high-profile conference presentations about how their scanner only takes four seconds to scan an entire class B address space. These scanners are actually trivial to write, since they omit all the congestion control and packet loss detection algorithms, leaving just a tight loop spewing probe packets as fast as the system can generate or the wire can bear. Such scanners are often promoted as stateless—meaning they have also omitted the code to track and retransmit probes. You can achieve similar behavior with Nmap by adding flags such as --min-rate 1000 to request that Nmap send at least 1,000 packets per second, and --max-retries 0 to disable retransmission of timed-out probes. Yet I rarely recommend this. Ninety-nine percent of the packets may be dropped by the next router upstream, and the scanner will never know the difference.

Unmetered packet blasting scanners such as Scanrand[1] are useful in some situations, but Nmap takes a much more conservative and accurate route. Nmap assumes the worst (high latency and packet loss) of the target networks at first, then speeds up as it gathers statistics showing that it can safely do so. While this happens automatically, an administrator can quicken the learning process by passing hints about the network to Nmap. An example of such a hint would be --max-rtt-timeout 200, which allows Nmap to assume that any responses to a target host probe will come within 200 milliseconds.

This chapter first discusses high-level methodologies for improving scan times. Then it covers how timing templates and low-level controls are used to speed up Nmap without impacting accuracy. It finishes with a tutorial by Jack Mogren of the Mayo Clinic, detailing how he improved scan time against his 676,352-IP network from nearly a week to 46 hours. Considering the huge importance of scanner performance, this chapter may seems short. This is because the chapter focuses on high-level general scanning performance tips, while tips for optimizing specific scan techniques are spread throughout this book where those techniques are covered.

6.2. Scan Time Reduction Techniques

The ideal solution to long scan times is to reduce them. This section offers many high-level tips for doing so. Unlike many circumstances in life, tuning your Nmap command line can make a huge difference.

---

[1] *http://sectools.org/tools4.html#scanrand*

Hot-rodding your Honda Accord with a coffee-can exhaust tip, a three-foot-high spoiler, and a big red "type R" sticker won't reduce your 0–60 time much. Yet Section 6.7, "Scanning 676,352 IP Addresses in 46 Hours" [143] describes how Jack Mogren shaved days off his Nmap runtime by simply adding a few stickers (I mean options) to his Nmap command line.

6.2.1. Omit Non-critical Tests

The electronic equivalent to buying a Hummer when you never leave the pavement or carry more than groceries is to launch an intense and comprehensive Nmap scan to obtain a relatively trivial amount of information. Wasting a few seconds per host rarely matters on a home network, but can make daily WAN scans infeasible for large enterprises. The following list details the most common over-scanning mistakes, starting with the most egregious newbie bloopers and followed by more subtle problems that even advanced users confront.

Specify ping scan (-sP) when you only need to determine what hosts are online.
> Some people determine whether a host is online using the command **nmap <hostname>**. While this works, it is overkill. Nmap will send two packets to determine that the host is up, then at least 1,000 to port scan the host. The problem is amplified when a whole network is scanned this way to find all online hosts, or one particular host.
>
> Rather than waste time port scanning, specify -sP to do a ping scan when all you wish to know is what hosts are up or what their MAC addresses are.

Limit the number of ports scanned.
> By default, Nmap scans the most common 1,000 ports. On a fast network of responsive machines, this may take a fraction of a second per host. But Nmap must slow down dramatically when it encounters rate limiting or firewalls that drop probe packets without responding. UDP scans can be agonizingly slow for these reasons. Yet the vast majority of open ports fall into just a few hundred port numbers. A port scan will be about 10 times as fast if you only scan 100 ports instead of the default 1,000. You can scan just the most popular 100 ports with the -F (fast scan) option, specify an arbitrary number of top ports with --top-ports, or provide a custom list of ports to -p.

Skip advanced scan types (-sC, -sV, -O, --traceroute, and -A).

> Some people regularly specify the -A Nmap option, which gives them the works. It causes Nmap to do OS detection, version detection, script scanning (NSE), and traceroute as well as the default port scan. Version detection can be extraordinarily useful, but can also bog down a large scan. So can NSE. When pressed for time, you can always skip -sC and -sV on the large scale scan and then perform them on individual ports as necessary later.
>
> OS detection is not nearly as slow as version detection, but it can still easily take up 5–10 seconds per online host. Even without this, you can often guess the OS based on the name, open ports, and MAC address on a LAN. And in many cases you may not care for the OS. So -O is another candidate for only-as-necessary use. As a compromise, you can specify --osscan-limit --max-os-tries 1 which tells Nmap not to retry OS detection attempts which fail to match, and also to skip OS detection against any online hosts that don't have at least one open TCP port and one closed TCP port. OS detection isn't as accurate against such hosts anyway.

Remember to turn off DNS resolution when it isn't necessary.

By default, Nmap performs reverse-DNS resolution against every host that is found to be online. It is done against all hosts if you skip the ping step with −PN or specify −R. This was a major bottleneck when host DNS libraries were used to look up one IP at a time.

While Nmap now has a fast parallel reverse-DNS system to speed queries, they still can take a substantial amount of time. Disable them with the −n option when you don't need the data. For simple scans (such as ping scans) against a large number of hosts, omitting DNS can sometimes reduce scan time by 20% or more. DNS time is not a major factor in more involved scans which probe thousands of ports or utilize intensive features such as version detection. If you want the Nmap host machine to handle name resolution (using the gethostbyaddr function), specify the −−system-dns option. Doing so can slow scans down dramatically.

6.2.2. Optimize Timing Parameters

Nmap offers dozens of options for providing hints and rules to control scan activity. These range from high level timing aggressiveness levels provided by the −T option (described in Section 6.6, "Timing Templates (-T)" [142]) to the finer-grained controls described in Section 6.5, "Low-Level Timing Controls" [141]. You can even combine the two. These options are particularly useful when scanning highly filtered networks where Nmap receives few responses to determine its own timing estimates. Scan time can often be safely cut in half. Most of these options will have little effect against a local LAN filled with responsive hosts, as Nmap can determine optimal values itself in that case.

6.2.3. Separate and Optimize UDP Scans

Scanning UDP ports is important because many vulnerable services use that protocol, but the timing characteristics and performance requirements of UDP scans are much different than TCP scans. Of particular concern is ICMP error rate-limiting, which is extremely common and affects UDP scans far more often than TCP.

For these reasons, I don't recommend combining TCP and UDP scans when performance is critical, even though Nmap supports doing so with options such as −sSU. You often want different timing flags for each protocol, requiring separate command lines. Section 5.4.2, "Speeding Up UDP Scans" [105] provides valuable tricks and real-life examples for improving UDP scan performance.

6.2.4. Upgrade Nmap

There have been many cases where I have investigated reports of poor Nmap performance only to find that the reporter used an ancient version that was many years out of date. The newest versions of Nmap have important algorithmic improvements, bug fixes, performance-enhancing features such as local network ARP scanning, and more. The first response to performance problems should be to compare your version of Nmap (run **nmap -V**) with the latest version available from *http://nmap.org*. Upgrade if necessary. If it is still not fast enough, try the other techniques in this chapter.

6.2.5. Execute Concurrent Nmap Instances

Some people try to speed up Nmap by executing many copies in parallel against one target each. For example, the Nessus scanner used to do this by default. This is usually much less efficient and slower than letting Nmap run against the whole network. Nmap has its own parallelization system that is customized to its needs, and Nmap is able to speed up as it learns about network reliability when it scans a large group. Further, there is substantial overhead in asking the OS to fork 65,536 separate Nmap instances just to scan a class B. Having dozens of copies of Nmap running in parallel is also a memory drain since each instance loads its own copy of the data files such as `nmap-services` and `nmap-os-db`.

While launching single-host Nmap scans in parallel is a bad idea, overall speed can usually be improved by dividing the scan into several large groups and executing those concurrently. Don't go overboard though. Five or ten Nmap processes are fine, but launching 100 Nmap processes at once is not recommended. Launching too many concurrent Nmap processes leads to resource contention. Another sort of concurrency is to run Nmap from different hosts at once. You can have **cron** (or **At** on Windows) schedule local hosts on each of your networks to start scanning machines local to them at the same time, then mail the results to a central data server. Scanning your Australian network from the U.S. will be slower than scanning it from a local machine on that network. The difference will be even greater if the U.S. machine must traverse extra firewalls to reach the distant network.

6.2.6. Scan From a Favorable Network Location

Restrictive firewalls can turn a five-second scan into a multi-hour chore. The latency and packet loss associated with some Internet routes doesn't help either. If you can run Nmap from host(s) local to the target network, do so. Of course if the goal is to view the network as an external attacker would, or to test the firewall, external scanning is required. On the other hand, scanning and securing the internal network provides defense in depth which is critical against internal threats and those wily attackers who circumvent the firewall (see Chapter 10, *Detecting and Subverting Firewalls and Intrusion Detection Systems* [257]).

When doing reverse DNS resolution, especially if you have a heavily burdened local nameserver, it can help to use a less busy nameserver or directly query the authoritative nameservers. This gain is usually slight and only worth doing for repeated or enormous scans. Of course, there are sometimes non-performance reasons for choosing nameservers.

6.2.7. Increase Available Bandwidth and CPU Time

You can occasionally improve Nmap scan times by increasing your available bandwidth or CPU power. This may be done either by installing a new data line or CPU, or by halting concurrently running applications which compete for these resources. For example, Nmap will run slower if you concurrently saturate your DSL line by downloading a pirate torrent of *The Matrix Reloaded*.

It is far more common that Nmap is constrained by its own congestion control algorithms than being CPU-bound or limited by the available local bandwidth. These controls help prevent network flooding and increase accuracy. Increasing CPU power and local bandwidth won't help this sort of self-limiting by Nmap—timing options must be adjusted instead. You can test whether Nmap is CPU constrained by monitoring your CPU load with an application such as top on Unix or the Task Manager on Windows. If your CPU spends most of its time idle, then upgrading won't help much. To test Nmap's bandwidth usage, run it in verbose mode (-v). Nmap will then report the number of bytes sent and received and its execution time, as shown in Example 6.1.

Example 6.1. Bandwidth usage over local 100 Mbps ethernet network

```
# nmap -v -n -p- sec.titan.net

Starting Nmap ( http://nmap.org )
[10 lines cut]
Interesting ports on 192.168.0.8:
Not shown: 65534 closed ports
PORT   STATE SERVICE
22/tcp open  ssh
MAC Address: 00:1A:6B:C1:33:37 (USI)

Nmap done: 1 IP address (1 host up) scanned in 2.20 seconds
          Raw packets sent: 65536 (2.884MB) | Rcvd: 65536 (2.621MB)
```

Multiply the byte values by eight and divide by the execution time to get the average bandwidth usage in bits per second. In Example 6.1, Nmap received 2,621,000 bytes (Nmap considers 1,000,000 bytes to be a MB) in 2.20 seconds. So receive traffic was about 9.5 Mbps (send rate was 10.5 Mbps). Therefore the 100 Mbps ethernet link isn't likely constraining Nmap, and upgrading to gigabit ethernet won't help much.

Some consumer broadband devices and other equipment has a hard time dealing with the rate of packets sent by Nmap, even though the small packet size (usually Nmap sends empty headers) keeps bandwidth low. In Example 6.1, "Bandwidth usage over local 100 Mbps ethernet network" [139], Nmap sent about 30,000 packets per second and received a similar number. Such high packet rates can cause problem with low-quality devices. In this case, we see that both send and receive packet counts were 65,536, which is the number of scanned ports (65,535) plus one for the initial ARP ping probe. Therefore Nmap did not encounter any packet drops requiring retransmission. This suggests again that the networking equipment was not a limiting factor—Nmap was probably CPU bound.

6.3. Coping Strategies for Long Scans

While optimizing scan options to speed up a scan can take you a long way, there is a limit to how fast Nmap can run while preserving accuracy and treating competing network flows fairly. Large scans involving thousands of hosts, all 65K ports, UDP, or version detection are likely to take a while even after optimization. This section provides powerful strategies for coping with these long scans.

6.3.1. Use a Multi-stage Approach

A comprehensive security audit will need to include UDP and TCP scanning of all 65,536 ports for each protocol, usually with -PN just in case a machine is up but heavily filtered. Yet fewer than 100 of those port numbers are commonly used and most hosts are responsive with moderate host discovery options. So specify -F to perform a quick scan popular ports on known-online hosts first. That lets you analyze the online hosts and most of the open ports while you start the huge -PN scan of all TCP and UDP ports with version and OS detection in the background. Short cut options for speeding up the quick scan are discussed in Section 6.2.1, "Omit Non-critical Tests" [136]. Once the slow scan is done, compare it to the earlier results to find any newly discovered hosts or ports.

6.3.2. Estimate and Plan for Scan Time

In many cases, the most frustrating aspect of long scans is having no idea when they will complete. Nmap is now more helpful than it used to be in that it provides regular scan time estimates as long as verbose mode (-v) is enabled.

Example 6.2. Estimating scan time

```
# nmap -T4 -sS -p0- -iR 500 -n --min-hostgroup 100 -v

Starting Nmap ( http://nmap.org )
Initiating SYN Stealth Scan against 29 hosts [65536 ports/host] at 23:27
[...]
SYN Stealth Scan Timing: About 0.30% done; ETC: 09:45 (10:15:45 remaining)
```

Example 6.2 shows us that the SYN scan is likely to take ten hours and eighteen minutes (23:27 to 9:45) to scan 29 hosts. So the total time Nmap will spend scanning the network can be roughly extrapolated by multiplying 21 minutes per host by the number of hosts online. If version detection or UDP are being done as well, you'll also have to watch the timing estimates for those.

Another option is to wait until Nmap has fully completed scanning its first group of hosts. Then extrapolate the time taken for the size of that set over the size of the entire target network. This is simpler because you don't need to worry about individual scan components. Basing your estimates on the number of target IP addresses finished versus the target IP space size can be misleading, as online hosts are rarely evenly distributed among that IP space. They are usually found in clumps, often near the beginning of the IP space. So if the scan itself includes host discovery (i.e. no -PN option), a more accurate measure is to ping scan the entire network first and then base your estimates on the number of online hosts Nmap has completed scanning versus the number found online by the ping scan.

While occasional estimates are printed automatically in verbose mode, you can always request the current estimate by pressing **<enter>** (see Section 15.15, "Runtime Interaction" [410]). If the estimate is within your timeframe, you can schedule something else to do while it proceeds. That beats checking whether Nmap is done every 20 minutes. An estimate showing that Nmap won't finish on time is even more valuable. You can immediately work on optimizing the scan or lengthening the engagement. Your options are much more limited if you only determine the scan is too slow after the deadline passes and Nmap is still running.

6.4. Port Selection Data and Strategies

Port scanning can be the most time consuming portion of an Nmap scan, even when the scan includes version detection or NSE scripts. Port scan time is roughly proportional to the number of ports scanned, so reducing the number of ports provides a significant performance boost. The down side is that reduced scans are less comprehensive, so you might miss open ports.

The reality is that there are 65,536 ports in each protocol, and most of them are almost never open. I spent a summer conducting large-scale scans to determine the prevalence of each TCP and UDP port. The results include data from scanning tens of millions of Internet IP addresses as well as enterprise networks scanned from within. This section provides empirical results you can rely on to strike the right balance between speed and effectiveness in your scans.

While more than a hundred thousand (total) TCP and UDP ports exist, the vast majority of open ports fall within a much smaller set. According to our research, the top 10 TCP ports and top 1,075 UDP ports represent half of the open ports for their protocol. To catch 90% of the open ports, you need to scan 576 TCP ports and 11,307 UDP ports. By default, Nmap scans the top 1,000 ports for each scan protocol requested. This catches roughly 93% of the TCP ports and 49% of the UDP ports. With the `-F` (fast) option, only the top 100 ports are scanned, providing 78% TCP effectiveness and 39% for UDP. To specify a different number of ports, specify that value to the `--top-ports` option. Table 6.1 provides an approximation of the number of TCP or UDP ports you must scan to reach a given effectiveness rate for that protocol.

Table 6.1. Required `--top-ports` values for reaching various effectiveness levels

Effectiveness	TCP ports required	UDP ports required
10%	1	5
20%	2	12
30%	4	27
40%	6	135
50%	10	1,075
60%	18	2,618
70%	44	5,157
80%	122	7,981
85%	236	9,623
90%	576	11,307
95%	1,558	13,035
99%	3,328	15,094
100%	65,536	65,536

While Nmap can handle port selection for you automatically (when you rely on defaults or use options such as `-F` or `--top-ports`), specifying ports explicitly with `-p` is often useful. In either case, familiarity with the most commonly seen open ports is important. The top ports according to our data are described in Section 4.1.2, "What Are the Most Popular Ports?" [75].

6.5. Low-Level Timing Controls

Nmap offers many fine-grained options for controlling scan speed. Most people use these options to speed Nmap up, but they can also be useful for slowing Nmap down. People do that to evade IDS systems, reduce network load, or even improve accuracy if network conditions are so bad that even Nmap's conservative default is too aggressive.

Table 6.2 lists each low-level timing control option by function. For detailed usage information on every option, read Section 15.11, "Timing and Performance" [394]. It is assumed that the reader is already familiar with the Nmap scanning algorithms described in Section 5.13, "Scan Code and Algorithms" [128].

Table 6.2. Low-level timing controls by function

Function	Options
Hostgroup (batch of hosts scanned concurrently) size	`--min-hostgroup, --max-hostgroup`
Number of probes launched in parallel	`--min-parallelism, --max-parallelism`
Probe timeout values	`--min-rtt-timeout, --max-rtt-timeout, --initial-rtt-timeout`
Maximum number of probe retransmissions allowed	`--max-retries`
Maximum time before giving up on a whole host	`--host-timeout`
Control delay inserted between each probe against an individual host	`--scan-delay, --max-scan-delay`
Rate of probe packets sent per second	`--min-rate, --max-rate`
Defeat RST packet response rate by target hosts	`--defeat-rst-ratelimit`

6.6. Timing Templates (-T)

While the fine-grained timing controls discussed in the previous section are powerful and effective, some people find them confusing. Moreover, choosing the appropriate values can sometimes take more time than the scan you are trying to optimize. So Nmap offers a simpler approach, with six timing templates. You can specify them with the -T option and their number (0–5) or their name. The template names are paranoid (0), sneaky (1), polite (2), normal (3), aggressive (4), and insane (5). The first two are for IDS evasion. Polite mode slows down the scan to use less bandwidth and target machine resources. Normal mode is the default and so -T3 does nothing. Aggressive mode speeds scans up by making the assumption that you are on a reasonably fast and reliable network. Finally insane mode assumes that you are on an extraordinarily fast network or are willing to sacrifice some accuracy for speed.

These templates allow the user to specify how aggressive they wish to be, while leaving Nmap to pick the exact timing values. The templates also make some minor speed adjustments for which fine-grained control options do not currently exist. For example, -T4 prohibits the dynamic scan delay from exceeding 10 ms for TCP ports and -T5 caps that value at 5 ms. Templates can be used in combination with fine-grained controls, and the granular options will override the general timing templates for those specific values. I recommend using -T4 when scanning reasonably modern and reliable networks. Keep that option (at the beginning of the command line) even when you add fine-grained controls so that you benefit from those extra minor optimizations that it enables.

Table 6.3 shows how the timing variables vary for each -T value. All time values are in milliseconds.

Table 6.3. Timing templates and their effects

	T0	T1	T2	T3	T4	T5
Name	Paranoid	Sneaky	Polite	Normal	Aggressive	Insane
`min-rtt-timeout`	100	100	100	100	100	50
`max-rtt-timeout`	300,000	15,000	10,000	10,000	1,250	300

	T0	T1	T2	T3	T4	T5
`initial-rtt-timeout`	300,000	15,000	1,000	1,000	500	250
`max-retries`	10	10	10	10	6	2
Initial (and minimum) scan delay (`--scan-delay`)	300,000	15,000	400	0	0	0
Maximum TCP scan delay	300,000	15,000	1,000	1,000	10	5
Maximum UDP scan delay	300,000	15,000	1,000	1,000	1,000	1,000
`host-timeout`	0	0	0	0	0	900,000
`min-parallelism`	Dynamic, not affected by timing templates					
`max-parallelism`	1	1	1	Dynamic	Dynamic	Dynamic
`min-hostgroup`	Dynamic, not affected by timing templates					
`max-hostgroup`	Dynamic, not affected by timing templates					
`min-rate`	No minimum rate limit					
`max-rate`	No maximum rate limit					
`defeat-rst-ratelimit`	Not enabled by default					

If you are on a decent broadband or ethernet connection, I would recommend always using −T4. Some people love −T5 though it is too aggressive for my taste. People sometimes specify −T2 because they think it is less likely to crash hosts or because they consider themselves to be polite in general. They often don't realize just how slow −T polite really is. They scan may take ten times longer than a default scan. Machine crashes and bandwidth problems are rare with the default timing options (−T3) and so I normally recommend that for cautious scanners. Omitting version detection is far more effective than playing with timing values for reducing these problems.

While −T0 and −T1 may be useful for avoiding IDS alerts, they will take an extraordinarily long time to scan thousands of machines or ports. For such a long scan, you may prefer to set the exact timing values you need rather than rely on the canned −T0 and −T1 values.

6.7. Scanning 676,352 IP Addresses in 46 Hours

This story was submitted by Jack L. Mogren of the Mayo Clinic. It functions as a tutorial, demonstrating the steps he took to implement a regular Nmap scanning regime and reduce scan time of this huge network from a week to 46 hours.

The Mayo Clinic has built a relatively large private network, with ARP tables indicating over 70,000 IP addresses in use. Our network management used to focus on creating and maintaining the physical architecture across three major campuses and several dozen satellites across the country. Our motto was "You need it? We'll build it". There was little regard for what was actually connected to the network. Network management conveniently ended at the data jack and suffered from the candy bar syndrome. It was crunchy and secure from the outside, but soft and chewy on the inside. We had well protected boundaries but few internal controls.

This attitude changed abruptly in January 2003 when the Slammer worm (W32.SQLExp) and its variants broke into our environment. Suddenly it became very important to know what was connected to our network. In the case of Slammer, we needed to know where all the devices running MS SQL Server 2000 or MSDE 2000 were located and who the administrators were. Lacking this information, the effort to eradicate Slammer lasted several months.

Thus was born the effort to "Know what's on the network". It sounds simplistic, but given size, complexity and network history, this was a major step forward and a new direction for our network management services.

Nmap has proven to be a valuable tool in this effort. You can't beat the price, and I appreciate the advantages that the open-source community brings to its development. Especially OS fingerprinting and the many contributions provided by end users.

I began experimenting with Nmap. My goal was to create a meaningful network inventory by using the Nmap -O option to quickly perform remote host identification via TCP/IP fingerprinting.

Let me start with a few words about our IP environment and my scanning platform. We currently own one class B and 44 class C ranges as well as using most of the private address space. That adds up to 676,352 possible IP addresses. I performed my scans from a Compaq DL380 running Red Hat Linux 8.0. My first attempt was this vanilla TCP SYN scan with OS detection (-O) and only ICMP echo requests for host discovery (-PE):

```
# nmap -O -PE -v -oX mayo.xml -iL ip_networks.txt
```

Unfortunately, that proceeded so slowly that it would have taken a week to scan our entire network. Given that all significant parts of our network were connected by at least a T1 line (1.54 Mbps), I added the insane canned timing policy (-T5). I also added fast scan mode (-F), which cut the number of ports scanned from about 1600 to 1200[2]. I also added --osscan-limit so that Nmap doesn't waste time OS scanning hosts with no ports open. This resulted in the following command:

```
# nmap -O -T5 -PE -F --osscan-limit -v -oX mayo.xml -iL ip_networks.txt
```

Unfortunately, this looked like it would still take a few days. So I edited the nmap-services file to trim down the number of ports to 270. The scan then finished in a little over 49 hours and found 66,558 devices. Tweaking the timing variables, removing the verbose option, and redirecting output to /dev/null reduced that time to 46 hours. That left me with this final command:

```
# nmap -O -T5 -PE -F --osscan-limit --max-rtt-timeout 100      \
      --max-parallelism 100 --min-hostgroup 100 -oX mayo.xml \
      -iL ip_networks.txt
```

I plan to perform this scan on a weekly basis and provide the output in the XML format to an MS SQL database. Our other scan methods already feed into this database and we are able to create reports that help us meet our original goal of knowing what's on the network. I may decide to distribute the load by running subsets of the scanning on several systems.

---

[2]With Nmap version 4.75 or higher, -F is even more effective in that it cuts the number of scanned ports to 100.

Chapter 7. Service and Application Version Detection

7.1. Introduction

While Nmap does many things, its most fundamental feature is port scanning. Point Nmap at a remote machine, and it might tell you that ports `25/tcp`, `80/tcp`, and `53/udp` are open. Using its `nmap-services` database of more than 2,200 well-known services, Nmap would report that those ports probably correspond to a mail server (SMTP), web server (HTTP), and name server (DNS) respectively. This lookup is usually accurate—the vast majority of daemons listening on TCP port 25 are, in fact, mail servers. However, you should not bet your security on this! People can and do run services on strange ports. Perhaps their main web server was already on port 80, so they picked a different port for a staging or test server. Maybe they think hiding a vulnerable service on some obscure port prevents "evil hackers" from finding it. Even more common lately is that people choose ports based not on the service they want to run, but on what gets through the firewall. When ISPs blocked port 80 after major Microsoft IIS worms CodeRed and Nimda, hordes of users responded by moving their personal web servers to another port. When companies block Telnet access due to its horrific security risks, I have seen users simply run telnetd on the Secure Shell (SSH) port instead.

Even if Nmap is right, and the hypothetical server above is running SMTP, HTTP, and DNS servers, that is not a lot of information. When doing vulnerability assessments (or even simple network inventories) of your companies or clients, you really want to know which mail and DNS servers and versions are running. Having an accurate version number helps dramatically in determining which exploits a server is vulnerable to. Do keep in mind that security fixes are often back-ported to earlier versions of software, so you cannot rely solely on the version number to prove a service is vulnerable. False negatives are rarer, but can happen when silly administrators spoof the version number of a vulnerable service to make it appear patched.

Another good reason for determining the service types and version numbers is that many services share the same port number. For example, port `258/tcp` is used by both the Checkpoint Firewall-1 GUI management interface and the yak Windows chat client. This makes a guess based on the `nmap-services` table even less accurate. Anyone who has done much scanning knows that you also often find services listening on unregistered ports—these are a complete mystery without version detection. A final problem is that filtered UDP ports often look the same to a simple port scanner as open ports (see Section 5.4, "UDP Scan (-sU)" [101]). But if they respond to the service-specific probes sent by Nmap version detection, you know for sure that they are open (and often exactly what is running).

Service scans sometimes reveal information about a target beyond the service type and version number. Miscellaneous information discovered about a service is collected in the "info" field. This is displayed in the `VERSION` column inside parentheses following the product name and version number. This field can include SSH protocol numbers, Apache modules, and much more.

Some services also report their configured hostnames, which differ from machines' reverse DNS hostnames surprisingly often. The hostname field is reported on a `Service Info` line following the port table. It sounds like a minor information leak, but can have consequences. One year at the CanSecWest security conference, I was huddled up in my room with my laptop. Suddenly the tcpdump window in the corner of my screen went wild and I realized my machine was under attack. I scanned back and found an unusual high port sitting open. Upon connecting, the port spewed a bunch of binary characters, but one ASCII field in the output gave a configured domain name. The domain was for a small enough security company that I knew exactly who was responsible. I had the front desk ring his hotel room, and boy was he surprised when I asked him to stop probing my box.

Two more fields that version detection can discover are operating system and device type. These are also reported on the `Service Info` line. We use two techniques here. One is application exclusivity. If we identify a service as Microsoft Exchange, we know the operating system is Windows since Exchange doesn't run on anything else. The other technique is to persuade more portable applications to divulge the platform information. Many servers (especially web servers) require very little coaxing. This type of OS detection is intended to complement Nmap's OS detection system (`-O`) and can sometimes report differing results. Consider a Microsoft Exchange server hidden behind a port-forwarding Unix firewall.

The Nmap version scanning subsystem obtains all of this data by connecting to open ports and interrogating them for further information using probes that the specific services understand. This allows Nmap to give a detailed assessment of what is really running, rather than just what port numbers are open. Example 7.1 shows the actual output.

Example 7.1. Simple usage of version detection

```
# nmap -A -T4 -F insecure.org

Starting Nmap ( http://nmap.org )
Interesting ports on insecure.org (205.217.153.53):
(The 1206 ports scanned but not shown below are in state: filtered)
PORT     STATE   SERVICE VERSION
22/tcp   open    ssh     OpenSSH 3.1p1 (protocol 1.99)
25/tcp   open    smtp    Qmail smtpd
53/tcp   open    domain  ISC BIND 9.2.1
80/tcp   open    http    Apache httpd 2.0.39 ((Unix) mod_perl/1.99_07-dev)
113/tcp  closed  auth
Device type: general purpose
Running: Linux 2.4.X|2.5.X
OS details: Linux Kernel 2.4.0 - 2.5.20

Nmap finished: 1 IP address (1 host up) scanned in 34.962 seconds
```

Nmap version detection offers the following advanced features (fully described later):

- High speed, parallel operation via non-blocking sockets and a probe/match definition grammar designed for efficient yet powerful implementation.

- Determines the application name and version number where available—not just the service protocol.

- Supports both the TCP and UDP protocols, as well as both textual ASCII and packed binary services.

- Multi-platform support, including Linux, Windows, Mac OS X, FreeBSD/NetBSD/OpenBSD, Solaris, and all the other platforms on which Nmap is known to work.

- If SSL is detected, Nmap connects using OpenSSL (if available) and tries to determine what service is listening behind that encryption layer. This allows it to discover services like HTTPS, POP3S, IMAPS, etc. as well as providing version details.

- If a SunRPC service is discovered, Nmap launches its brute-force RPC grinder to find the program number, name, and version number.

- IPv6 is supported, including TCP, UDP, and SSL over TCP.

- Community contributions: if Nmap gets data back from a service that it does not recognize, a *service fingerprint* is printed along with a submission URL. This system is patterned after the extremely successful Nmap OS Detection fingerprint submission process. New probes and corrections can also be submitted.

- Comprehensive database: Nmap recognizes more than one thousand service signatures, covering more than 180 unique service protocols from ACAP, AFP, and AIM to XML-RPC, Zebedee, and Zebra.

7.2. Usage and Examples

Before delving into the technical details of how version detection is implemented, here are some examples demonstrating its usage and capabilities. To enable version detection, just add −sV to whatever Nmap flags you normally use. Or use the −A option, which turns on version detection and other *A*dvanced and *A*ggressive features later. It is really that simple, as shown in Example 7.2.

Example 7.2. Version detection against www.microsoft.com

```
# nmap -A -T4 -F www.microsoft.com

Starting Nmap ( http://nmap.org )
Interesting ports on 80.67.68.30:
(The 1208 ports scanned but not shown below are in state: closed)
PORT      STATE     SERVICE       VERSION
22/tcp   open      ssh           Akamai-I SSH (protocol 1.5)
80/tcp   open      http          AkamaiGHost (Akamai's HTTP Acceleration service)
443/tcp  open      ssl/http      AkamaiGHost (Akamai's HTTP Acceleration service)
Device type: general purpose
Running: Linux 2.1.X|2.2.X
OS details: Linux 2.1.19 - 2.2.25

Nmap finished: 1 IP address (1 host up) scanned in 19.223 seconds
```

This preceding scan demonstrates a couple things. First of all, it is gratifying to see www.Microsoft.Com served off one of Akamai's Linux boxes. More relevant to this chapter is that the listed service for port 443 is ssl/http. That means that service detection first discovered that the port was SSL, then it loaded up OpenSSL and performed service detection again through SSL connections to discover a web server running AkamiGHost behind the encryption. Recall that −T4 causes Nmap to go faster (more aggressive timing) and −F tells Nmap to scan only ports registered in nmap-services.

Example 7.3 is a longer and more diverse example.

Example 7.3. Complex version detection

```
# nmap -A -T4 localhost

Starting Nmap ( http://nmap.org )
Interesting ports on felix (127.0.0.1):
(The 1640 ports scanned but not shown below are in state: closed)
PORT      STATE SERVICE      VERSION
21/tcp    open  ftp          WU-FTPD wu-2.6.1-20
22/tcp    open  ssh          OpenSSH 3.1p1 (protocol 1.99)
53/tcp    open  domain       ISC BIND 9.2.1
79/tcp    open  finger       Linux fingerd
111/tcp   open  rpcbind      2 (rpc #100000)
443/tcp   open  ssl/http     Apache httpd 2.0.39 ((Unix) mod_perl/1.99_04-dev)
515/tcp   open  printer
631/tcp   open  ipp          CUPS 1.1
953/tcp   open  rndc?
5000/tcp  open  ssl/ftp      WU-FTPD wu-2.6.1-20
5001/tcp  open  ssl/ssh      OpenSSH 3.1p1 (protocol 1.99)
5002/tcp  open  ssl/domain   ISC BIND 9.2.1
5003/tcp  open  ssl/finger   Linux fingerd
6000/tcp  open  X11          (access denied)
8000/tcp  open  http-proxy   Junkbuster webproxy
8080/tcp  open  http         Apache httpd 2.0.39 ((Unix) mod_perl/1.99_04-dev)
8081/tcp  open  http         Apache httpd 2.0.39 ((Unix) mod_perl/1.99_04-dev)
Device type: general purpose
Running: Linux 2.4.X|2.5.X
OS details: Linux Kernel 2.4.0 - 2.5.20

Nmap finished: 1 IP address (1 host up) scanned in 42.494 seconds
```

You can see here the way RPC services are treated, with the brute-force RPC scanner being used to determine that port 111 is rpcbind version 2. You may also notice that port 515 gives the service as `printer`, but that version column is empty. Nmap determined the service name by probing, but was not able to determine anything else. On the other hand, port 953 gives the service as "`rndc?`". The question mark tells us that Nmap was not even able to determine the service name through probing. As a fallback, rndc is mentioned because that has port 953 registered in `nmap-services`. Unfortunately, none of Nmap's probes elicited any sort of response from rndc. If they had, Nmap would have printed a service fingerprint and a submission URL so that it could be recognized in the next version. As it is, Nmap requires a special probe. One might even be available by the time you read this. Section 7.7, "Community Contributions" [164] provides details on writing your own probes.

It is also worth noting that some services provide much more information than just the version number. Examples above include whether X11 permits connections, the SSH protocol number, and the Apache module versions list. Some of the Apache modules even had to be cut from the output to fit on this page.

A few early reviewers questioned the sanity of running services such as SSH and finger over SSL. This was actually just fun with stunnel[1], in part to ensure that parallel SSL scans actually work.

---

[1] *http://www.stunnel.org/*

7.3. Technique Described

Nmap version scanning is actually rather straightforward. It was designed to be as simple as possible while still being scalable, fast, and accurate. The truly nitty-gritty details are best discovered by downloading and reviewing the source code, but a synopsis of the techniques used follows.

Nmap first does a port scan as per your instructions, and then passes all the `open` or `open|filtered` TCP and/or UDP ports to the service scanning module. Those ports are then interrogated in parallel, although a single port is described here for simplicity.

1. Nmap checks to see if the port is one of the ports to be excluded, as specified by the `Exclude` directive in `nmap-service-probes`. If it is, Nmap will not scan this port for reasons mentioned in Section 7.6, "nmap-service-probes File Format" [158].

2. If the port is TCP, Nmap starts by connecting to it. If the connection succeeds and the port had been in the `open|filtered` state, it is changed to `open`. This is rare (for TCP) since people trying to be so stealthy that they use a TCP scan type which produces `open|filtered` ports (such as FIN scan) generally know better than to blow all of their stealth by performing version detection.

3. Once the TCP connection is made, Nmap listens for roughly five seconds. Many common services, including most FTP, SSH, SMTP, Telnet, POP3, and IMAP servers, identify themselves in an initial welcome banner. Nmap refers to this as the "NULL probe", because Nmap just listens for responses without sending any probe data. If any data is received, Nmap compares it to hundreds of signature regular expressions in its `nmap-service-probes` file (described in Section 7.6, "nmap-service-probes File Format" [158]). If the service is fully identified, we are done with that port! The regular expression includes substrings that can be used to pick version numbers out of the response. In some cases, Nmap gets a "soft match" on the service type, but no version info. In that case, Nmap continues but only sends probes that are known to recognize the soft-matched service type.

4. At this point, Nmap UDP probes start, and TCP connections end up here if the NULL probe above fails or soft-matches. Since the reality is that most ports are used by the service they are registered to in `nmap-services`, every probe has a list of port numbers that are considered to be most effective. For example, the probe called GetRequest that recognizes web servers (among other services) lists 80-85, 8000-8010, and 8080-8085 as probable ports. Nmap sequentially executes the probe(s) that match the port number being scanned.

   Each probe includes a probe string (which can be arbitrary ASCII text or \xHH escaped binary), which is sent to the port. Responses that come back are compared to a list of regular expressions of the same type as discussed in the NULL probe description above. As with the NULL probe, these tests can either result in a full match (ends processing for the remote service), a soft match (limits future probes to those which match a certain service), or no match at all. The exact list of regular expressions that Nmap uses to test for a match depends on the probe fallback configuration. For instance, the data returned from the X11Probe is very unlikely to match any regular expressions crafted for the GetRequest probe. On the other hand, it is likely that results returned from a Probe such as RTSPRequest might match a regular expression crafted for GetRequest since the two protocols being tested for are closely related. So the RTSPRequest probe has a fallback to GetRequest matches. For a more comprehensive explanation, see Section 7.3.1, "Cheats and Fallbacks" [151].

If any response during version detection is ever received from a UDP port which was in the open|filtered state, that state is changed to open. This makes version detection an excellent complement to UDP scan, which is forced to label all scanned UDP ports as open|filtered when some common firewall rules are in effect. While combining UDP scanning with version detection can take many times as long as a plain UDP scan, it is an effective and useful technique. This method is described in Section 5.4.1, "Disambiguating Open from Filtered UDP Ports" [102].

5. In most cases, the NULL probe or the probable port probe(s) (there is usually only one) described above matches the service. Since the NULL probe shares its connection with the probable port probe, this allows service detection to be done with only one brief connection in most cases. With UDP only one packet is usually required. But should the NULL probe and probable port probe(s) fail, Nmap goes through all of the existing probes sequentially. In the case of TCP, Nmap must make a new connection for each probe to avoid having previous probes corrupt the results. This worst-case scenario can take a bit of time, especially since Nmap must wait about five seconds for the results from each probe because of slow network connections and otherwise slowly responding services. Fortunately, Nmap utilizes several automatic techniques to speed up scans:

   - Nmap makes most probes generic enough to match many services. For example, the GenericLines probe sends two blank lines ("\r\n\r\n") to the service. This matches daemons of many diverse service types, including FTP, ident, POP3, UUCP, Postgres, and whois. The GetRequest probe matches even more service types. Other examples include "help\r\n" and generic RPC and MS SMB probes.

   - If a service matches a softmatch directive, Nmap only needs to try probes that can potentially match that service.

   - All probes were not created equal! Some match many more services than others. Because of this, Nmap uses the rarity metric to avoid trying probes that are extremely unlikely to match. Experienced Nmap users can force all probes to be tried regardless or limit probe attempts even further than the default by using the --version-intensity, --version-all, and --version-light options discussed in Section 7.3.2, "Probe Selection and Rarity" [152].

6. One of the probes tests whether the target port is running SSL. If so (and if OpenSSL is available), Nmap connects back via SSL and restarts the service scan to determine what is listening behind the encryption. A special directive allows different probable ports for normal and SSL tunneled connections. For example, Nmap should start against port 443 (HTTPS) with an SSL probe. But after SSL is detected and enabled, Nmap should try the GetRequest probe against port 443 because that port usually has a web server listening behind SSL encryption.

7. Another generic probe identifies RPC-based services. When these are found, the Nmap RPC grinder (discussed later) is initiated to brute force the RPC program number/name and supported version numbers. Similarly, an SMB post-processor for fingerprinting Windows services may be added eventually.

8. If at least one of the probes elicits some sort of response, yet Nmap is unable to recognize the service, the response content is printed to the user in the form of a *fingerprint*. If users know what services are actually listening, they are encouraged to submit the fingerprint to Nmap developers for integration into Nmap, as described in Section 7.7.1, "Submit Service Fingerprints" [164].

7.3.1. Cheats and Fallbacks

Even though Nmap waits a generous amount of time for services to reply, sometimes an application is slow to respond to the NULL probe. This can occur for a number of reasons, including slow reverse DNS lookups performed by some services. Because of this, Nmap can sometimes match the results from a subsequent probe to a match line designed for the NULL probe.

For example, suppose we scan port 25 (SMTP) on a server to determine what is listening. As soon as we connect, that service may conduct a bunch of DNS blacklist lookups to determine whether we should be treated as spammers and denied service. Before it finishes that, Nmap gives up waiting for a NULL probe response and sends the next probe with port 25 registered, which is "HELP\r\n". When the service finally completes its anti-spam checks, it prints a greeting banner, reads the Help probe, and responds as shown in Example 7.4.

Example 7.4. NULL probe cheat example output

```
220 hcsw.org ESMTP Sendmail 8.12.3/8.12.3/Debian-7.1; Tue, [cut]
214-2.0.0 This is sendmail version 8.12.3
214-2.0.0 Topics:
214-2.0.0       HELO    EHLO    MAIL    RCPT    DATA
214-2.0.0       RSET    NOOP    QUIT    HELP    VRFY
214-2.0.0       EXPN    VERB    ETRN    DSN     AUTH
214-2.0.0       STARTTLS
214-2.0.0 For more info use "HELP <topic>".
214-2.0.0 To report bugs in the implementation send email to
214-2.0.0       sendmail-bugs@sendmail.org.
214-2.0.0 For local information send email to Postmaster at your site.
214 2.0.0 End of HELP info
```

Nmap reads this data from the socket and finds that no regular expressions from the Help probe match the data returned. This is because Nmap normally expects to receive the ESMTP banner during the NULL probe and match it there.

Because this is a relatively common scenario, Nmap "cheats" by trying to match responses to any of the NULL Probe match lines if none of the probe-specific lines match. In this case, a null match line exists which reports that the program is Sendmail, the version is 8.12.3/8.12.3/Debian-7.1, and the hostname is hcsw.org.

The NULL probe cheat is actually just a specific example of a more general Nmap feature: fallbacks. The fallback directive is described in detail in Section 7.6, "nmap-service-probes File Format" [158]. Essentially, any probe that is likely to encounter results that can be matched by regular expressions in other probes has a fallback directive that specifies these other probes.

For example, in some configurations of the popular Apache web server, Apache won't respond to the GetRequest ("GET / HTTP/1.0\r\n\r\n") probe because no virtual host name has been specified. Nmap is still able to correctly identify these servers because those servers usually respond to the HTTPOptions probe. That probe has a fallback to the GetRequest regular expressions, which are sufficiently general to recognize Apache's responses to the HTTPOptions probes.

7.3.2. Probe Selection and Rarity

In determining what probes to use, Nmap considers their `rarity`. This is an indication of how likely the probe is to return useful data. If a probe has a high rarity, it is considered less common and is less likely to be tried. Nmap users can specify which probes are tried by changing the intensity level of the version scan, as described below. The precise algorithm Nmap uses when determining which probes to use follows:

1. For TCP, the NULL probe is always tried first.

2. All probes that have the port being scanned listed as a probable port (see Section 7.6, "nmap-service-probes File Format" [158]) are tried in the order they appear in `nmap-service-probes`.

3. All other probes that have a rarity value less than or equal to the current intensity value of the scan are tried, also in the order they appear in `nmap-service-probes`.

Once a probe is found to match, the algorithm terminates and results are reported.

Because all of Nmap's probes (other than the NULL probe) have a rarity value associated with them, it is relatively easy to control how many of them are tried when performing a version scan. Simply choose an intensity level appropriate for a scan. The higher an intensity level, the more probes will be tried. So if a very comprehensive scan is desired, a high intensity level is appropriate—even though it may take longer than a scan conducted at a lower intensity level. Nmap's default intensity level is 7 but Nmap provides the following switches for different scanning needs:

`--version-intensity <intensity level between 0 and 9>`
> Sets the intensity level of a version scan to the specified value. If 0 is specified, only the NULL probe (for TCP) and probes that list the port as a probable port are tried. Example: **nmap -sV --version-intensity 3 scanme.nmap.org**

`--version-intensity`
> Sets the intensity level to 2. Example: **nmap -sV --version-light scanme.nmap.org**

`--version-all`
> Sets the intensity level to 9. Since all probes have a rarity level between 1 and 9, this tries all of the probes. Example: **nmap -sV --version-all scanme.nmap.org**

7.4. Technique Demonstrated

If the English description above is not clear enough, you can see for yourself how it works by adding the `--version-trace` (and usually `-d` (debugging)) options to your Nmap command line. This shows all the connection and data read/write activity of the service scan. An annotated real-world example follows.

```
# nmap -sSV -T4 -F -d --version-trace insecure.org

Starting Nmap ( http://nmap.org )
Host insecure.org (205.217.153.53) appears to be up ... good.
```

```
Initiating SYN Stealth Scan against insecure.org (205.217.153.53) at 19:53
Initiating service scan against 4 services on 1 host at 19:53
```

The SYN scan has found 4 open ports—now we are beginning a service scan against each of them in parallel. We start with a TCP connection for the NULL probe:

```
Starting probes against new service: 205.217.153.53:22 (tcp)
NSOCK (2.0750s) TCP connection requested to 205.217.153.53:22 (IOD #1) EID 8
Starting probes against new service: 205.217.153.53:25 (tcp)
NSOCK (2.0770s) TCP connection requested to 205.217.153.53:25 (IOD #2) EID 16
Starting probes against new service: 205.217.153.53:53 (tcp)
NSOCK (2.0830s) TCP connection requested to 205.217.153.53:53 (IOD #3) EID 24
Starting probes against new service: 205.217.153.53:80 (tcp)
NSOCK (2.0860s) TCP connection requested to 205.217.153.53:80 (IOD #4) EID 32
NSOCK (2.0870s) Callback: CONNECT SUCCESS for EID 32 [205.217.153.53:80]
NSOCK (2.0870s) Read request from IOD #4 [205.217.153.53:80]
                (timeout: 5000ms) EID 42
NSOCK (2.0870s) Callback: CONNECT SUCCESS for EID 24 [205.217.153.53:53]
NSOCK (2.0870s) Read request from IOD #3 [205.217.153.53:53]
                (timeout: 5000ms) EID 50
NSOCK (2.0870s) Callback: CONNECT SUCCESS for EID 16 [205.217.153.53:25]
NSOCK (2.0870s) Read request from IOD #2 [205.217.153.53:25]
                (timeout: 5000ms) EID 58
NSOCK (2.0870s) Callback: CONNECT SUCCESS for EID 8 [205.217.153.53:22]
NSOCK (2.0870s) Read request from IOD #1 [205.217.153.53:22]
                (timeout: 5000ms) EID 66
```

At this point, NULL probe connections have successfully been made to all four services. It starts at 2 seconds because that is how long the ping and SYN scans took.

```
NSOCK (2.0880s) Callback: READ SUCCESS for EID 66 [205.217.153.53:22]
                (23 bytes): SSH-1.99-OpenSSH_3.1p1.
Service scan match: 205.217.153.53:22 is ssh.
                Version: |OpenSSH|3.1p1|protocol 1.99|
```

SSH was nice enough to fully identify itself immediately upon connection as OpenSSH 3.1p1. One down, three to go.

```
NSOCK (2.0880s) Callback: READ SUCCESS for EID 58 [205.217.153.53:25]
                (27 bytes): 220 core.lnxnet.net ESMTP..
Service scan soft match: 205.217.153.53:25 is smtp
```

The mail server on port 25 also gave us a useful banner. We do not know what type of mail server it is, but starting with 220 and including the word ESMTP tells us it is a mail (SMTP) server. So Nmap softmatches smtp, meaning that only probes able to match SMTP servers are tried from now on. Note that non-printable characters are represented by dots—so the ". ." after ESMTP is really the "\r \n" line termination sequence.

```
NSOCK (2.0880s) Read request from IOD #2 [205.217.153.53:25]
                (timeout: 4996ms) EID 74
NSOCK (7.0880s) Callback: READ TIMEOUT for EID 74 [205.217.153.53:25]
NSOCK (7.0880s) Write request for 6 bytes to IOD #2 EID 83
                [205.217.153.53:25]: HELP..
```

```
NSOCK (7.0880s) Read request from IOD #2 [205.217.153.53:25]
                (timeout: 5000ms) EID 90
```

Nmap listens a little longer on the SMTP connection, just in case the server has more to say. The read request times out after five seconds. Nmap then finds the next probe which is registered to port 25 and has SMTP signatures. That probe simply consists of HELP\r\n, which Nmap writes into the connection.

```
NSOCK (7.0880s) Callback: READ TIMEOUT for EID 50 [205.217.153.53:53]
NSOCK (7.0880s) Write request for 32 bytes to IOD #3 EID 99
                [205.217.153.53:53]: ..............version.bind.....
NSOCK (7.0880s) Read request from IOD #3 [205.217.153.53:53]
                (timeout: 5000ms) EID 106
```

The DNS server on port 53 does not return anything at all. The first probe registered to port 53 in nmap-service-probes is DNSVersionBindReq, which queries a DNS server for its version number. This is sent onto the wire.

```
NSOCK (7.0880s) Callback: READ TIMEOUT for EID 42 [205.217.153.53:80]
NSOCK (7.0880s) Write request for 18 bytes to IOD #4 EID 115
                [205.217.153.53:80]: GET / HTTP/1.0....
NSOCK (7.0880s) Read request from IOD #4 [205.217.153.53:80]
                (timeout: 5000ms) EID 122
```

The port 80 NULL probe also failed to return any data. An HTTP GET request is sent, since that probe is registered to port 80.

```
NSOCK (7.0920s) Callback: READ SUCCESS for EID 122
                [205.217.153.53:80] [EOF](15858 bytes)
Service scan match: insecure.org (205.217.153.53):80 is http.
                Version: |Apache httpd|2.0.39|(Unix) mod_perl/1.99_07-dev..
```

Apache returned a huge (15KB) response, so it is not printed. That response provided detailed configuration information, which Nmap picks out of the response. There are no other probes registered for port 80. So if this had failed, Nmap would have tried the first TCP probe in nmap-service-probes. That probe simply sends blank lines ("\r\n\r\n"). A new connection would have been made in case the GET probe confused the service.

```
NSOCK (7.0920s) Callback: READ SUCCESS for EID 106 [205.217.153.53:53]
                (50 bytes): .0........version.bind.......9.2.1
Service scan match: insecure.org (205.217.153.53):53 is domain.
                Version: |ISC BIND|9.2.1||
```

Port 53 responded to our DNS version request. Most of the response (as with the probe) is binary, but you can clearly see the version 9.2.1 there. If this probe had failed, the next probe registered to port 53 is a DNS server status request (14 bytes: \0\x0C\0\0\x10\0\0\0\0\0\0\0\0\0). Having this backup probe helps because many more servers respond to a status request than a version number request.

```
NSOCK (7.0920s) Callback: READ SUCCESS for EID 90 [205.217.153.53:25]
                (55 bytes): 214 qmail home page: http...
```

```
Service scan match: insecure.org (205.217.153.53):25 is smtp.
                    Version: |qmail smtpd|||
```

Port 25 gives a very helpful response to the Help probe. Other SMTP servers such as Postfix, Courier, and Exim can often be identified by this probe as well. If the response did not match, Nmap would have given up on this service because it had already softmatched `smtp` and there are no more SMTP probes in `nmap-service-probes`.

```
The service scan took 5 seconds to scan 4 services on 1 host.
```

This service scan run went pretty well. No service required more than one connection. It took five seconds because Qmail and Apache hit the five-second NULL probe timeout before Nmap sent the first real probes. Here is the reward for these efforts:

```
Interesting ports on insecure.org (205.217.153.53):
(The 1212 ports scanned but not shown below are in state: closed)
PORT    STATE SERVICE VERSION
22/tcp open  ssh     OpenSSH 3.1p1 (protocol 1.99)
25/tcp open  smtp    qmail smtpd
53/tcp open  domain  ISC BIND 9.2.1
80/tcp open  http    Apache httpd 2.0.39 ((Unix) mod_perl/1.99_07-dev)

Nmap finished: 1 IP address (1 host up) scanned in 7.104 seconds
```

7.5. Post-processors

Nmap is usually finished working on a port once it has deduced the service and version information as demonstrated above. However, there are certain services for which Nmap performs additional work. The post-processors presently available are Nmap Scripting Engine integration, RPC grinding, and SSL tunneling. Windows SMB interrogation is under consideration.

7.5.1. Nmap Scripting Engine Integration

The regular-expression based approach of version detection is powerful, but it cannot recognize everything. Some services cannot be recognized by simply sending a standard probe and matching a pattern to the response. Some services require custom probe strings or a complex multi-step handshaking process. Others require more advanced processing than a regular expression to recognize a response. For example, the Skype v2 service was designed to be difficult to detect due to the risk that incumbent carriers (such as phone companies providing DSL lines) would consider them a competitor and degrade or block the service from their subscribers. The only way we could find to detect this service involved analyzing responses to two different probes. Similarly, we could recognize more SNMP services if we tried a few hundred different community names by brute force. Neither of these tasks are well suited to traditional Nmap version detection, but both are easily accomplished with the Nmap Scripting Language. For these reasons, version detection now calls NSE by default to handle some tricky services, as described in Section 9.10, "Version Detection Using NSE" [251].

7.5.2. RPC Grinding

SunRPC (Sun Remote Procedure Call) is a common Unix protocol used to implement many services including NFS. Nmap ships with an `nmap-rpc` database of almost 600 RPC programs. Many RPC services use high-numbered ports and/or the UDP transport protocol, making them available through many poorly configured firewalls. RPC programs (and the infrastructure libraries themselves) also have a long history of serious remotely exploitable security holes. So network administrators and security auditors often wish to learn more about any RPC programs on their networks.

If the portmapper (rpcbind) service (UDP or TCP port 111) is available, RPC services can be enumerated with the Unix **rpcinfo** command. Example 7.5 demonstrates this against a default Solaris 9 server.

Example 7.5. Enumerating RPC services with rpcinfo

```
> rpcinfo -p ultra
   program vers proto    port
    100000    4   tcp     111  rpcbind
    100000    4   udp     111  rpcbind
    100232   10   udp   32777  sadmind
    100083    1   tcp   32775  ttdbserverd
    100221    1   tcp   32777  kcms_server
    100068    5   udp   32778  cmsd
    100229    1   tcp   32779  metad
    100230    1   tcp   32781  metamhd
    100242    1   tcp   32783  rpc.metamedd
    100001    4   udp   32780  rstatd
    100002    3   udp   32782  rusersd
    100002    3   tcp   32785  rusersd
    100008    1   udp   32784  walld
    100012    1   udp   32786  sprayd
    100011    1   udp   32788  rquotad
    100024    1   udp   32790  status
    100024    1   tcp   32787  status
    100133    1   udp   32790  nsm_addrand
    100133    1   tcp   32787  nsm_addrand
 [ Dozens of lines cut for brevity ]
```

This example shows that hosts frequently offer many RPC services, which increases the probability that one is exploitable. You should also notice that most of the services are on strange high-numbered ports (which may change for any number of reasons) and split between UDP and TCP transport protocols.

Because the RPC information is so sensitive, many administrators try to obscure this information by blocking the portmapper port (111). Unfortunately, this does not close the hole. Nmap can determine all of the same information by directly communicating with open RPC ports through the following three-step process.

1. The TCP and/or UDP port scan finds all of the open ports.

2. Version detection determines which of the open ports use the SunRPC protocol.

3. The RPC brute force engine determines the program identity of each RPC port by trying a *null command* against each of the 600 programs numbers in `nmap-rpc`. Most of the time Nmap guesses wrong and

---

receives an error message stating that the requested program number is not listening on the port. Nmap continues trying each number in its list until success is returned for one of them. Nmap gives up in the unlikely event that it exhausts all of its known program numbers or if the port sends malformed responses that suggest it is not really RPC.

The RPC program identification probes are done in parallel, and retransmissions are handled for UDP ports. This feature is automatically activated whenever version detection finds any RPC ports. Or it can be performed without version detection by specifying the -sR option. Example 7.6 demonstrates direct RPC scanning done as part of version detection.

Example 7.6. Nmap direct RPC scan

```
# nmap -F -A -sSU ultra

Starting Nmap ( http://nmap.org )
Interesting ports on ultra.nmap.org (192.168.0.50):
(The 2171 ports scanned but not shown below are in state: closed)
PORT        STATE SERVICE          VERSION
[A whole bunch of ports cut for brevity]
32776/tcp open  kcms_server       1 (rpc #100221)
32776/udp open  sadmind           10 (rpc #100232)
32777/tcp open  kcms_server       1 (rpc #100221)
32777/udp open  sadmind           10 (rpc #100232)
32778/tcp open  metad             1 (rpc #100229)
32778/udp open  cmsd              2-5 (rpc #100068)
32779/tcp open  metad             1 (rpc #100229)
32779/udp open  rstatd            2-4 (rpc #100001)
32780/tcp open  metamhd           1 (rpc #100230)
32780/udp open  rstatd            2-4 (rpc #100001)
32786/tcp open  status            1 (rpc #100024)
32786/udp open  sprayd            1 (rpc #100012)
32787/tcp open  status            1 (rpc #100024)
32787/udp open  rquotad           1 (rpc #100011)
Device type: general purpose
Running: Sun Solaris 9
OS details: Sun Solaris 9

Nmap finished: 1 IP address (1 host up) scanned in 252.701 seconds
```

7.5.3. SSL Post-processor Notes

As discussed in the technique section, Nmap has the ability to detect the SSL encryption protocol and then launch an encrypted session through which it executes normal version detection. As with the RPC grinder discussed previously, the SSL post-processor is automatically executed whenever an appropriate (SSL) port is detected. This is demonstrated by Example 7.7.

Example 7.7. Version scanning through SSL

```
nmap -PN -sSV -T4 -F www.amazon.com

Starting Nmap ( http://nmap.org )
Interesting ports on 207-171-184-16.amazon.com (207.171.184.16):
(The 1214 ports scanned but not shown below are in state: filtered)
PORT     STATE SERVICE   VERSION
80/tcp  open  http      Apache Stronghold httpd 2.4.2 (based on Apache 1.3.6)
443/tcp open  ssl/http Apache Stronghold httpd 2.4.2 (based on Apache 1.3.6)

Nmap finished: 1 IP address (1 host up) scanned in 35.038 seconds
```

Note that the version information is the same for each of the two open ports, but the service is `http` on port 80 and `ssl/http` on port 443. The common case of HTTPS on port 443 is not hard-coded—Nmap should be able to detect SSL on any port and determine the underlying protocol for any service that Nmap can detect in clear-text. If Nmap had not detected the server listening behind SSL, the service listed would be `ssl/unknown`. If Nmap had not been built with SSL support, the service listed would have simply been `ssl`. The version column would be blank in both of these cases.

The SSL support for Nmap depends on the free OpenSSL library[2]. It is not included in the Linux RPM binaries, to avoid breaking systems which lack these libraries. The Nmap source code distribution attempts to detect OpenSSL on a system and link to it when available. See Chapter 2, *Obtaining, Compiling, Installing, and Removing Nmap* [25] for details on customizing the build process to include or exclude OpenSSL.

7.6. `nmap-service-probes` File Format

As with remote OS detection (`-O`), Nmap uses a flat file to store the version detection probes and match strings. While the version of `nmap-services` distributed with Nmap is sufficient for most users, understanding the file format allows advanced Nmap hackers to add their own services to the detection engine. Like many Unix files, `nmap-service-probes` is line-oriented. Lines starting with a hash (#) are treated as comments and ignored by the parser. Blank lines are ignored as well. Other lines must contain one of the directives described below. Some readers prefer to peek at the examples in Section 7.6.9, "Putting It All Together" [163] before tackling the following dissection.

7.6.1. `Exclude` Directive

Syntax: `Exclude <port specification>`

Examples:

```
Exclude 53,T:9100,U-30000-40000
```

This directive excludes the specified ports from the version scan. It can only be used once and should be near the top of the file, above any Probe directives. The Exclude directive uses the same format as the Nmap `-p` switch, so ranges and comma separated lists of ports are supported. In the `nmap-service-probes` included with Nmap the only ports excluded are TCP port 9100 through 9107. These are common ports for

---

[2] *http://www.openssl.org*

printers to listen on and they often print any data sent to them. So a version detection scan can cause them to print many pages full of probes that Nmap sends, such as SunRPC requests, help statements, and X11 probes.

This behavior is often undesirable, especially when a scan is meant to be stealthy. However, Nmap's default behavior of avoiding scanning this port can make it easier for a sneaky user to hide a service: simply run it on an excluded port such as 9100 and it is less likely to be identified by name. The port scan will still show it as open. Users can override the Exclude directive with the `--allports` option. This causes version detection to interrogate all open ports.

7.6.2. `Probe` Directive

Syntax: `Probe <protocol> <probename> <probesendstring>`

Examples:

```
Probe TCP GetRequest q|GET / HTTP/1.0\r\n\r\n|
Probe UDP DNSStatusRequest q|\0\0\x10\0\0\0\0\0\0\0\0\0|
Probe TCP NULL q||
```

The Probe directive tells Nmap what string to send to recognize various services. All of the directives discussed later operate on the most recent `Probe` statement. The arguments are as follows:

`<protocol>`

This must be either `TCP` or `UDP`. Nmap only uses probes that match the protocol of the service it is trying to scan.

`<probename>`

This is a plain English name for the probe. It is used in service fingerprints to describe which probes elicited responses.

`<probestring>`

Tells Nmap what to send. It must start with a `q`, then a delimiter character which begins and ends the string. Between the delimiter characters is the string that is actually sent. It is formatted similarly to a C or Perl string in that it allows the following standard escape characters: `\\ \0, \a, \b, \f, \n, \r, \t, \v, \xHH`. One `Probe` line in `nmap-service-probes` has an empty probe string, as shown in the third example above. This is the TCP NULL probe which just listens for the initial banners that many services send. If your delimiter character (`|` in these examples) is needed for your probe string, you need to choose a different delimiter.

7.6.3. `match` Directive

Syntax: `match <service> <pattern> [<versioninfo>]`

Examples:

```
match ftp m/^220.*Welcome to PureFTPd (\d\S+)/ p/PureFTPd/ v/$1/
match ssh m/^SSH-([.\d]+)-OpenSSH_(\S+)/ p/OpenSSH/ v/$2/ i/protocol $1/
match mysql m/^.\0\0\0\n(4\.[-.\w]+)\0...\0/s p/MySQL/ i/$1/
```

```
match chargen m|@ABCDEFGHIJKLMNOPQRSTUVWXYZ|
match uucp m|^login: Password: Login incorrect\.$| p/SunOS uucpd/ o/SunOS/
match printer m|^([\w-_.]+): lpd: Illegal service request\n$| p/lpd/ h/$1/
match afs m|^[\d\D]{28}\s*(OpenAFS)([\d\.]{3}[^\s\0]*)\0| p/$1/ v/$2/
```

The match directive tells Nmap how to recognize services based on responses to the string sent by the previous `Probe` directive. A single `Probe` line may be followed by dozens or hundreds of `match` statements. If the given pattern matches, an optional version specifier builds the application name, version number, and additional info for Nmap to report. The arguments to this directive follow:

`<service>`

  This is simply the service name that the pattern matches. Examples would be `ssh`, `smtp`, `http`, or `snmp`. As a special case, you can prefix the service name with `ssl/`, as in `ssl/vmware-auth`. In that case, the service would be stored as `vmware-auth` tunneled by SSL. This is useful for services which can be fully recognized without the overhead of making an SSL connection.

`<pattern>`

  This pattern is used to determine whether the response received matches the service given in the previous parameter. The format is like Perl, with the syntax being `m/[regex]/[opts]`. The "m" tells Nmap that a match string is beginning. The forward slash (`/`) is a delimiter, which can be substituted by almost any printable character as long as the second slash is also replaced to match. The regex is a Perl-style regular expression[3]. This is made possible by the excellent Perl Compatible Regular Expressions (PCRE) library (*http://www.pcre.org*). The only options currently supported are `'i'`, which makes a match case-insensitive and `'s'` which includes newlines in the `'.'` specifier. As you might expect, these two options have the same semantics as in Perl. Subexpressions to be captured (such as version numbers) are surrounded by parentheses as shown in most of the examples above.

`<versioninfo>`

  The `<versioninfo>` section actually contains six optional fields. Each field begins with an identifying letter (such as `h` for "hostname"). Next comes a delimiter character which the signature writer chooses. The preferred delimiter is slash (`'/'`) unless that is used in the field itself. Next comes the field value, followed by the delimiter character. The following table describes the six fields:

Table 7.1. `versioninfo` field formats and values

Field format	Value description
`p/vendorproductname/`	Includes the vendor and often service name and is of the form "Sun Solaris rexecd", "ISC BIND named", or "Apache httpd".
`v/version/`	The application version "number", which may include non-numeric characters and even multiple words.
`i/info/`	Miscellaneous further information which was immediately available and might be useful. Examples include whether an X server is open to unauthenticated connections, or the protocol number of SSH servers.
`h/hostname/`	The hostname (if any) offered up by a service. This is common for protocols such as SMTP and POP3 and is useful because these

---

[3] *http://www.perl.com/doc/manual/html/pod/perlre.html*

Field format	Value description
	hostnames may be for internal networks or otherwise differ from the straightforward reverse DNS responses.
o/operatingsystem/	The operating system the service is running on. This may legitimately be different than the OS reported by Nmap IP stack based OS detection. For example, the target IP might be a Linux box which uses network address translation to forward requests to an Microsoft IIS server in the DMZ. In this case, stack OS detection should report the OS as Linux, while service detection reports port 80 as being Windows.
d/devicetype/	The type of device the service is running on. Some services disclose this information, and it can be inferred in many more cases. For example, the HP-ChaiServer web server only runs on printers.

Any of the six fields can be omitted. In fact, all of the fields can be omitted if no further information on the service is available. Any of the version fields can include numbered strings such as $1 or $2, which are replaced (in a Perl-like fashion) with the corresponding parenthesized substring in the <pattern>.

In rare cases, a *helper function* can be applied to the replacement text before insertion. The $P() helper function will filter out unprintable characters. This is useful for converting Unicode UTF-16 encoded strings such as W\0O\0R\0K\0G\0R\0O\0U\0P\0 into the ASCII approximation WORKGROUP. It can be used in any versioninfo field by passing it the number of the match you want to make printable, like this: i/$P(3)/.

Another helper function is $SUBST(). This is used for making substitutions in matches before they are printed. It takes three arguments. The first is the substitution number in the pattern, just as you would use in a normal replacement variable such as $1 or $3. The second and third arguments specify a substring you wish to find and replace, respectively. All instances of the match string found in the substring are replaced, not just the first one. For example, the VanDyke VShell sshd gives its version number in a format such as 2_2_3_578. We use the versioninfo field v/$SUBST(1,"_",".")/ to convert it to the more conventional form 2.2.3.578.

7.6.4. softmatch Directive

Syntax: softmatch <service> <pattern>

Examples:

```
softmatch ftp m/^220 [-.\w ]+ftp.*\r\n$/i
softmatch smtp m|^220 [-.\w ]+SMTP.*\r\n|
softmatch pop3 m|^\+OK [-\[\]\(\)!,/+:<>@.\w ]+\r\n$|
```

The softmatch directive is similar in format to the match directive discussed above. The main difference is that scanning continues after a softmatch, but it is limited to probes that are known to match the given service. This allows for a normal ("hard") match to be found later, which may provide useful version information. See Section 7.3, "Technique Described" [149] for more details on how this works. Arguments are not defined here because they are the same as for match above, except that there is never a <versioninfo> argument. Also as with match, many softmatch statements can exist within a single Probe section.

7.6.5. `ports` and `sslports` Directives

Syntax: `ports <portlist>`

Examples:

```
ports 21,43,110,113,199,505,540,1248,5432,30444
ports 111,4045,32750-32810,38978
```

This line tells Nmap what ports the services identified by this probe are commonly found on. It should only be used once within each `Probe` section. The syntax is a slightly simplified version of that taken by the Nmap -p option. See the examples above. More details on how this works are in Section 7.3, "Technique Described" [149].

Syntax: `sslports <portlist>`

Example:

```
sslports 443
```

This is the same as 'ports' directive described above, except that these ports are often used to wrap a service in SSL. For example, the HTTP probe declares "sslports 443" and SMTP-detecting probes have an "sslports 465" line because those are the standard ports for HTTPS and SMTPS respectively. The `<portlist>` format is the same as with `ports`. This optional directive cannot appear more than once per `Probe`.

7.6.6. `totalwaitms` Directive

Syntax: `totalwaitms <milliseconds>`

Example:

```
totalwaitms 5000
```

This rarely necessary directive specifies the amount of time Nmap should wait before giving up on the most recently defined `Probe` against a particular service. The Nmap default is usually fine.

7.6.7. `rarity` Directive

Syntax: `rarity <value between 1 and 9>`

Example:

```
rarity 6
```

The rarity directive roughly corresponds to how frequently this probe can be expected to return useful results. The higher the number, the more rare the probe is considered and the less likely it is to be tried against a service. More details can be found in Section 7.3.2, "Probe Selection and Rarity" [152].

7.6.8. `fallback` Directive

Syntax: `fallback` `<Comma separated list of probes>`

Example:

```
fallback GetRequest,GenericLines
```

This optional directive specifies which probes should be used as fallbacks for if there are no matches in the current Probe section. For more information on fallbacks see Section 7.3.1, "Cheats and Fallbacks" [151]. For TCP probes without a fallback directive, Nmap first tries match lines in the probe itself and then does an implicit fallback to the NULL probe. If the fallback directive is present, Nmap first tries match lines from the probe itself, then those from the probes specified in the fallback directive (from left to right). Finally, Nmap will try the NULL probe. For UDP the behavior is identical except that the NULL probe is never tried.

7.6.9. Putting It All Together

Here are some examples from `nmap-service-probes` which put this all together (to save space many lines have been skipped). After reading this far into the section, the following should be understood.

```
# The Exclude directive takes a comma separated list of ports.
# The format is exactly the same as the -p switch.
Exclude T:9100-9107

# This is the NULL probe that just compares any banners given to us
##############################NEXT PROBE##############################
Probe TCP NULL q||
# Wait for at least 5 seconds for data.  Otherwise an Nmap default is used.
totalwaitms 5000
# Windows 2003
match ftp m/^220[ -]Microsoft FTP Service\r\n/ p/Microsoft ftpd/
match ftp m/^220 ProFTPD (\d\S+) Server/ p/ProFTPD/ v/$1/
softmatch ftp m/^220 [-.\w ]+ftp.*\r\n$/i
match ident m|^flock\(\) on closed filehandle .*midentd| p/midentd/ i/broken/
match imap m|^\* OK Welcome to Binc IMAP v(\d[-.\w]+)| p/Binc IMAPd/ v$1/
softmatch imap m/^\* OK [-.\w ]+imap[-.\w ]+\r\n$/i
match lucent-fwadm m|^0001;2$| p/Lucent Secure Management Server/
match meetingmaker m/^\xc1,$/ p/Meeting Maker calendaring/
# lopster 1.2.0.1 on Linux 1.1
match napster m|^1$| p/Lopster Napster P2P client/

Probe UDP Help q|help\r\n\r\n|
rarity 3
ports 7,13,37
```

```
match chargen m|@ABCDEFGHIJKLMNOPQRSTUVWXYZ|
match echo m|^help\r\n\r\n$|
```

7.7. Community Contributions

No matter how technically advanced a service detection framework is, it would be nearly useless without a comprehensive database of services against which to match. This is where the open source nature of Nmap really shines. The Insecure.Org lab is pretty substantial by geek standards, but it can never hope to run more than a tiny percentage of machine types and services that are out there. Fortunately experience with OS detection fingerprints has shown that Nmap users together run all of the common stuff, plus a staggering array of bizarre equipment as well. The Nmap OS fingerprint database contains more than a thousand entries, including all sorts of switches, WAPs, VoIP phones, game consoles, Unix boxes, Windows hosts, printers, routers, PDAs, firewalls, etc. Version detection also supports user submissions. Nmap users have contributed thousands of services. There are three primary ways that the Nmap community helps to make this an exceptional database: submitting service fingerprints, database corrections, and new probes.

7.7.1. Submit Service Fingerprints

If a service responds to one or more of Nmap's probes and yet Nmap is unable to identify that service, Nmap prints a *service fingerprint* like this one:

```
SF-Port21-TCP:V=3.40PVT16%D=9/6%Time=3F5A961C%r(NULL,3F,"220\x20stage\x20F
SF:TP\x20server\x20\(Version\x202\.1WU\(1\)\+SCO-2\.6\.1\+-sec\)\x20ready\
SF:.\r\n")%r(GenericLines,81,"220\x20stage\x20FTP\x20server\x20\(Version\x
SF:202\.1WU\(1\)\+SCO-2\.6\.1\+-sec\)\x20ready\.\r\n500\x20''\:\x20command\
SF:x20not\x20understood\.\r\n500\x20''\:\x20command\x20not\x20understood\.\
SF:r\n");
```

If you receive such a fingerprint, and are sure you know what daemon version is running on the target host, please submit the fingerprint at the URL Nmap gives you. The whole submission process is anonymous (unless you choose to provide identifying info) and should not take more than a couple minutes. If you are feeling particularly helpful, scan the system again using -d (Nmap sometimes gives longer fingerprints that way) and paste both fingerprints into the fingerprint box on the submission form. Sometimes people read the file format section and submit their own working match lines. This is OK, but please submit the service fingerprint(s) as well because existing scripts make integrating and testing them relatively easy.

For those who care, the information in the fingerprint above is port number (21), protocol (TCP), Nmap version (3.40PVT16), date (September 6), Unix time in hex, and a sequence of probe responses in the form r({<probename>}, {<responselength>}, "{<responsestring>}").

7.7.2. Submit Database Corrections

This is another easy way to help improve the database. When integrating a service fingerprint submitted for "chargen on Windows XP" or "FooBar FTP server 3.9.213", it is difficult to determine how general the match is. Will it also match chargen on Solaris or FooBar FTP 2.7? Since there is no good way to tell, a very specific name is used in the hope that people will report when the match needs to be generalized. The only reason the Nmap DB is so comprehensive is that thousands of users have spent a few minutes each to submit new information. If you scan a host and the service fingerprint gives an incorrect OS, version number, application name, or even service type, please let us know as described below:

Upgrade to the latest Nmap (Optional)
> Many Linux distributions and other operating systems ship with ancient versions of Nmap. The Nmap version detection database is improved with almost every release, so check your version number by running **nmap -V** and then compare that to the latest available from *http://nmap.org/download.html*. The problem you are seeing may have already been corrected. Installing the newest version takes only a few minutes on most platforms, and is valuable regardless of whether the version detection flaw you are reporting still exists. But even if you don't have time to upgrade right now, submissions from older releases are still valuable.

Be absolutely certain you know what is running
> Invalid "corrections" can corrupt the version detection DB. If you aren't certain exactly what is running on the remote machine, please find out before submitting.

Generate a fingerprint
> Run the command **nmap -O -PN -sSV -T4 -d --version-trace -p<port> <target>**, where *<port>* is the port running the misidentified service on the *<target>* host. If the service is UDP rather than TCP, substitute −sUV for −sSV.

Send us your correction
> Now simply submit your correction to us at *http://insecure.org/cgi-bin/submit.cgi?corr-service*. Thanks for contributing to the Nmap community and helping to make version detection even better!

7.7.3. Submit New Probes

Suppose Nmap fails to detect a service. If it received a response to any probes at all, it should provide a fingerprint that can be submitted as described above. But what if there is no response and thus a fingerprint is not available? Create and submit your own probe! These are very welcome. The following steps describe the process.

Steps for creating a new version detection probe

1. Download the latest version of Nmap from *http://nmap.org* and try again. You would feel a bit silly spending time developing a new probe just to find out that it has already been added. Make sure no fingerprint is available, as it is better to recognize services using existing probes if possible than to create too many new ones. If the service does not respond to any of the existing probes, there is no other choice.

2. Decide on a good probe string for recognizing the service. An ideal probe should elicit a response from as many instances of the service as possible, and ideally the responses should be unique enough to differentiate between them. This step is easiest if you understand the protocol very well, so consider reading the relevant RFCs and product documentation. One simple approach is to simply start a client for the given service and watch what initial handshaking is done by sniffing the network with Wireshark or tcpdump, or connecting to a listening Netcat.

3. Once you have decided on the proper string, add the appropriate new Probe line to Nmap (see Section 7.3, "Technique Described" [149] and Section 7.6, "nmap-service-probes File Format" [158]). Do not put in any match lines at first, although a `ports` directive to make this new test go first against the registered

---

ports is OK. Then scan the service with Nmap a few times. You should get a fingerprint back showing the service's response to your new probe. Send the new probe line and the fingerprints (against different machines if possible, but even a few against the same daemon helps to note differences) to Fyodor at <fyodor@insecure.org>. It will likely then be integrated into future versions of Nmap. Any details you can provide on the nature of your probe string is helpful as well. For custom services that only appear on your network, it is better to simply add them to your own nmap-service-probes rather than the global Nmap.

7.8. SOLUTION: Find All Servers Running an Insecure or Nonstandard Application Version

7.8.1. Problem

A common task is scanning a range of IP addresses to find all servers of a particular version or even satisfying a particular property. This is something that Nmap's version detection excels in.

One of the most popular database application is the open-source MySQL server. MySQL can be configured to disallow all remote logins from untrusted IPs. This is a good security practice when remote logins aren't required. A case in point: in 2005 a MySQL remote code execution vulnerability was discovered and published[4]. Fortunately, an attacker must be able to log in first—no doubt saving the Internet from yet another devastating worm. In light of problems like this and the fact that SQL logins and passwords are frequently guessable or discoverable through SQL injection attacks, intuition, and inside knowledge of the network, remote logins should be denied when possible.

The problem for a network administrator is to discover MySQL servers that needlessly allow logins from untrusted IPs and take appropriate defensive measures.

Note
This solution was contributed by Nmap developer Doug Hoyte.

7.8.2. Solution

Nmap's version detection comes in handy in this situation because it adds the word unauthorized to the service detection info line when the server forbids our host any access. If we want to scan the network of 10.0.0.0/24 a simple yet effective strategy is to run the following command from an untrusted source:

nmap -sV -p 3306 -oG 10.0.0-mysqls-032506.gnmap 10.0.0.0/24

Next we can use the Unix **grep** utility to find IPs that accept connections from our IP and don't disallow logins by default (**grep**'s −v switch specifies inverse results and only prints out lines that *don't* match the given pattern):

grep 'Ports: 3306/open/tcp//mysql' 10.0.0-mysqls-032506.gnmap | grep -v unauthorized

---

[4] *http://www.securityfocus.com/bid/12781*

The resulting output shows the MySQL servers that allow remote logins:

```
Host: 10.0.0.33 (foo.com) Ports: 3306/open/tcp//mysql//MySQL 4.1.11/
Host: 10.0.0.72 (bar.com) Ports: 3306/open/tcp//mysql//MySQL 4.0.24-standard/
Host: 10.0.0.99 () Ports: 3306/open/tcp//mysql//MySQL 4.1.11-Debian_4sarge2/
Host: 10.0.0.154 () Ports: 3306/open/tcp//mysql//MySQL 4.0.25-standard/
Host: 10.0.0.155 () Ports: 3306/open/tcp//mysql//MySQL 4.0.25-standard/
```

7.8.3. Discussion

The trick to this is understanding some MySQL protocol basics and knowing how to read the `nmap-service-probes` file. Grepping the file for `Probe` and `mysql` match lines leads to the following (line wrapped) output:

```
$ cat /usr/local/share/nmap/nmap-service-probes | egrep '^(Probe|match mysql)'
Probe TCP NULL q||
match mysql m/^.\0\0\0\xffj\x04.*Host .* is not allowed to connect to this
          MySQL server$/ p/MySQL/ i/unauthorized/
match mysql m|^.\0\0\0\xffj\x04Host hat keine Berechtigung, eine Verbindung
          zu diesem MySQL Server herzustellen\.| p/MySQL/
          i/unauthorized; German/
match mysql m/^.\0\0\0...Al sistema '[-.\w]+' non e` consentita la
          connessione a questo server MySQL$/ p/MySQL/
          i/unauthorized; Italian/
match mysql m|^.\0\0\0\xffi?\x04?Host .* is blocked because of many connection
          errors\.| p/MySQL/ i/blocked - too many connection errors/
match mysql m/^.\0\0\0.(3\.[-.\w]+)\0.*\x08\x02\0\0\0\0\0\0\0\0\0\0\0\0\0\0$/s
          p/MySQL/ v/$1/
match mysql m/^.\0\0\0\n(3\.[-.\w]+)\0...\0/s p/MySQL/ v/$1/
match mysql m/^.\0\0\0\n(4\.[-.\w]+)\0.../s p/MySQL/ v/$1/
match mysql m|^.\0\0\0\n(5\.[-.\w]+)\0...\0|s p/MySQL/ v/$1/
match mysql m|^.\0\0\0\xffj\x04'[\d.]+' .* MySQL|s p/MySQL/
Probe TCP GenericLines q|\r\n\r\n|
Probe TCP GetRequest q|GET / HTTP/1.0\r\n\r\n|
Probe TCP HTTPOptions q|OPTIONS / HTTP/1.0\r\n\r\n|
...
```

We see that the `mysql` match lines are designed to be triggered by the NULL probe so no custom probes are needed to determine which servers allow remote logins (for that see Section 7.9, "SOLUTION: Hack Version Detection to Suit Custom Needs, such as Open Proxy Detection" [168]). By looking at these `mysql` match lines that we discover MySQL services that don't allow remote logins will result in an info field containing the word `unauthorized`.

In addition to service types and version numbers, there are many cases where version detection is able to gather useful information on scan targets. The probes file is full of such gems that can turn a time-consuming task of protocol research, script coding, locating test servers, and debugging into a simple Nmap command. A few interesting tidbits of information that version detection can sometimes reveal are:

- SSH protocol versions

- Whether a CVS pserver is properly configured

- The usernames used by popular peer-to-peer file sharing clients

- Whether an X server is accepting connections

- Language and other localization parameters of many services

- The wordsize of the target's CPU

- The configured botnames of popular IRC bots such as eggdrop

- Whether posting is allowed on Internet news (NNTP) servers

The version detection database is constantly growing and being refined thanks to the amazing Nmap user community and their service fingerprint submissions. This solution is a good example of how investigating the capabilities of Nmap's service detection can provide elegant, sometimes non-obvious solutions to many diverse problems.

7.9. SOLUTION: Hack Version Detection to Suit Custom Needs, such as Open Proxy Detection

7.9.1. Problem

An important part of securing any network is identifying dangerous hosts. Nmap's service detection system is a flexible, reliable way to do this. It can help identify vulnerable versions of software, find misconfigured servers, and more. But sometimes actually trying to misuse services in ways the stock version scan doesn't dare to is the best way to determine if they are actually vulnerable.

Open proxies are servers that will blindly relay requests from untrusted hosts to servers of their choosing. Running these inside a network can be extremely dangerous for many reasons, as attackers can:

- Launch attacks that appear to come from your network

- Steal bandwidth or other network services from you

- Pretend to be an internal client to further escalate their privileges inside your organization

This provides good motivation for hacking version detection to specifically try to exploit open proxies. We could probably map out which ports are proxies by using Nmap's normal proxy match lines, but the best, and only real way to prove an application is vulnerable is to actually exploit it yourself.

 Note

This solution was contributed by Nmap developer Doug Hoyte.

7.9.2. Solution

The first thing we do is copy the `nmap-service-probes` file so we can work on a temporary copy:

```
mkdir ~/proxydetect
cp /usr/local/share/nmap/nmap-service-probes ~/proxydetect
```

Next we want to temporarily force Nmap to use our temporary file:

```
export NMAPDIR=$HOME/proxydetect
```

Now we need to add a probe and match line to the file, so open up your favorite editor and place the following text into your copy of `nmap-service-probes`. A good place to put it is after all the match lines in the NULL probe, but immediately before the next Probe line (GenericLines).

```
Probe TCP ProxyProbe q|GET http://insecure.org/ HTTP/1.1\r\nHost: insecure ↵
.org\r\n\r\n|
rarity 1
ports 1-65535
totalwaitms 20000
match proxy m|^HTTP/1.[01] 200 OK\r?\n.*TITLE>Insecure.O|s p/Open HTTP Proxy!!/
```

Now Nmap will actually try to request an HTTP download from `insecure.org` by treating any scanned ports as proxies. We will start to see the following in scans of networks containing open proxies:

```
PORT    STATE SERVICE VERSION
80/tcp open  proxy   Open HTTP Proxy!!
```

7.9.3. Discussion

The placement of our probe, the low `rarity` value, and extensive `ports` range help ensure that our custom probe is tried very soon into the service scan so that other probes like GetRequest don't simply identify this as a proxy before we've had a chance to use our active probe.

We also used a `totalwaitms` directive to make Nmap wait longer for this probe to time out. This can be necessary because not only are we dealing with the latency and unreliability of the connection between us and the proxy, but also the latency and unreliability of the connection between the proxy and the server containing the page we requested (`insecure.org`).

Keep in mind that many other protocols can be proxied in addition to HTTP. Version detection will identify proxies for many of them including FTP, POP3, IMAP, and SMTP. SOCKS proxies have special match lines that determine information on the authentication options the proxy has configured. As we did in this solution, often we can use version detection to tell whether such proxies are open or not by using custom probes files. However, more complicated tests are probably best done with NSE scripts.

Chapter 8. Remote OS Detection

8.1. Introduction

When exploring a network for security auditing or inventory/administration, you usually want to know more than the bare IP addresses of identified machines. Your reaction to discovering a printer may be very different than to finding a router, wireless access point, telephone PBX, game console, Windows desktop, or Unix server. Finer grained detection (such as distinguishing Mac OS X 10.4 from 10.3) is useful for determining vulnerability to specific flaws and for tailoring effective exploits for those vulnerabilities.

In part due to its value to attackers, many systems are tight-lipped about their exact nature and operating system configuration. Fortunately, Nmap includes a huge database of heuristics for identifying thousands of different systems based on how they respond to a selection of TCP/IP probes. Another system (part of version detection) interrogates open TCP or UDP ports to determine device type and OS details. Results of these two systems are reported independently so that you can identify combinations such as a Checkpoint firewall forwarding port 80 to a Windows IIS server.

While Nmap has supported OS detection since 1998, this chapter describes the 2nd generation system released in 2006.

8.1.1. Reasons for OS Detection

While some benefits of discovering the underlying OS and device types on a network are obvious, others are more obscure. This section lists the top reasons I hear for discovering this extra information.

Determining vulnerability of target hosts

It is sometimes very difficult to determine remotely whether an available service is susceptible or patched for a certain vulnerability. Even obtaining the application version number doesn't always help, since OS distributors often back-port security fixes without changing the version number. The surest way to verify that a vulnerability is real is to exploit it, but that risks crashing the service and can lead to wasted hours or even days of frustrating exploitation efforts if the service turns out to be patched.

OS detection can help reduce these false positives. For example, the Rwho daemon on unpatched Sun Solaris 7 through 9 may be remotely exploitable (Sun alert #57659). Remotely determining vulnerability is difficult, but you can rule it out by finding that a target system is running Solaris 10.

Taking this from the perspective of a systems administrator rather than a pen-tester, imagine you run a large Sun shop when alert #57659 comes out. Scan your whole network with OS detection to find machines which need patching before the bad guys do.

Tailoring exploits

Even after you discover a vulnerability in a target system, OS detection can be helpful in exploiting it. Buffer overflows, format-string exploits, and many other vulnerabilities often require custom-tailored shellcode with offsets and assembly payloads generated to match the target OS and hardware architecture. In some

---

cases, you only get one try because the service crashes if you get the shellcode wrong. Use OS detection first or you may end up sending Linux shellcode to a FreeBSD server.

Network inventory and support

While it isn't as exciting as busting root through a specially crafted format string exploit, there are many administrative reasons to keep track of what is running on your network. Before you renew that IRIX support contract for another year, scan to see if anyone still uses such machines. An inventory can also be useful for IT budgeting and ensuring that all company equipment is accounted for.

Detecting unauthorized and dangerous devices

With the ubiquity of mobile devices and cheap commodity networking equipment, companies are increasingly finding that employees are extending their networks in undesirable ways. They may install a $20 wireless access point (WAP) in their cubicle without realizing (or caring) that they just opened up the protected corporate network to potential attackers in the parking lot or nearby buildings. WAPs can be so dangerous that Nmap has a special category for detecting them, as demonstrated in Section 8.8, "SOLUTION: Detect Rogue Wireless Access Points on an Enterprise Network" [202]. Users may also cause sysadmins grief by connecting insecure and/or worm-infected laptops to the corporate network. Regular scanning can detect unauthorized devices for investigation and containment.

Social engineering

Another possible use is social engineering. Lets say that you are scanning a target company and Nmap reports a "Datavoice TxPORT PRISM 3000 T1 CSU/DSU 6.22/2.06". You could call up the target pretending to be Datavoice support and discuss some issues with their PRISM 3000. Tell them you are about to announce a big security hole, but are first providing the patch to valued customers. Some naive administrators might assume that only an authorized engineer from Datavoice would know so much about their CSU/DSU. Of course the patch you send them is a Trojan horse that gives you remote access to sniff and traipse through their network. Be sure to read the rest of this chapter for detection accuracy and verification advice before trying this. If you guess the target system wrong and they call the police, that will be an embarrassing story to tell your cellmates.

8.2. Usage and Examples

The inner workings of OS detection are quite complex, but it is one of the easiest features to use. Simply add -O to your scan options. You may want to also increase the verbosity with -v for even more OS-related details. This is shown in Example 8.1.

Example 8.1. OS detection with verbosity (−O −v)

```
# nmap -O -v scanme.nmap.org

Starting Nmap ( http://nmap.org )
Interesting ports on scanme.nmap.org (64.13.134.52):
Not shown: 994 filtered ports
PORT      STATE   SERVICE
22/tcp    open    ssh
25/tcp    closed  smtp
53/tcp    open    domain
70/tcp    closed  gopher
80/tcp    open    http
113/tcp   closed  auth
Device type: general purpose
Running: Linux 2.6.X
OS details: Linux 2.6.20-1 (Fedora Core 5)
Uptime guess: 11.433 days (since Thu Sep 18 13:13:01 2008)
TCP Sequence Prediction: Difficulty=204 (Good luck!)
IP ID Sequence Generation: All zeros

Nmap done: 1 IP address (1 host up) scanned in 6.21 seconds
          Raw packets sent: 2021 (90.526KB) | Rcvd: 23 (1326B)
```

Including the −O −v options caused Nmap to generate the following six extra line items:

Device type
:   All fingerprints are classified with one or more high-level device types, such as router, printer, firewall, or (as in this case) general purpose. These are further described in the section called "Device and OS classification (Class lines)" [196]. Several device types may be shown, in which case they will be separated with the pipe symbol as in "Device Type: router|firewall".

Running
:   This field is also related to the OS classification scheme described in the section called "Device and OS classification (Class lines)" [196]. It shows the OS Family (Linux in this case) and OS generation (2.6.X) if available. If there are multiple OS families, they are separated by commas. When Nmap can't narrow down OS generations to one specific choice, options are separated by the pipe symbol ('|') Examples include OpenBSD 3.X, NetBSD 3.X|4.X and Linux 2.4.X|2.5.X|2.6.X.

    If Nmap finds too many OS families to print concisely, it will omit this line. When there are no perfect matches, Nmap changes the field to Running (JUST GUESSING) and adds an accuracy percentage (100% is a perfect match) in parentheses after each candidate family name. If no fingerprints are close matches, the line is omitted.

OS details
:   This line gives the detailed description for each fingerprint that matches. While the Device type and Running lines are from predefined enumerated lists that are easy to parse by a computer, the OS details line contains free-form data which is useful to a human reading the report. This can include more exact version numbers, device models, and architectures specific to a given fingerprint. In this example, the only matching fingerprint was Linux 2.6.20-1 (Fedora Core 5). When there are multiple exact matches, they are comma-separated. If there aren't any perfect matches, but some close guesses,

---

the field is renamed `Aggressive OS guesses` and fingerprints are shown followed by a percentage in parentheses which specifies how close each match was.

Uptime guess

As part of OS detection, Nmap receives several SYN/ACK TCP packets in a row and checks the headers for a timestamp option. Many operating systems use a simple counter for this which starts at zero at boot time then increments at a constant rate such as twice per second. By looking at several responses, Nmap can determine the current values and rate of increase. Simple linear extrapolation determines boot time. The timestamp algorithm is used for OS detection too (see the section called "TCP timestamp option algorithm (TS)" [182]) since the increment rate on different systems varies from 2 Hz to 1,000 Hz.

The uptime guess is labeled a "guess" because various factors can make it completely inaccurate. Some operating systems do not start the timestamp counter at zero, but initialize it with a random value, making extrapolation to zero meaningless. Even on systems using a simple counter starting at zero, the counter eventually overflows and wraps around. With a 1,000 Hz counter increment rate, the counter resets to zero roughly every 50 days. So a host that has been up for 102 days will appear to have been up only two days. Even with these caveats, the uptime guess is accurate much of the time for most operating systems, so it is printed when available, but only in verbose mode. The uptime guess is omitted if the target gives zeros or no timestamp options in its SYN/ACK packets, or if it does not reply at all. The line is also omitted if Nmap cannot discern the timestamp increment rate or it seems suspicious (like a 30-year uptime).

Network Distance

A side effect of one of the OS detection tests allows Nmap to compute how many routers are between it and a target host. The distance is zero when you are scanning localhost, and one for a machine on the same network segment. Each additional router on the path adds one to the hop count. The `Network Distance` line is not printed in this example, since Nmap omits the line when it cannot be computed (no reply to the relevant probe).

TCP Sequence Prediction

Systems with poor TCP initial sequence number generation are vulnerable to blind TCP spoofing attacks. In other words, you can make a full connection to those systems and send (but not receive) data while spoofing a different IP address. The target's logs will show the spoofed IP, and you can take advantage of any trust relationship between them. This attack was all the rage in the mid-nineties when people commonly used rlogin to allow logins to their account without any password from trusted IP addresses. Kevin Mitnick is alleged to have used this attack to break into Tsutomu Shimomura's computers in December 1994.

The good news is that hardly anyone uses rlogin anymore, and many operating systems have been fixed to use unpredictable initial sequence numbers as proposed by RFC 1948. For these reasons, this line is only printed in verbose mode. Sadly, many vendors still ship vulnerable operating systems and devices[1]. Even the fixed ones often vary in implementation, which leaves them valuable for OS detection purposes. The class describes the ISN generation algorithm used by the target, and difficulty is a rough estimate of how hard the system makes blind IP spoofing (0 is the easiest). The parenthesized comment is based on the difficulty index and ranges from `Trivial joke` to `Easy`, `Medium`, `Formidable`, `Worthy challenge`, and finally `Good luck`! Further details about sequence tests are provided in the section called "TCP ISN greatest common divisor (GCD)" [180].

---

[1]A fascinating visual look at this is available from *http://lcamtuf.coredump.cx/newtcp/*

While the rlogin family is mostly a relic of the past, clever attackers can still find effective uses for blind TCP spoofing. For example, it allows for spoofed HTTP requests. You don't see the results, but just the URL (POST or GET request) can have dramatic side effects. The spoofing allows attackers to hide their identity, frame someone else, or exploit IP address restrictions.

IP ID sequence generation

Many systems unwittingly give away sensitive information about their traffic levels based on how they generate the lowly 16-bit ID field in IP packets. This can be abused to spoof a port scan against other systems and for other mischievous purposes discussed in Section 5.10, "TCP Idle Scan (-sI)" [117]. This field describes the ID generation algorithm that Nmap was able to discern. More information on how it classifies them is available in the section called "TCP IP ID sequence generation algorithm (TI)" [181]. Note that many systems use a different IP ID space for each host they communicate with. In that case, they may appear vulnerable (such as showing the Incremental class) while still being secure against attacks such as the idle scan. For this reason, and because the issue is rarely critical, the IP ID sequence generation line is only printed in verbose mode. If Nmap does not receive sufficient responses during OS detection, it will omit the whole line. The best way to test whether a host is vulnerable to being an idle scan zombie is to test it with -sI.

While TCP fingerprinting is a powerful method for OS detection, interrogating open ports for clues is another effective approach. Some applications, such as Microsoft IIS, only run on a single platform (thus giving it away), while many other apps divulge their platform in overly verbose banner messages. Adding the -sV option enables Nmap version detection, which is trained to look for these clues (among others). In Example 8.2, Nmap catches the platform details from an FTP server.

Example 8.2. Using version scan to detect the OS

```
# nmap -sV -O -v 129.128.X.XX
Starting Nmap ( http://nmap.org )
Interesting ports on [hostname] (129.128.X.XX):
Not shown: 994 closed ports
PORT         STATE     SERVICE        VERSION
21/tcp       open      ftp            HP-UX 10.x ftpd 4.1
22/tcp       open      ssh            OpenSSH 3.7.1p1 (protocol 1.99)
111/tcp      open      rpc
445/tcp      filtered  microsoft-ds
1526/tcp     open      oracle-tns     Oracle TNS Listener
32775/tcp open         rpc
No exact OS matches for host
TCP Sequence Prediction: Class=truly random
                         Difficulty=9999999 (Good luck!)
IP ID Sequence Generation: Incremental
Service Info: OS: HP-UX
```

In this example, the line "No exact OS matches for host" means that TCP/IP fingerprinting failed to find an exact match. Fortunately, the Service Info field a few lines down discloses that the OS is HP-UX. If several operating systems were detected (which can happen with NAT gateway boxes that redirect ports to several different machines), the field would be OSs and the values would be comma separated. The Service Info line can also contain hostnames and device types found during the version scan. The focus of this chapter is on TCP/IP fingerprinting though, since version detection was covered in Chapter 7, *Service and Application Version Detection* [145].

With two effective OS detection methods available, which one should you use? The best answer is usually both. In some cases, such as a proxy firewall forwarding to an application on another host, the answers may legitimately differ. TCP/IP fingerprinting will identify the proxy while version scanning will generally detect the server running the proxied application. Even when no proxying or port forwarding is involved, using both techniques is beneficial. If they come out the same, that makes the results more credible. If they come out wildly different, investigate further to determine what is going on before relying on either. Since OS and version detection go together so well, the -A option enables them both.

OS detection is far more effective if at least one open and one closed TCP port are found. Set the --osscan-limit option and Nmap will not even try OS detection against hosts which do not meet this criteria. This can save substantial time, particularly on -PN scans against many hosts. You still need to enable OS detection with -O (or -A) for this to have any effect.

Another OS detection option is --osscan-guess. When Nmap is unable to detect a perfect OS match, it sometimes offers up near-matches as possibilities. The match has to be very close for Nmap to do this by default. If you specify this option (or the equivalent --fuzzy option), Nmap will guess more aggressively. Nmap still tells you when an imperfect match is printed and display its confidence level (percentage) for each guess.

When Nmap performs OS detection against a target and fails to find a perfect match, it usually repeats the attempt. By default, Nmap tries five times if conditions are favorable for OS fingerprint submission, and twice when conditions aren't so good. The --max-os-tries option lets you change this maximum number of OS detection tries. Lowering it (usually to 1) speeds Nmap up, though you miss out on retries which could potentially identify the OS. Alternatively, a high value may be set to allow even more retries when conditions are favorable. This is rarely done, except to generate better fingerprints for submission and integration into the Nmap OS database.

Like just about every other part of Nmap, results ultimately come from the target machine itself. While rare, systems are occasionally configured to confuse or mislead Nmap. Several programs have even been developed specifically to trick Nmap OS detection (see Section 11.5.4, "OS Spoofing" [302]). Your best bet is to use numerous reconnaissance methods to explore a network, and don't trust any one of them.

TCP/IP fingerprinting requires collecting detailed information about the target's IP stack. The most commonly useful results, such as TTL information, are printed to Nmap output whenever they are obtained. Slightly less pertinent information, such as IP ID sequence generation and TCP sequence prediction difficulty, is only printed in verbose mode. But if you want all of the IP stack details that Nmap collected, you can find it in a compact form called a *subject fingerprint*. Nmap sometimes prints this (for user submission purposes) when it doesn't recognize a host. You can also force Nmap to print it (in normal, interactive, and XML formats) by enabling debugging with (-d). Then read Section 8.5, "Understanding an Nmap Fingerprint" [191] to interpret it.

8.3. TCP/IP Fingerprinting Methods Supported by Nmap

Nmap OS fingerprinting works by sending up to 15 TCP, UDP, and ICMP probes to known open and closed ports of the target machine. These probes are specially designed to exploit various ambiguities in the standard protocol RFCs. Then Nmap listens for responses. Dozens of attributes in those responses are analyzed and combined to generate a fingerprint. Every probe packet is tracked and resent at least once if there is no response. All of the packets are IPv4 with a random IP ID value. Probes to an open TCP port are skipped if no such port has been found. For closed TCP or UDP ports, Nmap will first check if such a port has been found. If not, Nmap will just pick a port at random and hope for the best.

The following sections are highly technical and reveal the hidden workings of Nmap OS detection. Nmap can be used effectively without understanding this, though the material can help you better understand remote networks and also detect and explain certain anomalies. Plus, some of the techniques are pretty cool. Readers in a hurry may skip to Section 8.7, "Dealing with Misidentified and Unidentified Hosts" [199]. But for those of you who are ready for a journey through TCP explicit congestion notification, reserved UDP header bits, initial sequence numbers, bogus flags, and Christmas tree packets: read on!

Even the best of us occasionally forget byte offsets for packet header fields and flags. For quick reference, the IPv4, TCP, UDP, and ICMP header layouts can be found in Section 7, "TCP/IP Reference" [xxvi]. The layout for ICMP echo request and destination unreachable packets are shown in Figure 8.1 and Figure 8.2.

Figure 8.1. ICMP echo request or reply header layout

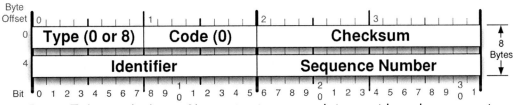

Data: Echo reply (type 0) must return any data sent in echo request

Figure 8.2. ICMP destination unreachable header layout

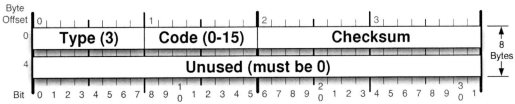

Data: Original (received) IP header, plus at least the first 8 data bytes

8.3.1. Probes Sent

This section describes each IP probe sent by Nmap as part of TCP/IP fingerprinting. It refers to Nmap response tests and TCP options which are explained in the following section.

Sequence generation (SEQ, OPS, WIN, and T1)

A series of six TCP probes is sent to generate these four test response lines. The probes are sent exactly 110 milliseconds apart so the total time taken is 550 ms. Exact timing is important as some of the sequence algorithms we detect (initial sequence numbers, IP IDs, and TCP timestamps) are time dependent. This

---

timing value was chosen to take above 500 ms so that we can reliably detect the common 2 Hz TCP timestamp sequences.

Each probe is a TCP SYN packet to a detected open port on the remote machine. The sequence and acknowledgment numbers are random (but saved so Nmap can differentiate responses). Detection accuracy requires probe consistency, so there is no data payload even if the user requested one with `--data-length`.

These packets vary in the TCP options they use and the TCP window field value. The following list provides the options and values for all six packets. The listed window field values do not reflect window scaling. EOL is the end-of-options-list option, which many sniffing tools don't show by default.

- **Packet #1:** window scale (10), NOP, MSS (1460), timestamp (TSval: 0xFFFFFFFF; TSecr: 0), SACK permitted. The window field is 1.

- **Packet #2:** MSS (1400), window scale (0), SACK permitted, timestamp (TSval: 0xFFFFFFFF; TSecr: 0), EOL. The window field is 63.

- **Packet #3:** Timestamp (TSval: 0xFFFFFFFF; TSecr: 0), NOP, NOP, window scale (5), NOP, MSS (640). The window field is 4.

- **Packet #4:** SACK permitted, Timestamp (TSval: 0xFFFFFFFF; TSecr: 0), window scale (10), EOL. The window field is 4.

- **Packet #5:** MSS (536), SACK permitted, Timestamp (TSval: 0xFFFFFFFF; TSecr: 0), window scale (10), EOL. The window field is 16.

- **Packet #6:** MSS (265), SACK permitted, Timestamp (TSval: 0xFFFFFFFF; TSecr: 0). The window field is 512.

The results of these tests include four result category lines. The first, SEQ, contains results based on sequence analysis of the probe packets. These test results are GCD, SP, ISR, TI, II, TS, and SS. The next line, OPS contains the TCP options received for each of the probes (the test names are O1 through O6). Similarly, the WIN line contains window sizes for the probe responses (named W1 through W6). The final line related to these probes, T1, contains various test values for packet #1. Those results are for the R, DF, T, TG, W, S, A, F, O, RD, and Q tests. These tests are only reported for the first probe since they are almost always the same for each probe.

ICMP echo (IE)

The IE test involves sending two ICMP echo request packets to the target. The first one has the IP DF bit set, a type-of-service (TOS) byte value of zero, a code of nine (even though it should be zero), the sequence number 295, a random IP ID and ICMP request identifier, and a random character repeated 120 times for the data payload.

The second ping query is similar, except a TOS of four (IP_TOS_RELIABILITY) is used, the code is zero, 150 bytes of data is sent, and the IP ID, request ID, and sequence numbers are incremented by one from the previous query values.

The results of both of these probes are combined into a IE line containing the R, DFI, T, TG, TOSI, CD, SI, and DLI tests. The R value is only true (Y) if both probes elicit responses. The T, and CD values are for the response to the first probe only, since they are highly unlikely to differ. The DFI, TOSI, SI, and DLI are custom tests for this special dual-probe ICMP case.

These ICMP probes follow immediately after the TCP sequence probes to ensure valid results of the shared IP ID sequence number test (see the section called "Shared IP ID sequence Boolean (SS)" [182]).

TCP explicit congestion notification (ECN)

This probe tests for explicit congestion notification (ECN) support in the target TCP stack. ECN is a method for improving Internet performance by allowing routers to signal congestion problems before they start having to drop packets. It is documented in RFC 3168. Nmap tests this by sending a SYN packet which also has the ECN CWR and ECE congestion control flags set. For an unrelated (to ECN) test, the urgent field value of 0xF7F5 is used even though the urgent flag is not set. The acknowledgment number is zero, sequence number is random, window size field is three, and the reserved bit which immediately precedes the CWR bit is set. TCP options are WScale (10), NOP, MSS (1460), SACK permitted, NOP, NOP. The probe is sent to an open port.

If a response is received, the R, DF, T, TG, W, O, CC, and Q tests are performed and recorded.

TCP (T2–T7)

The six T2 through T7 tests each send one TCP probe packet. With one exception, the TCP options data in each case is (in hex) 03030A0102040109080AFFFFFFFF000000000402. Those 20 bytes correspond to window scale (10), NOP, MSS (265), Timestamp (TSval: 0xFFFFFFFF; TSecr: 0), then SACK permitted. The exception is that T7 uses a Window scale value of 15 rather than 10. The variable characteristics of each probe are described below:

- **T2** sends a TCP null (no flags set) packet with the IP DF bit set and a window field of 128 to an open port.

- **T3** sends a TCP packet with the SYN, FIN, URG, and PSH flags set and a window field of 256 to an open port. The IP DF bit is not set.

- **T4** sends a TCP ACK packet with IP DF and a window field of 1024 to an open port.

- **T5** sends a TCP SYN packet without IP DF and a window field of 31337 to a closed port.

- **T6** sends a TCP ACK packet with IP DF and a window field of 32768 to a closed port.

- **T7** sends a TCP packet with the FIN, PSH, and URG flags set and a window field of 65535 to a closed port. The IP DF bit is not set.

In each of these cases, a line is added to the fingerprint with results for the R, DF, T, TG, W, S, A, F, O, RD, and Q tests.

UDP (U1)

This probe is a UDP packet sent to a closed port. The character 'C' (0x43) is repeated 300 times for the data field. The IP ID value is set to 0x1042 for operating systems which allow us to set this. If the port is truly closed and there is no firewall in place, Nmap expects to receive an ICMP port unreachable message in

---

return. That response is then subjected to the R, DF, T, TG, TOS, IPL, UN, RIPL, RID, RIPCK, RUCK, RUL, and RUD tests.

8.3.2. Response Tests

The previous section describes probes sent by Nmap, and this one completes the puzzle by describing the barrage of tests performed on responses. The short names (such as DF, R, and RIPCK) are those used in the nmap-os-db fingerprint database to save space. All numerical test values are given in hexadecimal notation, without leading zeros, unless noted otherwise. The tests are documented in roughly the order they appear in fingerprints.

TCP ISN greatest common divisor (GCD)

The SEQ test sends six TCP SYN packets to an open port of the target machine and collects SYN/ACK packets back. Each of these SYN/ACK packets contains a 32-bit initial sequence number (ISN). This test attempts to determine the smallest number by which the target host increments these values. For example, many hosts (especially old ones) always increment the ISN in multiples of 64,000.

The first step in calculating this is creating an array of differences between probe responses. The first element is the difference between the 1st and 2nd probe response ISNs. The second element is the difference between the 2nd and 3rd responses. There are five elements if Nmap receives responses to all six probes. Since the next couple of sections reference this array, we will call it diff1. If an ISN is lower than the previous one, Nmap looks at both the number of values it would have to subtract from the first value to obtain the second, and the number of values it would have to count up (including wrapping the 32-bit counter back to zero). The smaller of those two values is stored in diff1. So the difference between 0x20000 followed by 0x15000 is 0xB000. The difference between 0xFFFFFF00 and 0xC000 is 0xC0FF. This test value then records the greatest common divisor of all those elements. This GCD is also used for calculating the SP result.

TCP ISN counter rate (ISR)

This value reports the average rate of increase for the returned TCP initial sequence number. Recall that a difference is taken between each two consecutive probe responses and stored in the previously discussed diff1 array. Those differences are each divided by the amount of time elapsed (in seconds—will generally be about 0.1) between sending the two probes which generated them. The result is an array, which we'll call seq_rates containing the rates of ISN counter increases per second. The array has one element for each diff1 value. An average is taken of the array values. If that average is less than one (e.g. a constant ISN is used), ISR is zero. Otherwise ISR is eight times the binary logarithm (log base-2) of that average value, rounded to the nearest integer.

TCP ISN sequence predictability index (SP)

While the ISR test measures the average rate of initial sequence number increments, this value measures the ISN variability. It roughly estimates how difficult it would be to predict the next ISN from the known sequence of six probe responses. The calculation uses the difference array (seq_rates) and GCD values discussed in the previous section.

This test is only performed if at least four responses were seen. If the previously computed GCD value is greater than nine, The elements of the previously computed seq_rates array are divided by that value.

We don't do the division for smaller GCD values because those are usually caused by chance. A standard deviation of the array of the resultant values is then taken. If the result is one or less, SP is zero. Otherwise the binary logarithm of the result is computed, then it is multiplied by eight, rounded to the nearest integer, and stored as SP.

Please keep in mind that this test is only done for OS detection purposes and is not a full-blown audit of the target ISN generator. There are many algorithm weaknesses that lead to easy predictability even with a high SP value.

TCP IP ID sequence generation algorithm (TI)

This test examines the IP header ID field for every response to the TCP SEQ probes. The test is only included if at least three probes were returned. It then classifies the target IP ID generator based on the algorithm below. Note that difference values assume that the counter can wrap. So the difference between an IP ID of 65,100 followed by a value of 700 is 1136. The difference between 2,000 followed by 1,100 is 64,636. Here are the calculation details:

1. If all of the ID numbers are zero, TI is set to Z.

2. If the IP ID sequence ever increases by at least 20,000, TI is set to RD (random).

3. If all of the IP IDs are identical, TI is set to that value in hex.

4. If any of the differences between two consecutive IDs exceed 1000, and is not evenly divisible by 256, TI is set to RI (random positive increments). If the difference is evenly divisible by 256, it must be at least 256,000 to cause this RI result.

5. If all of the differences are divisible by 256 and no greater than 5120, TI is set to BI (broken increment). This happens on systems like Microsoft Windows where the IP ID is sent in host byte order rather than network byte order. It works fine and isn't any sort of RFC violation, though it does give away host architecture details which can be useful to attackers.

6. If all of the differences are less than ten, TI is set to I (incremental). We allow difference up to ten here (rather than requiring sequential ordering) because traffic from other hosts can cause sequence gaps.

7. If none of the previous steps identify the generation algorithm, the test is omitted from the fingerprint.

ICMP IP ID sequence generation algorithm (II)

This test is similar to TI above, except that it evaluates IP IDs from the ICMP responses to our two ping probes. It is only included if both responses are received. IP ID differences are absolute (assume wrapping) and are calculated as described in TI. The result is easier to calculate than TI. There is no RD result because there aren't enough samples to support it. II is calculated as follows:

1. If both ID numbers are zero, II is set to Z

2. If both IP IDs are identical, TI is set to that value in hex.

3. If the absolute difference IDs exceed 1000, and is not evenly divisible by 256, `II` is set to `RI` (random positive increments). If the difference is evenly divisible by 256, it must be at least 256,000 to cause this `RI` result.

4. If the IP ID difference is divisible by 256 and no greater than 5120, `II` is set to `BI` (broken increment). This happens on systems like Microsoft where the IP ID is sent in host byte order rather than network byte order. It works fine and isn't any sort of RFC violation, though it does give away host architecture details which can be useful to attackers.

5. If the difference is less than ten, `II` is set to `I` (incremental). We allow difference up to ten here (rather than requiring sequential ordering) because traffic from other hosts can cause sequence gaps.

6. If none of the previous steps identify the generation algorithm, the test is omitted from the fingerprint.

Shared IP ID sequence Boolean (`SS`)

This Boolean value records whether the target shares its IP ID sequence between the TCP and ICMP protocols. If our six TCP IP ID values are 117,118,119,120,121, and 122, then our ICMP results are 123 and 124, it is clear that not only are both sequences incremental, but they are both part of the same sequence. If, on the other hand, TCP IP ID values are 117-122 but the ICMP values are 32,917 and 32,918, a different sequence is being used.

This test is only included if `II` is `RI`, `BI`, or `I` and `TI` is the same. If `SS` is included, the result is `S` if the sequence is shared and `O` (other) if it is not. That determination is made by the following algorithm:

Let `avg` be the final TCP sequence response IP ID minus the first TCP sequence response IP ID, divided by the difference in probe numbers. If probe #1 returns an IP ID of 10,000 and probe #6 returns 20,000, `avg` would be (20,000 - 10,000) / (6 - 1), which equals 2,000.

If the first ICMP echo response IP ID is less than the final TCP sequence response IP ID plus three times `avg`, the `SS` result is `S`. Otherwise it is `O`.

TCP timestamp option algorithm (`TS`)

`TS` is another test which attempts to determine target OS characteristics based on how it generates a series of numbers. This one looks at the TCP timestamp option (if any) in responses to the `SEQ` probes. It examines the TSval (first four bytes of the option) rather than the echoed TSecr (last four bytes) value. It takes the difference between each consecutive TSval and divides that by the amount of time elapsed between Nmap sending the two probes which generated those responses. The resultant value gives a rate of timestamp increments per second. Nmap computes the average increments per second over all consecutive probes and then calculates the `TS` as follows:

1. If any of the responses have no timestamp option, `TS` is set to `U` (unsupported).

2. If any of the timestamp values are zero, `TS` is set to `0`.

3. If the average increments per second falls within the ranges `0-5.66`, `70-150`, or `150-350`, `TS` is set to 1, 7, or 8, respectively. These three ranges get special treatment because they correspond to the 2 Hz, 100 Hz, and 200 Hz frequencies used by many hosts.

4. In all other cases, Nmap records the binary logarithm of the average increments per second, rounded to the nearest integer. Since most hosts use 1,000 Hz frequencies, A is a common result.

TCP options (O, O1-O6)

This test records the TCP header options in a packet. It preserves the original ordering and also provides some information about option values. Because RFC 793 doesn't require any particular ordering, implementations often come up with unique orderings. Some platforms don't implement all options (they are, of course, optional). When you combine all of those permutations with the number of different option values that implementations use, this test provides a veritable trove of information. The value for this test is a string of characters representing the options being used. Several options take arguments that come immediately after the character. Supported options and arguments are all shown in Table 8.1.

Table 8.1. O test values

Option Name	Character	Argument (if any)
End of Options List (EOL)	L	
No operation (NOP)	N	
Maximum Segment Size (MSS)	M	The value is appended. Many systems echo the value used in the corresponding probe.
Window Scale (WS)	W	The actual value is appended.
Timestamp (TS)	T	The T is followed by two binary characters representing the TSval and TSecr values respectively. The characters are 0 if the field is zero and 1 otherwise.
Selective ACK permitted (SACK)	S	

As an example, the string M5B4NW3NNT11 means the packet includes the MSS option (value 0x5B4) followed by a NOP. Next comes a window scale option with a value of three, then two more NOPs. The final option is a timestamp, and neither of its two fields were zero. If there are no TCP options in a response, the test will exist but the value string will be empty. If no probe was returned, the test is omitted.

While this test is generally named O, the six probes sent for sequence generation purposes are a special case. Those are inserted into the special OPS test line and take the names O1 through O6 to distinguish which probe packet they relate to. The "O" stands for "options". Despite the different names, each test O1 through O6 is processed exactly the same way as the other O tests.

TCP initial window size (W, W1-W6)

This test simply records the 16-bit TCP window size of the received packet. It is quite effective, since there are more than 80 values that at least one OS is known to send. A down side is that some operating systems have more than a dozen possible values by themselves. This leads to false negative results until we collect all of the possible window sizes used by an operating system.

While this test is generally named W, the six probes sent for sequence generation purposes are a special case. Those are inserted into a special WIN test line and take the names W1 through W6. The window size is recorded for all of the sequence number probes because they differ in TCP MSS option values, which causes some operating systems to advertise a different window size. Despite the different names, each test is processed exactly the same way.

Responsiveness (R)

This test simply records whether the target responded to a given probe. Possible values are Y and N. If there is no reply, remaining fields for the test are omitted.

A risk with this test involves probes that are dropped by a firewall. This leads to R=N in the subject fingerprint. Yet the reference fingerprint in nmap-os-db may have R=Y if the target OS usually replies. Thus the firewall could prevent proper OS detection. To reduce this problem, reference fingerprints generally omit the R=Y test from the IE and U1 probes, which are the ones most likely to be dropped. In addition, if Nmap is missing a closed TCP port for a target, it will not set R=N for the T5, T6, or T7 tests even if the port it tries is non-responsive. After all, the lack of a closed port may be because they are all filtered.

IP don't fragment bit (DF)

The IP header contains a single bit which forbids routers from fragmenting a packet. If the packet is too large for routers to handle, they will just have to drop it (and ideally return a "destination unreachable, fragmentation needed" response). This test records Y if the bit is set, and N if it isn't.

Don't fragment (ICMP) (DFI)

This is simply a modified version of the DF test that is used for the special IE probes. It compares results of the don't fragment bit for the two ICMP echo request probes sent. It has four possible values, which are enumerated in Table 8.2.

Table 8.2. DFI test values

Value	Description
N	Neither of the ping responses have the DF bit set.
S	Both responses echo the DF value of the probe.
Y	Both of the response DF bits are set.
O	The one remaining other combination—both responses have the DF bit toggled.

IP initial time-to-live (T)

IP packets contain a field named time-to-live (TTL) which is decremented every time they traverse a router. If the field reaches zero, the packet must be discarded. This prevents packets from looping endlessly. Because operating systems differ on which TTL they start with, it can be used for OS detection. Nmap determines how many hops away it is from the target by examining the ICMP port unreachable response to the U1 probe. That response includes the original IP packet, including the already-decremented TTL field, received by the target. By subtracting that value from our as-sent TTL, we learn how many hops away the machine is. Nmap then adds that hop distance to the probe response TTL to determine what the initial TTL was when that ICMP probe response packet was sent. That initial TTL value is stored in the fingerprint as the T result.

Even though an eight-bit field like TTL can never hold values greater than 0xFF, this test occasionally results in values of 0x100 or higher. This occurs when a system (could be the source, a target, or a system in between) corrupts or otherwise fails to correctly decrement the TTL. It can also occur due to asymmetric routes.

Nmap can also learn from the system interface and routing tables when the hop distance is zero (localhost scan) or one (on the same network segment). This value is used when Nmap prints the hop distance for the user, but it is not used for T result computation.

IP initial time-to-live guess (TG)

It is not uncommon for Nmap to receive no response to the U1 probe, which prevents Nmap from learning how many hops away a target is. Firewalls and NAT devices love to block unsolicited UDP packets. But since common TTL values are spread well apart and targets are rarely more than 20 hops away, Nmap can make a pretty good guess anyway. Most systems send packets with an initial TTL of 32, 60, 64, 128, or 255. So the TTL value received in the response is rounded up to the next value out of 32, 64, 128, or 255. 60 is not in that list because it cannot be reliably distinguished from 64. It is rarely seen anyway. The resulting guess is stored in the TG field. This TTL guess field is not printed in a subject fingerprint if the actual TTL (T) value was discovered.

Explicit congestion notification (CC)

This test is only used for the ECN probe. That probe is a SYN packet which includes the CWR and ECE congestion control flags. When the response SYN/ACK is received, those flags are examined to set the CC (congestion control) test value as described in Table 8.3.

Table 8.3. CC test values

Value	Description
Y	Only the ECE bit is set (not CWR). This host supports ECN.
N	Neither of these two bits is set. The target does not support ECN.
S	Both bits are set. The target does not support ECN, but it echoes back what it thinks is a reserved bit.
O	The one remaining combination of these two bits (other).

TCP miscellaneous quirks (Q)

This tests for two quirks that a few implementations have in their TCP stack. The first is that the reserved field in the TCP header (right after the header length) is nonzero. This is particularly likely to happen in response to the ECN test as that one sets a reserved bit in the probe. If this is seen in a packet, an "R" is recorded in the Q string.

The other quirk Nmap tests for is a nonzero urgent pointer field value when the URG flag is not set. This is also particularly likely to be seen in response to the ECN probe, which sets a non-zero urgent field. A "U" is appended to the Q string when this is seen.

The Q string must always be generated in alphabetical order. If no quirks are present, the Q test is empty but still shown.

TCP sequence number (S)

This test examines the 32-bit sequence number field in the TCP header. Rather than record the field value as some other tests do, this one examines how it compares to the TCP acknowledgment number from the probe that elicited the response. It then records the appropriate value as shown in Table 8.4.

Table 8.4. S test values

Value	Description
Z	Sequence number is zero.
A	Sequence number is the same as the acknowledgment number in the probe.
A+	Sequence number is the same as the acknowledgment number in the probe plus one.
O	Sequence number is something else (other).

ICMP sequence number(SI)

This test looks at the sequence number in ICMP echo response packets. It is only used for the two IE echo request probes. The four values it can take are shown in Table 8.5.

Table 8.5. SI test values

Value	Description
Z	Both sequence numbers are set to 0.
S	Both sequence numbers echo the ones from the probes.
<NNNN>	When they both use the same non-zero number, it is recorded here.
O	Any other combination.

TCP acknowledgment number (A)

This test is the same as S except that it tests how the acknowledgment number in the response compares to the sequence number in the respective probe. The four possible values are given in Table 8.6.

Table 8.6. A test values

Value	Description
Z	Acknowledgment number is zero.
S	Acknowledgment number is the same as the sequence number in the probe.
S+	Acknowledgment number is the same as the sequence number in the probe plus one.
O	Acknowledgment number is something else (other).

TCP flags (F)

This field records the TCP flags in the response. Each letter represents one flag, and they occur in the same order as in a TCP packet (from high-bit on the left, to the low ones). So the value SA represents the SYN and ACK bits set, while the value AS is illegal (wrong order). The possible flags are shown in Table 8.7.

Table 8.7. F test values

Character	Flag name	Flag byte value
E	ECN Echo (ECE)	64
U	Urgent Data (URG)	32
A	Acknowledgment (ACK)	16
P	Push (PSH)	8
R	Reset (RST)	4
S	Synchronize (SYN)	2
F	Final (FIN)	1

TCP RST data checksum (RD)

Some operating systems return ASCII data such as error messages in reset packets. This is explicitly allowed by section 4.2.2.12 of RFC 1122. When Nmap encounters such data, it performs a CRC16 checksum and reports the results. When there is no data, RD is set to zero. Some of the few operating systems that may return data in their reset packets are HP-UX and versions of Mac OS prior to Mac OS X.

IP type of service (TOS)

This test simply records the type of service byte from the IP header of ICMP port unreachable packets. This byte is described in RFC 791. The value is not recorded for other responses (such as TCP or echo response packets) because variations there are usually caused by network devices or host services rather than reflecting the target OS itself.

IP type of service for ICMP responses (TOSI)

This test compares the IP type of service (TOS) bytes from the responses to both IE test ICMP echo request probes. The possible values are shown in Table 8.8.

Table 8.8. TOSI test values

Value	Description
Z	Both TOS values are zero.
S	Both TOS values are each the same as in the corresponding probe.
<NN>	When they both use the same non-zero number, it is recorded here.
O	Any other combination.

IP total length (`IPL`)

This test records the total length (in octets) of an IP packet. It is only used for the port unreachable response elicited by the `U1` test. That length varies by implementation because they are allowed to choose how much data from the original probe to include, as long as they meet the minimum RFC 792 requirement. That requirement is to include the original IP header and at least eight bytes of data.

Unused port unreachable field nonzero (`UN`)

An ICMP port unreachable message header is eight bytes long, but only the first four are used. RFC 792 states that the last four bytes must be zero. A few implementations (mostly ethernet switches and some specialized embedded devices) set it anyway. The value of those last four bytes is recorded in this field.

Returned probe IP total length value (`RIPL`)

ICMP port unreachable messages (as are sent in response to the `U1` probe) are required to include the IP header which generated them. This header should be returned just as they received it, but some implementations send back a corrupted version due to changes they made during IP processing. This test simply records the returned IP total length value. If the correct value of 0x148 (328) is returned, the value G (for good) is stored instead of the actual value.

Returned probe IP ID value (`RID`)

The `U1` probe has a static IP ID value of 0x1042. If that value is returned in the port unreachable message, the value G is stored for this test. Otherwise the exact value returned is stored. Some systems, such as Solaris, manipulate IP ID values for raw IP packets that Nmap sends. In such cases, this test is skipped. We have found that some systems, particularly HP and Xerox printers, flip the bytes and return 0x4210 instead.

Integrity of returned probe IP checksum value (`RIPCK`)

The IP checksum is one value that we *don't* expect to remain the same when returned in a port unreachable message. After all, each network hop during transit changes the checksum as the TTL is decremented. However, the checksum we receive should match the enclosing IP packet. If it does, the value G (good) is stored for this test. If the returned value is zero, then Z is stored. Otherwise the result is I (invalid).

Integrity of returned probe UDP length and checksum (`RUL` and `RUCK`)

The UDP header length and checksum values should be returned exactly as they were sent. If so, G is recorded for these tests. Otherwise the value actually returned is recorded. The proper length is 0x134 (308).

Integrity of returned UDP data (`RUD`)

If the UDP payload returned consists of 300 'C' (0x43) characters as expected, a G is recorded for this test. Otherwise I (invalid) is recorded.

ICMP response code (CD)

The code value of an ICMP echo reply (type zero) packet is supposed to be zero. But some implementations wrongly send other values, particularly if the echo request has a nonzero code (as one of the IE tests does). The response code values for the two probes are combined into a CD value as described in Table 8.9.

Table 8.9. CD test values

Value	Description
Z	Both code values are zero.
S	Both code values are the same as in the corresponding probe.
<NN>	When they both use the same non-zero number, it is shown here.
O	Any other combination.

IP data length for ICMP responses (DLI)

When data is included with an ICMP echo request packet, it is supposed to be returned intact in the corresponding echo response. But some implementations truncate the data anyway. This tests looks at both ICMP responses to the IE probes, and assigns a value as described in Table 8.10.

Table 8.10. DLI test values

Value	Description
Z	Neither response includes any data.
S	Both responses return all data sent in the corresponding request.
<NN>	If at least one of the responses truncates the data, the largest amount of data returned (in either packet) is stored here. When they both truncate the data length to the same non-zero number, it is shown here. This value only counts actual data, not the IP or ICMP headers.

8.4. Fingerprinting Methods Avoided by Nmap

Nmap supports many more OS detection techniques than any other program, and we are always interested in hearing about new ideas. Please send them to the Nmap development list (*nmap-dev*) for discussion. However there are some methods that just aren't a good fit. This section details some of the most interesting ones. While they aren't supported by Nmap, some are useful in combination with Nmap to verify findings or learn further details.

8.4.1. Passive Fingerprinting

Passive fingerprinting uses most of the same techniques as the active fingerprinting performed by Nmap. The difference is that a passive system simply sniffs the network, opportunistically classifying hosts as it observes their traffic. This is more difficult than active fingerprinting, since you have to accept whatever communication happens rather than designing your own custom probes. It is a valuable technique, but doesn't belong in a fundamentally active tool such as Nmap. Fortunately, Michal Zalewski has written the excellent p0f[2] passive OS fingerprinting tool. He also devised a couple of the current Nmap OS fingerprinting tests. Another option is SinFP[3] by GomoR, which supports both active and passive fingerprinting.

8.4.2. Exploit Chronology

TCP/IP fingerprinting works well for distinguishing different operating systems, but detecting different versions of the same operating system can be troublesome. The company must change their stack in some way we can differentiate. Fortunately, many OS vendors regularly update their systems to comply with the latest standards. But what about those who don't? Most of them at least get around to fixing exploitable stack bugs eventually. And those fixes are easy to detect remotely. First send the exploit payload, be it a land attack, teardrop, ping of death, SYN flood, or WinNuke. Send one attack at a time, then immediately try to contact the system again. If it is suddenly non-responsive, you have narrowed down the OS to versions which didn't ship with the fix.

Warning

If you use denial of service (DoS) exploits as part of your OS detection suite, remember to perform those tests last.

8.4.3. Retransmission Times

TCP implementations have significant leeway in exactly how long they wait before retransmitting packets. The proof-of-concept tools Ring and Cron-OS are available to exploit this. They send a SYN packet to an open port, then ignore the SYN/ACK they receive rather than acknowledging it with an ACK (to complete the connection) or a RST (to kill it). The target host will resend the SYN/ACK several more times, and these tools track every subsecond of the wait. While some information can indeed be gleaned from this technique, there are several reasons that I haven't incorporated the patch into Nmap:

- It usually requires modifying the source host firewall rules to prevent your system from replying with a RST packet to the SYN/ACK it receives. That is hard to do in a portable way. And even if it was easy, many users don't appreciate applications mucking with their firewall rules.

- It can be very slow. The retransmissions can go on for several minutes. That is a long time to wait for a test that doesn't give all that much information in the first place.

- It can be inaccurate because packet drops and latency (which you have to expect in real-world environments) can lead to bogus results.

I have enumerated these reasons here because they also apply to some other proposed OS detection methods. I would love to add new tests, but they must be quick and require few packets. Messing with host firewall is unacceptable. I try to avoid making full TCP connections for stack fingerprinting, though that is done for OS detection as part of the version scanning system.

---

[2] *http://lcamtuf.coredump.cx/p0f.shtml*
[3] *http://www.gomor.org/bin/view/Sinfp*

8.4.4. IP Fragmentation

IP fragmentation is a complex system and implementations are riddled with bugs and inconsistencies. Possible tests could examine how overlapping fragments are assembled or time the defragmentation timeouts. These tests are avoided for Nmap because many firewalls and other inline devices defragment traffic at gateways. Thus Nmap may end up fingerprinting the firewall rather than the true destination host. In addition, fragments are difficult to send on some operating systems. Linux 2.6 kernels have a tendency to queue the fragments you are trying to send and assemble them itself before transmission.

8.4.5. Open Port Patterns

The target host OS can often be guessed simply by looking at the ports which are open. Microsoft Windows machines often have TCP ports 135 and 139 open. Windows 2000 and newer also listen on port 445. Meanwhile, a machine running services on port 22 (ssh) and 631 (Internet Printing Protocol) is likely running Unix.

While this heuristic is often useful, it just isn't reliable enough for Nmap. Combinations of ports can be obscured by firewall rules, and most mainstream protocols are available on multiple platforms. OpenSSH servers can be run on Windows[4], and the "Windows SMB" ports can be serviced by Samba[5] running on a Unix machine. Port forwarding clouds the issue even further. A machine which appears to be running Microsoft IIS might be a Unix firewall simply forwarding port 80 to a Windows machine.

For these reasons, Nmap does not consider open port numbers during TCP/IP stack fingerprinting. However, Nmap can use version detection information (see Chapter 7, *Service and Application Version Detection* [145]) to separately discover operating system and device type information. By keeping the OS detection results discovered by OS detection and version detection separate, Nmap can gracefully handle a Checkpoint firewall which uses TCP port forwarding to a Windows web server. The stack fingerprinting results should be "Checkpoint Firewall-1" while version detection should suggest that the OS is Windows. Keep in mind that only a small fraction of version detection signatures include OS and device type information—we can only populate these fields when the application divulges the information or when it only runs on one OS or device type.

8.5. Understanding an Nmap Fingerprint

When Nmap stores a fingerprint in memory, Nmap uses a tree of attributes and values in data structures that users need not even be aware of. But there is also a special ASCII-encoded version which Nmap can print for users when a machine is unidentified. Thousands of these serialized fingerprints are also read back every time Nmap runs (with OS detection enabled) from the `nmap-os-db` database. The fingerprint format is a compromise between human comprehension and brevity. The format is so terse that it looks like line noise to many inexperienced users, but those who read this document should be able to decipher fingerprints with ease. There are actually two types of fingerprints, though they have the same general structure. The fingerprints of known operating systems that Nmap reads in are called *reference fingerprints*, while the fingerprint Nmap displays after scanning a system is a *subject fingerprint*. The reference fingerprints are a bit more complex since they can be tailored to match a whole class of operating systems by adding leeway to (or omitting)

---

[4] *http://sshwindows.sourceforge.net/*
[5] *http://www.samba.org/*

tests that aren't so reliable while allowing only a single possible value for other tests. The reference fingerprints also have OS details and classifications. Since the subject tests are simpler, we describe them first.

8.5.1. Decoding the Subject Fingerprint Format

If Nmap performs OS fingerprinting on a host and doesn't get a perfect OS matches despite promising conditions (such as finding both open and closed ports accessible on the target), Nmap prints a subject fingerprint that shows all of the test results that Nmap deems relevant, then asks the user to submit the data to Nmap.Org. Tests aren't shown when Nmap has no useful results, such as when the relevant probe responses weren't received. A special line named SCAN gives extra details about the scan (such as Nmap version number) that provide useful context for integrating fingerprint submissions into nmap-os-db. A typical subject fingerprint is shown in Example 8.3.

Example 8.3. A typical subject fingerprint

```
OS:SCAN(V=4.62%D=5/21%OT=80%CT=1%CU=36069%PV=Y%DS=1%G=Y%M=001839%TM=483466E
OS:0%P=i686-pc-linux-gnu)SEQ(SP=C9%GCD=1%ISR=CE%TI=Z%II=I%TS=8)OPS(O1=M5B4S
OS:T11NW0%O2=M5B4ST11NW0%O3=M5B4NNT11NW0%O4=M5B4ST11NW0%O5=M5B4ST11NW0%O6=M
OS:5B4ST11)WIN(W1=16A0%W2=16A0%W3=16A0%W4=16A0%W5=16A0%W6=16A0)ECN(R=Y%DF=Y
OS:%T=40%W=16D0%O=M5B4NNSNW0%CC=N%Q=)T1(R=Y%DF=Y%T=40%S=O%A=S+%F=AS%RD=0%Q=
OS:)T2(R=N)T3(R=Y%DF=Y%T=40%W=16A0%S=O%A=S+%F=AS%O=M5B4ST11NW0%RD=0%Q=)T4(R
OS:=Y%DF=Y%T=40%W=0%S=A%A=Z%F=R%O=%RD=0%Q=)T5(R=Y%DF=Y%T=40%W=0%S=Z%A=S+%F=
OS:AR%O=%RD=0%Q=)T6(R=Y%DF=Y%T=40%W=0%S=A%A=Z%F=R%O=%RD=0%Q=)T7(R=Y%DF=Y%T=
OS:40%W=0%S=Z%A=S+%F=AR%O=%RD=0%Q=)U1(R=Y%DF=N%T=40%TOS=C0%IPL=164%UN=0%RIP
OS:L=G%RID=G%RIPCK=G%RUCK=G%RUL=G%RUD=G)IE(R=Y%DFI=N%T=40%TOSI=S%CD=S%SI=S%
OS:DLI=S)
```

Now you may look at this fingerprint and immediately understand what everything means. If so, you can simply skip this section. But I have never seen such a reaction. Many people probably think some sort of buffer overflow or unterminated string error is causing Nmap to spew garbage data at them. This section helps you decode the information so you can immediately tell that blind TCP sequence prediction attacks against this machine are moderately hard, but it may make a good idle scan (-sI) zombie. The first step in understanding this fingerprint is to fix the line wrapping. The tests are all squished together, with each line wrapped at 71 characters. Then OS: is prepended to each line, raising the length to 74 characters. This makes fingerprints easy to cut and paste into the Nmap fingerprint submission form (see Section 8.7.2, "When Nmap Fails to Find a Match and Prints a Fingerprint" [201]). Removing the prefix and fixing the word wrapping (each line should end with a right parenthesis) leads to the cleaned-up version in Example 8.4.

Example 8.4. A cleaned-up subject fingerprint

```
SCAN(V=4.62%D=5/21%OT=80%CT=1%CU=36069%PV=Y%DS=1%G=Y%M=001839%
     TM=483466E0%P=i686-pc-linux-gnu)
SEQ(SP=C9%GCD=1%ISR=CE%TI=Z%II=I%TS=8)
OPS(O1=M5B4ST11NW0%O2=M5B4ST11NW0%O3=M5B4NNT11NW0%O4=M5B4ST11NW0%
    O5=M5B4ST11NW0%O6=M5B4ST11)
WIN(W1=16A0%W2=16A0%W3=16A0%W4=16A0%W5=16A0%W6=16A0)
ECN(R=Y%DF=Y%T=40%W=16D0%O=M5B4NNSNW0%CC=N%Q=)
T1(R=Y%DF=Y%T=40%S=O%A=S+%F=AS%RD=0%Q=)
T2(R=N)
T3(R=Y%DF=Y%T=40%W=16A0%S=O%A=S+%F=AS%O=M5B4ST11NW0%RD=0%Q=)
T4(R=Y%DF=Y%T=40%W=0%S=A%A=Z%F=R%O=%RD=0%Q=)
T5(R=Y%DF=Y%T=40%W=0%S=Z%A=S+%F=AR%O=%RD=0%Q=)
T6(R=Y%DF=Y%T=40%W=0%S=A%A=Z%F=R%O=%RD=0%Q=)
T7(R=Y%DF=Y%T=40%W=0%S=Z%A=S+%F=AR%O=%RD=0%Q=)
U1(R=Y%DF=N%T=40%TOS=C0%IPL=164%UN=0%RIPL=G%RID=G%RIPCK=G%RUCK=G%RUL=G%RUD=G)
IE(R=Y%DFI=N%T=40%TOSI=S%CD=S%SI=S%DLI=S)
```

While this still isn't the world's most intuitive format (we had to keep it short), the format is much clearer now. Every line is a category, such as SEQ for the sequence generation tests, T3 for the results from that particular TCP probe, and IE for tests related to the two ICMP echo probes.

Following each test name is a pair of parentheses which enclose results for individual tests. The tests take the format `<testname>=<value>`. All of the possible categories, tests, and values are described in Section 8.3, "TCP/IP Fingerprinting Methods Supported by Nmap" [176]. Each pair of tests are separated by a percentage symbol (%). Tests values can be empty, leading to a percentage symbol or category-terminating right-parenthesis immediately following the equal sign. The string "O=%RD=0%Q=)" in T4 of our example shows two of these empty tests. A blank test value must match another blank value, so this empty TCP quirks Q value wouldn't match a fingerprint with Q set to RU.

In some cases, a whole test is missing rather than just its value. For example, T2 of our sample fingerprint has no W (TCP window), S (sequence number), A (acknowledgment number), T (TTL), or TG (TTL guess) tests. This is because the one test and value it does include, R=N, means that no response was returned for the T2 probe. So including a window value or sequence number would make little sense. Similarly, tests which aren't well supported on the system running Nmap are skipped. An example is the RID (IP ID field returned in ICMP packet) test, which doesn't work well on Solaris because that system tends to corrupt the ID field Nmap sends out. Tests which are inconclusive (such as failing to detect the IP ID sequence for the TI and II tests) are also omitted.

Decoding the SCAN line of a subject fingerprint

The SCAN line is a special case in a subject fingerprint. Rather than describe the target system, these tests describe various conditions of the scan. These help us integrate fingerprints submitted to Nmap.Org. The tests in this line are:

- Nmap version number (V).

- Date of scan (D) in the form month/day.

- Open and closed TCP ports (on target) used for scan (OT and CT). Unlike most tests, these are printed in decimal format. If Nmap was unable to find an open or a closed port, the test is included with an empty value (even when Nmap guesses a possibly closed port and sends a probe there).

- Closed UDP port (CU). This is the same as CT, but for UDP. Since the majority of scans don't include UDP, this test's value is usually empty.

- Private IP space (PV) is Y if the target is on the 10.0.0.0/8, 172.16.0.0/12, or 192.168.0.0/16 private networks (RFC 1918). Otherwise it is N.

- Network distance (DS) is the network hop distance from the target. It is 0 if the target is localhost, 1 if directly connected on an ethernet network, or the exact distance if discovered by Nmap. If the distance is unknown, this test is omitted.

- Good results (G) is Y if conditions and results seem good enough to submit this fingerprint to Nmap.Org. It is N otherwise. Unless you force them by enabling debugging (-d) or extreme verbosity (-vv), G=N fingerprints aren't printed by Nmap.

- Target MAC prefix (M) is the first six hex digits of the target MAC address, which correspond to the vendor name. Leading zeros are not included. This field is omitted unless the target is on the same ethernet network (DS=1).

- The OS scan time (TM) is provided in Unix time_t format (in hexadecimal).

- The platform Nmap was compiled for is given in the P field.

8.5.2. Decoding the Reference Fingerprint Format

When Nmap scans a target to create a subject fingerprint, it then tries to match that data against the thousands of *reference fingerprints* in the nmap-os-db database. Reference fingerprints are initially formed from one or more subject fingerprints and thus have much in common. They do have a bit of extra information to facilitate matching and of course to describe the operating systems they represent. For example, the subject fingerprint we just looked at might form the basis for the reference fingerprint in Example 8.5.

Example 8.5. A typical reference fingerprint

```
Fingerprint Sony PlayStation 3 game console
Class Sony | embedded || game console
SEQ(SP=F7-101%GCD=<7%ISR=FC-106%TI=RD%TS=21)
OPS(O1=M5B4NNSNW1NNT11%O2=M5B4NNSNW1NNT11%O3=M5B4NW1NNT11%
    O4=M5B4NNSNW1NNT11%O5=M5B4NNSNW1NNT11%O6=M5B4NNSNNT11)
WIN(W1=FFFF%W2=FFFF%W3=FFFF%W4=FFFF%W5=FFFF%W6=FFFF)
ECN(R=Y%DF=N%T=41%TG=41%W=FFFF%O=M5B4NNSNW1%CC=N%Q=)
T1(R=Y%DF=N%T=41%TG=41%S=O%A=S+%F=AS%RD=0%Q=)
T2(R=Y%DF=N%T=41%TG=41%W=0%S=Z%A=O|S%F=AR%O=%RD=0%Q=)
T3(R=Y%DF=N%T=41%TG=41%W=FFFF%S=O%A=S+%F=AS%O=M5B4NNSNW1NNT11%RD=0%Q=)
T4(R=Y%DF=N%T=41%TG=41%W=0%S=A|O%A=Z%F=R%O=%RD=0%Q=)
T5(R=Y%DF=N%T=41%TG=40%W=0%S=Z%A=O|S+%F=AR%O=%RD=0%Q=)
T6(R=Y%DF=N%T=40%TG=40%W=0%S=A|O%A=Z%F=R%O=%RD=0%Q=)
T7(R=Y%DF=N%T=40%TG=40%W=0%S=Z%A=O|S%F=AR%O=%RD=0%Q=)
U1(DF=N%T=FF%TG=FF%TOS=0%IPL=38%UN=0%RIPL=G%RID=G%RIPCK=G%RUCK=G%RUL=G%RUD=G)
IE(DFI=N%T=FF%TG=FF%TOSI=S%CD=S%SI=S%DLI=S)
```

Some differences are immediately obvious. Line wrapping is not done because that is only important for the submission process. The SCAN line is also removed, since that information describes a specific scan instance rather than general target OS characteristics.

You probably also noticed the two new lines, Fingerprint and Class, which are new to this reference fingerprint. A more subtle change is that some of the individual test results have been removed while others have been enhanced with logical expressions.

Free-form OS description (Fingerprint line)

The Fingerprint line first serves as a token so Nmap knows to start loading a new fingerprint. Each fingerprint only has one such line. Immediately after the Fingerprint token (and a space) comes a textual description of the operating system(s) represented by this fingerprint. These are in free-form English text, designed for human interpretation rather than a machine parser. Nevertheless, Nmap tries to stick with a consistent format including the vendor, product name, and then version number. Version number ranges and comma-separated alternatives discussed previously can be found in this field. Here are some examples:

```
Fingerprint HP LaserJet printer (4050, 4100, 4200, or 8150)
Fingerprint Sun Solaris 9 or 10 (SPARC)
Fingerprint Linux 2.6.22 - 2.6.24
Fingerprint Microsoft Windows Server 2003 SP1
Fingerprint Microsoft Windows XP Professional SP1
Fingerprint Minolta Di550 laser printer
```

In an ideal world, every different OS would correspond to exactly one unique fingerprint. Unfortunately, OS vendors don't make life so easy for us. The same OS release may fingerprint differently based on what network drivers are in use, user-configurable options, patch levels, processor architecture, amount of RAM available, firewall settings, and more. Sometimes the fingerprints differ for no discernible reason. While the reference fingerprint format has an expression syntax for coping with slight variations, creating multiple fingerprints for the same OS is often preferable when major differences are discovered.

Just as multiple fingerprints are often needed for one OS, sometimes a single fingerprint describes several systems. If two systems give the exact same results for every single test, Nmap has little choice but to offer

---

up both as possibilities. This commonly occurs for several reasons. One is that vendors may release a new version of their OS without any significant changes to their IP stack. Maybe they made important changes elsewhere in the system, or perhaps they did little but want to make a bunch of money selling "upgrades". In these cases, Nmap often prints a range such as `Apple Mac OS X 10.4.8 - 10.4.11` or `Sun Solaris 9 or 10`.

Another cause of duplicate fingerprints is embedded devices which share a common OS. For example, a printer from one vendor and an ethernet switch from another may actually share an embedded OS from a third vendor. In many cases, subtle differences between the devices still allow them to be distinguished. But sometimes Nmap must simply list a group of possibilities such as `Cisco 1200-series WAP, HP ProCurve 2650 switch, or Xerox Phaser 7400N or 8550DT printer`.

There are also cases where numerous vendors private label the exact same OEM device with their own brand name and model number. Here again, Nmap must simply list the possibilities. But distinguishing these is less important because they are all fundamentally the same device.

Tip

If the description printed by Nmap (which comes from the `Fingerprint` line) isn't informative enough for you, more detailed information may be available in comments above the fingerprint itself in `nmap-os-db`. You can find it installed on your system as described in Chapter 14, *Understanding and Customizing Nmap Data Files* [363], or look up the latest version at *http://nmap.org/data/nmap-os-db*. Search for the exact OS description that Nmap gives you. Keep in mind that there may be several `Fingerprint` lines with exactly the same description, so you may have to examine them all. Or use the Nmap XML output, which shows the line number of each match.

Device and OS classification (`Class` lines)

While the `Fingerprint` description works great for analysts reading Nmap output directly, many people run Nmap from other scripts and applications. Those applications might use the OS information to check for OS-specific vulnerabilities or just create a pretty graph or report.

A more structured OS classification system exists for these purposes. It is also useful when there are multiple matches. If you only get a partial fingerprint (maybe no open ports were found on the target so many tests had to be skipped), it might match dozens of different fingerprints in the `nmap-os-db` database. Printing the details for all of those fingerprints would be a mess. But thanks to OS classification, Nmap can find commonality. If all of the matches are classified as Linux, Nmap will simply print that the target is a Linux box.

Every fingerprint has one or more `Class` lines. Each contains four well-defined fields: vendor, OS name, OS family, and device type. The fields are separated by the pipe symbol (|).

The device type is a broad classification such as `router`, `printer`, or `game console` and was discussed previously in this chapter. General-purpose operating systems such as `Linux` and `Windows` which can be used for just about anything are classified as `general purpose`.

The vendor is the company which makes an OS or device. Examples are `Apple`, `Cisco`, `Microsoft`, and `Linksys`. For community projects such as OpenBSD and Linux without a controlling vendor, the OS family name is repeated for the vendor column.

OS family includes products such as `Windows`, `Linux`, `IOS` (for Cisco routers), `Solaris`, and `OpenBSD`. There are also hundreds of devices such as switches, broadband routers, and printers which use undisclosed operating systems. When the underlying OS isn't clear, `embedded` is used.

OS generation is a more granular description of the OS. Generations of Linux include `2.4.X` and `2.6.X`, while Windows generations include `95`, `98`, `Me`, `2000`, `XP`, and `Vista`. FreeBSD uses generations such as `4.X` and `5.X`. For obscure operating systems which we haven't subdivided into generations (or whenever the OS is listed simply as `embedded`), this field is left blank.

Each field may contain just one value. When a fingerprint represents more than one possible combination of these four fields, multiple `Class` lines are used. Example 8.6 provides some example `Fingerprint` lines followed by their corresponding classifications.

Example 8.6. Some typical fingerprint descriptions and corresponding classifications

```
Fingerprint D-Link DSL-500G ADSL router
Class D-Link | embedded || broadband router

Fingerprint Linksys WRT54GC or TRENDnet TEW-431BRP WAP
Class Linksys | embedded || WAP
Class TRENDnet | embedded || WAP

Fingerprint Apple Mac OS X 10.3.9 (Panther) - 10.4.7 (Tiger)
Class Apple | Mac OS X | 10.3.X | general purpose
Class Apple | Mac OS X | 10.4.X | general purpose

Fingerprint Sony PlayStation 3 game console
Class Sony | embedded || game console
```

If these examples aren't enough, a listing of classifications recognized by the latest version of Nmap is maintained at *http://nmap.org/data/os-classes.txt*.

Test expressions

The test expressions don't have to change between a subject and reference fingerprint, but they almost always do. The reference fingerprint often needs to be generalized a little bit to match all instances of a particular OS, rather than just the machine you are scanning. For example, some Windows XP machines return a Window size of `F424` to the T1 probe, while others return `FAF0`. This may be due to the particular ethernet device driver in use, or maybe how much memory is available. In any case, we would like to detect Windows XP no matter which window size is used.

One way to generalize a fingerprint is to simply remove tests that produce inconsistent results. Remove all of the window size tests from a reference fingerprint, and systems will match that print no matter what size they use. The downside is that you can lose a lot of important information this way. If the only Window sizes that a particular system ever sends are `F424` and `FAF0`, you really only want to allow those two values, not all 65,536 possibilities.

While removing tests is overkill in some situations, it is useful in others. The R=Y test value, meaning there was a response, is usually removed from the U1 and IE tests before they are added to `nmap-os-db`. These probes are often blocked by a firewall, so the lack of a response should not count against the OS match.

When removing tests is undesirable, Nmap offers an expression syntax for allowing a test to match multiple values. For example, W=F424|FAF0 would allow those two Windows XP window values without allowing any others. Table 8.11 shows the permitted operators in test values.

Table 8.11. Reference fingerprint test expression operators

Op Name	Symbol	Example	Description
Or			O=|ME|MNNTNW	Matches if the corresponding subject fingerprint test takes the value of any of the clauses. In this example, the initial pipe symbol means that an empty options list will match too.
Range	–	SP=7-A	Matches if the subject fingerprint's corresponding test produces a numeric value which falls within the range specified.
Greater than	>	SP=>8	Matches if the subject fingerprint's corresponding test produces a numeric value which is greater than the one specified.
Less than	<	GCD=<5	Matches if the subject fingerprint's corresponding test produces a numeric value which is less than the one specified.

Expressions can combine operators, as in GCD=<7|64|256|>1024, which matches if the GCD is less than seven, exactly 64, exactly 256, or greater than 1024.

8.6. OS Matching Algorithms

Nmap's algorithm for detecting matches is relatively simple. It takes a subject fingerprint and tests it against every single reference fingerprint in `nmap-os-db`.

When testing against a reference fingerprint, Nmap looks at each probe category line from the subject fingerprint (such as SEQ or T1) in turn. Any probe lines which do *not* exist in the reference fingerprint are skipped. When the reference fingerprint does have a matching line, they are compared.

For a probe line comparison, Nmap examines every individual test (R, DF, W, etc.) from the subject category line in turn. Any tests which do *not* exist in the reference line are skipped. Whenever a matching test is found, Nmap increments the `PossiblePoints` accumulator by the number of points assigned to this test. Then the test values are compared. If the reference test has an empty value, the subject test only matches if its value is empty too. If the reference test is just a plain string or number (no operators), the subject test must match it exactly. If the reference string contains operators (|, –, >, or <), the subject must match as described in the section called "Test expressions" [197]. If a test matches, the `NumMatchPoints` accumulator is incremented by the test's point value.

Once all of the probe lines are tested for a fingerprint, Nmap divides `NumMatchPoints` by `PossiblePoints`. The result is a confidence factor describing the probability that the subject fingerprint matches that particular reference fingerprint. It is treated as a percentage, so `1.00` is a perfect match while `0.95` is very close.

Test point values are assigned by a special `MatchPoints` entry (which may only appear once) in `nmap-os-db`. This entry looks much like a normal fingerprint, but instead of providing results for each test, it provides point values (non-negative integers) for each test. Tests listed in the `MatchPoints` structure only apply when found in the same test they are listed in. So a value given for the `W` (Window size) test in `T1` doesn't affect the `W` test in `T3`. An example `MatchPoints` structure is given in Example 8.7.

Example 8.7. The MatchPoints structure

```
MatchPoints
SEQ(SP=25%GCD=75%ISR=25%TI=100%II=100%SS=80%TS=100)
OPS(O1=20%O2=20%O3=20%O4=20%O5=20%O6=20)
WIN(W1=15%W2=15%W3=15%W4=15%W5=15%W6=15)
ECN(R=100%DF=20%T=15%TG=15%W=15%O=15%CC=100%Q=20)
T1(R=100%DF=20%T=15%TG=15%S=20%A=20%F=30%RD=20%Q=20)
T2(R=80%DF=20%T=15%TG=15%W=25%S=20%A=20%F=30%O=10%RD=20%Q=20)
T3(R=80%DF=20%T=15%TG=15%W=25%S=20%A=20%F=30%O=10%RD=20%Q=20)
T4(R=100%DF=20%T=15%TG=15%W=25%S=20%A=20%F=30%O=10%RD=20%Q=20)
T5(R=100%DF=20%T=15%TG=15%W=25%S=20%A=20%F=30%O=10%RD=20%Q=20)
T6(R=100%DF=20%T=15%TG=15%W=25%S=20%A=20%F=30%O=10%RD=20%Q=20)
T7(R=80%DF=20%T=15%TG=15%W=25%S=20%A=20%F=30%O=10%RD=20%Q=20)
U1(R=50%DF=20%T=15%TG=15%TOS=50%IPL=100%UN=100%RIPL=100%RID=100%RIPCK=100% ↵
    RUCK=100%RUL=100%RUD=100)
IE(R=50%DFI=40%T=15%TG=15%TOSI=25%CD=100%SI=100%DLI=100)
```

Once all of the reference fingerprints have been evaluated, Nmap orders them and prints the perfect matches (if there aren't too many). If there are no perfect matches, but some are very close, Nmap may print those. Guesses are more likely to be printed if the `--osscan-guess` option is given.

8.7. Dealing with Misidentified and Unidentified Hosts

While Nmap has a huge database, it cannot detect everything. Nmap has no chance to detect most toasters, refrigerators, chairs, or automobiles because they have no IP stack. Yet I wouldn't rule any of these out, given the ever-expanding list of connected devices. The Nmap fingerprint DB includes plenty of game consoles, phones, thermometers, cameras, interactive toys, and media players.

Having an IP address is necessary but not sufficient to guarantee a proper fingerprint. Nmap may still guess wrong or fail to produce any guess at all. Here are some suggestions for improving your results:

Upgrade to the latest Nmap
> Many Linux distributions and other operating systems ship with ancient versions of Nmap. The Nmap OS database is improved with almost every release, so check your version number by running **nmap -V** and then compare that to the latest available from *http://nmap.org/download.html*. Installing the newest version takes only a few minutes on most platforms.

Scan all ports

When Nmap detects OS detection problems against a certain host, it will issue warnings. One of the most common is: "Warning: OS detection will be MUCH less reliable because we did not find at least 1 open and 1 closed TCP port". It is possible that such ports really are unavailable on the machine, but retrying your scan with -p- to scan all ports may find some that are responsive for OS detection. Doing a UDP scan (-sU) too can help even more, though it will slow the scan substantially.

Try a more aggressive guess

If Nmap says there are no matches close enough to print, something is probably wrong. Maybe a firewall or NAT box in the way is modifying the probe or response packets. This can cause a hybrid situation where one group of tests look like they are from one OS, while another set look completely different. Adding the --osscan-guess may give more clues as to what is running.

Scan from a different location

The more network hops your packet has to go through to reach its target, the greater the chances that a network device will modify (or drop) the probe or response. NAT gateways, firewalls, and especially port forwarding can confuse OS detection. If you are scanning the IP of a load balancing device which simply redirects packets to a diverse network of servers, it isn't even clear what the "correct" OS detection result would be.

Many ISPs filter traffic to "bad" ports, and others use transparent proxies to redirect certain ports to their own servers. The port 25 or 80 you think are open on your target may actually be spoofed from your ISP to connect to ISP proxy servers. Another behavior which can confuse OS detection is when firewalls spoof TCP reset packets as if they are coming from the destination host. This is particularly common from port 113 (identd). Both the reset spoofing and transparent proxies can often be detected by noticing that every machine on a target network seems to exhibit the behavior—even those which otherwise seem to be down. If you detect any such nonsense, be sure to exclude these ports from your scan so they don't taint your results. You may also want to try from a completely different network location. The closer you are to the target, the more accurate the results will be. In a perfect case, you would always scan the target from the same network segment it resides on.

8.7.1. When Nmap Guesses Wrong

Occasionally Nmap will report an OS guess which you know is wrong. The errors are usually minor (such as reporting a machine running Linux 2.4.16 as "Linux kernel 2.4.8 - 2.4.15"), but there have been reports of Nmap being completely off (such as reporting your web server as an AppleWriter printer). When you encounter such problems (minor or major), please report them so everyone can benefit. The only reason the Nmap DB is so comprehensive is that thousands of users have spent a few minutes each to submit new information. Please follow these instructions:

Have a recent version of Nmap

Run **nmap -V** to determine which version of Nmap you have. You don't need to be running the absolute latest version of Nmap (though that would be ideal), but make sure your version is 4.20 or higher because we only need second generation OS fingerprints, not the old style produced by previous versions. You can determine the latest available version of Nmap by visiting *http://nmap.org/download.html*. If you upgrade, you might find that the identification has already been fixed.

Be absolutely certain you know what is running

Invalid "corrections" can corrupt the OS DB. If you aren't certain exactly what is running on the remote machine, please find out before submitting.

Generate a fingerprint

Run the command **nmap -O -sSU -F -T4 -d `<target>`**, where *`<target>`* is the misidentified system in question. Look at the OS detection results to ensure that the misidentification is still present.

If the Nmap output for the host OS results says `(JUST GUESSING)`, it is expected that results may be a little off. Don't submit a correction in this case.

Otherwise, the map command should have produced results including the line `OS fingerprint:`. Below that is the fingerprint (a series of lines which each start with `OS:`).

Check that OS detection works against other hosts

Try scanning a couple other hosts on the target network which you know have a different OS. If they aren't detected properly, maybe there is some network obstruction between the systems which is corrupting the packets.

If you have gotten this far and are still able to submit, good for you! Please submit the information at *http://insecure.org/cgi-bin/submit.cgi?corr-os*

8.7.2. When Nmap Fails to Find a Match and Prints a Fingerprint

When Nmap detects that OS detection conditions seem ideal and yet it finds no exact matches, it will print out a message like this:

```
No OS matches for host (If you know what OS is running on it, see
http://nmap.org/submit/ ).
TCP/IP fingerprint:
OS:SCAN(V=4.62%D=5/20%OT=21%CT=1%CU=42293%PV=Y%DS=1%G=Y%M=008077%TM=48336D6
OS:D%P=i686-pc-linux-gnu)SEQ(SP=11%GCD=1E848%ISR=A4%TI=I%II=I%SS=S%TS=A)OPS
OS:(O1=M5B4NW0NNSNNT11%O2=M578NW0NNSNNT11%O3=M280NW0NNT11%O4=M5B4NW0NNSNNT1
OS:1%O5=M218NW0NNSNNT11%O6=M109NNSNNT11)WIN(W1=21F0%W2=2088%W3=2258%W4=21F0
OS:%W5=20C0%W6=209D)ECN(R=Y%DF=N%T=40%W=2238%O=M5B4NW0NNS%CC=N%Q=)T1(R=Y%DF
OS:=N%T=40%S=O%A=S+%F=AS%RD=0%Q=)T2(R=N)T3(R=Y%DF=N%T=40%W=209D%S=O%A=S+%F=
OS:AS%O=M109NW0NNSNNT11%RD=0%Q=)T4(R=Y%DF=N%T=40%W=0%S=A%A=Z%F=R%O=%RD=0%Q=
OS:)T5(R=Y%DF=N%T=40%W=0%S=Z%A=S+%F=AR%O=%RD=0%Q=)T6(R=Y%DF=N%T=40%W=0%S=A%
OS:A=Z%F=R%O=%RD=0%Q=)T7(R=Y%DF=N%T=40%W=0%S=Z%A=S+%F=AR%O=%RD=0%Q=)U1(R=Y%
OS:DF=N%T=FF%TOS=0%IPL=38%UN=0%RIPL=G%RID=G%RIPCK=G%RUCK=G%RUL=G%RUD=G)IE(R
OS:=Y%DFI=N%T=FF%TOSI=Z%CD=S%SI=S%DLI=S)
```

Please consider submitting the fingerprint so that all Nmap users can benefit. It only takes a minute or two and it may mean you don't need to see that ugly message again when you scan the host with the next Nmap version! Simply visit the URL Nmap provides for instructions.

If Nmap finds no matches and yet prints no fingerprint, conditions were not ideal. Even if you obtain the fingerprint through debug mode or XML output, please don't submit it unless Nmap asks you to (as in the previous example).

8.7.3. Modifying the `nmap-os-db` Database Yourself

People often ask about integrating a fingerprint themselves rather than (or in addition to) submitting it to Nmap.Org. While we don't offer detailed instructions or scripts for this, it is certainly possible after you become intimately familiar with Section 8.5, "Understanding an Nmap Fingerprint" [191]. I hope this is useful for your purposes, but there is no need to send your own reference fingerprint creations to us. We can only integrate raw subject fingerprint submissions from the web form.

8.8. SOLUTION: Detect Rogue Wireless Access Points on an Enterprise Network

8.8.1. Problem

With the ubiquity of mobile devices and cheap commodity networking equipment, companies are increasingly finding that employees are extending their networks in undesirable ways. Among the most dangerous devices are 802.11 wireless access points (WAPs). Users may install a $20 WAP in their cubicle so they can work from the break room, without realizing (or caring) that they just opened the protected corporate network to potential attackers in the parking lot or nearby buildings.

Some WAP installations are even worse than those installed by naive users. Breaching a building's security is much riskier for an attacker than accessing corporate data from far away through a network. It carries the risk of being arrested on the spot. So attackers have been known to install compact WAPs so they can then intrude on the network at will from the relative safety of a car down the street. A WAP taped under a desk or otherwise hidden is unlikely to be noticed for a while.

While the focus of this solution is finding WAPs, the same strategy can be used to find just about anything. You might need to locate all Cisco routers to apply a new patch or Solaris boxes to determine whether you have enough systems to warrant paying for support.

One way to find unauthorized wireless devices is to sweep the area with a wireless sniffer such as Kismet[6] or NetStumbler[7]. Another approach is to scan the wired side with Nmap. Not surprisingly, this solution focuses exclusively on the latter approach. Each technique can miss certain WAPs, so the best approach is to do both and merge the results.

8.8.2. Solution

Scan your whole address space using the -A option. You can speed it up by limiting scanned ports to 1–85, 113, 443, and 8080–8100. Those should find both an open and closed port on most WAPs, which improves OS detection accuracy. If your network spans multiple ethernet segments, scan each segment from a designated machine on the same segment. This speeds up the scan (especially since you can do them in parallel), and also gives you the MAC address of each device. Scanning from the same segment also allows you to spot stealth devices. Even a WAP with all ports filtered will generally respond to an ARP request. Results should be saved in at least normal and XML formats, so you might as well use -oA. Consider all of the

---

[6] *http://www.kismetwireless.net/*
[7] *http://www.netstumbler.com/*

---

performance-enhancing options described in Chapter 6, *Optimizing Nmap Performance* [135]. A good and relatively safe start for performance options is `-T4 --min-hostgroup 50 --max-rtt-timeout 1000 --initial-rtt-timeout 300 --max-retries 3 --host-timeout 20m --max-scan-delay 1000`. Put this all together for a command like:

nmap -A -oA ~/nmap-logs/wapscan -p 1-85,113,443,8080-8100 -T4 --min-hostgroup 50 --max-rtt-timeout 1000 --initial-rtt-timeout 300 --max-retries 3 --host-timeout 20m --max-scan-delay 1000 `<target_network>`

When the scan completes, search for WAP characteristics. On a network of fewer than a couple hundred live hosts, your best bet is to look at each one individually. For larger networks, you will likely need to automate the task. Searching for individual characteristics can be done with grep, though a Perl script which analyzes the XML output is preferable. This is pretty easy thanks to existing modules, such as Nmap::Scanner and Nmap::Parser, for parsing Nmap XML output. See Section 13.7, "Manipulating XML Output with Perl" [352] for examples.

Once you determine a list of candidates, it is probably best to open the normal Nmap output file and examine each one to eliminate false positives. For example, a Linksys device may be flagged as a possible WAP even though it could be one of their plain switches without any wireless functionality.

Once you find the WAPs, it is time to track them down. This can usually be done by querying the switch they connect to for their physical ethernet port number.

8.8.3. WAP Characteristics

Now it is time to discuss the WAP characteristics to look for. Understanding these is useful for manual inspections or for modifying the WAP finder script to search for something else. You will probably see many of them immediately by looking at the scan of a typical WAP in Example 8.8.

Example 8.8. Scan results against a consumer WAP

```
nmap -A -v wap.nmap.org

Starting Nmap ( http://nmap.org )
Interesting ports on wap.nmap.org (192.168.0.6):
Not shown: 999 closed ports
PORT    STATE SERVICE VERSION
80/tcp open  http    Netgear MR-series WAP (MR814; Embedded HTTPD 1.00)
MAC Address: 00:09:5B:3F:7D:5E (Netgear)
Device type: WAP
Running: Compaq embedded, Netgear embedded
OS details: WAP: Compaq iPAQ Connection Point or Netgear MR814
Service Info: Device: WAP

Nmap done: 1 IP address (1 host up) scanned in 10.90 seconds
          Raw packets sent: 1703 (75.706KB) | Rcvd: 1686 (77.552KB)
```

This device shows many obvious clues to being a WAP (`Device type: WAP` is pretty blatant) and some more subtle ones. But WAPs aren't always so easy to discover. This section provides a list of WAP characteristics, starting with the most powerful and ending with heuristics that are long shots or more likely to produce false positives. Each characteristic listed is accompanied by an XPath[8] expression that shows where to find it in Nmap XML output. Since this is security related, I suggest trying all of them and removing false positives manually.

TCP/IP fingerprinting device type

As described in the section called "Device and OS classification (Class lines)" [196], every reference fingerprint has at least one classification (which includes device type) associated with it. Because WAPs are so controversial, we try to use that (or give two classifications) when multiple types would fit. So devices like the D-Link DI-624 wireless broadband router is classified as `WAP` rather than `switch` or `router`. The device type can be found in XML output using the XPath expression `/nmaprun/host/os/osclass/@type`. (That is, the `type` attribute of the `osclass` element of the `os` element of any of the `host` elements inside the root `nmaprun` element).

TCP/IP fingerprinting details

While devices with Wireless capability *should* be classified as device type `WAP`, it is worth searching the detailed OS description for terms such as `wireless` or `wap` just to be sure. The description is in `/nmaprun/host/os/osmatch/@name` in XML output.

Version detection device type

Version detection also tries to determine device types, but by fingerprinting the target's running services rather than its IP stack. Check whether the XML `devicetype` attribute located at `/nmaprun/host/ports/port/service/@devicetype` is `WAP`. To be completely safe, checking the `/nmaprun/host/ports/port/service/@extrainfo` field for the substrings `wap` or `wireless` is worthwhile.

Vendor (from MAC address, TCP/IP fingerprinting, and version detection)

Certain vendors specialize in producing the low-cost consumer networking devices which are most likely to covertly find their way onto office networks. Examples are Linksys, Netgear, Belkin, SMC, D-Link, Motorola, Trendnet, Zyxel, and Gateway. You can check for these vendors based on the MAC address lookup (which is at `/nmaprun/host/address/@vendor` in XML output), OS detection (`/nmaprun/host/os/osclass/@vendor` in XML output), or version detection (`/nmaprun/host/ports/port/service/@product` in XML output) results. Be sure to search for the vendor as a substring of the fields, since the field may contain incorporation type (e.g. Inc.) or other information.

This test may lead to many false positives. If you use a vendor heavily for authorized devices, such as putting Netgear NICs in your desktop machines, you may have to remove that vendor and rerun the script.

Hostname

It doesn't hurt to check hostnames (reverse DNS resolution) for terms such as `wap`, `wireless`, or `airport`. These can be found at `/nmaprun/host/hostnames/hostname/@name` in XML output. Non-administrative employees rarely change DNS names, but this can be useful for pen-testers, new administrators, and others who may be scanning a new network looking for authorized access points.

---

[8] *http://www.w3.org/TR/xpath*

Chapter 9. Nmap Scripting Engine

9.1. Introduction

The Nmap Scripting Engine (NSE) is one of Nmap's most powerful and flexible features. It allows users to write (and share) simple scripts to automate a wide variety of networking tasks. Those scripts are then executed in parallel with the speed and efficiency you expect from Nmap. Users can rely on the growing and diverse set of scripts distributed with Nmap, or write their own to meet custom needs.

We designed NSE to be versatile, with the following tasks in mind:

Network discovery

> This is Nmap's bread and butter. Examples include looking up whois data based on the target domain, querying ARIN, RIPE, or APNIC for the target IP to determine ownership, performing identd lookups on open ports, SNMP queries, and listing available NFS/SMB/RPC shares and services.

More sophisticated version detection

> The Nmap version detection system (Chapter 7, *Service and Application Version Detection* [145]) is able to recognize thousands of different services through its probe and regular expression signature based matching system, but it cannot recognize everything. For example, identifying the Skype v2 service requires two independent probes, which version detection isn't flexible enough to handle. Nmap could also recognize more SNMP services if it tried a few hundred different community names by brute force. Neither of these tasks are well suited to traditional Nmap version detection, but both are easily accomplished with NSE. For these reasons, version detection now calls NSE by default to handle some tricky services. This is described in Section 9.10, "Version Detection Using NSE" [251].

Vulnerability detection

> When a new vulnerability is discovered, you often want to scan your networks quickly to identify vulnerable systems before the bad guys do. While Nmap isn't a comprehensive vulnerability scanner, NSE is powerful enough to handle even demanding vulnerability checks. Many vulnerability detection scripts are already available and we plan to distribute more as they are written.

Backdoor detection

> Many attackers and some automated worms leave backdoors to enable later reentry. Some of these can be detected by Nmap's regular expression based version detection. For example, within hours of the MyDoom worm hitting the Internet, Jay Moran posted an Nmap version detection probe and signature so that others could quickly scan their networks for MyDoom infections. NSE is needed to reliably detect more complex worms and backdoors.

Vulnerability exploitation

> As a general scripting language, NSE can even be used to exploit vulnerabilities rather than just find them. The capability to add custom exploit scripts may be valuable for some people (particularly penetration testers), though we aren't planning to turn Nmap into an exploitation framework such as Metasploit[1].

---

[1] *http://www.metasploit.com*

9.1. Introduction

These listed items were our initial goals, and we expect Nmap users to come up with even more inventive uses for NSE.

Scripts are written in the embedded Lua programming language[2]. The language itself is well documented in the books *Programming in Lua, Second Edition* and *Lua 5.1 Reference Manual*. The reference manual is also freely available online[3], as is the first edition of *Programming in Lua*[4]. Given the availability of these excellent general Lua programming references, this document only covers aspects and extensions specific to Nmap's scripting engine.

NSE is activated with the `-sC` option (or `--script` if you wish to specify a custom set of scripts) and results are integrated into Nmap normal and XML output. Two types of scripts are supported: service and host scripts. Service scripts relate to a certain open port (service) on the target host, and any results they produce are included next to that port in the Nmap output port table. Host scripts, on the other hand, run no more than once against each target IP and produce results below the port table. Example 9.1 shows a typical script scan. Service scripts producing output in this example are `ssh-hostkey`, which provides the system's RSA and DSA SSH keys, and `rpcinfo`, which queries portmapper to enumerate available services. The only host script producing output in this example is `smb-os-discovery`, which collects a variety of information from SMB servers. Nmap discovered all of this information in a third of a second.

Example 9.1. Typical NSE output

```
# nmap -sC -p22,111,139 -T4 localhost

Starting Nmap ( http://nmap.org )
Interesting ports on flog (127.0.0.1):
PORT     STATE SERVICE
22/tcp   open  ssh
|  ssh-hostkey: 1024 b1:36:0d:3f:50:dc:13:96:b2:6e:34:39:0d:9b:1a:38 (DSA)
|_ 2048 77:d0:20:1c:44:1f:87:a0:30:aa:85:cf:e8:ca:4c:11 (RSA)
111/tcp  open  rpcbind
|  rpcinfo:
|  100000  2,3,4    111/udp   rpcbind
|  100024  1      56454/udp   status
|_ 100000  2,3,4    111/tcp   rpcbind
139/tcp  open  netbios-ssn

Host script results:
|  smb-os-discovery: Unix
|  LAN Manager: Samba 3.0.31-0.fc8
|_ Name: WORKGROUP

Nmap done: 1 IP address (1 host up) scanned in 0.33 seconds
```

9.2. Usage and Examples

While NSE has a complex implementation for efficiency, it is strikingly easy to use. Simply specify `-sC` to enable the most common scripts. Or specify the `--script` option to choose your own scripts to execute

[2] *http://www.lua.org/*
[3] *http://www.lua.org/manual/5.1/*
[4] *http://www.lua.org/pil/*

by providing categories, script file names, or the name of directories full of scripts you wish to execute. You can customize some scripts by providing arguments to them via the `--script-args` option. The two remaining options, `--script-trace` and `--script-updatedb`, are generally only used for script debugging and development. Script scanning is also included as part of the -A (aggressive scan) option.

9.2.1. Script Categories

NSE scripts define a list of categories they belong to. Currently defined categories are `auth`, `default`, `discovery`, `external`, `intrusive`, `malware`, `safe`, `version`, and `vuln`. Category names are not case sensitive. The following list describes each category.

`auth`
These scripts try to determine authentication credentials on the target system, often through a brute-force attack. Examples include `snmp-brute`, `http-auth`, and `ftp-anon`.

`default`
These scripts are the default set and are run when using the -sC or -A options rather than listing scripts with `--script`. This category can also be specified explicitly like any other using `--script=default`. Many factors are considered in deciding whether a script should be run by default:

Speed
A default scan must finish quickly, which excludes brute force authentication crackers, web spiders, and any other scripts which can take minutes or hours to scan a single service.

Usefulness
Default scans need to produce valuable and actionable information. If even the script author has trouble explaining why an average networking or security professional would find the output valuable, the script should not run by default. The script may still be worth including in Nmap so that administrators can run for those occasions when they do need the extra information.

Verbosity
Nmap output is used for a wide variety of purposes and needs to be readable and concise. A script which frequently produces pages full of output should not be added to the `default` category. When there is no important information to report, NSE scripts (particularly default ones) should return nothing. Checking for an obscure vulnerability may be OK by default as long as it only produces output when that vulnerability discovered.

Reliability
Many scripts use heuristics and fuzzy signature matching to reach conclusions about the target host or service. Examples include `sniffer-detect` and `sql-injection`. If the script is often wrong, it doesn't belong in the `default` category where it may confuse or mislead casual users. Users who specify a script or category directly are generally more advanced and likely know how the script works or at least where to find its documentation.

Intrusiveness
Some scripts are very intrusive because they use significant resources on the remote system, are likely to crash the system or service, or are likely to be perceived as an attack by the remote administrators. The more intrusive a script is, the less suitable it is for the `default` category.

Privacy

Some scripts, particularly those in the `external` category described later, divulge information to third parties by their very nature. For example, the `whois` script must divulge the target IP address to regional whois registries. We have also considered (and decided against) adding scripts which check target SSH and SSL key fingerprints against Internet weak key databases. The more privacy-invasive a script is, the less suitable it is for `default` category inclusion.

We don't have exact thresholds for each of these criteria, and many of them are subjective. All of these factors are considered together when making a decision whether to promote a script into the `default` category. A few default scripts are `identd-owners` (determines the username running remote services using identd), `http-auth` (obtains authentication scheme and realm of web sites requiring authentication), and `ftp-anon` (tests whether an FTP server allows anonymous access).

discovery

These scripts try to actively discover more about the network by querying public registries, SNMP-enabled devices, directory services, and the like. Examples include `html-title` (obtains the title of the root path of web sites), `smb-enum-shares` (enumerates Windows shares), and `snmp-sysdescr` (extracts system details via SNMP).

external

Scripts in this category may send data to a third-party database or other network resource. An example of this is `whois`, which makes a connection to whois servers to learn about the address of the target. There is always the possibility that operators of the third-party database will record anything you send to them, which in many cases will include your IP address and the address of the target. Most scripts involve traffic strictly between the scanning computer and the client; any that do not are placed in this category.

intrusive

These are scripts that cannot be classified in the `safe` category because the risks are too high that they will crash the target system, use up significant resources on the target host (such as bandwidth or CPU time), or otherwise be perceived as malicious by the target's system administrators. Examples are `http-open-proxy` (which attempts to use the target server as an HTTP proxy) and `snmp-brute` (which tries to guess a device's SNMP community string by sending common values such as `public`, `private`, and `cisco`).

malware

These scripts test whether the target platform is infected by malware or backdoors. Examples include `smtp-strangeport`, which watches for SMTP servers running on unusual port numbers, and `auth-spoof`, which detects identd spoofing daemons which provide a fake answer before even receiving a query. Both of these behaviors are commonly associated with malware infections.

safe

Scripts which weren't designed to crash services, use large amounts of network bandwidth or other resources, or exploit security holes are categorized as `safe`. These are less likely to offend remote administrators, though (as with all other Nmap features) we cannot guarantee that they won't ever cause adverse reactions. Most of these perform general network discovery. Examples are `ssh-hostkey` (retrieves an SSH host key) and `html-title` (grabs the title from a web page).

version

The scripts in this special category are an extension to the version detection feature and cannot be selected explicitly. They are selected to run only if version detection (-sV) was requested. Their output cannot be distinguished from version detection output and they do not produce service or host script results. Examples are `skypev2-version`, `pptp-version`, and `iax2-version`.

vuln

These scripts check for specific known vulnerabilities and generally only report results if they are found. Examples include `realvnc-auth-bypass` and `xampp-default-auth`.

9.2.2. Command-line Arguments

These are the five command line arguments specific to script-scanning:

-sC

Performs a script scan using the default set of scripts. It is equivalent to `--script=default`. Some of the scripts in this `default` category are considered intrusive and should not be run against a target network without permission.

--script <script-categories>|<directory>|<filename>|all

Runs a script scan (like -sC) using the comma-separated list of script categories, individual scripts, or directories containing scripts, rather than the default set. Nmap first tries to interpret the arguments as categories, then (if that fails) as files or directories. A script or directory of scripts may be specified as an absolute or relative path. Absolute paths are used as supplied. Relative paths are searched for in the following places until found: --datadir/; $NMAPDIR/; ~/.nmap/ (not searched on Windows); NMAPDATADIR/ or ./. A `scripts/` subdirectory is also tried in each of these.

If a directory is specified and found, Nmap loads all NSE scripts (any filenames ending with .nse) from that directory. Filenames without the nse extension are ignored. Nmap does not search recursively into subdirectories to find scripts. If individual file names are specified, the file extension does not have to be nse.

Nmap scripts are stored in a `scripts` subdirectory of the Nmap data directory by default (see Chapter 14, *Understanding and Customizing Nmap Data Files* [363]). For efficiency, scripts are indexed in a database stored in `scripts/script.db`. which lists the category or categories in which each script belongs. Give the argument `all` to execute all scripts in the Nmap script database.

Scripts are not run in a sandbox and thus could accidentally or maliciously damage your system or invade your privacy. Never run scripts from third parties unless you trust the authors or have carefully audited the scripts yourself.

--script-args

provides arguments to the scripts. See Section 9.2.3, "Arguments to Scripts" [210] for a detailed explanation.

--script-trace

This option is similar to --packet-trace, but works at the application level rather than packet by packet. If this option is specified, all incoming and outgoing communication performed by scripts is printed. The displayed information includes the communication protocol, source and target addresses,

---

and the transmitted data. If more than 5% of transmitted data is unprintable, hex dumps are given instead. Specifying `--packet-trace` enables script tracing too.

`--script-updatedb`

This option updates the script database found in `scripts/script.db` which is used by Nmap to determine the available default scripts and categories. It is only necessary to update the database if you have added or removed NSE scripts from the default `scripts` directory or if you have changed the categories of any script. This option is used by itself without arguments: **nmap --script-updatedb**.

Some other Nmap options have effects on script scans. The most prominent of these is `-sV`. A version scan automatically executes the scripts in the `version` category. The scripts in this category are slightly different than other scripts because their output blends in with the version scan results and they do not produce any script scan output.

Another option which affects the scripting engine is `-A`. The aggressive Nmap mode implies the `-sC` option.

9.2.3. Arguments to Scripts

Arguments may be passed to NSE scripts using the `--script-args` option. The script arguments are generally name-value pairs. They are provided to scripts as a Lua table named `args` inside `nmap.registry`. The argument names are keys for the corresponding values. The values can be either strings or tables. Subtables can be used to pass arguments to scripts with finer granularity, such as passing different usernames for different scripts. Here is a typical Nmap invocation with script arguments:

```
$ nmap -sC --script-args user=foo,pass=bar,whois={whodb=nofollow+ripe}
```

The aforementioned command results in this Lua table:

```
{user="foo",pass="bar",whois={whodb="nofollow+ripe"}}
```

You could therefore access the username (`foo`) inside your script with this statement:

```
local username = nmap.registry.args.user
```

Subtables used to override options for scripts are usually named after the script to ease retrieval.

9.2.4. Usage Examples

A simple script scan using the default set of scripts:

```
$ nmap -sC example.com
```

Executing a specific script with tracing enabled:

```
$ nmap --script=./showSSHVersion.nse --script-trace example.com
```

Execute all scripts in the `mycustomscripts` directory as well as all default scripts in the `safe` category:

```
$ nmap --script=mycustomscripts,safe example.com
```

9.3. Script Format

NSE scripts consist of two–five descriptive fields along with either a port or host rule defining when the script should be executed and an action block containing the actual script instructions. Values can be assigned to the descriptive fields just as you would assign any other Lua variables. Their names must be lowercase as shown in this section.

9.3.1. `description` Field

The `description` field describes what a script is testing for and any important notes the user should be aware of. Depending on script complexity, the description may vary from a few sentences to a few paragraphs. The first paragraph should be a brief synopsis of the script function suitable for stand-alone presentation to the user. Further paragraphs may provide much more script detail.

9.3.2. `categories` Field

The `categories` field defines one or more categories to which a script belongs (see Section 9.2.1, "Script Categories" [207]). The categories are case-insensitive and may be specified in any order. They are listed in an array-style Lua table as in this example:

```
categories = {"default", "discovery", "safe"}
```

9.3.3. `author` Field

The `author` field contains the script authors' names and contact information. If you are worried about spam, feel free to omit or obscure your email address, or give your home page URL instead. This optional field is not used by NSE, but gives script authors due credit or blame.

9.3.4. `license` Field

Nmap is a community project and we welcome all sorts of code contributions, including NSE scripts. So if you write a valuable script, don't keep it to yourself! The optional `license` field helps ensure that we have legal permission to distribute all the scripts which come with Nmap. All of those scripts currently use the standard Nmap license (described in Section 15.19.1, "Nmap Copyright and Licensing" [412]). They include the following line:

```
license = "Same as Nmap--See http://nmap.org/book/man-legal.html"
```

The Nmap license is similar to the GNU GPL. Script authors may use a BSD-style license (no advertising clause) instead if they prefer that.

9.3.5. `runlevel` Field

This optional field determines script execution order. When this section is absent, the run level defaults to 1.0. Scripts with a given `runlevel` execute after any with a lower `runlevel` and before any scripts with a higher `runlevel` against a single target machine. The order of scripts with the same `runlevel` is

---

undefined and they often run concurrently. One application of run levels is allowing scripts to depend on each other. If `script A` relies on some information gathered by `script B`, give B a lower run level than A. `Script B` can store information in the NSE registry for A to retrieve later. For information on the NSE registry, see Section 9.7.5, "The Registry" [245].

9.3.6. Port and Host Rules

Nmap uses the script rules to determine whether a script should be run against a target. A script contains either a *port rule*, which governs which ports of a target the scripts may run against, or a *host rule*, which specifies that the script should be run only once against a target IP and only if the given conditions are met. A rule is a Lua function that returns either `true` or `false`. The script *action* is only performed if its rule evaluates to `true`. Host rules accept a host table as their argument and may test, for example, the IP address or hostname of the target. A port rule accepts both host and port tables as arguments for any TCP or UDP port in the `open`, `open|filtered`, or `unfiltered` port states. Port rules generally test factors such as the port number, port state, or listening service name in deciding whether to run against a port. Example rules are shown in Section 9.8.2, "The Rule" [246].

9.3.7. Action

The action is the heart of an NSE script. It contains all of the instructions to be executed when the script's port or host rule triggers. It is a Lua function which accepts the same arguments as the rule and can return either `nil` or a string. If a string is returned by a service script, the string and script's filename are printed in the Nmap port table output. A string returned by a host script is printed below the port table. No output is produced if the script returns `nil`. For an example of an NSE action refer to Section 9.8.3, "The Mechanism" [247].

9.4. Script Language

The core of the Nmap Scripting Engine is an embeddable Lua interpreter. Lua is a lightweight language designed for extensibility. It offers a powerful and well documented API for interfacing with other software such as Nmap.

The second part of the Nmap Scripting Engine is the NSE Library, which connects Lua and Nmap. This layer handles issues such as initialization of the Lua interpreter, scheduling of parallel script execution, script retrieval and more. It is also the heart of the NSE network I/O framework and the exception handling mechanism. It also includes utility libraries to make scripts more powerful and convenient. The utility library modules and extensions are described in Section 9.6, "NSE Libraries" [236].

9.4.1. Lua Base Language

The Nmap scripting language is an embedded Lua[5] interpreter which was extended with libraries for interfacing with Nmap. The Nmap API is in the Lua namespace `nmap`. This means that all calls to resources provided by Nmap have an `nmap` prefix. `nmap.new_socket()`, for example, returns a new socket wrapper object. The Nmap library layer also takes care of initializing the Lua context, scheduling parallel scripts and collecting the output produced by completed scripts.

---

[5] *http://www.lua.org/*

During the planning stages, we considered several programming languages as the base for Nmap scripting. Another option was to implement a completely new programming language. Our criteria were strict: NSE had to be easy to use, small in size, compatible with the Nmap license, scalable, fast and parallelizable. Several previous efforts (by other projects) to design their own security auditing language from scratch resulted in awkward solutions, so we decided early not to follow that route. First the Guile Scheme interpreter was considered, but the preference drifted towards the Elk interpreter due to its more favorable license. But parallelizing Elk scripts would have been difficult. In addition, we expect that most Nmap users prefer procedural programming over functional languages such as Scheme. Larger interpreters such as Perl, Python, and Ruby are well-known and loved, but are difficult to embed efficiently. In the end, Lua excelled in all of our criteria. It is small, distributed under the liberal MIT open source license, has coroutines for efficient parallel script execution, was designed with embeddability in mind, has excellent documentation, and is actively developed by a large and committed community. Lua is now even embedded in other popular open source security tools including the Wireshark sniffer and Snort IDS.

9.5. NSE Scripts

This section lists (alphabetically) all NSE scripts packaged with Nmap at the time of this writing. It comes straight from the script source code thanks to the NSEDoc documentation system described in Section 9.9, "Writing Script Documentation (NSEDoc)" [248]. Of course no paper documentation can stay current with software developed as actively as NSE is. For the most comprehensive and up-to-date documentation, see the online NSE Documentation Portal at *http://nmap.org/nsedoc/*.

asn-query.nse

Categories: discovery, external

Maps IP addresses to autonomous system (AS) numbers.

The script works by sending DNS TXT queries to a DNS server which in turn queries a third-party service provided by Team Cymru (team-cymru.org) using an in-addr.arpa style zone set up especially for use by Nmap.

The responses to these queries contain both Origin and Peer ASNs and their descriptions, displayed along with the BGP Prefix and Country Code.

The script caches results to reduce the number of queries and should perform a single query for all scanned targets in a BGP Prefix present in Team Cymru's database.

Be aware that any targets against which this script is run will be sent to and potentially recorded by one or more DNS servers and Team Cymru. In addition your IP address will be sent along with the ASN to a DNS server (your default DNS server, or whichever one you specified with the dns script argument).

Script Arguments

dns
    The address of a recursive nameserver to use (optional).

Usage

```
nmap --script asn-query.nse [--script-args dns=<DNS server>] <target>
```

Sample Output

```
Host script results:
|  asn-query:
|  BGP: 64.13.128.0/21 | Country: US
|    Origin AS: 10565 SVCOLO-AS - Silicon Valley Colocation, Inc.
|       Peer AS: 3561 6461
|  BGP: 64.13.128.0/18 | Country: US
|    Origin AS: 10565 SVCOLO-AS - Silicon Valley Colocation, Inc.
|_      Peer AS: 174 2914 6461
```

auth-owners.nse

Categories: default, safe

Attempts to find the owner of an open TCP port by querying an auth (identd - port 113) daemon which must also be open on the target system.

Sample Output

```
21/tcp   open     ftp          ProFTPD 1.3.1
|_ auth-owners: nobody
22/tcp   open     ssh          OpenSSH 4.3p2 Debian 9etch2 (protocol 2.0)
|_ auth-owners: root
25/tcp   open     smtp         Postfix smtpd
|_ auth-owners: postfix
80/tcp   open     http         Apache httpd 2.0.61 ((Unix) PHP/4.4.7 ...)
|_ auth-owners: dhapache
113/tcp  open     auth?
|_ auth-owners: nobody
587/tcp  open     submission Postfix smtpd
|_ auth-owners: postfix
5666/tcp open     unknown
|_ auth-owners: root
```

auth-spoof.nse

Categories: malware

Checks for an identd (auth) server which is spoofing its replies.

Tests whether an identd (auth) server responds with an answer before we even send the query. This sort of identd spoofing can be a sign of malware infection though it can also be used for legitimate privacy reasons.

daytime.nse

Categories: discovery

Retrieves the day and time from the UDP Daytime service.

dns-random-srcport.nse

Categories: external, intrusive

Checks a DNS server for the predictable-port recursion vulnerability. Predictable source ports can make a DNS server vulnerable to cache poisoning attacks (see CVE-2008-1447).

The script works by querying porttest.dns-oarc.net. Be aware that any targets against which this script is run will be sent to and potentially recorded by one or more DNS servers and the porttest server. In addition your IP address will be sent along with the porttest query to the DNS server running on the target.

dns-random-txid.nse

Categories: external, intrusive

Checks a DNS server for the predictable-TXID DNS recursion vulnerability. Predictable TXID values can make a DNS server vulnerable to cache poisoning attacks (see CVE-2008-1447).

The script works by querying txidtest.dns-oarc.net. Be aware that any targets against which this script is run will be sent to and potentially recorded by one or more DNS servers and the txidtest server. In addition your IP address will be sent along with the txidtest query to the DNS server running on the target.

dns-recursion.nse

Categories: default, intrusive

Checks if a DNS server allows queries for third-party names.

It is expected that recursion will be enabled on your own internal nameservers.

dns-zone-transfer.nse

Categories: default, intrusive, discovery

Requests a zone transfer (AXFR) from a DNS server.

The script sends an AXFR query to a DNS server. The domain to query is determined by examining the name given on the command line, the DNS server's hostname, or it can be specified with the `dnszonetransfer.domain` script argument. If the query is successful all domains and domain types are returned along with common type specific data (SOA/MX/NS/PTR/A).

If we don't have the "true" hostname for the DNS server we cannot determine a likely zone to perform the transfer on.

Useful resources

- DNS for rocket scientists: *http://www.zytrax.com/books/dns/*
- How the AXFR protocol works: *http://cr.yp.to/djbdns/axfr-notes.html*

Script Arguments

`dnszonetransfer.domain`
   Domain to transfer.

Usage

```
nmap --script dns-zone-transfer.nse \
    --script-args 'dnszonetransfer={domain=<domain>}'
```

Sample Output

```
53/tcp    open      domain
|  dns-zone-transfer:
|  foo.com.              SOA    ns2.foo.com. piou.foo.com.
|  foo.com.              TXT
|  foo.com.              NS     ns1.foo.com.
|  foo.com.              NS     ns2.foo.com.
|  foo.com.              NS     ns3.foo.com.
|  foo.com.              A      127.0.0.1
|  foo.com.              MX     mail.foo.com.
|  anansie.foo.com.      A      127.0.0.2
|  dhalgren.foo.com.     A      127.0.0.3
|  drupal.foo.com.       CNAME
|  goodman.foo.com.      A      127.0.0.4 i
|  goodman.foo.com.      MX     mail.foo.com.
|  isaac.foo.com.        A      127.0.0.5
|  julie.foo.com.        A      127.0.0.6
|  mail.foo.com.         A      127.0.0.7
|  ns1.foo.com.          A      127.0.0.7
|  ns2.foo.com.          A      127.0.0.8
|  ns3.foo.com.          A      127.0.0.9
|  stubing.foo.com.      A      127.0.0.10
|  vicki.foo.com.        A      127.0.0.11
|  votetrust.foo.com.    CNAME
|  www.foo.com.          CNAME
|_ foo.com.              SOA    ns2.foo.com. piou.foo.com.
```

finger.nse

Categories: default, discovery

Attempts to retrieve a list of usernames using the finger service.

ftp-anon.nse

Categories: default, auth, safe

Checks if an FTP server allows anonymous logins.

Sample Output

```
|_ ftp-anon: Anonymous FTP login allowed
```

ftp-bounce.nse

Categories: default, intrusive

Checks to see if an FTP server allows port scanning using the FTP bounce method.

html-title.nse

Categories: default, discovery, safe

Shows the title of the default page of a web server.

The script will follow no more than one HTTP redirect, and only if the redirection leads to the same host. The script may send a DNS query to determine whether the host the redirect leads to has the same IP address as the original target.

Sample Output

```
Interesting ports on scanme.nmap.org (64.13.134.52):
PORT   STATE SERVICE
80/tcp open  http
|_ html-title.nse: Go ahead and ScanMe!
```

http-auth.nse

Categories: default, auth, intrusive

Retrieves the authentication scheme and realm of a web service that requires authentication.

Sample Output

```
80/tcp open  http
|  http-auth: HTTP Service requires authentication
|    Auth type: Basic, realm = Password Required
|_   HTTP server may accept admin:admin combination for Basic authentication
```

http-open-proxy.nse

Categories: default, discovery, external, intrusive

Checks if an HTTP proxy is open.

The script attempts to connect to www.google.com through the (possible) proxy and checks for a `Server: gws` header field in the response.

If the target is an open proxy, this script causes the target to retrieve a web page from www.google.com.

http-passwd.nse

Categories: intrusive, vuln

Checks if a web server is vulnerable to directory traversal by attempting to retrieve /etc/passwd using various traversal methods such as requesting ../../../../etc/passwd.

http-trace.nse

Categories: discovery

Sends an HTTP TRACE request and shows header fields that were modified in the response.

Sample Output

```
80/tcp open   http
|  http-trace: Response differs from request.  First 5 additional lines:
|  Cookie: UID=d4287aa38d02f409841b4e0c0050c131...
|  Country: us
|  Ip_is_advertise_combined: yes
|  Ip_conntype-Confidence: -1
|_ Ip_line_speed: medium
```

iax2-version.nse

Categories: version

Detects the UDP IAX2 service.

The script sends an Inter-Asterisk eXchange (IAX) Revision 2 Control Frame POKE request and checks for a proper response. This protocol is used to enable VoIP connections between servers as well as client-server communication.

irc-info.nse

Categories: default, discovery

Gathers information from an IRC server.

It uses STATS, LUSERS, and other queries to obtain this information.

Sample Output

```
6665/tcp open     irc
|  irc-info: Server: target.example.org
|  Version: hyperion-1.0.2b(381). target.example.org
|  Lservers/Lusers: 0/4204
|  Uptime: 106 days, 2:46:30
|  Source host: source.example.org
|_ Source ident: OK n=nmap
```

ms-sql-info.nse

Categories: default, discovery, intrusive

Attempts to extract information from Microsoft SQL Server instances.

mysql-info.nse

Categories: default, discovery, safe

Connects to a MySQL server and prints information such as the protocol and version numbers, thread ID, status, capabilities, and the password salt.

If service detection is performed and the server appears to be blocking our host or is blocked because of too many connections, then this script isn't run (see the portrule).

Sample Output

```
3306/tcp open  mysql
|  mysql-info: Protocol: 10
|  Version: 5.0.51a-3ubuntu5.1
|  Thread ID: 7
|  Some Capabilities: Connect with DB, Transactions, Secure Connection
|  Status: Autocommit
|_ Salt: bYyt\NQ/4V6IN+*3`imj
```

nbstat.nse

Categories: default, discovery, safe

Attempts to retrieve the target's NetBIOS names and MAC address.

By default, the script displays the name of the computer and the logged-in user; if the verbosity is turned up, it displays all names the system thinks it owns.

Usage

```
sudo nmap -sU --script nbstat.nse -p137 <host>
```

Sample Output

```
(no verbose)
|_ nbstat: NetBIOS name: TST, NetBIOS user: RON, NetBIOS MAC: 00:0c:29:f9:d9:28

(verbose)
|  nbstat: NetBIOS name: TST, NetBIOS user: RON, NetBIOS MAC: 00:0c:29:f9:d9:28
|  Name: TST<00>            Flags: <unique><active>
|  Name: TST<20>            Flags: <unique><active>
|  Name: WORKGROUP<00>      Flags: <group><active>
|  Name: TST<03>            Flags: <unique><active>
|  Name: WORKGROUP<1e>      Flags: <group><active>
|  Name: RON<03>            Flags: <unique><active>
|  Name: WORKGROUP<1d>      Flags: <unique><active>
|_ Name: \x01\x02__MSBROWSE__\x02<01>  Flags: <group><active>
```

pop3-brute.nse

Categories: intrusive, auth

Tries to log into a POP3 account by guessing usernames and passwords.

pop3-capabilities.nse

Categories: default

Retrieves POP3 email server capabilities.

Sample Output

```
110/tcp open   pop3
|_ pop3-capabilities: USER CAPA RESP-CODES UIDL PIPELINING STLS TOP SASL(PLAIN)
```

pptp-version.nse

Categories: version

Attempts to extract system information from the point-to-point tunneling protocol (PPTP) service.

realvnc-auth-bypass.nse

Categories: default, vuln

Checks if a VNC server is vulnerable to the RealVNC authentication bypass (CVE-2006-2369).

robots.txt.nse

Categories: default, discovery, safe

Checks for disallowed entries in robots.txt.

The higher the verbosity or debug level, the more disallowed entries are shown.

Sample Output

```
80/tcp  open    http    syn-ack
|   robots.txt: has 156 disallowed entries (40 shown)
|   /news?output=xhtml& /search /groups /images /catalogs
|   /catalogues /news /nwshp /news?btcid=*& /news?btaid=*&
|   /setnewsprefs? /index.html? /? /addurl/image? /pagead/ /relpage/
|   /relcontent /sorry/ /imgres /keyword/ /u/ /univ/ /cobrand /custom
|   /advanced_group_search /googlesite /preferences /setprefs /swr /url /default
|   /m? /m/? /m/lcb /m/news? /m/setnewsprefs? /m/search? /wml?
|_ /wml/? /wml/search?
```

rpcinfo.nse

Categories: default, safe, discovery

Connects to portmapper and fetches a list of all registered programs.

Sample Output

```
111/tcp open   rpcbind
|  rpcinfo:
|  100000  2         111/udp  rpcbind
|  100005  1,2,3     705/udp  mountd
|  100003  2,3,4    2049/udp  nfs
|  100024  1       32769/udp  status
|  100021  1,3,4   32769/udp  nlockmgr
|  100000  2         111/tcp  rpcbind
|  100005  1,2,3     706/tcp  mountd
|  100003  2,3,4    2049/tcp  nfs
|  100024  1       50468/tcp  status
|_ 100021  1,3,4   50468/tcp  nlockmgr
```

skypev2-version.nse

Categories: version

Detects the Skype version 2 service.

smb-check-vulns.nse

Categories: intrusive

Checks if a host is vulnerable to MS08-067, a Windows RPC vulnerability that can allow remote code execution. This script is intended to check for more vulnerabilities in the future.

Checking for MS08-067 is very dangerous, as the check is likely to crash systems. On a fairly wide scan conducted by Brandon Enright, we determined that on average, a vulnerable system is more likely to crash than to survive the check. Out of 82 vulnerable systems, 52 crashed. As such, great care should be taken when using this check.

You have the option to supply a username and password, but it shouldn't be necessary for a default configuration.

Script Arguments

smb*
   This script supports the smbusername, smbpassword, smbhash, smbguest, and smbtype script arguments of the smb module.

9.5. NSE Scripts
221

Usage

```
nmap --script smb-check-vulns.nse -p445 <host>
sudo nmap -sU -sS --script smb-check-vulns.nse -p U:137,T:139 <host>
```

Sample Output

```
Host script results:
|_ smb-check-vulns: This host is vulnerable to MS08-067
```

`smb-enum-domains.nse`

Categories: discovery, intrusive

Attempts to enumerate domains on a system, along with their policies. This will likely only work without credentials against Windows 2000.

After the initial `bind` to SAMR, the sequence of calls is:

* `Connect4`: get a connect_handle
* `EnumDomains`: get a list of the domains (stop here if you just want the names).
* `QueryDomain`: get the SID for the domain.
* `OpenDomain`: get a handle for each domain.
* `QueryDomainInfo2`: get the domain information.
* `QueryDomainUsers`: get a list of the users in the domain.

Script Arguments

smb*

This script supports the `smbusername`, `smbpassword`, `smbhash`, `smbguest`, and `smbtype` script arguments of the `smb` module.

Usage

```
nmap --script smb-enum-domains.nse -p445 <host>
sudo nmap -sU -sS --script smb-enum-domains.nse -p U:137,T:139 <host>
```

Sample Output

```
Host script results:
|   smb-enum-domains:
|   Domain: LOCALSYSTEM
|    |_ SID: S-1-5-21-2956463495-2656032972-1271678565
|    |_ Users: Administrator, Guest, SUPPORT_388945a0
|    |_ Creation time: 2007-11-26 15:24:04
|    |_ Passwords: min length: 11 characters; min age: 5 days; max age: 63 days
|    |_ Password lockout: 3 attempts in under 15 minutes will lock the account u⌐
ntil manually reset
|    |_ Password history : 5 passwords
|    |_ Password properties:
|       |_  Password complexity requirements exist
|       |_  Administrator account cannot be locked out
|   Domain: Builtin
```

```
|      |_ SID: S-1-5-32
|      |_ Users:
|      |_ Creation time: 2007-11-26 15:24:04
|      |_ Passwords: min length: n/a; min age: n/a; max age: 42 days
|      |_ Account lockout disabled
|      |_ Password properties:
|         |_ Password complexity requirements do not exist
|_        |_ Administrator account cannot be locked out
```

smb-enum-sessions.nse

Categories: discovery, intrusive

Enumerates the users logged into a system either locally, through a remote desktop client (terminal services), or through a SMB share.

Enumerating the local and terminal services users is done by reading the remote registry. Keys under HKEY_USERS are SIDs that represent the currently logged in users, and those SIDs can be converted to proper names by using the LsaLookupSids function. Doing this requires any access higher than anonymous. Guests, users, or administrators are all able to perform this request on the operating systems I (Ron Bowes) tested.

Enumerating SMB connections is done using the srvsvc.netsessenum function, which returns who's logged in, when they logged in, and how long they've been idle for. Unfortunately, I couldn't find a way to get the user's domain with this function, so the domain isn't printed. The level of access required for this varies between Windows versions, but in Windows 2000 anybody (including the anonymous account) can access this, and in Windows 2003 a user or administrator account is required.

Since both of these are related to users being logged into the server, it seemed logical to combine them into a single script.

I learned the idea and technique for this from sysinternals' tool, PsLoggedOn.exe. I use similar function calls to what they use, so thanks go out to them. Thanks also to Matt, for giving me the idea to write this one.

Script Arguments

smb*

This script supports the smbusername, smbpassword, smbhash, smbguest, and smbtype script arguments of the smb module.

Usage

```
nmap --script smb-enum-sessions.nse -p445 <host>
sudo nmap -sU -sS --script smb-enum-sessions.nse -p U:137,T:139 <host>
```

Sample Output

```
Host script results:
|   smb-enum-sessions:
|   Users logged in:
|   |_ TESTBOX\Administrator since 2008-10-21 08:17:14
|   |_ DOMAIN\rbowes since 2008-10-20 09:03:23
```

```
| Active SMB Sessions:
|_ |_ ADMINISTRATOR is connected from 10.100.254.138 for [just logged in, it's ⌐
probably you], idle for [not idle]
```

smb-enum-shares.nse

Categories: discovery, intrusive

Attempts to list shares using the `srvsvc.NetShareEnumAll` MSRPC function, then retrieve more information about each share using `srvsvc.NetShareGetInfo`.

Running `NetShareEnumAll` will work anonymously on Windows 2000, and requires a user-level account on any other Windows version. Calling `NetShareGetInfo` requires an administrator account on every version of Windows I (Ron Bowes) tested.

Although `NetShareEnumAll` is restricted on certain systems, actually connecting to a share to check if it exists will always work. So, if `NetShareEnumAll` fails, a list of common shares will be attempted.

After a list of shares is found, whether or not it's complete, we attempt to connect to each of them anonymously, which lets us divide them into the classes "anonymous" and "restricted."

When possible, once the list of shares is determined, `NetShareGetInfo` is called to get additional information on the share. Odds are this will fail, unless we're doing an authenticated test.

Script Arguments

smb*
> This script supports the `smbusername`, `smbpassword`, `smbhash`, `smbguest`, and `smbtype` script arguments of the `smb` module.

Usage

```
nmap --script smb-enum-shares.nse -p445 <host>
sudo nmap -sU -sS --script smb-enum-shares.nse -p U:137,T:139 <host>
```

Sample Output

```
Standard:
|   smb-enum-shares:
|   Anonymous shares: IPC$
|_  Restricted shares: F$, ADMIN$, C$

Verbose:
Host script results:
|   smb-enum-shares:
|   Anonymous shares:
|      IPC$
|      |_ Type: STYPE_IPC_HIDDEN
|      |_ Comment: Remote IPC
|      |_ Users: 1, Max: <unlimited>
|      |_ Path:
|      test
|      |_ Type: STYPE_DISKTREE
```

```
|    |_ Comment: This is a test share, with a maximum of 7 users
|    |_ Users: 0, Max: 7
|    |_ Path: C:\Documents and Settings\Ron\Desktop\test
| Restricted shares:
|   ADMIN$
|    |_ Type: STYPE_DISKTREE_HIDDEN
|    |_ Comment: Remote Admin
|    |_ Users: 0, Max: <unlimited>
|    |_ Path: C:\WINNT
|   C$
|    |_ Type: STYPE_DISKTREE_HIDDEN
|    |_ Comment: Default share
|    |_ Users: 0, Max: <unlimited>
|_   |_ Path: C:\
```

smb-enum-users.nse

Categories: discovery, intrusive

Attempts to enumerate the users on a remote Windows system, with as much information as possible, through a variety of techniques (over SMB and MSRPC, which uses port 445 or 139). Some functions in SAMR are used to enumerate users, and some brute-force guessing using LSA functions is attempted.

One technique used is calling the `QueryDisplayInfo` function in the SAMR library. If this succeeds, it will return a detailed list of users. This can be done anonymously against Windows 2000, and with a user-level account on other Windows versions (but not with a guest-level account).

To perform this test, the following functions are used:

- `Bind`: bind to the SAMR service.
- `Connect4`: get a connect_handle.
- `EnumDomains`: get a list of the domains.
- `QueryDomain`: get the sid for the domain.
- `OpenDomain`: get a handle for each domain.
- `QueryDisplayInfo`: get the list of users in the domain.
- `Close`: Close the domain handle.
- `Close`: Close the connect handle.

The advantage of this technique is that a lot of details are returned, including the full name and description; the disadvantage is that it requires a user-level account on every system except for Windows 2000. Additionally, it only pulls actual user accounts, not groups or aliases.

Regardless of whether this succeeds, a second technique is used to pull user accounts, called LSA bruteforcing. LSA bruteforcing can be done anonymously against Windows 2000, and requires a guest account or better on other systems. It has the advantage of running with less permission, and will also find more account types (i.e., groups, aliases, etc.). The disadvantages is that it returns less information, and that, because it's a brute-force guess, it's possible to miss accounts.

This isn't a brute-force technique in the common sense, however: it's a brute-forcing of users' RIDs. A user's RID is a value (generally 500, 501, or 1000+) that uniquely identifies a user on a domain or system. An LSA

---

function is exposed which lets us convert the RID (say, 1000) to the username (say, "Ron"). So, the technique will essentially try converting 1000 to a name, then 1001, 1002, etc., until we think we're done.

Users are broken into groups of five RIDs, then checked individually (checking too many at once causes problems). We continue checking until we reach 1100, and get an empty group. This probably isn't the most effective way, but it seems to work. It might be a good idea to modify this, in the future, with some more intelligence. I (Ron Bowes) performed a test on an old server with a lot of accounts, and I got these results: 500, 501, 1000, 1030, 1031, 1053, 1054, 1055, 1056, 1057, 1058, 1059, 1060, 1061, 1062, 1063, 1064, 1065, 1066, 1067, 1070, 1075, 1081, 1088, 1090. The jump from 1000 to 1030 is quite large and can easily result in missing accounts, in an automated check.

Before attempting this conversion, the SID of the server has to be determined. The SID is determined by doing the reverse operation, that is, converting a name into a RID. The name is determined by looking up any name present on the system. We try:

- The computer name and domain name, returned in SMB_COM_NEGOTIATE;
- An nbstat query to get the server name and the user currently logged in; and
- Some common names: "administrator", "guest", and "test".

In theory, the computer name should be sufficient for this to always work, and so far has in my tests, but I included the rest of the names for good measure.

The names and details from both of these techniques are merged and displayed. If the output is verbose, then extra details are shown. The output is ordered alphabetically.

Credit goes out to the enum.exe, sid2user.exe, and user2sid.exe programs, the code I wrote for this is largely based on the techniques used by them.

Script Arguments

smb*

> This script supports the smbusername, smbpassword, smbhash, smbguest, and smbtype script arguments of the smb module.

Usage

```
nmap --script smb-enum-users.nse -p445 <host>
sudo nmap -sU -sS --script smb-enum-users.nse -p U:137,T:139 <host>
```

Sample Output

```
Host script results:
|   smb-enum-users:
|_  TESTBOX\Administrator, EXTERNAL\DnsAdmins, TESTBOX\Guest, EXTERNAL\HelpServi ⌐
cesGroup, EXTERNAL\PARTNERS$, TESTBOX\SUPPORT_388945a0

Host script results:
|   smb-enum-users:
|   Administrator
|     |_ Type: User
|     |_ Domain: LOCALSYSTEM
|     |_ Full name: Built-in account for administering the computer/domain
```

```
|     |_ Flags: Normal account, Password doesn't expire
|   DnsAdmins
|     |_ Type: Alias
|     |_ Domain: EXTRANET
|   EventViewer
|     |_ Type: User
|     |_ Domain: SHARED
|   ProxyUsers
|     |_ Type: Group
|     |_ Domain: EXTRANET
|   ComputerAccounts
|     |_ Type: Group
|     |_ Domain: EXTRANET
|   Helpdesk
|     |_ Type: Group
|     |_ Domain: EXTRANET
|   Guest
|     |_ Type: User
|     |_ Domain: LOCALSYSTEM
|     |_ Full name: Built-in account for guest access to the computer/domain
|     |_ Flags: Normal account, Disabled, Password not required, Password doesn' ⏎
t expire
|   Staff
|     |_ Type: Alias
|     |_ Domain: LOCALSYSTEM
|   Students
|     |_ Type: Alias
|_    |_ Domain: LOCALSYSTEM
```

smb-os-discovery.nse

Categories: default, discovery, safe

Attempts to determine the operating system over the SMB protocol (ports 445 and 139).

Although the standard smb* script arguments can be used, they likely won't change the outcome in any meaningful way.

Script Arguments

smb*

    This script supports the smbusername, smbpassword, smbhash, smbguest, and smbtype script arguments of the smb module.

Usage

```
nmap --script smb-os-discovery.nse -p445 127.0.0.1
sudo nmap -sU -sS --script smb-os-discovery.nse -p U:137,T:139 127.0.0.1
```

Sample Output

```
|   smb-os-discovery: Windows 2000
|   LAN Manager: Windows 2000 LAN Manager
```

```
|  Name: WORKGROUP\TEST1
|_ System time: 2008-09-09 20:55:55 UTC-5
```

smb-security-mode.nse

Categories: discovery, safe

Returns information about the SMB security level determined by SMB.

Here is how to interpret the output:

User-level authentication: Each user has a separate username/password that is used to log into the system. This is the default setup of pretty much everything these days.

Share-level authentication: The anonymous account should be used to log in, then the password is given (in plaintext) when a share is accessed. All users who have access to the share use this password. This was the original way of doing things, but isn't commonly seen, now. If a server uses share-level security, it is vulnerable to sniffing.

Challenge/response passwords supported: If enabled, the server can accept any type of password:

* Plaintext
* LM and NTLM
* LMv2 and NTLMv2

If it isn't set, the server can only accept plaintext passwords. Most servers are configured to use challenge/response these days. If a server is configured to accept plaintext passwords, it is vulnerable to sniffing. LM and NTLM are fairly secure, although there are some brute-force attacks against them.

Message signing: If required, all messages between the client and server must be signed by a shared key, derived from the password and the server challenge. If supported and not required, message signing is negotiated between clients and servers and used if both support and request it. By default, Windows clients don't sign messages, so if message signing isn't required by the server, messages probably won't be signed; additionally, if performing a man-in-the-middle attack, an attacker can negotiate no message signing. If message signing isn't required, the server is vulnerable to man-in-the-middle attacks.

This script will allow you to use the smb* script arguments (to set the username and password, etc.), but it probably won't ever require them.

Script Arguments

smb*
> This script supports the smbusername, smbpassword, smbhash, smbguest, and smbtype script arguments of the smb module.

Usage

```
nmap --script smb-security-mode.nse -p445 127.0.0.1
sudo nmap -sU -sS --script smb-security-mode.nse -p U:137,T:139 127.0.0.1
```

Sample Output

```
|  smb-security-mode: User-level authentication
|  smb-security-mode: Challenge/response passwords supported
|_ smb-security-mode: Message signing supported
```

smb-server-stats.nse

Categories: discovery, intrusive

Attempts to grab the server's statistics over SMB and MSRPC, which uses TCP ports 445 or 139.

An administrator account is required to pull these statistics on most versions of Windows, and Vista doesn't seem to let even the administrator account pull them.

Some of the numbers returned here don't feel right to me, but they're definitely the numbers that Windows returns. Take the values here with a grain of salt.

Script Arguments

smb*

> This script supports the smbusername, smbpassword, smbhash, smbguest, and smbtype script arguments of the smb module.

Usage

```
nmap --script smb-server-stats.nse -p445 <host>
sudo nmap -sU -sS --script smb-server-stats.nse -p U:137,T:139 <host>
```

Sample Output

```
Host script results:
|  smb-server-stats:
|  Server statistics collected since 2008-10-17 09:32:41 (4d0h24m29s):
|  |_ Traffic 133467 bytes (0.38b/s) sent, 167696 bytes (0.48b/s) received
|  |_ Failed logins: 5
|  |_ Permission errors: 1, System errors: 0
|  |_ Print jobs spooled: 0
|_ |_ Files opened (including pipes): 18
```

smb-system-info.nse

Categories: discovery, intrusive

Pulls back information about the remote system from the registry. Getting all of the information requires an administrative account, although a user account will still get a lot of it. Guest probably won't get any, nor will anonymous. This goes for all operating systems, including Windows 2000.

Windows Vista doesn't appear to have the WINREG binding (or it's different and I don't know it), so this doesn't support Vista at all.

Script Arguments

`smb*`

This script supports the `smbusername`, `smbpassword`, `smbhash`, `smbguest`, and `smbtype` script arguments of the `smb` module.

Usage

```
nmap --script smb-system-info.nse -p445 <host>
sudo nmap -sU -sS --script smb-system-info.nse -p U:137,T:139 <host>
```

Sample Output

```
Host script results:
|  smb-system-info:
|  OS Details
|  |_ Microsoft Windows Server 2003 Service Pack 2 (ServerNT 5.2 build 3790)
|  |_ Installed on 2007-11-26 23:40:40
|  |_ Registered to IPC (organization: MYCOMPANY)
|  |_ Path: %SystemRoot%\system32;%SystemRoot%;%SystemRoot%\System32\Wbem;C:\Pr
ogram Files\Microsoft SQL Server\90\Tools\binn\;C:\Program Files\IBM\Rational A
ppScan\
|  |_ Systemroot: C:\WINDOWS
|  |_ Page files: C:\pagefile.sys 2046 4092 (cleared at shutdown => 0)
|  Hardware
|  |_ CPU 0: Intel(R) Xeon(TM) CPU 2.80GHz [2780mhz GenuineIntel]
|  |_ Identifier 0: x86 Family 15 Model 2 Stepping 9
|  |_ CPU 1: Intel(R) Xeon(TM) CPU 2.80GHz [2780mhz GenuineIntel]
|  |_ Identifier 1: x86 Family 15 Model 2 Stepping 9
|  |_ CPU 2: Intel(R) Xeon(TM) CPU 2.80GHz [2780mhz GenuineIntel]
|  |_ Identifier 2: x86 Family 15 Model 2 Stepping 9
|  |_ CPU 3: Intel(R) Xeon(TM) CPU 2.80GHz [2780mhz GenuineIntel]
|  |_ Identifier 3: x86 Family 15 Model 2 Stepping 9
|  |_ Video driver: RAGE XL PCI Family (Microsoft Corporation)
|  Browsers
|  |_ Internet Explorer 7.0000
|_ |_ Firefox 3.0.3 (en-US)
```

smtp-commands.nse

Categories: default, discovery, safe

Attempts to use EHLO and HELP to gather the Extended commands supported by an SMTP server.

Sample Output

```
25/tcp open smtp
|  smtp-commands: EHLO uninvited.example.net Hello root at localhost [127.0.0.1
], SIZE 52428800, PIPELINING, HELP
|_ HELP Commands supported: AUTH HELO EHLO MAIL RCPT DATA NOOP QUIT RSET HELP
```

smtp-open-relay.nse

Categories: demo

Checks if an SMTP server is an open relay.

smtp-strangeport.nse

Categories: malware

Checks if SMTP is running on a non-standard port.

This may indicate that crackers or script kiddies have set up a backdoor on the system to send spam or control the machine.

Sample Output

```
22/tcp   open    smtp
|_ smtp-strangeport: Mail server on unusual port: possible malware
```

sniffer-detect.nse

Categories: discovery

Checks if a target on a local Ethernet has its network card in promiscuous mode.

The techniques used are described at *http://www.securityfriday.com/promiscuous_detection_01.pdf*.

Sample Output

```
Host script results:
|_ sniffer-detect: Likely in promiscuous mode (tests: "11111111")
```

snmp-brute.nse

Categories: intrusive, auth

Attempts to find an SNMP community string by brute force guessing.

snmp-sysdescr.nse

Categories: default, discovery, safe

Attempts to extract system information from an SNMP version 1 service.

Sample Output

```
|  snmp-sysdescr: HP ETHERNET MULTI-ENVIRONMENT,ROM A.25.80,JETDIRECT,JD117,EEP ↵
ROM V.28.22,CIDATE 08/09/2006
|_   System uptime: 28 days, 17:18:59 (248153900 timeticks)
```

sql-injection.nse

Categories: intrusive, vuln

Spiders an HTTP server looking for URLs containing queries vulnerable to an SQL injection attack.

The script spiders an HTTP server looking for URLs containing queries. It then proceeds to combine crafted SQL commands with susceptible URLs in order to obtain errors. The errors are analysed to see if the URL is vulnerable to attack. This uses the most basic form of SQL injection but anything more complicated is better suited to a standalone tool. Both meta-style and HTTP redirects are supported.

We may not have access to the target web server's true hostname, which can prevent access to virtually hosted sites. This script only follows absolute links when the host name component is the same as the target server's reverse-DNS name.

ssh-hostkey.nse

Categories: safe, default, intrusive

Shows SSH hostkeys.

Shows the target SSH server's key fingerprint and (with high enough verbosity level) the public key itself. It records the discovered host keys in `nmap.registry` for use by other scripts. Output can be controlled with the `ssh_hostkey` script argument.

Script Arguments

ssh_hostkey
  Controls the output format of keys. Multiple values may be given, separated by spaces. Possible values are
  - "full": The entire key, not just the fingerprint.
  - "bubble": Bubble Babble output,
  - "visual": Visual ASCII art representation.
  - "all": All of the above.

Usage

```
nmap host --script SSH-hostkey --script-args ssh_hostkey=full
nmap host --script SSH-hostkey --script-args ssh_hostkey=all
nmap host --script SSH-hostkey --script-args ssh_hostkey='visual bubble'
```

Sample Output

```
22/tcp open  ssh
| ssh-hostkey: 2048 f0:58:ce:f4:aa:a4:59:1c:8e:dd:4d:07:44:c8:25:11 (RSA)
22/tcp open  ssh
| ssh-hostkey: 2048 f0:58:ce:f4:aa:a4:59:1c:8e:dd:4d:07:44:c8:25:11 (RSA)
| +--[ RSA 2048]----+
| |         .E*+    |
| |          oo     |
| |         . o .   |
| |          O . .  |
```

```
|  |        o S o .   |
|  |        = o + .   |
|  |        . * o .   |
|  |        = .       |
|  |      o .         |
|_ +-----------------+
22/tcp open   ssh
|  ssh-hostkey: 2048 xuvah-degyp-nabus-zegah-hebur-nopig-bubig-difeg-hisym-rume ↵
f-cuxex (RSA)
|_ ssh-rsa AAAAB3NzaC1yc2EAAAABIwAAAQEAwVuv2gcr0maaKQ69VVIEv2ob4OxnuI64fkeOnCXD ↵
11Ux5tTA+vefXUWEMxgMuA7iX4irJHy2zer0NQ3Z3yJvr5scPgTYIaEOp5Uo/eGFG9Agpk5wE8CoF0e ↵
47iCAPHqzlmP2V7aNURLMODb3jVZuI07A2ZRrMGrD8d888E2ORVORv1rYeTYCqcMMoVFmX913gWEdk4 ↵
yx3w5sD8v5O1Iuyd1v19mPfyhrI5E1E1n1/Xjp5N0/xP2GUBrdkDMxKaxqTPMie/f0dXBUPQQN697a5 ↵
q+51BRPhKYOtn6yQKCd9s1Q22nxn72Jmi1RzbMyYJ52FosDT755Qmb46GLrDMaZMQ==
```

sshv1.nse

Categories: default, safe

Checks if an SSH server supports the obsolete and less secure SSH Protocol Version 1.

sslv2.nse

Categories: default, safe

Determines whether the server supports obsolete and less secure SSL-v2, and discovers which ciphers it supports.

Sample Output

```
443/tcp open    https    syn-ack
|  sslv2: server still supports SSLv2
|       SSL2_RC4_128_WITH_MD5
|       SSL2_DES_192_EDE3_CBC_WITH_MD5
|       SSL2_RC2_CBC_128_CBC_WITH_MD5
|       SSL2_DES_64_CBC_WITH_MD5
|       SSL2_RC4_128_EXPORT40_WITH_MD5
|_      SSL2_RC2_CBC_128_CBC_WITH_MD5
```

telnet-brute.nse

Categories: auth, intrusive

Tries to get Telnet login credentials by guessing usernames and passwords.

upnp-info.nse

Categories: default, safe

Attempts to extract system information from the UPnP service.

Sample Output

```
|  upnp-info:  System/1.0 UPnP/1.0 IGD/1.0
|_ Location: http://192.168.1.1:80/UPnP/IGD.xml
```

`whois.nse`

Categories: discovery, external, safe

Queries the WHOIS services of Regional Internet Registries (RIR) and attempts to retrieve information about the IP Address Assignment which contains the Target IP Address.

The fields displayed contain information about the assignment and the organisation responsible for managing the address space. When output verbosity is requested on the Nmap command line (-v) extra information about the assignment will be displayed.

To determine which of the RIRs to query for a given Target IP Address this script utilises Assignments Data hosted by IANA. The data is cached locally and then parsed for use as a lookup table. The locally cached files are refreshed periodically to help ensure the data is current. If, for any reason, these files are not available to the script then a default sequence of Whois services are queried in turn until: the desired record is found; or a referral to another (defined) Whois service is found; or until the sequence is exhausted without finding either a referral or the desired record.

The script will recognize a referral to another Whois service if that service is defined in the script and will continue by sending a query to the referred service. A record is assumed to be the desired one if it does not contain a referral.

To reduce the number unnecessary queries sent to Whois services a record cache is employed and the entries in the cache can be applied to any targets within the range of addresses represented in the record.

In certain circumstances, the ability to cache responses prevents the discovery of other, smaller IP address assignments applicable to the target because a cached response is accepted in preference to sending a Whois query. When it is important to ensure that the most accurate information about the IP address assignment is retrieved the script argument `whodb` should be used with a value of `"nocache"` (see script arguments). This reduces the range of addresses that may use a cached record to a size that helps ensure that smaller assignments will be discovered. This option should be used with caution due to the potential to send large numbers of whois queries and possibly be banned from using the services.

In using this script your IP address will be sent to iana.org. Additionally your address and the address of the target of the scan will be sent to one of the RIRs.

Script Arguments

`whodb`
> Takes any of the following values, which may be combined:
> - `whodb=nofile` Prevent the use of IANA assignments data and instead query the default services.
> - `whodb=nofollow` Ignore referrals and instead display the first record obtained.
> - `whodb=nocache` Prevent the acceptance of records in the cache when they apply to large ranges of addresses.
> - `whodb=[service-ids]` Redefine the default services to query. Implies `nofile`.

Usage

```
# Basic usage:
nmap target --script whois

# To prevent the use of IANA assignments data supply the nofile value
# to the whodb argument:
nmap target --script whois --script-args whodb=nofile
nmap target --script whois --script-args whois={whodb=nofile}

# Supplying a sequence of whois services will also prevent the use of
# IANA assignments data and override the default sequence:
nmap target --script whois --script-args whodb=arin+ripe+afrinic
nmap target --script whois --script-args whois={whodb=apnic*lacnic}
# The order in which the services are supplied is the order in which
# they will be queried. (N.B. commas or semi-colons should not be
# used to delimit argument values.)

# To return the first record obtained even if it contains a referral
# to another service, supply the nofollow value to whodb:
nmap target --script whois --script-args whodb=nofollow
nmap target --script whois --script-args whois={whodb=nofollow+ripe}
# Note that only one service (the first one supplied) will be used in
# conjunction with nofollow.

# To ensure discovery of smaller assignments even if larger ones
# exist in the cache, supply the nocache value to whodb:
nmap target --script whois --script-args whodb=nocache
nmap target --script whois --script-args whois={whodb=nocache}
```

Sample Output

```
Host script results:
|   whois: Record found at whois.arin.net
|   netrange: 64.13.134.0 - 64.13.134.63
|   netname: NET-64-13-143-0-26
|   orgname: Titan Networks
|   orgid: INSEC
|_  country: US stateprov: CA
```

`xampp-default-auth.nse`

Categories: auth, vuln

Check if an XAMP or XAMPP FTP server uses a default username and password.

XAMP is an Apache distribution designed for easy installation and administration.

Sample Output

```
21/tcp  open   ftp
|_ xampp-default-auth: Login success with u/p: nobody/xampp
```

9.6. NSE Libraries

In addition to the significant built-in capabilities of Lua, we have written or integrated many extension libraries which make script writing more powerful and convenient. These libraries (sometimes called modules) are compiled if necessary and installed along with Nmap. They have their own directory, `nselib`, which is installed in the configured datadir. Scripts need only `require` [6] the default libraries in order to use them.

9.6.1. List of All Libraries

This list is just an overview to give an idea of what libraries are available. Developers will want to consult the complete documentation at *http://nmap.org/nsedoc/*.

base64
: Base64 encoding and decoding. Follows RFC 4648.

bin
: Pack and unpack binary data.

bit
: Bitwise operations on integers.

comm
: Common communication functions for network discovery tasks like banner grabbing and data exchange.

datafiles
: Read and parse some of Nmap's data files: `nmap-protocols`, `nmap-rpc`, and `nmap-services`.

dns
: Simple DNS library supporting packet creation, encoding, decoding, and querying.

http
: Client-side HTTP library.

ipOps
: Utility functions for manipulating and comparing IP addresses.

listop
: Functional-style list operations.

match
: Buffered network I/O helper functions.

msrpc
: Call various MSRPC functions.

netbios
: Creates and parses NetBIOS traffic. The primary use for this is to send NetBIOS name requests.

---

[6] *http://www.lua.org/manual/5.1/manual.html#pdf-require*

---

nmap

Interface with Nmap internals.

openssl

OpenSSL bindings.

packet

Facilities for manipulating raw packets.

pcre

Perl Compatible Regular Expressions.

pop3

POP3 functions.

shortport

Functions for building short portrules.

smb

Server Message Block (SMB, also known as CIFS) traffic.

snmp

SNMP functions.

ssh1

Functions for the SSH-1 protocol.

ssh2

Functions for the SSH-2 protocol.

stdnse

Standard Nmap Scripting Engine functions.

strbuf

String buffer facilities.

tab

Arrange output into tables.

unpwdb

Username/password database library.

url

URI parsing, composition, and relative URL resolution.

9.6.2. Adding C Modules to Nselib

A few of the modules included in nselib are written in C or C++ rather than Lua. Two examples are `bit` and `pcre`. We recommend that modules be written in Lua if possible, but C and C++ may be more appropriate

---

if performance is critical or (as with the `pcre` and `openssl` modules) you are linking to an existing C library. This section describes how to write your own compiled extensions to nselib.

The Lua C API is described at length in *Programming in Lua, Second Edition*, so this is a short summary. C modules consist of functions that follow the protocol of the lua_CFunction[7] type. The functions are registered with Lua and assembled into a library by calling the `luaL_register` function. A special initialization function provides the interface between the module and the rest of the NSE code. By convention the initialization function is named in the form `luaopen_<module>`.

The smallest compiled module that comes with NSE is `bit`, and one of the most straightforward is `openssl`. These modules serve as good examples for a beginning module writer. The source code for `bit` is found in `nse_bit.cc` and `nse_bit.h`, while the `openssl` source is in `nse_openssl.cc` and `nse_openssl.h`. Most of the other compiled modules follow this `nse_<module name>.cc` naming convention.

Reviewing the `openssl` module shows that one of the functions in `nse_openssl.cc` is `l_md5`, which calculates an MD5 digest. Its function prototype is:

```
static int l_md5(lua_State *L);
```

The prototype shows that `l_md5` matches the lua_CFunction type. The function is static because it does not have to be visible to other compiled code. Only an address is required to register it with Lua. Later in the file, `l_md5` is entered into an array of type luaL_reg and associated with the name `md5`:

```
static const struct luaL_reg openssllib[] = {
  { "md5", l_md5 },
  { NULL, NULL }
};
```

This function will now be known as `md5` to NSE. Next the library is registered with a call to `luaL_register` inside the initialization function `luaopen_openssl`, as shown next. Some lines relating to the registration of OpenSSL BIGNUM types have been omitted:

```
LUALIB_API int luaopen_openssl(lua_State *L) {
  luaL_register(L, OPENSSLLIBNAME, openssllib);
  return 1;
}
```

The function `luaopen_openssl` is the only function in the file that is exposed in `nse_openssl.h`. `OPENSSLLIBNAME` is simply the string `"openssl"`.

After a compiled module is written, it must be added to NSE by including it in the list of standard libraries in `nse_init.cc`. Then the module's source file names must be added to `Makefile.in` in the appropriate places. For both these tasks you can simply follow the example of the other C modules. For the Windows build, the new source files must be added to the `mswin32/nmap.vcproj` project file using MS Visual Studio (see Section 2.4.4, "Compile from Source Code" [38]).

---

[7] *http://www.lua.org/manual/5.1/manual.html#lua_CFunction*

9.7. Nmap API

NSE scripts have access to several Nmap facilities for writing flexible and elegant scripts. The API provides target host details such as port states and version detection results. It also offers an interface to the Nsock library for efficient network I/O.

9.7.1. Information Passed to a Script

An effective Nmap scripting engine requires more than just a Lua interpreter. Users need easy access to the information Nmap has learned about the target hosts. This data is passed as arguments to the NSE script's `action` method. The arguments, `host` and `port`, are Lua tables which contain information on the target against which the script is executed. If a script matched a hostrule, it gets only the `host` table, and if it matched a portrule it gets both `host` and `port`. The following list describes each variable in these two tables.

host
> This table is passed as a parameter to the rule and action functions. It contains information on the operating system run by the host (if the -O switch was supplied), the IP address and the host name of the scanned target.

host.os
> The os entry in the host table is an array of strings. The strings (as many as eight) are the names of the operating systems the target is possibly running. Strings are only entered in this array if the target machine is a perfect match for one or more OS database entries. If Nmap was run without the -O option, then host.os is nil.

host.ip
> Contains a string representation of the IP address of the target host. If the scan was run against a host name and the reverse DNS query returned more than one IP addresses then the same IP address is used as the one chosen for the scan.

host.name
> Contains the reverse DNS entry of the scanned target host represented as a string. If the host has no reverse DNS entry, the value of the field is an empty string.

host.targetname
> Contains the name of the host as specified on the command line. If the target given on the command line contains a netmask or is an IP address the value of the field is nil.

host.directly_connected
> A Boolean value indicating whether or not the target host is directly connected to (i.e. on the same network segment as) the host running Nmap.

host.mac_addr
> MAC address of the destination host (six-byte long binary string) or nil, if the host is not directly connected.

`host.mac_addr_src`

Our own MAC address, which was used to connect to the host (either our network card's, or (with `--spoof-mac`) the spoofed address).

`host.interface`

A string containing the interface name (dnet-style) through which packets to the host are sent.

`host.bin_ip`

The target host's IPv4 address as a 32-bit binary value.

`host.bin_ip_src`

Our host's (running Nmap) source IPv4 address as a 32-bit binary value.

`port`

The port table is passed to an NSE service script (i.e. only those with a portrule rather than a hostrule) in the same fashion as the host table. It contains information about the port against which the script is running. While this table is not passed to host scripts, port states on the target can still be requested from Nmap using the `nmap.get_port_state()` call.

`port.number`

Contains the port number of the target port.

`port.protocol`

Defines the protocol of the target port. Valid values are `"tcp"` and `"udp"`.

`port.service`

Contains a string representation of the service running on `port.number` as detected by the Nmap service detection. If the `port.version` field is `nil`, Nmap has guessed the service based on the port number. Otherwise version detection was able to determine the listening service and this field is equal to `port.version.name`.

`port.version`

This entry is a table which contains information retrieved by the Nmap version scanning engine. Some of the values (such as service name, service type confidence, and the RPC-related values) may be retrieved by Nmap even if a version scan was not performed. Values which were not determined default to `nil`. The meaning of each value is given in the following table:

Table 9.1. `port.version` values

Name	Description
name	Contains the service name Nmap decided on for the port.
name_confidence	Evaluates how confident Nmap is about the accuracy of name, from 1 (least confident) to 10.
product, version, extrainfo, hostname, ostype, devicetype	These five variables are described in `<versioninfo>` [160].
service_tunnel	Contains the string `"none"` or `"ssl"` based on whether or not Nmap used SSL tunneling to detect the service.

Name	Description
service_fp	The service fingerprint, if any, is provided in this value. This is described in Section 7.7, "Community Contributions" [164].
rpc_status	Contains a string value of good_prog if we were able to determine the program number of an RPC service listening on the port, unknown if the port appears to be RPC but we couldn't determine the program number, not_rpc if the port doesn't appear be RPC, or untested if we haven't checked for RPC status.
rpc_program, rpc_lowver, rpc_highver	The detected RPC program number and the range of version numbers supported by that program. These will be nil if rpc_status is anything other than good_prog.

port.state

Contains information on the state of the port. Service scripts are only run against ports in the open or open|filtered states, so port.state generally contains one of those values. Other values might appear if the port table is a result of the get_port_state function. You can adjust the port state using the nmap.set_port_state() call. This is normally done when an open|filtered port is determined to be open.

9.7.2. Network I/O API

To allow for efficient and parallelizable network I/O, NSE provides an interface to Nsock, the Nmap socket library. The smart callback mechanism Nsock uses is fully transparent to NSE scripts. The main benefit of NSE's sockets is that they never block on I/O operations, allowing many scripts to be run in parallel. The I/O parallelism is fully transparent to authors of NSE scripts. In NSE you can either program as if you were using a single non-blocking socket or you can program as if your connection is blocking. Even blocking I/O calls return once a specified timeout has been exceeded. Two flavors of Network I/O are supported: connect-style and raw packet.

Connect-style network I/O

This part of the network API should be suitable for most classical network uses: Users create a socket, connect it to a remote address, send and receive data and finally close the socket. Everything up to the Transport layer (which is either TCP, UDP or SSL) is handled by the library.

An NSE socket is created by calling nmap.new_socket, which returns a socket object. The socket object supports the usual connect, send, receive, and close methods. Additionally the functions receive_bytes, receive_lines, and receive_buf allow greater control over data reception. Example 9.2 shows the use of connect-style network operations. The try function is used for error handling, as described in Section 9.7.4, "Exception Handling" [244].

Example 9.2. Connect-style I/O

```
require("nmap")

local socket = nmap.new_socket()
socket:set_timeout(1000)
try = nmap.new_try(function() socket:close() end)
try(socket:connect(host.ip, port.number))
try(socket:send("login"))
response = try(socket:receive())
socket:close()
```

Raw packet network I/O

For those cases where the connection-oriented approach is too high-level, NSE provides script developers with the option of raw packet network I/O.

Raw packet reception is handled through a Libpcap wrapper inside the Nsock library. The steps are to open a capture device, register listeners with the device, and then process packets as they are received.

The `pcap_open` method creates a handle for raw socket reads from an ordinary socket object. This method takes a callback function, which computes a packet hash from a packet (including its headers). This hash can return any binary string, which is later compared to the strings registered with the `pcap_register` function. The packet hash callback will normally extract some portion of the packet, such as its source address.

The pcap reader is instructed to listen for certain packets using the `pcap_register` function. The function takes a binary string which is compared against the hash value of every packet received. Those packets whose hashes match any registered strings will be returned by the `pcap_receive` method. Register the empty string to receive all packets.

A script receives all packets for which a listener has been registered by calling the `pcap_receive` method. The method blocks until a packet is received or a timeout occurs.

The more general the packet hash computing function is kept, the more scripts may receive the packet and proceed with their execution. To handle packet capture inside your script you first have to create a socket with `nmap.new_socket` and later close the socket with `socket_object:close`—just like with the connection-based network I/O.

Receiving raw packets is important, but sending them is a key feature as well. To accomplish this, NSE can access a wrapper around the `libdnet` library. Raw packet writes do not use a standard socket object like reads do. Instead, call the function `nmap.new_dnet` to create a dnet object with ethernet sending methods. Then open an interface with the `ethernet_open` method. Raw ethernet frames can then be sent with `ethernet_send`. When you're done, close the ethernet handle with `ethernet_close`.

Sometimes the easiest ways to understand complex APIs is by example. The `sniffer-detect.nse` script included with Nmap uses raw packet capture and sending in an attempt to detect promiscuous-mode machines on the network (those running sniffers).

9.7.3. Thread Mutexes

Each script execution thread (e.g. `ftp-anon` running against an FTP server on the target host) yields to other scripts whenever it makes a call on network objects (sending or receiving data). Some scripts require finer concurrency control over thread execution. An example is the `whois` script which queries whois servers for each target IP address. Because many concurrent queries often result in getting one's IP banned for abuse, and because a single query may return additional information for targets other threads are running against, it is useful to have other threads pause while one thread performs a query.

To solve this problem, NSE includes a `mutex` function which provides a mutex[8] (mutual exclusion object) usable by scripts. The mutex allows for only one thread to be working on an object. Competing threads waiting to work on this object are put in the waiting queue until they can get a "lock" on the mutex. A solution for the `whois` problem above is to have each thread block on a mutex using a common string, thus ensuring that only one thread is querying whois servers at once. That thread can store the results in the NSE registry before releasing unlocking the mutex. The next script in the waiting queue can then run. It will first check the registry and only query whois servers if the previous results were insufficient.

The first step is to create a mutex object using a statement such as:

```
mutexfn = nmap.mutex(object)
```

The `mutexfn` returned is a function which works as a mutex for the `object` passed in. This object can be any Lua data type except `nil`, `booleans`, and `numbers`. The returned function allows you to lock, try to lock, and release the mutex. Its first and only parameter must be one of the following:

`"lock"`
> Make a blocking lock on the mutex. If the mutex is busy (another thread has a lock on it), then the thread will yield and wait. The function returns with the mutex locked.

`"trylock"`
> Makes a non-blocking lock on the mutex. If the mutex is busy then it immediately returns with a return value of `false`. Otherwise the mutex locks the mutex and returns `true`.

`"done"`
> Releases the mutex and allows another thread to lock it. If the thread does not have a lock on the mutex, an error will be raised.

`"running"`
> Returns the thread locked on the mutex or `nil` if the mutex is not locked. This should only be used for debugging as it interferes with garbage collection of finished threads.

A simple example of using the API is provided in Example 9.3. For real-life examples, read the `asn-query.nse` and `whois.nse` scripts in the Nmap distribution.

---

[8] *http://en.wikipedia.org/wiki/Mutual_exclusion*

Example 9.3. Mutex manipulation

```
local mutex = nmap.mutex("My Script's Unique ID");
function action(host, port)
  mutex "lock";
  -- Do critical section work - only one thread at a time executes this.
  mutex "done";
  return script_output;
end
```

9.7.4. Exception Handling

NSE provides an exception handling mechanism which is not present in the base Lua language. It is tailored specifically for network I/O operations, and follows a functional programming paradigm rather than an object oriented one. The `nmap.new_try` API method is used to create an exception handler. This method returns a function which takes a variable number of arguments that are assumed to be the return values of another function. If an exception is detected in the return values (the first return value is false), then the script execution is aborted and no output is produced. Optionally, you can pass a function to `new_try` which will be called if an exception is caught. The function would generally perform any required cleanup operations.

Example 9.4 shows cleanup exception handling at work. A new function named `catch` is defined to simply close the newly created socket in case of an error. It is then used to protect connection and communication attempts on that socket. If no catch function is specified, execution of the script aborts without further ado—open sockets will remain open until the next run of Lua's garbage collector. If the verbosity level is at least one or if the scan is performed in debugging mode a description of the uncaught error condition is printed on standard output. Note that it is currently not easily possible to group several statements in one try block.

Example 9.4. Exception handling example

```
local result, socket, try, catch

result = ""
socket = nmap.new_socket()
catch = function()
socket:close()
end
try = nmap.new_try(catch)

try(socket:connect(host.ip, port.number))
result = try(socket:receive_lines(1))
try(socket:send(result))
```

Writing a function which is treated properly by the try/catch mechanism is straightforward. The function should return multiple values. The first value should be a Boolean which is `true` upon successful completion of the function and `false` otherwise. If the function completed successfully, the try construct consumes the indicator value and returns the remaining values. If the function failed then the second returned value must be a string describing the error condition. Note that if the value is not `nil` or `false` it is treated as `true` so you can return your value in the normal case and return `nil`, `<error description>` if an error occurs.

9.7.5. The Registry

The registry is a Lua table (accessible as `nmap.registry`) with the special property that it is visible by all scripts and retains its state between script executions. The registry is transient—it is not stored between Nmap executions. Every script can read and write to the registry. Scripts commonly use it to save information for other instances of the same script. For example, the `whois` and `asn-query` scripts may query one IP address, but receive information which may apply to tens of thousands of IPs on that network. Saving the information in the registry may prevent other script threads from having to repeat the query.

The registry may also be used to hand information to completely different scripts. For example, the `snmp-brute` script saves a discovered community name in the registry where it may be used by other SNMP scripts. Scripts which leave information behind for a second script must have a lower `runlevel` than that second script, or there is no guarantee that they will run first.

Because every script can write to the registry table, it is important to avoid conflicts by choosing keys wisely (uniquely).

9.8. Script Writing Tutorial

Suppose that you are convinced of the power of NSE. How do you go about writing your own script? Let's say that you want to extract information from an identification server to determine the owner of the process listening on a TCP port. This is not really the purpose of identd (it is meant for querying the owner of outgoing connections, not listening daemons), but many identd servers allow it anyway. Nmap used to have this functionality (called ident scan), but it was removed while transitioning to a new scan engine architecture. The protocol identd uses is pretty simple, but still too complicated to handle with Nmap's version detection language. First, you connect to the identification server and send a query of the form `<port-on-server>`, `<port-on-client>` and terminated with a newline character. The server should then respond with a string containing the server port, client port, response type, and address information. The address information is omitted if there is an error. More details are available in RFC 1413, but this description is sufficient for our purposes. The protocol cannot be modeled in Nmap's version detection language for two reasons. The first is that you need to know both the local and the remote port of a connection. Version detection does not provide this data. The second, more severe obstacle, is that you need two open connections to the target—one to the identification server and one to the listening port you wish to query. Both obstacles are easily overcome with NSE.

The anatomy of a script is described in Section 9.3, "Script Format" [211]. In this section we will show how the described structure is utilized.

9.8.1. The Head

The head of the script is essentially its meta information. This includes the fields: `description`, `categories`, `runlevel`, `author`, and `license` as well as initial NSEDoc information such as usage, args, and output tags (see Section 9.9, "Writing Script Documentation (NSEDoc)" [248]).

The description field should contain a paragraph or more describing what the script does. If anything about the script results might confuse or mislead users, and you can't eliminate the issue by improving the script or results text, it should be documented in the `description`. If there are multiple paragraphs, the first is

---

used as a short summary where necessary. Make sure that first paragraph can serve as a stand alone abstract. This description is short because it is such a simple script:

```
description = [[
Attempts to find the owner of an open TCP port by querying an auth
(identd - port 113) daemon which must also be open on the target system.
]]
```

Next comes NSEDoc information. This script is missing the common `@usage` and `@args` tags since it is so simple, but it does have an NSEDoc `@output` tag:

```
---
--@output
-- 21/tcp    open      ftp          ProFTPD 1.3.1
-- |_ auth-owners: nobody
-- 22/tcp    open      ssh          OpenSSH 4.3p2 Debian 9etch2 (protocol 2.0)
-- |_ auth-owners: root
-- 25/tcp    open      smtp         Postfix smtpd
-- |_ auth-owners: postfix
-- 80/tcp    open      http         Apache httpd 2.0.61 ((Unix) PHP/4.4.7 ...)
-- |_ auth-owners: dhapache
-- 113/tcp   open      auth?
-- |_ auth-owners: nobody
-- 587/tcp   open       submission Postfix smtpd
-- |_ auth-owners: postfix
-- 5666/tcp open       unknown
-- |_ auth-owners: root
```

Next come the `author`, `license`, and `categories` tags. This script belongs to the `safe` because we are not using the service for anything it was not intended for. Because this script is one that should run by default it is also in the `default` category. Here are the variables in context:

```
author = "Diman Todorov <diman.todorov@gmail.com>"

license = "Same as Nmap--See http://nmap.org/book/man-legal.html"

categories = {"default", "safe"}
```

9.8.2. The Rule

The rule section is a Lua method which decides whether to skip or execute the script's action method against a particular service or host. This decision is usually based on the host and port information passed to the rule function. In the case of the identification script, it is slightly more complicated than that. To decide whether to run the identification script against a given port we need to know if there is an auth server running on the target machine. In other words, the script should be run only if the currently scanned TCP port is open and TCP port 113 is also open. For now we will rely on the fact that identification servers listen on TCP port 113. Unfortunately NSE only gives us information about the currently scanned port.

To find out if port 113 is open, we use the `nmap.get_port_state` function. If the auth port was not scanned, the `get_port_state` function returns `nil`. So we check that the table is not `nil`. We also check that both ports are in the `open` state. If this is the case, the action is executed, otherwise we skip the action.

9.8. Script Writing Tutorial

```
portrule = function(host, port)
        local auth_port = { number=113, protocol="tcp" }
        local identd = nmap.get_port_state(host, auth_port)

        if
                identd ~= nil
                and identd.state == "open"
                and port.protocol == "tcp"
                and port.state == "open"
        then
                return true
        else
                return false
        end
end
```

9.8.3. The Mechanism

At last we implement the actual functionality! The script first connects to the port on which we expect to find the identification server, then it will connect to the port we want information about. Doing so involves first creating two socket options by calling nmap.new_socket. Next we define an error-handling catch function which closes those sockets if failure is detected. At this point we can safely use object methods such as open, close, send and receive to operate on the network socket. In this case we call connect to make the connections. NSE's exception handling mechanism. is used to avoid excessive error-handling code. We simply wrap the networking calls in a try call which will in turn call our catch function if anything goes wrong.

If the two connections succeed, we construct a query string and parse the response. If we received a satisfactory response, we return the retrieved information.

```
action = function(host, port)
        local owner = ""

        local client_ident = nmap.new_socket()
        local client_service = nmap.new_socket()

        local catch = function()
                client_ident:close()
                client_service:close()
        end

        local try = nmap.new_try(catch)

        try(client_ident:connect(host.ip, 113))
        try(client_service:connect(host.ip, port.number))

        local localip, localport, remoteip, remoteport =
                try(client_service:get_info())

        local request = port.number .. ", " .. localport .. "\n"

        try(client_ident:send(request))
```

```
        owner = try(client_ident:receive_lines(1))

        if string.match(owner, "ERROR") then
                owner = nil
        else
                owner = string.match(owner, "USERID : .+ : (.+)\n", 1)
        end

        try(client_ident:close())
        try(client_service:close())

        return owner
end
```

Note that because we know that the remote port is stored in `port.number`, we could have ignored the last two return values of `client_service:get_info()` like this:

```
local localip, localport = try(client_service:get_info())
```

In this example we exit quietly if the service responds with an error. This is done by assigning `nil` to the `owner` variable which will be returned. NSE scripts generally only return messages when they succeed, so they don't flood the user with pointless alerts.

9.9. Writing Script Documentation (NSEDoc)

Scripts are used by more than just their authors, so they require good documentation. NSE modules need documentation so developers can use them in their scripts. NSE's documentation system, described in this section, aims to meet both these needs. While reading this section, you may want to browse NSE's online documentation, which is generated using this system. It is at *http://nmap.org/nsedoc/*.

NSE uses a customized version of the LuaDoc[9] documentation system called NSEDoc. The documentation for scripts and modules is contained in their source code, as comments with a special form. Example 9.5 is an NSEDoc comment taken from the `stdnse.print_debug()` function.

Example 9.5. An NSEDoc comment for a function

```
--- Prints a formatted debug message if the current verbosity level is greater
-- than or equal to a given level.
--
-- This is a convenience wrapper around
-- <code>nmap.print_debug_unformatted()</code>. The first optional numeric
-- argument, <code>verbosity</code>, is used as the verbosity level necessary
-- to print the message (it defaults to 1 if omitted). All remaining arguments
-- are processed with Lua's <code>string.format()</code> function.
-- @param level Optional verbosity level.
-- @param fmt Format string.
-- @param ... Arguments to format.
```

Documentation comments start with three dashes: ---. The body of the comment is the description of the following code. The first paragraph of the description should be a brief summary, with the following paragraphs providing more detail. Special tags starting with @ mark off other parts of the documentation. In the above example you see @param, which is used to describe each parameter of a function. A complete list of the documentation tags is found in Section 9.9.1, "NSE Documentation Tags" [250].

Text enclosed in the HTML-like <code> and </code> tags will be rendered in a monospace font. This should be used for variable and function names, as well as multi-line code examples. When a sequence of lines start with the characters "* ", they will be rendered as a bulleted list.

It is good practice to document every public function and table in a script or module. Additionally every script and module should have its own file-level documentation. A documentation comment at the beginning of a file (one that is not followed by a function or table definition) applies to the entire file. File-level documentation can and should be several paragraphs long, with all the high-level information useful to a developer using a module or a user running a script. Example 9.6 shows documentation for the comm module (with a few paragraphs removed to save space).

Example 9.6. An NSEDoc comment for a module

```
--- Common communication functions for network discovery tasks like
-- banner grabbing and data exchange.
--
-- These functions may be passed a table of options, but it's not required. The
-- keys for the options table are <code>"bytes"</code>, <code>"lines"</code>,
-- <code>"proto"</code>, and <code>"timeout"</code>. <code>"bytes"</code> sets
-- a minimum number of bytes to read. <code>"lines"</code> does the same for
-- lines. <code>"proto"</code> sets the protocol to communicate with,
-- defaulting to <code>"tcp"</code> if not provided. <code>"timeout"</code>
-- sets the socket timeout (see the socket function <code>set_timeout()</code>
-- for details).
-- @author Kris Katterjohn 04/2008
-- @copyright Same as Nmap--See http://nmap.org/book/man-legal.html
```

There are some special considerations for documenting scripts rather than functions and modules. In particular, scripts have special variables for some information which would otherwise belongs in @-tag comments (script variables are described in Section 9.3, "Script Format" [211]). In particular, a script's description belongs in the description variable rather than in a documentation comment, and the information that would go in @author and @copyright belong in the variables author and license instead. NSEDoc

---

knows about these variables and will use them in preference to fields in the comments. Scripts should also have an `@output` tag showing sample output, as well as `@args` and `@usage` where appropriate. Example 9.7 shows proper form for script-level documentation, using a combination of documentation comments and NSE variables.

Example 9.7. An NSEDoc comment for a script

```
description = [[
Maps IP addresses to autonomous system (AS) numbers.

The script works by sending DNS TXT queries to a DNS server which in
turn queries a third-party service provided by Team Cymru
(team-cymru.org) using an in-addr.arpa style zone set up especially for
use by Nmap.
]]


---
-- @usage
-- nmap --script asn-query.nse [--script-args dns=<DNS server>] <target>
-- @args dns The address of a recursive nameserver to use (optional).
-- @output
-- Host script results:
-- |   AS Numbers:
-- |   BGP: 64.13.128.0/21 | Country: US
-- |     Origin AS: 10565 SVCOLO-AS - Silicon Valley Colocation, Inc.
-- |       Peer AS: 3561 6461
-- |   BGP: 64.13.128.0/18 | Country: US
-- |     Origin AS: 10565 SVCOLO-AS - Silicon Valley Colocation, Inc.
-- |_      Peer AS: 174 2914 6461

author = "jah, Michael"
license = "Same as Nmap--See http://nmap.org/book/man-legal.html"
categories = {"discovery", "external"}
```

Compiled NSE modules are also documented with NSEDoc, even though they have no Lua source code. Each compiled module has a file `<modulename>.luadoc` that is kept in the `nselib` directory alongside the Lua modules. This file lists and documents the functions and tables in the compiled module as though they were written in Lua. Only the name of each function is required, not its definition (not even `end`). You must use the `@name` and `@class` tags when documenting a table to assist the documentation parser in identifying it. There are several examples of this method of documentation in the Nmap source distribution (including `nmap.luadoc`, `bit.luadoc`, and `pcre.luadoc`).

9.9.1. NSE Documentation Tags

The following tags are understood by NSEDoc:

`@param`
> Describes a function parameter. The first word following `@param` is the name of the parameter being described. The tag should appear once for each parameter of a function.

`@see`
> Adds a cross-reference to another function or table.

`@return`
> Describes a return value of a function. `@return` may be used multiple times for multiple return values.

`@usage`
> Provides a usage example of a function or script. In the case of a function, the example is Lua code; for a script it is an Nmap command line. `@usage` may be given more than once.

`@name`
> Defines a name for the function or table being documented. This tag is normally not necessary because NSEDoc infers names through code analysis.

`@class`
> Defines the "class" of the object being modified: `function`, `table`, or `module`. Like `@name`, this is normally inferred automatically.

`@field`
> In the documentation of a table, `@field` describes the value of a named field.

`@args`
> Describes a script argument, as used with the `--script-args` option (see Section 9.2.3, "Arguments to Scripts" [210]). The first word after `@args` is the name of the argument, and everything following that is the description. This tag is special to script-level comments.

`@output`
> This tag, which is exclusive to script-level comments, shows sample output from a script.

`@author`
> This tag, which may be given multiple times, lists the authors of an NSE module. For scripts, use the `author` variable instead.

`@copyright`
> This tag describes the copyright status of a module. For scripts, use the `license` variable instead.

9.10. Version Detection Using NSE

The version detection system built into Nmap was designed to efficiently recognize the vast majority of protocols with a simple probe and pattern matching syntax. Some protocols require more complex communication than version detection can handle. A generalized scripting language as provided by NSE is perfect for these tough cases.

NSE's `version` category contains scripts that enhance standard version detection. Scripts in this category are run whenever you request version detection with `-sV`; you don't need to use `-sC` to run these. This cuts the other way too: if you use `-sC`, you won't get `version` scripts unless you also use `-sV`.

One protocol which we were unable to detect with normal version detection is Skype version 2. The protocol was likely designed to frustrate detection out of a fear that telecom-affiliated Internet service providers might consider Skype competition and interfere with the traffic. Yet we did find one way to detect it. If Skype receives an HTTP GET request, it pretends to be a web server and returns a 404 error. But for other requests, it sends back a chunk of random-looking data. Proper identification requires sending two probes and comparing the two responses—an ideal task for NSE. The simple NSE script which accomplishes this is shown in Example 9.8.

Example 9.8. A typical version detection script (Skype version 2 detection)

```
description = [[
Detects the Skype version 2 service.
]]
author = "Brandon Enright <bmenrigh@ucsd.edu>"
license = "Same as Nmap--See http://nmap.org/book/man-legal.html"
categories = {"version"}

require "comm"

portrule = function(host, port)
        return (port.number == 80 or port.number == 443 or
                port.service == nil or port.service == "" or
                port.service == "unknown")
                and port.protocol == "tcp" and port.state == "open"
                and port.service ~= "http" and port.service ~= "ssl/http"
end

action = function(host, port)
        local status, result = comm.exchange(host, port,
                "GET / HTTP/1.0\r\n\r\n", {bytes=26, proto=port.protocol})
        if (not status) then
                return
        end
        if (result ~= "HTTP/1.0 404 Not Found\r\n\r\n") then
                return
        end
        -- So far so good, now see if we get random data for another request
        status, result = comm.exchange(host, port,
                "random data\r\n\r\n", {bytes=15, proto=port.protocol})

        if (not status) then
                return
        end
        if string.match(result, "[^%s!-~].*[^%s!-~].*[^%s!-~]") then
                -- Detected
                port.version.name = "skype2"
                port.version.product = "Skype"
                nmap.set_port_version(host, port, "hardmatched")
                return
        end
        return
end
```

If the script detects Skype, it augments its `port` table with now-known `name` and `product` fields. It then sends this new information to Nmap by calling `nmap.set_port_version`. Several other version fields are available to be set if they are known, but in this case we only have the name and product. For the full list of version fields, refer to the `nmap.set_port_version` documentation.

Notice that this script does nothing unless it detects the protocol. A script shouldn't produce output (other than debug output) just to say it didn't learn anything.

9.11. Example Script: `finger.nse`

The finger script (`finger.nse`) is a perfect example of a short and simple NSE script.

First the information fields are assigned. A detailed description of what the script actually does goes in the `description` field.

```
description = [[
Attempts to get a list of usernames via the finger service.
]]
author = "Eddie Bell <ejlbell@gmail.com>"
license = "Same as Nmap--See http://nmap.org/book/man-legal.html"
```

The `categories` field is a table containing all the categories the script belongs to—These are used for script selection with the `--script` option:

```
categories = {"default", "discovery"}
```

You can use the facilities provided by the nselib (Section 9.6, "NSE Libraries" [236]) with `require`. Here we want to use common communication functions and shorter port rules:

```
require "comm"
require "shortport"
```

We want to run the script against the finger service. So we test whether it is using the well-known finger port (`79/tcp`), or whether the service is named "finger" based on version detection results or in the port number's listing in `nmap-services`:

```
portrule = shortport.port_or_service(79, "finger")
```

First, the script uses `nmap.new_try` to create an exception handler that will quit the script in case of an error. Next, it passes control to `comm.exchange`, which handles the network transaction. Here we have asked to wait in the communication exchange until we receive at least 100 lines, wait at least 5 seconds, or until the remote side closes the connection. Any errors are handled by the `try` exception handler. The script returns a string if the call to `comm.exchange()` was successful.

```
action = function(host, port)
 local try = nmap.new_try()

 return try(comm.exchange(host, port, "\r\n",
```

```
                {lines=100, proto=port.protocol, timeout=5000}))
end
```

9.12. Implementation Details

Now it is time to explore the NSE implementation details in depth. Understanding how NSE works is useful for designing efficient scripts and libraries. The canonical reference to the NSE implementation is the source code, but this section provides an overview of key details. It should be valuable to folks trying to understand and extend the NSE source code, as well as to script authors who want to better-understand how their scripts are executed.

9.12.1. Initialization Phase

During its initialization stage, Nmap loads the Lua interpreter and its provided libraries. These libraries are fully documented in the Lua Reference Manual[10]. Here is a summary of the libraries, listed alphabetically by their namespace name:

debug

> The debug library provides a low-level API to the Lua interpreter, allowing you to access functions along the execution stack, retrieve function closures and object metatables, and more.

io

> The Input/Output library offers functions such as reading from files or from the output from programs you execute.

math

> Numbers in Lua usually correspond to the double C type, so the math library provides access to rounding functions, trigonometric functions, random number generation, and more.

os

> The Operating System library provides system facilities such as filesystem operations (including file renaming or removal and temporary file creation) and system environment access.

package

> Among the functions provided by Lua's package-lib is require, which is used to load nselib modules.

string

> The string library provides functions for manipulating Lua strings, including printf-style string formatting, pattern matching using Lua-style patterns, substring extraction, and more.

table

> The table manipulation library is essential for operating on Lua's central data structure (tables).

In addition to loading the libraries provided by Lua, the nmap namespace functions are loaded. The search paths are the same directories that Nmap searches for its data files, except that the nselib directory is appended to each. At this stage any provided script arguments are stored inside the registry.

---

[10] *http://www.lua.org/manual/5.1/manual.html*

The next phase of NSE initialization is loading the selected scripts, based on the defaults or arguments provided to the `--script` option. The `version` category scripts are loaded as well if version detection was enabled. NSE first tries to interpret each `--script` argument as a category. This is done with a Lua C function in `nse_init.cc` named `entry` based on data from the `script.db` script categorization database. If the category is found, those scripts are loaded. Otherwise Nmap tries to interpret `--script` arguments as files or directories. If no files or directories with a given name are found in Nmap's search path, an error is raised and the Script Engine aborts.

If a directory is specified, all of the `.nse` files inside it are loaded. Each loaded file is executed by Lua. If a *portrule* is present, it is saved in the *porttests* table with a portrule key and file closure value. Otherwise, if the script has a *hostrule*, it is saved in the *hosttests* table in the same manner.

9.12.2. Matching Scripts with Targets

After initialization is finished, the `hostrules` and `portrules` are evaluated for each host in the current target group. The rules of every chosen script is tested against every host and (in the case of service scripts) each `open` and `open|filtered` port on the hosts. The combination can grow quite large, so portrules should be kept as simple as possible. Save any heavy computation for the script's `action`.

Next, a Lua thread[11] is created for each of the matching script-target combinations. Each thread is stored with pertinent information such as the runlevel, target, target port (if applicable), host and port tables (passed to the `action`), and the script type (service or host script). The `mainloop` function then processes each runlevel grouping of threads in order.

9.12.3. Script Execution

Nmap performs NSE script scanning in parallel by taking advantage of Nmap's Nsock parallel I/O library and the Lua coroutines [12] language feature. Coroutines offer collaborative multi-threading so that scripts can suspend themselves at defined points and allow other coroutines to execute. Network I/O, particularly waiting for responses from remote hosts, often involves long wait times, so this is when scripts yield to others. Key functions of the Nsock wrapper cause scripts to yield (pause). When Nsock finishes processing such a request, it makes a callback which causes the script to be pushed from the waiting queue back into the running queue so it can resume operations when its turn comes up again.

The `mainloop` function moves threads between the waiting and running queues as needed. A thread which yields is moved from the running queue into the waiting list. Running threads execute until they either yield, complete, or fail with an error. Threads are made ready to run (placed in the running queue) by calling `process_waiting2running`. This process of scheduling running threads and moving threads between queues continues until no threads exist in either queue.

---

[11] *http://www.lua.org/manual/5.1/manual.html#2.11*

[12] *http://www.lua.org/manual/5.1/manual.html#2.11*

Chapter 10. Detecting and Subverting Firewalls and Intrusion Detection Systems

10.1. Introduction

Many Internet pioneers envisioned a global open network with a universal IP address space allowing virtual connections between any two nodes. This allows hosts to act as true peers, serving and retrieving information from each other. People could access all of their home systems from work, changing the climate control settings or unlocking the doors for early guests. This vision of universal connectivity has been stifled by address space shortages and security concerns. In the early 1990s, organizations began deploying firewalls for the express purpose of reducing connectivity. Huge networks were cordoned off from the unfiltered Internet by application proxies, network address translation devices, and packet filters. The unrestricted flow of information gave way to tight regulation of approved communication channels and the content that passes over them.

Network obstructions such as firewalls can make mapping a network exceedingly difficult. It will not get any easier, as stifling casual reconnaissance is often a key goal of implementing the devices. Nevertheless, Nmap offers many features to help understand these complex networks, and to verify that filters are working as intended. It even supports mechanisms for bypassing poorly implemented defenses. One of the best methods of understanding your network security posture is to try to defeat it. Place yourself in the mind-set of an attacker and deploy techniques from this chapter against your networks. Launch an FTP bounce scan, idle scan, fragmentation attack, or try to tunnel through one of your own proxies.

In addition to restricting network activity, companies are increasingly monitoring traffic with intrusion detection systems (IDS). All of the major IDSs ship with rules designed to detect Nmap scans because scans are sometimes a precursor to attacks. Many of these products have morphed into intrusion *prevention* systems (IPS) that actively block traffic deemed malicious. Unfortunately for network administrators and IDS vendors, reliably detecting bad intentions by analyzing packet data is a tough problem. Attackers with patience, skill, and the help of certain Nmap options can usually pass by IDSs undetected. Meanwhile, administrators must cope with large numbers of false positive results where innocent activity is misdiagnosed and alerted on or blocked.

10.2. Why Would Ethical Professionals (White-hats) Ever Do This?

Some of you white-hat readers may be tempted to skip this chapter. For authorized use against your own networks, why would you ever want to evade your own security systems? Because it helps in understanding the danger of real attackers. If you can sneak around a blocked portmapper port using Nmap direct RPC scanning, then so can the bad guys. It is easy to make a mistake in configuring complex firewalls and other devices. Many of them even come with glaring security holes which conscientious users must find and close.

Regular network scanning can help find dangerous implicit rules (for example, in your Checkpoint Firewall-1 or Windows IPsec filters) before attackers do.

There are good reasons for evading IDSs as well. Product evaluation is one of the most common. If attackers can slide under the radar by simply adding an Nmap flag or two, the system is not offering much protection. It may still catch the script kiddies and worms, but they are usually blazingly obvious anyway.

Occasionally people suggest that Nmap should not offer features for evading firewall rules or sneaking past IDSs. They argue that these features are just as likely to be misused by attackers as used by administrators to enhance security. The problem with this logic is that these methods would still be used by attackers, who would just find other tools or patch the functionality into Nmap. Meanwhile, administrators would find it that much harder to do their jobs. Deploying only modern, patched FTP servers is a far more powerful defense than trying to prevent the distribution of tools implementing the FTP bounce attack.

10.3. Determining Firewall Rules

The first step toward bypassing firewall rules is to understand them. Where possible, Nmap distinguishes between ports that are reachable but closed, and those that are actively filtered. An effective technique is to start with a normal SYN port scan, then move on to more exotic techniques such as ACK scan and IP ID sequencing to gain a better understanding of the network.

10.3.1. Standard SYN Scan

One helpful feature of the TCP protocol is that systems are required by RFC 793 to send a negative response to unexpected connection requests in the form of a TCP RST (reset) packet. The RST packet makes closed ports easy for Nmap to recognize. Filtering devices such as firewalls, on the other hand, tend to drop packets destined for disallowed ports. In some cases they send ICMP error messages (usually port unreachable) instead. Because dropped packets and ICMP errors are easily distinguishable from RST packets, Nmap can reliably detect filtered TCP ports from open or closed ones, and it does so automatically. This is shown in Example 10.1.

Example 10.1. Detection of closed and filtered TCP ports

```
# nmap -sS -T4 scanme.nmap.org

Starting Nmap ( http://nmap.org )
Interesting ports on scanme.nmap.org (64.13.134.52):
Not shown: 994 filtered ports
PORT     STATE  SERVICE
22/tcp   open   ssh
25/tcp   closed smtp
53/tcp   open   domain
70/tcp   closed gopher
80/tcp   open   http
113/tcp  closed auth

Nmap done: 1 IP address (1 host up) scanned in 5.40 seconds
```

One of the most important lines in Example 10.1 is the parenthetical note "Not shown: 994 filtered ports". In other words, this host has a proper deny-by-default firewall policy. Only those ports the administrator explicitly allowed are reachable, while the default action is to deny (filter) them. Three of the enumerated ports are in the open state (22, 53, and 80), and another three are closed (25, 70, and 113). The remaining 994 tested ports are unreachable by this standard scan (filtered).

Sneaky firewalls that return RST

While the Nmap distinction between closed ports (which return a RST packet) and filtered ports (returning nothing or an ICMP error) is usually accurate, many firewall devices are now capable of forging RST packets as though they are coming from the destination host and claiming that the port is closed. One example of this capability is the Linux iptables system, which offers many methods for rejecting undesired packets. The iptables man page documents this feature as follows:

> --reject-with *type*
>
> The *type* given can be icmp-net-unreachable, icmp-host-unreachable, icmp-port-unreachable, icmp-proto-unreachable, icmp-net-prohibited or icmp-host-prohibited, which return the appropriate ICMP error message (port-unreachable is the default). The option tcp-reset can be used on rules which only match the TCP protocol: this causes a TCP RST packet to be sent back. This is mainly useful for blocking ident (`113/tcp`) probes which frequently occur when sending mail to broken mail hosts (which won't accept your mail otherwise).

Forging RST packets by firewalls and IDS/IPS is not particularly common outside of port 113, as it can be confusing to legitimate network operators and it also allows scanners to move on to the next port immediately without waiting on the timeout caused by dropped packets. Nevertheless, it does happen. Such forgery can usually be detected by careful analysis of the RST packet in comparison with other packets sent by the machine. Section 10.6, "Detecting Packet Forgery by Firewall and Intrusion Detection Systems" [289] describes effective techniques for doing so.

10.3.2. ACK Scan

As described in depth in Section 5.7, "TCP ACK Scan (-sA)" [113], the ACK scan sends TCP packets with only the ACK bit set. Whether ports are open or closed, the target is required by RFC 793 to respond with a RST packet. Firewalls that block the probe, on the other hand, usually make no response or send back an ICMP destination unreachable error. This distinction allows Nmap to report whether the ACK packets are being filtered. The set of filtered ports reported by an Nmap ACK scan is often smaller than for a SYN scan against the same machine because ACK scans are more difficult to filter. Many networks allow nearly unrestricted outbound connections, but wish to block Internet hosts from initiating connections back to them. Blocking incoming SYN packets (without the ACK bit set) is an easy way to do this, but it still allows any ACK packets through. Blocking those ACK packets is more difficult, because they do not tell which side started the connection. To block unsolicited ACK packets (as sent by the Nmap ACK scan), while allowing ACK packets belonging to legitimate connections, firewalls must statefully watch every established connection to determine whether a given ACK is appropriate. These stateful firewalls are usually more secure because they can be more restrictive. Blocking ACK scans is one extra available restriction. The downsides are that they require more resources to function, and a stateful firewall reboot can cause a device to lose state and terminate all established connections passing through it.

While stateful firewalls are widespread and rising in popularity, the stateless approach is still quite common. For example, the Linux Netfilter/iptables system supports the `--syn` convenience option to make the stateless approach described above easy to implement.

In the previous section, a SYN scan showed that all but six of 1,000 common ports on scanme.nmap.org were in the filtered state. Example 10.2 demonstrates an ACK scan against the same host to determine whether it is using a stateful firewall.

Example 10.2. ACK scan against Scanme

```
# nmap -sA -T4 scanme.nmap.org

Starting Nmap ( http://nmap.org )
Interesting ports on scanme.nmap.org (64.13.134.52):
Not shown: 994 filtered ports
PORT      STATE        SERVICE
22/tcp   unfiltered ssh
25/tcp   unfiltered smtp
53/tcp   unfiltered domain
70/tcp   unfiltered gopher
80/tcp   unfiltered http
113/tcp unfiltered auth

Nmap done: 1 IP address (1 host up) scanned in 5.96 seconds
```

The same six ports displayed in the SYN scan are shown here. The other 994 are still filtered. This is because Scanme is protected by this stateful iptables directive: **iptables -A INPUT -m state --state ESTABLISHED,RELATED -j ACCEPT**. This only accepts packets that are part of or related to an established connection. Unsolicited ACK packets sent by Nmap are dropped, except to the six special ports shown. Special rules allow all packets to the ports 22, 25, 53, 70, and 80, as well as sending a RST packet in response to port 113 probes. Note that the six shown ports are in the `unfiltered` state, since the ACK scan cannot further divide them into `open` (22, 53, and 80) or `closed` (25, 70, 113).

Now let us look at another example. A Linux host named Para on my local network uses the following (simplified to save space) firewall script:

```
#!/bin/sh
#
# A simple, stateless, host-based firewall script.

# First of all, flush & delete any existing tables
iptables -F
iptables -X

# Deny by default (input/forward)
iptables --policy INPUT DROP
iptables --policy OUTPUT ACCEPT
iptables --policy FORWARD DROP

# I want to make ssh and www accessible from outside
iptables -A INPUT -m multiport -p tcp --destination-port 22,80 -j ACCEPT

# Allow responses to outgoing TCP requests
iptables -A INPUT --proto tcp ! --syn -j ACCEPT
```

This firewall is stateless, as there is no sign of the `--state` option or the `-m state` module request. Example 10.3 shows SYN and ACK scans against this host.

Example 10.3. Contrasting SYN and ACK scans against Para

```
# nmap -sS -p1-100 -T4 para

Starting Nmap ( http://nmap.org )
Interesting ports on para (192.168.10.191):
Not shown: 98 filtered ports
PORT    STATE   SERVICE
22/tcp open    ssh
80/tcp closed http
MAC Address: 00:60:1D:38:32:90 (Lucent Technologies)

Nmap done: 1 IP address (1 host up) scanned in 3.81 seconds

# nmap -sA -p1-100 -T4 para

Starting Nmap ( http://nmap.org )
All 100 scanned ports on para (192.168.10.191) are: unfiltered
MAC Address: 00:60:1D:38:32:90 (Lucent Technologies)

Nmap done: 1 IP address (1 host up) scanned in 0.70 seconds
```

In the SYN scan, 98 of 100 ports are filtered. Yet the ACK scan shows every scanned port being `unfiltered`. In other words, all of the ACK packets are sneaking through unhindered and eliciting RST responses. These responses also make the scan more than five times as fast, since it does not have to wait on timeouts.

Now we know how to distinguish between stateful and stateless firewalls, but what good is that? The ACK scan of Para shows that some packets are probably reaching the destination host. I say probably because firewall forgery is always possible. While you may not be able to establish TCP connections to those ports, they can be useful for determining which IP addresses are in use, OS detection tests, certain IP ID shenanigans, and as a channel for tunneling commands to rootkits installed on those machines. Other scan types, such as FIN scan, may even be able to determine which ports are open and thus infer the purpose of the hosts. Such hosts may be useful as zombies for an IP ID idle scan.

This pair of scans also demonstrates that what we are calling a port state is not solely a property of the port itself. Here, the same port number is considered `filtered` by one scan type and `unfiltered` by another. What IP address you scan from, the rules of any filtering devices along the way, and which interface of the target machine you access can all affect how Nmap sees the ports. The port table only reflects what Nmap saw when running from a particular machine, with a defined set of options, at the given time.

10.3.3. IP ID Tricks

The humble identification field within IP headers can divulge a surprising amount of information. Later in this chapter it will be used for port scanning (idle scan technique) and to detect when firewall and intrusion detection systems are forging RST packets as though they come from protected hosts. Another neat trick is to discern what source addresses make it through the firewall. There is no point spending hours on a blind spoofing attack "from" 192.168.0.1 if some firewall along the way drops all such packets.

I usually test this condition with the free network probing tool **hping2**[1]. This is a rather complex technique, but it can be valuable sometimes. Here are the steps I take:

1. Find at least one accessible (open or closed) port of one machine on the internal network. Routers, printers, and Windows boxes often work well. Recent releases of Linux, Solaris, and OpenBSD have largely resolved the issue of predictable IP ID sequence numbers and will not work. The machine chosen should have little network traffic to avoid confusing results.

2. Verify that the machine has predictable IP ID sequences. The following command tests a Windows XP machine named Playground. The hping2 options request that five SYN packets be sent to port 80, one second apart.

```
# hping2 -c 5 -i 1 -p 80 -S playground
HPING playground (eth0 192.168.0.40): S set, 40 headers + 0 data bytes
len=46 ip=192.168.0.40 ttl=128 id=64473 sport=80 flags=RA seq=0 rtt=0.7 ms
len=46 ip=192.168.0.40 ttl=128 id=64474 sport=80 flags=RA seq=1 rtt=0.3 ms
len=46 ip=192.168.0.40 ttl=128 id=64475 sport=80 flags=RA seq=2 rtt=0.3 ms
len=46 ip=192.168.0.40 ttl=128 id=64476 sport=80 flags=RA seq=3 rtt=0.3 ms
len=46 ip=192.168.0.40 ttl=128 id=64477 sport=80 flags=RA seq=4 rtt=0.3 ms

--- playground hping statistic ---
5 packets transmitted, 5 packets received, 0% packet loss
round-trip min/avg/max = 0.3/0.3/0.7 ms
```

Since the IP ID fields are perfectly sequential, we can move on to the next test. If they were random or very far apart, we would have to find a new accessible host.

---

[1] *http://www.hping.org*

3. Start a flood of probes to the target from a host near your own (just about any host will do). An example command is **hping2 --spoof scanme.nmap.org --fast -p 80 -c 10000 -S playground**. Replace `scanme.nmap.org` with some other host of your choice, and `playground` with your target host. Getting replies back is not necessary, because the goal is simply to increment the IP ID sequences. Do not use the real address of the machine you are running hping2 from. Using a machine nearby on the network is advised to reduce the probability that your own ISP will block the packets.

While this is going on, redo the test from the previous step against your target machine.

```
# hping2 -c 5 -i 1 -p 80 -S playground
HPING playground (eth0 192.168.0.40): S set, 40 headers + 0 data bytes
len=46 ip=192.168.0.40 ttl=128 id=64672 sport=80 flags=RA seq=0 rtt=0.6 ms
len=46 ip=192.168.0.40 ttl=128 id=64683 sport=80 flags=RA seq=1 rtt=0.2 ms
len=46 ip=192.168.0.40 ttl=128 id=64694 sport=80 flags=RA seq=2 rtt=0.2 ms
len=46 ip=192.168.0.40 ttl=128 id=64705 sport=80 flags=RA seq=3 rtt=0.2 ms
len=46 ip=192.168.0.40 ttl=128 id=64716 sport=80 flags=RA seq=4 rtt=0.2 ms

--- playground hping statistic ---
5 packets transmitted, 5 packets received, 0% packet loss
round-trip min/avg/max = 0.2/0.3/0.6 ms
```

This time, the IP IDs are increasing by roughly 11 per second instead of one. The target is receiving our 10 forged packets per second, and responding to each of them. Each response increments the IP ID. Some hosts use a unique IP ID sequence for each IP address they communicate with. If that had been the case, we would not have seen the IP ID leaping like this and we would have to look for a different target host on the network.

4. Repeat step 3 using spoofed addresses that you suspect may be allowed through the firewall or trusted. Try addresses behind their firewall, as well as the RFC 1918 private networks such as 10.0.0.0/8, 192.168.0.0/16, and 172.16.0.0/12. Also try localhost (127.0.0.1) and maybe another address from 127.0.0.0/8 to detect cases where 127.0.0.1 is hard coded in. There have been many security holes related to spoofed localhost packets, including the infamous Land denial of service attack. Misconfigured systems sometimes trust these addresses without checking whether they came from the loopback interface. If a source address gets through to the end host, the IP ID will jump as seen in step 3. If it continues to increment slowly as in step 2, the packets were likely dropped by a firewall or router.

The end result of this technique is a list of source address netblocks that are permitted through the firewall, and those that are blocked. This information is valuable for several reasons. The IP addresses a company chooses to block or allow may give clues as to what addresses are used internally or trusted. For example, machines on a company's production network might trust IP addresses on the corporate network, or trust a system administrator's personal machine. Machines on the same production network also sometimes trust each other, or trust localhost. Common IP-based trust relationships are seen in NFS exports, host firewall rules, TCP wrappers, custom applications, rlogin, etc. Another example is SNMP, where a spoofed request to a Cisco router could cause the router to transfer (TFTP) its configuration data back to the attacker. Before spending substantial time trying to find and exploit these problems, use the test described here to determine whether the spoofed packets even get through.

A concrete example of this trusted-source-address problem is that I once found that a company's custom UDP service allowed users to skip authentication if they came from special netblocks entered into a configuration file. These netblocks corresponded to different corporate locations, and the feature was meant to ease administration and debugging. Their Internet-facing firewall smartly tried to block those addresses, as actual employees could access production from a private link instead. But by using the techniques described in this section, I found that the firewall was not perfectly synced with the config file. There were a few addresses from which I could successfully forge the UDP control messages and take over their application.

This technique of mapping out the firewall rules does not use Nmap, but the results are valuable for future runs. For example, this test can show whether to use certain decoys (-D). The best decoys will make it all the way to the target system. In addition, forged packets must get through for the IP ID idle scan (discussed later) to work. Testing potential source IPs with this technique is usually easier than finding and testing every potential idle proxy machine on a network. Potential idle proxies need only be tested if they pass step number two, above.

10.3.4. UDP Version Scanning

The previous sections have all focused on the prevalent TCP protocol. Working with UDP is often more difficult because the protocol does not provide acknowledgment of open ports like TCP does. Many UDP applications will simply ignore unexpected packets, leaving Nmap unsure whether the port is open or filtered. So Nmap places these ambiguous ports in the open|filtered state, as shown in Example 10.4.

Example 10.4. UDP scan against firewalled host

```
# nmap -sU -p50-59 scanme.nmap.org

Starting Nmap ( http://nmap.org )
Interesting ports on scanme.nmap.org (64.13.134.52):
PORT    STATE         SERVICE
50/udp open|filtered re-mail-ck
51/udp open|filtered la-maint
52/udp open|filtered xns-time
53/udp open|filtered domain
54/udp open|filtered xns-ch
55/udp open|filtered isi-gl
56/udp open|filtered xns-auth
57/udp open|filtered priv-term
58/udp open|filtered xns-mail
59/udp open|filtered priv-file

Nmap done: 1 IP address (1 host up) scanned in 1.38 seconds
```

This 10-port scan was not very helpful. No port responded to the probe packets, and so they are all listed as open or filtered. One way to better understand which ports are actually open is to send a whole bunch of UDP probes for dozens of different known UDP services in the hope of eliciting a response from any open ports. Nmap version detection (Chapter 7, *Service and Application Version Detection* [145]) does exactly that. Example 10.5 shows the same scan with the addition of version detection (-sV).

Example 10.5. UDP version scan against firewalled host

```
# nmap -sV -sU -p50-59 scanme.nmap.org

Starting Nmap ( http://nmap.org )
Interesting ports on scanme.nmap.org (64.13.134.52):
PORT    STATE         SERVICE      VERSION
50/udp  open|filtered re-mail-ck
51/udp  open|filtered la-maint
52/udp  open|filtered xns-time
53/udp  open          domain       ISC BIND 9.3.4
54/udp  open|filtered xns-ch
55/udp  open|filtered isi-gl
56/udp  open|filtered xns-auth
57/udp  open|filtered priv-term
58/udp  open|filtered xns-mail
59/udp  open|filtered priv-file

Nmap done: 1 IP address (1 host up) scanned in 56.59 seconds
```

Version detection shows beyond a doubt that port 53 (domain) is open, and even what it is running. The other ports are still `open|filtered` because they did not respond to any of the probes. They are probably filtered, though this is not guaranteed. They could be running a service such as SNMP which only responds to packets with the correct community string. Or they could be running an obscure or custom UDP service for which no Nmap version detection probe exists. Also note that this scan took more than 40 times as long as the previous scan. Sending all of those probes to each port is a relatively slow process. Adding the `--version-intensity 0` option would reduce scan time significantly by only sending the probes most likely to elicit a response from services at a given port number.

10.4. Bypassing Firewall Rules

While mapping out firewall rules can be valuable, bypassing rules is often the primary goal. Nmap implements many techniques for doing this, though most are only effective against poorly configured networks. Unfortunately, those are common. Individual techniques each have a low probability of success, so try as many different methods as possible. The attacker need only find one misconfiguration to succeed, while the network defenders must close every hole.

10.4.1. Exotic Scan Flags

The previous section discussed using an ACK scan to map out which target network ports are filtered. However, it could not determine which of the accessible ports were open or closed. Nmap offers several scan methods that are good at sneaking past firewalls while still providing the desired port state information. FIN scan is one such technique. In Section 10.3.2, "ACK Scan" [260], SYN and ACK scans were run against a machine named Para. The SYN scan showed only two open ports, perhaps due to firewall restrictions. Meanwhile, the ACK scan is unable to recognize open ports from closed ones. Example 10.6 shows another scan attempt against Para, this time using a FIN scan. Because a naked FIN packet is being set, this packet flies past the rules blocking SYN packets. While a SYN scan only found one open port below 100, the FIN scan finds both of them.

Example 10.6. FIN scan against stateless firewall

```
# nmap -sF -p1-100 -T4 para

Starting Nmap ( http://nmap.org )
Interesting ports on para (192.168.10.191):
Not shown: 98 filtered ports
PORT     STATE           SERVICE
22/tcp open|filtered ssh
53/tcp open|filtered domain
MAC Address: 00:60:1D:38:32:90 (Lucent Technologies)

Nmap done: 1 IP address (1 host up) scanned in 1.61 seconds
```

Many other scan types are worth trying, since the target firewall rules and target host type determine which techniques will work. Some particularly valuable scan types are FIN, Maimon, Window, SYN/FIN, and NULL scans. These are all described in Chapter 5, *Port Scanning Techniques and Algorithms* [95].

10.4.2. Source Port Manipulation

One surprisingly common misconfiguration is to trust traffic based only on the source port number. It is easy to understand how this comes about. An administrator will set up a shiny new firewall, only to be flooded with complains from ungrateful users whose applications stopped working. In particular, DNS may be broken because the UDP DNS replies from external servers can no longer enter the network. FTP is another common example. In active FTP transfers, the remote server tries to establish a connection back to the client to transfer the requested file.

Secure solutions to these problems exist, often in the form of application-level proxies or protocol-parsing firewall modules. Unfortunately there are also easier, insecure solutions. Noting that DNS replies come from port 53 and active FTP from port 20, many administrators have fallen into the trap of simply allowing incoming traffic from those ports. They often assume that no attacker would notice and exploit such firewall holes. In other cases, administrators consider this a short-term stop-gap measure until they can implement a more secure solution. Then they forget the security upgrade.

Overworked network administrators are not the only ones to fall into this trap. Numerous products have shipped with these insecure rules. Even Microsoft has been guilty. The IPsec filters that shipped with Windows 2000 and Windows XP contain an implicit rule that allows all TCP or UDP traffic from port 88 (Kerberos). Apple fans shouldn't get too smug about this because the firewall which shipped with Mac OS X Tiger is just as bad. Jay Beale discovered that even if you enable the "Block UDP Traffic" box in the firewall GUI, packets from port 67 (DHCP) and 5,353 (Zeroconf) pass right through. Yet another pathetic example of this configuration is that Zone Alarm personal firewall (versions up to 2.1.25) allowed any incoming UDP packets with the source port 53 (DNS) or 67 (DHCP).

Nmap offers the -g and --source-port options (they are equivalent) to exploit these weaknesses. Simply provide a port number, and Nmap will send packets from that port where possible. Nmap must use different port numbers for certain OS detection tests to work properly. Most TCP scans, including SYN scan, support the option completely, as does UDP scan. In May 2004, JJ Gray posted example Nmap scans to Bugtraq that demonstrate exploitation of the Windows IPsec source port 88 bug against one of his clients. A normal scan, followed by a -g 88 scan are shown in Example 10.7. Some output has been removed for brevity and clarity.

Example 10.7. Bypassing Windows IPsec filter using source port 88

```
# nmap -sS -v -v -PN 172.25.0.14

Starting Nmap ( http://nmap.org )
Interesting ports on 172.25.0.14:
Not shown: 1658 filtered ports
PORT    STATE  SERVICE
88/tcp closed kerberos-sec

Nmap done: 1 IP address (1 host up) scanned in 7.02 seconds

# nmap -sS -v -v -PN -g 88 172.25.0.14

Starting Nmap ( http://nmap.org )
Interesting ports on 172.25.0.14:
Not shown: 1653 filtered ports
PORT       STATE SERVICE
135/tcp   open  msrpc
139/tcp   open  netbios-ssn
445/tcp   open  microsoft-ds
1025/tcp  open  NFS-or-IIS
1027/tcp  open  IIS
1433/tcp  open  ms-sql-s

Nmap done: 1 IP address (1 host up) scanned in 0.37 seconds
```

Note that the closed port 88 was the hint that lead JJ to try using it as a source port. For further information on this vulnerability, see Microsoft Knowledge Base Article 811832.

10.4.3. IPv6 Attacks

While IPv6 has not exactly taken the world by storm, it is reasonably popular in Japan and certain other regions. When organizations adopt this protocol, they often forget to lock it down as they have instinctively learned to do with IPv4. Or they may try to, but find that their hardware does not support IPv6 filtering rules. Filtering IPv6 can sometimes be more critical than IPv4 because the expanded address space often allows the allocation of globally addressable IPv6 addresses to hosts that would normally have to use the private IPv4 addresses specified by RFC 1918.

Performing an IPv6 scan rather than the IPv4 default is often as easy as adding -6 to the command line. Certain features such as OS detection and UDP scanning are not yet supported for this protocol, but the most popular features work. Example 10.8 demonstrates IPv4 and IPv6 scans, performed long ago, of a well-known IPv6 development and advocacy organization.

Example 10.8. Comparing IPv4 and IPv6 scans

```
> nmap www.kame.net

Starting Nmap ( http://nmap.org )
Interesting ports on kame220.kame.net (203.178.141.220):
Not shown: 984 closed ports
Port        State       Service
19/tcp      filtered    chargen
21/tcp      open        ftp
22/tcp      open        ssh
53/tcp      open        domain
80/tcp      open        http
111/tcp     filtered    sunrpc
137/tcp     filtered    netbios-ns
138/tcp     filtered    netbios-dgm
139/tcp     filtered    netbios-ssn
513/tcp     filtered    login
514/tcp     filtered    shell
2049/tcp    filtered    nfs
2401/tcp    open        cvspserver
5999/tcp    open        ncd-conf
7597/tcp    filtered    qaz
31337/tcp   filtered    Elite

Nmap done: 1 IP address (1 host up) scanned in 34.47 seconds

> nmap -6 www.kame.net

Starting Nmap ( http://nmap.org )
Interesting ports on 3ffe:501:4819:2000:210:f3ff:fe03:4d0:
Not shown: 994 closed ports
Port        State       Service
21/tcp      open        ftp
22/tcp      open        ssh
53/tcp      open        domain
80/tcp      open        http
111/tcp     open        sunrpc
2401/tcp    open        cvspserver

Nmap done: 1 IP address (1 host up) scanned in 19.01 seconds
```

The first scan shows numerous filtered ports, including frequently exploitable services such as SunRPC, Windows NetBIOS, and NFS. Yet scanning the same host with IPv6 shows no filtered ports! Suddenly SunRPC (port 111) is available, and waiting to be queried by an IPv6-enabled **rpcinfo** or by Nmap version detection, which supports IPv6. They fixed the issue shortly after I notified them of it.

In order to perform an IPv6 scan, a system must be configured for IPv6. It must have an IPv6 address and routing information. Since my ISPs do not provide IPv6 addresses, I use the free IPv6 tunnel broker service at *http://www.tunnelbroker.net*. Other tunnel brokers are listed at Wikipedia[2]. 6to4 tunnels are another popular, free approach. Of course, this technique also requires that the target use IPv6.

---

[2] *http://en.wikipedia.org/wiki/List_of_IPv6_tunnel_brokers*

10.4.4. IP ID Idle Scanning

The IP ID idle scan has a reputation for being one of the most stealthy scan types, since no packets are sent to the target from your real address. Open ports are inferred from the IP ID sequences of a chosen zombie machine. A less recognized feature of idle scan is that the results obtained are actually those you would get if the zombie was to scan the target host directly. In a similar way that the -g option allows exploitation of trusted source ports, idle scan can sometimes exploit trusted source IP addresses. This ingenious scan type, which was originally conceived by security researcher Antirez, is described fully in Section 5.10, "TCP Idle Scan (-sI)" [117].

10.4.5. Multiple Ping Probes

A common issue when trying to scan through firewalled networks is that dropped ping probes can lead to missed hosts. To reduce this problem, Nmap allows a very wide variety of probes to be sent in parallel. Hopefully at least one will get through. Chapter 3, *Host Discovery (Ping Scanning)* [47] discusses these techniques in depth, including empirical data on the best firewall-busting techniques.

10.4.6. Fragmentation

Some packet filters have trouble dealing with IP packet fragments. They could reassemble the packets themselves, but that requires extra resources. There is also the possibility that fragments will take different paths, preventing reassembly. Due to this complexity, some filters ignore all fragments, while others automatically pass all but the first fragment. Interesting things can happen if the first fragment is not long enough to contain the whole TCP header, or if the second packet partially overwrites it. The number of filtering devices vulnerable to these problems is shrinking, though it never hurts to try.

An Nmap scan will use tiny IP fragments if the -f is specified. By default Nmap will include up to eight bytes of data in each fragment, so a typical 20 or 24 byte (depending on options) TCP packet is sent in three tiny fragments. Every instance of -f adds eight to the maximum fragment data size. So -f -f allows up to 16 data bytes within each fragment. Alternatively, you can specify the --mtu option and give the maximum data bytes as an argument. The --mtu argument must be a multiple of eight, and cannot be combined with the -f option.

Some source systems defragment outgoing packets in the kernel. Linux with the iptables connection tracking module is one such example. Do a scan while a sniffer such as Wireshark is running to ensure that sent packets are fragmented. If your host OS is causing problems, try the --send-eth option to bypass the IP layer and send raw ethernet frames.

Fragmentation is only supported for Nmap's raw packet features, which includes TCP and UDP port scans (except connect scan and FTP bounce scan) and OS detection. Features such as version detection and the Nmap Scripting Engine generally don't support fragmentation because they rely on your host's TCP stack to communicate with target services.

Out-of-order and partially overlapping IP fragments can be useful for Network research and exploitation, but that calls for an even lower-level networking tool than Nmap. Nmap sends fragments in order without any overlaps.

If a fragmented port scan gets through, a tool such as Fragroute[3] can be used to fragment other tools and exploits used to attack the host.

10.4.7. Proxies

Application-level proxies, particularly for the Web, have become popular due to perceived security and network efficiency (through caching) benefits. Like firewalls and IDS, misconfigured proxies can cause far more security problems than they solve. The most frequent problem is a failure to set appropriate access controls. Hundreds of thousands of wide-open proxies exist on the Internet, allowing anyone to use them as anonymous hopping points to other Internet sites. Dozens of organizations use automated scanners to find these open proxies and distribute the IP addresses. Occasionally the proxies are used for arguably positive things, such as escaping the draconian censorship imposed by the Chinese government on its residents. This "great firewall of China" has been known to block the New York Times web site as well as other news, political, and spiritual sites that the government disagrees with. Unfortunately, the open proxies are more frequently abused by more sinister folks who want to anonymously crack into sites, commit credit card fraud, or flood the Internet with spam.

While hosting a wide-open proxy to Internet resources can cause numerous problems, a more serious condition is when the open proxies allow connections back into the protected network. Administrators who decide that internal hosts must use a proxy to access Internet resources often inadvertently allow traffic in the opposite direction as well. The hacker Adrian Lamo is famous for breaking into Microsoft, Excite, Yahoo, WorldCom, the New York Times, and other large networks, usually by exploiting this reverse-proxy technique.

Nmap does not presently offer a proxy scan-through option, though it is high on the priority list. Section 7.9, "SOLUTION: Hack Version Detection to Suit Custom Needs, such as Open Proxy Detection" [168] discusses a way to find open proxies using Nmap version detection. In addition, plenty of dedicated free proxy scanners are available on Internet sites such as Packet Storm[4]. Lists of thousands of open proxies are widespread as well.

10.4.8. MAC Address Spoofing

Ethernet devices (including Wi-Fi) are identified by a unique six-byte media access control (MAC) address. The first three bytes make up an organizationally unique identifier (OUI). This prefix is assigned to a vendor by the IEEE. The vendor is then responsible for assigning the remaining three bytes uniquely in the adapters and devices it sells. Nmap includes a database which maps OUIs to the vendor names they are assigned to. This helps in identifying devices while scanning a network, though this section describes why it can't be completely trusted. The OUI database file, `nmap-mac-prefixes`, is described in Section 14.6, "MAC Address Vendor Prefixes: nmap-mac-prefixes" [368].

While MAC addresses are pre-assigned to ethernet devices, they can be changed with a driver on most current hardware. But since few people change their MAC address (or even know they have one), many networks use them for identification and authorization purposes. For example, most wireless access points provide a configuration option for limiting access to a certain set of MAC addresses. Similarly, some paid or private networks will force you to authenticate or pay after you connect using a web form. Then they will allow you access to the rest of the network based on your MAC address. Given that it is generally easy to sniff MAC addresses (they must be sent in every frame sent and received), and then to spoof that MAC to gain

---

[3] *http://www.monkey.org/~dugsong/fragroute/*
[4] *http://packetstormsecurity.nl/*

---

unauthorized access to the network, this form of access control is rather weak. It is also only effective at the edges of a network, since an end-host's MAC address is replaced when traversing a router.

In addition to access control, MAC addresses are sometimes used for accountability. Network admins will record MAC addresses when they obtain a DHCP lease or when a new machine communicates on the network. If network abuse or piracy complaints are received later, they figure out the MAC address based on the IP address and incident time. Then they use the MAC to track down the responsible machine and its owner. The ease of MAC address spoofing undermines this approach to some degree. Even when users are guilty, they may raise the specter of MAC address spoofing to deflect responsibility.

Nmap supports MAC address spoofing with the `--spoof-mac` option. The argument given can take several forms. If it is simply the number 0, Nmap chooses a completely random MAC address for the session. If the given string is an even number of hex digits (with the pairs optionally separated by a colon), Nmap will use those as the MAC. If fewer than 12 hex digits are provided, Nmap fills in the remainder of the six bytes with random values. If the argument isn't a zero or hex string, Nmap looks through `nmap-mac-prefixes` to find a vendor name containing the given string (it is case insensitive). If a match is found, Nmap uses the vendor's OUI and fills out the remaining three bytes randomly. Valid `--spoof-mac` argument examples are `Apple`, `0`, `01:02:03:04:05:06`, `deadbeefcafe`, `0020F2`, and `Cisco`. This option implies `--send-eth` to ensure that Nmap actually sends ethernet-level packets. This option only affects raw packet scans such as SYN scan or OS detection, not connection-oriented features such as version detection or the Nmap Scripting Engine.

Even when MAC address spoofing isn't needed for network access, it can be used for deception. If I'm at a conference and launch a scan from my Thinkpad with `--spoof-mac Apple`, suspicious eyes may turn to the MacBook users in the room.

10.4.9. Source Routing

This old-school technique is still effective in some cases. If a particular router on the path is causing you trouble, try to find a route around it. Effectiveness of this technique is limited because packet filtering problems usually occur on or near the target network. Those machines are likely to either drop all source routed packets or to be the only way into the network. Nmap supports both loose and strict source routing using the `--ip-options` option. For example, specifying `--ip-options "L 192.168.0.7 192.168.30.9"` requests that the packet be loose source routed through those two given IP way points. Specify `S` instead of `L` for strict source routing. If you choose strict source routing, keep in mind that you will have to specify every single hop along the path.

For a real-life example of source routing used to evade filtering policies on a modern network, see Section 10.4.12, "A Practical Real-life Example of Firewall Subversion" [272]. While IPv4 source routing is very commonly blocked, the IPv6 form of source routing is much more pervasive. An interesting article on that problem is available at *http://lwn.net/Articles/232781/*.

If a source routed path to a target machine is discovered with Nmap, exploitability is not limited to port scanning. Hobbit's Netcat[5] is a classic tool for enabling TCP and UDP communication over source routed paths (use the `-g` option).

---

[5] *http://sectools.org/#netcat*

10.4.10. FTP Bounce Scan

While only a small percentage of FTP servers are still vulnerable, it is worth checking all of your clients' systems for this problem. At a minimum, it allows outside attackers to utilize vulnerable systems to scan other parties. Worse configurations even allow attackers to bypass the organization's firewalls. Details and examples of this technique are provided in Section 5.12, "TCP FTP Bounce Scan (-b)" [127]. Example 10.9 shows an HP printer being used to relay a port scan. If this printer is behind the organization's firewall, it can be used to scan normally inaccessible (to the attacker) internal addresses as well.

Example 10.9. Exploiting a printer with the FTP bounce scan

```
felix~> nmap -p 22,25,135 -PN -v -b XXX.YY.111.2 scanme.nmap.org

Starting Nmap ( http://nmap.org )
Attempting connection to ftp://anonymous:-wwwuser@@XXX.YY.111.2:21
Connected:220 JD FTP Server Ready
Login credentials accepted by ftp server!
Initiating TCP ftp bounce scan against scanme.nmap.org (64.13.134.52)
Adding open port 22/tcp
Adding open port 25/tcp
Scanned 3 ports in 12 seconds via the Bounce scan.
Interesting ports on scanme.nmap.org (64.13.134.52):
PORT    STATE    SERVICE
22/tcp  open     ssh
25/tcp  open     smtp
135/tcp filtered msrpc

Nmap done: 1 IP address (1 host up) scanned in 21.79 seconds
```

10.4.11. Take an Alternative Path

I hate to overuse the "think outside the box" cliché, but continually banging on the front door of a well-secured network is not always the best approach. Look for other ways in. Wardial their phone lines, attack subsidiaries who may have special network access, or show up at their offices with Wi-Fi sniffing equipment, or even sneak in and plug into a convenient ethernet jack. Nmap works well through all of these connections. Just make sure that your penetration-testing contract covers these methods before your client catches you in a ninja suit grappling onto their datacenter rooftop.

10.4.12. A Practical Real-life Example of Firewall Subversion

Now that many individual techniques for bypassing firewall rules have been covered, it is time to put them together in a real-life penetration testing scenario. It all started with a post[6] to the SecurityFocus *pen-test* list from security pro Michael Cain. He and coworker Demetris Papapetrou were penetration testing the internal network of a large corporation and had just bypassed firewall rules meant to prevent one VLAN from accessing another. I was pleased to read that they performed this feat using Nmap, and I wrote them for the whole

---

[6] *http://seclists.org/pen-test/2008/Mar/0010.html*

---

story. It is both instructional and inspirational in that it demonstrates the value of perseverance and trying every technique you know, even after the most common exploits fail. Don't let that firewall beat you!

The story starts with Michael and Demetris performing an Nmap scan which shows that they are stuck on a heavily filtered network. They can reach some corporate servers, but not any of the (potentially vulnerable) desktop client machines which have to exist somewhere on the network. Perhaps they are on a restricted conference room or lobby network, or maybe a wireless access point set up for corporate guests. Some of the discovered hosts and networks are shown in Example 10.10. A few details in this story (such as IP addresses) have been changed for confidentiality reasons. I will call the target corporation Megacorp.

Example 10.10. Some interesting hosts and networks at Megacorp

```
10.10.5.1   - A router/firewall which will give us grief later
10.10.5.42 - Our protagonists are scanning from this machine
10.10.6.30 - files2.megacorp.com; Nmap shows this is a Windows machine
             with port 445 open.
10.10.6.60 - mail.megacorp.com; Nmap OS detection shows that it is
             Solaris 8. Port 25 is open and accessible.
10.10.10.0/24 - Nothing shows up here, but many of the IPs have
             reverse-DNS names, so Demetris suspects that a
             firewall may be blocking his probes.  The goal is to
             reach any available hosts on this subnet.
```

Given the goal of determining if any hosts are hiding on the 10.10.10.0/24 network, Demetris starts with a simple ping scan using ICMP echo request queries (-PE). The results are shown in Example 10.11.

Example 10.11. Ping scan against the target network

```
# nmap -n -sP -PE -T4 10.10.10.0/24
Starting Nmap ( http://nmap.org )
Nmap done: 256 IP addresses (0 hosts up) scanned in 26.167 seconds
```

The ping scan fails to find any responsive hosts. Demetris is understandably disappointed, but at least it makes this section more interesting and instructive. Perhaps the network truly is empty, but it could also be packed with vulnerable machines which Demetris is blocked from accessing. He needs to dig deeper. In Example 10.12, Demetris chooses one IP on that network and performs a ping scan. He specifies the packet tracing (--packet-trace) and extra verbosity (-vv) options to determine what is going on at the packet level. The reason for choosing just one IP is to avoid a confusing flood of hundreds of packets.

Example 10.12. Packet trace against a single IP

```
# nmap -vv -n -sP -PE -T4 --packet-trace 10.10.10.7
Starting Nmap ( http://nmap.org )
SENT (0.3130s) ICMP 10.10.5.42 > 10.10.10.7 echo request (type=8/code=0)
             ttl=41 id=7193 iplen=28
RCVD (0.3130s) ICMP 10.10.5.1 > 10.10.5.42 host 10.10.10.7 unreachable
             (type=3/code=1) ttl=255 id=25980 iplen=56
Nmap done: 1 IP address (0 hosts up) scanned in 0.313 seconds
```

It seems that Demetris is receiving ICMP host unreachable messages when trying to scan these IPs (or at least this one). Routers commonly do that when a host is unavailable and so they can't determine a MAC address. It is also occasionally caused by filtering. Demetris scans the other hosts on the network and verifies that they behave the same way. It is possible that only ICMP packets are filtered, so Demetris decides to try a TCP SYN scan. He runs the command **nmap -vv -n -sS -T4 -PN --reason 10.10.10.0/24**. All ports are shown as filtered, and the `--reason` results blame some host unreachable messages and some nonresponsive ports. The nonresponsive ports may be due to rate limiting of host unreachable messages sent by the router. Many routers will only send one of these every few seconds. Demetris can verify whether rate limiting is the cause by running the scan again and seeing if the host unreachable messages come for exactly the same set of ports. If the ports are the same, it may be a specific port-based filter. If Nmap receives host-unreachable messages for different ports each time, rate limiting is likely the cause.

If a filter is causing the problem, it could be a simple stateless firewall as is commonly available on routers and switches. As discussed in previous sections, these sometimes allow TCP ACK packets through unmolested. Demetris repeats the scan, but specifies `-sA` for an ACK scan rather than `-sS`. Any `unfiltered` ports found by the scan would suggest that the ACK packets made it through and elicited a TCP RST response from the target host. Unfortunately, the results were all `filtered` in this case, just as with the SYN scan.

Demetris decides to try something more advanced. He already knows that port 445 is open on the Windows machine at 10.10.6.30 (files2.megacorp.com) from his initial Nmap scan. While Demetris hasn't been able to reach the 10.10.10.0/24 network directly, perhaps files2 (being an important company file server) is able to access that IP range. Demetris decides to try bouncing his scans off files2 using the IPID Idle scan. First he wants to ensure that files2 works as a zombie by testing it against 10.10.6.60—a known-responsive machine with port 25 open. The results of this test are shown in Example 10.13.

Example 10.13. Testing an idle scan

```
# nmap -vv -n -PN -sI 10.10.6.30:445 -p 25 10.10.6.60

Starting Nmap ( http://nmap.org )

Initiating idle scan against 10.10.6.60 at 13:10
Idle scan using zombie 10.10.6.30 (10.10.6.30:445); Class: Incremental
Even though your Zombie (10.10.6.30) appears to be vulnerable to IP ID
sequence prediction (class: Incremental), our attempts have failed.  This
generally means that either the Zombie uses a separate IP ID base for each
host (like Solaris), or because you cannot spoof IP packets (perhaps your ISP
has enabled egress filtering to prevent IP spoofing), or maybe the target
network recognizes the packet source as bogus and drops them
QUITTING!
```

Using 10.10.6.30 as an Idle Zombie didn't work out well. If the problem was due to heavy traffic, he could try again in the middle of the night. The `--packet-trace` option combined with thorough reading of Section 5.10, "TCP Idle Scan (-sI)" [117] could help determine why 10.10.6.30 isn't working as a zombie. Demetris tries the handful of other hosts he has found on the network, and none work as zombies.

Demetris begins to worry about whether he will ever crack into the 10.10.10.0/24 network. Fortunately, he is an old hand at this and has another trick up his sleeve—IP source routing. In the early days of the Internet (and even today with IPv6), source routing was an important and widely deployed network diagnosis feature. It allows you to specify the hops you want a packet to take to its target rather than relying on normal routing rules. With strict source routing, you must specify every hop. Loose source routing allows you to fill in key IP way points, while normal Internet routing fills in hop details between those way points.

Long ago the networking community reached consensus that source routing is more trouble (particularly for security) than it is worth. Many (if not most) routers are configured to drop source routed IPv4 packets, so some folks have considered the problem fixed since the early 90's. Yet source routing, like SYN flooding and Telnet password sniffing, continues as a rare but potent risk. Demetris tests this attack by ping-scanning files2 (10.10.6.30) using packets loose-source-routed through the 10.10.6.60 mail server. Results are shown in Example 10.14.

Example 10.14. Testing source routing

```
# nmap -n -sP -PE --ip-options "L 10.10.6.60" --reason 10.10.6.30
Starting Nmap ( http://nmap.org )
Host 10.10.6.30 appears to be up, received echo-reply.
Nmap done: 1 IP address (1 host up) scanned in .313 seconds
```

Demetris is both surprised and delighted that the test works. He immediately turns his attention to his true target network, repeating his initial ping scan with an additional option: --ip-options "L 10.10.6.60". This time, Nmap reports that the machine at 10.10.10.7 is responsive. Demetris learns that it wasn't reachable before because the 10.10.10.0/24 and 10.10.5.0/24 subnets are on different router VLANs configured to prevent them from communicating to each other. Demetris' source routing technique opened a big loophole in that policy! Demetris follows up with a SYN scan of the 10.10.10.7 machine, as shown in Example 10.15.

Example 10.15. Success at last

```
# nmap -vv -n -sS -PN --ip-options "L 10.10.6.60" --reason 10.10.10.7
Starting Nmap ( http://nmap.org )
Interesting ports on 10.10.10.7:
Not shown: 988 closed ports
Reason: 988 resets
PORT       STATE      SERVICE              REASON
21/tcp     filtered   ftp                  no-response
23/tcp     filtered   telnet               no-response
25/tcp     open       smtp                 syn-ack
80/tcp     open       http                 syn-ack
135/tcp    open       msrpc                syn-ack
139/tcp    open       netbios-ssn          syn-ack
443/tcp    open       https                syn-ack
445/tcp    open       microsoft-ds         syn-ack
515/tcp    open       printer              syn-ack
1032/tcp   open       iad3                 syn-ack
1050/tcp   open       java-or-OTGfileshare syn-ack
3372/tcp   open       msdtc                syn-ack
Nmap done: 1 IP address (1 host up) scanned in 21.203 seconds
```

Demetris omitted OS detection and version detection from this initial scan, but this looks like a Windows machine from the open port profile. Demetris can now connect to and access these ports as long as he uses tools such as Netcat which offer source routing options. I don't know what happens next in the story, but I'm guessing that it involves Demetris fully penetrating the network and then helping the company redesign it more securely.

10.5. Subverting Intrusion Detection Systems

Firewalls are not the only obstacle that modern attackers face. Intrusion detection and prevention systems can be problematic as well. Network administration staff do not always take well to a flood of 2:00 A.M. intrusion alert pages from the IDS. Considerate hackers take pains to prevent their actions from causing all of these alerts in the first place. A first step is to detect whether an IDS is even present—many small companies do not use them. If an IDS is suspected or detected, there are many effective techniques for subverting it. They fall into three categories that vary by intrusiveness: avoiding the IDS as if the attacker is not there, confusing the IDS with misleading data, and exploiting the IDS to gain further network privilege or just to shut it down. Alternatively, attackers who are not concerned with stealth can ignore the IDS completely as they pound away at the target network.

10.5.1. Intrusion Detection System Detection

Early on in the never-ending battle between network administrators and malicious hackers, administrators defended their turf by hardening systems and even installing firewalls to act as a perimeter barrier. Hackers developed new tools to penetrate or sneak around the firewalls and exploit vulnerable hosts. The arms race escalated with administrators introducing intrusion detection systems that constantly watch for devious activity. Attackers responded, of course, by devising systems for detecting and deceiving the IDS. While intrusion detection systems are meant to be passive devices, many can be detected by attackers over the network.

The least conspicuous IDS is one that passively listens to network traffic without ever transmitting. Special network tap hardware devices are available to ensure that the IDS *cannot* transmit, even if it is compromised by attackers. Despite the security advantages of such a setup, it is not widely deployed due to practical considerations. Modern IDSs expect to be able send alerts to central management consoles and the like. If this was all the IDS transmitted, the risk would be minimal. But to provide more extensive data on the alert, they often initiate probes that may be seen by attackers.

Reverse probes

One probe commonly initiated by IDSs is reverse DNS query of the attacker's IP address. A domain name in an alert is more valuable than just an IP address, after all. Unfortunately, attackers who control their own rDNS (quite common) can watch the logs in real time and learn that they have been detected. This is a good time for attackers to feed misinformation, such as bogus names and cache entries to the requesting IDS.

Some IDSs go much further and send more intrusive probes to the apparent attackers. When an attacker sees his target scan him back, there is no question that he has set off alarms. Some IDSs send Windows NetBIOS information requests back to the attacker. ISS BlackICE Defender is one vendor that does (or at least did) this by default. I wrote a small tool called icepick which sends a simple packet that generates an alert from listening BlackICE instances. Then it watches for telltale NetBIOS queries and reports any BlackICE installations found. One could easily scan large networks looking for this IDS and then attempt to exploit them using holes discussed later in this chapter.

Not content with simply locating BlackICE installations or detecting them during penetration tests, I wrote a simple Unix program called windentd which replies to the probe with misinformation. Figure 10.1 shows a BlackICE console where the Intruder is listed as "Your Mother" thanks to windentd and icepick. Those

---

simple tools are available from *http://insecure.org/presentations/CanSecWest01/*, though they are not supported.

Figure 10.1. BlackICE discovers an unusual intruder

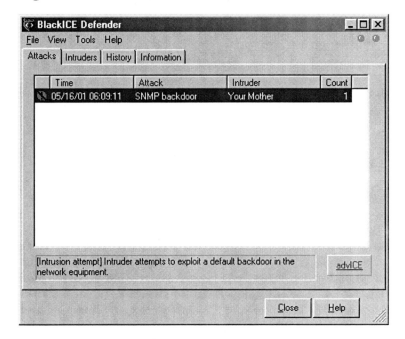

Sudden firewall changes and suspicious packets

Many intrusion detection systems have morphed into what marketing departments label intrusion prevention systems. Some can only sniff the network like a normal IDS and send triggered packet responses. The best IPS systems are inline on the network so that they can restrict packet flow when suspicious activity is detected. For example, an IPS may block any further traffic from an IP address that they believe has port scanned them, or that has attempted a buffer overflow exploit. Attackers are likely to notice this if they port scan a system, then are unable to connect to the reported open ports. Attackers can confirm that they are blocked by trying to connect from another IP address.

Suspicious response packets can also be a tip-off that an attacker's actions have been flagged by an IDS. In particular, many IDSs that are *not* inline on the network will forge RST packets in an attempt to tear down connections. Ways to determine that these packets are forged are covered in Section 10.6, "Detecting Packet Forgery by Firewall and Intrusion Detection Systems" [289].

Naming conventions

Naming conventions can be another giveaway of IDS presence. If an Nmap list scan returns host names such as realsecure, ids-monitor, or dragon-ids, you may have found an intrusion detection system. The administrators might have given away that information inadvertently, or they may think of it like the alarm stickers on house and car windows. Perhaps they think that the script kiddies will be scared away by IDS-related names. It could also be misinformation. You can never fully trust DNS names. For example, you might assume that bugzilla.securityfocus.com is a web server running the popular Bugzilla web-based bug tracking software.

Not so. The Nmap scan in Example 10.16 shows that it is probably a Symantec Raptor firewall instead. No web server is accessible, though there may be one hidden behind the Raptor.

Example 10.16. Host names can be deceiving

```
# nmap -sS -sV -T4 -p1-24 bugzilla.securityfocus.com

Starting Nmap ( http://nmap.org )
Interesting ports on 205.206.231.82:
Not shown: 21 closed ports
PORT    STATE SERVICE    VERSION
21/tcp open  ftp-proxy Symantec Enterprise Firewall FTP proxy
22/tcp open  ssh?
23/tcp open  telnet     Symantec Raptor firewall secure gateway telnetd

Nmap done: 1 IP address (1 host up) scanned in 0.94 seconds
```

Unexplained TTL jumps

One more way to detect certain IDSs is to watch for unexplained gaps (or suspicious machines) in traceroutes. While most operating systems include a **traceroute** command (it is abbreviated to **tracert** on Windows), Nmap offers a faster and more effective alternative with the --traceroute option. Unlike standard **traceroute**, Nmap sends its probes in parallel and is able to determine what sort of probe will be most effective based on scan results. In Example 10.17, which was contrived for simplicity, traceroute locates nothing at hop five. That may be an inline IDS or firewall protecting the target company. Of course, this can only detect inline IDSs as opposed to those which passively sniff the network without being part of the route. Even some inline devices may not be spotted because they fail to decrement the TTL or refuse to pass ICMP ttl-exceeded messages back from the protected network.

Example 10.17. Noting TTL gaps with traceroute

```
# nmap --traceroute www.target.com
Interesting ports on orestes.red.target.com (10.0.0.6)
Not shown: 996 filtered ports
PORT     STATE  SERVICE
22/tcp   open   ssh
53/tcp   open   domain
80/tcp   open   http
113/tcp  closed auth

TRACEROUTE (using port 22/tcp)
HOP RTT    ADDRESS
1   1.10   gw (205.217.153.49)
2   10.40  metro1-ge-152.pa.meer.net (205.217.152.1)
3   12.02  208.185.168.171 (208.185.168.171)
4   14.74  p4-2-0-0.r06.us.bb.verio.net (129.250.9.129)
5   ...
6   15.07  orestes.red.target.com (10.0.0.6)

Nmap done: 1 IP address (1 host up) scanned in 4.35 seconds
```

While traceroute is the best-known method for obtaining this information, it isn't the only one. IPv4 offers an obscure option called record route for gathering this information. Due to the maximum IP header size, a maximum of nine hops can be recorded. In addition, some hosts and routers drop packets with this option set. It is still a handy trick for those times when traditional traceroute fails. This option can be specified with Nmap using `--ip-options R` to set the option and `--packet-trace` to read it from the response. It is generally used in conjunction with an ICMP ping scan (`-sP -PE`). Most operating systems offer an `-R` option to their ping command, which is easier to use than Nmap for this purpose. An example of this technique is provided in Example 10.18.

Example 10.18. Using the IP record route option

```
> ping -R 151.164.184.68
PING 151.164.184.68 (151.164.184.68) 56(124) bytes of data.
64 bytes from 151.164.184.68: icmp_seq=1 ttl=126 time=11.7 ms
NOP
RR:     192.168.0.100
        69.232.194.10
        192.168.0.6
        192.168.0.100

--- 151.164.184.68 ping statistics ---
1 packets transmitted, 1 received, 0% packet loss, time 0ms
rtt min/avg/max/mdev = 11.765/11.765/11.765/0.000 ms
```

10.5.2. Avoiding Intrusion Detection Systems

The most subtle way to defeat intrusion detection systems is to avoid their watchful gaze entirely. The reality is that rules governing IDSs are pretty brittle in that they can often be defeated by manipulating the attack slightly. Attackers have dozens of techniques, from URL encoding to polymorphic shellcode generators for escaping IDS detection of their exploits. This section focuses on stealthy port scanning, which is even easier than stealthily exploiting vulnerabilities.

Slow down

When it comes to avoiding IDS alerts, patience is a virtue. Port scan detection is usually threshold based. The system watches for a given number of probes in a certain timeframe. This helps prevent false positives from innocent users. It is also essential to save resources—saving connection probes forever would consume memory and make real-time list searching too slow. The downside to this threshold approach is that attackers can evade it by keeping their scan rate just below the threshold. Nmap offers several canned timing modes that can be selected with the `-T` option to accomplish this. For example, the `-T paranoid` option causes Nmap to send just one probe at a time, waiting five minutes between them. A large scan may take weeks, but at least it probably will not be detected. The `-T sneaky` option is similar, but it only waits 15 seconds between probes.

Rather than specify canned timing modes such as `sneaky`, timing variables can be customized precisely with options such as `--max-parallelism`, `--min-rtt-timeout`, and `--scan-delay`. Chapter 6, *Optimizing Nmap Performance* [135] describes these in depth.

A practical example: bypassing default Snort 2.2.0 rules

Examining the handy open-source Snort IDS provides a lesson on sneaking under the radar. Snort has had several generations of port scan detectors. The Flow-Portscan module is quite formidable. A scan that slips by this is likely to escape detection by many other IDSs as well.

Flow-portscan is made up of two detection systems that can work in concert (or be enabled individually) to detect port scanners. The system and its dozens of configuration variables are documented in `docs/README.flow-portscan` in the Snort distribution, but I'll provide a quick summary.

The simpler detection method in Flow-portscan is known as the *fixed time scale*. This simply watches for `scanner-fixed-threshold` probe packets in `scanner-fixed-window` seconds. Those two variables, which are set in `snort.conf`, each default to 15. Note that the counter includes any probes sent from a single machine to any host on the protected network. So quickly scanning a single port on each of 15 protected machines will generate an alert just as surely as scanning 15 ports on a single machine.

If this were the only detection method, the solution would be pretty easy. Pass the `--scan-delay 1075` option to ensure that Nmap waits 1.075 seconds between sending probes. The intuitive choice might be a one second wait between packets to avoid 15 packets in 15 seconds, but that is not enough. There are only 14 waits between sending the first packet and the fifteenth, so the wait must be at least 15/14, or 1.07143 seconds. Some poor sap who chooses `--scan-delay 1000` would slow the scan down dramatically, while still triggering the alarm. If multiple hosts on the network are being probed, they must be scanned separately to avoid triggering the alarm. The option `--max-hostgroup 1` would ensure that only one host at a time is scanned, but is not completely safe because it will not enforce the `--scan-delay` between the last probe sent to one host, and the first sent to the next. As long as at least 15 ports per host are being scanned, you could compensate by making the `--scan-delay` at least 1155 ms, or simply start single-target Nmap instances from a shell script, waiting 1075 ms between them. Example 10.19 shows such a stealthy scan of several machines on a network. Multiple Nmap instances are handled using the Bash shell syntax. Here the IPs are specified manually. If many targets were desired, they could be enumerated into a file with the `-iL` (list scan) option, then Nmap started against each using a normal shell loop. The reason these scans took more than 1.075 seconds per port is that retransmissions were required for the filtered ports to ensure that they were not dropped due to network congestion.

Example 10.19. Slow scan to bypass the default Snort 2.2.0 Flow-portscan fixed time scan detection method

```
felix~# for target in 205.217.153.53 205.217.153.54 205.217.153.62; \
do nmap --scan-delay 1075 -p21,22,23,25,53 $target; \
usleep 1075000; \
done

Starting Nmap ( http://nmap.org )
Interesting ports on insecure.org (205.217.153.53):
PORT    STATE    SERVICE
21/tcp filtered ftp
22/tcp open     ssh
23/tcp filtered telnet
25/tcp open     smtp
53/tcp open     domain

Nmap done: 1 IP address (1 host up) scanned in 10.75 seconds

Starting Nmap ( http://nmap.org )
Interesting ports on lists.insecure.org (205.217.153.54):
PORT    STATE    SERVICE
21/tcp filtered ftp
22/tcp open     ssh
23/tcp filtered telnet
25/tcp open     smtp
53/tcp open     domain

Nmap done: 1 IP address (1 host up) scanned in 10.78 seconds

Starting Nmap ( http://nmap.org )
Interesting ports on scanme.nmap.org (205.217.153.62):
PORT    STATE    SERVICE
21/tcp filtered ftp
22/tcp open     ssh
23/tcp filtered telnet
25/tcp open     smtp
53/tcp open     domain

Nmap done: 1 IP address (1 host up) scanned in 10.80 seconds
```

Unfortunately for port scanning enthusiasts, defeating Snort is not so simple. It has another detection method, known as *sliding time scale*. This method is similar to the fixed-window method just discussed, except that it increases the window whenever a new probe from a host is detected. An alarm is raised if `scanner-sliding-threshold` probes are detected during the window. The window starts at `scanner-sliding-window` seconds, and increases for each probe detected by the amount of time elapsed so far in the window times `scanner-sliding-scale-factor`. Those three variables default to 40 probes, 20 seconds, and a factor of 0.5 in `snort.conf`.

The sliding scale is rather insidious in the way it grows continually as new packets come in. The simplest (if slow) solution would be to send one probe every 20.1 seconds. This would evade both the default fixed and sliding scales. This could be done just as in Example 10.19, but using a higher value. You could speed this up by an order of magnitude by sending 14 packets really fast, waiting 20 seconds for the window to expire, then repeating with another 14 probes. You may be able to do this with a shell script controlling Nmap, but writing your own simple SYN scanning program for this custom job may be preferable.

Scatter probes across networks rather than scanning hosts consecutively

As discussed in the previous section, IDSs are often programmed to alarm only after a threshold of suspicious activity has been reached. This threshold is often global, applying to the whole network protected by the IDS rather than just a single host. Occasionally they specifically watch for traffic from a given source address to consecutive hosts. If a host sends a SYN packet to port 139 of host 10.0.0.1, that isn't too suspicious by itself. But if that probe is followed by similar packets to 10.0.0.2, .3, .4, and .5, a port scan is clearly indicated.

One way to avoid triggering these alarms is to scatter probes among a large number of hosts rather than scanning them consecutively. Sometimes you can avoid scanning very many hosts on the same network. If you are only conducting a research survey, consider scattering probes across the whole Internet with −iR rather than scanning one large network. The results are likely to be more representative anyway.

In most cases, you want to scan a particular network and Internet-wide sampling isn't enough. Avoiding the consecutive-host probe alarms is easy. Nmap offers the --randomize-hosts option which splits up the target networks into blocks of 16384 IPs, then randomizes the hosts in each block. If you are scanning a huge network, such as class B or larger, you may get better (more stealthy) results by randomizing larger blocks. You can achieve this by increasing PING_GROUP_SZ in nmap.h and then recompiling. The block size used in a --randomize-hosts scan is four times the value of PING_GROUP_SZ. Note that higher values of PING_GROUP_SZ eat up more host memory. An alternative solution is to generate the target IP list with a list scan (−sL −n −oN <filename>), randomize it with a Perl script, then provide the whole list to Nmap with −iL. You will probably have to use this approach if you are scanning a huge network such as 10.0.0.0/8 and want all 16 million IP addresses randomized.

Fragment packets

IP fragments can be a major problem for intrusion detection systems, particularly because the handling of oddities such as overlapping fragments and fragmentation assembly timeouts are ambiguous and differ substantially between platforms. Because of this, the IDS often has to guess at how the remote system will interpret a packet. Fragment assembly can also be resource intensive. For these reasons, many intrusion detection systems still do not support fragmentation very well. Specify the −f to specify that a port scan use tiny (8 data bytes or fewer) IP fragments. See Section 10.4.6, "Fragmentation" [269] for more important details.

Evade specific rules

Most IDS vendors brag about how many alerts they support, but many (if not most) are easy to bypass. The most popular IDS among Nmap users is the open-source Snort[7]. Example 10.20 shows all of the default rules in Snort 2.0.0 that reference Nmap.

Example 10.20. Default Snort rules referencing Nmap

```
felix~/src/snort-2.0.0/rules>grep -i nmap *
icmp.rules:alert icmp $EXTERNAL_NET any -> $HOME_NET any (msg:"ICMP PING NMAP";
 dsize:0;itype: 8;reference:arachnids,162;
 classtype:attempted-recon;sid:469;rev:1;)
scan.rules:alert tcp $EXTERNAL_NET any -> $HOME_NET any (msg:"SCAN nmap XMAS";
 flags:FPU;reference:arachnids,30;classtype:attempted-recon; sid:1228;rev:1;)
scan.rules:alert tcp $EXTERNAL_NET any -> $HOME_NET any (msg:"SCAN nmap TCP";
 flags:A;ack:0;reference:arachnids,28;classtype:attempted-recon;sid:628;rev:1;)
scan.rules:alert tcp $EXTERNAL_NET any ->
 $HOME_NET any (msg:"SCAN nmap fingerprint attempt";
 flags:SFPU;reference:arachnids,05;classtype:attempted-recon; sid:629; rev:1;)
web-attacks.rules:alert tcp $EXTERNAL_NET any -> $HTTP_SERVERS $HTTP_PORTS
 (msg:"WEB-ATTACKS nmap command attempt";
 flow:to_server,established;content:"nmap%20";
 nocase;sid:1361;classtype:web-application-attack; rev:4;)
```

Now let us look at these rules through the eyes of an attacker. The first rule looks for an ICMP ping packet without any payload (`dsize:0`). Simply specifying a non-zero `--data-length` option will defeat that rule. Or the user could specify a different type of ping scan entirely, such as TCP SYN ping.

The next rule searches for TCP packets with the FIN, PSH, and URG flags set (flags:FPU) and signals an Nmap Xmas scan alert. Adding the option `--scanflags FINPSH` to the Xmas scan options will remove the URG flag. The scan will still work as expected, but the rule will fail to trigger.

The third rule in the list looks for TCP packets with the ACK bit set but an acknowledgment number of zero (flags:A;ack:0). Ancient versions of Nmap had this behavior, but it was fixed in 1999 in response to the Snort rule.

Rule number four looks for TCP packets with the SYN, FIN, PSH, and URG flags set (flags:SFPU). It then declares an Nmap OS fingerprinting attempt. An attacker can avoid flagging this by omitting the `-O` flag. If he really wishes to do OS detection, that single test can be commented out in `osscan2.cc`. The OS detection will still be quite accurate, but the IDS alert will not flag.

The final rule looks for people sending the string "`nmap `" to web servers. They are looking for attempts to execute commands through the web server. An attacker could defeat this by renaming Nmap, using a tab character instead of a space, or connecting with SSL encryption if available.

Of course there are other relevant rules that do not have Nmap in the name but could still be flagged by intrusive port scans. Advanced attackers install the IDS they are concerned with on their own network, then alter and test scans in advance to ensure that they do not trigger alarms.

---

[7] *http://www.snort.org*

Snort was only chosen for this example because its rules database is public and it is a fellow open-source network security tool. Commercial IDSs suffer from similar issues.

Avoid easily detected Nmap features

Some features of Nmap are more conspicuous than others. In particular, version detection connects to many different services, which will often leave logs on those machines and set off alarms on intrusion detection systems. OS detection is also easy to spot by intrusion detection systems, because a few of the tests use rather unusual packets and packet sequences. The Snort rules shown in Example 10.20, "Default Snort rules referencing Nmap" [283] demonstrate a typical Nmap OS detection signature.

One solution for pen-testers who wish to remain stealthy is to skip these conspicuous probes entirely. Service and OS detection are valuable, but not essential for a successful attack. They can also be used on a case-by-case basis against machines or ports that look interesting, rather than probing the whole target network with them.

10.5.3. Misleading Intrusion Detection Systems

The previous section discussed using subtlety to avoid the watchful eye of intrusion detection systems. An alternative approach is to actively mislead or confuse the IDS with packet forgery. Nmap offers numerous options for effecting this.

Decoys

Street criminals know that one effective means for avoiding authorities after a crime is to blend into any nearby crowds. The police may not be able to tell the purse snatcher from all of the innocent passersby. In the network realm, Nmap can construct a scan that appears to be coming from dozens of hosts across the world. The target will have trouble determining which host represents the attackers, and which ones are innocent decoys. While this can be defeated through router path tracing, response-dropping, and other active mechanisms, it is generally an effective technique for hiding the scan source. Figure 10.2 shows a BlackICE report screen that is inundated with decoys. The administrator cannot complain to the providers for every ISP on the list. It would take a long time, and all but one of the hosts are innocent.

Figure 10.2. An attacker masked by dozens of decoys

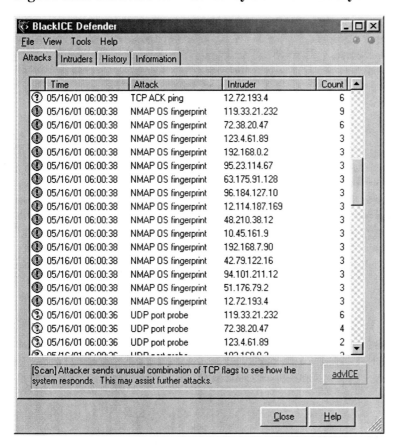

Warning

Many retail (dialup, cable modem, DSL, etc.) ISPs filter out most spoofed packets, though spoofed packets from the same network range as yours may get through. Do some tests first against some machine you control across the Internet, or you could even test this against 3rd party servers using IP ID tricks similar to those discussed in Section 10.3.3, "IP ID Tricks" [262].

Decoys are added with the -D option. The argument is a list of hosts, separated by commas. The string ME can be used as one of the decoys to represent where the true source host should appear in the scan order. Otherwise it will be a random position. Including ME in the 6th position or further in the list prevents some common port scan detectors from reporting the activity. For example, Solar Designer's excellent Scanlogd only reports the first five scan sources to avoid flooding its logs with decoys.

You can also use RND to request a random, non-reserved IP address, or RND:<number> to generate <number> random addresses.

Note that the hosts used as decoys should be up and running. It would be pretty easy to determine which host is scanning if only one is actually up on the network. Using too many down decoys can also cause target ports to become temporarily unresponsive, due to a condition known as a SYN flood. Using IP addresses instead of names is advised to avoid appearing in the decoy networks' nameserver logs. The targets themselves should ideally be expressed by IP addresses too.

Decoys are used both in the initial ping scan (using ICMP, SYN, ACK, or whatever) and during the actual port scanning phase. Decoys are also used during remote OS detection. They are not used for DNS queries or service/version detection, so you will give yourself away if you use options such as -sV or -A. Using too many decoys can slow a scan dramatically, and sometimes even make it less accurate.

Port scan spoofing

While a huge group of decoys is quite effective at hiding the true source of a port scan, the IDS alerts will make it obvious that someone is using decoys. A more subtle, but limited, approach is to spoof a port scan from a single address. Specify -S followed by a source IP, and Nmap will launch the requested port scan from that given source. No useful Nmap results will be available since the target will respond to the spoofed IP, and Nmap will not see those responses. IDS alarms at the target will blame the spoofed source for the scan. You may have to specify -e <interfacename> to select the proper interface name (such as eth0, ppp0, etc.) for Nmap to send the spoofed packets through. This can be useful for framing innocent parties, casting doubt in the administrator's mind about the accuracy of his IDS, and denial of service attacks that will be discussed in Section 10.5.4, "DoS Attacks Against Reactive Systems" [287].

Idle scan

Idle scan is a clever technique that allows for spoofing the source IP address, as discussed in the previous section, while still obtaining accurate TCP port scan results. This is done by abusing properties of the IP identification field as implemented by many systems. It is described in much more depth in Section 5.10, "TCP Idle Scan (-sI)" [117].

DNS proxying

Even the most carefully laid plans can be foiled by one little overlooked detail. If the plan involves ultra-stealth port scanning, that little detail can be DNS. As discussed in Section 3.4, "DNS Resolution" [56], Nmap performs reverse-DNS resolution by default against every responsive host. If the target network administrators are the paranoid log-everything type or they have an extremely sensitive IDS, these DNS lookup probes could be detected. Even something as unintrusive as a list scan (-sL) could be detected this way. The probes will come from the DNS server configured for the machine running Nmap. This is usually a separate machine maintained by your ISP or organization, though it is sometimes your own system.

The most effective way to eliminate this risk is to specify -n to disable all reverse DNS resolution. The problem with this approach is that you lose the valuable information provided by DNS. Fortunately, Nmap offers a way to gather this information while concealing the source. A substantial percentage of DNS servers on the Internet are open to recursive queries from anyone. Specify one or more of those name servers to the --dns-servers option of Nmap, and all rDNS queries will be proxied through them. Example 10.21 demonstrates this technique by conducting a list scan of some SecurityFocus IPs while using the public recursive DNS servers 4.2.2.1 and 4.2.2.2 to cover any tracks. Keep in mind that forward DNS still uses your host's configured DNS server, so specify target IP addresses rather than domain names to prevent even that tiny potential information leak. For this reason, Example 10.21 first shows the Linux host command being used to look up www.securityfocus.com rather than specifying that host name in the Nmap command line. To avoid IDS thresholds based on the number of requests from a single DNS server, you may

---

specify dozens of comma-separated DNS servers to `--dns-servers` and Nmap will round-robin its requests among them.

Example 10.21. Using DNS Proxies (Recursive DNS) for a Stealth List Scan of SecurityFocus

```
# host www.securityfocus.com 4.2.2.1
Using domain server:
Address: 4.2.2.1#53

www.securityfocus.com has address 205.206.231.12
www.securityfocus.com has address 205.206.231.15
www.securityfocus.com has address 205.206.231.13

# nmap --dns-servers 4.2.2.1,4.2.2.2 -sL 205.206.231.12/28

Starting Nmap ( http://nmap.org )
Host 205.206.231.0 not scanned
Host mail2.securityfocus.com (205.206.231.1) not scanned
Host ns1.securityfocus.com (205.206.231.2) not scanned
Host sgs1.securityfocus.com (205.206.231.3) not scanned
Host sgs2.securityfocus.com (205.206.231.4) not scanned
Host 205.206.231.5 not scanned
Host adserver.securityfocus.com (205.206.231.6) not scanned
Host datafeeds.securityfocus.com (205.206.231.7) not scanned
Host sfcm.securityfocus.com (205.206.231.8) not scanned
Host mail.securityfocus.com (205.206.231.9) not scanned
Host www.securityfocus.com (205.206.231.10) not scanned
Host www1.securityfocus.com (205.206.231.11) not scanned
Host www2.securityfocus.com (205.206.231.12) not scanned
Host www3.securityfocus.com (205.206.231.13) not scanned
Host media.securityfocus.com (205.206.231.14) not scanned
Host www5.securityfocus.com (205.206.231.15) not scanned
Nmap done: 16 IP addresses (0 hosts up) scanned in 0.27 seconds
```

10.5.4. DoS Attacks Against Reactive Systems

Many vendors are pushing what they call intrusion *prevention* systems. These are basically IDSs that can actively block traffic and reset established connections that are deemed malicious. These are usually inline on the network or host-based, for greater control over network activity. Other (non-inline) systems listen promiscuously and try to deal with suspicious connections by forging TCP RST packets. In addition to the traditional IPS vendors that try to block a wide range of suspicious activity, many popular small programs such as Port Sentry[8] are designed specifically to block port scanners.

While blocking port scanners may at first seem like a good idea, there are many problems with this approach. The most obvious one is that port scans are usually quite easy to forge, as previous sections have demonstrated. It is also usually easy for attackers to tell when this sort of scan blocking software is in place, because they will not be able to connect to purportedly open ports after doing a port scan. They will try again from another system and successfully connect, confirming that the original IP was blocked. Attackers can then use the

---

[8] *http://sourceforge.net/projects/sentrytools/*

host spoofing techniques discussed previously (-S option) to cause the target host to block any systems the attacker desires. This may include important DNS servers, major web sites, software update archives, mail servers, and the like. It probably would not take long to annoy the legitimate administrator enough to disable reactive blocking. While most such products offer a whitelist option to prevent blocking certain important hosts, enumerating them all is extraordinarily difficult. Attackers can usually find a new commonly used host to block, annoying users until the administrator determines the problem and adjusts the whitelist accordingly.

10.5.5. Exploiting Intrusion Detection Systems

The most audacious way to subvert intrusion detection systems is to hack them. Many commercial and open source vendors have pitiful security records of product exploitability. Internet Security System's flagship RealSecure and BlackICE IDS products had a vulnerability which allowed the Witty worm to compromise more than ten thousand installations, then disabled the IDSs by corrupting their filesystems. Other IDS and firewall vendors such as Cisco, Checkpoint, Netgear, and Symantec have suffered serious remotely exploitable vulnerabilities as well. Open source sniffers have not done much better, with exploitable bugs found in Snort, Wireshark, tcpdump, FakeBO, and many others. Protocol parsing in a safe and efficient manner is extremely difficult, and most of the applications need to parse hundreds of protocols. Denial of service attacks that crash the IDS (often with a single packet) are even more common than these privilege escalation vulnerabilities. A crashed IDS will not detect any Nmap scans.

Given all of these vulnerabilities, exploiting the IDS may be the most viable way into the target network. A nice aspect of this approach is that you do not even have to find the IDS. Sending a rogue packet to any "protected" machine on the network is usually enough to trigger these IDS bugs.

10.5.6. Ignoring Intrusion Detection Systems

While advanced attackers will often employ IDS subversion techniques described in this chapter, the much more common novice attackers (script kiddies) rarely concern themselves with IDSs. Many companies do not even deploy an IDS, and those that do often have them misconfigured or pay little attention to the alerts. An Internet-facing IDS will see so many attacks from script kiddies and worms that a few Nmap scans to locate a vulnerable service are unlikely to raise any flags.

Even if such an attacker compromises the network, is detected by a monitored IDS, and then kicked out of the systems, that is a small loss. Hacking is often a numbers game for them, so losing one compromised network out of thousands is inconsequential. Such a well-patrolled network would have likely quickly noticed their usage (such as denial of service attacks, mass scanning, or spam sending) and shut them down anyway. Hackers want to compromise negligently administered and poorly monitored networks that will provide long-lasting nodes for criminal activity.

Being tracked down and prosecuted is rarely a concern of the IDS-ignoring set. They usually launch attacks from other compromised networks, which are often several globe-spanning hops away from their true location. Or they may use anonymous connectivity such as provided by some Internet cafes, school computer labs, libraries, or the prevalent open wireless access points. Throwaway dialup accounts are also commonly used. Even if they get kicked off, signing up again with another (or the same) provider takes only minutes. Many attackers come from Romania, China, South Korea, and other countries where prosecution is highly unlikely.

Internet worms are another class of attack that rarely bothers with IDS evasion. Shameless scanning of millions of IP addresses is preferred by both worms and script kiddies as it leads to more compromises per hour than a careful, targeted approach that emphasizes stealth.

While most attacks make no effort at stealth, the fact that most intrusion detection systems are so easily subverted is a major concern. Skilled attackers are a small minority, but are often the greatest threat. Do not be lulled into complacency by the large number of alerts spewed from IDSs. They cannot detect everything, and often miss what is most important.

Even skilled hackers sometimes ignore IDS concerns for initial reconnaissance. They simply scan away from some untraceable IP address, hoping to blend in with all of the other attackers and probe traffic on the Internet. After analyzing the results, they may launch more careful, stealthy attacks from other systems.

10.6. Detecting Packet Forgery by Firewall and Intrusion Detection Systems

Previous sections mentioned that some firewall and intrusion detection systems can be configured to forge packets as if they came from one of the protected systems behind the device. TCP RST packets are a frequent example. Load balancers, SSL accelerators, network address translation devices, and certain honeynets can also lead to confusing or inconsistent results. Understanding how Nmap interprets responses helps a great deal in piecing together complex remote network topologies. When Nmap reports unusual or unexpected results, you can add the `--packet-trace` option to see the raw packets upon which Nmap based its conclusions. In perplexing situations, you may have to go even further and launch custom probes and analyze packets with other tools such as hping2 and Wireshark. The goal is often to find inconsistencies that help you understand the actual network setup. The following sections describe several useful techniques for doing so. While most of these tests do not involve Nmap directly, they can be useful for interpreting unexpected Nmap results.

10.6.1. Look for TTL Consistency

Firewalls, load balancers, NAT gateways, and similar devices are usually located one or more hops in front of the machines they are protecting. In this case, packets can be created with a TTL such that they reach the network device but not the end host. If a RST is received from such a probe, it must have been sent by the device.

During one informal assessment, I scanned the network of a large magazine publisher over the Internet (you may remember them from Section 4.5, "SOLUTION: Scan a Large Network for a Certain Open TCP Port" [88]). Almost every IP address showed port 113 closed. Suspecting RST forgery by a firewall, I dug a bit deeper. Because it contained open, closed, and filtered ports, I decided to focus on this host in particular:

```
# nmap -sS -PN -T4 mx.chi.playboy.com
Starting Nmap ( http://nmap.org )
Interesting ports on mx.chi.playboy.com (216.163.143.4):
Not shown: 998 filtered ports
PORT    STATE   SERVICE
25/tcp  open    smtp
113/tcp closed  auth
```

```
Nmap done: 1 IP address (1 host up) scanned in 53.20 seconds
```

Is port 113 really closed, or is the firewall spoofing RST packets? I counted the distance (in network hops) to ports 25 and 113 using the custom traceroute mode of the free hping2 utility, as shown in Example 10.22. I could have used the faster Nmap `--traceroute` option to do this, but that option did not exist at the time.

Example 10.22. Detection of closed and filtered TCP ports

```
# hping2 -t 5 --traceroute -p 25 -S mx.chi.playboy.com
[combined with results from hping2 -i 1 --ttl \* -p 25 -S mx.chi.playboy.com]
5->TTL 0 during transit from 64.159.2.97 (ae0-54.mp2.SanJose1.Level3.net)
6->TTL 0 during transit from 64.159.1.34 (so-3-0-0.mp2.Chicago1.Level3.net)
7->TTL 0 during transit from 200.247.10.170 (pos9-0.core1.Chicago1.level3.net)
8->TTL 0 during transit from 200.244.8.42 (gige6-0.ipcolo1.Chicago1.Level3.net)
9->TTL 0 during transit from 166.90.73.205 (ge1-0.br1.ord.playboy.net)
10->TTL 0 during transit from 216.163.228.247 (f0-0.b1.chi.playboy.com)
11->No response
12->TTL 0 during transit from 216.163.143.130 (fw.chi.playboy.com)
13->46 bytes from 216.163.143.4: flags=SA seq=0 ttl=52 id=48957 rtt=75.8 ms

# hping2 -t 5 --traceroute -p 113 -S mx.chi.playboy.com
[ results augmented again ]
5->TTL 0 during transit from 64.159.2.97 (ae0-54.mp2.SanJose1.Level3.net)
6->TTL 0 during transit from 64.159.1.34 (so-3-0-0.mp2.Chicago1.Level3.net)
7->TTL 0 during transit from 200.247.10.170 (pos9-0.core1.Chicago1.level3.net)
8->TTL 0 during transit from 200.244.8.42 (gige6-0.ipcolo1.Chicago1.Level3.net)
9->TTL 0 during transit from 166.90.73.205 (ge1-0.br1.ord.playboy.net)
10->TTL 0 during transit from 216.163.228.247 (f0-0.b1.chi.playboy.com)
11->Nothing
12->46 bytes from 216.163.143.4: flags=RA seq=0 ttl=48 id=53414 rtt=75.0 ms
```

This custom traceroute shows that reaching open port 25 requires 13 hops. 12 hops away is a firewall in Chicago, helpfully named fw.chi.playboy.com. One would expect different ports on the same machine to be the same hop-distance away. Yet port 113 responds with a RST after only 12 hops. That RST is being forged by fw.chi.playboy.com. Since the firewall is known to forge port 113 responses, those packets should not be taken as an indicator that a host is available at a given IP address. I found available hosts by ping scanning the network again, using common probe types such as ICMP echo requests (`-PE`) and SYN packets to ports 22 and 80 (`-PS22,80`), but omitting any ping probes involving TCP port 113.

10.6.2. Look for IP ID and Sequence Number Consistency

Every IP packet contains a 16-bit identification field that is used for defragmentation. It can also be exploited to gain a surprising amount of information on remote hosts. This includes port scanning using the Nmap idle scan technique, traffic estimation, host alias detection, and much more. It can also help to detect many network devices, such as load balancers. I once noticed strange OS detection results when scanning beta.search.microsoft.com. So I launched hping2 SYN probes against TCP port 80 to learn what was going on. Example 10.23 shows the results.

Example 10.23. Testing IP ID sequence number consistency

```
# hping2 -c 10 -i 1 -p 80 -S beta.search.microsoft.com
HPING beta.search.microsoft.com. (eth0 207.46.197.115): S set, 40 headers
46 bytes from 207.46.197.115: flags=SA seq=0 ttl=56 id=57645 win=16616
46 bytes from 207.46.197.115: flags=SA seq=1 ttl=56 id=57650 win=16616
46 bytes from 207.46.197.115: flags=RA seq=2 ttl=56 id=18574 win=0
46 bytes from 207.46.197.115: flags=RA seq=3 ttl=56 id=18587 win=0
46 bytes from 207.46.197.115: flags=RA seq=4 ttl=56 id=18588 win=0
46 bytes from 207.46.197.115: flags=SA seq=5 ttl=56 id=57741 win=16616
46 bytes from 207.46.197.115: flags=RA seq=6 ttl=56 id=18589 win=0
46 bytes from 207.46.197.115: flags=SA seq=7 ttl=56 id=57742 win=16616
46 bytes from 207.46.197.115: flags=SA seq=8 ttl=56 id=57743 win=16616
46 bytes from 207.46.197.115: flags=SA seq=9 ttl=56 id=57744 win=16616
```

Looking at the sequence of IP ID numbers (in bold), it is clear that there are really two machines sharing this IP address through some sort of load balancer. One has IP ID sequences in the range of 57K, while the other is using 18K. Given this information, it is no wonder that Nmap had trouble settling on a single operating system guess. They may be running on very different systems.

Similar tests can be performed on other numeric fields, such as the TCP timestamp option or the initial sequence number returned by open ports. In this particular case, you can see that the TCP window size and TCP flags also give the hosts away.

10.6.3. The Bogus TCP Checksum Trick

Another handy trick for determining whether an IDS or firewall is spoofing response packets is to send probes with a bogus TCP checksum. Essentially all end hosts check the checksum before further processing and will not respond to these corrupt packets. Firewalls, on the other hand, often omit this check for performance reasons. We can detect this behavior the --badsum option, as shown in Example 10.24.

Example 10.24. Finding a firewall with bad TCP checksums

```
# nmap -sS -p 113 -PN --badsum google.com

Starting Nmap ( http://nmap.org )
Warning: Hostname google.com resolves to 3 IPs. Using 64.233.187.99.
Interesting ports on jc-in-f99.google.com (64.233.187.99):
PORT    STATE  SERVICE
113/tcp closed auth

Nmap done: 1 IP address (1 host up) scanned in 0.44 seconds
```

From Example 10.24 we can infer that there is some sort of network device, perhaps a firewall, that is handling packets destined to google.com on port 113 without verifying TCP checksums. Normally, an end host will silently drop packets with bad TCP checksums and we will see a filtered port instead of a closed one. --badsum will also use bad checksums for other protocols on top of IP, including UDP, ICMP, and IGMP.

This technique, along with other reasons for deliberately sending packets with malformed checksums, is further described in *Phrack* 60, article 12[9] by Ed3f. While this is sometimes a useful technique, there are several caveats to consider:

1. Many modern firewalls now verify TCP checksums (at least when determining whether to respond to a packet) to avoid leaking this information. So this technique is more useful for proving that a --badsum probe response was sent by a firewall (or other device with an incomplete TCP stack) than for proving that a filtered --badsum probe was dropped by an end host.

2. Using --badsum does not guarantee that packets will be sent with bad checksums on all platforms. On a few systems, the kernel or the network card performs the checksum calculation and insert the correct value, overwriting the desired bad value. One way to make sure this isn't happening to you is to use a remote machine to sniff the packets you are sending. For example, when sniffing with tcpdump, packets with bad TCP checksums will be indicated like [bad tcp cksum aa79 (->ab79)!]. Another approach is to do a normal SYN scan against one of your hosts (with at least one open port). Then do the same scan with --badsum. If the same ports are still shown as open, then --badsum probably isn't working for you. Please report the problem as described in Section 15.17, "Bugs" [411].

10.6.4. Round Trip Times

When a firewall forges a probe response, that response usually returns slightly sooner than a response from the true destination host would. After all, the firewall is usually at least one hop closer. It is also optimized for quickly parsing and processing packets, and does little else. The destination host, on the other hand, may be so busy running applications that it takes several milliseconds longer to respond to a probe. Thus, a close comparison of round trip times can often give away firewall shenanigans.

A challenge with this technique is that the time discrepancy between a firewall response and a true target response may be a fraction of a millisecond. Normal round trip time variances may be greater than that, so sending just two probes (one that solicits a response known to be from the target host, and one suspect response that may be from the firewall) is rarely enough. Sending a thousand of each probe type cancels out most of the RTT variance so that fundamental differences can be discerned. This doesn't need to take all that long—**hping2** with the -c 1000 -i u50000 sends a thousand probes in less than a minute. From those results, calculate the median rather than using the average it gives you. This prevents enormous times (such as from a lost response that is retransmitted two seconds later) from skewing the data. Do the thousand probes once or twice more to determine how consistent the results are. Then try the same with the suspect probe and compare the two. If the times are exactly the same to the last significant digit, the same host is likely sending both responses. If you consistently see that one probe type responds more quickly than the other, packet forgery may be responsible.

This method isn't perfect. A time discrepancy could be caused by any number of other factors than a firewall. It is still a valuable technique, as detecting network anomalies such as packet forgery is like proving a court case. Every little bit of evidence helps toward reaching a conclusion. The discrepancy may even lead to more interesting discoveries than firewall forgery. Maybe certain ports on the target are being redirected to a honeynet to better study attacks.

---

[9] *http://nmap.org/p60-12.html*

10.6.5. Close Analysis of Packet Headers and Contents

It is surprising how many elements can differ in even a small TCP header. Refer to Chapter 8, *Remote OS Detection* [171] for dozens of subtle details that can be indicative of a different OS. For example, different systems respond with different TCP options, RST packet text, type of service values, etc. If there are several systems behind a load balancer, or the packets are being sent by firewall or intrusion detection systems, the packets will rarely match exactly.

An excellent tool for dissecting packet headers is Wireshark because it can break the header out into individual fields and provide textual descriptions of the binary contents of the packet. The trick to comparing packets is to collect one packet you think may be from a firewall and another packet of the same type from the target host or target operating system. Two packet types you are likely to be able to collect are TCP reset packets and ICMP error packets. By using hping2 or the `--scanflags` Nmap option it should be possible to elicit responses with different IP, TCP, or ICMP headers.

10.6.6. Unusual Network Uniformity

When response packets are sent by a firewall, they are often more uniform than would be expected from clusters of individual machines. While scanning the magazine company discussed in the previous TTL-checking section, I found that hundreds of sequential-IP machines responded with a RST to port 113. In a real cluster of machines, you would expect at least a couple to be offline at a given time. Additionally, I was unable to elicit any other type of response from most of these addresses. This suspicious result led me to do the TTL tests which showed that the `fw.chi` host was actually spoofing the RST packets.

A firewall doesn't even have to spoof packets to give itself away. Another common firewall configuration is to drop packets to specific ports. Many ISPs filter Windows ports 135, 139, and 445 to reduce the spread of worms. If a large number of adjacent live hosts show up with the same set of filtered ports, a network firewall is the likely culprit. After determining which ports are being filtered by a firewall, you can often map out how many hosts are protected by those firewall rules by scanning many netblocks for those filtered ports. This can lead to the discovery of any accidental holes or the organization's DMZ (demilitarized zone) which typically hosts public services and has far looser firewall rules.

Chapter 11. Defenses Against Nmap

11.1. Introduction

Chapter 10, *Detecting and Subverting Firewalls and Intrusion Detection Systems* [257] discussed the myriad ways that Nmap (along with a few other open-source security tools) can be used to slip through firewalls and outsmart intrusion detection systems. Now we look at the situation from the other side of the fence: How technology such as firewalls and IDSs can defend against Nmap. Possible defenses include blocking the probes, restricting information returned, slowing down the Nmap scan, and returning misleading information. The dangers of some defenses are covered as well. Obfuscating your network to the extent that attackers cannot understand what is going on is not a net win if your administrators no longer understand it either. Similarly, defensive software meant to confuse or block port scanners is not beneficial if it opens up more serious vulnerabilities itself. Many of the techniques described herein protect against active probes in general, not just those produced with Nmap.

11.2. Scan Proactively, Then Close or Block Ports and Fix Vulnerabilities

It is often said that the best defense is a good offense. An excellent way to defend against attackers is to think like them. Scan your networks regularly and carefully analyze the output for vulnerabilities. Use crontab on Unix, or the Task Scheduler on Windows, with a system such as Ndiff[1] or nmap-report (see Section 1.2.3, "MadHat in Wonderland" [9]) to notify you of any changes.

Proactive scanning provides the opportunity to find and fix vulnerabilities before attackers do. Equally important is closing and blocking unnecessarily available ports to prevent exploitation by vulnerabilities you don't yet know about. Proactive scanning also makes you better aware of what information attackers can obtain. When you have reviewed the results yourself for weaknesses and are comfortable with your security posture, port scanners become much less threatening. The people who are most paranoid about port scanners and employ the most defensive and detection software are often those who have the least confidence in their network security. I do not want to dissuade anyone from using the techniques described throughout this chapter, but only to suggest that they first seek out and fix any existing network risks and vulnerabilities. Fixing a hole is far more effective than trying to hide it. That approach is also less stressful than constantly worrying that attackers may find the vulnerabilities.

Once proactive scanning is in place, the first step is to fix any known vulnerabilities. Next comes audit every open port available externally through the firewall or on the internal network. Services which the public doesn't need to reach should be blocked at the firewall. If employees need to reach them, perhaps they can use the VPN instead. Internal services are often listening even when they aren't being used. They might have been installed or enabled by default, or were enabled due to past use and never disabled. Such unnecessary services should be disabled. Even if you don't know of a vulnerability in the service, attackers might. Security bugs might be found for the service in the future too. A closed ports is a much smaller risk than an open one. Once known holes are fixed, private services are blocked by the firewall, and unnecessary services disabled,

---

[1] *http://nmap.org/ndiff/*

further defensive technology such as intrusion prevention systems may be warranted to protect against zero-day exploits, internal threats, and any holes that your vulnerability analysis system misses.

Proactive network scanning and auditing should become a routine rather than a one-off audit. On any complex network, hosts and services are added and changed regularly. You must keep on top of these if the network is to remain secure.

Remember that some poorly implemented and tested systems may react adversely to port scans, OS detection, or version detection. This is rarely a problem when scanning across the Internet, because machines that crash when scanned do not last long in such a hostile environment. Internal machines are often more fragile. When beginning a proactive scanning program, ensure that it is approved and communicated to affected parties in advance. Start with a relatively small part of the network and ensure there are no problems, then take it further in stages. You may want to start with simple port scanning, then move on to OS detection or version detection later as desired.

11.3. Block and Slow Nmap with Firewalls

One of the best defensive measures against scanning is a well-configured firewall. Rather than simply obfuscate the network configuration, as some techniques described later do, well-configured firewalls can effectively block many avenues of attack.

Any decent firewall book emphasizes this cardinal rule: deny by default. Rather than trying to block suspected malicious traffic, block everything first, then specifically override that to allow essential traffic. It is much easier to overlook blocking something malicious than to accidentally explicitly allow the same. Additionally, failing to block bad traffic may not be noticed until it is exploited by an attacker, while failing to allow legitimate traffic is usually quickly discovered by the affected users. And they will keep reminding you until it is fixed.

The two preceding reasons should be enough to convince anyone to go with deny-by-default, but there are other benefits as well. One is to slow down large scale reconnaissance from tools like Nmap. When an Nmap TCP SYN scan encounters a closed port, the target machine sends back a RST packet and that port's status is determined within the space of only one round-trip-time. That is under a quarter of a second, even across the world from my web server in California to an ISP in Moscow. If a firewall filters the port by dropping the probe, on the other hand, Nmap has to wait for a worst-case timeout before giving up. Nmap then makes several retransmissions just in case the packet was dropped by some router due to overcapacity rather than by a firewall rule. In large-scale scans, the difference can be quite significant. For example, a 1,000-port TCP SYN scan against a machine on my wireless network (**nmap -sS -T4 para**) takes only five seconds when all ports are open or closed. Filtering a dozen or so commonly exploited ports increases the scan time to 12 seconds. Moving to default-deny (filtering all ports except the five open ones) nearly triples the scan time to 33 seconds. A 28-second difference may not sound meaningful, but it can add up to extra days for large-scale scans.

Filtered ports are even more frustrating to attackers when the UDP protocol is used. When firewalling is not involved, virtually all systems respond with an ICMP port unreachable when Nmap probes a closed port. Open ports usually do not respond at all. So if a deny-by-default firewall drops a probe packet, Nmap cannot tell if the port is open or filtered. Retransmissions do not help here, as the port will never respond. Attackers must then resort to slower and much more conspicuous techniques such as Nmap version detection and SNMP community string brute forcing to make sense of the UDP ports.

To actually slow Nmap down, make sure the firewall is dropping the packets rather than responding with an ICMP error or TCP RST. Otherwise Nmap will run just as fast and accurately as if the ports were closed, though you still reap the benefit of blocking the probes. As an example of this distinction, the Linux iptables firewall offers the target actions DROP and REJECT. As the names imply, DROP does nothing beyond blocking the packet, while REJECT sends an error message back. The former is better for slowing down reconnaissance and is usually recommended, though REJECT can ease network trouble diagnosis by making it crystal clear that the firewall is blocking certain traffic.

Another tenet of firewalls is *defense in depth*. Even though ports are blocked by the firewall, make sure they are closed (no application is listening) anyway. Assume that a determined attacker will eventually breach the firewall. Even if they get through using a technique from Chapter 10, *Detecting and Subverting Firewalls and Intrusion Detection Systems* [257], the individual machines should be locked down to present a strong defense. This reduces the scope and damage of mistakes, which everyone makes on occasion. Attackers will need to find weaknesses in both the firewall and individual machines. A port scanner is pretty impotent against ports that are both closed and filtered. Using private address space (such as with network address translation) and additional firewalls provide even more protection.

11.4. Detect Nmap Scans

Some people believe that detecting port scans is a waste of time. They are so common that any organization connected to the Internet will be regularly scanned. Very few of these represent targeted attacks. Many are Internet worms endlessly pounding away seeking some Windows vulnerability or another. Some scans come from Internet research projects, others from curious or bored individuals exploring the Internet. I scanned tens of thousands of IPs seeking good examples and empirical data for this book. Other scans actually are malicious. Script kiddies regularly scan huge ranges for systems susceptible to their exploit du jour. While these folks have bad intentions, they are likely to move along on their own after finding no vulnerable services on your network. The biggest threat are attackers specifically targeting your organization, though those represent such a small percentage of detected scans that they are extremely tough to distinguish. So many administrators do not even bother recording port scans.

Other administrators take a different view. They contend that port scans are often precursors to attacks, and should at least be logged if not responded to. They often place detection systems on internal networks to reduce the flood of Internet port scan activity. The logs are sometimes analyzed for trends, or submitted to 3rd parties such as Dshield for world-wide correlation and analysis. Sometimes extensive logs and scary graphs measuring attacks are submitted to management to justify adequate budgets.

System logs alone are rarely sufficient for detecting port scans. Usually only scan types that establish full TCP connections are logged, while the default Nmap SYN scan sneaks through. Even full TCP connections are only logged if the particular application explicitly does so. Such error messages, when available, are often cryptic. However, a bunch of different services spouting error messages at the same time is a common indicator of scanning activity. Intrusive scans, particularly those using Nmap version detection, can often be detected this way. But only if the administrators actually read the system logs regularly. The vast majority of log messages go forever unread. Log monitoring tools such as Logwatch[2] and Swatch[3] can certainly help, but the reality is that system logs are only marginally effective at detecting Nmap activity.

---

[2] *http://www.logwatch.org*
[3] *http://swatch.sourceforge.net/*

Special purpose port scan detectors are a more effective approach to detecting Nmap activity. Two common examples are PortSentry[4] and Scanlogd[5]. Scanlogd has been around since 1998 and was carefully designed for security. No vulnerabilities have been reported during its lifetime. PortSentry offers similar features, as well as a reactive capability that blocks the source IP of suspected scanners. Note that this reactive technique can be dangerous, as demonstrated in Section 11.5.6, "Reactive Port Scan Detection" [304].

Despite being subject to threshold-based attacks discussed in Section 10.5.2, "Avoiding Intrusion Detection Systems" [279], these port scan detection tools work pretty well. Yet the type of administrator who cares enough to keep tabs on port scans will also want to know about more serious attacks such as exploit attempts and installed backdoors. For this reason, intrusion detection systems that alert on a wide range of suspicious behavior are more popular than these special-purpose tools.

Many vendors now sell intrusion detection systems, but Nmap users gravitate to an open-source lightweight IDS named Snort. It ranked as the third most popular security tool among a survey group of 3,243 Nmap users (*http://sectools.org*). Like Nmap, Snort is improved by a global community of developers. It supports more than two thousand rules for detecting all sorts of suspicious activity, including port scans.

A properly installed and monitored IDS can be a tremendous security asset, but do not forget the risks discussed in Section 10.5, "Subverting Intrusion Detection Systems" [276]. Snort has had multiple remotely exploitable vulnerabilities, and so have many of its commercial competitors. Additionally, a skilled attacker can defeat most IDS rules, so do not let your guard down. IDSs too often lead to a false sense of security.

11.5. Clever Trickery

Nmap, like other active probing tools, obtains its information by sending out packets to target systems and then trying to interpret and organize any responses into useful reports. Nmap must rely on information from systems and networks that may be downright hostile environments. Some administrators take offense at being scanned, and a small percentage try to confuse or slow Nmap with active measures beyond the firewall and IDS techniques discussed previously.

Many of these active response methods are quite clever. I would argue that many are too clever, causing more problems than they solve. One such problem is exploitability. Much of this custom active response software is just a quick hack, written without careful security consideration. For example, an administrator friend of mine named Paul was quite proud of installing FakeBO on his machine. He laughed at the prospect of fooling script kiddies into thinking they found a Back Orifice infected machine to commandeer, when Paul was really just logging their attempts. The joke was on Paul when a FakeBO buffer overflow was discovered and an attacker used it to compromise his box and install a real backdoor.

The other major risk common to these technologies is displacement of time that is better spent elsewhere. Confusing attackers can be fun and gratifying, and in some cases even hampers attacks. In the end, however, these techniques are mostly security by obscurity. While they can still be beneficial, they aren't as important as more resilient technologies such as firewalls and vulnerability patching. Advanced attackers will likely see through the obfuscation anyway, and the script kiddies and worms rarely bother with reconnaissance. The daily attempted IIS exploits against my Apache web server are testament to that. These techniques should be considered only when you are already highly confident of your security posture. Too many people use them as a substitute to truly securing their networks.

---

[4] *http://sourceforge.net/projects/sentrytools/*
[5] *http://www.openwall.com/scanlogd/*

11.5.1. Hiding Services on Obscure Ports

Occasionally administrators advocate running services on unusual ports to make it harder for attackers to find them. In particular, they note the frequency of single-port sweeps across their address space from attackers seeking out a vulnerable version of some software. Autonomous worms frequently do the same thing.

It is true that this sort of obfuscation may prevent some worms and script kiddies from finding services, but they are rarely more than a marginal threat to companies that quickly patch vulnerabilities. And companies who do not patch quickly will not be saved by this simple port obfuscation. Proponents often argue that even more skillful attackers will fall for this. Some have even posted to security lists that scanning all 65,536 TCP ports is inconceivable. They are wrong. Attackers can and do scan all TCP ports. In addition, techniques such as Nmap version detection make it easy to determine what service is listening on an unusual port. Example 11.1 shows such a scan. Notable is that it only takes eight minutes, and this is from a slow residential aDSL line in another state. From a faster machine, the same scan takes only three minutes. If the default state had been filtered, the scan would have been slower but not unreasonably so. Even if a scan takes 10 or 20 minutes, an attacker does not have to sit around watching. A targeted attack against a company can easily be left overnight, and mass attackers may leave a scanner running for weeks, periodically downloading the latest data files.

Example 11.1. An all-TCP-port version scan

```
# nmap -sSV -T4 -O -p0-65535 apollo.sco.com

Starting Nmap ( http://nmap.org )
Interesting ports on apollo.sco.com (216.250.128.35):
Not shown: 65524 closed ports
PORT        STATE       SERVICE VERSION
0/tcp       filtered    unknown
21/tcp      open        ftp      WU-FTPD 2.1WU(1)+SCO-2.6.1+-sec
22/tcp      open        ssh      SSH 1.2.22 (protocol 1.5)
199/tcp     open        smux?
457/tcp     open        http     NCSA httpd 1.3
615/tcp     open        http     NCSA httpd 1.5
1035/tcp    filtered    unknown
1521/tcp    open        oracle   Oracle DB Listener 2.3.4.0.0 (for SCO System V/386)
13722/tcp   open        inetd    inetd exec err /usr/openv/netbackup/bin/bpjava-msvc
13782/tcp   open        inetd    inetd exec err /usr/openv/netbackup/bin/bpcd
13783/tcp   open        inetd    inetd exec err /usr/openv/bin/vopied
64206/tcp   open        unknown
Device type: general purpose
Running: SCO UnixWare
OS details: SCO UnixWare 7.0.0 or OpenServer 5.0.4-5.0.6

Nmap done: 1 IP address (1 host up) scanned in 501.90 seconds
#
```

The biggest downside to this approach is a major inconvenience to legitimate users. Some services, such as SMTP and DNS, almost always have to run on their well-known ports for practical reasons. Even for services such as HTTP and SSH that can be more easily changed, doing so means that all users must remember an unusual port number such as 52,147 whenever they connect to the service. When there are several "hidden" services, it is particularly difficult to remember which is which. Using different ports on each machine

---

becomes even more confusing, but standardizing on unusual port mappings across the organization reduces the purported benefit of this scheme. Attackers may notice that SSH is always at 52,147. The end result is that all-port Nmap scans against your servers may increase, as frustrated legitimate users try to find where essential services are hidden. Less savvy users may flood you with phone calls instead.

11.5.2. Port Knocking

A technique called port knocking has recently become popular as a way to hide services from potential attackers. The method is well described on the front page of *http://www.portknocking.org/*:

> Port knocking is a method of establishing a connection to a networked computer that has no open ports. Before a connection is established, ports are opened using a port knock sequence, which is a series of connection attempts to closed ports. A remote host generates and sends an authentic knock sequence in order to manipulate the server's firewall rules to open one or more specific ports. These manipulations are mediated by a port knock daemon, running on the server, which monitors the firewall log file for connection attempts that can be translated into authentic knock sequences. Once the desired ports are opened, the remote host can establish a connection and begin a session. Another knock sequence may be used to trigger the closing of the port.

This method is not brand new, but it exploded in popularity in 2003 when Martin Krzywinski coined the phrase port knocking, wrote an implementation, created the extensive web site, and wrote articles about it for Sys Admin and Linux Journal magazines. Port knocking adds a second layer of protection to services, though authentication is usually weaker than that provided by primary services such as SSH. Implementations are usually subject to sniffing and replay attacks, and often suffer from brute force and denial of service threats as well.

The upside is a service concealment which is much stronger than the simple and ineffective obscure ports technique described previously. A port competently hidden through port knocking is nearly impossible to discover using active probes such as those sent by Nmap. On the other hand, sniffer-based systems such as intrusion detection systems and passive network mappers trivially detect this scheme.

Deciding whether to implement port knocking requires an analysis of the benefits and costs applicable to the proposed implementation. Service concealment is only beneficial for a small set of applications. The motivation is to prevent attackers from connecting to (and exploiting) vulnerable services, while still allowing connections from authorized users all over the world. If only certain IP addresses need to connect, firewall restrictions limiting connections to those specific IPs are usually a better approach. In an ideal world, applications would securely handle authentication themselves and there would be no need to hide them to prevent exploitation. Unfortunately, even security-conscious programs such as SSH have suffered numerous remotely exploitable pre-authentication flaws. While these bugs should be fixed as soon as possible in any case, port knocking may provide an extra window of time before a new bug is exploited. After all, some SSH exploits spread underground long before official patches were available. Then when a bug is announced, even the most conscientious administrator may require several hours or days to learn about the bug, test the fix, and locate and patch all vulnerable instances. The response time of a home computer owner may be even longer. After all, the vast majority of computer users do not subscribe to Bugtraq.

The good guys are not the only ones who benefit from service concealment. It is at least as popular (if not more so) for gray hat and downright criminal uses. Many ISPs restrict users from running any server daemons such as web or SSH services. Customers could hide a personal SSH daemon or web server (only for very limited use, as the public could not easily connect) using port knocking technology. Similarly, my friend Tom's employer only permitted connections from home using a Windows-only VPN client. Tom responded by setting up a port knocking system (before it was called that) which, upon receiving the appropriate probes, set up a reverse SSH tunnel from his work server back to his home Linux box. This allowed him to work from home with full access to the work network and without having to suffer the indignities of using Windows. It is worth re-iterating that the service provider in both the ISP and employer examples could have detected the subterfuge using a sniffer or netflow. Segueing into even darker uses, computer criminals frequently use techniques like these to hide backdoors in systems that they have compromised. Script kiddies may just leave a blatant SSH daemon or even raw root shell listening on some high port, vulnerable to detection by the next Nmap scan. More cautious attackers use concealment techniques including port knocking in their backdoors and rootkits.

While the service concealment provided by this system can be valuable, it comes with many limitations. Services intended for public use are inappropriate, since no one is going to install a special knock client just to visit your web site. In addition, publicizing the access instructions would defeat the system's primary purpose. Non-public service should usually be blocked by a firewall rather than shielded with port knocking. When a group of people need access, VPNs are often a better solution as they offer encryption and user-level access control. VPNs are also built to handle real-world networks, where packets can be dropped, duplicated, and re-ordered. A relatively simple probe using the Portknocking.Org implementation can require more than 30 port probes, all of which must arrive at the destination in order. For this many probes, you will need a special client. Using **telnet** or a web browser is too tedious. Additionally, all firewalls in the path must allow you to connect to these unusual ports. Given these restrictions and hassles, using a VPN may be just as convenient.

An additional risk is that port knocking implementations are still immature. The best-known one, written by Martin Krzywinski, warns on the download page that "this is a prototype and includes the bare minimum to get started. Do not use this for production environments." Also remember that proactive scanning to inventory your own network will be more difficult with programs such as this installed.

Do not let this long list of limitations dissuade you from even considering port knocking. It may be appropriate for specific circumstances, particularly those related to hidden backdoors or remote administration of a personal machine.

11.5.3. Honeypots and Honeynets

An increasingly popular method for confusing attackers is to place bait systems on a network and monitor them for attacks. These are known as honeypots. I am a member of the Honeynet Project[6], which installs networks of these for research purposes. Many corporations have deployed these systems for corporate security purposes, though doing so is risky. The extensive monitoring required makes them high-maintenance and there is always a risk that attackers will break in and use the machines to commit serious crimes. Lower maintenance solutions, such as Honeyd described in the next section, or even an IDS, may be more appropriate. In any case, honeypots are designed to catch more invasive attacks than simple Nmap scans, so they are not discussed further.

---

[6] *http://www.honeynet.org*

11.5.4. OS Spoofing

Several programs have been developed specifically to trick Nmap OS detection. They manipulate the host operating system to support custom responses to Nmap probes. In this way, a Linux PC can be made to resemble an Apple LaserWriter printer or even a webcam. IP Personality[7], released in 2000, is one of the most popular systems. It extends the Linux Netfilter framework to support these shenanigans. Unfortunately, it has not been updated since April 2002 and may not work on kernel versions beyond 2.4.18.

Tool availability alone does not make OS spoofing a good idea. One has to justify the effort somehow. The IP Personality FAQ avoids the question "Why would you need this?" by responding that "If you ask this, then you don't". Nevertheless, some people find it valuable enough to write and use these tools. One reason is that specific OS information makes it easier for attackers to infer vulnerabilities on your network, and also helps decide what sort of exploit to run. Of course the vulnerability itself is the real problem there, and should be fixed. Other people run this sort of tool because they are embarrassed about the OS they run, or they are extremely privacy conscious. If your operating system is in a legal gray area because some company is claiming IP infringement and filing suits against users, OS spoofing might protect against such a nuisance suit.

One serious problem with masking a host OS this way is that it can cause security and functionality problems. Nmap tests for several important security properties, such as TCP initial sequence number and IP identification number predictability. Emulating a different system, such as a printer, may require weakening these number sequences so that they are predictable and vulnerable to all the attacks that implies. The obscurity gained by spoofing your operating system fingerprint is not worth sacrificing valuable security mechanisms. This sort of spoofing can also cripple functionality. Many Nmap OS detection tests involve asking the system what TCP options are supported. Pretending not to support certain options such as timestamps and window scaling will remove the efficiency benefits of those options. Pretending to support unavailable options can be disastrous.

In Example 11.2, Nmap is fooled by IP Personality into believing a Linux box is really a Sega Dreamcast game console. It is from a paper entitled *A practical approach for defeating Nmap OS-Fingerprinting*[8] by David Barroso Berrueta. That excellent paper includes far more examples, as well as detailed configuration instructions. It also describes many similar systems, with handy warnings such as "the code is not very stable. I loaded the module and in a few moments my Linux box got frozen."

---

[7] *http://ippersonality.sourceforge.net/*
[8] *http://nmap.org/misc/defeat-nmap-osdetect.html*

Example 11.2. Deceiving Nmap with IP Personality

```
# nmap -sS -O -oN nmap2.log 192.168.0.19

Interesting ports on 192.168.0.19:
(The 1597 ports scanned but not shown below are in state: closed)
Port       State      Service
22/tcp     open       ssh
25/tcp     open       smtp
80/tcp     open       http
143/tcp    open       imap
Remote operating system guess: Sega Dreamcast
Nmap finished: 1 IP address (1 host up) scanned in 5.886 seconds
```

A newer and more popular program for operating system spoofing (among other features) is Honeyd[9]. It is actively maintained by author Niels Provos and offers several major benefits over IP Personality. One is that it is much easier to configure. Almost 100 configuration lines were required for the Dreamcast spoofing using IP Personality, above. Honeyd, on the other hand, simply reads the Nmap OS detection database and emulates any OS the user chooses. (Be aware that Honeyd uses a database from Nmap's 1st generation OS detection, which was discontinued in 2007.) Honeyd also solves the security and functionality problems of OS spoofing by creating synthetic hosts for the emulation. You can ask Honeyd to take over hundreds of unused IP addresses in an organization. It responds to probes sent to those IPs based on its configuration. This eliminates the security and functionality risks of trying to mask a host's own TCP stack. You are creating a bunch of synthetic hosts instead, so this does not help obscure the OS of existing hosts. The synthetic hosts basically constitute a low-maintenance honeynet that can be watched for attacks. It is mostly intended for research purposes, such as using the worldwide network of Honeyd installations to identify new worms and track spammer activity.

As with other techniques in this section, I recommend experimenting with OS spoofing only when completely satisfied by your security posture. Spoofing a single OS, or even adding hundreds of decoy Honeyd instances, is no substitute for patching vulnerable systems. Many attackers (and especially worms) do not even bother with OS detection before sending exploit code.

It is also worth noting that these systems are easy to detect by skilled attackers. It is extraordinarily hard to present a convincing facade, given all of application and TCP stack differences between operating systems. Nobody will believe that the system in Example 11.2, "Deceiving Nmap with IP Personality" [303] offering IMAP, SMTP, and SSH is really a Dreamcast running its native OS. In addition, a bug in all versions up to 0.8 allowed for simple Honeyd identification with a single probe packet. There are also many TCP characteristics that Honeyd cannot yet handle. Those can be used to detect Honeyd, though Nmap does not automate this work. If Honeyd becomes widespread, detection functionality will likely be added to Nmap.

Deception programs such as Honeyd are just one reason that Nmap users should interpret Nmap results carefully and watch for inconsistencies, particularly when scanning networks that you do not control.

11.5.5. Tar Pits

Rather than trick attackers, some people aim for just slowing them down. Tar pits have long been popular methods for slowing Internet worms and spammers. Some administrators use TCP techniques such as

---

[9] *http://www.honeyd.org*

zero-sized receive windows or slowly trickling data back byte by byte. LaBrea[10] is a popular implementation of this. Others use application-level techniques such as long delays before responding to SMTP commands. While these are mostly used by anti-spammers, similar techniques can be used to slow Nmap scans. For example, limiting the rate of RST packets sent by closed ports can dramatically slow scanners down.

11.5.6. Reactive Port Scan Detection

We previously discussed scan detection using tools such as Scanlogd. Other tools go much further than that, and actually respond to the scans. Some people propose attacking back by launching exploits or denial of service attacks against the scan source. This is a terrible idea for many reasons. For one, scans are often forged. If the source address is accurate, it may be a previous victim that the attacker is using as a scapegoat. Or the scan may be part of an Internet research survey or come from a legitimate employee or customer. Even if the source address is a computer belonging to an actual attacker, striking back may disrupt innocent systems and routers along the path. It may also be illegal.

While the idea of attacking back is widely shunned in the security community, there is much more interest in responding to detected attacks by adjusting firewall rules to block the offending IP address. The idea is to prevent them from following up on the scan with an actual attack. There are several risks in this approach. One is that you show your hand. It will be obvious to attackers that they have been blocked, and most have plenty of other IP addresses they can use to continue probing. They will then know about your reactive system, and could escalate their own attacks. A more important problem is that scans are so easily forged. Section 10.5.3, "Misleading Intrusion Detection Systems" [284] describes several methods for doing so. When an attacker notices the block, he may spoof scans from important systems, such as major web sites and DNS servers. A target network which then blocks those IPs will be committing a denial of service attack on itself. Restricting firewall blocks to scans that initiate a full TCP connection reduces the spoofing problem, but that fails to stop even the default Nmap SYN scan.

11.5.7. Escalating Arms Race

While the primary focus of this book is on open-source tools, a number of commercial vendors have introduced products that attempt to deceive Nmap. One example is the Cisco Security Agent. The evaluation guide claims the following protections against Nmap.

> Network Mapper (Nmap) identifies which devices are present on a network and what operating system and services they are running by sending out a series of network probes. The presence of a device on the network and the ports it is running are both announced by its response to Nmap probes. The pattern of error messages returned identifies the operating system. Nmap is surprisingly accurate. It is frequently used at the initial stage of an attack or investigation to determine which systems might respond to an attacker's exploits.

> Expected outcome of Nmap scan against Cisco Security Agent protected systems: Nmap is unable to identify the target operating system of systems running the default server or default desktop policies. Nmap scans appear to hang while its security tests timeout. Nmap scans against systems not protected by Cisco Security Agent report results very quickly

I am investigating how CSA works, and whether Nmap can automatically detect and adjust for it. Scanning technology is an arms race. Open source and commercial companies will continue to create products designed

---

[10] *http://labrea.sourceforge.net/*

to slow down, block, or deceive Nmap and other tools. Meanwhile, Nmap continually improves, developing resiliency in the face of these challenges.

Chapter 12. Zenmap GUI Users' Guide

12.1. Introduction

Zenmap is the official graphical user interface (GUI) for the Nmap Security Scanner. It is a multi-platform, free and open-source application designed to make Nmap easy for beginners to use while providing advanced features for experienced Nmap users. Frequently used scans can be saved as profiles to make them easy to run repeatedly. A command creator allows interactive creation of Nmap command lines. Scan results can be saved and viewed later. Saved scans can be compared with one another to see how they differ. The results of recent scans are stored in a searchable database. A typical Zenmap screen shot is shown in Figure 12.1. See the official Zenmap web page[1] for more screen shots.

Figure 12.1. Typical Zenmap screen shot

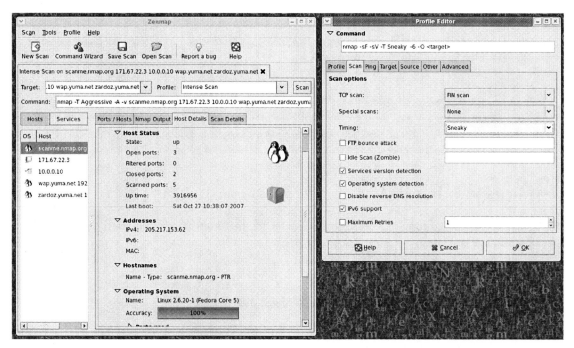

This guide is meant to make Nmap and Zenmap easy to use together, even if you haven't used either before. For the parts of this guide that deal specifically with Nmap (command-line options and such), refer to Chapter 15, *Nmap Reference Guide* [373].

12.1.1. The Purpose of a Graphical Frontend for Nmap

No frontend can replace good old command-line Nmap. The nature of a frontend is that it depends on another tool to do its job. Therefore the purpose of Zenmap is not to replace Nmap, but to make Nmap *more useful*. Here are some of the advantages Zenmap offers over plain Nmap.

---

[1] *http://nmap.org/zenmap/*

Interactive and graphical results viewing

In addition to showing Nmap's normal output, Zenmap can arrange its display to show all ports on a host or all hosts running a particular service. It summarizes details about a single host or a complete scan in a convenient display. Zenmap can even draw a topology map of discovered networks. The results of several scans may be combined together and viewed at once.

Comparison

Zenmap has the ability to graphically show the differences between two scans. You can see what changed between the same scan run on different days, between scans of two different hosts, between scans of the same hosts with different options, or any other combination. This allows administrators to easily track new hosts or services appearing on their networks, or existing ones going down.

Convenience

Zenmap keeps track of your scan results until you choose to throw them away. That means you can run a scan, see the results, and then decide whether to save them to a file. There is no need to think of a file name in advance.

Repeatability

Zenmap's command profiles make it easy to run the exact same scan more than once. There's no need to set up a shell script to do a common scan.

Discoverability

Nmap has literally hundreds of options, which can be daunting for beginners. Zenmap's interface is designed to always show the command that will be run, whether it comes from a profile or was built up by choosing options from a menu. This helps beginners learn and understand what they are doing. It also helps experts double-check exactly what will be run before they press "Scan".

12.2. Scanning

Begin Zenmap by typing **zenmap** in a terminal or by clicking the Zenmap icon in the desktop environment. The main window, as shown in Figure 12.2, is displayed.

Figure 12.2. Zenmap's main window

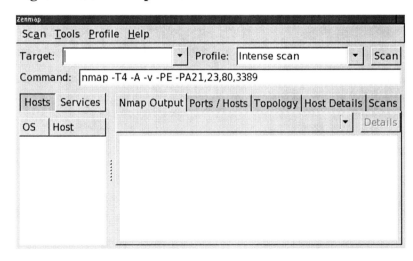

One of Zenmap's goals is to make security scanning easy for beginners and for experts. Running a scan is as simple as typing the target in the "Target" field, selecting the "Intense scan" profile, and clicking the "Scan" button. This is shown in Figure 12.3.

Figure 12.3. Target and profile selection

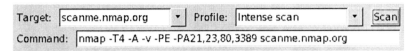

While a scan is running (and after it completes), the output of the Nmap command is shown on the screen.

Any number of targets, separated by spaces, may be entered in the target field. All the target specifications supported by Nmap are also supported by Zenmap, so targets such as `192.168.0.0/24` and `10.0.0-5.*` work. Zenmap remembers the targets scanned most recently. To re-scan a host, select the host from the combo box attached to the "Target" text field.

12.2.1. Profiles

The "Intense scan" is just one of several scan profiles that come with Zenmap. Choose a profile by selecting it from the "Profile" combo box. Profiles exist for several common scans. After selecting a profile the Nmap command line associated with it is displayed on the screen. Of course, it is possible to edit these profiles or create new ones. This is covered in Section 12.7, "The Profile Editor" [323].

It is also possible to type in an Nmap command and have it executed without using a profile. Just type in the command and press return or click "Scan". When you do this the "Profile" entry becomes blank to indicate that the scan is not using any profile—it comes directly from the command field.

12.2.2. Scan Aggregation

Zenmap has the ability to combine the results of many Nmap scans into one view, a feature known as *scan aggregation*. When one scan is finished, you may start another in the same window. When the second scan is finished, its results are merged with those from the first. The collection of scans that make up an aggregated view is called a *network inventory*.

An example of aggregation will make the concept clearer. Let's run a quick scan against scanme.nmap.org.

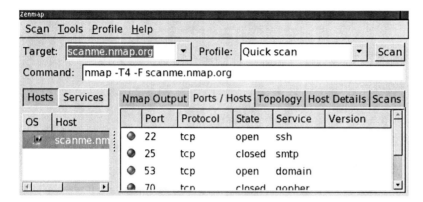

Now do the same against localhost:

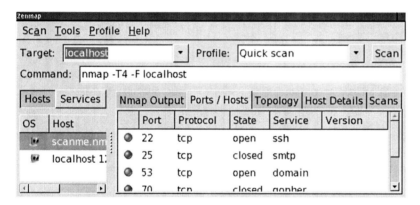

Now results for both scanme and localhost are shown. This is something you could have done with one Nmap scan, giving both targets, although it's convenient not to have to think of all the targets in advance. Now suppose we want some more information about scanme, so we launch an intense scan on it.

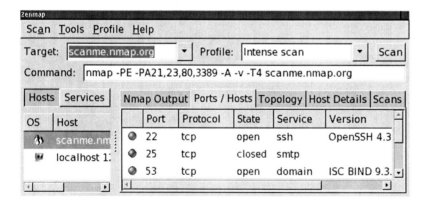

Now scanme has a little penguin icon showing that its operating system has been detected as Linux. Additionally some of its services have been identified. Now we're doing something you can't do with a single Nmap scan, because you can't single out a host for more intense scanning like we did. The results for localhost are still present, though we won't know more about it than we did before unless we decide to do a more in-depth scan.

It is not necessary to wait for one scan to finish before starting another. Several scans may run concurrently. As each one finishes its results are added to the inventory. Any number of scans may make up an inventory; the collection of scans is managed in the "Scans" scan results tab, as fully described in the section called "The Scans tab" [315].

It is possible to have more than one inventory open at the same time. Zenmap uses the convention that one window represents one network inventory. To start a new inventory, select "New Window" from the "Scan" menu or use the **ctrl+N** keyboard shortcut. Starting a scan with the "Scan" button will append the scan to the inventory in the current window. To put it in a different inventory open up a separate window and run the scan from there. Loading scan results from a file or directory will start a new inventory, unless you use the "Open Scan in This Window" menu item. For more on saving and loading network inventories and individual scans see Section 12.4, "Saving and Loading Scan Results" [316].

To close a window choose "Close Window" from the "Scan" menu or press **ctrl+W**. When all open windows are closed the application will terminate. To close all open windows select "Quit" or press **ctrl+Q**.

12.3. Interpreting Scan Results

Nmap's output is displayed during and after a scan. This output will be familiar to Nmap users. Except for Zenmap's color highlighting, this doesn't offer any visualization advantages over running Nmap in a terminal. However, other parts of Zenmap's interface interpret and aggregate the terminal output in a way that makes scan results easier to understand and use.

12.3.1. Scan Results Tabs

Each scan window contains five tabs which each display different aspects of the scan results. They are: "Nmap Output", "Ports / Hosts", "Topology", "Host Details", and "Scans". Each of these are discussed in this section.

The "Nmap Output" tab

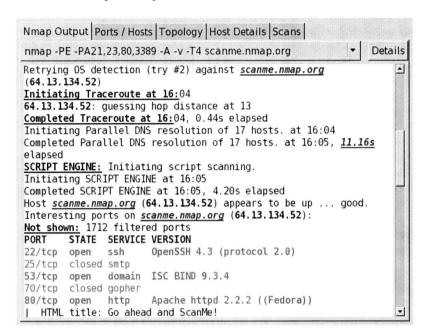

The "Nmap Output" tab is displayed by default when a scan is run. It shows the familiar Nmap terminal output. The display highlights parts of the output according to their meaning; for example, open and closed ports are displayed in different colors. Custom highlights can be configured in `zenmap.conf` (see Section 12.11, "Description of zenmap.conf" [333]).

Recall that the results of more than one scan may be shown in a window (see Section 12.2.2, "Scan Aggregation" [309]). The drop-down combo box at the top of the tab allows you to select the scan to display. The "Details" button brings up a window showing miscellaneous information about the scan, such as timestamps, command-line options, and the Nmap version number used.

The "Ports / Hosts" tab

	Port	Protocol	State	Service	Version
●	22	tcp	open	ssh	OpenSSH 4.3 (protocol 2.0)
●	25	tcp	closed	smtp	
●	53	tcp	open	domain	ISC BIND 9.3.4
●	70	tcp	closed	gopher	
●	80	tcp	open	http	Apache httpd 2.2.2 ((Fedora))
●	113	tcp	closed	auth	

The "Ports / Hosts" tab's display differs depending on whether a host or a service is currently selected. When a host is selected, it shows all the interesting ports on that host, along with version information when available. Host selection is further described in Section 12.3.2, "Sorting by Host" [315].

12.3. Interpreting Scan Results

	Hostname	Port	Protocol	State	Version
●	home.domain.actdsltmp 192.168.0.1	80	tcp	open	Vonage ht
●	scanme.nmap.org 64.13.134.52	80	tcp	open	Apache ht

Nmap Output | Ports / Hosts | Topology | Host Details | Scans

When a service is selected, the "Ports / Hosts" tab shows all the hosts which have that port open or filtered. This is a good way to quickly answer the question "What computers are running HTTP?" Service selection is further described in Section 12.3.3, "Sorting by Service" [316].

The "Topology" tab

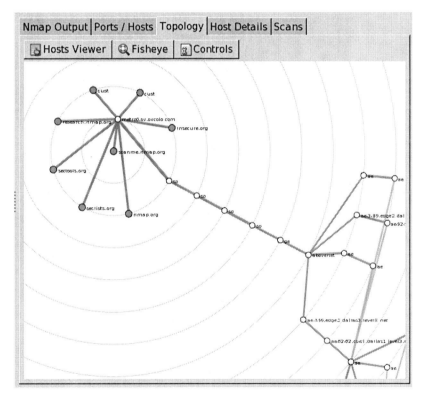

The "Topology" tab is an interactive view of the connections between hosts in a network. Hosts are arranged in concentric rings. Each ring represents an additional network hop from the center node. Clicking on a node brings it to the center. Because it shows a representation of the network paths between hosts, the "Topology" tab benefits from the use of the `--traceroute` option. Topology view is discussed in more detail in Section 12.5, "Surfing the Network Topology" [317].

The "Host Details" tab

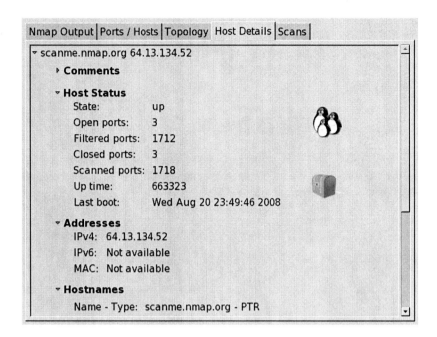

The "Host Details" tab breaks all the information about a single host into a hierarchical display. Shown are the host's names and addresses, its state (up or down), and the number and status of scanned ports. The host's uptime, operating system, OS icon (see Figure 12.5, "OS icons" [316]), and other associated details are shown when available. When no exact OS match is found, the closest matches are displayed. There is also a collapsible text field for storing a comment about the host which will be saved when the scan is saved to a file (see Section 12.4, "Saving and Loading Scan Results" [316]).

Each host has an icon that provides a very rough "vulnerability" estimate, which is based solely on the number of open ports. The icons and the numbers of open ports they correspond to are

   0–2 open ports,

   3–4 open ports,

   5–6 open ports,

   7–8 open ports, and

   9 or more open ports.

The "Scans" tab

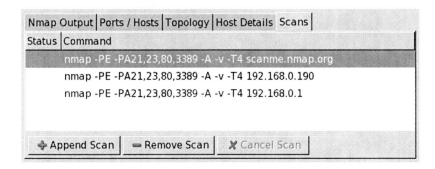

The "Scans" tab shows all the scans that are aggregated to make up the network inventory. From this tab you can add scans (from a file or directory) and remove scans.

While a scan is executing and not yet complete, its status is "Running". You may cancel a running scan by clicking the "Cancel Scan" button.

12.3.2. Sorting by Host

Figure 12.4. Host selection

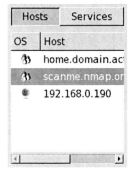

On the left side of Zenmap's main window is a column headed by two buttons labeled "Hosts" and "Services". Clicking the "Hosts" button will bring up a list of all hosts that were scanned, as in Figure 12.4. Commonly this contains just a single host, but it can contain thousands in a large scan. The host list can be sorted by OS or host name/IP address by clicking the headers at the top of the list. Selecting a host will cause the "Ports / Hosts" tab to display the interesting ports on that host.

Each host is labeled with its host name or IP address and has an icon indicating the operating system that was detected for that host. The icon is meaningful only if OS detection (-O) was performed. Otherwise, the icon will be a default one indicating that the OS is unknown. Figure 12.5 shows all possible icons. Note that Nmap's OS detection cannot always provide the level of specificity implied by the icons; for example a Red Hat Linux host will often be displayed with the generic Linux icon.

Figure 12.5. OS icons

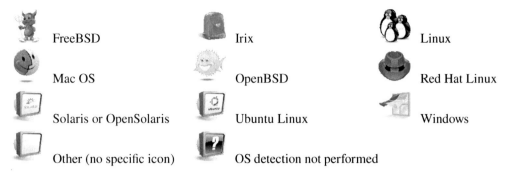

FreeBSD   Irix   Linux

Mac OS   OpenBSD   Red Hat Linux

Solaris or OpenSolaris   Ubuntu Linux   Windows

Other (no specific icon)   OS detection not performed

12.3.3. Sorting by Service

Figure 12.6. Service selection

Above the same list that contains all the scanned hosts is a button labeled "Services". Clicking that will change the list into a list of all ports that are open, filtered, or open|filtered on any of the targets, as shown in Figure 12.6. (Ports that were not listed explicitly in Nmap output are not included.) The ports are identified by service name (http, ftp, etc.). The list can be sorted by clicking the header of the list.

Selecting a host will cause the "Ports / Hosts" tab to display all the hosts that have that service open or filtered.

12.4. Saving and Loading Scan Results

To save an individual scan to a file, choose "Save Scan" from the "Scan" menu (or use the keyboard shortcut **ctrl+S**). If there is more than one scan into the inventory you will be asked which one you want to save. Results are saved in Nmap XML format, which is discussed in Section 13.6, "XML Output (-oX)" [348].

You can save every scan in an inventory with "Save to Directory" under the "Scan" menu (**ctrl+alt+S**). When saving an inventory for the first time, you will commonly create a new directory using the "Create Folder" button in the save dialog. In subsequent saves you can continue saving to the same directory. To reduce the chance of overwriting unrelated scan files, the save-to-directory function will refuse to continue if the chosen directory contains a file that doesn't belong to the inventory. If you are sure you want to save to that directory, delete any offending files and then save again.

Saved results are loaded by choosing "Open Scan" from the "Scan" menu, or by typing the **ctrl+O** keyboard shortcut. In the file selector, the "Open" button opens a single scan, while the "Open Directory" button opens every file in the chosen directory (perhaps created using "Save to Directory").

"Open Scan" opens loaded scans in a new window, thereby creating a new inventory. To merge loaded scans into the current inventory instead, use "Open Scan in This Window".

12.4.1. The Recent Scans Database

Scan results that are not saved to a file are automatically stored in a database. Scan results that are loaded from a file, and are then modified (such as by the addition of a host comment) but not re-saved, are also stored in the database. The database is stored in a file called `zenmap.db` and its location is platform-dependent (see Section 12.10, "Files Used by Zenmap" [330]). By default, scans are kept in the database for 60 days and then removed. This time interval can be changed by modifying the value of the `save_time` variable in the `[search]` section of `zenmap.conf` (see Section 12.11, "Description of zenmap.conf" [333]).

Zenmap's search interface, because it searches the contents of the recent scans database by default, doubles as a database viewer. On opening the search window every scan in the database is shown. The list of scans may then be filtered by a search string. See Section 12.8, "Searching Saved Results" [325].

12.5. Surfing the Network Topology

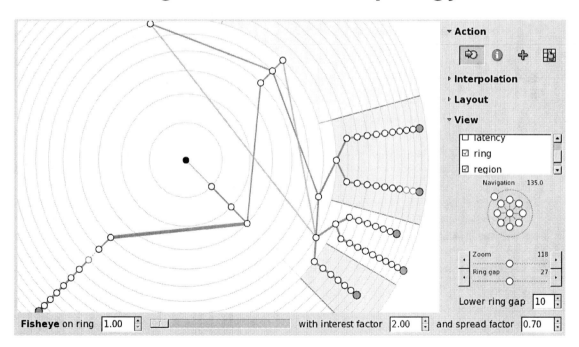

12.5.1. An Overview of the "Topology" Tab

Zenmap's "Topology" tab provides an interactive, animated visualization of the connections between hosts on a network. Hosts are shown as nodes on a graph that extends radially from the center. Click and drag to pan the display, and use the controls provided to zoom in and out. Click on a host and it becomes the new center. The graph rearranges itself in a smooth animation to reflect the new view of the network. Run a new scan and every new host and network path will be added to the topology automatically.

The topology view is most useful when combined with Nmap's `--traceroute` option, because that's the option that discovers the network path to a host. You can view a network inventory that doesn't have traceroute information in the topology, but network paths will not be visible. Remember, though, that you can add traceroute information to a network inventory just by running another scan thanks to Zenmap's scan aggregation.

Initially the topology is shown from the point of view of localhost, with you at the center. Click on a host to move it to the center and see what the network looks like from its point of view.

The topology view is an adaptation of the RadialNet program by João Paulo S. Medeiros.

12.5.2. Legend

The topology view uses many symbols and color conventions. This section explains what they mean.

Each regular host in the network is represented by a little circle. The color and size of the circle is determined by the number of open ports on the host. The more open ports, the larger the circle. A white circle represents an intermediate host in a network path that was not port scanned. If a host has fewer than three open ports, it will be green; between three and six open ports, yellow; more than six open ports; red.

If a host is a router, switch, or wireless access point, it is drawn with a square rather than a circle.

Network distance is shown as concentric gray rings. Each additional ring signifies one more network hop from the center host.

Connections between hosts are shown with colored lines. Primary traceroute connections are shown with blue lines. Alternate paths (paths between two hosts where a different path already exists) are drawn in orange. Which path is primary and which paths are alternates is arbitrary and controlled by the order in which paths were recorded. The thickness of a line is proportional to its round-trip time; hosts with a higher RTT have a thicker line. Hosts with no traceroute information are clustered around localhost, connected with a dashed black line.

If there is no RTT for a hop (a missing traceroute entry), the connection is shown with a blue dashed line and the unknown host that makes the connection is shown with a blue outline.

Some special-purpose hosts may carry one or more icons describing what type of host they are:

⊞ A router.

⊠ A switch.

🔊 A wireless access point.

⊟ A firewall.

⊟ A host with some ports filtered.

12.5.3. Controls

The controls appear in a column when the "Controls" button is clicked. The controls are divided into sections.

Action controls

The controls in the "Action" section control what happens when you click on a host. The buttons in this section are, from left to right, "Change focus", "Show information", "Group children", and "Fill region". When the mode is "Change focus", clicking on a host rearranges the display to put the selected host at the center. When the mode is "Show information", clicking on a host brings up a window with information about it.

When the mode is "Group children", clicking a host collapses into it all of its children—those nodes that are farther from the center. When a host is grouped it appears thus: ◎. Clicking on a grouped node ungroups it again. This diagram shows the process of grouping.

Figure 12.7. Grouping a host's children

When the mode is "Fill region", clicking a host highlights the region of the display occupied by the host and its children. The highlighted hosts are exactly the same as those that would be grouped in "Group children" mode. You can choose different colors to highlight different regions. This diagram shows an example of several regions highlighted in different colors.

Figure 12.8. Highlighting regions of the topology

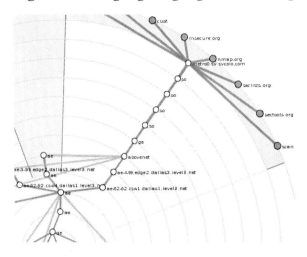

Interpolation controls

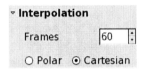

The controls in the "Interpolation" section control how quickly the animation proceeds when part of the graph changes.

Layout controls

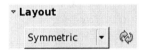

There are two options for the automatic layout of nodes. Symmetric mode gives each subtree of a host an equal-sized slice of the graph. It shows the network hierarchy well but hosts far from the center can be squeezed close together. Weighted mode gives hosts with more children a larger piece of the graph.

View controls

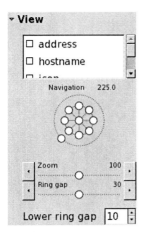

The checkboxes in the "View" section enable and disable parts of the display. For example, disable "hostname" to show only an IP address for each host, or disable "address" to use no labels at all. The "latency" option enables and disables the display of the round-trip times to each host, as determined by Nmap's `--traceroute` option. If "slow in/out" is checked, the animation will not be linear, but will go faster in the middle of the animation and slower at the beginning and end.

The compass-like widget pans the screen in eight directions. Click the center to return to the center host. The ring around the outside controls the rotation of the entire graph.

"Zoom" and "Ring gap" both control the overall size of the graph. "Zoom" changes the size of everything—hosts, labels, connecting lines. "Ring gap" just increases the spacing between the concentric rings, keeping everything else the same size. "Lower ring gap" gives a minimum spacing for the rings, useful mainly when fisheye is enabled.

Fisheye controls

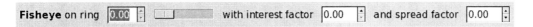

The fisheye controls give more space to a selected ring, compressing all the others. The slider controls which ring gets the most attention. The "interest factor" is how many times greater the ring spacing is for the chosen ring than it would be with no fisheye. The "spread factor" ranges from −1 to 1. It controls how many adjacent rings are expanded around the selected ring, with higher numbers meaning more spread.

12.5.4. Keyboard Shortcuts

The topology display recognizes these keyboard shortcuts:

Key	Function
c	Return the display to the center host.
a	Show or hide host addresses.
h	Show or hide hostnames.
i	Show or hide host icons.
l	Show or hide latency.
r	Show or hide the rings.

12.5.5. The Hosts Viewer

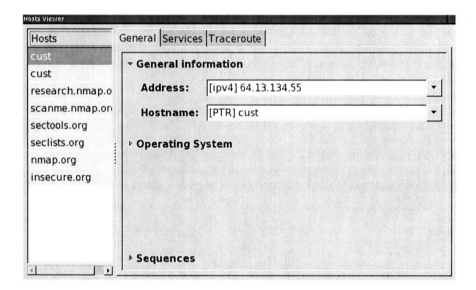

The host viewer is an alternative way to get details about hosts. Activate the viewer by clicking the "Hosts Viewer" button. All the hosts in the inventory are presented in a list. Select any host to get details about it.

12.6. The Nmap Command Constructor Wizard

The Nmap command constructor wizard allows the interactive creation of Nmap command lines without having to remember, for example, that -sS means "SYN scan". Start the wizard by selecting "Command Wizard" from the "Tools" menu or by typing the **ctrl+I** keyboard shortcut. The start page of the wizard will be shown.

You must decide whether you wish to save the scan description as a profile to run it again, or just make the command and run it once. If you choose to create a profile, you will be prompted to enter the profile's name and description.

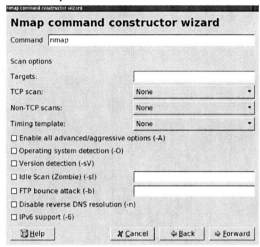

Next you are presented with a series of pages that prompt you interactively for Nmap options. Making a selection from the menus or check boxes will change the command to reflect the selection. For example, choosing a scan type of "TCP SYN Scan" will add -sS to the command line. Checking "Operating system detection" will add -O to the command, and unchecking it will remove it again.

When you get to the end of wizard, click "Apply". If you chose to create a new profile, it will be created and available in the profile combo box. If you chose to create the command and run it once, it will begin to run immediately.

12.7. The Profile Editor

It is common with Nmap to want to run the same scan repeatedly. For example, a system administrator may run a scan of an entire network once a month to keep track of things. Zenmap's mechanism for facilitating this is called profiles.

Figure 12.9. Choosing a profile

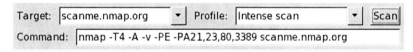

Each window contains a combo box labeled "Profile". Opening it shows what profiles are available. Selecting a profile will cause the "Command" field to display the command line that will be executed. The profiles that come with Zenmap are sufficient for many scanning purposes, but sooner or later you will want to create your own.

12.7.1. Creating a New Profile

The commands for working with profiles are under the "Profile" menu. To create a new profile, select "New Profile" from the "Profile" menu or use the **ctrl+P** keyboard shortcut. You will see a dialog like Figure 12.10.

Figure 12.10. The profile editor

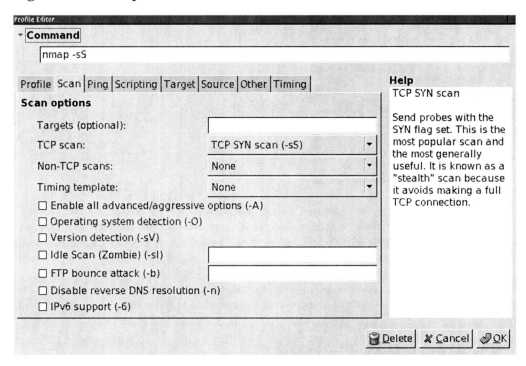

The profile editor starts by displaying a tab called "Profile" which asks for the new profile's name and description. The "Profile name" field is how the scan will be identified in the drop-down combo box in the scan interface. The text in the "Description" field is a description of the purpose of the profile.

The rest of the tabs allow you to specify Nmap options, either by typing them directly in the "Command" field or by clicking on the checkboxes. Hover the mouse pointer over an option to get a description of what the option does and what kind of input it expects.

A profile may or may not include scan targets. If you often run the same scan against the same set of targets, you will find it convenient to list the targets within the profile. If you plan to run the same scan against different targets, leave the "Targets" field blank, and fill in the targets later, when you run the scan.

12.7.2. Editing a Profile

To edit a profile, select the profile you want to edit, then choose "Edit Selected Profile" from the "Profile" menu or use the **ctrl+E** keyboard shortcut. The profile editor will open, this time with the name and description filled from the profile selected. Making a change to the profile here will modify the profile permanently.

To delete a profile, click the "Delete" button within the profile editor after opening the profile you want to delete as if to edit it. Zenmap will present a warning before deleting the profile. To leave the editor without modifying the profile, use the "Cancel" button.

12.7.3. Deriving a New Profile from an Old One

To create a new profile using another profile as a template, select the template profile, then select "New Profile with Selected" from the "Profile" menu or use the **ctrl+R** keyboard shortcut. This will set all the options based on the selected profile while leaving the name and description blank for you to fill in. Any changes made to the options will affect only the newly created profile, not the original profile from which it was derived.

To leave the editor without creating the derived profile, use the "Cancel" button.

12.8. Searching Saved Results

Zenmap allows you to search saved scan results files and the database of recent scans. To begin searching, select "Search Scan Results" from the "Tools" menu or use the **ctrl+F** keyboard shortcut. The search dialog appears as shown in Figure 12.11.

Figure 12.11. The search dialog

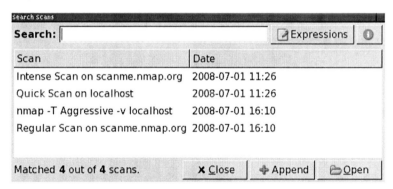

The search interface initially shows all the scans in the recent scans database (for which see Section 12.4.1, "The Recent Scans Database" [317]). The reason all the scans are shown is simple—no restrictions have yet been placed on the search, so every possible result is returned.

Searches may be given in terms of several search criteria, however the simplest search is just a keyword search. Just type a word like scanme in the "Search" field to find all scans that have that word as part of their output, whether as a host name, operating system name, profile, or anything else. An example of this is shown in Figure 12.12.

Figure 12.12. Keyword search

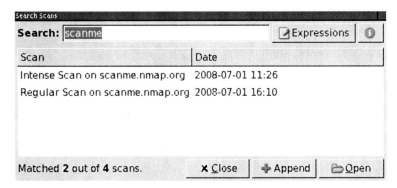

Searches happen live, as you type. When you have found the scan you want click the "Open" button or double-click on the scan name.

More complicated searches can be built up using the "Expressions" interface. Click the "Expressions" button and graphical representation of the current search will appear. Modify the search by selecting from the combo boxes displayed. Click "+" to add a criterion and "−" to remove one. Click the "Expressions" button again to hide the criteria (they are still present in the search string). Editing of the search text is disabled while the expressions are shown. An example of a more complicated search is shown in Figure 12.13.

Figure 12.13. Expressions search

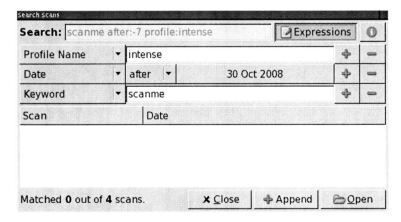

Searches are and-based, meaning that all the criteria must be true for a scan to match and appear in the results list. Most searches are case-insensitive. (The only case-sensitive criterion is option:.) By default only the scans in the recent scans database are searched. To recursively search files in a directory, use the "Include Directory" expression.

You will have noticed that whenever you choose a search expression a text representation of it appears in the search entry. The string in the "Search" field is what really controls the search; the "Expressions" interface is just a convenient way to set it. When you have learned what search strings correspond to what expressions, you may skip the expressions interface and just type in a search string directly.

The following is a list of all the textual search criteria recognized by the search interface. Most criteria have a short form: `d:-5` is the same as `date:-5` and `op:80` is the same as `open:80`. The short form of each criterion is given in the list below.

`<keyword>`
> An unadorned word matches anything in a scan. For example, `apache` will match all Apache servers and `linux` will match all Linux hosts. There is a chance of false positives when using the keyword search, like if a host happens to be named `apache` or `linux`.

Port states
> Every possible port state is also a search criterion. They are
>
> `open:<ports>` (`op:` for short)
> `closed:<ports>` (`cp:` for short)
> `filtered:<ports>` (`fp:` for short)
> `unfiltered:<ports>` (`ufp:` for short)
> `open|filtered:<ports>` (`ofp:` for short)
> `closed|filtered:<ports>` (`cfp:` for short)
>
> Use `open:80` to match scans that have a host with port 80 open. The `<ports>` argument may also be a comma-separated list.
>
> Additionally the `scanned:` (`sp:`) criterion matches scans in which the given ports were scanned, whatever their final state.

`date:<YYYY-MM-DD>` or `date:-<n>` (`d:` for short)
> Matches scans that occurred on the given date in `<YYYY-MM-DD>` format. Or use `date:-<n>` to match scans that occurred any on the day `<n>` days ago. Use `date:-1` to find scans performed yesterday.
>
> When using the `<YYYY-MM-DD>` format, the date may be followed by one or more `~`, each of which widens the range of dates matched by one day on both sides. `date:2007-12-23` matches scans that occurred between 00:00 and 24:00 on December 23, 2007. `date:2007-12-23~` matches scans that took place between 00:00 on December 22 and 24:00 on December 24. This "fuzzy" date matching is useful when you can't remember exactly when you ran a scan.

`after:<YYYY-MM-DD>` or `after:-<n>` (`a:` for short)
> Matches scans that occurred on or after the given date in `<YYYY-MM-DD>` format. Or use `after:-<n>` to match scans that occurred within the last `<n>` days. For example, `after:-7` matches scans that happened in the last week.

`before:<YYYY-MM-DD>` or `before:-<n>` (`b:` for short)
> Matches scans that occurred on or before the given date in `<YYYY-MM-DD>` format. Or use `before:-<n>` to match scans that occurred any time before `<n>` days ago.

`target:<name>` (`t:` for short)
> Matches scans of any hosts with the given name. The name may be either the name specified in the scan or the reverse-DNS name of any host.

`option:<option>` (`o:` for short)

Matches scans that used the given command-line option. Omit any leading – or --: `option:A` matches scans that used the `-A` option.

This criterion matches only literally. `option:O` will not match scans that used `-A`, even though `-A` implies `-O`. Similarly `option:sU` will not match scans that used `-sSU`. Option matching is case-sensitive.

`os:<string>`

Matches scans of hosts with the given string in any part of their OS description. `os:windows` will return scans of Microsoft Windows hosts broadly.

`service:<string>` (`s:` for short)

Matches scans of hosts with the given string in any part of the service description of any of their ports. `service:ssh` will return scans of hosts running any type of SSH.

`profile:<name>` (`pr:` for short)

Matches scans that used the named profile, for example `profile:"intense scan"`.

`inroute:<host>` (`ir:` for short)

Matches scans where the given host appears as an intermediate router in `--traceroute` output.

`dir:<directory>`

`dir:` is not really a search criterion. Rather it is the way to search a directory in the filesystem in addition to those in the recent scans database. Directories are searched recursively for files ending with certain extensions, `xml` only by default. To match more file names modify the `file_extension` variable of the `[search]` section of `zenmap.conf` according to the instructions in Section 12.11.1, "Sections of zenmap.conf" [333].

12.9. Comparing Results

It is a common desire to run the same scan twice at different times, or run two slightly different scans at the same time, and see how they differ. Zenmap provides an interface for comparing scan results, shown in Figure 12.14. Open the comparison tool by selecting "Compare Results" from the "Tools" menu or by using the **ctrl+D** (think "diff") keyboard shortcut. Zenmap supports comparing two scan results at a time.

Figure 12.14. Comparison tool

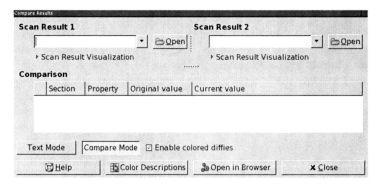

The first step in performing a comparison is selecting the two scans to compare. The combo boxes under "Scan Result 1" and "Scan Result 2" allow you to choose from open scans. Or click the "Open" buttons to get scan results from a file. To compare results from the recent scans database, you must first open those scans using the search interface (see Section 12.8, "Searching Saved Results" [325]).

The distinction between Scan Result 1 and Scan Result 2 is important. Comparison are always done from Scan Result 1 to Scan Result 2, that is, how Scan Result 2 differs from Scan Result 1. Once the two results have been chosen the comparison is done immediately.

12.9.1. Graphical Comparison

Figure 12.15 shows a comparison of a regular scan and an intense scan of the same host.

Figure 12.15. Graphical comparison

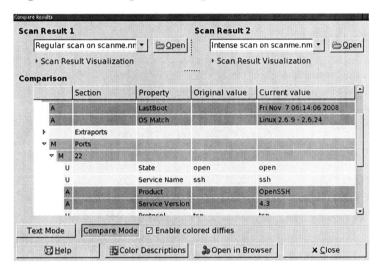

The differences and similarities of the two scans is shown hierarchically and in colors. Each color also has a letter code that describes how that part of the scan changed (or not). The codes are: U for unchanged, A for added, M for modified, and N for not present (or deleted). The colors can be modified by clicking the "Color Descriptions" button.

12.9.2. Text Comparison

An alternative view of the comparison is the text mode, which is activated by clicking the "Text Mode" button. A text mode comparison of the same two scans is shown in Figure 12.16. An advantage of the text mode output is that it can be copied and pasted into a file or an email message.

Figure 12.16. Text mode comparison

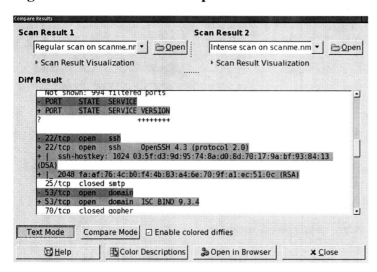

The output of a text mode comparison is similar to that of the Unix diff tool. Each line begins with a character indicating the meaning of the line. The possible character codes are shown in Table 12.1.

Table 12.1. Text diff character codes

Code	Meaning
" " (space)	The line is identical in both scans.
+	The line was added in the second scan.
−	The line was removed in the second scan.
?	^, +, and − characters on the remainder of the line indicate which characters were modified, added, or removed, respectively, in the line immediately above.

An HTML rendering of the text difference can be viewed by clicking the "Open in Browser" button. This view is meant to be saved for archival purposes or printed for a report.

12.10. Files Used by Zenmap

Zenmap uses a number of configuration and control files, and of course requires Nmap to be installed. Where the files are stored depends on the platform and how Zenmap was configured. The configuration files are divided into two categories: system files and per-user files.

12.10.1. The `nmap` Executable

Zenmap depends on the `nmap` command-line executable being installed. The program is first searched for in all of the directories specified in the `PATH` environment variable.

On some platforms the `nmap` command isn't commonly installed in any of the directories in `PATH`. As a convenience for those platforms, the following additional directories will be searched if the command is not found in the `PATH`:

- On Mac OS X, the directory `/usr/local/bin` is searched.

- On Windows, the directory containing the Zenmap executable is searched.

To use an absolute path to the executable, or if the executable is installed under a name other than `nmap`, modify the `nmap_command_path` variable in the `[paths]` section of `zenmap.conf`. For example, if you have installed nmap in `/opt/bin`, use

```
[paths]
nmap_command_path = /opt/bin/nmap
```

Or if you have a custom-compiled version of Nmap called `nmap-custom`, use

```
[paths]
nmap_command_path = nmap-custom
```

See Section 12.11, "Description of zenmap.conf" [333].

12.10.2. System Configuration Files

These files affect the installation of Zenmap across an entire installation. On Unix and Mac OS X, they are in `<prefix>/share/zenmap`, where `<prefix>` is the filesystem prefix Zenmap was compiled with. The prefix is likely `/usr` or `/usr/local`, so Zenmap's file are probably in `/usr/share/zenmap` or `/usr/local/share/zenmap`. On Windows, the location also depends on where Zenmap was installed. They are probably in `C:\Program Files\Nmap\share\zenmap`. The Zenmap system configuration directory contains the following:

`config/`
The files under `config` are copied to per-user configuration directories. See Section 12.10.3, "Per-user Configuration Files" [332].

`docs/`
The files in the `docs` subdirectory are Zenmap's documentation files.

`locale/`
The files in the `locale/` subdirectory contain translations of the text used by Zenmap into other languages.

`misc/profile_editor.xml`
This file defines what options are presented by the profile editor (see Section 12.7, "The Profile Editor" [323]). It can be edited with care to alter the profile editor system-wide.

`misc/wizard.xml`
This file defines what options are presented by the command constructor wizard (see Section 12.6, "The Nmap Command Constructor Wizard" [322]). It can be edited with care to alter the wizard system-wide.

12.10.3. Per-user Configuration Files

These files affect only one user of Zenmap. Some of them are copied from the `config` subdirectory of the system files when Zenmap is run for the first time. Per-user files are in *<HOME>*/`.zenmap` on Unix and Mac OS X, where *<HOME>* is the current user's home directory. They are in `C:\Users\`*<USER>*`\.zenmap` on Windows Vista and `C:\Documents and Settings\`*<USER>*`\.zenmap` on previous versions of Windows, where *<USER>* is the name of the current user.

`recent_scans.txt`
> This contains a list of file names of recently saved scans. These scans are shown under the "Scan" menu. Scans must have been saved to a file to appear here. See Section 12.4, "Saving and Loading Scan Results" [316]. If this file doesn't exist it is created when Zenmap is run.

`scan_profile.usp`
> This file contains descriptions of scan profiles, including the defaults and user-created profiles. I recommend using the profile editor (see Section 12.7, "The Profile Editor" [323]) to make changes to this file. This file is copied from the system configuration directory the first time Zenmap is run.

`target_list.txt`
> This file contains a list of recently scanned targets. If it doesn't exist it is created when Zenmap is run.

`zenmap.conf`
> This is Zenmap's main configuration file. It holds the settings for a particular user's copy of Zenmap and is discussed in more detail in Section 12.11, "Description of zenmap.conf" [333].

`zenmap.db`
> This is the database of recent scans, as described in Section 12.4.1, "The Recent Scans Database" [317]. It is created if it doesn't already exist.

`zenmap_version`
> This file contains the version of Zenmap that was used to create this per-user configuration directory. It may be helpful to compare the version number in this file with the file of the same name in the system configuration directory if you suspect a version conflict. It is simply copied from the system configuration the first time Zenmap is run.

12.10.4. Output Files

Whenever a scan is run, Zenmap instructs Nmap to put XML output in a temporary file so that Zenmap can parse it. Normally the XML output file is deleted when the scan is finished. However, if the command line in Zenmap contains an `-oX` or `-oA` option, XML output is written to the named file instead, and that file isn't deleted when the scan completes. In other words, `-oX` and `-oA` work the way you would expect. `-oG`, `-oN`, and `-oS` work too, even though Zenmap doesn't use the output files produced by those options.

There is one important thing to note in Zenmap's handling of these filenames. Percent characters (%) are escaped to keep them from being interpreted as `strftime`-like format specifiers (see Section 13.2.1, "Controlling Output Type" [338]). This is because Zenmap must know exactly what name Nmap will use for its output file. If in Zenmap you type `-oX scan-%T-%D.xml`, the output file will be saved in the file scan-%T-%D.xml, not scan-144840-121307.xml or whatever it would have been based on the current time and date if you were executing Nmap directly.

12.11. Description of `zenmap.conf`

`zenmap.conf` is the user-specific configuration file for Zenmap. It is a plain text file located in the per-user configuration directory (see Section 12.10.3, "Per-user Configuration Files" [332]). The syntax is that recognized by the Python ConfigParser[2] module, which is similar to that of Windows INI files. Sections are delimited by titles in square brackets. Within sections are lines containing *<name>=<value>* or *<name>: <value>* pairs. An excerpt from a `zenmap.conf` is shown.

```
[output_highlight]
enable_highlight = True

[paths]
nmap_command_path = nmap

[search]
search_db = 1
file_extension = xml
store_results = 1
directory =
save_time = 60;days
```

Some of these settings can be controlled from within Zenmap without editing the configuration file directly.

12.11.1. Sections of `zenmap.conf`

Boolean values are normalized from `True`, `true`, or `1` to true or anything else to false.

`[paths]`
> The `[paths]` section defines important paths used by Zenmap. Only one is defined, `nmap_command_path`, which is the path to the Nmap executable. Whatever the first word is in a command line executed by Zenmap will be replaced by the value of this variable. Its default value of `nmap` is appropriate for most systems. See Section 12.10.1, "The nmap Executable" [330] for examples.

`[search]`
> The `[search]` section defines how the search tool (see Section 12.8, "Searching Saved Results" [325]) behaves. The names in this section correspond to the options in the "Search options" tab of the search dialog. It has the following names defined.

`directory`
> The directory to search for saved scan results files.

`file_extension`
> A semicolon-separated list of file name extensions to search.

---

[2] *http://docs.python.org/lib/module-ConfigParser.html*

search_db
: A Boolean controlling whether to search the recent scans database.

store_results

: A Boolean controlling whether to store scan results in the recent scans database. See Section 12.4.1, "The Recent Scans Database" [317].

save_time
: How long to keep scan results in the recent scans database. Results older than this are deleted when Zenmap is closed. The format is a number and a time interval separated by semicolons, for example 60;days or 1;years.

[diff]
: The [diff] section defines how the comparison tool (see Section 12.9, "Comparing Results" [328]) behaves. It has the following names defined.

diff_mode
: Controls whether comparisons are shown by default in graphical or text mode. Must be either compare for graphical mode or text.

colored_diff
: A Boolean that controls if comparisons use color.

[diff_colors]
: The [diff_colors] section defines the colors used by the comparison tool. It has the following names defined: unchanged, added, not_present, and modified, the meanings of which are defined in Section 12.9, "Comparing Results" [328]. The value of each of these is a list of three integers in the range 0–65535 representing red, green, and blue in the format [<red>, <green>, <blue>]. For example, [65535, 0, 0] specifies red.

[output_highlight]
: The [output_highlight] section contains a single Boolean variable enable_highlight, which enables output highlighting when True and disables it if False.

[date_highlight], [hostname_highlight], [ip_highlight], [port_list_highlight], [open_port_highlight], [closed_port_highlight], [filtered_port_highlight], [details_highlight]
: These sections all define the nature of Nmap output highlighting, which is discussed in the section called "The Nmap Output tab" [312]. These are best edited from within Zenmap. Within each of these sections, the following names are defined.

regex
: The regular expression that matches the relevant part of the output.

bold
: A Boolean controlling whether to make this highlight bold.

italic
: A Boolean controlling whether to make this highlight italic.

```
underline
```
A Boolean controlling whether to underline this highlight.

```
text
```
The color of the text in this highlight. The syntax is a list of three integers in the range 0–65535 representing red, green, and blue in the format `[<red>, <green>, <blue>]`. For example, `[65535, 0, 0]` for a red highlight.

```
highlight
```
The color of the background in this highlight. The syntax is the same as for `text`.

12.12. Command-line Options

Being a graphical application, most of Zenmap's functionality is exposed through its graphical interface. Zenmap's command-line options are given here for completeness and because they are sometimes useful. In particular, it's good to know that the command **zenmap <results file>** starts Zenmap with the results in `<results file>` already open.

12.12.1. Synopsis

```
zenmap [ <options> ] [ <results file> ]
```

12.12.2. Options Summary

```
-f, --file <results file>
```
Open the given results file for viewing. The results file may be an Nmap XML output file (`.xml`, as produced by **nmap -oX**), or a file previously saved by Zenmap.

```
-h, --help
```
Show a help message and exit.

```
-n, --nmap <Nmap command line>
```
Run the given Nmap command within the Zenmap interface. After `-n` or `--nmap`, every remaining command line argument is read as the command line to execute. This means that `-n` or `--nmap` must be given last, after any other options. Note that the command line must include the **nmap** executable name: **zenmap -n nmap -sS target**.

```
-p, --profile <profile>
```
Start with the given profile selected. The profile name is just a string: `"Regular scan"`. If combined with `-t`, begin a scan with the given profile against the specified target.

```
-t, --target <target>
```
Start with the given target. If combined with `-p`, begin a scan with the given profile against the specified target.

```
-v, --verbose
```
Increase verbosity (of Zenmap, not Nmap). This option may be given multiple times for even more verbosity printed to the console window used to start Zenmap.

12.12.3. Error Output

If Zenmap happens to crash, it normally helps you send a bug report with a stack trace. Set the environment variable `ZENMAP_DEVELOPMENT` (the value doesn't matter) to disable automatic crash reporting and have errors printed to the console. Try the Bash shell command **ZENMAP_DEVELOPMENT=1 zenmap -v -v -v** to get a useful debugging output.

On Windows, standard error is redirected to the file `zenmap.exe.log` in the same directory as `zenmap.exe` rather than being printed to the console.

12.13. History

Zenmap was originally derived from Umit[3], an Nmap GUI created during the Google-sponsored Nmap Summer of Code in 2005 and 2006. The primary author of Umit was Adriano Monteiro Marques. When Umit was modified and integrated into Nmap in 2007, it was renamed Zenmap.

---

[3] *http://www.umitproject.org*

Chapter 13. Nmap Output Formats

13.1. Introduction

A common problem with open-source security tools is confusing and disorganized output. They often spew out many lines of irrelevant debugging information, forcing users to dig through pages of output trying to discern important results from the noise. Program authors often devote little effort to organizing and presenting results effectively. The output messages can be difficult to understand and poorly documented. This shouldn't be too surprising—writing clever code to exploit some TCP/IP weakness is usually more gratifying than documentation or UI work. Since open source authors are rarely paid, they do what they enjoy.

At the risk of offending my friend Dan Kaminsky, I'll name his Scanrand[1] port scanner as an example of a program that was clearly developed with far more emphasis on neat technical tricks than a user friendly UI. The sample output in Example 13.1 is from the Scanrand documentation page.

Example 13.1. Scanrand output against a local network

```
bash-2.05a# scanrand 10.0.1.1-254:quick
    UP:        10.0.1.38:80      [01]    0.003s
    UP:       10.0.1.110:443     [01]    0.017s
    UP:       10.0.1.254:443     [01]    0.021s
    UP:        10.0.1.57:445     [01]    0.024s
    UP:        10.0.1.59:445     [01]    0.024s
    UP:        10.0.1.38:22      [01]    0.047s
    UP:       10.0.1.110:22      [01]    0.058s
    UP:       10.0.1.110:23      [01]    0.058s
    UP:       10.0.1.254:22      [01]    0.077s
    UP:       10.0.1.254:23      [01]    0.077s
    UP:        10.0.1.25:135     [01]    0.088s
    UP:        10.0.1.57:135     [01]    0.089s
    UP:        10.0.1.59:135     [01]    0.090s
    UP:        10.0.1.25:139     [01]    0.097s
    UP:        10.0.1.27:139     [01]    0.098s
    UP:        10.0.1.57:139     [01]    0.099s
    UP:        10.0.1.59:139     [01]    0.099s
    UP:        10.0.1.38:111     [01]    0.127s
    UP:        10.0.1.57:1025    [01]    0.147s
    UP:        10.0.1.59:1025    [01]    0.147s
    UP:        10.0.1.57:5000    [01]    0.156s
    UP:        10.0.1.59:5000    [01]    0.157s
    UP:        10.0.1.53:111     [01]    0.182s
bash-2.05a#
```

While this does get the job done, it is difficult to interpret. Output is printed based on when the response was received, without any option for sorting the port numbers or even grouping all open ports on a target host together. A bunch of space is wasted near the beginning of each line and no summary of results is provided.

---

[1] *http://sectools.org/tools4.html#scanrand*

Nmap's output is also far from perfect, though I do try pretty hard to make it readable, well-organized, and flexible. Given the number of ways Nmap is used by people and other software, no single format can please everyone. So Nmap offers several formats, including the interactive mode for humans to read directly and XML for easy parsing by software.

In addition to offering different output formats, Nmap provides options for controlling the verbosity of output as well as debugging messages. Output types may be sent to standard output or to named files, which Nmap can append to or clobber. Output files may also be used to resume aborted scans. This chapter includes full details on these options and every output format.

13.2. Command-line Flags

As with almost all other Nmap capabilities, output behavior is controlled by command-line flags. These flags are grouped by category and described in the following sections.

13.2.1. Controlling Output Type

The most fundamental output control is designating the format(s) of output you would like. Nmap offers five types, as summarized in the following list and fully described in later sections.

Output formats supported by Nmap

Interactive output
> This is the output that Nmap sends to the standard output stream (stdout) by default. So it has no special command-line option. Interactive mode caters to human users reading the results directly and it is characterized by a table of interesting ports that is shown in dozens of examples throughout this book.

Normal output (-oN)
> This is very similar to interactive output, and is sent to the file you choose. It does differ from interactive output in several ways, which derive from the expectation that this output will be analyzed after the scan completes rather than interactively. So interactive output includes messages (depending on verbosity level specified with -v) such as scan completion time estimates and open port alerts. Normal output omits those as unnecessary once the scan completes and the final interesting ports table is printed. This output type prints the nmap command-line used and execution time and date on its first line.

XML output (-oX)
> XML offers a stable format that is easily parsed by software. Free XML parsers are available for all major computer languages, including C/C++, Perl, Python, and Java. In almost all cases that a non-trivial application interfaces with Nmap, XML is the preferred format. This chapter also discusses how XML results can be transformed into other formats, such as HTML reports and database tables.

Grepable output (-oG)
> This simple format is easy to manipulate on the command line with simple Unix tools such as grep, awk, cut, and diff. Each host is listed on one line, with the tab, slash, and comma characters used to delimit output fields. While this can be handy for quickly grokking results, the XML format is preferred for more significant tasks as it is more stable and contains more information.

sCRiPt KiDDi3 0utPU+ (-oS)

This format is provided for the l33t haXXorZ!

While interactive output is the default and has no associated command-line options, the other four format options use the same syntax. They take one argument, which is the filename that results should be stored in. Multiple formats may be specified, but each format may only be specified once. For example, you may wish to save normal output for your own review while saving XML of the same scan for programmatic analysis. You might do this with the options -oX myscan.xml -oN myscan.nmap. While this chapter uses the simple names like myscan.xml for brevity, more descriptive names are generally recommended. The names chosen are a matter of personal preference, though I use long ones that incorporate the scan date and a word or two describing the scan, placed in a directory named after the company I'm scanning. As a convenience, you may specify -oA <basename> to store scan results in normal, XML, and grepable formats at once. They are stored in <basename>.nmap, <basename>.xml, and <basename>.gnmap, respectively. As with most programs, you can prefix the filenames with a directory path, such as ~/nmaplogs/foocorp/ on Unix or c:\hacking\sco on Windows.

While these options save results to files, Nmap still prints interactive output to stdout as usual. For example, the command **nmap -oX myscan.xml target** prints XML to myscan.xml and fills standard output with the same interactive results it would have printed if -oX wasn't specified at all. You can change this by passing a hyphen character as the argument to one of the format types. This causes Nmap to deactivate interactive output, and instead print results in the format you specified to the standard output stream. So the command nmap -oX - target will send only XML output to stdout. Serious errors may still be printed to the normal error stream, stderr.

When you specify a filename to an output format flag such as -oN, that file is overwritten by default. If you prefer to keep the existing content of the file and append the new results, specify the --append-output option. All output filenames specified in that Nmap execution will then be appended to rather than clobbered. This doesn't work well for XML (-oX) scan data as the resultant file generally won't parse properly until you fix it up by hand.

Unlike some Nmap arguments, the space between the logfile option flag (such as -oX) and the filename or hyphen is mandatory. If you omit the flags and give arguments such as -oG- or -oXscan.xml, a backwards compatibility feature of Nmap will cause the creation of *normal format* output files named G- and Xscan.xml respectively.

All of these arguments support strftime-like conversions in the filename. %H, %M, %S, %m, %d, %y, and %Y are all exactly the same as in strftime. %T is the same as %H%M%S, %R is the same as %H%M, and %D is the same as %m%d%y. A % followed by any other character just yields that character (%% gives you a percent symbol). So -oX 'scan-%T-%D.xml' will use an XML file in the form of scan-144840-121307.xml.

13.2.2. Controlling Verbosity of Output

After deciding which format(s) you wish results to be saved in, you can decide how detailed those results should be. The first -v option enables verbosity with a level of one. Specify -v twice for a slightly greater effect. Verbosity levels greater than two aren't useful. Most changes only effect interactive output, and some also affect normal and script kiddie output. The other output types are meant to be processed by machines, so Nmap can give substantial detail by default in those formats without fatiguing a human user. However, there are a few changes in other modes where output size can be reduced substantially by omitting some detail. For example, a comment line in the grepable output that provides a list of all ports scanned is only printed in verbose mode because it can be quite long. The following list describes the major changes you get with at least one -v option.

Scan completion time estimates

On scans that take more than a minute or two, you will see occasional updates like this in interactive output mode:

```
SYN Stealth Scan Timing: About 30.01% done; ETC: 16:04
(0:01:09 remaining)
```

New updates are given if the estimates change significantly. All port scanning techniques except for idle scan and FTP bounce scan support completion time estimation, and so does version scanning.

Open ports reported when discovered

When verbosity is enabled, open ports are printed in interactive mode as they are discovered. They are still reported in the final interesting ports table as well. This allows users to begin investigating open ports before Nmap even completes. Open port alerts look like this:

```
Discovered open port 53/tcp on 64.13.134.52
```

Additional warnings

Nmap always prints warnings about obvious mistakes and critical problems. That standard is lowered when verbosity is enabled, allowing more warnings to be printed. There are dozens of these warnings, covering topics from targets experiencing excessive drops or extraordinarily long latency, to ports which respond to probes in unexpected ways. Rate limiting prevents these warnings from flooding the screen.

Additional notes

Nmap prints many extra informational notes when in verbose mode. For example, it prints out the time when each port scan is started along with the number of hosts and ports scanned. It later prints out a concluding line disclosing how long the scan took and briefly summarizing the results.

Extra OS detection information

With verbosity, results of the TCP ISN and IP ID sequence number predictability tests are shown. These are done as a byproduct of OS detection. With verbosity greater than one, the actual OS detection fingerprint is shown in more cases.

Down hosts are printed in ping scan

During a ping scan with verbosity enabled, down hosts will be printed, rather than just up ones.

Birthday wishes

Nmap wishes itself a happy birthday when run in verbose mode on September 1.

The changes that are usually only useful until Nmap finishes and prints its report are only sent to interactive output mode. If you send normal output to a file with -oN, that file won't contain open port alerts or completion time estimates, though they are still printed to stdout. The assumption is that you will review the file when Nmap is done and don't want a lot of extra cruft, while you might watch Nmap's execution progress on standard output and care about runtime progress. If you really want everything printed to stdout sent to a file, use the output stream redirection provided by your shell (e.g. **nmap -v scanme.nmap.org > scanoutput.nmap**).

The dozens of small changes contingent on verbosity (mostly extra messages) are too numerous to cover here. They are also always subject to change. An effective way to see them all is to unpack the latest Nmap tarball and grep for them with a command such as **grep -A1 o.verbose *.cc**. Representative excerpts from the output are shown in Example 13.2.

Example 13.2. Grepping for verbosity conditionals

```
idle_scan.cc: if (o.debugging || o.verbose) {
idle_scan.cc-   log_write(LOG_STDOUT, "Initiating Idlescan against %s\n",
                        target->NameIP());
--
nmap.cc: if (o.verbose)
nmap.cc-   output_ports_to_machine_parseable_output(ports, o.TCPScan(),
                                        o.udpscan, o.ipprotscan);
--
nmap_rpc.cc: if (o.debugging || o.verbose)
nmap_rpc.cc-   gh_perror("recvfrom in get_rpc_results");
--
osscan.cc: if (o.verbose && openport != (unsigned long) -1)
osscan.cc-   log_write(LOG_STDOUT, "For OSScan assuming port %d is open, %d..."
--
output.cc: if (o.verbose)
output.cc-   log_write(LOG_NORMAL|LOG_SKID|LOG_STDOUT,
                        "IP ID Sequence Generation: %s\n",...
```

The following two examples put all of this together. Example 13.3 shows the output of a normal scan without the −v option.

Example 13.3. Interactive output without verbosity enabled

```
# nmap -T4 -A -p- scanme.nmap.org

Starting Nmap ( http://nmap.org )
Interesting ports on scanme.nmap.org (64.13.134.52):
Not shown: 65529 filtered ports
PORT    STATE  SERVICE VERSION
22/tcp  open   ssh      OpenSSH 4.3 (protocol 2.0)
25/tcp  closed smtp
53/tcp  open   domain  ISC BIND 9.3.4
70/tcp  closed gopher
80/tcp  open   http     Apache httpd 2.2.2 ((Fedora))
|_ HTML title: Go ahead and ScanMe!
113/tcp closed auth
Device type: general purpose
Running: Linux 2.6.X
OS details: Linux 2.6.17 - 2.6.21, Linux 2.6.23

TRACEROUTE (using port 22/tcp)
HOP RTT   ADDRESS
1   16.92 nodem-msfc-vl245-act-security-gw-1-113.ucsd.edu (132.239.1.113)
[... nine similar lines cut ...]
11  21.97 scanme.nmap.org (64.13.134.52)

OS and Service detection performed. Please report any incorrect results ⏎
 at http://nmap.org/submit/ .
Nmap done: 1 IP address (1 host up) scanned in 168.10 seconds
```

Example 13.4 is the output of the same scan with verbosity enabled. Features such as the extra OS identification data, completion time estimates, open port alerts, and extra informational messages are easily identified in the latter output. This extra info is often helpful during interactive scanning, so I always specify -v when scanning a single machine unless I have a good reason not to.

Example 13.4. Interactive output with verbosity enabled

```
# nmap -v -T4 -A -p- scanme.nmap.org
Starting Nmap ( http://nmap.org )
Initiating Ping Scan at 00:12
Completed Ping Scan at 00:12, 0.02s elapsed (1 total hosts)
Initiating SYN Stealth Scan at 00:12
Scanning scanme.nmap.org (64.13.134.52) [65535 ports]
Discovered open port 80/tcp on 64.13.134.52
Discovered open port 53/tcp on 64.13.134.52
Discovered open port 22/tcp on 64.13.134.52
SYN Stealth Scan Timing: About 16.66% done; ETC: 00:15 (0:02:30 remaining)
Completed SYN Stealth Scan at 00:14, 125.13s elapsed (65535 total ports)
Scanning 3 services on scanme.nmap.org (64.13.134.52)
Completed Service scan at 00:14, 6.05s elapsed (3 services on 1 host)
Initiating OS detection (try #1) against scanme.nmap.org (64.13.134.52)
[Removed some verbose traceroute and parallel DNS related messages]
Initiating SCRIPT ENGINE at 00:14
Completed SCRIPT ENGINE at 00:14, 4.09s elapsed
Host scanme.nmap.org (64.13.134.52) appears to be up ... good.
Interesting ports on scanme.nmap.org (64.13.134.52):
Not shown: 65529 filtered ports
PORT     STATE   SERVICE VERSION
22/tcp   open    ssh      OpenSSH 4.3 (protocol 2.0)
25/tcp   closed  smtp
53/tcp   open    domain   ISC BIND 9.3.4
70/tcp   closed  gopher
80/tcp   open    http     Apache httpd 2.2.2 ((Fedora))
|_ HTML title: Go ahead and ScanMe!
113/tcp  closed  auth
Device type: general purpose
Running: Linux 2.6.X
OS details: Linux 2.6.17 - 2.6.21, Linux 2.6.23
Uptime guess: 12.476 days (since Wed Jul  2 12:48:56 2008)
TCP Sequence Prediction: Difficulty=198 (Good luck!)
IP ID Sequence Generation: All zeros

TRACEROUTE (using port 22/tcp)
HOP RTT    ADDRESS
1   0.25   nodem-msfc-vl245-act-security-gw-1-113.ucsd.edu (132.239.1.113)
[... nine similar lines cut ...]
11  20.67 scanme.nmap.org (64.13.134.52)

OS and Service detection performed. Please report any incorrect results⏎
 at http://nmap.org/submit/ .
Nmap done: 1 IP address (1 host up) scanned in 147.462 seconds
         Raw packets sent: 131128 (5.771MB) | Rcvd: 283637 (12.515MB)
```

13.2.3. Enabling Debugging Output

When even verbose mode doesn't provide sufficient data for you, debugging is available to flood you with much more! As with the verbosity option (-v), debugging is enabled with a command-line flag (-d) and the debug level can be increased by specifying it multiple times. Alternatively, you can set a debug level by giving an argument to -d. For example, -d9 sets level nine. That is the highest effective level and will produce thousands of lines unless you run a very simple scan with very few ports and targets.

Debugging output is useful when a bug is suspected in Nmap, or if you are simply confused as to what Nmap is doing and why. As this feature is mostly intended for developers, debug lines aren't always self-explanatory. If you don't understand a line, your only recourses are to ignore it, look it up in the source code, or request help from the development list (*nmap-dev*). Some lines are self explanatory, but messages become more obscure as the debug level is increased. Example 13.5 shows a few different debugging lines that resulted from a -d5 scan of Scanme.

Example 13.5. Some representative debugging lines

```
Timeout vals: srtt: 27495 rttvar: 27495 to: 137475 delta -2753
              ==> srtt: 27150 rttvar: 21309 to: 112386
RCVD (15.3330s) TCP 64.13.134.52:25 > 132.239.1.115:50122 RA ttl=52
              id=0 iplen=40 seq=0 win=0 ack=4222318673
**TIMING STATS** (15.3350s): IP, probes active/freshportsleft/retry_stack/
                               outstanding/retranwait/onbench,
                               cwnd/ccthresh/delay, timeout/srtt/rttvar/
   Groupstats (1/1 incomplete): 83/*/*/*/*/* 82.80/75/* 100000/25254/4606
   64.13.134.52: 83/60836/0/777/316/4295 82.80/75/0 100000/26200/4223
Current sending rates: 711.88 packets / s, 31322.57 bytes / s.
Overall sending rates: 618.24 packets / s, 27202.62 bytes / s.
Discovered filtered port 10752/tcp on 64.13.134.52
Packet capture filter (device eth0): dst host 132.239.1.115 and
                               (icmp or ((tcp or udp) and
                               (src host 64.13.134.52)))
SCRIPT ENGINE: TCP 132.239.1.115:59045 > 64.13.134.52:53 | CLOSE
```

No full example is given here because debug logs are so long. A scan against Scanme used 32 lines of text without verbosity (Example 13.3, "Interactive output without verbosity enabled" [342]), and 61 with it (Example 13.4, "Interactive output with verbosity enabled" [343]). The same scan with -d instead of -v took 113 lines. With -d2 it ballooned to 65,731 lines, and -d5 output 396,879 lines! The debug option implicitly enables verbosity, so there is no need to specify them both.

Determining the best output level for a certain debug task is a matter of trial and error. I try a low level first to understand what is going on, then increase it as necessary. As I learn more, I may be able to better isolate the problem or question. I then try to simplify the command in order to offset some increased verbiage of the higher debug level.

Just as **grep** can be useful to identify the changes and levels associated with verbosity, it also helps with investigating debug output. I recommend running this command from the nmap-<VERSION> directory in the Nmap source tarball:

> **grep -A1 o.debugging *.cc**

13.2.4. Handling Error and Warning Messages

Warnings and errors printed by Nmap usually go only to the screen (interactive output), leaving any normal-format output files (usually specified with -oN) uncluttered. When you do want to see those messages in the normal output file you specified, use the --log-errors option. It is useful when you aren't watching the interactive output or when you want to record errors while debugging a problem. The error and warning messages will still appear in interactive mode too. This won't work for most errors related to bad command-line arguments because Nmap may not have initialized its output files yet. In addition, some Nmap error and warning messages use a different system which does not yet support this option.

An alternative to `--log-errors` is redirecting interactive output (including the standard error stream) to a file. Most Unix shells make this approach easy. For example, tcsh uses the format **nmap \<options\> \>&** **alloutput.nmap**. Bash uses a slightly different syntax: **nmap \<options\> &\> alloutput.nmap**. The Windows cmd.exe syntax for doing this is so convoluted that `--log-errors` is recommended instead. For example, you can run **nmap --log-errors -oN alloutput.nmap \<options\>**.

13.2.5. Enabling Packet Tracing

The `--packet-trace` option causes Nmap to print a summary of every packet it sends and receives. This can be extremely useful for debugging or understanding Nmap's behavior, as examples throughout this book demonstrate. Example 13.6 shows a simple ping scan of Scanme with packet tracing enabled.

Example 13.6. Using `--packet-trace` to detail a ping scan of Scanme

```
# nmap --packet-trace -n -sP scanme.nmap.org

Starting Nmap ( http://nmap.org )
SENT (0.0230s) ICMP 132.239.1.115 > 64.13.134.52 echo request
                (type=8/code=0) ttl=38 id=5420 iplen=28
SENT (0.0230s) TCP 132.239.1.115:43743 > 64.13.134.52:80 A ttl=57
                id=29415 iplen=40  seq=2799605278 win=2048 ack=2120834905
RCVD (0.0380s) TCP 64.13.134.52:80 > 132.239.1.115:43743 R ttl=52
                id=0 iplen=40  seq=2120834905 win=0
Host 64.13.134.52 appears to be up.
Nmap done: 1 IP address (1 host up) scanned in 0.04 seconds
```

This Nmap execution shows three extra lines caused by packet tracing (each have been wrapped for readability). Each line contains several fields. The first is whether a packet is sent or received by Nmap, as abbreviated to SENT and RCVD. The next field is a time counter, providing the elapsed time since Nmap started. The time is in seconds, and in this case Nmap only required a tiny fraction of one. The next field is the protocol: TCP, UDP, or ICMP. Next comes the source and destination IP addresses, separated with a directional arrow. For TCP or UDP packets, each IP is followed by a colon and the source or destination port number.

The remainder of each line is protocol specific. As you can see, ICMP provides a human-readable type if available (echo request in this case) followed by the ICMP type and code values. The ICMP packet logs end with the IP TTL, ID, and packet length field. TCP packets use a slightly different format after the destination IP and port number. First comes a list of characters representing the set TCP flags. The flag characters are SAFRPUEC, which stand for SYN, ACK, FIN, RST, PSH, URG, ECE, and CWR, respectively. The latter two flags are part of TCP explicit congestion notification, described in RFC 3168.

Because packet tracing can lead to thousands of output lines, it helps to limit scan intensity to the minimum that still serves your purpose. A scan of a single port on a single machine won't bury you in data, while the output of a `--packet-trace` scan of a whole network can be overwhelming. Packet tracing is automatically enabled when the debug level (`-d`) is at least three.

Sometimes `--packet-trace` provides specialized data that Nmap never shows otherwise. For example, Example 13.6, "Using --packet-trace to detail a ping scan of Scanme" [345] shows ICMP and TCP ping packets sent to the target host. The target responds to the ICMP echo request, which can be valuable information that Nmap doesn't otherwise show. It is possible that the target host replied to the TCP packet as well—Nmap stops listening once it receives one response to a ping scan since that is all it takes to determine that a host is online.

13.2.6. Resuming Aborted Scans

Some extensive Nmap runs take a very long time—on the order of days. Such scans don't always run to completion. Restrictions may prevent Nmap from being run during working hours, the network could go down, the machine Nmap is running on might suffer a planned or unplanned reboot, or Nmap itself could crash. The administrator running Nmap could cancel it for any other reason as well, by pressing **ctrl-C**. Restarting the whole scan from the beginning may be undesirable. Fortunately, if normal (-oN) or grepable (-oG) logs were kept, the user can ask Nmap to resume scanning with the target it was working on when execution ceased. Simply specify the `--resume` option and pass the normal/grepable output file as its argument. No other arguments are permitted, as Nmap parses the output file to use the same ones specified previously. Simply call Nmap as **nmap --resume <logfilename>**. Nmap will append new results to the data files specified in the previous execution. Resumption does not support the XML output format because combining the two runs into one valid XML file would be difficult.

13.3. Interactive Output

Interactive output is what Nmap prints to the stdout stream, which usually appears on the terminal window you executed Nmap from. In other circumstances, you might have redirected stdout to a file or another application such as Nessus or an Nmap GUI may be reading the results. If a larger application is interpreting the results rather than printing Nmap output directly to the user, then using the XML output discussed in Section 13.6, "XML Output (-oX)" [348] would be more appropriate.

This format has but one goal: to present results that will be valuable to a human reading over them. No effort is made to make these easily machine parsable or to maintain a stable format between Nmap versions. Better formats exist for these things. The toughest challenge is deciding which information is valuable enough to print. Omitting data that a user wants is a shame, though flooding the user with pages of mostly irrelevant output can be even worse. The verbosity, debugging, and packet tracing flags are available to shift this balance based on individual users' preferences.

This output format needs no extensive description here, as most Nmap examples in this book already show it. To understand Nmap's interactive output for a certain feature, see the section of this book dedicated to that feature. Typical examples of interactive output are given in Example 13.3, "Interactive output without verbosity enabled" [342] and Example 13.4, "Interactive output with verbosity enabled" [343].

13.4. Normal Output (-oN)

Normal output is printed to a file when the -oN option is specified with a filename argument. It is similar to interactive output, except that notes which lose relevance once a scan completes are removed. It is assumed that the file will be read after Nmap completes, so estimated completion times and new open port alerts are redundant to the actual completion time and the ordered port table. Since output may be saved a long while

---

and reviewed among many other logs, Nmap prints the execution time, command-line arguments, and Nmap version number on the first line. A similar line at the end of a scan divulges final timing and a host count. Those two lines begin with a pound character to identify them as comments. If your application must parse normal output rather than XML/grepable formats, ensure that it ignores comments that it doesn't recognize rather than treating them as an error and aborting. Example 13.7 is a typical example of normal output. Note that −oN − was used to prevent interactive output and send normal output straight to stdout.

Example 13.7. A typical example of normal output

```
# nmap -T4 -A -p- -oN - scanme.nmap.org

# Nmap 4.68 scan initiated Tue Jul 15 07:27:26 2008 as: nmap -T4 -A -p- ↵
-oN - scanme.nmap.org
Interesting ports on scanme.nmap.org (64.13.134.52):
Not shown: 65529 filtered ports
PORT     STATE   SERVICE VERSION
22/tcp   open    ssh     OpenSSH 4.3 (protocol 2.0)
25/tcp   closed  smtp
53/tcp   open    domain  ISC BIND 9.3.4
70/tcp   closed  gopher
80/tcp   open    http    Apache httpd 2.2.2 ((Fedora))
|_ HTML title: Go ahead and ScanMe!
113/tcp closed auth
Device type: general purpose
Running: Linux 2.6.X
OS details: Linux 2.6.17 - 2.6.21, Linux 2.6.23

TRACEROUTE (using port 22/tcp)
HOP RTT    ADDRESS
1   2.98   nodem-msfc-vl245-act-security-gw-1-113.ucsd.edu (132.239.1.113)
[... nine similar lines cut ...]
11  13.34 scanme.nmap.org (64.13.134.52)

OS and Service detection performed. Please report any incorrect results ↵
at http://nmap.org/submit/ .
# Nmap done at Tue Jul 15 07:29:45 2008 -- 1 IP address (1 host up) ↵
scanned in 138.938 seconds
```

13.5. $crIpT kIddI3 0uTPut (−oS)

Script kiddie output is like interactive output, except that it is post-processed to better suit the 'l33t HaXXorZ! They previously looked down on Nmap due to its consistent capitalization and spelling. It is best understood by example, as given in Example 13.8.

Example 13.8. A typical example of $crIpt KiDDi3 0utPut

```
# nmap -T4 -A -oS - scanme.nmap.org

StaRtIng NMap ( httP://nmap.Org )
Int3rest|ng pOrtz On $CAnme.nmap.Org (64.13.134.52):
NOt ShOwn: 65529 FilterEd pOrt$
PORT    $TATE  $ERVIC3 V3R$IoN
22/tcP  Op3n   s$h     Open$$H 4.3 (prOtOcol 2.0)
25/TcP  closEd $mtp
53/tcp  op3n   dOma!n  I$C BIND 9.3.4
70/tcp  clo$ed GOph3r
80/tcp  Op3n   htTP    4pach3 httpd 2.2.2 ((F3d0ra))
|_ HTML tITl3: gO aheAD And $canM3!
113/tcp cl0$Ed auTh
DeviCe type: g3NeraL purp0$3
RUnning: L1Nux 2.6.X
oS detAIlz: LinUx 2.6.17 - 2.6.21, L1nux 2.6.23
[Many lines cut for brevity]
NmAp doNe: 1 ip addre$z (1 HO$t up) $canneD iN 138.94 $ecONdS
```

Some humor-impaired people take this option far too seriously, and scold me for catering to script kiddies. It is simply a joke *making fun* of the script kiddies—they don't actually use this mode (I hope).

13.6. XML Output (–oX)

XML, the *extensible markup language*, has its share of critics as well as plenty of zealous proponents. I was long in the former group, and only grudgingly incorporated XML into Nmap after volunteers performed most of the work. Since then, I have learned to appreciate the power and flexibility that XML offers, and even wrote this book in the DocBook XML format. I strongly recommend that programmers interact with Nmap through the XML interface rather than trying to parse the normal, interactive, or grepable output. That format includes more information than the others and is extensible enough that new features can be added without breaking existing programs that use it. It can be parsed by standard XML parsers, which are available for all popular programming languages, usually for free. Editors, validators, transformation systems, and many other applications already know how to handle the format. Normal and interactive output, on the other hand, are custom to Nmap and subject to regular changes as I strive for a clearer presentation to end users. Grepable output is also Nmap-specific and tougher to extend than XML. It is considered deprecated, and many Nmap features such as MAC address detection are not presented in this output format.

An example of Nmap XML output is shown in Example 13.9. Whitespace has been adjusted for readability. In this case, XML was sent to stdout thanks to the –oX – construct. Some programs executing Nmap opt to read the output that way, while others specify that output be sent to a filename and then they read that file after Nmap completes.

Example 13.9. An example of Nmap XML output

```
# nmap -T4 -A -p- -oX - scanme.nmap.org
<?xml version="1.0" encoding="utf-8"?>
<?xml-stylesheet href="/usr/share/nmap/nmap.xsl" type="text/xsl"?>
<!-- Nmap 4.68 scan initiated Tue Jul 15 07:27:26 2008 as:
          nmap -T4 -A -p- -oX - scanme.nmap.org -->
<nmaprun scanner="nmap" args="nmap -T4 -A -p- -oX - scanme.nmap.org"
         start="1216106846" startstr="Tue Jul 15 07:27:26 2008"
         version="4.68" xmloutputversion="1.02">
  <scaninfo type="syn" protocol="tcp" numservices="65535" services="1-65535" />
  <verbose level="0" /> <debugging level="0" />
   <host starttime="1216106846" endtime="1216106985">
    <status state="up" reason="reset" />
    <address addr="64.13.134.52" addrtype="ipv4" />
    <hostnames><hostname name="scanme.nmap.org" type="PTR" /></hostnames>
    <ports><extraports state="filtered" count="65529">
        <extrareasons reason="no-responses" count="65529" /></extraports>
      <port protocol="tcp" portid="22">
        <state state="open" reason="syn-ack" reason_ttl="52" />
        <service name="ssh" product="OpenSSH" version="4.3"
                 extrainfo="protocol 2.0" method="probed" conf="10" /> </port>
      <!-- Several port elements removed for brevity -->
      <port protocol="tcp" portid="80">
        <state state="open" reason="syn-ack" reason_ttl="52" />
        <service name="http" product="Apache httpd" version="2.2.2"
                 extrainfo="(Fedora)" method="probed" conf="10" />
        <script id="HTML title" output="Go ahead and ScanMe!" /> </port>
      <port protocol="tcp" portid="113">
        <state state="closed" reason="reset" reason_ttl="52" />
        <service name="auth" method="table" conf="3" /> </port> </ports>
    <os>
      <portused state="open" proto="tcp" portid="22" />
      <portused state="closed" proto="tcp" portid="25" />
      <osclass type="general purpose" vendor="Linux" osfamily="Linux"
               osgen="2.6.X" accuracy="100" />
      <osmatch name="Linux 2.6.17 - 2.6.21" accuracy="100" line="11886" />
      <osmatch name="Linux 2.6.23" accuracy="100" line="13895" /> </os>
    <uptime seconds="1104050" lastboot="Wed Jul  2 12:48:55 2008" />
    <tcpsequence index="203" difficulty="Good luck!"
         values="31F88BFB,327D2AA6,329B817C,329D4191,321A15D3,32B3D917" />
    <ipidsequence class="All zeros" values="0,0,0,0,0,0" />
    <tcptssequence class="1000HZ"
         values="41CE58DD,41CE5941,41CE59A5,41CE5A09,41CE5A6D,41CE5AD5" />
    <trace port="22" proto="tcp">
      <hop ttl="1" rtt="2.98" ipaddr="132.239.1.113"
           host="nodem-msfc-vl245-act-security-gw-1-113.ucsd.edu" />
      <!-- Several hop elements removed for brevity -->
      <hop ttl="11" rtt="13.34" ipaddr="64.13.134.52"
           host="scanme.nmap.org" /> </trace>
    <times srtt="14359" rttvar="1215" to="100000" /> </host>
  <runstats><finished time="1216106985" timestr="Tue Jul 15 07:29:45 2008" />
   <hosts up="1" down="0" total="1" />
   <!-- Nmap done at Tue Jul 15 07:29:45 2008;
            1 IP address (1 host up) scanned in 138.938 seconds -->
  </runstats>
</nmaprun>
```

Another advantage of XML is that its verbose nature makes it easier to read and understand than other formats. Readers familiar with Nmap in general can likely understand most of the XML output in Example 13.9, "An example of Nmap XML output" [349] without further documentation. The grepable output format, on the other hand, is tough to decipher without its own reference guide.

There are a few aspects of the example XML output which may not be self-explanatory. For example, look at the two `port` elements in Example 13.10

Example 13.10. Nmap XML port elements

```
<port protocol="tcp" portid="80">
  <state state="open" reason="syn-ack" reason_ttl="52" />
  <service name="http" product="Apache httpd" version="2.2.2"
           extrainfo="(Fedora)" method="probed" conf="10" />
  <script id="HTML title" output="Go ahead and ScanMe!" />
</port>
<port protocol="tcp" portid="113">
  <state state="closed" reason="reset" reason_ttl="52" />
  <service name="auth" method="table" conf="3" />
</port>
```

The port protocol, ID (port number), state, and service name are the same as would be shown in the interactive output port table. The service `product`, `version`, and `extrainfo` attributes come from version detection and are combined together into one field of the interactive output port table. The `method` and `conf` attributes aren't present in any other output types. The method can be `table`, meaning the service name was simply looked up in `nmap-services` based on the port number and protocol, or it can be `probed`, meaning that it was determined through the version detection system. The `conf` attribute measures the confidence Nmap has that the service name is correct. The values range from one (least confident) to ten. Nmap only has a confidence level of three for ports determined by table lookup, while it is highly confident (level 10) that port 80 of Example 13.10, "Nmap XML port elements" [350] is Apache httpd, because Nmap connected to the port and found a server exhibiting the HTTP protocol with Apache banners.

One other aspect that some users find confusing is that the attributes `/nmaprun/@start` and `/nmaprun/runstats/finished/@time` hold timestamps given in Unix time, the number of seconds January 1, 1970. This is often easier for programs to handle. For the convenience of human readers, versions 3.78 and newer include the equivalent calendar time written out in the attributes `/nmaprun/@startstr` and `/nmaprun/runstats/finished/@endstr`.

Nmap includes a document type definition (DTD) which allows XML parsers to validate Nmap XML output. While it is primarily intended for programmatic use, it can also help humans interpret Nmap XML output. The DTD defines the legal elements of the format, and often enumerates the attributes and values they can take on. It is reproduced in Appendix A, *Nmap XML Output DTD* [415].

13.6.1. Using XML Output

The Nmap XML format can be used in many powerful ways, though few users actually take any advantage of it. I believe this is due to inexperience of many users with XML, combined with a lack of practical, solution-oriented documentation on using the Nmap XML format. This chapter provides several practical examples, including Section 13.7, "Manipulating XML Output with Perl" [352], Section 13.8, "Output to a Database" [354], and Section 13.9, "Creating HTML Reports" [355].

A key advantage of XML is that you do not need to write your own parser as you do for specialized Nmap output types such as grepable and interactive output. Any general XML parser should do.

The XML parser that people are most familiar with is the one in your web browser. Both IE and Mozilla/Firefox include capable parsers that can be used to view Nmap XML data. Using them is as simple as typing the XML filename or URL into the address bar. Figure 13.1 shows an example of XML output rendered by a web browser. How this automatic rendering works and how to save a permanent copy of an HTML report is covered in Section 13.9, "Creating HTML Reports" [355].

Figure 13.1. XML output in a web browser

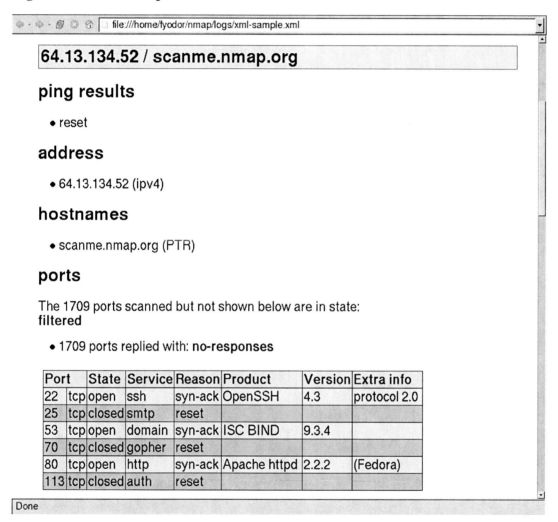

Nmap XML output can of course be viewed in any text editor or XML editor. Some spreadsheet programs, including Microsoft Excel, are able to import Nmap XML data directly for viewing. These general-purpose XML processors share the limitation that they treat Nmap XML generically, just like any other XML file. They don't understand the relative importance of elements, nor how to organize the data for a more useful presentation. The use of specialized XML processors that make sense of Nmap XML output is the subject of the following sections.

13.7. Manipulating XML Output with Perl

Generic XML parsers are available for all popular programming languages, often for free. Examples are the libxml C library and the Apache Xerces parser for Java and C++ (with Perl and COM bindings). While these parsers are sufficient for handling Nmap XML output, developers have created custom modules for several languages which can make the task of interoperating with Nmap XML even easier.

The language with the best custom Nmap XML support is Perl. Max Schubert (affectionately known as Perldork) has created a module named Nmap::Scanner[2] while Anthony Persaud created Nmap::Parser[3]. These two modules have many similarities: they can execute Nmap themselves or read from an output file, are well documented, come with numerous example scripts, are part of the Comprehensive Perl Archive Network (CPAN), and are popular with users. They each offer both a callback based parser for interpreting data as Nmap runs as well as an all-at-once parser for obtaining a fully parsed document once Nmap finishes executing. Their APIs are a bit different—Nmap::Scanner relies on type-safe classes while Nmap::Parser relies on lighter-weight native Perl arrays. I recommend looking at each to decide which best meets your needs and preferences.

Example 13.11 is a simple demonstration of Nmap::Parser. It comes from the module's documentation (which contains many other examples as well). It performs a quick scan, then prints overall scan statistics as well as information on each available target host. Notice how readable it is compared to scripts using other Nmap output formats that are dominated by parsing logic and regular expressions. Even people with poor Perl skills could use this as a starting point to create simple programs to automate their Nmap scanning needs.

---

[2] *http://sourceforge.net/projects/nmap-scanner/*
[3] *http://nmapparser.wordpress.com/*

Example 13.11. Nmap::Parser sample code

```perl
use Nmap::Parser;

      #PARSING
my $np = new Nmap::Parser;

$nmap_exe = '/usr/bin/nmap';
$np->parsescan($nmap_exe,'-sT -p1-1023', @ips);

#or

$np->parsefile('nmap_output.xml'); #using filenames

      #GETTING SCAN INFORMATION

print "Scan Information:\n";
$si = $np->get_scaninfo();
#get scan information by calling methods
print
'Number of services scanned: '.$si->num_of_services()."\n",
'Start Time: '.$si->start_time()."\n",
'Scan Types: ',(join ' ',$si->scan_types())."\n";

      #GETTING HOST INFORMATION

print "Hosts scanned:\n";
for my $host_obj ($np->get_host_objects()){
  print
  'Hostname   : '.$host_obj->hostname()."\n",
  'Address    : '.$host_obj->ipv4_addr()."\n",
  'OS match   : '.$host_obj->os_match()."\n",
  'Open Ports: '.(join ',',$host_obj->tcp_ports('open'))."\n";
      #... you get the idea...
}

#frees memory--helpful when dealing with memory intensive scripts
$np->clean();
```

For comparison, Example 13.12 is a sample Perl script using Nmap::Scanner, copied from its documentation. This one uses an event-driven callback approach, registering the functions `scan_started` and `port_found` to print real-time alerts when a host is found up and when each open port is discovered on the host.

Example 13.12. Nmap::Scanner sample code

```perl
my $scanner = new Nmap::Scanner;
$scanner->register_scan_started_event(\&scan_started);
$scanner->register_port_found_event(\&port_found);
$scanner->scan('-sS -p 1-1024 -O --max-rtt-timeout 200 somehost.org.net.it');

sub scan_started {
    my $self      = shift;
    my $host      = shift;

    my $hostname = $host->name();
    my $addresses = join(', ', map {$_->address()} $host->addresses());
    my $status = $host->status();

    print "$hostname ($addresses) is $status\n";
}

sub port_found {
    my $self      = shift;
    my $host      = shift;
    my $port      = shift;

    my $name = $host->name();
    my $addresses = join(', ', map {$_->addr()} $host->addresses());

    print "On host $name ($addresses), found ",
          $port->state()," port ",
          join('/',$port->protocol(),$port->portid()),"\n";
}
```

13.8. Output to a Database

A common desire is to output Nmap results to a database for easier queries and tracking. This allows users from an individual penetration tester to an international enterprise to store all of their scan results and easily compare them. The enterprise might run large scans daily and schedule queries to mail administrators of newly open ports or available machines. The penetration tester might learn of a new vulnerability and search all of his old scan results for the affected application so that he can warn the relevant clients. Researchers may scan millions of IP addresses and keep the results in a database for easy real-time queries.

While these goals are laudable, Nmap offers no direct database output functionality. Not only are there too many different database types for me to support them all, but user's needs vary so dramatically that no single database schema is suitable. The needs of the enterprise, pen-tester, and researcher all call for different table structures.

For projects large enough to require a database, I recommend deciding on an optimal DB schema first, then writing a simple program or script to import Nmap XML data appropriately. Such scripts often take only minutes, thanks to the wide availability of XML parsers and database access modules. Perl often makes a good choice, as it offers a powerful database abstraction layer and also custom Nmap XML support. Section 13.7, "Manipulating XML Output with Perl" [352] shows how easily Perl scripts can make use of Nmap XML data.

Another option is to use a custom Nmap database support patch. One example is nmap-sql[4], which adds MySQL logging functionality into Nmap itself. The downsides are that it currently only supports the MySQL database and it must be frequently ported to new Nmap versions. An XML-based approach, on the other hand, is less likely to break when new Nmap versions are released.

Another option is PBNJ[5], a suite of tools for monitoring changes to a network over time. It stores scan data such as online hosts and open ports to a database (SQLite, MySQL or Postgres). It offers a flexible querying and alerting system for accessing that data or displaying changes.

13.9. Creating HTML Reports

Nmap does not have an option for saving scan results in HTML, however it is easy to get an HTML view of Nmap XML output just by opening the XML file in a web browser. An example is shown in Figure 13.1, "XML output in a web browser" [351].

How does the web browser know how to convert XML to HTML? An Nmap XML output file usually contains a reference to an XSL[6] stylesheet called nmap.xsl that describes how the transformation takes place.

The XML processing instruction that says where the stylesheet can be found will look something like

```
<?xml-stylesheet href="/usr/share/nmap/nmap.xsl" type="text/xsl"?>
```

The exact location may be different depending on the platform and how Nmap was configured.

Such a stylesheet reference will work fine when viewing scan results on the same machine that initiated the scan, but it will not work if the XML file is transferred to another machine where the nmap.xsl file is in a different place or absent entirely. To make the XML styling portable, give the --webxml option to Nmap. This will change the processing instruction to read

```
<?xml-stylesheet href="http://nmap.org/data/nmap.xsl" type="text/xsl"?>
```

The resultant XML output file will render as HTML on any web-connected machine. Using the network location in this fashion is often more useful, but the local copy of nmap.xsl is used by default for privacy reasons.

To use a different stylesheet, use the --stylesheet <file> option. Note that --webxml is an alias for --stylesheet http://nmap.org/data/nmap.xsl.

To omit the stylesheet entirely, use the option --no-stylesheet. This will cause web browsers to show the output as a plain, uninterpreted XML tree.

13.9.1. Saving a Permanent HTML Report

While web browsers can display an HTML view of Nmap XML, they don't usually make it easy to save the generated HTML to a file. For that a standalone XSLT processor is required. Here are commands that turn an Nmap XML output file into an HTML file using common XSLT processors.

---

[4] *http://sourceforge.net/projects/nmapsql*
[5] *http://pbnj.sourceforge.net/*
[6] *http://www.w3.org/Style/XSL/*

Saxon[7]

> **java -jar saxon.jar -a `<nmap-output.xml>` -o `<nmap-output.html>`**

Xalan[8]

> **Xalan -a `<nmap-output.xml>` -o `<nmap-output.html>`** (using Xalan C++)

> **java -jar xalan.jar -IN `<nmap-output.xml>` -OUT `<nmap-output.html>`** (using Xalan Java)

xsltproc[9]

> **xsltproc `<nmap-output.xml>` -o `<nmap-output.html>`**

13.10. Grepable Output (–oG)

This output format is covered last because it is deprecated. The XML output format is far more powerful, and is nearly as convenient for experienced users. XML is a standard for which dozens of excellent parsers are available, while grepable output is my own simple hack. XML is extensible to support new Nmap features as they are released, while I often must omit those features from grepable output for lack of a place to put them.

Nevertheless, grepable output is still quite popular. It is a simple format that lists each host on one line and can be trivially searched and parsed with standard Unix tools such as grep, awk, cut, sed, diff, and Perl. Even I usually use it for one-off tests done at the command line. Finding all the hosts with the SSH port open or that are running Solaris takes only a simple grep to identify the hosts, piped to an awk or cut command to print the desired fields. One grepable output aficionado is MadHat (madhat@unspecific.com), who contributed to this section.

Example 13.13 shows a typical example of grepable output. Normally each host takes only one line, but I split this entry into seven lines to fit on the page. There are also three lines starting with a hash prompt (not counting the Nmap command line). Those are comments describing when Nmap started, the command line options used, and completion time and statistics. One of the comment lines enumerates the port numbers that were scanned. I shortened it to avoid wasting dozens of lines. That particular comment is only printed in verbose (–v) mode. Increasing the verbosity level beyond one –v will not further change the grepable output. The times and dates have been replaced with [time] to reduce line length.

---

[7] *http://saxon.sourceforge.net/*
[8] *http://xalan.apache.org/*
[9] *http://xmlsoft.org/XSLT/*

Example 13.13. A typical example of grepable output

```
# nmap -oG - -T4 -A -v scanme.nmap.org
# Nmap 4.68 scan initiated [time] as: nmap -oG - -T4 -A -v scanme.nmap.org
# Ports scanned: TCP(1715;1-1027,1029-1033,...,65301) UDP(0;) PROTOCOLS(0;)
Host: 64.13.134.52 (scanme.nmap.org)    Ports: 22/open/tcp//ssh//OpenSSH 4.3 ⏎
(protocol 2.0)/, 25/closed/tcp//smtp///, 53/open/tcp//domain//ISC BIND ⏎
9.3.4/,70/closed/tcp//gopher///, 80/open/tcp//http//Apache httpd 2.2.2 ⏎
((Fedora))/,113/closed/tcp//auth/// Ignored State: filtered (1709)  OS: ⏎
Linux 2.6.20-1 (Fedora Core 5) Seq Index: 203  IP ID Seq: All zeros
# Nmap done at [time] -- 1 IP address (1 host up) scanned in 34.96 seconds
```

The command-line here requested that grepable output be sent to standard output with the - argument to
-oG. Aggressive timing (-T4) as well as OS and version detection (-A) were requested. The comment lines
are self-explanatory, leaving the meat of grepable output in the Host line. Had I scanned more hosts, each
of the available ones would have its own Host line.

13.10.1. Grepable Output Fields

The host line is split into fields, each of which consist of a field name followed by a colon and space, then
the field content. The fields are separated by tab characters (ASCII number nine, '\t'). Example 13.13, "A
typical example of grepable output" [357] shows six fields: Host, Ports, Ignored State, OS, Seq Index, and
IP ID. A Status section is included in list (-sL) and ping (-sP) scans, and a Protocols section is included
in IP protocol (-sO) scans. The exact fields given depend on Nmap options used. For example, OS detection
triggers the OS, Seq Index, and IP ID fields. Because they are tab delimited, you might split up the fields
with a Perl line such as:

```
@fields = split("\t", $host_line);
```

In the case of Example 13.13, "A typical example of grepable output" [357], the array @fields would
contain six members. $fields[0] would contain "Host: 64.13.134.52 (scanme.nmap.org)",
and $fields[1] would contain the long Ports field. Scripts that parse grepable output should ignore fields
they don't recognize, as new fields may be added to support Nmap enhancements.

The eight possible fields are described in the following sections.

Host field

Example: Host: 64.13.134.52 (scanme.nmap.org)

The Host field always comes first and is included no matter what Nmap options are chosen. The contents
are the IP address (an IPv6 address if -6 was specified), a space, and then the reverse DNS name in
parentheses. If no reverse name is available, the parentheses will be empty.

Ports field

Example: Ports: 111/open/tcp//rpcbind (rpcbind V2)/(rpcbind:100000*2-2)/2 (rpc #100000)/,
113/closed/tcp//auth///

The Ports field is by far the most complex, as can be seen in Example 13.13, "A typical example of grepable output" [357]. It includes entries for every interesting port (the ones which would be included in the port table in normal Nmap output). The port entries are separated with a comma and a space character. Each port entry consists of seven subfields, separated by a forward slash (/). The subfields are: port number, state, protocol, owner, service, SunRPC info, and version info. Some subfields may be empty, particularly for basic port scans without OS or version detection. The consecutive slashes in Example 13.13, "A typical example of grepable output" [357] reveal empty subfields. In Perl, you might split them up as so:

```
($port, $state, $protocol, $owner, $service, $rpc_info, $version) =
        split('/', $ports);
```

Alternatively, you could grab the information from the command line using commands such as these:

```
cut -d/ -f<fieldnumbers>
awk -F/ '{print $<fieldnumber>}'
```

Certain subfields can contain a slash in other output modes. For example, an SSL-enabled web server would show up as ssl/http and the version info might contain strings such as mod_ssl/2.8.12. Since a slash is the subfield delimiter, this would screw up parsing. To avoid this problem, slashes are changed into the pipe character (|) when they would appear anywhere in the Port field.

Parsers should be written to allow more than seven slash-delimited subfields and to simply ignore the extras because future Nmap enhancements may call for new ones. The following list describes each of the seven currently defined Port subfields.

Port number
: This is simply the numeric TCP or UDP port number.

State
: The same port state which would appear in the normal output port table is shown here.

Protocol
: This is tcp or udp.

Owner
: This used to specify the username that the remote server is running under based on results from querying an identd (auth) server of the target host. The ident scan (-I) is no longer available with Nmap, so this field is always empty. Ident data can still be obtained using the identd-owners.nse NSE script, though results are not placed in this field.

Service
: The service name, as obtained from an nmap-services lookup, or (more reliably) through version detection (-sV) if it was requested and succeeded. With version detection enabled, compound entries such as ssl|http and entries with a trailing question mark may be seen. The meaning is the same as for normal output, as discussed in Chapter 7, *Service and Application Version Detection* [145].

SunRPC info
: If version detection (-sV) or RPC scan (-sR) were requested and the port was found to use the SunRPC protocol, the RPC program number and accepted version numbers are included here. A typical example is "(rpcbind:100000*2-2)". The data is always returned inside parentheses. It starts with the program name, then a colon and the program number, then an asterisk followed by the low and high

supported version numbers separated by a hyphen. So in this example, rpcbind (program number 100,000) is listening on the port for rpcbind version 2 requests.

Version info

If version detection is requested and succeeds, the results are provided here in the same format used in interactive output. For SunRPC ports, the RPC data is printed here too. The format for RPC results in this column is *<low version number>-<high version number>* (rpc #*<rpc program number>*). When only one version number is supported, it is printed by itself rather than as a range. A port which shows (rpcbind:100000*2-2) in the SunRPC info subfield would show 2 (rpc #100000) in the version info subfield.

Protocols field

Example: Protocols: 1/open/icmp/, 2/open|filtered/igmp/

The IP protocol scan (-sO) has a Protocols field rather than Ports. Its contents are quite similar to the Ports field, but it has only three subfields rather than seven. They are delimited with slashes, just as with the Ports field. Any slashes that would appear in a subfield are changed into pipes (|), also as done in the Ports field. The subfields are protocol number, state, and protocol name. These correspond to the three fields shown in interactive output for a protocol scan. An example of IP protocol scan grepable output is shown in Example 13.14. The Host line, which would normally be all one line, is here wrapped for readability.

Example 13.14. Grepable output for IP protocol scan

```
# nmap -v -oG - -sO localhost
# Nmap 4.68 scan initiated [time] as: nmap -v -oG - -sO localhost
# Ports scanned: TCP(0;) UDP(0;) PROTOCOLS(256;0-255)
Host: 127.0.0.1 (localhost)
      Protocols: 1/open/icmp/, 2/open|filtered/igmp/, 6/open/tcp/,
                17/open/udp/, 136/open|filtered/udplite/, 255/open|filtered//
      Ignored State: closed (250)
# Nmap done at [time] -- 1 IP address (1 host up) scanned in 2.345 seconds
```

Ignored State field

Example: Ignored State: filtered (1658)

To save space, Nmap may omit ports in one non-open state from the list in the Ports field. Nmap does this in interactive output too. Regular Nmap users are familiar with the lines such as "The 1658 ports scanned but not shown below are in state: filtered". For grepable mode, that state is given in the Ignored State field. Following the state name is a space, then in parentheses is the number of ports found in that state.

OS field

Example: OS: Linux 2.4.0 - 2.5.20

Any perfect OS matches are listed here. If there are multiple matches, they are separated by a pipe character as shown in Example 13.13, "A typical example of grepable output" [357]. Only the free-text descriptions are provided. Grepable mode does not provide the vendor, OS family, and device type classification shown in other output modes.

Seq Index field

Example: Seq Index: 3004446

This number is an estimate of the difficulty of performing TCP initial sequence number prediction attacks against the remote host. These are also known as blind spoofing attacks, and they allow an attacker to forge a full TCP connection to a remote host as if it was coming from some other IP address. This can always help an attacker hide his or her tracks, and it can lead to privilege escalation against services such as rlogin that commonly grant extra privileges to trusted IP addresses. The `Seq Index` value is only available when OS detection (`-O`) is requested and succeeds in probing for this. It is reported in interactive output when verbosity (`-v`) is requested. More details on the computation and meaning of this value are provided in Chapter 8, *Remote OS Detection* [171].

IP ID Seq field

Example: IP ID Seq: All zeros

This simply describes the remote host's IP ID generation algorithm. It is only available when OS detection (`-O`) is requested and succeeds in probing for it. Interactive mode reports this as well, and it is discussed in Chapter 8, *Remote OS Detection* [171].

Status field

Example: Status: Up

Ping and list scans contain only two fields in grepable mode: Host and Status. Status describes the target host as either Up, Down, or Unknown. List scan always categorizes targets as Unknown because it does not perform any tests. Ping scan lists a host as up if it responds to at least one ping probe, and down if no responses are received. It used to also report `Smurf` if ping probes sent to the target resulted in one or more responses from other hosts, but that is no longer done. Down hosts are only shown when verbosity is enabled with `-v`. Example 13.15 demonstrates a ping scan of 100 random hosts, while Example 13.16 demonstrates a list scan of five hosts.

Example 13.15. Ping scan grepable output

```
# nmap -sP -oG - -iR 100
# nmap [version] scan initiated [time] as: nmap -sP -oG - -iR 100
Host: 67.101.77.102 (h-67-101-77-102.nycmny83.covad.net)        Status: Up
Host: 219.93.164.197 () Status: Up
Host: 222.113.158.200 ()        Status: Up
Host: 66.130.155.190 (modemcable190.155-130-66.mc.videotron.ca) Status: Up
# Nmap done at [time] -- 100 IP addresses (4 hosts up) scanned in 13.22 seconds
```

Example 13.16. List scan grepable output

```
# nmap -sL -oG - -iR 5
# nmap [version] scan initiated [time] as: nmap -sL -oG - -iR 5
Host: 199.223.2.1 ()      Status: Unknown
Host: 191.222.112.87 () Status: Unknown
Host: 62.23.21.157 (host.157.21.23.62.rev.coltfrance.com)      Status: Unknown
Host: 138.217.47.127 (CPE-138-217-47-127.vic.bigpond.net.au)      Status: Unknown
Host: 8.118.0.91 ()      Status: Unknown
# Nmap done at [time] -- 5 IP addresses (0 hosts up) scanned in 1.797 seconds
```

13.10.2. Parsing Grepable Output on the Command Line

Grepable output really shines when you want to gather information quickly without the overhead of writing a script to parse XML output. Example 13.17 shows a typical example of this. The goal is to find all hosts on a class C sized network with port 80 open. Nmap is told to scan just that port of each host (skipping the ping stage) and to output a grepable report to stdout. The results are piped to a trivial awk command which finds lines containing /open/ and outputs fields two and three for each matching line. Those fields are the IP address and hostname (or empty parentheses if the hostname is unavailable).

Example 13.17. Parsing grepable output on the command line

```
> nmap -p80 -PN -oG - 10.1.1.0/24 | awk '/open/{print $2 " " $3}'
10.1.1.72 (userA.corp.foocompany.biz)
10.1.1.73 (userB.corp.foocompany.biz)
10.1.1.75 (userC.corp.foocompany.biz)
10.1.1.149 (admin.corp.foocompany.biz)
10.1.1.152 (printer.corp.foocompany.biz)
10.1.1.160 (10-1-1-160.foocompany.biz)
10.1.1.161 (10-1-1-161.foocompany.biz)
10.1.1.201 (10-1-1-201.foocompany.biz)
10.1.1.254 (10-1-1-254.foocompany.biz)
```

Chapter 14. Understanding and Customizing Nmap Data Files

14.1. Introduction

Nmap relies on six data files for port scanning and other operations, all of which have names beginning with `nmap-`. One example is `nmap-services`, a registry of port names to their corresponding port number and protocol. The others, which this chapter describes one by one, are `nmap-service-probes` (version detection probe database), `nmap-rpc` (SunRPC program name to number database for direct RPC scanning), `nmap-os-db` (OS detection database), `nmap-mac-prefixes` (ethernet MAC address prefix (OUI) to vendor lookup table), and `nmap-protocols` (list of IP protocols for protocol scan). Additionally this chapter covers certain files related to scripting with the Nmap Scripting Engine. The source distribution installs these files in `/usr/local/share/nmap/` and the official Linux RPMs put them in `/usr/share/nmap/`. Other distributions may install them elsewhere.

The latest versions of these files are kept at *http://nmap.org/data/*, though it is strongly recommended that users upgrade to the most recent Nmap version rather than grabbing newer data files à la carte. There are no guarantees that newer files will work with older versions of Nmap (though they almost always do), and the resulting Frankenstein versions of Nmap can confuse the operating system and service fingerprint submission process.

Most users never change the data files, but it can be handy for advanced users who might want to add a version fingerprint or port assignment for a custom daemon running at their company. This section provides a description of each file and how they are commonly changed. The general mechanism for replacing Nmap data files with custom versions is then discussed. A couple of the files don't relate to port scanning directly, but they are all discussed here for convenience.

14.2. Well Known Port List: `nmap-services`

The `nmap-services` file is a registry of port names to their corresponding number and protocol. Each entry has a number representing how likely that port is to be found open. Most lines have a comment as well. Nmap ignores the comments, but users sometimes grep for them in the file when Nmap reports an open service of a type that the user does not recognize. Example 14.1 shows a typical excerpt from the file. Some padding whitespace has been added for readability.

Example 14.1. Excerpt from `nmap-services`

```
qotd        17/tcp      0.002346   # Quote of the Day
qotd        17/udp      0.009209   # Quote of the Day
msp         18/udp      0.000610   # Message Send Protocol
chargen     19/tcp      0.002559   # ttytst source Character Generator
chargen     19/udp      0.015865   # ttytst source Character Generator
ftp-data    20/tcp      0.001079   # File Transfer [Default Data]
ftp-data    20/udp      0.001878   # File Transfer [Default Data]
ftp         21/tcp      0.197667   # File Transfer [Control]
ftp         21/udp      0.004844   # File Transfer [Control]
ssh         22/tcp      0.182286   # Secure Shell Login
ssh         22/udp      0.003905   # Secure Shell Login
telnet      23/tcp      0.221265
telnet      23/udp      0.006211
priv-mail   24/tcp      0.001154   # any private mail system
priv-mail   24/udp      0.000329   # any private mail system
smtp        25/tcp      0.131314   # Simple Mail Transfer
smtp        25/udp      0.001285   # Simple Mail Transfer
```

This file was originally based off the IANA assigned ports list at *http://www.iana.org/assignments/port-numbers*, though many other ports have been added over the years. The IANA does not track trojans, worms and the like, yet discovering them is important for many Nmap users.

The grammar of this file is pretty simple. There are three whitespace-separated columns. The first is the service name or abbreviation, as seen in the SERVICE column of Nmap output. The second column gives the port number and protocol, separated by a slash. That syntax is seen in the PORT column of Nmap output. The third column is the "port frequency", a measure of how often the port was found open during research scans of the Internet. If omitted, the frequency is zero. Nmap disregards anything beyond the third column, but most lines continue with whitespace then and a pound ('#') character, followed by a comment. Lines may be blank or contain just a pound character followed by comments.

Astute readers notice the similarity in structure between `nmap-services` and `/etc/services` (usually found at `C:\windows\system32\drivers\etc\services` on Windows). This is no coincidence. The format was kept to allow systems administrators to copy in any custom entries from their own `/etc/services`, or even to substitute their own version of that file entirely. The `/etc/services` format allows a third column providing alias names for a service. This would conflict with the third column being used for the port frequency, so the contents of that column are ignored if they are not numeric.

Example 14.1 shows that UDP ports are often registered for TCP-only services such as SSH and FTP. This was inherited from the IANA, who tend to always register services for both protocols. Having the extra entries doesn't hurt, because by default Nmap scans ports with the highest frequencies and low-frequency ports are simply skipped. And, though it may be unexpected, the excerpt shows that sometimes the UDP counterparts of popular TCP ports are found open.

Administrators sometimes change this file to reflect custom services running on their network. For example, an online services company I once consulted for had dozens of different custom daemons running on high-numbered ports. Doing this allows Nmap to display results for these ports using their proper names rather than `unknown`. Remember that if you add entries without a port frequency figure, the frequency is taken to be zero, so the port will not be scanned by default. Use an option like -p [1-65535] to ensure that all named ports are scanned.

Similarly, a certain registered port may be frequently wrong for a certain organization. nmap-services can only handle one service name per port number and protocol combination, yet sometimes several different types of applications end up using the same default port number. In that case, I try to choose the most popular one for nmap-services. Organizations which commonly use another service on such a port number may change the file accordingly.

Services specific to a single organization should generally stay in their own nmap-services, but other port registrations can benefit everyone. If you find that the default port for a major worm, trojan, file sharing application, or other service is missing from the latest nmap-services, please send it to me (<fyodor@insecure.org>) for inclusion in the next release. This helps all users while preventing you from having to maintain and update your own custom version of nmap-services.

Another common customization is to strip nmap-services down to only the most common, essential services for an organization. Without a port specification, Nmap will not scan any ports not listed in the services file, so this is a way to limit the number of ports scanned without using a long argument to the -p option. The stripped-down file should normally be placed in a custom location accessible with the --datadir or --servicedb option rather than where Nmap will use it by default. Advice for customizing these files, including ways to prevent Nmap upgrades from wiping out your modified versions can be found in Section 14.9, "Using Customized Data Files" [370].

14.3. Version Scanning DB: `nmap-service-probes`

This file contains the probes that the Nmap service/version detection system (-sV or -A options) uses during port interrogation to determine what program is listening on a port. Example 14.2 offers a typical excerpt.

Example 14.2. Excerpt from `nmap-service-probes`

```
##############################NEXT PROBE##############################
# DNS Server status request: http://www.rfc-editor.org/rfc/rfc1035.txt
Probe UDP DNSStatusRequest q|\0\0\x10\0\0\0\0\0\0\0\0\0\0\0|
ports 53,135
match domain m|^\0\0\x90\x04\0\0\0\0\0\0\0\0|
# This one below came from 2 tested Windows XP boxes
match msrpc m|^\x04\x06\0\0\x10\0\0\0\0\0\0\0|
[...]
###########################NEXT PROBE############################
Probe UDP Help q|help\r\n\r\n|
ports 7,13,37
match chargen m| @ABCDEFGHIJKLMNOPQRSTUVWXYZ|
match echo m|^help\r\n\r\n$|
match time m|^[\xc0-\xc5]...$|
```

The grammar of this file is fully described in Chapter 7, *Service and Application Version Detection* [145]. While nmap-service-probes is more complex than nmap-services, the benefits of improving it can also be greater. Nmap can be taught to actually recognize a company's custom services, rather than simply guessed based on `nmap-services` port registration.

Additionally, some administrators have been using version detection for tasks well beyond its original intended purpose. A short probe can cause Nmap to print the title of web pages, recognize worm-infected machines, locate open proxies, and more. A practical example of this is provided in Section 7.9, "SOLUTION: Hack Version Detection to Suit Custom Needs, such as Open Proxy Detection" [168].

14.4. SunRPC Numbers: `nmap-rpc`

As with `nmap-services`, `nmap-rpc` simply maps numbers to names. In this case, SunRPC program numbers are mapped to the program name which uses them. Example 14.3 offers a typical excerpt.

Example 14.3. Excerpt from `nmap-rpc`

```
rpcbind        100000   portmap sunrpc rpcbind
rstatd         100001   rstat rup perfmeter rstat_svc
rusersd        100002   rusers
nfs            100003   nfsprog nfsd
ypserv         100004   ypprog
mountd         100005   mount showmount
rpc.operd      100080   opermsg         # Sun Online-Backup
# DMFE/DAWS (Defense Automated Warning System)
#
Gqsrv          200034   gqsrv
Ppt            200035   ppt
Pmt            200036   pmt
```

Nmap only cares about the first two whitespace-separated columns—the program name and number. It doesn't look at any aliases or comments that may appear beyond that. Blank lines and those starting with pound comments are permitted. This format is the same as used by `/etc/rpc` on Unix, so administrators may use that file instead if they desire.

`nmap-rpc` is only used by the RPC grinding feature of Nmap version descriptions. That feature is covered in Section 7.5.2, "RPC Grinding" [156].

Users rarely change `nmap-rpc`. When they do, it is usually to add a custom service or a public one that is missing from the latest `nmap-rpc`. In the latter case, please send a note to me at `<fyodor@insecure.org>` so that I can add it to the next version. As with `nmap-services`, some administrators strip the file down, removing obscure RPC programs to save scan time. The same warning applies: specify your stripped `nmap-rpc` with the `--datadir` option rather than installing it where it will be used implicitly.

14.5. Nmap OS Detection DB: `nmap-os-db`

The `nmap-os-db` data file contains hundreds of examples of how different operating systems respond to Nmap's specialized OS detection probes. It is divided into blocks known as *fingerprints*, with each fingerprint containing an operating system's name, its general classification, and response data. Example 14.4 is an excerpt from the file showing a couple of typical fingerprints.

Example 14.4. Excerpt from `nmap-os-db`

```
Fingerprint FreeBSD 7.0-CURRENT
Class FreeBSD | FreeBSD | 7.X | general purpose
SEQ(SP=101-10D%GCD=<7%ISR=108-112%TI=RD%II=RI%TS=20|21|22)
OPS(O1=M5B4NW8NNT11%O2=M578NW8NNT11%O3=M280NW8NNT11%O4=M5B4NW8NNT11% ⏎
    O5=M218NW8NNT11%O6=M109NNT11)
WIN(W1=FFFF%W2=FFFF%W3=FFFF%W4=FFFF%W5=FFFF%W6=FFFF)
ECN(R=Y%DF=Y%T=40%TG=40%W=FFFF%O=M5B4NW8%CC=N%Q=)
T1(R=Y%DF=Y%T=40%TG=40%S=O%A=S+%F=AS%RD=0%Q=)
T2(R=N)
T3(R=Y%DF=Y%T=40%TG=40%W=FFFF%S=O%A=S+%F=AS%O=M109NW8NNT11%RD=0%Q=)
T4(R=Y%DF=Y%T=40%TG=40%W=0%S=A%A=Z%F=R%O=%RD=0%Q=)
T5(R=Y%DF=Y%T=40%TG=40%W=0%S=Z%A=S+%F=AR%O=%RD=0%Q=)
T6(R=Y%DF=Y%T=40%TG=40%W=0%S=A%A=Z%F=R%O=%RD=0%Q=)
T7(R=Y%DF=Y%T=40%TG=40%W=0%S=Z%A=S%F=AR%O=%RD=0%Q=)
U1(DF=N%T=40%TG=40%TOS=0%IPL=38%UN=0%RIPL=G%RID=G%RIPCK=G%RUCK=G%RUL=G%RUD=G)
IE(DFI=S%T=40%TG=40%TOSI=S%CD=S%SI=S%DLI=S)

Fingerprint Linux 2.6.11 - 2.6.20
Class Linux | Linux | 2.6.X | general purpose
SEQ(SP=B9-CF%GCD=<7%ISR=C4-D7%TI=Z%II=I%TS=7)
OPS(O1=M5B4ST11NW1%O2=M5B4ST11NW1%O3=M5B4NNT11NW1%O4=M5B4ST11NW1% ⏎
    O5=M5B4ST11NW1%O6=M5B4ST11)
WIN(W1=16A0%W2=16A0%W3=16A0%W4=16A0%W5=16A0%W6=16A0)
ECN(R=Y%DF=Y%T=40%TG=40%W=16D0%O=M5B4NNSNW1%CC=N%Q=)
T1(R=Y%DF=Y%T=40%TG=40%S=O%A=S+%F=AS%RD=0%Q=)
T2(R=N)
T3(R=Y%DF=Y%T=40%TG=40%W=16A0%S=O%A=S+%F=AS%O=M5B4ST11NW1%RD=0%Q=)
T4(R=Y%DF=Y%T=40%TG=40%W=0%S=A%A=Z%F=R%O=%RD=0%Q=)
T5(R=Y%DF=Y%T=40%TG=40%W=0%S=Z%A=S+%F=AR%O=%RD=0%Q=)
T6(R=Y%DF=Y%T=40%TG=40%W=0%S=A%A=Z%F=R%O=%RD=0%Q=)
T7(R=Y%DF=Y%T=40%TG=40%W=0%S=Z%A=S+%F=AR%O=%RD=0%Q=)
U1(DF=N%T=40%TG=40%TOS=C0%IPL=164%UN=0%RIPL=G%RID=G%RIPCK=G%RUCK=G%RUL=G%RUD=G)
IE(DFI=N%T=40%TG=40%TOSI=S%CD=S%SI=S%DLI=S)
```

The `nmap-os-db` OS database is consulted when remote OS detection is requested with the `-O` option. In short, Nmap sends special probes to a target system and compares the responses with the entries in the OS database. If there is a match, the database entry likely describes the target system. The process of OS detection is described fully in Chapter 8, *Remote OS Detection* [171]. See Section 8.5.1, "Decoding the Subject Fingerprint Format" [192] for a detailed description of the reference fingerprint format.

`nmap-os-db` is rarely changed by users. Adding or modifying a fingerprint is a moderately complex process and there is usually no reason ever to remove one. The best way to get an updated version of the OS database is to get the latest release of Nmap.

The OS database does not (yet) have information on every networked operating system ever made. The database grows through the contributions of Nmap users. If Nmap can't guess an OS but you know what it is, please submit the fingerprint, following the instructions in Section 8.7.2, "When Nmap Fails to Find a Match and Prints a Fingerprint" [201]. Occasionally fingerprints have errors or become out of date. If you see this, consider submitting a correction as described in Section 8.7.1, "When Nmap Guesses Wrong" [200].

Everyone benefits when the database is improved, and submitting your improvements keeps you from having to maintain your own fork of the file.

14.6. MAC Address Vendor Prefixes: `nmap-mac-prefixes`

Users rarely modify this file, which maps MAC address prefixes to vendor names. Read on for the complete treatment.

Ethernet devices, which have become the dominant network interface type, are each programmed with a unique 48-bit identifier known as a MAC address. This address is placed in ethernet headers to identify which machine on a local network sent a packet, and which machine the packet is destined for. Humans usually represent it as a hex string, such as `00:60:1D:38:32:90`.

To assure that MAC addresses are unique in a world with thousands of vendors, the IEEE assigns an Organizationally Unique Identifier (OUI) to each company manufacturing ethernet devices. The company must use its own OUI for the first three bytes of MAC addresses for equipment it produces. For example, the OUI of `00:60:1D:38:32:90` is `00601D`. It can choose the remaining three bytes however it wishes, as long as they are unique. A counter is the simple approach. Companies that assign all 16.8 million possible values can obtain more OUIs. `nmap-mac-prefixes` maps each assigned OUI to the name of the vendor that sells them. Example 14.5 is a typical excerpt.

Example 14.5. Excerpt from `nmap-mac-prefixes`

```
006017 Tokimec
006018 Stellar ONE
006019 Roche Diagnostics
00601A Keithley Instruments
00601B Mesa Electronics
00601C Telxon
00601D Lucent Technologies
00601E Softlab
00601F Stallion Technologies
006020 Pivotal Networking
006021 DSC
006022 Vicom Systems
006023 Pericom Semiconductor
006024 Gradient Technologies
006025 Active Imaging PLC
006026 Viking Components
```

The first value is the three-byte OUI as 6 hex digits. It is followed by the company name. This file is created, using a simple Perl script, from the complete list of OUIs available from *http://standards.ieee.org/regauth/oui/oui.txt*. The IEEE also offers an OUI FAQ at *http://standards.ieee.org/faqs/OUI.html*.

Nmap can determine the MAC address of hosts on a local ethernet LAN by reading the headers off the wire. It uses this table to look up and report the manufacturer name based on the OUI. This can be useful for roughly identifying the type of machine you are dealing with. A device with a Cisco, Hewlett Packard, or

Sun OUI probably identifies a router, printer, or SPARCstation, respectively. Example 14.5, "Excerpt from nmap-mac-prefixes" [368] shows that the device at `00:60:1D:38:32:90` was made by Lucent. It is in fact the Lucent Orinoco wireless card in my laptop.

14.7. IP Protocol Number List: `nmap-protocols`

This file maps the one-byte IP protocol number in the IP header into the corresponding protocol name. Example 14.6 is a typical excerpt.

Example 14.6. Excerpt from `nmap-protocols`

```
hopopt        0      HOPOPT     # IPv6 Hop-by-Hop Option
icmp          1      ICMP       # Internet Control Message
igmp          2      IGMP       # Internet Group Management
ggp           3      GGP        # Gateway-to-Gateway
ip            4      IP         # IP in IP (encapsulation)
st            5      ST         # Stream
tcp           6      TCP        # Transmission Control
cbt           7      CBT        # CBT
egp           8      EGP        # Exterior Gateway Protocol
[ ... ]
chaos        16      CHAOS      # Chaos
udp          17      UDP        # User Datagram
```

The first two fields are the protocol name or abbreviation and the number in decimal format. Nmap doesn't care about anything after the protocol number. It is used for IP protocol scanning, as described at Section 5.11, "IP Protocol Scan (-sO)" [125]. Less than 140 protocols are defined and users almost never modify this file. The raw data is made available by the IANA at *http://www.iana.org/assignments/protocol-numbers*

14.8. Files Related to Scripting

The scripts used by the Nmap Scripting Engine may be considered another kind of data file. Scripts are stored in a `scripts` subdirectory of one of the directories listed in Section 14.9, "Using Customized Data Files" [370]. The name of each script file ends in `.nse`. For all the details on scripts see Chapter 9, *Nmap Scripting Engine* [205].

All of the files in the script directory are executable scripts, except for one: `script.db`. This file is a plain-text cache of which categories each script belongs to. It should not be edited directly; use the `--script-updatedb` option instead.

Each of NSE's extension modules (see Section 9.6, "NSE Libraries" [236]) is stored in one of two places. Pure Lua extensions are kept in the `nselib` subdirectory of the Nmap data directory, normally the same one `scripts` is in. This is where modules like `shortport` and `stdnse` are kept, in files whose names end in `.lua`.

14.9. Using Customized Data Files

Any or all of the Nmap data files may be replaced with versions customized to the user's liking. They can only be replaced in whole—you can not specify changes that will be merged with the original files at runtime. When Nmap looks for each file, it searches by name in many directories and selects the first one found. This is the analogous to the way your Unix shell finds programs you ask to execute by searching through the directories in your PATH one at a time in order. The following list gives the Nmap directory search order. It shows that an nmap-services found in the directory specified by --datadir will be used in preference to one found in ~/.nmap/ because the former is searched first.

Nmap data file directory search order

1. If --datadir option was specified, check the directory given as its argument.

2. If the NMAPDIR environmental variable is set, check that directory.

3. If Nmap is not running on Windows, search in ~/.nmap of the user running Nmap. It tries the real user ID's home directory, and then the effective UID's if they differ.

4. If Nmap *is* running on Windows, check the directory in which the Nmap binary resides.

5. Check the compiled in NMAPDATADIR directory. That value is defined to c:\nmap on Windows, and <$prefix>/share/nmap on Unix. <$prefix> is /usr/local for the default source build and /usr for the Linux RPMs. The <$prefix> can be changed by giving **./configure** the --prefix option when compiling the source.

6. As a last resort, the current working directory of your shell (.) is tried. This is done last for the same security reasons that . should not appear first on your shell execution PATH. On a shared system, a malicious user could place bogus data files in a shared directory such as /tmp. Those files could be malformed, causing Nmap to complain and exit, or they could cause Nmap to skip important ports. If Nmap tried . first, other users who happened to run Nmap in that shared directory would get the bogus versions. This could also happen by accident if you inadvertently ran Nmap in a directory that happened to have a file named nmap-services (or one of the other ones). Users who really want Nmap to try the current directory early may set the environment variable NMAPDIR to . at their own risk.

This list shows the many choices users have when deciding how to replace a file with their own customized version. The option I usually recommend is to place the customized files in a special directory named appropriately for the change. For example, an nmap-services stripped to contain just the hundred most common ports could be placed in ~/nmap-fewports. Then specify this directory with the --datadir option. This ensures that the customized files are only used intentionally. Since the Nmap output-to-file formats include the Nmap command-line used, you will know which files were used when reviewing the logs later.

Another option is to simply edit the original in NMAPDATADIR. This is rarely recommended, as the edited file will likely be overwritten the next time Nmap is upgraded. Additionally, this makes it hard to use the original files if you suspect that your replacements are causing a problem. This also makes it difficult to compare your version with the original to recall what you changed.

A third option is to place the customized files in your Unix ~/.nmap directory. Of course you should only insert files that you have changed. The others will still be retrieved from NMAPDATADIR as usual. This is very convenient, as Nmap will use the customized files implicitly whenever you run it. That can be a disadvantage as well. Users sometimes forget the files exist. When they upgrade Nmap to a version with newer data files, the old copies in ~/.nmap will still be used, reducing the quality of results.

Setting the NMAPDIR environment variable to the directory with files is another alternative. This can be useful when testing a new version of Nmap. Suppose you obtain Nmap version 4.68, notice the huge list of changes, and decide to test it out before replacing your current known-working version. You might compile it in ~/src/nmap-4.68, but execute it there and Nmap tries to read the data files from /usr/local/share/nmap. Those are the old versions, since Nmap 4.68 has not yet been installed. Simply set NMAPDIR to ~/src/nmap-4.68, test to your heart's content, and then perform the **make install**. A disadvantage to using NMAPDIR regularly is that the directory name is not recorded in Nmap output files like it is when --datadir is used instead.

Chapter 15. Nmap Reference Guide

Name

nmap — Network exploration tool and security / port scanner

Synopsis

nmap [*<Scan Type>* ...] [*<Options>*] { *<target specification>* }

15.1. Description

Nmap ("Network Mapper") is an open source tool for network exploration and security auditing. It was designed to rapidly scan large networks, although it works fine against single hosts. Nmap uses raw IP packets in novel ways to determine what hosts are available on the network, what services (application name and version) those hosts are offering, what operating systems (and OS versions) they are running, what type of packet filters/firewalls are in use, and dozens of other characteristics. While Nmap is commonly used for security audits, many systems and network administrators find it useful for routine tasks such as network inventory, managing service upgrade schedules, and monitoring host or service uptime.

The output from Nmap is a list of scanned targets, with supplemental information on each depending on the options used. Key among that information is the "interesting ports table". That table lists the port number and protocol, service name, and state. The state is either open, filtered, closed, or unfiltered. Open means that an application on the target machine is listening for connections/packets on that port. Filtered means that a firewall, filter, or other network obstacle is blocking the port so that Nmap cannot tell whether it is open or closed. Closed ports have no application listening on them, though they could open up at any time. Ports are classified as unfiltered when they are responsive to Nmap's probes, but Nmap cannot determine whether they are open or closed. Nmap reports the state combinations open|filtered and closed|filtered when it cannot determine which of the two states describe a port. The port table may also include software version details when version detection has been requested. When an IP protocol scan is requested (-sO), Nmap provides information on supported IP protocols rather than listening ports.

In addition to the interesting ports table, Nmap can provide further information on targets, including reverse DNS names, operating system guesses, device types, and MAC addresses.

A typical Nmap scan is shown in Example 15.1. The only Nmap arguments used in this example are -A, to enable OS and version detection, script scanning, and traceroute; -T4 for faster execution; and then the two target hostnames.

Example 15.1. A representative Nmap scan

```
# nmap -A -T4 scanme.nmap.org

Starting Nmap ( http://nmap.org )
Interesting ports on scanme.nmap.org (64.13.134.52):
Not shown: 994 filtered ports
PORT     STATE  SERVICE VERSION
22/tcp   open   ssh       OpenSSH 4.3 (protocol 2.0)
25/tcp   closed smtp
53/tcp   open   domain  ISC BIND 9.3.4
70/tcp   closed gopher
80/tcp   open   http      Apache httpd 2.2.2 ((Fedora))
|_ HTML title: Go ahead and ScanMe!
113/tcp closed auth
Device type: general purpose
Running: Linux 2.6.X
OS details: Linux 2.6.20-1 (Fedora Core 5)

TRACEROUTE (using port 80/tcp)
HOP RTT    ADDRESS
[Cut first seven hops for brevity]
8    10.59 so-4-2-0.mpr3.pao1.us.above.net (64.125.28.142)
9    11.00 metro0.sv.svcolo.com (208.185.168.173)
10   9.93  scanme.nmap.org (64.13.134.52)

Nmap done: 1 IP address (1 host up) scanned in 17.00 seconds
```

The newest version of Nmap can be obtained from *http://nmap.org*. The newest version of the man page is available at *http://nmap.org/book/man.html*.

15.2. Options Summary

This options summary is printed when Nmap is run with no arguments, and the latest version is always available at *http://nmap.org/data/nmap.usage.txt*. It helps people remember the most common options, but is no substitute for the in-depth documentation in the rest of this manual. Some obscure options aren't even included here.

Nmap 4.76 (http://nmap.org)
Usage: nmap [Scan Type(s)] [Options] {target specification}
TARGET SPECIFICATION:
  Can pass hostnames, IP addresses, networks, etc.
  Ex: scanme.nmap.org, microsoft.com/24, 192.168.0.1; 10.0.0-255.1-254
  -iL <inputfilename>: Input from list of hosts/networks
  -iR <num hosts>: Choose random targets
  --exclude <host1[,host2][,host3],...>: Exclude hosts/networks
  --excludefile <exclude_file>: Exclude list from file
HOST DISCOVERY:
  -sL: List Scan - simply list targets to scan
  -sP: Ping Scan - go no further than determining if host is online
  -PN: Treat all hosts as online -- skip host discovery
  -PS/PA/PU [portlist]: TCP SYN/ACK or UDP discovery to given ports

-PE/PP/PM: ICMP echo, timestamp, and netmask request discovery probes
-PO [protocol list]: IP Protocol Ping
-n/-R: Never do DNS resolution/Always resolve [default: sometimes]
--dns-servers <serv1[,serv2],...>: Specify custom DNS servers
--system-dns: Use OS's DNS resolver

SCAN TECHNIQUES:
-sS/sT/sA/sW/sM: TCP SYN/Connect()/ACK/Window/Maimon scans
-sU: UDP Scan
-sN/sF/sX: TCP Null, FIN, and Xmas scans
--scanflags <flags>: Customize TCP scan flags
-sI <zombie host[:probeport]>: Idle scan
-sO: IP protocol scan
-b <FTP relay host>: FTP bounce scan
--traceroute: Trace hop path to each host
--reason: Display the reason a port is in a particular state

PORT SPECIFICATION AND SCAN ORDER:
-p <port ranges>: Only scan specified ports
  Ex: -p22; -p1-65535; -p U:53,111,137,T:21-25,80,139,8080
-F: Fast mode - Scan fewer ports than the default scan
-r: Scan ports consecutively - don't randomize
--top-ports <number>: Scan <number> most common ports
--port-ratio <ratio>: Scan ports more common than <ratio>

SERVICE/VERSION DETECTION:
-sV: Probe open ports to determine service/version info
--version-intensity <level>: Set from 0 (light) to 9 (try all probes)
--version-light: Limit to most likely probes (intensity 2)
--version-all: Try every single probe (intensity 9)
--version-trace: Show detailed version scan activity (for debugging)

SCRIPT SCAN:
-sC: equivalent to --script=default
--script=<Lua scripts>: <Lua scripts> is a comma separated list of
        directories, script-files or script-categories
--script-args=<n1=v1,[n2=v2,...]>: provide arguments to scripts
--script-trace: Show all data sent and received
--script-updatedb: Update the script database.

OS DETECTION:
-O: Enable OS detection
--osscan-limit: Limit OS detection to promising targets
--osscan-guess: Guess OS more aggressively

TIMING AND PERFORMANCE:
Options which take <time> are in milliseconds, unless you append 's'
(seconds), 'm' (minutes), or 'h' (hours) to the value (e.g. 30m).
-T[0-5]: Set timing template (higher is faster)
--min-hostgroup/max-hostgroup <size>: Parallel host scan group sizes
--min-parallelism/max-parallelism <time>: Probe parallelization
--min-rtt-timeout/max-rtt-timeout/initial-rtt-timeout <time>: Specifies
    probe round trip time.
--max-retries <tries>: Caps number of port scan probe retransmissions.
--host-timeout <time>: Give up on target after this long

--scan-delay/--max-scan-delay <time>: Adjust delay between probes
--min-rate <number>: Send packets no slower than <number> per second
--max-rate <number>: Send packets no faster than <number> per second
FIREWALL/IDS EVASION AND SPOOFING:
-f; --mtu <val>: fragment packets (optionally w/given MTU)
-D <decoy1,decoy2[,ME],...>: Cloak a scan with decoys
-S <IP_Address>: Spoof source address
-e <iface>: Use specified interface
-g/--source-port <portnum>: Use given port number
--data-length <num>: Append random data to sent packets
--ip-options <options>: Send packets with specified ip options
--ttl <val>: Set IP time-to-live field
--spoof-mac <mac address/prefix/vendor name>: Spoof your MAC address
--badsum: Send packets with a bogus TCP/UDP checksum
OUTPUT:
-oN/-oX/-oS/-oG <file>: Output scan in normal, XML, s|<rIpt kIddi3,
   and Grepable format, respectively, to the given filename.
-oA <basename>: Output in the three major formats at once
-v: Increase verbosity level (use twice or more for greater effect)
-d[level]: Set or increase debugging level (Up to 9 is meaningful)
--open: Only show open (or possibly open) ports
--packet-trace: Show all packets sent and received
--iflist: Print host interfaces and routes (for debugging)
--log-errors: Log errors/warnings to the normal-format output file
--append-output: Append to rather than clobber specified output files
--resume <filename>: Resume an aborted scan
--stylesheet <path/URL>: XSL stylesheet to transform XML output to HTML
--webxml: Reference stylesheet from Nmap.Org for more portable XML
--no-stylesheet: Prevent associating of XSL stylesheet w/XML output
MISC:
-6: Enable IPv6 scanning
-A: Enables OS detection and Version detection, Script scanning and Traceroute
--datadir <dirname>: Specify custom Nmap data file location
--send-eth/--send-ip: Send using raw ethernet frames or IP packets
--privileged: Assume that the user is fully privileged
--unprivileged: Assume the user lacks raw socket privileges
-V: Print version number
-h: Print this help summary page.
EXAMPLES:
nmap -v -A scanme.nmap.org
nmap -v -sP 192.168.0.0/16 10.0.0.0/8
nmap -v -iR 10000 -PN -p 80
SEE THE MAN PAGE FOR MANY MORE OPTIONS, DESCRIPTIONS, AND EXAMPLES

15.3. Target Specification

Everything on the Nmap command-line that isn't an option (or option argument) is treated as a target host specification. The simplest case is to specify a target IP address or hostname for scanning.

Sometimes you wish to scan a whole network of adjacent hosts. For this, Nmap supports CIDR-style addressing. You can append /`<numbits>` to an IP address or hostname and Nmap will scan every IP address for which the first `<numbits>` are the same as for the reference IP or hostname given. For example, 192.168.10.0/24 would scan the 256 hosts between 192.168.10.0 (binary: `11000000 10101000 00001010 00000000`) and 192.168.10.255 (binary: `11000000 10101000 00001010 11111111`), inclusive. 192.168.10.40/24 would do exactly the same thing. Given that the host scanme.nmap.org is at the IP address 64.13.134.52, the specification scanme.nmap.org/16 would scan the 65,536 IP addresses between 64.13.0.0 and 64.13.255.255. The smallest allowed value is /0, which scans the whole Internet. The largest value is /32, which scans just the named host or IP address because all address bits are fixed.

CIDR notation is short but not always flexible enough. For example, you might want to scan 192.168.0.0/16 but skip any IPs ending with .0 or .255 because they are commonly broadcast addresses. Nmap supports this through octet range addressing. Rather than specify a normal IP address, you can specify a comma separated list of numbers or ranges for each octet. For example, 192.168.0-255.1-254 will skip all addresses in the range that end in .0 and or .255. Ranges need not be limited to the final octets: the specifier 0-255.0-255.13.37 will perform an Internet-wide scan for all IP addresses ending in 13.37. This sort of broad sampling can be useful for Internet surveys and research.

IPv6 addresses can only be specified by their fully qualified IPv6 address or hostname. CIDR and octet ranges aren't supported for IPv6 because they are rarely useful.

Nmap accepts multiple host specifications on the command line, and they don't need to be the same type. The command **nmap scanme.nmap.org 192.168.0.0/16 10.0.0,1,3-7.0-255** does what you would expect.

While targets are usually specified on the command lines, the following options are also available to control target selection:

`-iL <inputfilename>` (Input from list)
> Reads target specifications from `<inputfilename>`. Passing a huge list of hosts is often awkward on the command line, yet it is a common desire. For example, your DHCP server might export a list of 10,000 current leases that you wish to scan. Or maybe you want to scan all IP addresses *except* for those to locate hosts using unauthorized static IP addresses. Simply generate the list of hosts to scan and pass that filename to Nmap as an argument to the `-iL` option. Entries can be in any of the formats accepted by Nmap on the command line (IP address, hostname, CIDR, IPv6, or octet ranges). Each entry must be separated by one or more spaces, tabs, or newlines. You can specify a hyphen (–) as the filename if you want Nmap to read hosts from standard input rather than an actual file.

`-iR <num hosts>` (Choose random targets)
> For Internet-wide surveys and other research, you may want to choose targets at random. The `<num hosts>` argument tells Nmap how many IPs to generate. Undesirable IPs such as those in certain private, multicast, or unallocated address ranges are automatically skipped. The argument 0 can be specified for a never-ending scan. Keep in mind that some network administrators bristle at unauthorized scans of their networks and may complain. Use this option at your own risk! If you find yourself really bored one rainy afternoon, try the command **nmap -sS -PS80 -iR 0 -p 80** to locate random web servers for browsing.

`--exclude <host1>[,<host2>[,...]]` (Exclude hosts/networks)
> Specifies a comma-separated list of targets to be excluded from the scan even if they are part of the overall network range you specify. The list you pass in uses normal Nmap syntax, so it can include hostnames, CIDR netblocks, octet ranges, etc. This can be useful when the network you wish to scan

---

includes untouchable mission-critical servers, systems that are known to react adversely to port scans, or subnets administered by other people.

`--excludefile <exclude_file>` (Exclude list from file)
> This offers the same functionality as the `--exclude` option, except that the excluded targets are provided in a newline, space, or tab delimited `<exclude_file>` rather than on the command line.

15.4. Host Discovery

One of the very first steps in any network reconnaissance mission is to reduce a (sometimes huge) set of IP ranges into a list of active or interesting hosts. Scanning every port of every single IP address is slow and usually unnecessary. Of course what makes a host interesting depends greatly on the scan purposes. Network administrators may only be interested in hosts running a certain service, while security auditors may care about every single device with an IP address. An administrator may be comfortable using just an ICMP ping to locate hosts on his internal network, while an external penetration tester may use a diverse set of dozens of probes in an attempt to evade firewall restrictions.

Because host discovery needs are so diverse, Nmap offers a wide variety of options for customizing the techniques used. Host discovery is sometimes called ping scan, but it goes well beyond the simple ICMP echo request packets associated with the ubiquitous ping tool. Users can skip the ping step entirely with a list scan (`-sL`) or by disabling ping (`-PN`), or engage the network with arbitrary combinations of multi-port TCP SYN/ACK, UDP, and ICMP probes. The goal of these probes is to solicit responses which demonstrate that an IP address is actually active (is being used by a host or network device). On many networks, only a small percentage of IP addresses are active at any given time. This is particularly common with private address space such as 10.0.0.0/8. That network has 16 million IPs, but I have seen it used by companies with less than a thousand machines. Host discovery can find those machines in a sparsely allocated sea of IP addresses.

If no host discovery options are given, Nmap sends a TCP ACK packet destined for port 80 and an ICMP echo request query to each target machine. An exception to this is that an ARP scan is used for any targets which are on a local ethernet network. For unprivileged Unix shell users, a SYN packet is sent instead of the ACK using the `connect` system call. These defaults are equivalent to the `-PA -PE` options. This host discovery is often sufficient when scanning local networks, but a more comprehensive set of discovery probes is recommended for security auditing.

The `-P*` options (which select ping types) can be combined. You can increase your odds of penetrating strict firewalls by sending many probe types using different TCP ports/flags and ICMP codes. Also note that ARP discovery (`-PR`) is done by default against targets on a local ethernet network even if you specify other `-P*` options, because it is almost always faster and more effective.

By default, Nmap does host discovery and then performs a port scan against each host it determines is online. This is true even if you specify non-default host discovery types such as UDP probes (`-PU`). Read about the `-sP` option to learn how to perform only host discovery, or use `-PN` to skip host discovery and port scan all target hosts. The following options control host discovery:

`-sL` (List Scan)
> The list scan is a degenerate form of host discovery that simply lists each host of the network(s) specified, without sending any packets to the target hosts. By default, Nmap still does reverse-DNS resolution on the hosts to learn their names. It is often surprising how much useful information simple hostnames give

out. For example, `fw.chi` is the name of one company's Chicago firewall. Nmap also reports the total number of IP addresses at the end. The list scan is a good sanity check to ensure that you have proper IP addresses for your targets. If the hosts sport domain names you do not recognize, it is worth investigating further to prevent scanning the wrong company's network.

Since the idea is to simply print a list of target hosts, options for higher level functionality such as port scanning, OS detection, or ping scanning cannot be combined with this. If you wish to disable ping scanning while still performing such higher level functionality, read up on the `-PN` option.

`-sP` (Ping Scan)

This option tells Nmap to only perform a ping scan (host discovery), then print out the available hosts that responded to the scan. Traceroute and NSE host scripts are also run if requested, but no further testing (such as port scanning or OS detection) is performed. This is by default one step more intrusive than the list scan, and can often be used for the same purposes. It allows light reconnaissance of a target network without attracting much attention. Knowing how many hosts are up is more valuable to attackers than the list provided by list scan of every single IP and host name.

Systems administrators often find this option valuable as well. It can easily be used to count available machines on a network or monitor server availability. This is often called a ping sweep, and is more reliable than pinging the broadcast address because many hosts do not reply to broadcast queries.

The `-sP` option sends an ICMP echo request and a TCP ACK packet to port 80 by default. When executed by an unprivileged user, only a SYN packet is sent (using a `connect` call) to port 80 on the target. When a privileged user tries to scan targets on a local ethernet network, ARP requests are used unless `--send-ip` was specified. The `-sP` option can be combined with any of the discovery probe types (the `-P*` options, excluding `-PN`) for greater flexibility. If any of those probe type and port number options are used, the default probes (ACK and echo request) are overridden. When strict firewalls are in place between the source host running Nmap and the target network, using those advanced techniques is recommended. Otherwise hosts could be missed when the firewall drops probes or their responses.

`-PN` (No ping)

This option skips the Nmap discovery stage altogether. Normally, Nmap uses this stage to determine active machines for heavier scanning. By default, Nmap only performs heavy probing such as port scans, version detection, or OS detection against hosts that are found to be up. Disabling host discovery with `-PN` causes Nmap to attempt the requested scanning functions against *every* target IP address specified. So if a class B sized target address space (/16) is specified on the command line, all 65,536 IP addresses are scanned. Proper host discovery is skipped as with the list scan, but instead of stopping and printing the target list, Nmap continues to perform requested functions as if each target IP is active. For machines on a local ethernet network, ARP scanning will still be performed (unless `--send-ip` is specified) because Nmap needs MAC addresses to further scan target hosts. This option flag used to be `P0` (uses zero), but was renamed to avoid confusion with protocol ping's `PO` (uses the letter O) flag.

`-PS <port list>` (TCP SYN Ping)

This option sends an empty TCP packet with the SYN flag set. The default destination port is 80 (configurable at compile time by changing `DEFAULT_TCP_PROBE_PORT_SPEC` in `nmap.h`). Alternate ports can be specified as a parameter. The syntax is the same as for the `-p` except that port type specifiers like `T:` are not allowed. Examples are `-PS22` and `-PS22-25,80,113,1050,35000`. Note that there can be no space between `-PS` and the port list. If multiple probes are specified they will be sent in parallel.

The SYN flag suggests to the remote system that you are attempting to establish a connection. Normally the destination port will be closed, and a RST (reset) packet sent back. If the port happens to be open, the target will take the second step of a TCP three-way-handshake by responding with a SYN/ACK TCP packet. The machine running Nmap then tears down the nascent connection by responding with a RST rather than sending an ACK packet which would complete the three-way-handshake and establish a full connection. The RST packet is sent by the kernel of the machine running Nmap in response to the unexpected SYN/ACK, not by Nmap itself.

Nmap does not care whether the port is open or closed. Either the RST or SYN/ACK response discussed previously tell Nmap that the host is available and responsive.

On Unix boxes, only the privileged user `root` is generally able to send and receive raw TCP packets. For unprivileged users, a workaround is automatically employed whereby the `connect` system call is initiated against each target port. This has the effect of sending a SYN packet to the target host, in an attempt to establish a connection. If `connect` returns with a quick success or an ECONNREFUSED failure, the underlying TCP stack must have received a SYN/ACK or RST and the host is marked available. If the connection attempt is left hanging until a timeout is reached, the host is marked as down. This workaround is also used for IPv6 connections, as raw IPv6 packet building support is not yet available in Nmap.

`-PA <port list>` (TCP ACK Ping)

The TCP ACK ping is quite similar to the just-discussed SYN ping. The difference, as you could likely guess, is that the TCP ACK flag is set instead of the SYN flag. Such an ACK packet purports to be acknowledging data over an established TCP connection, but no such connection exists. So remote hosts should always respond with a RST packet, disclosing their existence in the process.

The `-PA` option uses the same default port as the SYN probe (80) and can also take a list of destination ports in the same format. If an unprivileged user tries this, or an IPv6 target is specified, the `connect` workaround discussed previously is used. This workaround is imperfect because `connect` is actually sending a SYN packet rather than an ACK.

The reason for offering both SYN and ACK ping probes is to maximize the chances of bypassing firewalls. Many administrators configure routers and other simple firewalls to block incoming SYN packets except for those destined for public services like the company web site or mail server. This prevents other incoming connections to the organization, while allowing users to make unobstructed outgoing connections to the Internet. This non-stateful approach takes up few resources on the firewall/router and is widely supported by hardware and software filters. The Linux Netfilter/iptables firewall software offers the `--syn` convenience option to implement this stateless approach. When stateless firewall rules such as this are in place, SYN ping probes (`-PS`) are likely to be blocked when sent to closed target ports. In such cases, the ACK probe shines as it cuts right through these rules.

Another common type of firewall uses stateful rules that drop unexpected packets. This feature was initially found mostly on high-end firewalls, though it has become much more common over the years. The Linux Netfilter/iptables system supports this through the `--state` option, which categorizes packets based on connection state. A SYN probe is more likely to work against such a system, as unexpected ACK packets are generally recognized as bogus and dropped. A solution to this quandary is to send both SYN and ACK probes by specifying `-PS` and `-PA`.

`-PU <port list>` (UDP Ping)

Another host discovery option is the UDP ping, which sends an empty (unless `--data-length` is specified) UDP packet to the given ports. The port list takes the same format as with the previously discussed `-PS` and `-PA` options. If no ports are specified, the default is 31338. This default can be configured at compile-time by changing `DEFAULT_UDP_PROBE_PORT_SPEC` in `nmap.h`. A highly uncommon port is used by default because sending to open ports is often undesirable for this particular scan type.

Upon hitting a closed port on the target machine, the UDP probe should elicit an ICMP port unreachable packet in return. This signifies to Nmap that the machine is up and available. Many other types of ICMP errors, such as host/network unreachables or TTL exceeded are indicative of a down or unreachable host. A lack of response is also interpreted this way. If an open port is reached, most services simply ignore the empty packet and fail to return any response. This is why the default probe port is 31338, which is highly unlikely to be in use. A few services, such as the Character Generator (chargen) protocol, will respond to an empty UDP packet, and thus disclose to Nmap that the machine is available.

The primary advantage of this scan type is that it bypasses firewalls and filters that only screen TCP. For example, I once owned a Linksys BEFW11S4 wireless broadband router. The external interface of this device filtered all TCP ports by default, but UDP probes would still elicit port unreachable messages and thus give away the device.

`-PE`; `-PP`; `-PM` (ICMP Ping Types)

In addition to the unusual TCP and UDP host discovery types discussed previously, Nmap can send the standard packets sent by the ubiquitous ping program. Nmap sends an ICMP type 8 (echo request) packet to the target IP addresses, expecting a type 0 (echo reply) in return from available hosts. Unfortunately for network explorers, many hosts and firewalls now block these packets, rather than responding as required by RFC 1122. For this reason, ICMP-only scans are rarely reliable enough against unknown targets over the Internet. But for system administrators monitoring an internal network, they can be a practical and efficient approach. Use the `-PE` option to enable this echo request behavior.

While echo request is the standard ICMP ping query, Nmap does not stop there. The ICMP standard (RFC 792) also specifies timestamp request, information request, and address mask request packets as codes 13, 15, and 17, respectively. While the ostensible purpose for these queries is to learn information such as address masks and current times, they can easily be used for host discovery. A system that replies is up and available. Nmap does not currently implement information request packets, as they are not widely supported. RFC 1122 insists that "a host SHOULD NOT implement these messages". Timestamp and address mask queries can be sent with the `-PP` and `-PM` options, respectively. A timestamp reply (ICMP code 14) or address mask reply (code 18) discloses that the host is available. These two queries can be valuable when administrators specifically block echo request packets while forgetting that other ICMP queries can be used for the same purpose.

`-PO <protocol list>` (IP Protocol Ping)

The newest host discovery option is the IP protocol ping, which sends IP packets with the specified protocol number set in their IP header. The protocol list takes the same format as do port lists in the previously discussed TCP and UDP host discovery options. If no protocols are specified, the default is to send multiple IP packets for ICMP (protocol 1), IGMP (protocol 2), and IP-in-IP (protocol 4). The default protocols can be configured at compile-time by changing `DEFAULT_PROTO_PROBE_PORT_SPEC` in `nmap.h`. Note that for the ICMP, IGMP, TCP (protocol

6), and UDP (protocol 17), the packets are sent with the proper protocol headers while other protocols are sent with no additional data beyond the IP header (unless the `--data-length` option is specified).

This host discovery method looks for either responses using the same protocol as a probe, or ICMP protocol unreachable messages which signify that the given protocol isn't supported on the destination host. Either type of response signifies that the target host is alive.

`-PR` (ARP Ping)

One of the most common Nmap usage scenarios is to scan an ethernet LAN. On most LANs, especially those using private address ranges specified by RFC 1918, the vast majority of IP addresses are unused at any given time. When Nmap tries to send a raw IP packet such as an ICMP echo request, the operating system must determine the destination hardware (ARP) address corresponding to the target IP so that it can properly address the ethernet frame. This is often slow and problematic, since operating systems weren't written with the expectation that they would need to do millions of ARP requests against unavailable hosts in a short time period.

ARP scan puts Nmap and its optimized algorithms in charge of ARP requests. And if it gets a response back, Nmap doesn't even need to worry about the IP-based ping packets since it already knows the host is up. This makes ARP scan much faster and more reliable than IP-based scans. So it is done by default when scanning ethernet hosts that Nmap detects are on a local ethernet network. Even if different ping types (such as `-PE` or `-PS`) are specified, Nmap uses ARP instead for any of the targets which are on the same LAN. If you absolutely don't want to do an ARP scan, specify `--send-ip`.

`--traceroute` (Trace path to host)

Traceroutes are performed post-scan using information from the scan results to determine the port and protocol most likely to reach the target. It works with all scan types except connect scans (`-sT`) and idle scans (`-sI`). All traces use Nmap's dynamic timing model and are performed in parallel.

Traceroute works by sending packets with a low TTL (time-to-live) in an attempt to elicit ICMP Time Exceeded messages from intermediate hops between the scanner and the target host. Standard traceroute implementations start with a TTL of 1 and increment the TTL until the destination host is reached. Nmap's traceroute starts with a high TTL and then decrements the TTL until it reaches zero. Doing it backwards lets Nmap employ clever caching algorithms to speed up traces over multiple hosts. On average Nmap sends 5–10 fewer packets per host, depending on network conditions. If a single subnet is being scanned (i.e. 192.168.0.0/24) Nmap may only have to send a single packet to most hosts.

`-n` (No DNS resolution)

Tells Nmap to *never* do reverse DNS resolution on the active IP addresses it finds. Since DNS can be slow even with Nmap's built-in parallel stub resolver, this option can slash scanning times.

`-R` (DNS resolution for all targets)

Tells Nmap to *always* do reverse DNS resolution on the target IP addresses. Normally reverse DNS is only performed against responsive (online) hosts.

`--system-dns` (Use system DNS resolver)

By default, Nmap resolves IP addresses by sending queries directly to the name servers configured on your host and then listening for responses. Many requests (often dozens) are performed in parallel to improve performance. Specify this option to use your system resolver instead (one IP at a time via the `getnameinfo` call). This is slower and rarely useful unless you find a bug in the Nmap parallel resolver (please let us know if you do). The system resolver is always used for IPv6 scans.

`--dns-servers <server1>[,<server2>[,...]]` (Servers to use for reverse DNS queries)

By default, Nmap determines your DNS servers (for rDNS resolution) from your resolv.conf file (Unix) or the Registry (Win32). Alternatively, you may use this option to specify alternate servers. This option is not honored if you are using `--system-dns` or an IPv6 scan. Using multiple DNS servers is often faster, especially if you choose authoritative servers for your target IP space. This option can also improve stealth, as your requests can be bounced off just about any recursive DNS server on the Internet.

This option also comes in handy when scanning private networks. Sometimes only a few name servers provide proper rDNS information, and you may not even know where they are. You can scan the network for port 53 (perhaps with version detection), then try Nmap list scans (`-sL`) specifying each name server one at a time with `--dns-servers` until you find one which works.

15.5. Port Scanning Basics

While Nmap has grown in functionality over the years, it began as an efficient port scanner, and that remains its core function. The simple command **nmap <target>** scans more than 1660 TCP ports on the host `<target>`. While many port scanners have traditionally lumped all ports into the open or closed states, Nmap is much more granular. It divides ports into six states: `open`, `closed`, `filtered`, `unfiltered`, `open|filtered`, or `closed|filtered`.

These states are not intrinsic properties of the port itself, but describe how Nmap sees them. For example, an Nmap scan from the same network as the target may show port `135/tcp` as open, while a scan at the same time with the same options from across the Internet might show that port as `filtered`.

The six port states recognized by Nmap

open

> An application is actively accepting TCP connections or UDP packets on this port. Finding these is often the primary goal of port scanning. Security-minded people know that each open port is an avenue for attack. Attackers and pen-testers want to exploit the open ports, while administrators try to close or protect them with firewalls without thwarting legitimate users. Open ports are also interesting for non-security scans because they show services available for use on the network.

closed

> A closed port is accessible (it receives and responds to Nmap probe packets), but there is no application listening on it. They can be helpful in showing that a host is up on an IP address (host discovery, or ping scanning), and as part of OS detection. Because closed ports are reachable, it may be worth scanning later in case some open up. Administrators may want to consider blocking such ports with a firewall. Then they would appear in the filtered state, discussed next.

filtered

> Nmap cannot determine whether the port is open because packet filtering prevents its probes from reaching the port. The filtering could be from a dedicated firewall device, router rules, or host-based firewall software. These ports frustrate attackers because they provide so little information. Sometimes they respond with ICMP error messages such as type 3 code 13 (destination unreachable: communication administratively prohibited), but filters that simply drop probes without responding are far more common. This forces Nmap to retry several times just in case the probe was dropped due to network congestion rather than filtering. This slows down the scan dramatically.

unfiltered

The unfiltered state means that a port is accessible, but Nmap is unable to determine whether it is open or closed. Only the ACK scan, which is used to map firewall rulesets, classifies ports into this state. Scanning unfiltered ports with other scan types such as Window scan, SYN scan, or FIN scan, may help resolve whether the port is open.

open|filtered

Nmap places ports in this state when it is unable to determine whether a port is open or filtered. This occurs for scan types in which open ports give no response. The lack of response could also mean that a packet filter dropped the probe or any response it elicited. So Nmap does not know for sure whether the port is open or being filtered. The UDP, IP protocol, FIN, NULL, and Xmas scans classify ports this way.

closed|filtered

This state is used when Nmap is unable to determine whether a port is closed or filtered. It is only used for the IP ID idle scan.

15.6. Port Scanning Techniques

As a novice performing automotive repair, I can struggle for hours trying to fit my rudimentary tools (hammer, duct tape, wrench, etc.) to the task at hand. When I fail miserably and tow my jalopy to a real mechanic, he invariably fishes around in a huge tool chest until pulling out the perfect gizmo which makes the job seem effortless. The art of port scanning is similar. Experts understand the dozens of scan techniques and choose the appropriate one (or combination) for a given task. Inexperienced users and script kiddies, on the other hand, try to solve every problem with the default SYN scan. Since Nmap is free, the only barrier to port scanning mastery is knowledge. That certainly beats the automotive world, where it may take great skill to determine that you need a strut spring compressor, then you still have to pay thousands of dollars for it.

Most of the scan types are only available to privileged users. This is because they send and receive raw packets, which requires root access on Unix systems. Using an administrator account on Windows is recommended, though Nmap sometimes works for unprivileged users on that platform when WinPcap has already been loaded into the OS. Requiring root privileges was a serious limitation when Nmap was released in 1997, as many users only had access to shared shell accounts. Now, the world is different. Computers are cheaper, far more people have always-on direct Internet access, and desktop Unix systems (including Linux and Mac OS X) are prevalent. A Windows version of Nmap is now available, allowing it to run on even more desktops. For all these reasons, users have less need to run Nmap from limited shared shell accounts. This is fortunate, as the privileged options make Nmap far more powerful and flexible.

While Nmap attempts to produce accurate results, keep in mind that all of its insights are based on packets returned by the target machines (or firewalls in front of them). Such hosts may be untrustworthy and send responses intended to confuse or mislead Nmap. Much more common are non-RFC-compliant hosts that do not respond as they should to Nmap probes. FIN, NULL, and Xmas scans are particularly susceptible to this problem. Such issues are specific to certain scan types and so are discussed in the individual scan type entries.

This section documents the dozen or so port scan techniques supported by Nmap. Only one method may be used at a time, except that UDP scan (-sU) may be combined with any one of the TCP scan types. As a memory aid, port scan type options are of the form -s<C>, where <C> is a prominent character in the scan name, usually the first. The one exception to this is the deprecated FTP bounce scan (-b). By default, Nmap performs a SYN Scan, though it substitutes a connect scan if the user does not have proper privileges to send

---

raw packets (requires root access on Unix) or if IPv6 targets were specified. Of the scans listed in this section, unprivileged users can only execute connect and FTP bounce scans.

-sS (TCP SYN scan)

SYN scan is the default and most popular scan option for good reasons. It can be performed quickly, scanning thousands of ports per second on a fast network not hampered by restrictive firewalls. SYN scan is relatively unobtrusive and stealthy, since it never completes TCP connections. It also works against any compliant TCP stack rather than depending on idiosyncrasies of specific platforms as Nmap's FIN/NULL/Xmas, Maimon and idle scans do. It also allows clear, reliable differentiation between the open, closed, and filtered states.

This technique is often referred to as half-open scanning, because you don't open a full TCP connection. You send a SYN packet, as if you are going to open a real connection and then wait for a response. A SYN/ACK indicates the port is listening (open), while a RST (reset) is indicative of a non-listener. If no response is received after several retransmissions, the port is marked as filtered. The port is also marked filtered if an ICMP unreachable error (type 3, code 1, 2, 3, 9, 10, or 13) is received.

-sT (TCP connect scan)

TCP connect scan is the default TCP scan type when SYN scan is not an option. This is the case when a user does not have raw packet privileges or is scanning IPv6 networks. Instead of writing raw packets as most other scan types do, Nmap asks the underlying operating system to establish a connection with the target machine and port by issuing the connect system call. This is the same high-level system call that web browsers, P2P clients, and most other network-enabled applications use to establish a connection. It is part of a programming interface known as the Berkeley Sockets API. Rather than read raw packet responses off the wire, Nmap uses this API to obtain status information on each connection attempt.

When SYN scan is available, it is usually a better choice. Nmap has less control over the high level connect call than with raw packets, making it less efficient. The system call completes connections to open target ports rather than performing the half-open reset that SYN scan does. Not only does this take longer and require more packets to obtain the same information, but target machines are more likely to log the connection. A decent IDS will catch either, but most machines have no such alarm system. Many services on your average Unix system will add a note to syslog, and sometimes a cryptic error message, when Nmap connects and then closes the connection without sending data. Truly pathetic services crash when this happens, though that is uncommon. An administrator who sees a bunch of connection attempts in her logs from a single system should know that she has been connect scanned.

-sU (UDP scans)

While most popular services on the Internet run over the TCP protocol, UDP services are widely deployed. DNS, SNMP, and DHCP (registered ports 53, 161/162, and 67/68) are three of the most common. Because UDP scanning is generally slower and more difficult than TCP, some security auditors ignore these ports. This is a mistake, as exploitable UDP services are quite common and attackers certainly don't ignore the whole protocol. Fortunately, Nmap can help inventory UDP ports.

UDP scan is activated with the -sU option. It can be combined with a TCP scan type such as SYN scan (-sS) to check both protocols during the same run.

UDP scan works by sending an empty (no data) UDP header to every targeted port. If an ICMP port unreachable error (type 3, code 3) is returned, the port is closed. Other ICMP unreachable errors (type 3, codes 1, 2, 9, 10, or 13) mark the port as filtered. Occasionally, a service will respond with a

UDP packet, proving that it is open. If no response is received after retransmissions, the port is classified as open|filtered. This means that the port could be open, or perhaps packet filters are blocking the communication. Version detection (-sV) can be used to help differentiate the truly open ports from the filtered ones.

A big challenge with UDP scanning is doing it quickly. Open and filtered ports rarely send any response, leaving Nmap to time out and then conduct retransmissions just in case the probe or response were lost. Closed ports are often an even bigger problem. They usually send back an ICMP port unreachable error. But unlike the RST packets sent by closed TCP ports in response to a SYN or connect scan, many hosts rate limit ICMP port unreachable messages by default. Linux and Solaris are particularly strict about this. For example, the Linux 2.4.20 kernel limits destination unreachable messages to one per second (in net/ipv4/icmp.c).

Nmap detects rate limiting and slows down accordingly to avoid flooding the network with useless packets that the target machine will drop. Unfortunately, a Linux-style limit of one packet per second makes a 65,536-port scan take more than 18 hours. Ideas for speeding your UDP scans up include scanning more hosts in parallel, doing a quick scan of just the popular ports first, scanning from behind the firewall, and using --host-timeout to skip slow hosts.

-sN; -sF; -sX (TCP NULL, FIN, and Xmas scans)
   These three scan types (even more are possible with the --scanflags option described in the next section) exploit a subtle loophole in the TCP RFC to differentiate between open and closed ports. Page 65 of RFC 793 says that "if the [destination] port state is CLOSED .... an incoming segment not containing a RST causes a RST to be sent in response." Then the next page discusses packets sent to open ports without the SYN, RST, or ACK bits set, stating that: "you are unlikely to get here, but if you do, drop the segment, and return."

When scanning systems compliant with this RFC text, any packet not containing SYN, RST, or ACK bits will result in a returned RST if the port is closed and no response at all if the port is open. As long as none of those three bits are included, any combination of the other three (FIN, PSH, and URG) are OK. Nmap exploits this with three scan types:

Null scan (-sN)
   Does not set any bits (TCP flag header is 0)

FIN scan (-sF)
   Sets just the TCP FIN bit.

Xmas scan (-sX)
   Sets the FIN, PSH, and URG flags, lighting the packet up like a Christmas tree.

These three scan types are exactly the same in behavior except for the TCP flags set in probe packets. If a RST packet is received, the port is considered closed, while no response means it is open|filtered. The port is marked filtered if an ICMP unreachable error (type 3, code 1, 2, 3, 9, 10, or 13) is received.

The key advantage to these scan types is that they can sneak through certain non-stateful firewalls and packet filtering routers. Another advantage is that these scan types are a little more stealthy than even a SYN scan. Don't count on this though—most modern IDS products can be configured to detect them. The big downside is that not all systems follow RFC 793 to the letter. A number of systems send RST responses to the probes regardless of whether the port is open or not. This causes all of the ports to be labeled `closed`. Major operating systems that do this are Microsoft Windows, many Cisco devices, BSDI, and IBM OS/400. This scan does work against most Unix-based systems though. Another downside of these scans is that they can't distinguish `open` ports from certain `filtered` ones, leaving you with the response `open|filtered`.

-sA (TCP ACK scan)

This scan is different than the others discussed so far in that it never determines `open` (or even `open|filtered`) ports. It is used to map out firewall rulesets, determining whether they are stateful or not and which ports are filtered.

The ACK scan probe packet has only the ACK flag set (unless you use `--scanflags`). When scanning unfiltered systems, `open` and `closed` ports will both return a RST packet. Nmap then labels them as `unfiltered`, meaning that they are reachable by the ACK packet, but whether they are `open` or `closed` is undetermined. Ports that don't respond, or send certain ICMP error messages back (type 3, code 1, 2, 3, 9, 10, or 13), are labeled `filtered`.

-sW (TCP Window scan)

Window scan is exactly the same as ACK scan except that it exploits an implementation detail of certain systems to differentiate open ports from closed ones, rather than always printing `unfiltered` when a RST is returned. It does this by examining the TCP Window field of the RST packets returned. On some systems, open ports use a positive window size (even for RST packets) while closed ones have a zero window. So instead of always listing a port as `unfiltered` when it receives a RST back, Window scan lists the port as `open` or `closed` if the TCP Window value in that reset is positive or zero, respectively.

This scan relies on an implementation detail of a minority of systems out on the Internet, so you can't always trust it. Systems that don't support it will usually return all ports `closed`. Of course, it is possible that the machine really has no open ports. If most scanned ports are `closed` but a few common port numbers (such as 22, 25, 53) are `filtered`, the system is most likely susceptible. Occasionally, systems will even show the exact opposite behavior. If your scan shows 1000 open ports and three closed or filtered ports, then those three may very well be the truly open ones.

-sM (TCP Maimon scan)

The Maimon scan is named after its discoverer, Uriel Maimon. He described the technique in *Phrack* Magazine issue #49 (November 1996). Nmap, which included this technique, was released two issues later. This technique is exactly the same as NULL, FIN, and Xmas scans, except that the probe is FIN/ACK. According to RFC 793 (TCP), a RST packet should be generated in response to such a probe whether the port is open or closed. However, Uriel noticed that many BSD-derived systems simply drop the packet if the port is open.

--scanflags (Custom TCP scan)

Truly advanced Nmap users need not limit themselves to the canned scan types offered. The `--scanflags` option allows you to design your own scan by specifying arbitrary TCP flags. Let your creative juices flow, while evading intrusion detection systems whose vendors simply paged through the Nmap man page adding specific rules!

The `--scanflags` argument can be a numerical flag value such as 9 (PSH and FIN), but using symbolic names is easier. Just mash together any combination of URG, ACK, PSH, RST, SYN, and FIN. For

---

example, --scanflags URGACKPSHRSTSYNFIN sets everything, though it's not very useful for scanning. The order these are specified in is irrelevant.

In addition to specifying the desired flags, you can specify a TCP scan type (such as -sA or -sF). That base type tells Nmap how to interpret responses. For example, a SYN scan considers no-response to indicate a filtered port, while a FIN scan treats the same as open|filtered. Nmap will behave the same way it does for the base scan type, except that it will use the TCP flags you specify instead. If you don't specify a base type, SYN scan is used.

-sI <zombie host>[:<probeport>] (idle scan)

This advanced scan method allows for a truly blind TCP port scan of the target (meaning no packets are sent to the target from your real IP address). Instead, a unique side-channel attack exploits predictable IP fragmentation ID sequence generation on the zombie host to glean information about the open ports on the target. IDS systems will display the scan as coming from the zombie machine you specify (which must be up and meet certain criteria). Full details of this fascinating scan type are in Section 5.10, "TCP Idle Scan (-sI)" [117].

Besides being extraordinarily stealthy (due to its blind nature), this scan type permits mapping out IP-based trust relationships between machines. The port listing shows open ports *from the perspective of the zombie host*. So you can try scanning a target using various zombies that you think might be trusted (via router/packet filter rules).

You can add a colon followed by a port number to the zombie host if you wish to probe a particular port on the zombie for IP ID changes. Otherwise Nmap will use the port it uses by default for TCP pings (80).

-sO (IP protocol scan)

IP protocol scan allows you to determine which IP protocols (TCP, ICMP, IGMP, etc.) are supported by target machines. This isn't technically a port scan, since it cycles through IP protocol numbers rather than TCP or UDP port numbers. Yet it still uses the -p option to select scanned protocol numbers, reports its results within the normal port table format, and even uses the same underlying scan engine as the true port scanning methods. So it is close enough to a port scan that it belongs here.

Besides being useful in its own right, protocol scan demonstrates the power of open-source software. While the fundamental idea is pretty simple, I had not thought to add it nor received any requests for such functionality. Then in the summer of 2000, Gerhard Rieger conceived the idea, wrote an excellent patch implementing it, and sent it to the *nmap-hackers* mailing list. I incorporated that patch into the Nmap tree and released a new version the next day. Few pieces of commercial software have users enthusiastic enough to design and contribute their own improvements!

Protocol scan works in a similar fashion to UDP scan. Instead of iterating through the port number field of a UDP packet, it sends IP packet headers and iterates through the eight-bit IP protocol field. The headers are usually empty, containing no data and not even the proper header for the claimed protocol. The three exceptions are TCP, UDP, and ICMP. A proper protocol header for those is included since some systems won't send them otherwise and because Nmap already has functions to create them. Instead of watching for ICMP port unreachable messages, protocol scan is on the lookout for ICMP *protocol* unreachable messages. If Nmap receives any response in any protocol from the target host, Nmap marks that protocol as open. An ICMP protocol unreachable error (type 3, code 2) causes the protocol to be marked as closed Other ICMP unreachable errors (type 3, code 1, 3, 9, 10, or 13) cause the protocol to be marked `filtered` (though they prove that ICMP is `open` at the same time). If no response is received after retransmissions, the protocol is marked `open|filtered`

`-b <FTP relay host>` (FTP bounce scan)

An interesting feature of the FTP protocol (RFC 959) is support for so-called proxy FTP connections. This allows a user to connect to one FTP server, then ask that files be sent to a third-party server. Such a feature is ripe for abuse on many levels, so most servers have ceased supporting it. One of the abuses this feature allows is causing the FTP server to port scan other hosts. Simply ask the FTP server to send a file to each interesting port of a target host in turn. The error message will describe whether the port is open or not. This is a good way to bypass firewalls because organizational FTP servers are often placed where they have more access to other internal hosts than any old Internet host would. Nmap supports FTP bounce scan with the `-b` option. It takes an argument of the form `<username>:<password>@<server>:<port>`. `<Server>` is the name or IP address of a vulnerable FTP server. As with a normal URL, you may omit `<username>:<password>`, in which case anonymous login credentials (user: `anonymous` password:`-wwwuser@`) are used. The port number (and preceding colon) may be omitted as well, in which case the default FTP port (21) on `<server>` is used.

This vulnerability was widespread in 1997 when Nmap was released, but has largely been fixed. Vulnerable servers are still around, so it is worth trying when all else fails. If bypassing a firewall is your goal, scan the target network for open port 21 (or even for any FTP services if you scan all ports with version detection), then try a bounce scan using each. Nmap will tell you whether the host is vulnerable or not. If you are just trying to cover your tracks, you don't need to (and, in fact, shouldn't) limit yourself to hosts on the target network. Before you go scanning random Internet addresses for vulnerable FTP servers, consider that sysadmins may not appreciate you abusing their servers in this way.

15.7. Port Specification and Scan Order

In addition to all of the scan methods discussed previously, Nmap offers options for specifying which ports are scanned and whether the scan order is randomized or sequential. By default, Nmap scans all ports up to and including 1024 as well as higher numbered ports listed in the `nmap-services` file for the protocol(s) being scanned.

`-p <port ranges>` (Only scan specified ports)

This option specifies which ports you want to scan and overrides the default. Individual port numbers are OK, as are ranges separated by a hyphen (e.g. `1-1023`). The beginning and/or end values of a range may be omitted, causing Nmap to use 1 and 65535, respectively. So you can specify `-p-` to scan ports from 1 through 65535. Scanning port zero is allowed if you specify it explicitly. For IP protocol scanning (`-sO`), this option specifies the protocol numbers you wish to scan for (0-255).

When scanning both TCP and UDP ports, you can specify a particular protocol by preceding the port numbers by `T:` or `U:`. The qualifier lasts until you specify another qualifier. For example, the argument `-p U:53,111,137,T:21-25,80,139,8080` would scan UDP ports 53,111,and 137, as well as the listed TCP ports. Note that to scan both UDP and TCP, you have to specify `-sU` and at least one TCP scan type (such as `-sS`, `-sF`, or `-sT`). If no protocol qualifier is given, the port numbers are added to all protocol lists.

Ports can also be specified by name according to what the port is referred to in the `nmap-services`. You can even use the wildcards * and ? with the names. For example, to scan FTP and all ports whose names begin with "http", use `-p ftp,http*`. Be careful about shell expansions and quote the argument to `-p` if unsure.

Ranges of ports can be surrounded by square brackets to indicate ports inside that range that appear in `nmap-services`. For example, the following will scan all ports in `nmap-services` equal to or below 1024: `-p [-1024]`. Be careful with shell expansions and quote the argument to `-p` if unsure.

`-F` (Fast (limited port) scan)

Specifies that you wish to scan fewer ports than the default. Normally Nmap scans the most common 1,000 ports for each scanned protocol. With `-F`, this is reduced to 100.

Nmap needs an `nmap-services` file with frequency information in order to know which ports are the most common (see Section 14.2, "Well Known Port List: nmap-services" [363] for more about port frequencies). If port frequency information isn't available, perhaps because of the use of a custom `nmap-services` file, `-F` means to scan only ports that are named in the services file (normally Nmap scans all named ports plus ports 1–1024).

`-r` (Don't randomize ports)

By default, Nmap randomizes the scanned port order (except that certain commonly accessible ports are moved near the beginning for efficiency reasons). This randomization is normally desirable, but you can specify `-r` for sequential port scanning instead.

`--port-ratio <decimal number between 0 and 1>`

Scans all ports in `nmap-services` file with a ratio greater than the number specified as the argument. (new format `nmap-services` only.)

`--top-ports <integer of 1 or greater>`

Scans the N highest-ratio ports found in `nmap-services` file. (new format `nmap-services` only.)

15.8. Service and Version Detection

Point Nmap at a remote machine and it might tell you that ports `25/tcp`, `80/tcp`, and `53/udp` are open. Using its `nmap-services` database of about 2,200 well-known services, Nmap would report that those ports probably correspond to a mail server (SMTP), web server (HTTP), and name server (DNS) respectively. This lookup is usually accurate—the vast majority of daemons listening on TCP port 25 are, in fact, mail servers. However, you should not bet your security on this! People can and do run services on strange ports.

Even if Nmap is right, and the hypothetical server above is running SMTP, HTTP, and DNS servers, that is not a lot of information. When doing vulnerability assessments (or even simple network inventories) of your companies or clients, you really want to know which mail and DNS servers and versions are running. Having an accurate version number helps dramatically in determining which exploits a server is vulnerable to. Version detection helps you obtain this information.

After TCP and/or UDP ports are discovered using one of the other scan methods, version detection interrogates those ports to determine more about what is actually running. The `nmap-service-probes` database

---

contains probes for querying various services and match expressions to recognize and parse responses. Nmap tries to determine the service protocol (e.g. FTP, SSH, Telnet, HTTP), the application name (e.g. ISC BIND, Apache httpd, Solaris telnetd), the version number, hostname, device type (e.g. printer, router), the OS family (e.g. Windows, Linux) and sometimes miscellaneous details like whether an X server is open to connections, the SSH protocol version, or the KaZaA user name). Of course, most services don't provide all of this information. If Nmap was compiled with OpenSSL support, it will connect to SSL servers to deduce the service listening behind that encryption layer. When RPC services are discovered, the Nmap RPC grinder (`-sR`) is automatically used to determine the RPC program and version numbers. Some UDP ports are left in the `open|filtered` state after a UDP port scan is unable to determine whether the port is open or filtered. Version detection will try to elicit a response from these ports (just as it does with open ports), and change the state to open if it succeeds. `open|filtered` TCP ports are treated the same way. Note that the Nmap `-A` option enables version detection among other things. Version detection is described in detail in Chapter 7, *Service and Application Version Detection* [145].

When Nmap receives responses from a service but cannot match them to its database, it prints out a special fingerprint and a URL for you to submit if to if you know for sure what is running on the port. Please take a couple minutes to make the submission so that your find can benefit everyone. Thanks to these submissions, Nmap has about 3,000 pattern matches for more than 350 protocols such as SMTP, FTP, HTTP, etc.

Version detection is enabled and controlled with the following options:

`-sV` (Version detection)

    Enables version detection, as discussed above. Alternatively, you can use `-A`, which enables version detection among other things.

`--allports` (Don't exclude any ports from version detection)

    By default, Nmap version detection skips TCP port 9100 because some printers simply print anything sent to that port, leading to dozens of pages of HTTP GET requests, binary SSL session requests, etc. This behavior can be changed by modifying or removing the `Exclude` directive in `nmap-service-probes`, or you can specify `--allports` to scan all ports regardless of any `Exclude` directive.

`--version-intensity <intensity>` (Set version scan intensity)

    When performing a version scan (`-sV`), Nmap sends a series of probes, each of which is assigned a rarity value between one and nine. The lower-numbered probes are effective against a wide variety of common services, while the higher numbered ones are rarely useful. The intensity level specifies which probes should be applied. The higher the number, the more likely it is the service will be correctly identified. However, high intensity scans take longer. The intensity must be between 0 and 9. The default is 7. When a probe is registered to the target port via the `nmap-service-probes ports` directive, that probe is tried regardless of intensity level. This ensures that the DNS probes will always be attempted against any open port 53, the SSL probe will be done against 443, etc.

`--version-light` (Enable light mode)

    This is a convenience alias for `--version-intensity 2`. This light mode makes version scanning much faster, but it is slightly less likely to identify services.

`--version-all` (Try every single probe)

    An alias for `--version-intensity 9`, ensuring that every single probe is attempted against each port.

`--version-trace` (Trace version scan activity)

This causes Nmap to print out extensive debugging info about what version scanning is doing. It is a subset of what you get with `--packet-trace`.

`-sR` (RPC scan)

This method works in conjunction with the various port scan methods of Nmap. It takes all the TCP/UDP ports found open and floods them with SunRPC program NULL commands in an attempt to determine whether they are RPC ports, and if so, what program and version number they serve up. Thus you can effectively obtain the same info as **rpcinfo -p** even if the target's portmapper is behind a firewall (or protected by TCP wrappers). Decoys do not currently work with RPC scan. This is automatically enabled as part of version scan (`-sV`) if you request that. As version detection includes this and is much more comprehensive, `-sR` is rarely needed.

15.9. OS Detection

One of Nmap's best-known features is remote OS detection using TCP/IP stack fingerprinting. Nmap sends a series of TCP and UDP packets to the remote host and examines practically every bit in the responses. After performing dozens of tests such as TCP ISN sampling, TCP options support and ordering, IP ID sampling, and the initial window size check, Nmap compares the results to its `nmap-os-db` database of more than a thousand known OS fingerprints and prints out the OS details if there is a match. Each fingerprint includes a freeform textual description of the OS, and a classification which provides the vendor name (e.g. Sun), underlying OS (e.g. Solaris), OS generation (e.g. 10), and device type (general purpose, router, switch, game console, etc).

If Nmap is unable to guess the OS of a machine, and conditions are good (e.g. at least one open port and one closed port were found), Nmap will provide a URL you can use to submit the fingerprint if you know (for sure) the OS running on the machine. By doing this you contribute to the pool of operating systems known to Nmap and thus it will be more accurate for everyone.

OS detection enables some other tests which make use of information that is gathered during the process anyway. One of these is TCP Sequence Predictability Classification. This measures approximately how hard it is to establish a forged TCP connection against the remote host. It is useful for exploiting source-IP based trust relationships (rlogin, firewall filters, etc) or for hiding the source of an attack. This sort of spoofing is rarely performed any more, but many machines are still vulnerable to it. The actual difficulty number is based on statistical sampling and may fluctuate. It is generally better to use the English classification such as "worthy challenge" or "trivial joke". This is only reported in normal output in verbose (`-v`) mode. When verbose mode is enabled along with `-O`, IP ID sequence generation is also reported. Most machines are in the "incremental" class, which means that they increment the ID field in the IP header for each packet they send. This makes them vulnerable to several advanced information gathering and spoofing attacks.

Another bit of extra information enabled by OS detection is a guess at a target's uptime. This uses the TCP timestamp option (RFC 1323) to guess when a machine was last rebooted. The guess can be inaccurate due to the timestamp counter not being initialized to zero or the counter overflowing and wrapping around, so it is printed only in verbose mode.

OS detection is covered in Chapter 8, *Remote OS Detection* [171].

OS detection is enabled and controlled with the following options:

-O (Enable OS detection)

Enables OS detection, as discussed above. Alternatively, you can use -A to enable OS detection along with other things.

--osscan-limit (Limit OS detection to promising targets)

OS detection is far more effective if at least one open and one closed TCP port are found. Set this option and Nmap will not even try OS detection against hosts that do not meet this criteria. This can save substantial time, particularly on -PN scans against many hosts. It only matters when OS detection is requested with -O or -A.

--osscan-guess; --fuzzy (Guess OS detection results)

When Nmap is unable to detect a perfect OS match, it sometimes offers up near-matches as possibilities. The match has to be very close for Nmap to do this by default. Either of these (equivalent) options make Nmap guess more aggressively. Nmap will still tell you when an imperfect match is printed and display its confidence level (percentage) for each guess.

--max-os-tries (Set the maximum number of OS detection tries against a target)

When Nmap performs OS detection against a target and fails to find a perfect match, it usually repeats the attempt. By default, Nmap tries five times if conditions are favorable for OS fingerprint submission, and twice when conditions aren't so good. Specifying a lower --max-os-tries value (such as 1) speeds Nmap up, though you miss out on retries which could potentially identify the OS. Alternatively, a high value may be set to allow even more retries when conditions are favorable. This is rarely done, except to generate better fingerprints for submission and integration into the Nmap OS database.

15.10. Nmap Scripting Engine (NSE)

The Nmap Scripting Engine (NSE) is one of Nmap's most powerful and flexible features. It allows users to write (and share) simple scripts (using the Lua programming language[1],) to automate a wide variety of networking tasks. Those scripts are executed in parallel with the speed and efficiency you expect from Nmap. Users can rely on the growing and diverse set of scripts distributed with Nmap, or write their own to meet custom needs.

Tasks we had in mind when creating the system include network discovery, more sophisticated version detection, vulnerability detection. NSE can even be used for vulnerability exploitation.

To reflect those different uses and to simplify the choice of which scripts to run, each script contains a field associating it with one or more categories. Currently defined categories are safe, intrusive, malware, version, discovery, vuln, auth, and default. These are all described in Section 9.2.1, "Script Categories" [207].

The Nmap Scripting Engine is described in detail in Chapter 9, *Nmap Scripting Engine* [205] and is controlled by the following options:

-sC

Performs a script scan using the default set of scripts. It is equivalent to --script=default. Some of the scripts in this category are considered intrusive and should not be run against a target network without permission.

---

[1] *http://lua.org*

`--script` `<script-categories>`|`<directory>`|`<filename>`|`all`

Runs a script scan (like `-sC`) using the comma-separated list of script categories, individual scripts, or directories containing scripts, rather than the default set. Nmap first tries to interpret the arguments as categories, then (if that fails) as files or directories. A script or directory of scripts may be specified as an absolute or relative path. Absolute paths are used as supplied. Relative paths are searched for in the following places until found: `--datadir/`; `$NMAPDIR/`; `~/.nmap/` (not searched on Windows); NMAPDATADIR/ or `./`. A `scripts/` subdirectory is also tried in each of these.

If a directory is specified and found, Nmap loads all NSE scripts (any filenames ending with `.nse`) from that directory. Filenames without the `nse` extension are ignored. Nmap does not search recursively into subdirectories to find scripts. If individual file names are specified, the file extension does not have to be `nse`.

Nmap scripts are stored in a `scripts` subdirectory of the Nmap data directory by default (see Chapter 14, *Understanding and Customizing Nmap Data Files* [363]). For efficiency, scripts are indexed in a database stored in `scripts/script.db`. which lists the category or categories in which each script belongs. Give the argument `all` to execute all scripts in the Nmap script database.

Malicious scripts are not run in a sandbox and thus could damage your system or invade your privacy. Never run scripts from third parties unless you trust the authors or have carefully audited the scripts yourself.

`--script-args` `<name1>=<value1>,<name2>={<name3>=<value3>},<name4>=<value4>`

Lets you provide arguments to NSE scripts. Arguments are passed as `name=value` pairs. The provided argument is processed and stored inside a Lua table, to which all scripts have access. The names are taken as strings (which must be alphanumeric values) and used as keys inside the `argument-table`. Values are either strings or tables themselves (surrounded by '`{`' and '`}`'). For example, you could pass the comma-separated arguments: `user=bar,pass=foo,whois={whodb=nofollow+ripe}`. String arguments are potentially used by several scripts; subtables are normally used by only one script. In scripts that take a subtable, the subtable is usually named after the script (like `whois` in this example).

`--script-trace`

This option does what `--packet-trace` does, just one ISO layer higher. If this option is specified all incoming and outgoing communication performed by a script is printed. The displayed information includes the communication protocol, the source, the target and the transmitted data. If more than 5% of all transmitted data is not printable, then the trace output is in a hex dump format. Specifying `--packet-trace` enables script tracing too.

`--script-updatedb`

This option updates the script database found in `scripts/script.db` which is used by Nmap to determine the available default scripts and categories. It is only necessary to update the database if you have added or removed NSE scripts from the default `scripts` directory or if you have changed the categories of any script. This option is generally used by itself: **nmap --script-updatedb**.

15.11. Timing and Performance

One of my highest Nmap development priorities has always been performance. A default scan (**nmap <hostname>**) of a host on my local network takes a fifth of a second. That is barely enough time to blink, but adds up when you are scanning hundreds or thousands of hosts. Moreover, certain scan options such as UDP scanning and version detection can increase scan times substantially. So can certain firewall configurations, particularly response rate limiting. While Nmap utilizes parallelism and many advanced algorithms to accelerate these scans, the user has ultimate control over how Nmap runs. Expert users carefully craft Nmap commands to obtain only the information they care about while meeting their time constraints.

Techniques for improving scan times include omitting non-critical tests, and upgrading to the latest version of Nmap (performance enhancements are made frequently). Optimizing timing parameters can also make a substantial difference. Those options are listed below.

Some options accept a `time` parameter. This is specified in milliseconds by default, though you can append 's', 'm', or 'h' to the value to specify seconds, minutes, or hours. So the `--host-timeout` arguments `900000`, `900s`, and `15m` all do the same thing.

`--min-hostgroup` *<numhosts>*; `--max-hostgroup` *<numhosts>* (Adjust parallel scan group sizes)

> Nmap has the ability to port scan or version scan multiple hosts in parallel. Nmap does this by dividing the target IP space into groups and then scanning one group at a time. In general, larger groups are more efficient. The downside is that host results can't be provided until the whole group is finished. So if Nmap started out with a group size of 50, the user would not receive any reports (except for the updates offered in verbose mode) until the first 50 hosts are completed.

> By default, Nmap takes a compromise approach to this conflict. It starts out with a group size as low as five so the first results come quickly and then increases the groupsize to as high as 1024. The exact default numbers depend on the options given. For efficiency reasons, Nmap uses larger group sizes for UDP or few-port TCP scans.

> When a maximum group size is specified with `--max-hostgroup`, Nmap will never exceed that size. Specify a minimum size with `--min-hostgroup` and Nmap will try to keep group sizes above that level. Nmap may have to use smaller groups than you specify if there are not enough target hosts left on a given interface to fulfill the specified minimum. Both may be set to keep the group size within a specific range, though this is rarely desired.

> These options do not have an effect during the host discovery phase of a scan. This includes plain ping scans (`-sP`). Host discovery always works in large groups of hosts to improve speed and accuracy.

> The primary use of these options is to specify a large minimum group size so that the full scan runs more quickly. A common choice is 256 to scan a network in Class C sized chunks. For a scan with many ports, exceeding that number is unlikely to help much. For scans of just a few port numbers, host group sizes of 2048 or more may be helpful.

`--min-parallelism` *<numprobes>*; `--max-parallelism` *<numprobes>* (Adjust probe parallelization)

> These options control the total number of probes that may be outstanding for a host group. They are used for port scanning and host discovery. By default, Nmap calculates an ever-changing ideal parallelism based on network performance. If packets are being dropped, Nmap slows down and allows fewer outstanding probes. The ideal probe number slowly rises as the network proves itself worthy. These options place minimum or maximum bounds on that variable. By default, the ideal parallelism can drop to one if the network proves unreliable and rise to several hundred in perfect conditions.

The most common usage is to set `--min-parallelism` to a number higher than one to speed up scans of poorly performing hosts or networks. This is a risky option to play with, as setting it too high may affect accuracy. Setting this also reduces Nmap's ability to control parallelism dynamically based on network conditions. A value of ten might be reasonable, though I only adjust this value as a last resort.

The `--max-parallelism` option is sometimes set to one to prevent Nmap from sending more than one probe at a time to hosts. This can be useful in combination with `--scan-delay` (discussed later), although the latter usually serves the purpose well enough by itself.

`--min-rtt-timeout` `<time>`, `--max-rtt-timeout` `<time>`, `--initial-rtt-timeout` `<time>` (Adjust probe timeouts)

Nmap maintains a running timeout value for determining how long it will wait for a probe response before giving up or retransmitting the probe. This is calculated based on the response times of previous probes. The exact formula is given in Section 5.13, "Scan Code and Algorithms" [128]. If the network latency shows itself to be significant and variable, this timeout can grow to several seconds. It also starts at a conservative (high) level and may stay that way for a while when Nmap scans unresponsive hosts.

Specifying a lower `--max-rtt-timeout` and `--initial-rtt-timeout` than the defaults can cut scan times significantly. This is particularly true for pingless (-PN) scans, and those against heavily filtered networks. Don't get too aggressive though. The scan can end up taking longer if you specify such a low value that many probes are timing out and retransmitting while the response is in transit.

If all the hosts are on a local network, 100 milliseconds is a reasonable aggressive `--max-rtt-timeout` value. If routing is involved, ping a host on the network first with the ICMP ping utility, or with a custom packet crafter such as **hping2** that is more likely to get through a firewall. Look at the maximum round trip time out of ten packets or so. You might want to double that for the `--initial-rtt-timeout` and triple or quadruple it for the `--max-rtt-timeout`. I generally do not set the maximum RTT below 100 ms, no matter what the ping times are. Nor do I exceed 1000 ms.

`--min-rtt-timeout` is a rarely used option that could be useful when a network is so unreliable that even Nmap's default is too aggressive. Since Nmap only reduces the timeout down to the minimum when the network seems to be reliable, this need is unusual and should be reported as a bug to the *nmap-dev* mailing list.

`--max-retries` `<numtries>` (Specify the maximum number of port scan probe retransmissions)

When Nmap receives no response to a port scan probe, it could mean the port is filtered. Or maybe the probe or response was simply lost on the network. It is also possible that the target host has rate limiting enabled that temporarily blocked the response. So Nmap tries again by retransmitting the initial probe. If Nmap detects poor network reliability, it may try many more times before giving up on a port. While this benefits accuracy, it also lengthen scan times. When performance is critical, scans may be sped up by limiting the number of retransmissions allowed. You can even specify `--max-retries` `0` to prevent any retransmissions, though that is only recommended for situations such as informal surveys where occasional missed ports and hosts are acceptable.

The default (with no -T template) is to allow ten retransmissions. If a network seems reliable and the target hosts aren't rate limiting, Nmap usually only does one retransmission. So most target scans aren't even affected by dropping `--max-retries` to a low value such as three. Such values can substantially speed scans of slow (rate limited) hosts. You usually lose some information when Nmap gives up on ports early, though that may be preferable to letting the `--host-timeout` expire and losing all information about the target.

`--host-timeout <time>` (Give up on slow target hosts)

Some hosts simply take a *long* time to scan. This may be due to poorly performing or unreliable networking hardware or software, packet rate limiting, or a restrictive firewall. The slowest few percent of the scanned hosts can eat up a majority of the scan time. Sometimes it is best to cut your losses and skip those hosts initially. Specify `--host-timeout` with the maximum amount of time you are willing to wait. For example, specify `30m` to ensure that Nmap doesn't waste more than half an hour on a single host. Note that Nmap may be scanning other hosts at the same time during that half an hour, so it isn't a complete loss. A host that times out is skipped. No port table, OS detection, or version detection results are printed for that host.

`--scan-delay <time>`; `--max-scan-delay <time>` (Adjust delay between probes)

This option causes Nmap to wait at least the given amount of time between each probe it sends to a given host. This is particularly useful in the case of rate limiting. Solaris machines (among many others) will usually respond to UDP scan probe packets with only one ICMP message per second. Any more than that sent by Nmap will be wasteful. A `--scan-delay` of `1s` will keep Nmap at that slow rate. Nmap tries to detect rate limiting and adjust the scan delay accordingly, but it doesn't hurt to specify it explicitly if you already know what rate works best.

When Nmap adjusts the scan delay upward to cope with rate limiting, the scan slows down dramatically. The `--max-scan-delay` option specifies the largest delay that Nmap will allow. A low `--max-scan-delay` can speed up Nmap, but it is risky. Setting this value too low can lead to wasteful packet retransmissions and possible missed ports when the target implements strict rate limiting.

Another use of `--scan-delay` is to evade threshold based intrusion detection and prevention systems (IDS/IPS). This technique is used in the section called "A practical example: bypassing default Snort 2.2.0 rules" [280] to defeat the default port scan detector in Snort IDS. Most other intrusion detection systems can be defeated in the same way.

`--min-rate <number>`; `--max-rate <number>` (Directly control the scanning rate)

Nmap's dynamic timing does a good job of finding an appropriate speed at which to scan. Sometimes, however, you may happen to know an appropriate scanning rate for a network, or you may have to guarantee that a scan will be finished by a certain time. Or perhaps you must keep Nmap from scanning too quickly. The `--min-rate` and `--max-rate` options are designed for these situations.

When the `--min-rate` option is given Nmap will do its best to send packets as fast as or faster than the given rate. The argument is a positive real number representing a packet rate in packets per second. For example, specifying `--min-rate 300` means that Nmap will try to keep the sending rate at or above 300 packets per second. Specifying a minimum rate does not keep Nmap from going faster if conditions warrant.

Likewise, `--max-rate` limits a scan's sending rate to a given maximum. Use `--max-rate 100`, for example, to limit sending to 100 packets per second on a fast network. Use `--max-rate 0.1` for a slow scan of one packet every ten seconds. Use `--min-rate` and `--max-rate` together to keep the rate inside a certain range.

These two options are global, affecting an entire scan, not individual hosts. They only affect port scans and host discovery scans. Other features like OS detection implement their own timing.

There are two conditions when the actual scanning rate may fall below the requested minimum. The first is if the minimum is faster than the fastest rate at which Nmap can send, which is dependent on hardware. In this case Nmap will simply send packets as fast as possible, but be aware that such high rates are likely to cause a loss of accuracy. The second case is when Nmap has nothing to send, for example at the end of a scan when the last probes have been sent and Nmap is waiting for them to time out or be responded to. It's normal to see the scanning rate drop at the end of a scan or in between hostgroups. The sending rate may temporarily exceed the maximum to make up for unpredictable delays, but on average the rate will stay at or below the maximum.

Specifying a minimum rate should be done with care. Scanning faster than a network can support may lead to a loss of accuracy. In some cases, using a faster rate can make a scan take *longer* than it would with a slower rate. This is because Nmap's adaptive retransmission algorithms will detect the network congestion caused by an excessive scanning rate and increase the number of retransmissions in order to improve accuracy. So even though packets are sent at a higher rate, more packets are sent overall. Cap the number of retransmissions with the `--max-retries` option if you need to set an upper limit on total scan time.

`--defeat-rst-ratelimit`

Many hosts have long used rate limiting to reduce the number of ICMP error messages (such as port-unreachable errors) they send. Some systems now apply similar rate limits to the RST (reset) packets they generate. This can slow Nmap down dramatically as it adjusts its timing to reflect those rate limits. You can tell Nmap to ignore those rate limits (for port scans such as SYN scan which *don't* treat non-responsive ports as `open`) by specifying `--defeat-rst-ratelimit`.

Using this option can reduce accuracy, as some ports will appear non-responsive because Nmap didn't wait long enough for a rate-limited RST response. With a SYN scan, the non-response results in the port being labeled `filtered` rather than the `closed` state we see when RST packets are received. This optional is useful when you only care about open ports, and distinguishing between `closed` and `filtered` ports isn't worth the extra time.

`-T paranoid|sneaky|polite|normal|aggressive|insane` (Set a timing template)

While the fine-grained timing controls discussed in the previous section are powerful and effective, some people find them confusing. Moreover, choosing the appropriate values can sometimes take more time than the scan you are trying to optimize. So Nmap offers a simpler approach, with six timing templates. You can specify them with the `-T` option and their number (0–5) or their name. The template names are `paranoid` (0), `sneaky` (1), `polite` (2), `normal` (3), `aggressive` (4), and `insane` (5). The first two are for IDS evasion. Polite mode slows down the scan to use less bandwidth and target machine resources. Normal mode is the default and so `-T3` does nothing. Aggressive mode speeds scans up by making the assumption that you are on a reasonably fast and reliable network. Finally insane mode assumes that you are on an extraordinarily fast network or are willing to sacrifice some accuracy for speed.

These templates allow the user to specify how aggressive they wish to be, while leaving Nmap to pick the exact timing values. The templates also make some minor speed adjustments for which fine-grained control options do not currently exist. For example, `-T4` prohibits the dynamic scan delay from exceeding 10 ms for TCP ports and `-T5` caps that value at 5 ms. Templates can be used in combination with fine-grained controls, and the fine-grained controls will you specify will take precedence over the timing template default for that parameter. I recommend using `-T4` when scanning reasonably modern and

---

reliable networks. Keep that option even when you add fine-grained controls so that you benefit from those extra minor optimizations that it enables.

If you are on a decent broadband or ethernet connection, I would recommend always using -T4. Some people love -T5 though it is too aggressive for my taste. People sometimes specify -T2 because they think it is less likely to crash hosts or because they consider themselves to be polite in general. They often don't realize just how slow -T polite really is. Their scan may take ten times longer than a default scan. Machine crashes and bandwidth problems are rare with the default timing options (-T3) and so I normally recommend that for cautious scanners. Omitting version detection is far more effective than playing with timing values at reducing these problems.

While -T0 and -T1 may be useful for avoiding IDS alerts, they will take an extraordinarily long time to scan thousands of machines or ports. For such a long scan, you may prefer to set the exact timing values you need rather than rely on the canned -T0 and -T1 values.

The main effects of T0 are serializing the scan so only one port is scanned at a time, and waiting five minutes between sending each probe. T1 and T2 are similar but they only wait 15 seconds and 0.4 seconds, respectively, between probes. T3 is Nmap's default behavior, which includes parallelization. -T4 does the equivalent of --max-rtt-timeout 1250 --initial-rtt-timeout 500 --max-retries 6 and sets the maximum TCP scan delay to 10 milliseconds. T5 does the equivalent of --max-rtt-timeout 300 --min-rtt-timeout 50 --initial-rtt-timeout 250 --max-retries 2 --host-timeout 15m as well as setting the maximum TCP scan delay to 5 ms.

15.12. Firewall/IDS Evasion and Spoofing

Many Internet pioneers envisioned a global open network with a universal IP address space allowing virtual connections between any two nodes. This allows hosts to act as true peers, serving and retrieving information from each other. People could access all of their home systems from work, changing the climate control settings or unlocking the doors for early guests. This vision of universal connectivity has been stifled by address space shortages and security concerns. In the early 1990s, organizations began deploying firewalls for the express purpose of reducing connectivity. Huge networks were cordoned off from the unfiltered Internet by application proxies, network address translation, and packet filters. The unrestricted flow of information gave way to tight regulation of approved communication channels and the content that passes over them.

Network obstructions such as firewalls can make mapping a network exceedingly difficult. It will not get any easier, as stifling casual reconnaissance is often a key goal of implementing the devices. Nevertheless, Nmap offers many features to help understand these complex networks, and to verify that filters are working as intended. It even supports mechanisms for bypassing poorly implemented defenses. One of the best methods of understanding your network security posture is to try to defeat it. Place yourself in the mind-set of an attacker, and deploy techniques from this section against your networks. Launch an FTP bounce scan, idle scan, fragmentation attack, or try to tunnel through one of your own proxies.

In addition to restricting network activity, companies are increasingly monitoring traffic with intrusion detection systems (IDS). All of the major IDSs ship with rules designed to detect Nmap scans because scans are sometimes a precursor to attacks. Many of these products have recently morphed into intrusion *prevention* systems (IPS) that actively block traffic deemed malicious. Unfortunately for network administrators and

IDS vendors, reliably detecting bad intentions by analyzing packet data is a tough problem. Attackers with patience, skill, and the help of certain Nmap options can usually pass by IDSs undetected. Meanwhile, administrators must cope with large numbers of false positive results where innocent activity is misdiagnosed and alerted on or blocked.

Occasionally people suggest that Nmap should not offer features for evading firewall rules or sneaking past IDSs. They argue that these features are just as likely to be misused by attackers as used by administrators to enhance security. The problem with this logic is that these methods would still be used by attackers, who would just find other tools or patch the functionality into Nmap. Meanwhile, administrators would find it that much harder to do their jobs. Deploying only modern, patched FTP servers is a far more powerful defense than trying to prevent the distribution of tools implementing the FTP bounce attack.

There is no magic bullet (or Nmap option) for detecting and subverting firewalls and IDS systems. It takes skill and experience. A tutorial is beyond the scope of this reference guide, which only lists the relevant options and describes what they do.

-f (fragment packets); --mtu (using the specified MTU)
> The -f option causes the requested scan (including ping scans) to use tiny fragmented IP packets. The idea is to split up the TCP header over several packets to make it harder for packet filters, intrusion detection systems, and other annoyances to detect what you are doing. Be careful with this! Some programs have trouble handling these tiny packets. The old-school sniffer named Sniffit segmentation faulted immediately upon receiving the first fragment. Specify this option once, and Nmap splits the packets into eight bytes or less after the IP header. So a 20-byte TCP header would be split into three packets. Two with eight bytes of the TCP header, and one with the final four. Of course each fragment also has an IP header. Specify -f again to use 16 bytes per fragment (reducing the number of fragments). Or you can specify your own offset size with the --mtu option. Don't also specify -f if you use --mtu. The offset must be a multiple of eight. While fragmented packets won't get by packet filters and firewalls that queue all IP fragments, such as the CONFIG_IP_ALWAYS_DEFRAG option in the Linux kernel, some networks can't afford the performance hit this causes and thus leave it disabled. Others can't enable this because fragments may take different routes into their networks. Some source systems defragment outgoing packets in the kernel. Linux with the iptables connection tracking module is one such example. Do a scan while a sniffer such as Wireshark is running to ensure that sent packets are fragmented. If your host OS is causing problems, try the --send-eth option to bypass the IP layer and send raw ethernet frames.

> Fragmentation is only supported for Nmap's raw packet features, which includes TCP and UDP port scans (except connect scan and FTP bounce scan) and OS detection. Features such as version detection and the Nmap Scripting Engine generally don't support fragmentation because they rely on your host's TCP stack to communicate with target services.

-D <decoy1>[,<decoy2>][,ME][,...] (Cloak a scan with decoys)
> Causes a decoy scan to be performed, which makes it appear to the remote host that the host(s) you specify as decoys are scanning the target network too. Thus their IDS might report 5–10 port scans from unique IP addresses, but they won't know which IP was scanning them and which were innocent decoys. While this can be defeated through router path tracing, response-dropping, and other active mechanisms, it is generally an effective technique for hiding your IP address.

> Separate each decoy host with commas, and you can optionally use ME as one of the decoys to represent the position for your real IP address. If you put ME in the sixth position or later, some common port scan

detectors (such as Solar Designer's excellent Scanlogd) are unlikely to show your IP address at all. If you don't use ME, Nmap will put you in a random position. You can also use RND to generate a random, non-reserved IP address, or RND:<number> to generate <number> addresses.

Note that the hosts you use as decoys should be up or you might accidentally SYN flood your targets. Also it will be pretty easy to determine which host is scanning if only one is actually up on the network. You might want to use IP addresses instead of names (so the decoy networks don't see you in their nameserver logs).

Decoys are used both in the initial ping scan (using ICMP, SYN, ACK, or whatever) and during the actual port scanning phase. Decoys are also used during remote OS detection (-O). Decoys do not work with version detection or TCP connect scan. When a scan delay is in effect, the delay is enforced between each batch of spoofed probes, not between each individual probe. Because decoys are sent as a batch all at once, they may temporarily violate congestion control limits.

It is worth noting that using too many decoys may slow your scan and potentially even make it less accurate. Also, some ISPs will filter out your spoofed packets, but many do not restrict spoofed IP packets at all.

-S <IP_Address> (Spoof source address)
In some circumstances, Nmap may not be able to determine your source address (Nmap will tell you if this is the case). In this situation, use -S with the IP address of the interface you wish to send packets through.

Another possible use of this flag is to spoof the scan to make the targets think that *someone else* is scanning them. Imagine a company being repeatedly port scanned by a competitor! The -e option and -PN are generally required for this sort of usage. Note that you usually won't receive reply packets back (they will be addressed to the IP you are spoofing), so Nmap won't produce useful reports.

-e <interface> (Use specified interface)
Tells Nmap what interface to send and receive packets on. Nmap should be able to detect this automatically, but it will tell you if it cannot.

--source-port <portnumber>; -g <portnumber> (Spoof source port number)
One surprisingly common misconfiguration is to trust traffic based only on the source port number. It is easy to understand how this comes about. An administrator will set up a shiny new firewall, only to be flooded with complains from ungrateful users whose applications stopped working. In particular, DNS may be broken because the UDP DNS replies from external servers can no longer enter the network. FTP is another common example. In active FTP transfers, the remote server tries to establish a connection back to the client to transfer the requested file.

Secure solutions to these problems exist, often in the form of application-level proxies or protocol-parsing firewall modules. Unfortunately there are also easier, insecure solutions. Noting that DNS replies come from port 53 and active FTP from port 20, many administrators have fallen into the trap of simply allowing incoming traffic from those ports. They often assume that no attacker would notice and exploit such firewall holes. In other cases, administrators consider this a short-term stop-gap measure until they can implement a more secure solution. Then they forget the security upgrade.

Overworked network administrators are not the only ones to fall into this trap. Numerous products have shipped with these insecure rules. Even Microsoft has been guilty. The IPsec filters that shipped with

Windows 2000 and Windows XP contain an implicit rule that allows all TCP or UDP traffic from port 88 (Kerberos). In another well-known case, versions of the Zone Alarm personal firewall up to 2.1.25 allowed any incoming UDP packets with the source port 53 (DNS) or 67 (DHCP).

Nmap offers the `-g` and `--source-port` options (they are equivalent) to exploit these weaknesses. Simply provide a port number and Nmap will send packets from that port where possible. Nmap must use different port numbers for certain OS detection tests to work properly, and DNS requests ignore the `--source-port` flag because Nmap relies on system libraries to handle those. Most TCP scans, including SYN scan, support the option completely, as does UDP scan.

`--data-length <number>` (Append random data to sent packets)

Normally Nmap sends minimalist packets containing only a header. So its TCP packets are generally 40 bytes and ICMP echo requests are just 28. This option tells Nmap to append the given number of random bytes to most of the packets it sends. OS detection (`-O`) packets are not affected because accuracy there requires probe consistency, but most pinging and portscan packets support this. It slows things down a little, but can make a scan slightly less conspicuous.

`--ip-options <S|R [route]|L [route]|T|U ... >`; `--ip-options <hex string>` (Send packets with specified ip options)

The IP protocol offers several options which may be placed in packet headers. Unlike the ubiquitous TCP options, IP options are rarely seen due to practicality and security concerns. In fact, many Internet routers block the most dangerous options such as source routing. Yet options can still be useful in some cases for determining and manipulating the network route to target machines. For example, you may be able to use the record route option to determine a path to a target even when more traditional traceroute-style approaches fail. Or if your packets are being dropped by a certain firewall, you may be able to specify a different route with the strict or loose source routing options.

The most powerful way to specify IP options is to simply pass in values as the argument to `--ip-options`. Precede each hex number with `\x` then the two digits. You may repeat certain characters by following them with an asterisk and then the number of times you wish them to repeat. For example, `\x01\x07\x04\x00*36\x01` is a hex string containing 36 NUL bytes.

Nmap also offers a shortcut mechanism for specifying options. Simply pass the letter `R`, `T`, or `U` to request record-route, record-timestamp, or both options together, respectively. Loose or strict source routing may be specified with an `L` or `S` followed by a space and then a space-separated list of IP addresses.

If you wish to see the options in packets sent and received, specify `--packet-trace`. For more information and examples of using IP options with Nmap, see *http://seclists.org/nmap-dev/2006/q3/0052.html*.

`--ttl <value>` (Set IP time-to-live field)

Sets the IPv4 time-to-live field in sent packets to the given value.

`--randomize-hosts` (Randomize target host order)

Tells Nmap to shuffle each group of up to 16384 hosts before it scans them. This can make the scans less obvious to various network monitoring systems, especially when you combine it with slow timing options. If you want to randomize over larger group sizes, increase `PING_GROUP_SZ` in `nmap.h` and recompile. An alternative solution is to generate the target IP list with a list scan (`-sL -n -oN <filename>`), randomize it with a Perl script, then provide the whole list to Nmap with `-iL`.

`--spoof-mac <MAC address, prefix, or vendor name>` (Spoof MAC address)

Asks Nmap to use the given MAC address for all of the raw ethernet frames it sends. This option implies `--send-eth` to ensure that Nmap actually sends ethernet-level packets. The MAC given can take several formats. If it is simply the number 0, Nmap chooses a completely random MAC address for the session. If the given string is an even number of hex digits (with the pairs optionally separated by a colon), Nmap will use those as the MAC. If fewer than 12 hex digits are provided, Nmap fills in the remainder of the six bytes with random values. If the argument isn't a zero or hex string, Nmap looks through `nmap-mac-prefixes` to find a vendor name containing the given string (it is case insensitive). If a match is found, Nmap uses the vendor's OUI (three-byte prefix) and fills out the remaining three bytes randomly. Valid `--spoof-mac` argument examples are `Apple`, `0`, `01:02:03:04:05:06`, `deadbeefcafe`, `0020F2`, and `Cisco`. This option only affects raw packet scans such as SYN scan or OS detection, not connection-oriented features such as version detection or the Nmap Scripting Engine.

`--badsum` (Send packets with bogus TCP/UDP checksums)

Asks Nmap to use an invalid TCP or UDP checksum for packets sent to target hosts. Since virtually all host IP stacks properly drop these packets, any responses received are likely coming from a firewall or IDS that didn't bother to verify the checksum. For more details on this technique, see *http://nmap.org/p60-12.html*

15.13. Output

Any security tools is only as useful as the output it generates. Complex tests and algorithms are of little value if they aren't presented in an organized and comprehensible fashion. Given the number of ways Nmap is used by people and other software, no single format can please everyone. So Nmap offers several formats, including the interactive mode for humans to read directly and XML for easy parsing by software.

In addition to offering different output formats, Nmap provides options for controlling the verbosity of output as well as debugging messages. Output types may be sent to standard output or to named files, which Nmap can append to or clobber. Output files may also be used to resume aborted scans.

Nmap makes output available in five different formats. The default is called *interactive output*, and it is sent to standard output (stdout). There is also *normal output*, which is similar to interactive except that it displays less runtime information and warnings since it is expected to be analyzed after the scan completes rather than interactively.

XML output is one of the most important output types, as it can be converted to HTML, easily parsed by programs such as Nmap graphical user interfaces, or imported into databases.

The two remaining output types are the simple *grepable output* which includes most information for a target host on a single line, and *sCRiPt KiDDi3 0utPUt* for users who consider themselves l<-r4d.

While interactive output is the default and has no associated command-line options, the other four format options use the same syntax. They take one argument, which is the filename that results should be stored in. Multiple formats may be specified, but each format may only be specified once. For example, you may wish to save normal output for your own review while saving XML of the same scan for programmatic analysis. You might do this with the options `-oX myscan.xml -oN myscan.nmap`. While this chapter uses the simple names like `myscan.xml` for brevity, more descriptive names are generally recommended. The names chosen are a matter of personal preference, though I use long ones that incorporate the scan date and a word or two describing the scan, placed in a directory named after the company I'm scanning.

While these options save results to files, Nmap still prints interactive output to stdout as usual. For example, the command **nmap -oX myscan.xml target** prints XML to `myscan.xml` and fills standard output with the same interactive results it would have printed if `-oX` wasn't specified at all. You can change this by passing a hyphen character as the argument to one of the format types. This causes Nmap to deactivate interactive output, and instead print results in the format you specified to the standard output stream. So the command **nmap -oX - target** will send only XML output to stdout. Serious errors may still be printed to the normal error stream, stderr.

Unlike some Nmap arguments, the space between the logfile option flag (such as `-oX`) and the filename or hyphen is mandatory. If you omit the flags and give arguments such as `-oG-` or `-oXscan.xml`, a backwards compatibility feature of Nmap will cause the creation of *normal format* output files named `G-` and `Xscan.xml` respectively.

All of these arguments support `strftime`-like conversions in the filename. `%H`, `%M`, `%S`, `%m`, `%d`, `%y`, and `%Y` are all exactly the same as in `strftime`. `%T` is the same as `%H%M%S`, `%R` is the same as `%H%M`, and `%D` is the same as `%m%d%y`. A `%` followed by any other character just yields that character (`%%` gives you a percent symbol). So `-oX 'scan-%T-%D.xml'` will use an XML file in the form of `scan-144840-121307.xml`.

Nmap also offers options to control scan verbosity and to append to output files rather than clobbering them. All of these options are described below.

Nmap Output Formats

`-oN <filespec>` (normal output)
> Requests that `normal output` be directed to the given filename. As discussed above, this differs slightly from `interactive output`.

`-oX <filespec>` (XML output)
> Requests that `XML output` be directed to the given filename. Nmap includes a document type definition (DTD) which allows XML parsers to validate Nmap XML output. While it is primarily intended for programmatic use, it can also help humans interpret Nmap XML output. The DTD defines the legal elements of the format, and often enumerates the attributes and values they can take on. The latest version is always available from *http://nmap.org/data/nmap.dtd*.
>
> XML offers a stable format that is easily parsed by software. Free XML parsers are available for all major computer languages, including C/C++, Perl, Python, and Java. People have even written bindings for most of these languages to handle Nmap output and execution specifically. Examples are Nmap::Scanner[2] and Nmap::Parser[3] in Perl CPAN. In almost all cases that a non-trivial application interfaces with Nmap, XML is the preferred format.
>
> The XML output references an XSL stylesheet which can be used to format the results as HTML. The easiest way to use this is simply to load the XML output in a web browser such as Firefox or IE. By default, this will only work on the machine you ran Nmap on (or a similarly configured one) due to the hard-coded `nmap.xsl` filesystem path. Use the `--webxml` or `--stylesheet` options to create portable XML files that render as HTML on any web-connected machine.

---

[2] *http://sourceforge.net/projects/nmap-scanner/*
[3] *http://nmapparser.wordpress.com/*

-oS `<filespec>` (ScRipT KIdd|3 oUTpuT)

Script kiddie output is like interactive output, except that it is post-processed to better suit the 133t HaXXorZ who previously looked down on Nmap due to its consistent capitalization and spelling. Humor impaired people should note that this option is making fun of the script kiddies before flaming me for supposedly "helping them".

-oG `<filespec>` (grepable output)

This output format is covered last because it is deprecated. The XML output format is far more powerful, and is nearly as convenient for experienced users. XML is a standard for which dozens of excellent parsers are available, while grepable output is my own simple hack. XML is extensible to support new Nmap features as they are released, while I often must omit those features from grepable output for lack of a place to put them.

Nevertheless, grepable output is still quite popular. It is a simple format that lists each host on one line and can be trivially searched and parsed with standard Unix tools such as grep, awk, cut, sed, diff, and Perl. Even I usually use it for one-off tests done at the command line. Finding all the hosts with the SSH port open or that are running Solaris takes only a simple grep to identify the hosts, piped to an awk or cut command to print the desired fields.

Grepable output consists of comments (lines starting with a pound (#)) and target lines. A target line includes a combination of six labeled fields, separated by tabs and followed with a colon. The fields are `Host`, `Ports`, `Protocols`, `Ignored State`, `OS`, `Seq Index`, `IP ID`, and `Status`.

The most important of these fields is generally `Ports`, which gives details on each interesting port. It is a comma separated list of port entries. Each port entry represents one interesting port, and takes the form of seven slash (/) separated subfields. Those subfields are: `Port number`, `State`, `Protocol`, `Owner`, `Service`, `SunRPC info`, and `Version info`.

As with XML output, this man page does not allow for documenting the entire format. A more detailed look at the Nmap grepable output format is available in Section 13.10, "Grepable Output (-oG)" [356].

-oA `<basename>` (Output to all formats)

As a convenience, you may specify `-oA` `<basename>` to store scan results in normal, XML, and grepable formats at once. They are stored in `<basename>`.nmap, `<basename>`.xml, and `<basename>`.gnmap, respectively. As with most programs, you can prefix the filenames with a directory path, such as `~/nmaplogs/foocorp/` on Unix or `c:\hacking\sco` on Windows.

Verbosity and debugging options

-v (Increase verbosity level)

Increases the verbosity level, causing Nmap to print more information about the scan in progress. Open ports are shown as they are found and completion time estimates are provided when Nmap thinks a scan will take more than a few minutes. Use it twice or more for even greater verbosity.

Most changes only affect interactive output, and some also affect normal and script kiddie output. The other output types are meant to be processed by machines, so Nmap can give substantial detail by default in those formats without fatiguing a human user. However, there are a few changes in other modes where output size can be reduced substantially by omitting some detail. For example, a comment line in the grepable output that provides a list of all ports scanned is only printed in verbose mode because it can be quite long.

`-d [level]` (Increase or set debugging level)

When even verbose mode doesn't provide sufficient data for you, debugging is available to flood you with much more! As with the verbosity option (`-v`), debugging is enabled with a command-line flag (`-d`) and the debug level can be increased by specifying it multiple times. Alternatively, you can set a debug level by giving an argument to `-d`. For example, `-d9` sets level nine. That is the highest effective level and will produce thousands of lines unless you run a very simple scan with very few ports and targets.

Debugging output is useful when a bug is suspected in Nmap, or if you are simply confused as to what Nmap is doing and why. As this feature is mostly intended for developers, debug lines aren't always self-explanatory. You may get something like: `Timeout vals: srtt: -1 rttvar: -1 to: 1000000 delta 14987 ==> srtt: 14987 rttvar: 14987 to: 100000`. If you don't understand a line, your only recourses are to ignore it, look it up in the source code, or request help from the development list (*nmap-dev*). Some lines are self explanatory, but the messages become more obscure as the debug level is increased.

`--reason` (Host and port state reasons)

Shows the reason each port is set to a specific state and the reason each host is up or down. This option displays the type of the packet that determined a port or hosts state. For example, A `RST` packet from a closed port or an echo reply from an alive host. The information Nmap can provide is determined by the type of scan or ping. The SYN scan and SYN ping (`-sS` and `-PS`) are very detailed, but the TCP connect scan (`-sT`) is limited by the implementation of the `connect` system call. This feature is automatically enabled by the debug option (`-d`) and the results are stored in XML log files even if this option is not specified.

`--packet-trace` (Trace packets and data sent and received)

Causes Nmap to print a summary of every packet sent or received. This is often used for debugging, but is also a valuable way for new users to understand exactly what Nmap is doing under the covers. To avoid printing thousands of lines, you may want to specify a limited number of ports to scan, such as `-p20-30`. If you only care about the goings on of the version detection subsystem, use `--version-trace` instead. If you only care about script tracing, specify `--script-trace`. With `--packet-trace`, you get all of the above.

`--open` (Show only open (or possibly open) ports)

Sometimes you only care about ports you can actually connect to (open ones), and don't want results cluttered with `closed`, `filtered`, and `closed|filtered` ports. Output customization is normally done after the scan using tools such as grep, awk, and Perl, but this feature was added due to overwhelming requests. Specify `--open` to only see `open`, `open|filtered`, and `unfiltered` ports. These three ports are treated just as they normally are, which means that `open|filtered` and `unfiltered` may be condensed into counts if there are an overwhelming number of them.

`--iflist` (List interfaces and routes)

Prints the interface list and system routes as detected by Nmap. This is useful for debugging routing problems or device mischaracterization (such as Nmap treating a PPP connection as ethernet).

`--log-errors` (Log errors/warnings to normal mode output file)

Warnings and errors printed by Nmap usually go only to the screen (interactive output), leaving any normal-format output files (usually specified with `-oN`) uncluttered. When you do want to see those messages in the normal output file you specified, add this option. It is useful when you aren't watching the interactive output or when you want to record errors while debugging a problem. The error and warning messages will still appear in interactive mode too. This won't work for most errors related to bad command-line arguments because Nmap may not have initialized its output files yet. In addition, some Nmap error and warning messages use a different system which does not yet support this option.

An alternative to `--log-errors` is redirecting interactive output (including the standard error stream) to a file. Most Unix shells make this approach easy, though it can be difficult on Windows.

Miscellaneous output options

`--append-output` (Append to rather than clobber output files)
When you specify a filename to an output format flag such as `-oX` or `-oN`, that file is overwritten by default. If you prefer to keep the existing content of the file and append the new results, specify the `--append-output` option. All output filenames specified in that Nmap execution will then be appended to rather than clobbered. This doesn't work well for XML (`-oX`) scan data as the resultant file generally won't parse properly until you fix it up by hand.

`--resume <filename>` (Resume aborted scan)
Some extensive Nmap runs take a very long time—on the order of days. Such scans don't always run to completion. Restrictions may prevent Nmap from being run during working hours, the network could go down, the machine Nmap is running on might suffer a planned or unplanned reboot, or Nmap itself could crash. The administrator running Nmap could cancel it for any other reason as well, by pressing **ctrl-C**. Restarting the whole scan from the beginning may be undesirable. Fortunately, if normal (`-oN`) or grepable (`-oG`) logs were kept, the user can ask Nmap to resume scanning with the target it was working on when execution ceased. Simply specify the `--resume` option and pass the normal/grepable output file as its argument. No other arguments are permitted, as Nmap parses the output file to use the same ones specified previously. Simply call Nmap as **nmap --resume <logfilename>**. Nmap will append new results to the data files specified in the previous execution. Resumption does not support the XML output format because combining the two runs into one valid XML file would be difficult.

`--stylesheet <path or URL>` (Set XSL stylesheet to transform XML output)
Nmap ships with an XSL stylesheet named `nmap.xsl` for viewing or translating XML output to HTML. The XML output includes an `xml-stylesheet` directive which points to `nmap.xml` where it was initially installed by Nmap (or in the current working directory on Windows). Simply load Nmap's XML output in a modern web browser and it should retrieve `nmap.xsl` from the filesystem and use it to render results. If you wish to use a different stylesheet, specify it as the argument to `--stylesheet`. You must pass the full pathname or URL. One common invocation is `--stylesheet http://nmap.org/data/nmap.xsl`. This tells a browser to load the latest version of the stylesheet from Nmap.Org. The `--webxml` option does the same thing with less typing and memorization. Loading the XSL from Nmap.Org makes it easier to view results on a machine that doesn't have Nmap (and thus `nmap.xsl`) installed. So the URL is often more useful, but the local filesystem location of `nmap.xsl` is used by default for privacy reasons.

`--webxml` (Load stylesheet from Nmap.Org)
This convenience option is simply an alias for `--stylesheet http://nmap.org/data/nmap.xsl`.

`--no-stylesheet` (Omit XSL stylesheet declaration from XML)

Specify this option to prevent Nmap from associating any XSL stylesheet with its XML output. The `xml-stylesheet` directive is omitted.

15.14. Miscellaneous Options

This section describes some important (and not-so-important) options that don't really fit anywhere else.

`-6` (Enable IPv6 scanning)

Since 2002, Nmap has offered IPv6 support for its most popular features. In particular, ping scanning (TCP-only), connect scanning, and version detection all support IPv6. The command syntax is the same as usual except that you also add the `-6` option. Of course, you must use IPv6 syntax if you specify an address rather than a hostname. An address might look like `3ffe:7501:4819:2000:210:f3ff:fe03:14d0`, so hostnames are recommended. The output looks the same as usual, with the IPv6 address on the "interesting ports" line being the only IPv6 give away.

While IPv6 hasn't exactly taken the world by storm, it gets significant use in some (usually Asian) countries and most modern operating systems support it. To use Nmap with IPv6, both the source and target of your scan must be configured for IPv6. If your ISP (like most of them) does not allocate IPv6 addresses to you, free tunnel brokers are widely available and work fine with Nmap. I use the free IPv6 tunnel broker service at *http://www.tunnelbroker.net*. Other tunnel brokers are listed at Wikipedia[4]. 6to4 tunnels are another popular, free approach.

`-A` (Aggressive scan options)

This option enables additional advanced and aggressive options. I haven't decided exactly which it stands for yet. Presently this enables OS detection (`-O`), version scanning (`-sV`), script scanning (`-sC`) and traceroute (`--traceroute`). More features may be added in the future. The point is to enable a comprehensive set of scan options without people having to remember a large set of flags. However, because script scanning with the default set is considered intrusive, you should not use `-A` against target networks without permission. This option only enables features, and not timing options (such as `-T4`) or verbosity options (`-v`) that you might want as well.

`--datadir <directoryname>` (Specify custom Nmap data file location)

Nmap obtains some special data at runtime in files named `nmap-service-probes`, `nmap-services`, `nmap-protocols`, `nmap-rpc`, `nmap-mac-prefixes`, and `nmap-os-db`. If the location of any of these files has been specified (using the `--servicedb` or `--versiondb` options), that location is used for that file. After that, Nmap searches these files in the directory specified with the `--datadir` option (if any). Any files not found there, are searched for in the directory specified by the NMAPDIR environmental variable. Next comes `~/.nmap` for real and effective UIDs (POSIX systems only) or location of the Nmap executable (Win32 only), and then a compiled-in location such as `/usr/local/share/nmap` or `/usr/share/nmap` . As a last resort, Nmap will look in the current directory.

---

[4] *http://en.wikipedia.org/wiki/List_of_IPv6_tunnel_brokers*

`--servicedb <services file>` (Specify custom services file)

Asks Nmap to use the specified services file rather than the `nmap-services` data file that comes with Nmap. Using this option also causes a fast scan (`-F`) to be used. See the description for `--datadir` for more information on Nmap's data files.

`--versiondb <service probes file>` (Specify custom service probes file)

Asks Nmap to use the specified service probes file rather than the `nmap-service-probes` data file that comes with Nmap. See the description for `--datadir` for more information on Nmap's data files.

`--send-eth` (Use raw ethernet sending)

Asks Nmap to send packets at the raw ethernet (data link) layer rather than the higher IP (network) layer. By default, Nmap chooses the one which is generally best for the platform it is running on. Raw sockets (IP layer) are generally most efficient for Unix machines, while ethernet frames are required for Windows operation since Microsoft disabled raw socket support. Nmap still uses raw IP packets on Unix despite this option when there is no other choice (such as non-ethernet connections).

`--send-ip` (Send at raw IP level)

Asks Nmap to send packets via raw IP sockets rather than sending lower level ethernet frames. It is the complement to the `--send-eth` option discussed previously.

`--privileged` (Assume that the user is fully privileged)

Tells Nmap to simply assume that it is privileged enough to perform raw socket sends, packet sniffing, and similar operations that usually require root privileges on Unix systems. By default Nmap quits if such operations are requested but `geteuid` is not zero. `--privileged` is useful with Linux kernel capabilities and similar systems that may be configured to allow unprivileged users to perform raw-packet scans. Be sure to provide this option flag before any flags for options that require privileges (SYN scan, OS detection, etc.). The `NMAP_PRIVILEGED` environmental variable may be set as an equivalent alternative to `--privileged`.

`--unprivileged` (Assume that the user lacks raw socket privileges)

This option is the opposite of `--privileged`. It tells Nmap to treat the user as lacking network raw socket and sniffing privileges. This is useful for testing, debugging, or when the raw network functionality of your operating system is somehow broken. The `NMAP_UNPRIVILEGED` environmental variable may be set as an equivalent alternative to `--unprivileged`.

`--release-memory` (Release memory before quitting)

This option is only useful for memory-leak debugging. It causes Nmap to release allocated memory just before it quits so that actual memory leaks are easier to spot. Normally Nmap skips this as the OS does this anyway upon process termination.

`--interactive` (Start in interactive mode)

Starts Nmap in interactive mode, which offers an interactive Nmap prompt allowing easy launching of multiple scans (either synchronously or in the background). This is useful for people who scan from multi-user systems as they often want to test their security without letting everyone else on the system know exactly which systems they are scanning. Use `--interactive` to activate this mode and then type **h** for help. This option is rarely used because proper shells are usually more familiar and feature-complete. This option includes a bang (!) operator for executing shell commands, which is one of many reasons not to install Nmap setuid root.

-V; --version (Print version number)
> Prints the Nmap version number and exits.

-h; --help (Print help summary page)
> Prints a short help screen with the most common command flags. Running Nmap without any arguments does the same thing.

15.15. Runtime Interaction

During the execution of Nmap, all key presses are captured. This allows you to interact with the program without aborting and restarting it. Certain special keys will change options, while any other keys will print out a status message telling you about the scan. The convention is that *lowercase letters increase* the amount of printing, and *uppercase letters decrease* the printing. You may also press '*?*' for help.

v / V
> Increase / decrease the verbosity level

d / D
> Increase / decrease the debugging Level

p / P
> Turn on / off packet tracing

?
> Print a runtime interaction help screen

Anything else
> Print out a status message like this:
>
> Stats: 0:00:08 elapsed; 111 hosts completed (5 up), 5 undergoing Service Scan
>
> Service scan Timing: About 28.00% done; ETC: 16:18 (0:00:15 remaining)

15.16. Examples

Here are some Nmap usage examples, from the simple and routine to a little more complex and esoteric. Some actual IP addresses and domain names are used to make things more concrete. In their place you should substitute addresses/names from *your own network.*. While I don't think port scanning other networks is or should be illegal, some network administrators don't appreciate unsolicited scanning of their networks and may complain. Getting permission first is the best approach.

For testing purposes, you have permission to scan the host scanme.nmap.org. This permission only includes scanning via Nmap and not testing exploits or denial of service attacks. To conserve bandwidth, please do not initiate more than a dozen scans against that host per day. If this free scanning target service is abused, it will be taken down and Nmap will report Failed to resolve given hostname/IP: scanme.nmap.org. These permissions also apply to the hosts scanme2.nmap.org, scanme3.nmap.org, and so on, though those hosts do not currently exist.

nmap -v scanme.nmap.org

This option scans all reserved TCP ports on the machine `scanme.nmap.org` . The `-v` option enables verbose mode.

nmap -sS -O scanme.nmap.org/24

Launches a stealth SYN scan against each machine that is up out of the 255 machines on "class C" network where Scanme resides. It also tries to determine what operating system is running on each host that is up and running. This requires root privileges because of the SYN scan and OS detection.

nmap -sV -p 22,53,110,143,4564 198.116.0-255.1-127

Launches host enumeration and a TCP scan at the first half of each of the 255 possible eight-bit subnets in the 198.116 class B address space. This tests whether the systems run SSH, DNS, POP3, or IMAP on their standard ports, or anything on port 4564. For any of these ports found open, version detection is used to determine what application is running.

nmap -v -iR 100000 -PN -p 80

Asks Nmap to choose 100,000 hosts at random and scan them for web servers (port 80). Host enumeration is disabled with `-PN` since first sending a couple probes to determine whether a host is up is wasteful when you are only probing one port on each target host anyway.

nmap -PN -p80 -oX logs/pb-port80scan.xml -oG logs/pb-port80scan.gnmap 216.163.128.20/20

This scans 4096 IPs for any web servers (without pinging them) and saves the output in grepable and XML formats.

15.17. Bugs

Like its author, Nmap isn't perfect. But you can help make it better by sending bug reports or even writing patches. If Nmap doesn't behave the way you expect, first upgrade to the latest version available from *http://nmap.org*. If the problem persists, do some research to determine whether it has already been discovered and addressed. Try searching for the error message on our search page at *http://insecure.org/search.html* or at Google. Also try browsing the *nmap-dev* archives at *http://seclists.org/*. Read this full manual page as well. If nothing comes of this, mail a bug report to `<nmap-dev@insecure.org>`. Please include everything you have learned about the problem, as well as what version of Nmap you are running and what operating system version it is running on. Problem reports and Nmap usage questions sent to `<nmap-dev@insecure.org>` are far more likely to be answered than those sent to Fyodor directly. If you subscribe to the nmap-dev list before posting, your message will bypass moderation and get through more quickly. Subscribe at *http://cgi.insecure.org/mailman/listinfo/nmap-dev*.

Code patches to fix bugs are even better than bug reports. Basic instructions for creating patch files with your changes are available at *http://nmap.org/data/HACKING*. Patches may be sent to *nmap-dev* (recommended) or to Fyodor directly.

15.18. Author

Fyodor `<fyodor@insecure.org>` (*http://insecure.org*)

Hundreds of people have made valuable contributions to Nmap over the years. These are detailed in the CHANGELOG file which is distributed with Nmap and also available from *http://nmap.org/changelog.html*.

15.19. Legal Notices

15.19.1. Nmap Copyright and Licensing

The Nmap Security Scanner is (C) 1996-2008 Insecure.Com LLC. Nmap is also a registered trademark of Insecure.Com LLC. This program is free software; you may redistribute and/or modify it under the terms of the GNU General Public License as published by the Free Software Foundation; Version 2 with the clarifications and exceptions described below. This guarantees your right to use, modify, and redistribute this software under certain conditions. If you wish to embed Nmap technology into proprietary software, we sell alternative licenses (contact <sales@insecure.com>). Dozens of software vendors already license Nmap technology such as host discovery, port scanning, OS detection, and version detection.

Note that the GPL places important restrictions on "derived works", yet it does not provide a detailed definition of that term. To avoid misunderstandings, we consider an application to constitute a "derivative work" for the purpose of this license if it does any of the following:

- Integrates source code from Nmap

- Reads or includes Nmap copyrighted data files, such as nmap-os-db or nmap-service-probes.

- Executes Nmap and parses the results (as opposed to typical shell or execution-menu apps, which simply display raw Nmap output and so are not derivative works.)

- Integrates/includes/aggregates Nmap into a proprietary executable installer, such as those produced by InstallShield.

- Links to a library or executes a program that does any of the above.

The term "Nmap" should be taken to also include any portions or derived works of Nmap. This list is not exclusive, but is just meant to clarify our interpretation of derived works with some common examples. These restrictions only apply when you actually redistribute Nmap. For example, nothing stops you from writing and selling a proprietary front-end to Nmap. Just distribute it by itself, and point people to *http://nmap.org* to download Nmap.

We don't consider these to be added restrictions on top of the GPL, but just a clarification of how we interpret "derived works" as it applies to our GPL-licensed Nmap product. This is similar to the way Linus Torvalds has announced his interpretation of how "derived works" applies to Linux kernel modules. Our interpretation refers only to Nmap—we don't speak for any other GPL products.

If you have any questions about the GPL licensing restrictions on using Nmap in non-GPL works, we would be happy to help. As mentioned above, we also offer alternative license to integrate Nmap into proprietary applications and appliances. These contracts have been sold to many security vendors, and generally include a perpetual license as well as providing for priority support and updates as well as helping to fund the continued development of Nmap technology. Please email <sales@insecure.com> for further information.

As a special exception to the GPL terms, Insecure.Com LLC grants permission to link the code of this program with any version of the OpenSSL library which is distributed under a license identical to that listed in the included `COPYING.OpenSSL` file, and distribute linked combinations including the two. You must obey the GNU GPL in all respects for all of the code used other than OpenSSL. If you modify this file, you may extend this exception to your version of the file, but you are not obligated to do so.

If you received these files with a written license agreement or contract stating terms other than the terms above, then that alternative license agreement takes precedence over these comments.

15.19.2. Creative Commons License for this Nmap Guide

This *Nmap Reference Guide* is (C) 2005-2008 Insecure.Com LLC. It is hereby placed under version 2.5 of the Creative Commons Attribution License[5]. This allows you redistribute and modify the work as you desire, as long as you credit the original source. Alternatively, you may choose to treat this document as falling under the same license as Nmap itself (discussed previously).

15.19.3. Source Code Availability and Community Contributions

Source is provided to this software because we believe users have a right to know exactly what a program is going to do before they run it. This also allows you to audit the software for security holes (none have been found so far).

Source code also allows you to port Nmap to new platforms, fix bugs, and add new features. You are highly encouraged to send your changes to <fyodor@insecure.org> for possible incorporation into the main distribution. By sending these changes to Fyodor or one of the Insecure.Org development mailing lists, it is assumed that you are offering Fyodor and Insecure.Com LLC the unlimited, non-exclusive right to reuse, modify, and relicense the code. Nmap will always be available Open Source, but this is important because the inability to relicense code has caused devastating problems for other Free Software projects (such as KDE and NASM). We also occasionally relicense the code to third parties as discussed above. If you wish to specify special license conditions of your contributions, just say so when you send them.

15.19.4. No Warranty

This program is distributed in the hope that it will be useful, but WITHOUT ANY WARRANTY; without even the implied warranty of MERCHANTABILITY or FITNESS FOR A PARTICULAR PURPOSE. See the GNU General Public License v2.0 for more details at *http://www.gnu.org/licenses/gpl-2.0.html*, or in the `COPYING` file included with Nmap.

It should also be noted that Nmap has occasionally been known to crash poorly written applications, TCP/IP stacks, and even operating systems. While this is extremely rare, it is important to keep in mind. *Nmap should never be run against mission critical systems* unless you are prepared to suffer downtime. We acknowledge here that Nmap may crash your systems or networks and we disclaim all liability for any damage or problems Nmap could cause.

---

[5] *http://creativecommons.org/licenses/by/2.5/*

15.19.5. Inappropriate Usage

Because of the slight risk of crashes and because a few black hats like to use Nmap for reconnaissance prior to attacking systems, there are administrators who become upset and may complain when their system is scanned. Thus, it is often advisable to request permission before doing even a light scan of a network.

Nmap should never be installed with special privileges (e.g. suid root) for security reasons.

15.19.6. Third-Party Software

This product includes software developed by the Apache Software Foundation. A modified version of the Libpcap portable packet capture library is distributed along with Nmap. The Windows version of Nmap utilized the Libpcap-derived WinPcap library instead. Regular expression support is provided by the PCRE library, which is open-source software, written by Philip Hazel. Certain raw networking functions use the Libdnet networking library, which was written by Dug Song. A modified version is distributed with Nmap. Nmap can optionally link with the OpenSSL cryptography toolkit for SSL version detection support. The Nmap Scripting Engine uses an embedded version of the Lua programming language. All of the third-party software described in this paragraph is freely redistributable under BSD-style software licenses.

15.19.7. United States Export Control Classification

U.S. Export Control: Insecure.Com LLC believes that Nmap falls under U.S. ECCN (export control classification number) 5D992. This category is called "Information Security software not controlled by 5D002". The only restriction of this classification is AT (anti-terrorism), which applies to almost all goods and denies export to a handful of rogue nations such as Iran and North Korea. Thus exporting Nmap does not require any special license, permit, or other governmental authorization.

Appendix A. Nmap XML Output DTD

A.1. Purpose

This document type definition (DTD) is used by XML parsers to validate Nmap XML output. The latest version is always available at *http://nmap.org/data/nmap.dtd*. While it is primarily intended for programmatic use, it is included here due to its value in helping humans interpret Nmap XML output. The DTD defines the legal elements of the format, and often enumerates the attributes and values they can take on. Using the DTD is discussed further in Section 13.6, "XML Output (-oX)" [348].

A.2. The Full DTD

```
<!--
nmap.dtd
This is the DTD for Nmap's XML output (-oX) format.
$Id: nmap.dtd 11010 2008-11-10 19:05:12Z david $

Originally written by:
William McVey <wam@cisco.com> <wam+nmap@wamber.net>

Now maintained by Fyodor <fyodor@insecure.org> as part of Nmap.

To validate using this file, simply add a DOCTYPE line similar to:
<!DOCTYPE nmaprun SYSTEM "nmap.dtd">
to the nmap output immediately below the prologue (the first line).  This
should allow you to run a validating parser against the output (so long
as the DTD is in your parser's DTD search path).

Bugs:
Most of the elements are "locked" into the specific order that nmap
generates, when there really is no need for a specific ordering.
This is primarily because I don't know the xml DTD construct to
specify "one each of this list of elements, in any order".  If there
is a construct similar to SGML's '&' operator, please let me know.

Portions Copyright (c) 2001-2008 Insecure.Com LLC
Portions Copyright (c) 2001 by Cisco systems, Inc.

Permission to use, copy, modify, and distribute modified and
unmodified copies of this software for any purpose and without fee is
hereby granted, provided that (a) this copyright and permission notice
appear on all copies of the software and supporting documentation, (b)
the name of Cisco Systems, Inc. not be used in advertising or
publicity pertaining to distribution of the program without specific
prior permission, and (c) notice be given in supporting documentation
that use, modification, copying and distribution is by permission of
```

Cisco Systems, Inc.

```
<!-- parameter entities to specify common "types" used elsewhere in the DTD -->
<!ENTITY % attr_alpha "CDATA" >
<!ENTITY % attr_numeric "CDATA" >
<!ENTITY % attr_ipaddr "CDATA" >
<!ENTITY % attr_percent "CDATA" >
<!ENTITY % attr_type "(ipv4 | ipv6 | mac)" >

<!ENTITY % host_states "(up|down|unknown|skipped)" >

<!-- see: nmap.c:statenum2str for list of port states -->
<!-- Maybe they should be enumerated as in scan_types below , but I -->
<!-- don't know how to escape states like open|filtered -->
<!ENTITY % port_states "CDATA" >

<!ENTITY % hostname_types "(PTR)" >

<!-- see output.c:output_xml_scaninfo_records for scan types -->
<!ENTITY % scan_types "(syn|ack|bounce|connect|null|xmas|window|maimon|fin|udp|ipproto)" >

<!-- <!ENTITY % ip_versions "(ipv4)" > -->

<!ENTITY % port_protocols "(ip|tcp|udp)" >

<!-- I don't know exactly what these are, but the values were enumerated via:
   grep "conf=" *
-->
<!ENTITY % service_confs  "( 0 | 3 | 5 | 10)" >

<!-- This element was started in nmap.c:nmap_main().
   It represents to the topmost element of the output document.
-->
<!ELEMENT nmaprun     (scaninfo*, verbose, debugging,
            ((taskbegin, taskprogress*, taskend) | host | output)*,
            runstats) >
<!ATTLIST nmaprun
  scanner (nmap) #REQUIRED
  args CDATA #IMPLIED
  start %attr_numeric; #IMPLIED
  startstr CDATA        #IMPLIED
  version CDATA #REQUIRED
```

```
  profile_name CDATA  #IMPLIED
  xmloutputversion CDATA  #REQUIRED
>


<!-- this element is written in output.c:doscaninfo() -->
<!ELEMENT scaninfo EMPTY >
<!ATTLIST scaninfo
  type %scan_types; #REQUIRED
  scanflags CDATA  #IMPLIED
  protocol %port_protocols; #REQUIRED
  numservices %attr_numeric; #REQUIRED
  services CDATA  #REQUIRED
>


<!-- these elements are written in nmap.c:nmap_main() -->
<!ELEMENT verbose EMPTY >
<!ATTLIST verbose level %attr_numeric; #IMPLIED >


<!ELEMENT debugging  EMPTY >
<!ATTLIST debugging level %attr_numeric; #IMPLIED >

<!-- this element is written in timing.c:beginOrEndTask() -->
<!ELEMENT taskbegin EMPTY >
<!ATTLIST taskbegin
  task  CDATA  #REQUIRED
  time  %attr_numeric; #REQUIRED
  extrainfo CDATA  #IMPLIED
>


<!-- this element is written in timing.c:printStats() -->
<!ELEMENT taskprogress EMPTY >
<!ATTLIST taskprogress
  task  CDATA  #REQUIRED
  time  %attr_numeric; #REQUIRED
  percent %attr_percent; #REQUIRED
  remaining %attr_numeric; #REQUIRED
  etc %attr_numeric; #REQUIRED
>


<!-- this element is written in timing.c:beginOrEndTask() -->
<!ELEMENT taskend EMPTY >
<!ATTLIST taskend
  task  CDATA  #REQUIRED
  time  %attr_numeric; #REQUIRED
  extrainfo CDATA  #IMPLIED
>

<!--
```

```
        this element is started in nmap.c:nmap_main() and filled by
        output.c:write_host_status(), output.c:printportoutput(), and
        output.c:printosscanoutput()
-->
<!ELEMENT host  ( status, address , (address | hostnames |
                  smurf | ports | os | distance | uptime |
                  tcpsequence | ipidsequence | tcptssequence |
                  hostscript | trace)*, times ) >
<!ATTLIST host
  starttime %attr_numeric; #IMPLIED
  endtime  %attr_numeric; #IMPLIED
  comment  CDATA  #IMPLIED
>

<!-- these elements are written by output.c:write_xml_initial_hostinfo() -->
<!ELEMENT status EMPTY >
<!ATTLIST status state %host_states; #REQUIRED
  reason CDATA  #REQUIRED
>

<!ELEMENT address EMPTY >
<!ATTLIST address
  addr %attr_ipaddr; #REQUIRED
  addrtype %attr_type; "ipv4"
  vendor  CDATA #IMPLIED
>

<!ELEMENT hostnames (hostname)* >
<!ELEMENT hostname EMPTY >
<!ATTLIST hostname
  name  CDATA  #IMPLIED
  type  %hostname_types; #IMPLIED
>

<!-- this element is written by output.c:write_host_status() -->
<!ELEMENT smurf  EMPTY >
<!ATTLIST smurf  responses %attr_numeric; #REQUIRED >

<!-- these elements are written by output.c:printportoutput() -->

<!ELEMENT ports  (extraports* , port*) >

<!ELEMENT extraports (extrareasons)* >
<!ATTLIST extraports
  state  %port_states; #REQUIRED
  count  %attr_numeric; #REQUIRED
>
```

```
<!ELEMENT extrareasons EMPTY >
<!ATTLIST extrareasons
  reason  CDATA #REQUIRED
  count  CDATA #REQUIRED
>


<!ELEMENT port  (state , owner? , service?, script*) >
<!ATTLIST port
  protocol %port_protocols; #REQUIRED
  portid %attr_numeric; #REQUIRED
>


<!ELEMENT state  EMPTY >
<!ATTLIST state
 state %port_states; #REQUIRED
 reason  CDATA #REQUIRED
 reason_ttl CDATA #REQUIRED
 reason_ip CDATA #IMPLIED
>


<!ELEMENT owner  EMPTY >
<!ATTLIST owner  name  CDATA #REQUIRED >


<!ELEMENT service EMPTY >
<!ATTLIST service
  name  CDATA  #REQUIRED
  conf %service_confs; #REQUIRED
             method        (table|detection|probed) #REQUIRED
             version       CDATA       #IMPLIED
             product       CDATA       #IMPLIED
             extrainfo     CDATA       #IMPLIED
  tunnel  (ssl) #IMPLIED
  proto  (rpc) #IMPLIED
  rpcnum  %attr_numeric; #IMPLIED
  lowver  %attr_numeric; #IMPLIED
  highver  %attr_numeric; #IMPLIED
             hostname      CDATA       #IMPLIED
             ostype        CDATA      #IMPLIED
             devicetype    CDATA       #IMPLIED
             servicefp     CDATA       #IMPLIED
>


<!ELEMENT script EMPTY >
<!ATTLIST script
 id CDATA #REQUIRED
 output CDATA #REQUIRED
>


<!ELEMENT os  ( portused* , osclass*, osmatch*, osfingerprint* ) >
```

```
<!ELEMENT portused EMPTY >
<!ATTLIST portused
  state  %port_states; #REQUIRED
  proto  %port_protocols; #REQUIRED
  portid  %attr_numeric; #REQUIRED
>
<!ELEMENT osclass    EMPTY >
<!ATTLIST osclass
              vendor      CDATA      #REQUIRED
              osgen       CDATA      #IMPLIED
              type        CDATA      #IMPLIED
              accuracy    CDATA      #REQUIRED
              osfamily    CDATA      #REQUIRED
>


<!ELEMENT osmatch EMPTY >
<!ATTLIST osmatch
  name  CDATA  #REQUIRED
  accuracy %attr_numeric; #REQUIRED
  line    %attr_numeric; #REQUIRED
>

<!ELEMENT osfingerprint EMPTY >
<!ATTLIST osfingerprint
  fingerprint CDATA  #REQUIRED
>

<!ELEMENT distance EMPTY >
<!ATTLIST distance
  value %attr_numeric; #REQUIRED
>

<!ELEMENT uptime EMPTY >
<!ATTLIST uptime
  seconds  %attr_numeric; #REQUIRED
  lastboot CDATA  #IMPLIED
>

<!ELEMENT tcpsequence EMPTY >
<!ATTLIST tcpsequence
  index %attr_numeric; #REQUIRED
  difficulty CDATA  #REQUIRED
  values CDATA  #REQUIRED
>

<!ELEMENT ipidsequence EMPTY >
<!ATTLIST ipidsequence
```

```
   class  CDATA  #REQUIRED
   values  CDATA  #REQUIRED
>


<!ELEMENT tcptssequence EMPTY >
<!ATTLIST tcptssequence
   class  CDATA  #REQUIRED
   values  CDATA  #IMPLIED
>


<!ELEMENT trace (hop*, error?) >
<!ATTLIST trace
     proto  CDATA  #REQUIRED
     port   CDATA  #REQUIRED
>


<!ELEMENT hop EMPTY>
<!ATTLIST hop
     ttl    CDATA  #REQUIRED
     rtt    CDATA  #IMPLIED
     ipaddr CDATA  #IMPLIED
     host   CDATA  #IMPLIED
>


<!ELEMENT error EMPTY>
<!ATTLIST error
     errorstr   CDATA #IMPLIED
>


<!ELEMENT times EMPTY>
<!ATTLIST times
 srtt CDATA #REQUIRED
 rttvar CDATA #REQUIRED
 to CDATA #REQUIRED
>


<!-- For embedding another type of output (screen output) like Zenmap does. -->
<!ELEMENT output (#PCDATA)>
<!ATTLIST output type  (interactive)  #IMPLIED>


<!-- these elements are generated in output.c:printfinaloutput() -->
<!ELEMENT runstats (finished, hosts) >


<!ELEMENT finished EMPTY >
<!ATTLIST finished time  %attr_numeric; #REQUIRED
                timestr  CDATA       #IMPLIED
>


<!ELEMENT hosts  EMPTY >
```

```
<!ATTLIST hosts
  up  %attr_numeric; "0"
  down  %attr_numeric; "0"
  total  %attr_numeric; #REQUIRED
>

<!ELEMENT hostscript ( script+ )>
```

Index

Options

A

ACK scan, 83, 113-115, 260, 387
    (see also -sA)
"action" script variable, 212, 239, 247
adaptive retransmission (see retransmission)
address ranges, 4, 48, 377
administrator privileges (see privileged users)
after: (Zenmap search criterion), 327
aggregated results (Zenmap), 309, 315, 318
aggressive (-T4) timing template, 4, 67, 142, 143, 398
"Aggressive OS guesses:", 174
AmigaOS, installing on, 44
Antirez, 117
Apple Developer Connection, 42
Apple Mac OS X (see Mac OS X)
apt-get, 35
ARIN (American Registry for Internet Numbers), 2, 54, 89
ARP ping, 64, 382
    (see also -PR)
    overriding other ping types, 59, 65
AS number (see autonomous system number)
"auth" script category, 207
auth service, 69, 71, 200, 245, 290
auth-owners script, 246
"author" script variable, 211, 253
authorized users (see privileged users)
autonomous system (AS) number, 56

B

b: (Zenmap search criterion, short for before:), 327
Beale, Jay, 266
before: (Zenmap search criterion), 327
Bell, Eddie, 253
Berrueta, David Barroso, 302
BGP (see Border Gateway Protocol)
binary packages, 32
bit NSE module, 238
black hat, 16, 97
blind TCP spoofing, 174, 192, 360
Border Gateway Protocol (BGP), 55
broken IP ID increment, 181
BSDs, 43
bugs, reporting, 411

C

Cain, Michael, 272
Casorran, Diego, 44
"categories" script variable, 211, 246
CC (OS detection response test), 179, 185
CD (OS detection response test), 178, 189
cfp: (Zenmap search criterion, short for closed|filtered:), 327
changelog, 20, 25, 412

cheats (version detection), 151
checksums, 291, 403
    (see also --badsum)
    and OS detection, 188
    of RST data, 187
Christensen, Steven, 40
CIDR (Classless Inter-Domain Routing), 2, 5, 17, 47, 377
Cisco Security Agent, 304
Classless Inter-Domain Routing (see CIDR)
closed port state, 6, 77, 98, 327, 373, 383
closed: (Zenmap search criterion), 327
closed|filtered port state, 78, 118, 122, 327, 373, 384
closed|filtered: (Zenmap search criterion), 327
command constructor wizard (Zenmap), 322
command-line options
    of Nmap, 374-376
    of Zenmap, 335
comparing results (Zenmap), 328-330
compilation, 29
    problems with, 32
Computer Fraud and Abuse Act, 15
Computer Misuse Act, 16
concurrent execution, 138
configure directives, 30
congestion control, 130, 135, 138
connect scan, 83, 100-101, 385
    (see also -sT)
conspicuous scans, 284, 297
copyright, 1, 20, 412
    of scripts, 211
cp: (Zenmap search criterion, short for closed:), 327
crashing targets, 19, 296, 413
CT (SCAN line test), 193
CU (SCAN line test), 193
Cygwin, 37, 38

D

D (SCAN line test), 193
d// (device type) version detection field, 161
d: (Zenmap search criterion, short for date:), 327
data files, 363-371
    customizing, 370-371
    directory search order, 209, 370, 394
    used by Zenmap, 330-333
database, output to, 354
date: (Zenmap search criterion), 327
Debian, installing on, 35
debugging, 343, 406
    (see also -d)
    Zenmap, 336
decoys, 119, 264, 284, 400
    which scans use, 286, 392
default ports, 75, 80, 83, 136, 389

K

Kaminsky, Dan, 337
keys, cryptographic, 26
keyword search in Zenmap, 325, 327
Kismet, 202
Krzywinski, Martin, 300, 301

L

LaBrea, 304
  (see also tar pits)
Lamo, Adrian, 270
latency, 90, 132, 138
  estimating with hping2, 92
  estimating with ping, 90
legal advice, 14
legal issues, 13-20
Lei, Zhao, 22
libdnet, 240, 242, 414
libpcap, 242, 414
license (see copyright)
"license" script variable, 211, 253
Linux
  compiling on, 29
  installing on, with apt-get, 35
  installing on, with RPM, 33
  installing on, with Yum, 34
list scan, 2, 12, 57, 378
  (see also -sL)
  purpose of, 57
loading scan results, 317
logging tools, 297
loopback interface, 36, 263
Low-level timing controls, 142
.lua filename extension, 369
Lua programming language, 206, 212, 393, 414
  (see also Nmap Scripting Engine)
LuaDoc, 248
.luadoc filename extension, 250
luaL_register, 238
Lutomirski, Andy, 21, 37

M

M (SCAN line test), 193
MAC address, 202, 239, 368, 403
  spoofing, 270
    (see also --spoof-mac)
Mac OS X, 41-43
  compiling on, 41
  executable installer, 41
  installing from third-party packages, 42
  running Nmap on, 42
machine output (see grepable output)

MacPorts, 42
MadHat, 9, 356
Maimon scan, 83, 116, 266, 387
  (see also -sM)
Maimon, Uriel, 116, 387
"malware" script category, 208
man page (see reference guide)
Mandrake (Linux distribution)
  installing on, with RPM, 33
  installing on, with Yum, 34
Marques, Adriano Monteiro, 22, 336
match directive (nmap-service-probes), 159, 163
MatchPoints (nmap-os-db), 199
Matrix, the, 8, 21
ME (decoy address), 285, 400
Medeiros, Joãa Paulo S., 318
"Medium" TCP sequence generation class, 174
Metasploit, 205
Microsoft Windows (see Windows)
Mitnick, Kevin, 174
Mizrahi, Avi, 16
Mogren, Jack, 135, 143
Moran, Jay, 205
Moulton, Scott, 15, 18
mutexes in NSE, 243
MySQL, 355

N

Ndiff, 295
Nessus, 20, 138
NetBSD, installing on, 44
Netcat, 271
Netcraft, 53
Netfilter (see iptables)
NetStumbler, 202
network address translation, 257, 297
network distance, 174, 184, 194
network inventory, 172
network inventory (Zenmap), 309
Network Mapper (see Nmap)
Nmap
  birthday of, 340
  checking if installed, 25
  description of, 373
  history of, 20-24
  uses of, 1
.nmap directory, 209, 370, 371, 394, 408
.nmap filename extension, 339
nmap NSE module, 212, 239-245
"Nmap Output" scan results tab, 312
Nmap Project Signing Key, 26
Nmap Scripting Engine (NSE), 13, 82, 205-255, 393-394
  API, 239
  C modules, 237

O

Q

Q (OS detection response test), 178, 179, 185

R

R (OS detection response test), 178, 179, 184
RadialNet, 318
random targets, 48, 377
   (see also -iR)
randomization of hosts, 67, 402
   (see also --randomize-hosts)
randomization of ports, 390
rarity directive (nmap-service-probes), 162, 163
rarity of version detection probes, 150, 152
rate limiting, 105, 126, 132, 304, 386, 397, 398
   detection of, 133
raw packets, 82, 95, 380, 384
   in NSE, 242
raw sockets, 409
RD (OS detection response test), 178, 179, 187
reason reporting (see --reason)
recent scans database, 317
record route IP option, 279, 402
record timestamp IP option, 402
Red Hat (Linux distribution)
   installing on, with RPM, 33
   installing on, with Yum, 34
reference guide (man page), 373-414
registered ports, 74
registry (NSE), 245, 254
regular expressions, 149, 160
   (see also Perl Compatible Regular Expressions)
   for syntax highlighting in Zenmap, 334
removal, 45
reserved ports, 73
resuming scans, 346, 407
retransmission, 132, 398
   number of retransmissions, 132
reverse DNS, 3, 12, 52, 56, 57, 80, 89, 145, 204, 286, 327
   disabling with -n, 382
   from an IDS, 276
   omitting to save time, 137
reverse probes, 276
RID (OS detection response test), 180, 188
   omission of, 188, 193
Rieger, Gerhard, 21, 126, 388
RIPCK (OS detection response test), 180, 188
RIPE (Réseaux IP Européens), 54
RIPL (OS detection response test), 180, 188
RND (decoy address), 285, 401
root (see privileged users)
rootkits, 79, 262, 301
round trip time (RTT), 292
   estimating, 130
RPC, 150, 268
   bypassing filtered portmapper port (see RPC grinder)
RPC grinder, 147, 148, 156-157, 257, 366, 391, 392
RPC scan (see RPC grinder)
rpcbind, 148, 156
rpcinfo, 156, 268
RPM, 33, 45
   installing from, 33
RTT (see round trip time)
RUCK (OS detection response test), 180, 188
RUD (OS detection response test), 180, 188
RUL (OS detection response test), 180, 188
rules in NSE (see "portrule" and "hostrule")
run level of scripts, 211, 245
"runlevel" script variable, 211
"Running:", 173
runtime interaction, 82, 140, 410

S

S (OS detection response test), 178, 179, 186
"safe" script category, 208, 246
saving scan results, 316
Saxon, 356
SCAN (subject OS fingerprint line), 192, 193
scan delay, 132
scan profiles (see Zenmap: scan profiles)
Scanlogd, 285, 298, 401
scanme.nmap.org, 18, 47
Scanrand, 135, 337
"Scans" scan results tab, 315
Schubert, Max, 352
SCO Corporation, 21
script arguments, 210, 394
   (see also --script-args)
script categories, 207
scR1pT kIddI3 output, 347, 403, 405
script kiddies, 8, 258, 277, 288, 297, 298, 339, 384
script names, examples of, 206
script.db, 209, 255, 369, 394
   (see also --script-updatedb)
scripting (see Nmap Scripting Engine)
scripts, location of, 209, 369, 394
security by obscurity, 298
SEQ (OS fingerprint category line), 177
SERVICE column, 364
service detection (see version detection)
service fingerprint, 147, 150
   example of, 164
   submission of, 147, 164
"Service Info:", 146, 175
service: (Zenmap search criterion), 328
setuid, why Nmap shouldn't be, 409, 414
Shimomura, Tsutomu, 174